Effective Teaching Methods

RESEARCH-BASED PRACTICE

Eighth Edition

Effective Teaching Methods
RESEARCH-BASED PRACTICE

Gary D. Borich

The University of Texas at Austin

PEARSON

Boston   Columbus   Indianapolis   New York   San Francisco   Upper Saddle River
Amsterdam   Cape Town   Dubai   London   Madrid   Milan   Munich   Paris   Montreal   Toronto
Delhi   Mexico City   São Paulo   Sydney   Hong Kong   Seoul   Singapore   Taipei   Tokyo

Vice President/Editorial Director: Jeffery Johnston
Executive Editor: Linda Bishop
Editorial Assistant: Laura Marenghi
Senior Marketing Manager: Darcy Betts
Production Editor: Karen Mason
Production Coordination, Editorial Services, and Text Design: Electronic Publishing Services, Inc., NYC
Art Rendering and Electronic Page Makeup: Jouve
Image Researcher: Jorgensen Fernandez
Cover Designer: Laura Gardner
Cover Photos: Nicole Hill/Rubberball/Getty Images; Ariel Skelley/Blend Images/Getty Images; Jack Hollingsworth/Photodisc/Getty Images

Credits and acknowledgments borrowed from other sources and reproduced, with permission, in this textbook appear here or on appropriate page within text. **Text Credits:** InTASC standards, www.ccsso.org. Used with permission from Council of Chief State School Officers; p. 25, Reprinted with permission from the National Board for Professional Teaching Standards, www.nbpts.org. All rights reserved; p. 341, Based on Nunn, G., & Kimberly, R. (2000, December). **Photo Credits:** Background Design: Vic&dd/Fotolia; In Practice icon, Minerva Studio/Fotolia; p. v, Courtesy of Gary Borich; pp. xii (bottom), xxi, 2, 30, 130, 155, 359, Monkey Business Images/Shutterstock; pp. x, 36, 63, Rob Marmion/Shutterstock; pp. xi, 68, 96, Jasmin Merda/Fotolia; pp. xii (top), 102, 124, Poznyakov/Shutterstock; pp. xiii, 160, 198, Michaeljung/Fotolia; pp. xiv, 204, 219, Robert Kneschke/Fotolia; pp. xv, 224, 247, Pressmaster/Shutterstock; pp. xvi (top), 252, 279, Krivosheev Vitaly/Shutterstock; pp. xvi (bottom), 284, 308, 316, 329, Monkey Business/Fotolia; pp. xvii, 322, 347, Anatoliy Samara/Shutterstock; pp. xviii, 352, 373, Eléonore H/Fotolia; pp. xix, 378, 418, Lisa F. Young/Fotolia; p. 11, Iofoto/Shutterstock; p. 20, Anthony Magnacca/Pearson Education; p. 21, Rob/Fotolia; p. 47, Dotshock/Shutterstock; p. 53, Golden Pixels LLC/Shutterstock; p. 55, Shock/Fotolia; p. 79, Neo Edmund/Fotolia; p. 86, Auremar/Shutterstock; p. 106, Lydmila/Fotolia; p. 116, Michaeljung/Shutterstock; p. 134, Oliveromg/Shutterstock; p. 144, AISPIX by Image Source/Shutterstock; p. 182, Monkey Business Images/Fotolia; p. 185, Annie Fuller/Pearson Education; p. 207, Karelnoppe/Fotolia; pp. 215, 371, Auremar/Fotolia; p. 238, Micromonkey/Fotolia; p. 239, Andres Rodriguez/Fotolia; p. 265, Petro Feketa/Fotolia; p. 275, Alexander Raths/Fotolia; p. 305, Jacek Chabraszewski/Shutterstock; p. 334, Jacek Chabraszewski/Fotolia; p. 381, Scott Cunningham/Pearson Education; p. 398, Michal Kowalski/Shutterstock

Library of Congress Cataloging-in-Publication Data

Borich, Gary D.
   Effective teaching methods : research-based practice / Gary Borich. — 8th ed.
     pages cm
   ISBN 978-0-13-284960-9
   1. Effective teaching—United States.   2. Lesson planning—United States.   I. Title.
   LB1025.3.B67 2013
   371.102—dc23   2012051575

10   9   8   7   6   5   4   3   2   1

PEARSON

ISBN-10: 0-13-284960-7
ISBN-13: 978-0-13-284960-9

Gary Borich grew up on the south side of Chicago, where he attended Mendel High School and later taught in the public school system of Niles, Illinois. He received his doctoral degree from Indiana University, where he was director of evaluation at the Institute for Child Study. Dr. Borich is a professor in the College of Education at the University of Texas at Austin and a past member of the board of examiners of the National Council for the Accreditation of Teacher Education (NCATE).

Dr. Borich's other books include *Observation Skills for Effective Teaching*, sixth edition; *Educational Assessment for the Elementary and Middle School Classroom*, second edition (with M. Tombari); *Clearly Outstanding: Making Each Day Count in Your Classroom*; *Becoming a Teacher: An Inquiring Dialogue for the Beginning Teacher*; *Educational Psychology: A Contemporary Approach*, second edition (with M. Tombari); *Educational Testing and Measurement*, tenth edition (with T. Kubiszyn); and *The Appraisal of Teaching: Concepts and Process*.

Dr. Borich lives in Austin, Texas, with his wife, Kathy. His interests include training and riding Arabian horses and he is the author of *An Illustrated Introduction to Classical Horsemanship*.

Brief Contents

Contents

2 Understanding Your Students   36

3 Classroom Management I: Establishing the Learning Climate 68

4 Classroom Management II: Promoting Student Engagement   102

5 Goals, Standards, and Objectives   130

6   *Unit and Lesson Planning   160*

7 *Technology Integration in Instruction*   204

9 Teaching Strategies for Direct Instruction 252

10 Teaching Strategies for Indirect Instruction 284

11 *Self-Directed Learning*   322

12 Cooperative Learning and the Collaborative Process   352

13 *Assessing Learners*   378

Preface

State curriculum standards and testing, differentiated instruction, new educational technologies for delivering lesson content, special populations in the general education classroom, new teacher certification and assessment requirements, and legislative initiatives, such No Child Left Behind and Response to Intervention, are but a few of the factors that continue to change the face of American schools and classroom teaching. This book has been written to help you prepare to meet these challenges and to discover the opportunities for professional growth and advancement they provide.

This eighth edition of *Effective Teaching Methods: Research-based Practice* continues to strengthen the four goals of previous editions. The first goal is to present teaching practices derived from nearly four decades of classroom research selected for their effectiveness with learners. The results have made it possible to replace many age-old anecdotal suggestions for good teaching with modern-day research-based teaching practices that are empirically related to positive outcomes in learners. Describing these teaching practices and how to use them to become an effective teacher is a major focus of this book.

Second, this text describes these effective teaching practices in a friendly, conversational manner. The language of classrooms is informal, and there is no reason a book about teachers in classrooms should not use the same language. Therefore, this book talks straight, avoiding complicated prescriptions, rambling discussions, or pseudo-scholarly language. The intent is to get the point across quickly and in a user-friendly style so that you can immediately apply what is presented in the classroom.

The third goal of this book is to be practical. Positive prescriptions for your classroom teaching show you how to engage students in the learning process, manage your classroom, and increase student achievement in today's heterogeneous classrooms. This book not only tells you what to do to obtain these results, it also shows you how to obtain them with extensive examples from classroom videos, written classroom dialogues, and case studies.

The final goal of this book is to be realistic. Some of the literature on effective teaching is theoretical and speculative. This book, in contrast, describes what the research says real teachers do in real classrooms to be effective, identifying which teaching practices they have found to be effective. Nothing in this book is pie-in-the-sky theorizing about effective teaching, because most of what is presented results directly from years of research and observation of effective teaching practices in actual classrooms.

These, then, are this book's four goals: to illustrate how to apply effective, research-based teaching practices, presented in a conversational style, that are practical and realistic in today's heterogeneous classrooms.

New to This Edition

Users of earlier editions of *Effective Teaching Methods* will notice that each chapter has been revised. The rapid pace of change and new research occurring in nearly every aspect of teaching has resulted in an eighth edition that considerably updates and extends earlier editions and provides an extensive complement of features to get beginning teachers confident and up to speed on their very first day of classroom observation and practice teaching.

- A new chapter organization, requested by text reviewers, present most of the chapters in a new order. For example, the parameters for classroom management and the learning environment now appear before the discussions of goals and objectives for learning and unit and daily lesson planning. The critical chapter on Questioning is positioned earlier in the text, allowing students to posit the role of questioning as they compare strategies for direct and indirect instruction and self-directed learning.

- Expanded sections on Multiple Intelligences in Chapter 2, including "Misconceptions about Intelligence," "General versus Specific Intellignce," "Socio-Emotional Intelligence," and Characteristics of intelligent behavior

- New section on Connecting with Students (Chapter 3), including information on mutual trust, confidence, identifying potential for learning, and identifying opportunities for exploration and discovery. In addition, instructional information on turning the classroom into a Professional Learning Community is provided.

- Expanded information on working with families in Chapter 4, including the influence of home and family on students and classroom behavior as well as preparing for, conducting, and evaluating the Teacher-Family conference. This section also contains a new "In Practice" feature: Focus on Getting Parents Involved in School Crises.

- New section in Chapter 5 on the rigor and relevance framework

- New Chapter 7, Technology Integration in Instruction that includes twenty-first century technologies such as Web 2.0, classroom management technology, and classroom applications for online learning and digital gaming

- New discussions for systematic and explicit Direct Instruction Strategies, including monitoring and diagnosing to gauge learner progress, presenting and structuring the delivery of new content, guiding student practice, offering feedback and correction for errors, leading students to mastery, and reviewing learned content and skills over time

- Revised description of Cognitive Strategies to promote lifelong learning

How This Book Is Organized

- **Chapter 1** introduces the characteristics of an effective teacher and what an effective teacher does in the classroom. This chapter also acquaints you with the NBPTS and InTASC standards that will be important for your certification and licensing.

- **Chapter 2** provides a discussion on understanding adaptive teaching, differentiated instruction, and how individual differences and learner diversity (prior achievement, learning style, culture and language, and home and family life) affect student learning needs and classroom management. This chapter will introduce you to the real nature and challenges of today's multicultural, heterogeneous classrooms and the teaching of English-language learners, immigrant populations, at-risk learners, and special-needs learners, including how to close the achievement gap among students of different socioeconomic levels.

- **Chapters 3 and 4** delve into classroom management and provide a complement of techniques and strategies that can quickly change your beginning days in the classroom from a concern for your own survival to a concern for the impact you are having on your learners.

- **Chapter 5** on goals, standards, and objectives shows you how to assess the extent to which you are achieving knowledge, thinking, and problem-solving behaviors in your classroom. This chapter expands the traditional taxonomies of cognitive and affective behavior to include the important higher-order objectives of metacognition, problem solving, decision making, critical thinking, and valuing. It also makes clear the important relationship between state standards and your classroom goals and objectives.

- **Chapter 6** on unit and lesson planning will improve your skills in linking subject-matter content to teaching methods and student outcomes in a continuous process of lesson planning. The chapter shows you how to compose thematic and interdisciplinary lessons to promote higher order thought processes and problem-solving behavior in your learners. It also provides some of the tools you can use to differentiate your instruction in a heterogeneous classroom.

- **NEW! Chapter 7** is a new chapter and describes how to effectively integrate educational and web-based instructional technologies into your lesson plans. Chapter graphics show you how online resources can be seamlessly integrated into every step of the lesson planning process. With the many examples provided for integrating technology into your lesson planning you should be well informed in using a wide variety of online tools and resources to enrich and add an exciting contructivist addition to your lessons.

- **Chapter 8** on teacher questioning shows you how to raise questions at different levels of cognitive complexity and how to use probes and follow-up questions to promote higher order thinking and problem-solving behavior. This chapter will help you ask questions that prepare your learners not only to engage in quick, firm, and correct responses during direct instruction but also to ask and respond to higher order questions during indirect instruction.

- **Chapters 9 and 10** provide you with an interchangeable menu of instructional activities that can be mixed and matched to the needs of your learners and objectives of your lesson to help you better implement the goals of differentiating instruction in a heterogeneous classroom. Chapter 9 offers teaching strategies that explain how to use direct instructional methods (such as explaining, presenting, drill and practice, and recitation), while Chapter 10 explores indirect instructional methods (group discussion, concept-learning, inquiry, and problem-solving activities).

- **Chapter 11** focuses on self-directed learning and how to use metacognitive techniques, teacher mediation, and the social dialogue of the classroom to help learners control, regulate, and take responsibility for their own learning. You will learn to unleash your learners' intuitive and imaginative capacities to learn on their own, with you as a resource, leaving them with a sense of ownership in what they have explored and discovered. This chapter offers specific tools and techniques that effective teachers use to get their students to become agents of their own learning.

- **Chapter 12** discusses cooperative learning and the collaborative process for productively organizing and managing group and team activities to promote communication skills, self-esteem, and problem solving. It will introduce you to the enthusiasm, motivation, and creativity that can result from learners working together on real-world projects and performances to form a partnership of ideas and a learning community, and how to teach your students the democratic and collaborative skills they will need in and beyond your classroom.

- **Chapter 13** offers an updated and expanded treatment of standardized tests that includes what you will need to know to assess the learners with special needs in your classroom. No other development in education during the last decade has generated more controversy than the use of standardized tests for making high-stakes decisions involving grade promotion, the selection of students for advanced academic programs, high school graduation, and assessing special populations, as called for by recently authorized and updated federal legislation. The chapter explores the assessment of student achievement and interpreting student progress using the Response to Intervention model and teacher-made objective tests, essays, performance assessments, and portfolios. This chapter will not only help you assess the day-to-day understanding of *all* learners, but it will help you bridge the gap between your learners' daily performance and their standardized test results.

Special Features of This Text

Features that can be found in the eighth edition include:

- **Chapter opening questions** and **new InTASC standards** focus you on the key aspects of each chapter.
- **In Practice** features offer practical teaching tips, strategies, and techniques that can help new teachers extend their textbook knowledge to their very first lesson plans, showing them tangible approaches to putting theory into practice and offering practical tips, strategies, and techniques. They include how to apply constructivist principles, use differentiated instruction, teach learners with special needs in a heterogeneous classroom, integrate technology and web based instruction into lesson plans, apply the concept of multiple intelligences, write

interdisciplinary unit plans, achieve mastery learning, initiate project- and problem-based learning, and use portfolios and performance assessments to provide learners an opportunity to participate in their own assessment. Several new In Practice features appear in this edition, including Focus on Applications for Online Learning, Focus on Digital Gaming in the Classroom, and Focus on Cooperative Learning.

- **A self-report survey instrument** is included in Chapter 1 and Appendix A for measuring the concerns you have about yourself as a teacher, concerns about the teaching task, and concerns about your impact on students, which can be used to chart your growth and development as a teacher over time.

- **A practical visual format** is included in Chapter 4 for organizing your unit and lesson plans, letting you graphically visualize the relationship between lessons and units and better prepare for meeting state standards and preparing your learners for their standardized assessments.

- **A Higher Order Thinking and Problem-Solving Checklist** is introduced in Chapters 5, 11, and 12 and included in Appendix C to help you achieve a curriculum in your classroom that encourages your students to problem solve, make decisions, and think critically.

- **End-of-chapter Practice OR End-of-chapter Application**

  - **End-of-chapter Summing Up** sections restate key concepts in an easy-to-follow outline format for easy reference during field experiences, observation assignments, and practice teaching. **Discussion and Practice Questions** review the most important content of each chapter, with keyed answers presented in Appendix B.

  - **NEW! Professional Practice** sections at the ends of chapters provide hands-on opportunities to engage you in decision making and problem solving as they are carried out in a real classroom. Together, all three sets of activities provide a menu of opportunities from which you can practice and advance the skills learned in each chapter.

  - **Field Experience and Practice Activities** at the end of each chapter encourage you to make decisions and solve practical classroom problems related to the content within each chapter with regard to lesson planning, classroom management, cultural diversity, and project-based learning.

  - **Digital Portfolio Activities** guide you in creating a professional portfolio of accomplishments with entries related to the content of each chapter. This portfolio will be a vehicle with which you can put your best foot forward to future instructors in your teacher preparation program, cooperating or supervisory teachers during student teaching, professional colleagues, and, most importantly, future employers. The portfolio will chronicle your best accomplishments in this course and beyond.

- **A glossary of key terms and definitions** recaps all of the major definitions, concepts, and teaching practices that you will need to review for the Praxis exams and your state's certification requirements.

Resources for Students and Instructors

MyEducationLab™

MyEducationLab is an online homework, tutorial, and assessment product designed to improve results by helping students quickly master concepts, and by providing educators with a robust set of tools for easily gauging and addressing the performance of individuals and classrooms.

MyEducationLab engages students with high-quality multimedia learning experiences that help them build critical teaching skills and prepare them for real-world practice. In practice exercises, students receive immediate feedback so they see mistakes right away, learn precisely which concepts are holding them back, and master concepts through targeted practice.

For educators, MyEducationLab provides highly-visual data and performance analysis to help them quickly identify gaps in student learning and make a clear connection among coursework, concept mastery, and national teaching standards. And because MyEducationLab comes from Pearson, it's developed by an experienced partner committed to providing content, resources, and expertise for the best digital learning experiences.

In *Preparing Teachers for a Changing World,* Linda Darling-Hammond and her colleagues point out that grounding teacher education in real classrooms—among real teachers and students and among actual examples of students' and teachers' work—is an important, and perhaps even an essential, part of training teachers for the complexities of teaching in today's classrooms.

In the MyEducationLab for this course, educators will find the following features and resources.

Advanced Data and Performance Reporting Aligned to National Standards. Advanced data and performance reporting helps educators quickly identify gaps in student learning and gauge and address individual and classroom performance. Educators easily see the connection among coursework, concept mastery, and national teaching standards with highly-visual views of performance reports. Data and assessments align directly to InTASC's Model Core Teaching Standards to support reporting for state and accreditation requirements.

Study Plan Specific to Your Text. MyEducationLab gives students the opportunity to test themselves on key concepts and skills, track their own progress through the course, and access personalized Study Plan activities.

The customized Study Plan is generated based on students' pretest results. Incorrect questions from the pretest indicate specific textbook learning outcomes the student is struggling with. The customized Study Plan suggests specific enriching activities for particular learning outcomes, helping students focus. Personalized Study Plan activities may include eBook reading assignments, and review, practice, and enrichment activities.

After students complete the enrichment activities, they take a posttest to see the concepts they've mastered or areas where they still may need extra help.

MyEducationLab then reports the Study Plan results to the instructor. Based on these reports, the instructor can adapt course material to suit the needs of individual students or the entire class.

Assignments and Activities. Designed to enhance students' understanding of concepts covered in class, these assignable exercises show concepts in action (through videos, cases, and/or student and teacher artifacts). They help students deepen content knowledge and synthesize and apply concepts and strategies they have read about in the book. (Correct answers for these assignments are available to the instructor only.)

Building Teaching Skills and Dispositions. These unique learning units help students practice and strengthen skills that are essential to effective teaching. After examining the steps involved in a core teaching process, students are given an opportunity to practice applying this skill via videos, student and teacher artifacts, and/or case studies of authentic classrooms. Providing multiple opportunities to practice a single teaching concept, each activity encourages a deeper understanding and application of concepts, as well as the use of critical thinking skills. After practice, students take a quiz that is reported to the instructor gradebook and performance reporting.

Course Resources. The Course Resources section of MyEducationLab is designed to help students prepare for and begin a career, navigate the first year of teaching, and understand key educational standards, policies, and laws. It includes the following:

- **The Certification and Licensure** section is designed to help you pass licensure exams by giving you access to state test requirements, overviews of what tests cover, and sample test items. The Certification and Licensure section includes the following:
  - **State Certification Test Requirements:** Here, you can click on a state and be taken to a list state certification tests. You can also click on the **Licensure Exams** to find:
    - ○ Basic information about each test
    - ○ Descriptions of what is covered on each test
    - ○ Sample test questions with explanations of correct answers

- National Evaluation Series™ by Pearson: Here, you can see the tests in the NES, learn what is covered on each exam, and access sample test items with descriptions and rationales of correct answers. You can also purchase interactive online tutorials developed by Pearson Evaluation Systems and the Pearson Teacher Education and Development group.
- ETS Online Praxis Tutorials: Here you can purchase interactive online tutorials developed by ETS and by the Pearson Teacher Education and Development group. Tutorials are available for the Praxis I exams and for select Praxis II exams.

The **Licensure and Standards** section provides access to current state and national standards.

- The **Preparing a Portfolio** section provides guidelines for creating a high-quality teaching portfolio.
- **Beginning Your Career** offers tips, advice, and other valuable information on:
  - Resume Writing and Interviewing: Includes expert advice on how to write impressive resumes and prepare for job interviews.
  - Your First Year of Teaching: Provides practical tips to set up a first classroom, manage student behavior, and more easily organize for instruction and assessment.
  - Law *and Public Policies:* Details specific directives and requirements needed to understand under the No Child Left Behind Act and the Individuals with Disabilities Education Improvement Act of 2004.
- The **Multimedia Index** aggregates resources in MyEducationLab by asset type (for example, video or artifact) for easy location and retrieval.

Visit **www.myeducationlab.com** for a demonstration of this exciting online teaching resource.

Support Materials for Instructors

The following resources are available for instructors to download on **www.pearsonhighered.com/educators**. Instructors enter the author or title of this book, select this particular edition of the book, and then click on the "Resources" tab to log in and download textbook supplements.

Instructor's Resource Manual and Test Bank
The Instructor's Resource Manual and Test Bank includes an overview of chapter content and related instructional activities for the college classroom and for practice the field as well as a robust collection of chapter-by-chapter test items.

PowerPoint™ Slides
The PowerPoint™ slides include key concept summarizations, diagrams, and other graphic aids to enhance learning. They are designed to help students understand, organize, and reinforce core concepts and theories.

MyEducationLab Correlation Guide
This guide connects chapter sections with appropriate assignable exercises on MyEducationLab.

TestGen
TestGen is a powerful test generator that instructors install on a computer and use in conjunction with the TestGen testbank file for the text. Assessments, including equations, graphs, and scientific notation, may be created for both print or testing online.

TestGen is available exclusively from Pearson Education publishers. Instructors install TestGen on a personal computer (Windows or Macintosh) and create tests for classroom testing and for other specialized delivery options, such as over a local area network or on the web. A test bank, which is also called a Test Item File (TIF), typically contains a large set of test items, organized by chapter and ready for use in creating a test, based on the associated textbook material.

Also Available . . . Pearson etext

Did you know this book is also available as an enhanced Pearson eText? The affordable, interactive version of this text includes 3-5 videos per chapter that exemplify, model, or expand upon chapter concepts. Look for the play button in the margins to see where video is available in the affordable enhanced eText version of this text.

To learn more about the enhanced Pearson eText, go to www.pearsonhighered.com/etextbooks

Additional Resources

The companion volume to this text, *Observation Skills for Effective Teaching,* Sixth Edition (also from Pearson Education), is intended to be used either in a preteaching observation experience or as an applications resource to the present volume. *Observation Skills for Effective Teaching* provides extensive examples, entertaining and instructional classroom dialogues, and practical observation and recording instruments keyed to and coordinated with the effective teaching methods presented in this text. Together, these texts provide a sequence of learning for the preservice and beginning teacher. For more information please visit **www.pearsonhighered.com** or contact your local Pearson Representative and reference ISBN 0137039727.

Acknowledgments

Many individuals contributed to the preparation of this book. Not the least significant are the many professionals whose studies of classroom life have contributed to the effective teaching methods described in this text.

I also extend my gratitude to Yungwei Hao for coauthoring Chapter 7 and bringing her state of the art expertise to the lesson planning process. I would also like to thank my good friends and colleagues Marty Tombari and Tom Kubiszyn for contributing their thoughts and ideas from earlier writings to this book. And, thanks to those educators who gave their time to review this eighth edition and guide this revision: Madeline A. Berry, State University College at Oneonta; Gail Luera, University of Michigan at Dearborn; Martha Jo Minus, The University Of West Alabama; Jane Z. Murphy, Middlesex Community College; Lois Paretti, University of Nevada, Las Vegas; and Scott K. Scheuerell, Loras College.

I also wish to acknowledge those teachers who over the years have shared their insights about the teaching process with me. Among them have been teachers in the Austin, Texas, Independent School District—especially William B. Travis High School and Travis Heights Elementary School, who provided the opportunity to observe many of the effective teaching methods described herein.

GDB
Austin, Texas

Effective Teaching Methods

RESEARCH-BASED PRACTICE

1

The Effective Teacher

This chapter will help you answer these questions and meet the following InTASC standards for effective teaching.

- What is an effective teacher?
- How can I become an effective teacher?
- Are there different definitions of effective teaching?
- What are some of the teaching practices used by effective teachers?
- How will I know if I am an effective teacher?

InTASC

STANDARD 1 **Learner Development.** The teacher understands how learners grow and develop, recognizing that patterns of learning and development vary individually within and across the cognitive, linguistic, social, emotional, and physical areas, and designs and implements developmentally appropriate and challenging learning experiences.

STANDARD 4 **Content Knowledge.** The teacher understands the central concepts, tools of inquiry, and structures of the discipline(s) he or she teaches and creates learning experiences that make these aspects of the discipline accessible and meaningful for learners to assure mastery of the content.

STANDARD 6 **Assessment.** The teacher understands and uses multiple methods of assessment to engage learners in their own growth, to monitor learner progress, and to guide the teacher's and learner's decision making.

How easily or quickly could you answer the question, "What is an effective teacher?" This question has been asked by every teacher, young and old. It is a deceptively simple question that has many different answers. Teaching is a complex and difficult task that demands extraordinary abilities. After decades of experience and research, one of the most important questions in education today still is, "What is an effective teacher?"

This chapter offers no single definition of an effective teacher. Instead, its goal is to introduce you to practices used by effective teachers that are related to positive outcomes in learners. These effective teaching practices do not tell the whole story of what an effective teacher is, but they do form an important foundation to help you become an effective teacher and profit from reading the chapters ahead. Subsequent chapters blend these practices with classroom management, lesson planning, problem-based learning, questioning strategies, learner assessment, and the attitudes and dispositions you will need to build a warm and nurturing relationship with your students. These topics will give you a rich and comprehensive picture of an effective teacher and, most importantly, help you become one.

MyEducationLab

Visit the MyEducationLab for *Effective Teaching Methods: Research-Based Practice,* 8/e to enhance your understanding of chapter concepts with a personalized Study Plan. You'll also have the opportunity to hone your teaching skills through video-based Assignments and Activities as well as Building Teaching Skills and Dispositions lessons.

What Is an Effective Teacher?

If you had grown up a century ago, you would have been able to answer the question of "What is an effective teacher?" very simply: A good teacher is a good person—a role model who meets the community ideal for a good citizen, good parent, and good employee. At that time, teachers were judged primarily on their goodness as people and only secondarily on their behavior in the classroom. They were expected to be honest, hardworking, generous, friendly, and considerate and to demonstrate these qualities in their classrooms by being organized, disciplined, insightful, and committed. Practically speaking, this meant that to be effective, all a teacher needed was King Solomon's wisdom, Sigmund Freud's insight, Albert Einstein's knowledge, and Florence Nightingale's dedication!

It soon became evident that this definition of an ideal teacher lacked clear, objective standards of performance that could be consistently applied and that could be used to train future teachers.

A New Direction

Over the past several decades, a revolution has occurred in defining good teaching. We have seen that defining good teachers by community ideals proved unrealistic and were poorly related to what teachers actually do in the classroom. This directed researchers to study the impact of specific teacher activities on the specific cognitive and affective behaviors of their students. The term *good teaching* changed to *effective teaching,* and the research focus shifted from studying teachers exclusively to including teachers' effects on students. These new ways of studying classroom behavior have made the student and teacher–student relationship in the classroom the focus of modern definitions of effective teaching.

Linking Teacher Behavior with Student Performance. During the past few decades, researchers developed new methods for studying the classroom interaction patterns of teachers and students. Their goal was to discover which patterns of teacher behavior promote desirable student performance. But before unveiling the findings of this research and their implications for effective teaching, let's see how this research was performed.

Patterns of Classroom Interaction. To collect data on the classroom interaction patterns of teachers and students, researchers often used instruments like those shown in Figures 1.1, 1.2, and 1.3. These particular instruments, devised by Good and Brophy (2007) for their research on effective teaching, record patterns of student–teacher interaction. Using the coding guide in Figure 1.1 and the response form in Figure 1.2, an observer codes both student responses to questions and the teacher's reaction and feedback. For example, in the tenth interchange recorded on Figure 1.2, a male student fails to answer a question (coded "0" under "Student Response"), is criticized by the teacher for not answering ("--"), and then is given the answer by the teacher ("Gives Ans."). Numbers for the interchanges are assigned as they occur, allowing the pattern of question–answer–feedback to be recorded over an entire class period across many classrooms.

On the Coding Form for Measuring Individual Praise (Figure 1.3), the observer codes the positive behavior being praised by the teacher (perseverance, progress, success, good thinking, and so

Figure 1.1 **Coding Categories for Question–Answer–Feedback Sequences**

Student Gender	Definition	Explanation
Symbol Label		
M	Male	The student answering the question is male.
F	Female	The student answering the question is female.
Student Response		
+	Right	The teacher accepts the student's response as correct or satisfactory.
±	Part right	The teacher considers the student's response to be only partially correct or to be correct but incomplete.
−	Wrong	The teacher considers the student's response to be incorrect.
0	No answer	The student makes no response or says he doesn't know (code student's answer here if teacher gives feedback reaction before he is able to respond).
Teacher Feedback Reaction		
++	Praise	Teacher praises student either in words ("fine," "good," "wonderful," "good thinking") or by expressing verbal affirmation in a notably warm, joyous, or excited manner.
+	Affirm	Teacher simply affirms that the student's response is correct (nods, repeats answer, says "Yes," "OK," etc.).
0	No reaction	Teacher makes no response whatever to student's response—he or she simply goes on to something else.
−	Negate	Teacher simply indicates that the student's response is incorrect (shakes head, says "No," "That's not right," "Hm-mm," etc.).
− −	Criticize	Teacher criticizes student, either in words ("You should know better than that," "That doesn't make any sense—you better pay close attention," etc.) or by expressing verbal negation in a frustrated, angry, or disgusted manner.
Gives Ans.	Teacher gives answer	Teacher provides the correct answer for the student.
Ask Other	Teacher asks another student	Teacher redirects the question, asking a different student to try to answer it.
Other Calls	Another student calls out answer	Another student calls out the correct answer, and the teacher acknowledges that it is correct.
Repeat	Repeats question	Teacher repeats the original question, either in its entirety or with a prompt ("Well?" "Do you know?" "What's the answer?").
Clue	Rephrase or clue	Teacher makes original question easier for student to answer by rephrasing it or by giving a clue.
New Ques.	New question	Teacher asks a new question (i.e., a question that calls for a different answer than the original question called for).

Source: Good, Thomas L., Looking in Class, 5th Ed., © 1990. Reprinted and electronically reproduced by permission of Pearson Education, Inc., Upper Saddle River, New Jersey.

on.). Individual students are identified by assigning each a unique number such as 14, 23, 6, and so on. This form records not only the praise behavior of the teacher in relation to individual student behavior but also the overall pattern or sequence of action. For example, student 23 is praised twice in a row, the first time for "Success" and the second time for "Good thinking."

Figure 1.2 Coding Response Form

Stu. No.	Sex		Student Response				Teacher Feedback Reaction					Gives Ans.	Ask Other	Other Calls	Repeat	Clue	New Ques.
	M	F	+	±	−	0	++	+	0	−	−−						
1		✓	✓					✓									
2	✓		✓					✓									
3	✓					✓										✓	
4	✓		✓				✓										
5	✓		✓					✓									
6		✓		✓						✓							✓
7	✓		✓				✓										
8	✓		✓						✓								
9	✓		✓						✓								
10	✓					✓					✓	✓					
11																	
12																	
13																	
14																	
15																	

Source: Good, Thomas L., Looking in Class, 5th Ed., © 1990. Reprinted and electronically reproduced by permission of Pearson Education, Inc., Upper Saddle River, New Jersey.

With instruments such as these, a rich and varied picture of classroom activity can be captured over the course of a research study and related to various measures of school achievement. Obviously, a single observation of a single class would provide too little data to reveal a consistent pattern of interaction. However, multiple observations extending across different days, teachers, or schools could reveal consistent patterns of teacher–student interactions. These patterns of classroom behavior

Figure 1.3 Coding Form for Measuring Individual Praise

USE: Whenever the teacher praises an individual student

PURPOSE: To see what behaviors the teacher reinforces through praises, and to see how the teacher's praise is distributed among the students.

Behavior Categories	Student Number		Codes
1. Perseverance or effort; worked long or hard	14	1.	3
2. Progress (relative to the past) toward achievement	23	2.	3,4
3. Success (right answer, high score) achievement	6	3.	3
4. Good thinking, good suggestions, good guess, or nice try	18	4.	3
5. Imagination, creativity, originality	8	5.	1
6. Neatness, careful work	8	6.	1
7. Good or compliant behavior, follows rules, pays attention	8	7.	1
8. Thoughtfulness, courtesy, offering to share, prosocial behavior		8.	
9. Other (specify)		9.	

NOTES:

All answers occurred during social studies discussion.

Was particularly concerned about #8, a low-achieving male.

10. _____
11. _____
12. _____
13. _____
14. _____
15. _____
16. _____
17. _____
18. _____
19. _____
20. _____
21. _____
22. _____
23. _____
24. _____
25. _____

Source: Good, Thomas L., Looking in Class, 5th Ed., (c) 1990. Reprinted and electronically reproduced by permission of Pearson Education, Inc., Upper Saddle River, New Jersey.

then can be related to student outcomes—such as classroom tests, student projects, oral performances, portfolio assessments, and standardized tests—to determine their effects on student performance.

It was in this manner that patterns of effective teaching began to emerge in studies conducted by different researchers. As in all research, some studies provided contradictory results or found no relationships among certain types of classroom interactions and student outcomes. But many studies found patterns of interaction between teacher and learner that consistently produced desirable student outcomes in the form of greater motivation to learn, higher achievement, increased problem solving, and improved learning skills.

Now that you know how the research was conducted, let's look at a preview of the teaching strategies and methods that researchers generally agree contribute to effective teaching and that will be addressed in the following chapters.

Key Behaviors Contributing to Effective Teaching

From this research, approximately ten teacher behaviors have been identified that show promising relationships to desirable student performance, primarily as measured by classroom assessments and standardized tests. Five of these behaviors have been consistently supported by research studies over the past three decades (Borich, 2008a; Brophy, 2002; Brophy & Good, 1986; Cantrell, 1998/1999; Dunkin & Biddle, 1974; Marzano, Pickering, & Pollock, 2004; McNary, Glasgow, & Hicks, 2005; Rosenshine, 1971; Saunders, 2005; Taylor, Pearson, Clark, & Walpole, 1999; Teddlie & Stringfield, 1993; Walberg, 1986; Willis, 2006). Another five have had some support and appear logically related to effective teaching. The first five are called **key behaviors**, because they are considered essential for effective teaching. The second five are called **helping behaviors**, because they can be used in combinations to implement the key behaviors. Following are the five key behaviors essential for effective teaching:

1. Lesson clarity
2. Instructional variety

3. Teacher task orientation
4. Engagement in the learning process
5. Student success rate

Let's take a closer look at each of these.

Lesson Clarity

Lesson clarity refers to how clear a teacher's presentation is to the class, as indicated in the following points:

More Effective Teachers

- Make ideas clear to learners who may be at different levels of understanding.
- Explain concepts in ways that help students follow along in a logical, step-by-step order.
- Have an oral delivery that is direct, audible to all students, and free of distracting mannerisms.

Less Effective Teachers

- Use vague, ambiguous, or indefinite language, such as "might probably be," "tends to suggest," and "could possibly happen."
- Use overly complicated sentences, such as "There are many important reasons for the start of World War II, but some are more important than others, so let's start with those that are thought to be important, but really aren't."
- Give directions that often result in student requests for clarification.

One result from research on lesson clarity is that teachers vary considerably in this behavior. Not all teachers are able to communicate clearly and directly to their students without wandering, speaking above students' levels of comprehension, or using speech patterns that impair their presentation's clarity (Brophy, 2002; Brown & Wragg, 1993; Cruickshank & Metcalf, 1994; Fasset & Warren, 2010; Muijs & Reynolds, 2005; Popham, 2009).

If you teach with a high degree of clarity, you will spend less time going over material. Your questions will be answered correctly the first time, allowing more time for instruction. Clarity is a complex behavior because it is related to many others, such as your organization of the content, lesson familiarity, and delivery strategies (whether you use a discussion, recitation, question–and–answer, or small-group format). Research shows that both the cognitive and oral clarity of presentations vary substantially among teachers. This in turn produces differences in student performance on cognitive tests of achievement (Marx & Walsh, 1988; Muijs & Reynolds, 2005). Table 1.1 summarizes some of the indicators of lesson clarity and teaching strategies you will learn about in this text, especially in Chapters 8 (on questioning strategies), 9 (on direct instruction), and 10 (on indirect instruction).

Instructional Variety

In this **video**, the teacher uses a variety of strategies to provide instruction. Listen as the narrator discusses the brain and how it works to integrate instruction.

The term **instructional variety** refers to your variability or flexibility of delivery during the presentation of a lesson (Brophy, 2002; Brophy & Good, 1986; Marzano, Pickering, & Pollock, 2004; Marzano, 2009; Rohrkemper & Corno, 1988). One of the most effective ways of creating variety during instruction is to ask questions. As you will learn in Chapter 8, many different types of questions can be integrated into the pacing and sequencing of a lesson to create meaningful variation (Chuska, 2003; Falk & Blumenreich, 2005; Wilen, 1991). Therefore, the effective teacher needs to know the art of asking questions and how to discriminate among different question formats—fact questions, process questions, convergent questions, and divergent questions. These question types are introduced in Chapter 8 and expanded on in Chapter 10.

Another aspect of instructional variety in teaching is perhaps the most obvious: the use of supplemental learning materials, computer software, displays, the Internet, and space in your classroom. The physical texture and visual variety of your classroom can also contribute to

Table 1.1 Indicators for Clarity

Being Clear (An effective teacher . . .)	Examples of Teaching Strategies
1. Informs learners of the lesson objective (e.g., describes what behaviors will be tested or required on future assignments as a result of the lesson)	Prepare a behavioral objective for the lesson at the desired level of complexity (e.g., knowledge, comprehension, etc.). Indicate to learners at the start of the lesson in what ways the behavior will be used in the future.
2. Provides learners with an advance organizer (e.g., that places the lesson in the perspective of past and/or future lessons)	Consult or prepare a unit plan to determine what task-relevant prior learning is required for this lesson and what task-relevant prior learning this lesson represents for future lessons. Begin the lesson by informing the learner that the content to be taught is part of this larger context.
3. Checks for task-relevant prior learning at the beginning of the lesson (e.g., determines the level of understanding of prerequisite facts or concepts and reteaches if necessary)	Ask questions of students at the beginning of a lesson or check assignments regularly to determine if task-relevant prior knowledge has been acquired.
4. Gives directives slowly and distinctly (e.g., repeats directives when needed or divides them into smaller pieces)	Organize procedures for lengthy assignments in step-by-step order, and give them as a handout as well as orally.
5. Knows ability levels and teaches at or slightly above learners' current level of understanding (e.g., knows learners' attention spans)	Determine learners' ability level from standardized tests, previous assignments, and interests, and retarget instruction accordingly.
6. Uses examples, illustrations, and demonstrations to explain and clarify (e.g., uses visuals to help interpret and reinforce main points)	Restate main points in at least one modality other than the one in which students were initially taught (e.g., visual vs. auditory).
7. Provides a review or summary at the end of each lesson	Use key phrases, repetition, or easy to memorize symbols to help students efficiently store and later recall content.

instructional variety. This has been shown to influence student engagement and the motivation to learn, and achievement on end-of-unit tests and performance assessments (Walqui, 2000). For example, some studies found the amount of disruptive behavior to be less in classrooms that had more varied activities and materials (Emmer & Evertson, 2012; Evertson & Emmer, 2012). Others have shown variety to be related to student attention (Borich, 2004, 2008a; Lysakowski & Walberg, 1981).

Some ways to incorporate variety into your teaching are presented in Chapter 7 (on technology integration), Chapter 9 (on direct instruction), Chapter 10 (on indirect instruction), and Chapter 12 (on cooperative learning and the collaborative process). Table 1.2 summarizes some of the indicators of instructional variety and teaching strategies covered in these chapters.

Teacher Task Orientation

Teacher task orientation is a key behavior that refers to the amount of classroom time the teacher devotes to teaching an academic subject. The more time allocated to teaching a specific topic, the greater the opportunity students have to learn.

For example, Table 1.3 shows the results achieved in a second-grade reading classroom when the teacher's task orientation—or time teaching an academic subject—was increased over a five-week period. Increasing the time devoted to this instructional objective from 4 minutes to 52 minutes a day, over an average of only 25 school days, yielded an increase of 27 percentile points (from 39 to 66) on a standardized achievement test. The researchers who recorded these data indicated that although such large increases in instructional time might appear unusual, they actually were achieved by teachers in these elementary school classrooms and that improvements in standardized achievement can be achieved with even small increments of a teacher's task orientation.

Table 1.2 Indicators for Variety

Using Variety (An effective teacher . . .)	Examples of Teaching Strategies
1. Uses attention gaining devices (e.g., begins with a challenging question, visual, or example)	Begin the lesson with an activity in a modality that is different from the last lesson or activity (e.g., change from listening to seeing).
2. Shows enthusiasm and animation through variation in eye contact, voice, and gestures (e.g., changes pitch and volume, moves about during the transition to a new activity)	Change position at regular intervals (e.g., every ten minutes). Change speed or volume to indicate that a change in content or activity has occurred.
3. Varies modes of presentation (e.g., presents, asks questions, then provides for independent practice [daily])	Establish an order of daily activities that rotates cycles of seeing, listening, and doing.
4. Uses a mix of rewards and reinforcers (e.g., extra credit, verbal praise, independent study, etc. [weekly, monthly])	Establish lists of rewards and expressions of verbal praise, and choose among them randomly. Provide reasons for praise along with the expression of it.
5. Incorporates student ideas or participation in some aspects of instruction (e.g., uses indirect instruction or divergent questioning [weekly, monthly])	Occasionally plan instruction in which student opinions are used to begin the lesson (e.g., "What would you do if . . .").
6. Varies types of questions (e.g., divergent, convergent, [weekly]) and probes (e.g., to clarify, to solicit, to redirect [daily])	Match questions to the behavior and complexity of the lesson objective. Vary the complexity of the lesson objectives in accord with the unit plan.

Table 1.3 Learning Time and Student Achievement: Example from Second-Grade Reading

Reading Score at First Testing (October)		Student Engaged Time in Reading with High Success Rate		Estimated Reading Score, Second Testing (December)	
Raw Score (out of 100)	Percentile	Total Time over 5 Weeks (Minutes)	Average Daily Time (Minutes)	Raw Score (out of 100)	Percentile
36	50	100	4	37	39
36	50	573	23	43	50
36	50	1,300	52	52	66

Note: An average of 25 school days occurred between the first and second testing.

Source: From *Teaching and Learning in the Elementary School: A Summary of the Beginning Teacher Evaluation Study,* Beginning Teacher Evaluation Study Report VII-I, by Charles W. Fisher et al., 1978. San Francisco: Far West Laboratory for Research and Development.

Some task-related questions a teacher must answer are (1) How much time do I spend planning for teaching and getting my students ready to learn? (2) How much time do I spend presenting, asking questions, and encouraging students to inquire or think independently? and (3) How much time do I spend assessing my learners' performance?

These questions pertain to how much content is presented, learned, and assessed, as opposed to how much time is delegated to procedural matters (for example, taking attendance, distributing handouts, collecting homework, checking for materials). All teachers need to prepare their students to learn and want them to enjoy learning. However, most researchers agree that student performance is higher in classrooms with teachers who spend the maximum amount of time available teaching

Table 1.4 Indicators for Teacher Task Orientation

Being Task Oriented (An effective teacher . . .)	Examples of Teaching Strategies
1. Develops unit and lesson plans that reflect the most relevant features of the curriculum guide or adopted text (e.g., each unit and lesson objective can be referenced back to the curriculum guide or text)	Key each lesson to a unit plan, the curriculum guide, and the text to test its relevance. Confer with other teachers concerning the most relevant portions of the text and curriculum guide.
2. Handles administrative and clerical interruptions efficiently (e.g., visitors, announcements, collection of money, dispensing of materials and supplies) by anticipating and organizing some tasks and deferring others to noninstructional time	Establish a five to ten minute restriction on how much time per every hour of instruction you will devote to noninstructional tasks. Defer all other tasks to before or after the lesson.
3. Stops or prevents misbehavior with a minimum of class disruption (e.g., has established academic and work rules to prevent intrusions into instructional time)	Establish rules for the most common misbehaviors, and post them conspicuously. Identify only the offender and offense during instructional time, deferring the consequence to later.
4. Selects the most appropriate instructional model for the objectives being taught (e.g., primarily uses direct instruction for knowledge and comprehension objectives and indirect instruction for inquiry and problem solving objectives)	Using your unit plan, curriculum guide, or adopted text, divide the content to be taught into (a) facts, rules, and action sequences, and (b) concepts, patterns, and abstractions. Generally, plan to use direct instruction for the former content and indirect instruction for the latter.
5. Builds to unit outcomes with clearly definable events (e.g., weekly and monthly review, feedback, and testing sessions)	Establish a schedule in which major classroom activities begin and end with clearly visible events (e.g., minor and major tests, review and feedback sessions).

subject specific content, as opposed to devoting large amounts of time to the process and materials needed to acquire that content. It follows that classrooms in which teacher–student interactions focus efficiently on subject matter content, which allows students the maximum opportunity to learn and to practice what was taught, are more likely to have higher rates of achievement. But these classrooms also are those in which the relationship between the teacher and learners provides the energy to motivate and challenge learners to reach increasingly higher levels of understanding (Berliner & Biddle, 1995; Brophy, 2002; Jones, Jones, Jones, & Jones, 2007; Tileston, 2010).

These topics are covered in Chapter 5, which prepares you to set goals and prepare objectives, and Chapter 6, which prepares you to execute them in your classroom with unit and lesson plans. Table 1.4 summarizes some of the indicators of a teacher's task orientation and the effective teaching strategies that are covered in these chapters.

Engagement in the Learning Process

Student engagement in the learning process, called **engaged learning time,** is a key behavior that refers to the amount of time students devote to learning in your classroom. Student engagement is related to but different from a teacher's task orientation. We learned in the previous section that a teacher's task orientation should provide students the greatest possible opportunity to learn and to practice the material being taught.

Distinct from your task orientation—or the amount of time you devote to teaching a topic—is the time your students are actively engaged in learning the material being taught. This has been called their *engagement rate,* or the percentage

An important key behavior for effective teaching is the variability or flexibility of delivery during the presentation of a lesson.

of time devoted to learning when your students are actually on task, attentive to, and engaged with the instructional materials, and benefiting from the activities being presented. Even though a teacher may be task oriented, providing maximum content coverage, the students may be disengaged. This means they are not actively thinking about, working with, or using what is being presented (Borich, 2008a; Borich & Tombari, 1997; Jones et al., 2007; Marx & Walsh, 1988; Riggs & Gholar, 2008).

Such disengagement can involve an emotional or mental detachment from the lesson that may or may not be obvious. When students jump out of their seats, talk, read a magazine, or leave for the restroom, they obviously are not engaged in instruction. Students also can be disengaged in far more subtle ways, such as looking attentive while their thoughts are many miles away. An unpleasant fact of life is that one-quarter of a class may be off task at any time, distracted for personal reasons that are often amplified by an impending lunch period, a Friday afternoon, or the day before a holiday. Correcting this type of disengagement may be difficult, requiring changes in the structure of the task itself and the cognitive demands being placed on the learner (Baum, Viens, & Slatin, 2005; Bennett & Desforges, 1988; Brophy, 1996; Doyle, 1983). Strategies for composing tasks and activities that elicit the active participation of your learners are presented in Chapters 8 through 12.

Several authors (Brophy, 2010; Evertson, 1995; Kuh, Kinzie, Smith, & Whitt, 2005; Meichenbaum & Biemiller, 1998; Tauber, 1990) have contributed useful suggestions for increasing learning time and, more importantly, student engagement during learning. Their work, updated by Emmer and Evertson (2012) and Evertson and Emmer (2012), provides the following suggestions for teachers for promoting student engagement:

1. Set rules that let pupils attend to their personal needs and work routines without obtaining your permission each time.

2. Move around the room to monitor pupils' seatwork and to communicate your awareness of students' progress.

3. Ensure that independent assignments are interesting, worthwhile, and easy enough to be completed by each pupil without your direction.

4. Minimize time-consuming activities, such as giving directions and organizing the class for instruction, by writing the daily schedule on the board. This will ensure that pupils know where to go and what to do.

5. Make abundant use of resources and activities that are at or slightly above a student's current level of understanding.

6. Avoid timing errors. Act promptly to prevent misbehaviors from occurring or increasing in severity so they do not influence others in the class.

These teaching practices have also been found to be beneficial for small groups and independent seatwork (Anderson, Stevens, Prawat, & Nickerson, 1988; Jones et al., 2007). These and other more specific ways of increasing your students' engagement rate are explored in Chapters 11 and 12 which cover strategies for self-directed learning and cooperative and collaborative learning. Table 1.5 summarizes some of the indicators of student engagement and effective teaching strategies covered in these chapters.

Student Success Rate

Our final key effective teaching behavior is student success rate. The term **student success rate** refers to the rate at which your students understand and correctly complete exercises and assignments.

A crucial aspect of the previously cited research on teacher task orientation and student engagement has been the level of difficulty of the material being presented. In some of these studies, level of difficulty was measured by the rate at which students understood and correctly answered questions on tests, exercises, and assignments. Three levels of difficulty are as follow:

- *High success.* The student understands the subject matter taught and makes only occasional careless errors.
- *Moderate success.* The student has partial understanding but makes some substantive errors.
- *Low success.* The student has little or no understanding of the subject matter.

Table 1.5 **Indicators for Engaging Students in the Learning Process**

Engaging Students Effectively in the Learning Process (An effective teacher . . .)	Examples of Teaching Strategies
1. Elicits the desired behavior immediately after the instructional stimuli (e.g., provides exercise or workbook problems to practice the desired behavior)	Schedule practice exercises or questions to immediately follow each set of instructional stimuli.
2. Provides opportunities for feedback in a nonevaluative atmosphere (e.g., asks students to respond as a group or covertly the first time through the material)	Require covert responding or nonevaluative (e.g., group) feedback at the start of a guided practice session.
3. Uses individual and group activities when needed (e.g., performance contracts, CD-ROMs, games and simulations, and learning centers as motivational aids)	Have individualized instructional materials available (e.g., remedial exercises or supplemental texts) for those students who may need them.
4. Uses meaningful verbal praise to get and keep students actively participating in the learning process	Maintain a warm and nurturing atmosphere by providing verbal praise and encouragement that is meaningful (e.g., explain why the answer was correct). Praise partially correct answers, with qualification.
5. Monitors seatwork and frequently checks progress during independent practice	Limit contact with individual students during seatwork to about 30 seconds each, providing instructionally relevant answers. Circulate among the entire class.

Not surprisingly, Berliner (1979), Good and Brophy (2007), Karweit and Slavin (1981), and Marzano, Pickering, and Heflebower (2010), found that student engagement—the time the learner is actively engaged with, thinking about, and working with the content being taught—was closely related to student success rate, as shown in Figure 1.4. Instruction that produces a moderate to high success rate results in increased performance because more content is covered at the learner's current level of understanding. This result was initially found for expository or didactic forms of instruction, with which learners are taught basic academic skills that are most easily learned through practice and repetition (Rosenshine, 1986). But more recent research has extended these findings to thinking skills instruction (Beyer, 1995) and project-based learning (Blumenfeld et al., 1991; Costa & Kallick, 2004a,b). Research has also shown that instruction promoting low error rates (high success) can contribute to increased levels of student self-esteem and positive attitudes toward the

Figure 1.4 **Levels of Time**

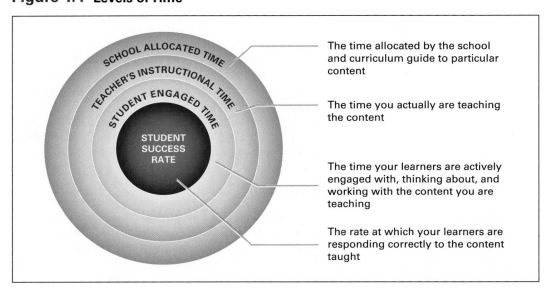

Table 1.6 Indicators for Student Success

Moderate to High Rates of Success (An effective teacher . . .)	Examples of Teaching Strategies
1. Establishes unit and lesson content that reflects prior learning (e.g., planning lesson sequences that consider task-relevant prior information)	Create a top-down unit plan, in which all the lesson outcomes at the bottom of the hierarchy that are needed to achieve unit outcomes at the top of the hierarchy are identified. Arrange lessons in the order most logical for achieving unit outcomes.
2. Administers correctives immediately after the initial response (e.g., shows a model of the correct answer and how to attain it after the first crude response is given)	Provide for guided practice prior to independent practice, and provide a means of self-checking (e.g., a handout with the correct answers) at intervals of practice.
3. Divides instructional stimuli into small chunks (e.g., establishes discrete, focused lessons that can be easily understood by learners at their current level of functioning)	Plan interdisciplinary thematic units to emphasize relationships and connections that are easily remembered.
4. Plans transitions to new material in easy to grasp steps (e.g., changes instructional stimuli according to an established thematic pattern so that each new lesson is seen as an extension of previous lessons)	Extend the unit plan hierarchy downward to more specific lessons that are tied together above with a single unit theme and outcome.
5. Varies the pace at which stimuli are presented and continually builds toward a climax or key event	Use review, feedback, and testing sessions to form intervals of increasing and decreasing intensity and expectation.

subject matter and the school (Brophy, 2010), which provide the motivation to move toward higher levels of achievement.

The average student in a typical classroom spends about half of the time working on tasks that provide the opportunity for high success. But researchers have found that students who spend more than the average time in high-success activities have higher achievement, better retention, and more positive attitudes toward school. These findings have led to the suggestion that students should spend about 60 percent to 70 percent of their time on tasks that allow almost complete understanding of the material being taught with only occasional errors (Brophy, 2002; Rosenshine, 1986).

Moderate to high success rates can produce mastery of lesson content. But they can also provide the foundation for your students to apply what they have learned and to reason, problem solve, and think critically and independently about the content (Chaffee, 2010; Duffy & Roehler, 1989; Meichenbaum & Biemiller, 1998; Rohrkemper & Corno, 1988). Many teachers devote insufficient time to this stage of learning, which is particularly crucial for attaining the goals of problem solving and critical thinking. A key activity for the effective teacher is organizing and planning instruction that yields moderate to high success rates but then challenges learners to go beyond the information given to construct their own understandings and meanings from lesson content.

We will learn more about this approach to learning, called *constructivism* (Chaille, 2007; Fosnot, 2005; Richardson, 1997), in this chapter and Chapters 10 and 11. Table 1.6 summarizes some of the indicators of student success and the teaching strategies covered in these chapters.

Summary of Five Key Behaviors

All five key behaviors—lesson clarity, instructional variety, teacher task orientation, student engagement, and success rate—are essential for effective teaching. Classroom researchers continue to study other effective teaching behaviors and to attain a more thorough understanding of those already described. However, for the first time, research has provided a basis for more clearly defining effective teaching and for training teachers. These five behaviors are the skeleton of the effective teacher, and the remainder of this text will use these to construct the heart and the mind of an effective teacher.

You learned earlier there is no simple answer to the question, "What is an effective teacher?" Many activities must be orchestrated into patterns of behavior for your teaching to be effective. The identification of only five behaviors makes teaching appear deceptively simple. However, as you will see in the following section, your success in implementing these five key behaviors in your classroom will be assisted by other helping behaviors.

Some Helping Behaviors Related to Effective Teaching

To complete our picture of an effective teacher, you will also need to know about some behaviors that can help you implement the five key behaviors in your classroom. These can be thought of as helping behaviors for performing the five key behaviors.

Research findings for helping behaviors, although promising, are not as strong and consistent as those that identified the five key behaviors. This is why helping behaviors need to be employed in the context of other behaviors to be effective, making them catalysts rather than agents by themselves (Marzano, Pickering, & Pollock, 2004; Saunders, 2005). Among these helping behaviors are the following:

1. Using student ideas and contributions
2. Structuring lesson content
3. Questioning
4. Probing
5. Teacher affect (developing the teacher–learner relationship)

Using Student Ideas and Contributions

Using student ideas and contributions is a behavior that includes acknowledging, modifying, applying, comparing, and summarizing student responses to promote the goals of a lesson and encourage student participation. Note how any one of these activities (Flanders, 1970) could be used to achieve one or more of the five key behaviors:

- *Acknowledging:* Taking a student's correct response and repeating it to the class (to increase lesson clarity)
- *Modifying:* Using a student's idea by rephrasing it or conceptualizing it in your words or another student's words (to create instructional variety)
- *Applying:* Using a student's idea to teach an inference or take the next step in a logical analysis of a problem (to increase success rate)
- *Comparing:* Taking a student's idea and drawing a relationship between it and ideas expressed earlier by the student or another student (to encourage engagement in the learning process)
- *Summarizing:* Using what was said by a student or a group of students as a recapitulation or review of concepts taught (to enhance task orientation)

More recently, the use of student ideas and student contributions has been extended to reasoning, problem solving, and independent thinking. This has been achieved through **teacher-mediated dialogue** that helps learners restructure what is being learned using their own ideas, experiences, and thought patterns. Teacher-mediated dialogue asks learners not just to respond with a correct answer but also to internalize the meaning of what was learned by elaborating, extending, and commenting on it using their own thoughts. In this manner, learners are encouraged to communicate the processes by which they are learning, thereby helping them to construct their own meanings and understandings of the content (Chaille, 2007; Fosnot, 2005; Henson, 2009; Phillips, 2000;

Richardson, 1997). We will present strategies for constructivist teaching and teacher-mediated dialogue in Chapters 10 and 11.

Use of student ideas and contributions also can increase a student's engagement in the learning process. Thus it has become a frequently used catalyst for helping achieve that key behavior (Emmer & Evertson, 2012; Evertson & Emmer, 2012). Consider this brief instructional dialogue, which uses student ideas to promote engagement:

> *Teacher:* Tom, what is the formula for the Pythagorean theorem?
>
> *Tom:* $c^2 = a^2 + b^2$.

At this point, the teacher simply could have said "Good!" and gone on to the next question. Instead, the teacher continues:

> *Teacher:* Let's show that on the board. Here is a triangle; now let's do exactly as Tom said. He said that squaring the altitude, which is *a,* and adding it to the square of the base, which is *b,* should give us the square of the hypotenuse, which is *c.* Carl, would you like to come up and show us how you would find the length of *c,* using the formula Tom just gave us?
>
> *Carl:* Well if *a* were equal to three and *b* equal to four, the way I would solve this problem would be to add the squares of both of them together and then find the square root—that would be *c.*
>
> *Teacher:* So, we square the three, square the four, add them together, and take the square root. This gives us five, the length of the hypotenuse.

Which of the five ways of using student ideas are in this dialogue? First, by putting Tom's response graphically on the board, this teacher applies Tom's answer by taking it to the next step, constructing a proof. Second, by repeating orally what Tom said, the teacher acknowledges to the entire class the value of Tom's contribution. And third, by having another student prove the correctness of Tom's response, a summary of the concept is provided. All this is accomplished from Tom's simple (and only) utterance: $c^2 = a^2 + b^2$.

Research indicates that student ideas and contributions, especially when used in the context of the naturally occurring dialogue of the classroom, are more strongly and consistently related to student engagement than simply approving a student's answer with "Good!" (Brophy, 2010; Good & Brophy, 2007). The standard phrases we use to acknowledge and reward students ("Correct," "Good," "Right") are so overused that they may not always convey the reward intended.

Although the use of student ideas looks simple, it takes skill and planning. Even when you have not planned your response, you should be prepared to seize opportunities to incorporate student ideas and contributions into your lesson.

Structuring Lesson Content

Teacher comments made for the purpose of organizing what is to come or summarizing what has gone before are called *structuring.* Used before an instructional activity or question, structuring assists learners in bridging the gap between what they are capable of doing on their own and what they are capable of doing with help from the teacher, thereby aiding their understanding and use of the material to be taught. Used at the conclusion of an instructional activity or question, structuring reinforces learned content and places it in proper relation to other content already taught. Both forms of structuring are related to student achievement and serve as effective catalysts for performing the five key behaviors (Meichenbaum & Biemiller, 1998; Rogoff, 1990; Rosenshine & Meister, 1992; Wormeli, 2004).

Typically, before and after structuring takes the following form:

> *Teacher:* [At beginning of lesson] OK, now that we have studied how the pipefish change their color and movements to blend in with their surroundings, we will study how the pipefish gathers its food. Most important, we will learn how the pipefish grow and provide the means for other fish, like the kind we eat for food, to flourish deep below the ocean's surface.

Teacher: [At end of lesson] So we have discovered that the pipefish protects itself by changing colors to blend in with plants on the ocean's floor and by swaying back and forth to fool its enemies. We might conclude from this that the pipefish evade rather than capture their natural enemies and feed close to the ocean's floor, where they can't be noticed. Can you think of when this clever strategy might not work, making the pipefish prey to other fish deep below the ocean's surface? (Palincsar & Brown, 1989)

This sequence illustrates some of the many ways you can use structuring. One way is to *signal* that a shift in direction or content is about to occur. A clear signal alerts students to the impending change. Without such a signal, students may confuse new content with old, missing the differences. Signals such as "Now that we have studied how the pipefish change their color and movements, . . . we will learn . . ." help students switch gears and provide a perspective that makes new content more meaningful.

Another type of structuring uses *emphasis*. Can you find a point of emphasis in the previous dialogue? By using the phrase "Most important," this teacher alerts students to the knowledge and understanding expected at the conclusion of this activity. This structuring helps the student to organize what is to follow, called an *advance organizer*.

In this instance, the students are clued to consider the factors that extend beyond the color and movement of the pipefish to include how they grow and provide the means for other fish to flourish. This makes the teacher's final question more meaningful ("Can you think of when this clever strategy might not work, making the pipefish prey to other fish deep below the ocean's surface?"). The students have been clued that such a question might be raised and that generalizations beyond the concepts discussed will be expected. Phrases such as "Now this is important," "We will return to this point later," and "Remember this" are called *verbal markers*. They can be used to emphasize your most important points.

In addition to verbal markers and advance organizers, the effective teacher organizes a lesson into an activity structure. An *activity structure* is a set of related tasks that differ in cognitive complexity and that, to some degree, may be placed under the control of the learner. Activity structures can be built in many ways (for example, cooperatively, competitively, independently) to vary the cognitive demands they make on the learner and to give tempo and momentum to a lesson. For the effective teacher, they are an important means for engaging students in the learning process and moving them from simple recall of facts to the higher response levels that require reasoning, critical thinking, and problem solving behavior.

Questioning

Questioning is another important helping behavior. Few other topics have been researched as much as the teacher's use of questions (Dantonio & Beisenherz, 2000; Falk & Blumenreich, 2005; Lewin, 2009; Power & Hubbard, 1999). One of the most important outcomes of research on questioning has been the distinction between *content questions* and *process questions*.

Content Questions.   Teachers pose content questions to have the student deal directly with the content taught. An example is when a teacher asks a question to see whether students can recall and understand specific material. The correct answer is known well in advance by the teacher. It also has been conveyed directly in class, in the text, or both. Few if any interpretations or alternative meanings of the question are possible.

Researchers have used various terms to describe content questions, such as the following:

Types of Content Questions

- *Direct:* The question requires no interpretation or alternative meanings.
  Example: What is the meaning of the word *ancient* in the story just read?

- *Lower order:* The question requires the recall only of readily available facts, as opposed to generalizations and inferences.
  Example: What was the mechanical breakthrough that gave the cotton gin superiority over all previous machines of its type?

- *Convergent:* Different data sources lead to the same answer.
  Example: What is one of the chemical elements in the air we breathe?

- *Closed:* The question has no possible alternative answers or interpretations.
  Example: What is the function of the central processing unit, or CPU, in a computer?
- *Fact:* The question requires the recall only of discrete pieces of well-accepted knowledge.
  Example: What is the result of dividing the number 47 by 6?

Some estimates have suggested that up to 80 percent of the questions teachers ask refer directly to specific content and have readily discernible and unambiguous correct answers (Gall & Gall, 1990). Perhaps even more important is the fact that approximately the same percentage of teacher made test items (and behavioral objectives) are written at the level of recall, knowledge, or fact (Borich & Tombari, 1997, 2004). Therefore, test items, behavioral objectives, and most instruction seem to emphasize readily known facts as they are presented in curriculum guides, workbooks, and texts, leaving much less time for encouraging higher-order thinking, such as problem solving, decision making, and valuing.

The art of questioning will become one of your most important skills as a teacher. The variety you convey to your students will be determined in large measure by your flexible use of questions. Asking questions is rarely an end in itself but rather a means of engaging students in the learning process by getting them to act on, work through, or think about the material presented.

Process Questions.   From the previous discussion, you can see why not all questions should be content questions. There are different purposes for which questions can be asked, with the intent of encouraging different mental processes. To problem solve, to guide, to arouse curiosity, to encourage creativity, to analyze, to synthesize, and to judge also are goals of instruction that should be reflected in your questioning strategies. For these purposes, learning content is not a goal by itself but a means of achieving higher-order goals.

Researchers have used various terms to describe process questions, such as the following:

Types of Process Questions

- *Indirect:* The question has various possible interpretations and alternative meanings.
  Example: What are some of the ways you have used the word *ancient*?

- *Higher order:* The question requires more complex mental processes than simple recall of facts (e.g., making generalizations and inferences).
  Example: What were the effects of the invention of the cotton gin on attitudes in the North?

- *Divergent:* Different data sources will lead to different correct answers.
  Example: From what we know about the many forms of pollution today, what would be one of the first things we have to do to clean the air we breathe?

- *Open:* A single correct answer is not expected or even possible.
  Example: How have recent advances in computer technology influenced your life?

- *Concept:* The question requires the processes of abstraction, generalization, and inference.
  Example: Using examples of your own choosing, what are some of the ways division and subtraction are similar?

Can you see the difference between this set of process questions and the set of content questions that preceded it? Notice that the process questions encourage more thinking and problem solving by requiring the learner to use personal sources of knowledge to actively construct her or his own interpretations and meanings, rather than acquiring understanding by giving back knowledge already organized in the form in which it was told.

As we saw earlier, this view of teaching and learning represents a movement in education called *constructivism.* **Constructivist teaching strategies** emphasize the learner's direct experience and the dialogue of the classroom as instructional tools while deemphasizing lecturing and telling (Chaille, 2007; Fosnot, 2005; Henson, 2009; Phillips, 2000; Richardson, 1997). See In Practice: Focus on Constructivism.

In Practice

Focus on Constructivism

Constructivism is a philosophy of learning that explains how people come to understand or know. In the late 1980s and early 1990s, many psychologists began to turn their attention to the constructivist view of learning, which assumes that learning is an active process in which learners internally construct knowledge from interactions with their physical and social environments. Constructivists believe that many of the things we know are influenced by context and prior experiences. Conceptual growth, from a constructivist perspective, results from sharing multiple perspectives and refining our interpretations in response to other perspectives.

Constructivists focus on engaging learners in richly textured contexts that are reflective of the natural environment. In such an environment, learners have opportunities to negotiate meanings and collaborate with each other. As a result, learners gain exposure to multiple perspectives and have opportunities to actively construct, refine, and take ownership of what they see and the meanings they derive from it. The knowledge constructed from this context is complex, personal, and insightful, which more easily allows learners to transfer it beyond textbook and classroom. By being able to construct meaning for themselves, students take ownership of their learning and teachers serve as facilitators who help students grow. Teachers are no longer information transmitters; instead, they provide guidance and scaffolding with which students can discover knowledge for themselves. In a constructivist learning environment, teachers promote a learning climate and context that extends students' experiences and interests, thus providing students with the opportunity to see multiple perspectives and develop their own understandings.

Savery and Duffy (1995) identify three essential attributes of constructivism:

1. Cognitive conflict or confusion is the stimulus for learning and influences the reorganization and nature of what is learned. According to Dewey (1938), it is the problem that leads to and is the organizer for learning, and according to Piaget (1977), it leads to a need for accommodation when the current experience cannot be assimilated into the learner's existing schema.

> Constructivism plays a significant role in student-centered teaching. The teacher in this **video** uses a variety of techniques aligned with constructivism.

2. Knowledge evolves through negotiation and contributing to how reality is constructed for each individual. Collaborative groups are important because learners can test their own understanding and examine the understanding and viewpoints of others.

3. Understanding comes from one's interactions with the environment. Cognition is not only within the individual but also comes from perceptions and experiences that are distributed across the entire context in which the learner is situated.

By examining the perspectives of constructivism, we can recognize that learning is an ongoing and active process and inquiry is an appropriate vehicle for facilitating the cognitively based constructivist approach to learning. In an inquiry based learning environment, students are engaged in a hands-on, subject related questioning, problem solving, or investigation, during which they observe, question, and gather information to test their understanding in an ongoing and active process (Henson, 2009; Chaille, 2007; Llewellyn, 2002).

Process questions and the use of probes, our next helping behavior, are important aids in constructivist thinking and activities in the classroom. We will have more to say about the role of direct experience and the use of constructivist strategies in the classroom in the chapters ahead, especially Chapters 10 and 11.

Probing

Another helping behavior is *probing,* which refers to teacher statements that encourage students to elaborate on an answer—either their own or another student's. Probing may take the form of a general question or can include other expressions that *elicit* clarification of an answer, *solicit* additional information about a response, or *redirect* a student's response in a more fruitful direction. Probing often is used to shift a discussion to some higher thought level.

Constructivist teaching strategies emphasize the learner's direct experience and the dialogue of the classroom as instructional tools.

Generally, student achievement is highest when the eliciting, soliciting, and (if necessary) redirecting occur in cycles. This systematically leads the discussion to a higher level of complexity, as when interrelationships, generalizations, and problem solutions are being sought. In this manner, you may begin a lesson with a simple fact question; then by eliciting clarification of student responses, soliciting new information, or redirecting an answer, you can move to a higher level of questioning.

A typical cycle might occur in the following manner:

Teacher:　Bobby, what is a scientific experiment?

Bobby:　Well, it's when you test something.

Teacher:　But what do you test? [Elicit]

Bobby:　Mmm, something you believe in and want to find out if it's really true.

Teacher:　What do you mean by that? [Solicit]

Mary:　He means you make a prediction.

Teacher:　What's another word for *prediction*? [Redirect]

Tom:　Hypothesis. You make a hypothesis and then go into the laboratory to see if it comes true.

Now find the teacher's soliciting, eliciting, and redirecting behaviors in the remainder of the dialogue:

Teacher:　OK. So a scientist makes a prediction or hypothesis and follows up with an experiment to see if it can be made to come true. Then what?

Billy:　That's the end!

Teacher:　[No comment for ten seconds; then discussion continues.] Is the laboratory like the real world?

David:　The scientist tries to make it like the real world, but it's much smaller, like the greenhouse pictured in our book.

Teacher:　So what must the scientist do with the findings from the experiment, if they are to be useful? [No one answers, so the teacher continues.] If something important happens in my experiment, wouldn't I argue that what happened could also happen in the real world?

Bobby:　You mean, if it's true in a specific situation, it will also be true in a more general situation?

Betty Jo:　That's making a generalization.

Teacher:　Good. So we see that a scientific investigation usually ends with a generalization. Let's summarize. What three things does a scientific investigation require?

Class:　A prediction, an experiment, and a generalization.

Teacher:　Good work, class.

Notice that all of the ingredients in this teacher's lesson were provided by the class. The concepts of hypothesis, experiment, and generalization were never defined for the class. The students defined these concepts for themselves with only an occasional "OK" or "Good" from the teacher to let them know they were on track. The teacher's role was limited to *eliciting* clarification, *soliciting* additional information, and *redirecting* the discussion. The purpose of this cycle of eliciting, soliciting, and redirecting is to promote inquiry and independent discovery of the content of the lesson. Generally, retention of material learned has been shown to be greater from inquiry teaching than from formal lecturing methods (Conant and Carin, 2008; Llewllyn, 2002; Paul, 1990).

Teacher Affect

Anyone who has ever been in a classroom where the teacher's presentation was lifeless, static, and without vocal variety can appreciate the commonsense value of the affective side of teaching. However, unlike the behaviors discussed previously, affect cannot be captured in transcripts of teaching or by classroom interaction instruments. Narrowly focused research instruments often miss a teacher's affective nature, which emerges from a more holistic view of the classroom. This affective nature is the foundation on which you can build a warm and nurturing relationship with your learners.

Effective teachers provide a warm and encouraging classroom climate by letting students know help is available.

What the instruments miss, the students see clearly. Students are good perceivers of the emotions and intentions underlying a teacher's actions, and they often respond accordingly. A teacher who is excited about the subject being taught and shows it by facial expression, voice inflection, gesture, and movement—thus communicating respect and caring for the learner—is more likely to hold the attention of students and motivate them to higher levels of achievement than one who does not exhibit these behaviors.

Students take their cues from these affective signs and lower or heighten their engagement with the lesson accordingly. Enthusiasm is an important aspect of a teacher's affect. *Enthusiasm* is the teacher's vigor, power, involvement, excitement, and interest during a classroom presentation and willingness to share this emotion with learners, who will want to respond in kind. We know from experience that enthusiasm is contagious. It can be displayed to your students in many ways, the most common being vocal inflection, gesture, eye contact, and animation. Most important, however, is how you coordinate these signs to communicate that you care about and respect the experiences, knowledge, and understandings your students bring to the classroom. Research has found a teacher's enthusiasm to be related to student achievement (Bettencourt, Gillett, Gall, & Hull, 1983; Cabello & Terrell, 1994; Tischler, 2005). And as noted earlier, teachers' enthusiasm is believed to be important in promoting student engagement as well as achievement (Kuh, Kinzie, Smith, & Whitt, 2005).

Obviously, no one can maintain a heightened state of enthusiasm for very long without becoming exhausted emotionally. Nor is this what is meant by the word *enthusiasm*. A proper level of enthusiasm is far more subtle, and perhaps that is why it has been so difficult to research. A proper level of enthusiasm involves a delicate balance of vocal inflection, gesturing, eye contact, and movement. In combination, these behaviors send to students a unified signal of vigor, involvement, and interest that conveys the message that you care. Timing and the ability to incorporate these behaviors into a consistent pattern make possible an unspoken behavioral dialogue with your students that is every bit as important as your spoken words.

Teaching Effectively with Diverse Learners and Content

Researchers have also uncovered behaviors of special importance to specific types of students and content. The two areas of findings that have had the most consistent results are these:

1. Teaching behaviors that affect learners of lower and higher socioeconomic status
2. Teaching behaviors that affect the teaching of reading and mathematics

How Does Effective Teaching Differ among Learners Who Have Different Socioeconomic Levels, Cultures, and Ethnicities?

Diversity plays a major role in how to prepare lessons effectively. This **video** discusses some strategies to meet the needs of diverse learners.

The term **socioeconomic status (SES)** can mean different things, but generally, it is an approximate index of one's income and education level. For the classroom researcher, the SES of students is determined directly by the income and education of their parents or indirectly by the nature of the school the students attend. For example, a school in which a high percentage of students qualify for a nationally sponsored free or reduced price lunch program due to the income level of their parents may be considered a lower-SES school.

Some schools are in impoverished areas, where the overall income and education levels of the community are low, whereas other schools are located in more affluent communities. Many schools in impoverished areas qualify for special financial assistance from the federal government, based on the median income of the students' parents. These schools are called *Title I* schools, and the majority of their students come from lower-SES homes and may be disadvantaged, at risk of school failure, have limited English proficiency, and/or belong to a cultural or ethnic minority. In our nation's 25 largest cities, SES is strongly tied to culture or ethnicity.

Because the conditions to which lower- and higher-SES students are tied, such as access to books, computers and other resources in the home, they are likely to exist for some time. Classroom researchers have studied the teacher practices that promote the most achievement in these different settings. Researchers such as Arizsa, 2010, Bowers and Flinders (1991), Dilworth and Brown (2001), Good and Brophy (2007), Kennedy (1991), Hoover (2011), McNary, Glasgow, and Hicks (2005), and Nieto and Bode (2012) have provided suggestions for teaching these student populations, while the research of others has helped teachers understand the learning needs of these and other special populations (Delpit & Dowdy, 2008; Diaz-Rico, 2012; Egbert & Ernst-Slavit, 2010; Echevarria & Graves, 2011). Some important teaching behaviors to emphasize for higher- and lower-SES learners are summarized in Table 1.7.

Notice in the table that, although each behavior is applicable to both lower- and higher-SES students, teacher affect is particularly important in lower-SES classrooms. Also notice that some of these teaching behaviors received little or no mention in our preceding discussions, because those discussions applied to students generally. Four of the behaviors shown for lower-SES classrooms (student responses, content organization, classroom instruction, and individualization) can be seen as special ways of creating student engagement at high rates of success for these learners. This presents a particular challenge when teaching lower-SES students who may lack some of the learning resources in the home available to higher-SES students and may be at risk of school failure.

Also, frequently correcting wrong answers in the absence of support or encouragement could be construed more often as a personal criticism by lower-SES students, who may already have a poor self-concept, than by higher-SES students. Therefore, feedback that could be construed as personal criticism would need to be provided in a consistently supportive and encouraging context (Brookhart, 2008).

Because much of the research on SES has been conducted in elementary classrooms, it is as yet uncertain to what extent the teaching practices in Table 1.7 apply to secondary classrooms. However, many of the learning characteristics of higher-SES and lower-SES students appear to be similar across grade levels. Your success as a teacher in a predominantly lower-SES or higher-SES classroom will therefore depend on your ability to vary the extent to which you emphasize the behaviors in Table 1.7.

How Does Effective Teaching Differ across Content Areas?

Another set of findings pertains to the different teaching behaviors that distinguish reading and language arts from basic mathematics instruction (Ball, Lubienski, & Mewborn, 2001; Barr, 2001; Kaplan, Rogers, & Webster, 2008). Although not all teachers will teach either reading or

Table 1.7 Important Teaching Behaviors for Lower-SES and Higher-SES Students

Teaching Behaviors	Examples
Helping Lower-SES Populations Achieve Success	
Teacher affect	Provide a warm and encouraging classroom climate by consistently letting students know help is available.
Student responses	Encourage an initial response from one student before moving to the next student.
Content organization	Present material with the opportunity to practice what has been learned immediately afterward.
	Show how related pieces of information fit together and are to be applied before beginning each new segment of instruction.
Classroom instruction	Emphasize applications before teaching patterns and abstractions. Present the most concrete material first.
	Monitor each student's progress at regular intervals. Use progress charts to help record learner improvement.
	Help students who need help immediately. Use peer and cross-age tutors, if necessary.
	Maintain the structure and flow between activities to maintain momentum. Organize and plan transitions in advance.
Individualization	Supplement the standard curriculum with specialized materials to meet the needs of individual students.
	Emphasize the importance of students' personal experiences to promote interest and attention.
Helping Higher-SES Populations Achieve Success	
Correcting	Check right answers by requiring extended oral or written reasoning.
Thinking and decision making	Supplement the curriculum with individualized material, some of which is slightly above students' current level of attainment.
	Assign homework and/or extended projects that require students to obtain original sources of information from outside the classroom.
Classroom interaction	Encourage student-to-student and student-to-teacher interactions in which students take responsibility for evaluating their own learning.
Verbal activities	Consistently engage students in verbal questions and answers that go beyond the text and workbook content.

Source: Based on information from Bowers and Flinders (1991); Good and Brophy (2007); Hill (1989); Irvine and York (2001); Kennedy (1991); Knapp and Woolverton (2001); Levine and Lezotte (2001); Nieto and Bode (2012); McNary, Glasgow, and Hicks (2005).

mathematics, this set of findings may be generalized to some extent to other types of content that are similar in form and structure.

For example, social studies, history, and language instruction all involve high reading content and share some of the same problem solving features as reading. General science, biology, physics, and chemistry are similar to the science of mathematics in that concepts, principles, and laws play a prominent role. Also, visual forms and symbolic expressions are at least as important in understanding scientific subjects as is the written word. Therefore, some cautious generalizations can be made about the teaching practices that are important for reading and basic mathematics instruction and subjects similar to each.

Some important findings are summarized in Table 1.8. Notice the two different approaches implied by the practices listed. For basic mathematics instruction, at first a formal, direct approach

Table 1.8 Important Teaching Behaviors for Reading and Mathematics Instruction

Teaching Behaviors	Examples
Findings for Reading Instruction	
Instructional activity	Devote sufficient time during reading instruction to discussing, explaining, and questioning to stimulate cognitive processes and promote learner responses.
Interactive technique	Use cues and questions that require every student to attempt a response during reading instruction.
Questions	Pose thought-provoking questions during reading instruction that require the student to predict, question, summarize, and clarify what he or she has read.
Findings for Basic Mathematics Instruction	
Instructional materials	Use application- and experience-oriented activities and media during mathematics instruction to foster task persistence.
Instructional content	Maximize coverage of instructional applications during mathematics instruction through the use of activity sheets, handouts, and problem sets at graduated levels of difficulty.
Instructional organization	Initially, emphasize full-class or large-group instruction during mathematics instruction. Gradually, transition to less guided and independent work, when it does not interfere with on-task behavior and learner persistence.

Source: Based on information from Akhavan (2008); Carpenter, Dossey, and Koehler (2004); English (2002); Grouws (1992); Kilpatrick, Martin, and Schifter (2003); National Council of Teachers of English (1996); Ronis (2007); and Stone (2007).

appears to be most effective. This approach includes maintaining structure through close adherence to texts, workbooks, and application oriented activities. This approach also maximizes instructional coverage by minimizing unstructured work that could diminish engaged learning time. In contrast, reading instruction allows for a more interactive and indirect approach, using more classroom discussions and experience oriented questions and answers.

These approaches are not mutually exclusive, however. What the research shows is that at first a more direct approach during basic mathematics instruction tends to result in greater student progress than would, say, the exclusive use of an inquiry approach. For reading, the reverse appears to be true: At first an exploratory, interactive approach, which encourages the use of classroom dialogue and student ideas, tends to result in greater student progress over time.

These different approaches represent degrees of emphasis, not exclusive practices. Clearly, teaching the basics of mathematics will at times require an inquiry approach, just as reading sometimes requires a presentation or telling approach. More important than either of these approaches, along with the practices in Tables 1.7 and 1.8 that represent them, is the ability of the teacher to be flexible. From these research studies, the message is clear: There are not only effective and ineffective ways to teach, but the effectiveness of any method will likely depend on the content being taught and the learners to whom it is being taught. The effective teacher is sensitive to when a change from one emphasis to another is necessary, regardless of the content or learner being taught.

The Complexity of Teaching

At this point, you might think an effective teacher simply is one who has mastered all of the key behaviors and helping behaviors. But teaching involves more than knowledge of how to perform individual behaviors. Much like an artist, who blends color and texture into a painting to produce a coherent impression, so must an effective teacher blend individual behaviors into teaching practices that promote student achievement. Teaching practices are larger than individual teaching behaviors that blend key and helping behaviors in different degrees. To be effective requires the orchestration and integration of the key and helping behaviors into meaningful patterns and rhythms that can achieve the goals of instruction within your classroom.

The truly effective teacher, then, knows how to execute individual behaviors with a larger purpose in mind. This larger purpose requires placing behaviors in sequences and patterns that accumulate to create an effect greater than can be achieved by any single behavior or small set of behaviors. This is why teaching involves a sense of timing and pacing that cannot be conveyed by any list of behaviors. The interrelationships among these behaviors, giving each its proper emphasis in the context of your classroom, are important to the effective teacher. And it is the combination of curriculum, learning objectives, instructional materials, and learners that provides the context for the proper blend. We will have more to say about these patterns of teaching effectiveness in the chapters ahead.

Professional Teaching Standards

The effective teaching methods described in this book draw on more than 30 years of research on effective teaching and on national and state standards for the teaching profession that have been closely aligned with current views of how and what students and teachers should learn.

For decades, American teaching reflected a direct instruction model. Teachers were expected to present or transmit knowledge to students, who were expected to receive, store, and return that knowledge upon request (Weiss & Weiss, 1998). Many researchers and educators have challenged this view, suggesting that learners do not simply receive knowledge; rather, they actively construct knowledge through interacting with the social, cultural, and linguistic context in which an experience occurs (Chaille, 2007; Fosnot, 2005; Henson, 2009; Nieto & Bode, 2012; Phillips, 2000; Richardson, 1997). Effective teachers function as able facilitators, coaches, and guides for students' knowledge-building processes. In other words, students can and should be taught to become agents of their own learning.

Reflecting this more interactive view of teaching, the National Board for Professional Teaching Standards (NBPTS) was formed in 1987 with the goal of achieving three major outcomes:

1. To establish high and rigorous standards for what effective teachers should know and be able to do
2. To develop and operate a national, voluntary system to assess and certify teachers who meet these standards
3. To advance related education reforms for the purpose of improving student learning in American schools

Governed by a board of directors, the majority of whom are classroom teachers, the NBPTS (2001) lists five propositions essential to accomplished teaching:

1. Teachers are committed to students and their learning.
2. Teachers know the subjects they teach and how to teach those subjects to students.
3. Teachers are responsible for managing and mentoring student learning.
4. Teachers think systematically about their practice and learn from experience.
5. Teachers are members of learning communities.

During the same year that the NBPTS was formed (1987), the Interstate New Teacher Assessment and Support Consortium (InTASC) was formed to create standards that could be reviewed by professional organizations and state agencies as a basis for licensing beginning teachers. The **InTASC standards** (Miller, 1992) were written as ten principles, which were then further described in terms of teacher knowledge, dispositions, and performances—in other words, what a beginning teacher should know and be able to do.

In 2011 the Council of Chief State School Officers (CCSSO) updated the InTASC Core Teaching Standards making them applicable to the growth and development of all, not just beginning, teachers. These updated standards were also written to be compatible with the Common Core

State Standards for students in math and English language arts, thereby providing a single coherent system by which teachers can be prepared, supported, and licensed.

Because you will probably work with the InTASC standards during your professional development program (and perhaps with the NBPTS standards for advanced certification later in your career), this text discusses research based practices used by effective teachers to achieve the InTASC and NBPTS standards. At the end of each chapter are test preparation exercises aligned with these standards to help you prepare for licensure examination. The end-of-chapter case histories and web based self-assessments on MyEducationLab provide a targeted rehearsal preparing you for the level of pedagogical knowledge that may be expected of you at the end of your teacher preparation program and for teacher certification and licensing.

The following sections outline the ten InTASC standards, each tagged with the chapters and appendices in this text that will provide you with the effective teaching methods for attaining them.

The Learner and Learning

Standard #1: Learner Development. The teacher understands how learners grow and develop, recognizing that patterns of learning and development vary individually within and across the cognitive, linguistic, social, emotional, and physical areas, and designs and implements developmentally appropriate and challenging learning experiences. [Chapters 2, 6, 7, 11]

Standard #2: Learning Differences. The teacher uses understanding of individual differences and diverse cultures and communities to ensure inclusive learning environments that enable each learner to meet high standards. [Chapters 1, 2, 11, 12]

Standard #3: Learning Environments. The teacher works with others to create environments that support individual and collaborative learning, and that encourage positive social interaction, active engagement in learning, and self-motivation. [Chapters 3, 7, 8, 10, 11]

Content Knowledge

Standard #4: Content Knowledge. The teacher understands the central concepts, tools of inquiry, and structures of the discipline(s) he or she teaches and creates learning experiences that make the discipline accessible and meaningful for learners to assure mastery of the content. [Chapters 5, 6, 9, 13]

Standard #5: Application of Content. The teacher understands how to connect concepts and use differing perspectives to engage learners in critical thinking, creativity, and collaborative problem solving related to authentic local and global issues. [Chapters 1, 2, 10, 12]

Instructional Practice

Standard #6: Assessment. The teacher understands and uses multiple methods of assessment to engage learners in their own growth, to monitor learner progress, and to guide the teacher's and learner's decision making. [Chapters 5, 6, 13]

Standard #7: Planning for Instruction. The teacher plans instruction that supports every student in meeting rigorous learning goals by drawing upon knowledge of content areas, curriculum, cross-disciplinary skills, and pedagogy, as well as knowledge of learners and the community context. [Chapters 2, 5, 6 , 7]

Standard #8: Instructional Strategies. The teacher understands and uses a variety of instructional strategies to encourage learners to develop deep understanding of content areas and their connections, and to build skills to apply knowledge in meaningful ways. [Chapters 8, 9, 10, 11, 12]

Professional Responsibility

Standard #9: Professional Learning and Ethical Practice. The teacher engages in ongoing professional learning and uses evidence to continually evaluate his/her practice, particularly the effects of his/her choices and actions on others (learners, families, other professionals, and the community), and adapts practice to meet the needs of each learner. [Chapters 1, 2, 4, 6]

Standard #10: Leadership and Collaboration. The teacher seeks appropriate leadership roles and opportunities to take responsibility for student learning, to collaborate with learners, families, colleagues, other school professionals, and community members to ensure learner growth, and to advance the profession. [Chapters 2, 3, 4, 13]

Each standard is accompanied by specific professional attitudes and dispositions that can assure its smooth and seamless application. For example, the teacher is expected to implement Standard 2, Learning Differences, in the context of the belief or disposition that all children can learn at high levels, that diverse family backgrounds and the abilities and interests of all learners are to be respected and integrated into instructional practice to better engage students in the learning process.

The above standards will be an important guide for you in preparing for exit tests for your teacher preparation program and licensure, such as the Praxis Series: Professional Assessments for Beginning Teachers (www.ets.org/praxis) (see Figure 1.5). The Praxis II examines your understanding of human growth and development, classroom management, instructional design

Figure 1.5 About the Praxis

The Praxis™ Series: Professional Assessments for Beginning Teachers is a set of validated assessments that provide information to colleges, state education agencies, and school districts for graduation, licensing, and hiring decisions. In addition, colleges and universities may use the basic academic skills component of the Praxis Series to qualify individuals for entry into teacher education programs.

The three areas of assessment in the Praxis Series are addressed as follows:

1. For entering a teacher training program: Praxis I: Pre-Professional Skills Tests
2. For licensure into the teaching profession: Praxis II: Subject Assessments
3. For the first year of teaching: Praxis III: Teacher Performance Assessments

The Praxis I: Pre-Professional Skills Tests measure basic skills in reading, writing, and math. The assessments serve as an opportunity for those seeking teacher training to demonstrate competence with the academic skills needed for a career in education. The test for each skill domain is 1 hour in duration and questions are in multiple-choice format, with the exception of the writing test which includes an essay section.

The Praxis II: Subjects Assessments include specialty area tests in over 120 subject areas taught in grades PreK-12 designed to assess content knowledge at the end of your teacher preparation program in the areas for which you are being trained and licensed to teach. The number and content of the tests taken are indicated by the subject areas and/or grade levels for which you wish to receive certification and determined by the state or other licensing agency from which you seek certification. Although formats vary among tests, most of the tests are from 1 to 2 hours in duration and include a combination of short-answer essay questions based on a specific teaching situation or passage and/or multiple-choice questions. Some typical content tests are Early Childhood Education; Biology; Physics; Business Education; General Science, English Language, Literature and Composition; Physical Education; Social Studies; and Art. In addition to specific subject assessments the Praxis II offers:

- **Principles of Learning and Teaching (PLT) Tests** which assess general pedagogical knowledge related particular grade ranges: Early Childhood, K-6, 5-9, and 7-12.
- **Teaching Foundations Exams (TFE)** which assess pedagogical knowledge related to broad content areas: multi-subject (elementary), English Language Arts, Mathematics, and Science.

The Praxis III: Teacher Performance Assessments are designed to evaluate the instructional skills of beginning teachers within the classroom context. Assessment is conducted through direct observation of teaching, review of documentation provided by the teacher, and structured interviews. Assessment criteria is organized under four domains:

- Instructional Planning
- The Classroom Environment
- Delivering Instruction
- Teacher Professionalism

Visit www.ets.org for more information.

and delivery, evaluation and assessment, and curriculum-specific knowledge. To prepare you for this examination, example case histories incorporating each of the InTASC ten standards are provided at the end of each chapter. Constructed-response and multiple-choice questions and answers corresponding to each case history following the format of the Praxis exam can be accessed on MyEducationLab. Figure 1.5 provides an overview of the Praxis exam and the remainder of this text will prepare you for it.

Your Transition to the Real World of Teaching

An important question for you as a prospective teacher is, "What type of knowledge and experiences will be needed to pass successfully into the real world of teaching?" The chapters ahead convey the types of knowledge that should move you quickly up the ladder of knowledge and experiences that make an effective teacher. But before learning about the tools and techniques that will help you progress up this ladder, you should take a moment to reflect on your own concerns about teaching at this point in your career.

Appendix A contains the Teacher Concerns Checklist, which is a 45-item self-report instrument for assessing the stages of concern with which teachers, like you, most strongly identify at different periods in their careers. Using the Teacher Concerns Checklist, you can rank your own level of teaching concerns and, using the scoring instructions provided, express the concerns with which you identify most closely. After reviewing the Checklist, return to this chapter and read further to learn more about this interesting facet of your growth and development as a teacher.

STOP now and complete the Teacher Concerns Checklist in Appendix A.

Now that you have ranked your most important teaching concerns, let's see what it means for your teaching. Your transition to the real world of teaching will usher in the first stage of teacher development, sometimes called the *survival stage* (Borich, 1993; Borich & Tombari, 1997; Burden, 1986; Fuller, 1969; Ryan, 1992). The distinguishing feature of this first stage of teaching is that your **teaching concerns** and plans focus on your own well-being more than on the teaching task or your learners. Bullough (1989) has described this stage as "the fight for one's professional life." During it, your concerns may include the following:

- Will my learners like me?
- Will they listen to what I say?
- What will parents and other teachers think of me?
- Will I do well when I'm being observed?

During this time, behavior management concerns will become a major focus of your planning efforts. For most teachers, survival, or *self,* concerns begin to diminish rapidly during the first months of teaching, but there is no precise time when they end. What signals their end is the transition to a new set of concerns and planning priorities. This new set of priorities focuses on how best to deliver instruction. Various labels have been used to describe this second stage, such as the *mastery stage of teaching* (Ryan, 1992), *consolidation and exploration* (Burden, 1986), and *trial and error* (Sacks & Harrington, 1982). Fuller (1969) has described this stage as one marked by concerns about the teaching *task*. At this stage, you are beginning to feel confident that you can manage the day-to-day routines of the classroom and deal with a variety of behavior problems. You are at the point where you now can plan your lessons without an exclusive focus on managing your classroom. Your planning turns instead toward improving your teaching skills and achieving greater mastery over the content you are teaching. Typically, your concerns during this stage may include:

- Where can I find individualized instructional materials?
- Will I have enough time to cover the content?

- Where can I get ideas for an interdisciplinary thematic unit?
- What is the best way to teach writing skills in a heterogeneous class?

The third and highest level of teacher planning is characterized by concerns that have less to do with management and lesson delivery and more with the impact of your teaching on learners. This stage of planning is sometimes referred to as the *impact stage.* At this stage, you will naturally view learners as individuals and will be concerned that each of your students fulfills her or his potential to learn. At this, the most advanced stage, your principal concerns may include:

- How can I increase my learners' feelings of accomplishment?
- How do I meet my learners' social and emotional needs?
- What is the best way to challenge my unmotivated learners?
- What skills do my learners need to best prepare them for the next grade?

Fuller (1969) speculated that concerns for *self, task,* and *impact* are the natural stages that most teachers pass through, representing a developmental growth pattern extending over months and even years of a teacher's career. Although some teachers may pass through these stages more quickly than others and at different levels of intensity, Fuller suggests that almost all teachers can be expected to move from one to another, with the most effective and experienced teachers expressing student-centered (impact) concerns at a high level of commitment.

Fuller's concerns theory has several other interesting implications. A teacher might return to an earlier stage of concern—for instance, moving from a concern for students back to a concern for task as a result of having to teach a new grade or subject or moving from a concern for task back to a concern for self as a result of having to teach different and unfamiliar students. The second time spent in a stage might be expected to be shorter than the first.

Finally, the three stages of concern need not be exclusive of one another. A teacher could have concerns predominantly in one area while still having concerns at lesser levels of intensity in the other stages.

Record your scores on the Teacher Concerns Checklist that you have just completed, and compare them with your scores at the end of this course to find out in what direction your concerns may have changed.

For Further Information

During the past decade, a number of national and state efforts—such as those by the National Council of Teachers of Mathematics (NCTM), the International Reading Association (IRA), and others—have sought to define the knowledge and performance for students or teachers in particular subject areas. The Mid-continent Regional Educational Laboratory (McREL) has created a large database that synthesizes many of these efforts. Visit their website at www.mcrel.org to learn more about standards.

The following is a case history and test preparation exercise intended to help you prepare for the licensure exam, which may be required by your teacher preparation program and your state for certification and licensing. You will find similar case histories at the end of each chapter. Based on the objectives and content of the Praxis II: Principles of Learning and Teaching exam and the InTASC and NBPTS standards, these in-depth case histories represent key concepts in the chapter. A short-answer question requiring analysis of the case history and discrete multiple-choice questions pertaining to typical licensure test content in this chapter are provided on MyEducationLab. (See Figure 1.5 for the composition of the Praxis II.) When you have completed the test preparation exercises, you will find a rubric and examples of scored student responses for the short-answer question. The correct answer and an explanation for each multiple-choice question, and additional questions pertaining to licensure test content. Although not intended as a comprehensive assessment of chapter content, these questions provide a targeted rehearsal for preparing you for the level of pedagogical knowledge and question formats that will be expected of you on the Praxis II exam and other exams that may be required at the end of your teacher preparation program.

Case History and Licensure Preparation

DIRECTIONS: *The following case history pertains to this chapter's content. After reading the case history, go to Chapter 1 in the Book Specific Resources section in the MyEducationLab for your course. Open the Case History and Licensure Preparation activity and complete the questions that follow. Upon completion of the test, scored answers to the short-answer question pertaining to the case history and multiple choice questions will be provided*

Case History

Mrs. Travis teaches seventh-grade English to a class of 29 students. In this class, there is a balance of boys and girls from low to high performing. Several students are mainstreamed, a few have limited English-speaking skills, and several are designated gifted. The majority perform at the average level. This case focuses in particular on the following three students.

Brady is a mainstreamed special education student new to the district. Her official classification is "emotionally disturbed," but some of her standardized test scores—particularly those for reading comprehension and vocabulary—put her near the gifted level. Her assigned seat is in the rear corner of the classroom, and she seems to enjoy the detachment it offers. Much of the time, Brady is reading a novel; her current choice is Franz Kafka's *Metamorphosis.*

Dalia is an honor roll student whose high motivation and study habits, rather than her test scores, underlie her achievement. She is always the first to class and begins on the daily warm-up even before the bell rings. Dalia is painstaking about her writing and anxious to get everything right. Often she stays after class or school to ask additional questions about an upcoming assignment. She is intent on becoming the first of her family to go to college.

Jim, an average student, is tall and outgoing and very excited that he has made the school football team. He has a good sense of humor and often jokes with fellow classmates. Although he has good attendance and is never late for class, his study habits are not very good. Sometimes he forgets his book or brings the wrong notebook, which he often uses as an excuse to "take the day off." And when he is on task, he often talks without raising his hand or interrupts other students in a burst of enthusiasm.

During the first several minutes of class, Mrs. Travis takes the roll while the class completes its usual warm-up, writing down the quote of the day, looking up synonyms for key underlined words, and finally paraphrasing the quote. Students also copy the daily lesson and homework assignment from the front board. A few students who have been absent go to the class calendar on the bulletin board to learn about makeup assignments.

Mrs. Travis asks Jim to read the quote: "The <u>roots</u> of <u>education</u> are <u>bitter,</u> but the <u>fruit</u> is <u>sweet</u>. Aristotle."

Jim reads from the board rather than his notebook, which he has forgotten today. Since he has not written down a synonym for the word *roots,* Mrs. Travis waits for him to look one up in the thesaurus. Jim takes his time but finally says "Base."

"That's a good choice," Mrs. Travis tells Jim. While she calls on others, she quietly slips Jim a blank page and suggests he write down the warm-up now so he can transfer it to his notebook at home. She remains standing next to his desk as she asks for more synonyms from the class. Reluctantly, Jim begins to write.

Throughout the discussion of the quotation, Brady has been reading her novel. When Mrs. Travis asks her to read her paraphrase of the quote, she replies without hesitation: "The underlying foundation of learning can be difficult or harsh, but the rewards are immense and joyous." Brady is about to go back to her book, but Mrs. Travis probes.

"Can you give some examples of those 'bitter roots,' Brady?"

"Well, having to do lesson warm-ups, for example, keeping a notebook, and putting up with someone who can hardly read." She stares at Jim.

Mrs. Travis admits that schoolwork can be difficult. "Those are some examples, Brady. Now tell us about some of the 'sweet fruit.'"

There is no reply. After about ten seconds, Mrs. Travis probes, "Is reading a Kafka book sweet fruit?"

Brady responds with only a shrug. Mrs. Travis continues, "Well, if you like *The Metamorphosis,* I'd recommend you read *The Judgment* next." Brady looks up from her reading and stares at Mrs. Travis, a look of surprise stamped on her face. Then she writes down the title on her hand.

After a discussion, the class gives several examples of the "bitter roots" of education they would rather do without. The examples of the "sweet fruits" are a little more difficult to elicit, so Mrs. Travis changes gears.

"Well, maybe now you don't see too much 'sweet fruit' because you are in the midst of it, but what about when you graduate from high school or college? What rewards will your education provide?"

"I want to be first in my family to go to college," Dalia says.

"I'm going to get a football scholarship," adds Jim. Several others mention the cars they plan to buy when they finish their education. Just as the shared enthusiasm is on the edge of getting too noisy, Mrs. Travis directs students to a ten minute writing assignment on today's lesson: The Rewards of Education.

For the next ten minutes, students write while Mrs. Travis walks around the room to monitor their progress and make suggestions. Even Brady lays aside the novel she has been reading to write.

Summing Up

This chapter introduced you to definitions of effective teaching and key behaviors that help achieve it. The main points in this chapter include the following:

What Is an Effective Teacher?

1. Early definitions of effective teaching focused primarily on a teacher's goodness as a person and only secondarily on his or her behavior in the classroom.

2. Most modern definitions of effective teaching identify patterns of teacher–student interaction in the classroom that influence the cognitive and affective performance of students.

3. Classroom interaction analysis is a research methodology in which the verbal interaction patterns of teachers and students are systematically observed, recorded, and related to student performance.

Key Behaviors Contributing to Effective Teaching

4. Five key behaviors for effective teaching and some indicators pertaining to them are the following:

   - *Lesson clarity:* Logical, step-by-step order; clear and audible delivery free of distracting mannerisms

   - *Instructional variety:* Variability in instructional materials, questioning, types of feedback, and teaching strategies

   - *Task orientation:* Achievement (content) orientation as opposed to process orientation, maximum content coverage, and time devoted to instruction

   - *Student engagement:* Limiting opportunities for distraction and getting students to work on, think through, and inquire about the content

   - *Success rate:* An estimated 60 percent to 70 percent of time spent on tasks that afford moderate to high levels of success, especially during expository or didactic instruction

Some Helping Behaviors Related to Effective Teaching

5. Five helping behaviors for effective teaching and some indicators pertaining to them are the following:

   - *Using student ideas and contributions:* Using students' responses to foster the goals of the lesson and getting students to elaborate on and extend learned content using their own ideas, experiences, and thought patterns

   - *Structuring:* Providing advance organizers and cognitive or mental strategies at the beginning of a lesson and creating activity structures with varied demands

   - *Questioning:* Using both content (direct) and process (indirect) questions to convey facts and to encourage inquiry and problem solving

   - *Probing:* Eliciting clarification, soliciting additional information, and redirecting when needed

   - *Teacher affect:* Exhibiting vigor, involvement, excitement, and interest during classroom presentations through vocal inflection, gesturing, eye contact, and animation, all of which communicate a warm and nurturing relationship to the learner

Teaching Effectively with Diverse Learners and Content

6. The key behaviors—such as lesson clarity, instructional variety, and teacher's task orientation—appear to be effective across all or most teaching contexts.

7. The helping behaviors—such as use of student ideas and contributions, structuring, and questioning—can be thought of as helping to perform the five key behaviors. These behaviors may be applied differently to help lower- and higher-SES students achieve success across areas of instruction, such as the teaching of reading and mathematics.

The Complexity of Teaching

8. Effective teaching involves the orchestration and integration of key and helping behaviors into meaningful patterns to create effective teaching practices.

Professional Teaching Standards

9. Governed by a board of directors, the majority of whom are classroom teachers, the National Board for Professional Teaching Standards (NBPTS) offers five propositions essential to effective teaching.

10. The Interstate New Teacher Assessment and Support Consortium (InTASC) standards are written as ten standards, which are further described in terms of teacher knowledge, dispositions, and performances to indicate what a beginning teacher should know and be able to do.

Your Transition to the Real World of Teaching

11. Fuller (1969) postulated three stages of concerns through which teachers pass on the way to becoming a professional: concern for self, concern for the teaching task, and concern for their impact on learners.

Key Terms

Constructivist teaching strategies
Engaged learning time
Helping behaviors
Instructional variety

InTASC standards
Key behaviors
Lesson clarity
Socioeconomic status (SES)

Student success rate
Teacher-mediated dialogue
Teacher task orientation
Teaching concerns

Discussion and Practice Questions

Questions marked with an asterisk are answered in Appendix B. Go to the Assignments and Activities section of the various topics on the MyEducationLab for your course to complete additional practice activities related to this chapter's content.

*1. In the following list, write the number 1 beside each indicator that likely would appear in an early definition of effective teaching based on either the characteristics of a good person or on the perceived psychological characteristics of a good teacher. Write the number 2 beside each indicator that likely would appear in the modern definition of effective teaching, based on the interaction patterns of teachers and students.

_____ Is always on time for work

_____ Is "intelligent"

_____ Stays after class to help students

_____ Works well with those in authority

_____ Has plenty of experience at his or her grade level

_____ Varies higher-level with lower-level questions

_____ Likes his or her job

_____ Uses attention gaining devices to engage students in the learning task

_____ Is open to criticism

_____ Shows vitality when presenting

_____ Has worked with difficult students before

_____ Always allows students to experience moderate to high levels of success

_____ Matches the class content closely with the curriculum guide

2. In your opinion, which of the following helping behaviors on the right would be most helpful in implementing the key behaviors on the left? More than a single helping behavior may be used for a given key behavior. Compare your results with those of a classmate, and discuss the reasons for any differences.

1. _____ Lesson clarity   a. Student ideas
2. _____ Instructional variety   b. Structuring
3. _____ Task orientation   c. Questioning
4. _____ Engagement in   d. Probing
         the learning task   e. Enthusiasm
5. _____ Success rate

3. Identify two behaviors for effective teaching that you would emphasize if you were teaching fifth-grade mathematics. Identify two you would emphasize when teaching fifth-grade reading. Justify your choices using the summary research tables in this chapter.

4. Indicate your perceived strengths in exhibiting the five key and five helping behaviors, using the following technique. First, notice the number assigned to each of the key behaviors:

1 lesson clarity
2 instructional variety
3 teacher task orientation
4 student engagement in the learning process
5 student success rate

Now for each of the following rows of numbers listed, circle the number representing the key behavior in which you perceive yourself to have the greater strength:

1 versus 2	2 versus 4
1 versus 3	2 versus 5
1 versus 4	3 versus 4
1 versus 5	3 versus 5
2 versus 3	4 versus 5

Count how many times you circled a 1, how many times you circled a 2, and so on, and write the frequencies on the following lines:

_____ 1
_____ 2
_____ 3
_____ 4
_____ 5

Your perceived greatest strength is the key behavior that has the highest frequency. Your perceived least strength is the key behavior with the lowest frequency.

5. Repeat the paired comparison technique (see item 4) in the same manner for the five helping behaviors.

1 use of student ideas
2 structuring
3 questioning
4 probing
5 enthusiasm

1 versus 2	2 versus 4
1 versus 3	2 versus 5
1 versus 4	3 versus 4
1 versus 5	3 versus 5
2 versus 3	4 versus 5

_____ 1
_____ 2
_____ 3
_____ 4
_____ 5

Professional Practice

Field Experience and Practice Activities

1. Recall a particularly effective teacher you had during your high school years—and a less effective one. Try to form a mental image of each teacher. Now rate each teacher on the five key behaviors in the following list. Use 1 to indicate strength in that behavior, 2 to indicate average performance, and 3 to indicate weakness in that behavior. Are the behavioral profiles of the two teachers different? How?

Behavior	Teacher X (more effective)	Teacher Y (less effective)
Lesson clarity	_____	_____
Instructional variety	_____	_____
Task orientation	_____	_____
Engagement in the learning process	_____	_____
Success rate	_____	_____

2. Now rate the same two teachers across the five helping behaviors. Is the pattern the same? What differences in ratings, if any, do you find across key and helping behaviors for the same teacher? How would you account for any differences that occurred?

Digital Portfolio Activities

The following digital portfolio activities relate to InTASC Standard 9:

- *What is a digital portfolio?* A digital portfolio contains the same materials that are placed in a traditional portfolio, but the materials are captured, organized, saved, and presented in a digital format. There are many advantages to being able to save and present important information relevant to your professional development in a digital format. First, a digital portfolio of your professional development can contain all the entries you might want to show a prospective employer in a fraction of the space that an accordion file, file box, or even binder would consume. Second, it can provide immediate access to exactly what you need at the time you need it to respond to a specific request for information without your having to clumsily rummage through reams of information. And, third, it can place audio, video, graphics, as well as text at your fingertips in seconds. Accessibility, ease of duplication, minimal storage space, and portability make a digital portfolio the most advanced and efficient means of saving and displaying your professional accomplishments. Each chapter of this text will suggest what you should consider placing in your digital portfolio to present your professional skills and experiences and start you toward your first teaching job.

- *How do I start a digital portfolio?* You can start your digital portfolio using your personal computer and commonly available software, such as Microsoft PowerPoint. However, using any of several specific software applications for a professional portfolio, identified on the Web or in Costantino, De Lorenzo, and Tirrell-Corbin (2008) and Adams-Bullock and Hawk (2010), can make the task even easier.

Now here are some suggestions for creating your first portfolio entries that relate to InTASC Standard 9:

1. This activity is designed to give you experience in creating a two minute video in which you state your philosophy of teaching—often required for your first job interview. This will give you the opportunity to introduce yourself on your laptop, rather than having to speak unrehearsed at what might be a stressful moment in an interview. You will need an inexpensive web camera, which will come with appropriate software. You may want to write out your two minute talk and use it as a guide to what you will say extemporaneously. Your objectives are to look natural and relaxed, to speak clearly, and to look directly into the camera. View your first trial and repeat the process as necessary until you give a confident picture of yourself. If you do not have the opportunity to use a web cam, simply save your statement in a folder on your computer labeled "Teaching Philosophy."

2. Complete the Teacher Concerns Checklist in Appendix A, if you have not already done so. Set up and date a new computer folder with the name "Teacher Concerns," and place it in a file with your scores for concerns for self, concerns for task, and concerns for impact. As your professional experience grows, retake the Teacher Concerns Checklist (for example, at the end of this course and occasionally thereafter) and place your new scores for these dimensions side by side with your previous scores. Over time, note how your scores shift from self-concerns to concerns for the teaching task and finally to concerns about your impact on students.

MyEducationLab™

Go to MyEducationLab (www.myeducationlab.com) for Effective Teaching Methods: Research-Based Practice where you can:

- Find learning outcomes for the various course topics course along with national standards that connect to these outcomes.

- Complete **Assignments and Activities** that can help you more deeply understand the chapter content.

- Apply and practice your understanding of the core teaching skills identified in the chapter with **Building Teaching Skills and Dispositions** coaching activities.

- Check your comprehension of the content covered in the chapter with a book specific **Study Plan**. Here you will be able to take a chapter **pretest**, receive feedback on your answers, and then access personalized **Review, Practice, and Enrichment exercises** to enhance your understanding of chapter content. After you complete the exercises, take a **posttest** to confirm your comprehension.

- Learn how to address common classroom management issues in the **Simulations in Classroom Management**.

- Access video clips of CCSSO **National Teachers of the Year award winners** responding to the question, "Why Do I Teach?" in the Teacher Talk section.

- Create, update, and share quality lesson plans with the **Lesson Plan Builder**.

- Access state licensure test requirements, overviews of what tests cover, and sample test items in the **Certification and Licensure** section.

- Learn how to create a high quality teaching portfolio in the **Preparing a Portfolio** section.

- Access tips, advice, and other information on resume writing and interviewing, your first year of teaching, and law and public policies in the Beginning Your Career section.

2 Understanding Your Students

This chapter will help you answer these questions and meet the following InTASC standards for effective teaching.

- What is a reflective teacher?
- What is differentiated instruction?
- What are some of the ways I can adapt my teaching to special populations?
- How can I use peer-group membership to foster the goals of my instruction?
- How can I help my learners acquire a positive self-concept?
- What are some ways I can promote family–school partnerships in my classroom?

InTASC

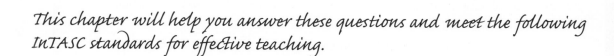 **STANDARD 1** **Learning Differences.** The teacher uses understanding of individual differences and diverse cultures and communities to ensure inclusive learning environments that enable each learner to meet high standards.

STANDARD 3 **Learning Environments.** The teacher works with others to create environments that support individual and collaborative learning, and that encourage positive social interaction, active engagement in learning, and self motivation.

STANDARD 4 **Content Knowledge.** The teacher understands how children learn and develop, recognizing that patterns of learning and development vary individually within and across the cognitive, linguistic, social, emotional, and physical areas, and designs and implements developmentally appropriate and challenging learning experiences.

STANDARD 9 **Professional Learning and Ethical Practice.** The teacher engages in ongoing professional learning and uses evidence to continually evaluate his/her practice, particularly the effects of his/her choices and actions on others (learners, families, other professionals, and the community), and adapts practice to meet the needs of each learner.

*C*hapter 1 explained that teaching is not simply the transmission of knowledge from teacher to learner but rather is the interaction of teacher with learner. This chapter discusses the decisions you must make about whom you will teach. In subsequent chapters, we will consider the decisions you must make about what and how you will teach.

Not so long ago, students were viewed as empty vessels into which the teacher poured the contents of the day's lesson. Teachers perceived their task to be the skilled transmission of appropriate grade-level content as it appeared in texts, curriculum guides, workbooks, and the academic disciplines.

Contradictions arose from such a simplistic definition of teaching and learning. For example, this definition could not explain why some students get poor grades and others good ones even when the teacher is skilled at transmitting the contents of the day's lesson. Nor could the definition explain why some students want to learn, whereas others do not even want to come to school; why some students do extra work and others do little at all; or why some students are actively engaged in the learning process while others are not.

These are just some of the individual differences that exist in every classroom and that can influence the outcome of your teaching, regardless of how adept you may be at transmitting the contents of the day's lesson. Adapting your teaching to individual differences will require you to make many decisions about your learners that cannot be reduced to simple formulas or rules. It will require that you become a **reflective teacher** (Hartman, 2009; York-Barr, Sommers, Ghere, & Montie, 2006), which means you take the time to ask tough questions about the success of your teaching efforts and the individual differences among your learners.

Reflective teachers are thoughtful and self-critical about their teaching. That is, they take the time necessary to adapt and differentiate their lessons to fit their learners' needs, prior histories, and experiences and to analyze and critique the success of their lessons afterward.

To help adapt subject-matter content to the world of their learners, reflective teachers use their learners' prior experiences and what they already know as instructional tools. By deemphasizing lecturing and telling, reflective teachers encourage their learners to use their own experiences to actively construct understandings that make sense to them and for which they can take ownership. In other words, reflective teachers bridge the gap between teaching and learning by actively engaging students in building a partnership of ideas from lesson content and encouraging them to gradually accept greater responsibility for their own learning.

In the chapters ahead, we will have more to say about how you can become a reflective teacher who adapts subject matter to the individual differences of learners in the heterogeneous classroom and who uses student experiences and the dialogue of the classroom to actively engage students in the learning process. In this chapter, we provide some important facts about the special needs of your learners that will help you understand and appreciate their individual differences and adapt your instruction to them.

Not All Learners Are Alike

MyEducationLab™

Visit the MyEducationLab for *Effective Teaching Methods: Research-Based Practice*, 8/e to enhance your understanding of chapter concepts with a personalized Study Plan. You'll also have the opportunity to hone your teaching skills through video-based Assignments and Activities as well as Building Teaching Skills and Dispositions lessons.

Any observer in any classroom will quickly notice that schoolchildren vary in experience, socioeconomic status (SES), culture and ethnicity, language, and learning style. In addition, many classrooms have learners with disabilities, representing **special populations**, that without the teacher's help could have limited academic success. As a general education teacher, the Individuals with Disabilities Education Improvement Act of 2004 (Federal Education Budget Project: Individuals with Disabilities Act Overview, 2011) requires you to actively contribute to the education of learners who have been identified as having physical, hearing, visual, mental, behavioral, learning, communication, or other-health-impaired disabilities.

These special learner needs, differences in SES, culture/ethnicity, language, abilities, and learning style will influence what your students learn as well as what and how you teach. Of what consequence is such an obvious observation? After all, you must teach all the students assigned to you, regardless of their differences or special needs. Two of the reasons for being aware of individual differences and special needs among your learners are these:

1. By recognizing students' individual differences and special needs, you will be better able to help them use their own experiences and learning histories to derive meaning and understanding from what you are teaching. With that knowledge, you will be better able to adapt your instructional methods to the learning needs of your students and employ different instructional methods with different learners.

2. When counseling students and talking with parents about the achievement and performance of your learners, you will be able to convey some of the reasons for their behavior. Understanding your students' individual differences and special learning needs can provide important information to parents, counselors, and other teachers when they wonder why, for instance, Jared is not learning, why Anita learns without studying, or why Angela does not want to learn.

Researchers have discovered that different instructional methods, when matched to the individual strengths and needs of learners, can significantly improve their achievement (Cronbach & Snow, 1981; Mayer, 2002; Tomlinson, 2010; Tomlinson & McTighe, 2006). For example, student-centered discussions improve the achievement of highly anxious students by providing a more informal, nurturing climate, whereas teacher-centered lectures increase the achievement of low-anxiety students by allowing for a more efficient and faster pace. The linguistic approach to teaching reading results in higher vocabulary achievement for students high in auditory ability and who learn best by hearing, whereas the whole-word approach is more effective for students low in auditory ability and who learn best by seeing. Researchers have found that achievement can be increased when the instructional method reflects the learners' favored modalities for learning (Cushner, McClelland, & Safford, 2008; D'Amico & Gallaway, 2008; Darling-Hammond & Bransford, 2005; Messick, 1995).

Adaptive Teaching

One approach to achieving a common instructional goal with learners whose individual differences—such as prior achievement, aptitude, or special needs—differ is called **adaptive teaching**. Adaptive teaching techniques apply different instructional strategies to different groups of learners so the natural diversity prevailing in the classroom does not prevent any learner from achieving success. Two approaches to adaptive teaching have been reported to be effective. They are the remediation approach and the compensatory approach.

The Remediation Approach. The **remediation approach** provides the learner with the prerequisite knowledge, skill, or behavior needed to benefit from the planned instruction. For example, you might attempt to lower the anxiety of highly anxious students with a student-centered discussion before an important presentation, so the presentation will equally benefit all students. Or you might teach listening skills to students low in auditory ability before using a linguistic approach to reading, so both groups will profit equally from this instructional approach.

The remediation approach to adaptive teaching will be successful to the extent that the desired prerequisite information, skill, or behavior can be taught within a reasonable period of time. When this is not possible or represents an inefficient use of classroom time, the compensatory approach to adaptive teaching can be taken.

The Compensatory Approach.   Using the **compensatory approach**, the teacher chooses an instructional method to compensate for the lack of information, skill, or ability known to exist among learners by altering the content presentation to circumvent a weakness and promote a strength. This is accomplished by using alternate modalities (pictures versus words) or by supplementing the content with additional learning resources (instructional games and simulations) and activities (group discussions or experience-oriented activities). Doing so may involve modifying the instructional technique to focus on known strengths. Techniques include the visual representation of content, using more flexible instructional presentations (films, pictures, illustrations), shifting to alternate instructional formats (self-paced texts, simulations, experience-oriented workbooks), and using performance-based assessment procedures that might require students to respond orally or assemble a portfolio of experiences, ideas, and products pertaining to a topic. For example, students who are slower to develop their reading comprehension and lack a technical math vocabulary might be taught a geometry unit supplemented with visual handouts. Portraying each theorem and axiom graphically emphasizes the visual modality.

Benefits of Adaptive Teaching.   Notice that adaptive teaching goes beyond the simple process of ability grouping, in which learners are divided into groups and then presented with approximately the same material at different rates. Some researchers have suggested that differences in academic performance between high and low achievers may actually increase with the use of ability grouping by creating a loss of self-esteem and motivation for the low group.

Adaptive teaching, in contrast, works to achieve success with all students, regardless of their individual differences. It does so either by remediation (building the knowledge, skills, or abilities required to profit from the planned instruction) or by compensation (emphasizing instructional methods/materials that rely on learner abilities that may be more highly developed). Therefore adaptive teaching requires an understanding of your students' learning strengths and experience with regard to specific lesson content and the alternative instructional methods that can maximize their strongest receptive modalities (such as visual versus auditory; discussion versus presentation; student experience driven versus text driven).

Some of the most promising instructional alternatives in adaptive teaching include:

- Cooperative grouping versus whole-class instruction
- Inquiry versus expository presentation
- Rule-example versus example-rule ordering
- Teacher-centered versus student-centered presentation
- Direct versus indirect instruction
- Examples from experience versus examples from text
- Group phonics versus individualized phonics instruction
- Individual responses versus choral responses
- Subvocal responses versus vocal responses
- Self-directed learning versus whole-group instruction
- Computer-driven text versus teacher presentation

Each of these teaching methods has been found more effective for some types of learners than for others. The research literature and curriculum texts in your teaching area offer many examples of specific content areas in which a particular instructional method—in association with a particular student characteristic—has enhanced student performance. However, your classroom experience will suggest many other ways in which you can alter your teaching to fit the individual needs of your learners. By knowing your students and by having knowledge of a variety of instructional methods, you can adapt your instruction to the learning needs of your students.

Differentiated Instruction

A related approach to responding to your learners' individual differences is called **differentiated instruction**. While the methods of adaptive teaching can be effective in responding to the whole class or groups of learners in the same classroom who may differ, for example, in English proficiency, number skills, or task-relevant prior knowledge, differentiated instruction focuses on the academic success of individual learners or small groups of learners. Although similar to models of adaptive teaching in overall theory, differentiated instruction is based on the premise that instructional approaches should also vary according to the individual whose academic success is or could be enhanced by a more targeted and individualized approach. To differentiate instruction is to recognize an individual student's learning history, background, readiness to learn, interests, and acquired skill set, and then choose instructional strategies more tailored to an individual learner or small group of learners to speed academic success, which might be slowed if only large-group instruction is available. The goal of differentiated instruction, therefore, is to maximize each student's personal growth and academic success by meeting each student at his or her individual level and providing the needed instruction and resources to lift him or her to the next step on the learning ladder.

Tomlinson (2004, 2010) identifies three elements of the curriculum—content, process, and products—that can be differentiated to make instruction more responsive to the individual needs of learners:

1. *Content.* Differentiation can take the form of varying the modalities in which students gain access to important learning, for example, by: (a) listening, reading, and doing; (b) presenting content in incremental steps, like rungs on a ladder, resulting in a continuum of skill-building tasks; and (c) offering learners a choice in the complexity of content with which they will begin a learning task that matches their current level of understanding and from which every learner can experience academic success.

2. *Process.* Differentiation takes the form of grouping flexibly, for example, by (a) varying from whole class, to collaborative groups, to small groups, to individuals and (b) providing incentives to learn based on a student's individual interests and current level of understanding.

3. *Products.* Tomlinson (2010) and Stiggens and Chappuis (2012) suggest varying assessment methods by: (a) providing teachers a menu of choices that may include oral responses, interviews, demonstrations and reenactments, portfolios, and formal tests; (b) keeping each learner challenged at his or her level of understanding with content at or slightly above his or her current level of functioning; and (c) allowing students to have some choice in the means in which they may express what they know—for example, writing a story, drawing a picture, or telling about a real-life experience that involves what is being taught.

But most important, differentiated instruction provides the opportunity for the teacher to consider multiple characteristics of the learner *simultaneously* while choosing an instructional strategy for a particular learner and learning objective. Therefore, differentiated instruction is ideally suited for a heterogeneous classroom, in which learning histories, learning styles, learner interests, and skills as well as disabilities representing special populations may impair learning. Overall, the goal of differentiated instruction is to give learners alternate paths with which to learn. Students working below grade level may be given resources that retrace major objectives that have already been taught, whereas learners above grade level may be asked to produce work that requires more complex and advanced thinking. By varying teaching strategies, the teacher makes sure that each student has the opportunity to learn in a manner compatible with his or her own learning strengths and preferences. The curriculum is no longer defined in terms of what a teacher will teach but rather in terms of what a student will be able to demonstrate.

We will have more to say about how to implement and manage a differentiated curriculum in your classroom in Chapter 6 on lesson planning.

Now let's look at some of the individual differences that can influence your students' learning and your teaching.

This **video** explains the concept of differentiated instruction. Pay attention to how DI is applied in the classroom.

The Effects of General Ability on Learning

One thing everyone remembers about elementary school is how some students seemed to learn so easily while others had to work so hard. In high school, the range of student ability seemed even greater. In a practical sense, we associate descriptors such as *smart, bright, able to solve problems, learns quickly,* and *can figure things out* with intelligence. Both in the classroom and in life, it seems that some have more ability than others. This observation often has been a source of anxiety, concern, and jealousy among learners. Perhaps because the topic of intelligence can so easily elicit emotions like these, it is one of the most talked about yet least understood aspects of student behavior.

Misconceptions about Intelligence

One of the greatest misconceptions that some teachers, parents, and learners have about intelligence is that it is a single, unified dimension. Such a belief is often expressed by the use of word pairs such as *slow/fast* and *bright/dull* when referring to different kinds of learners. Unfortunately, these phrases indicate that a student is either fast or slow, bright or dull; in fact, each of us, regardless of our intelligence, may be all of these at one time or another. On a particular task of a certain nature, you may appear to be slow, but given another task requiring different abilities, you may be fast. How do such vast differences occur within a single individual?

Everyone knows from personal experience in school, hobbies, sports, and interpersonal relationships that the degree of intelligence depends on the circumstances and conditions under which the intelligence is exhibited. Observations such as this have led researchers to study and identify more than one kind of intelligence. This new way of looking at intelligence has led to a better understanding of classic contradictions, like why Carlos is good in vocabulary but not in spelling, why Angela is good in social studies but poor at reading maps, and why Tamara is good at analyzing the reasons behind historical events but not at memorizing the names and dates that go along with them. Each of these seemingly contradictory behaviors can be explained by the special abilities required by each task. These specific abilities, in which we all differ, are the most useful aspects for understanding the learning needs of your students.

General versus Specific Abilities

Common sense tells us that some abilities can be inherited while others are learned. However, despite how parents, other teachers, and even your own students may feel, these positions are highly dependent on the notion of a *general,* or overall, intelligence that becomes less relevant in the context of specific abilities. General intelligence only moderately predicts school grades, whereas specific abilities tend to predict not only school grades but also the more important real-life performances that school grades are supposed to represent (Borich & Tombari, 2004).

If we think of school learning as a pie and general intelligence as a piece of it, we can ask: How large a piece of the classroom learning pie is taken up by general ability? The answer, illustrated in Figure 2.1, is that only about 25 percent can be attributed to general intelligence; about 75 percent must be assigned to **social competence**. So knowing your learners' specific strengths and altering your instructional goals and activities accordingly will contribute far more to your effective teaching than will categorizing your students' performances in ways that indicate only their general intelligence.

The Effects of Specific Abilities on Learning

Specific definitions of intelligence and the behaviors they represent commonly are called *aptitudes.* As a teacher, you are unlikely to measure aptitudes in your classroom, but you need to know of their influence on the performance of your students. Your students' aptitudes may already have been assessed in a district-wide testing program, or you can ask the school counselor or psychologist to measure a specific aptitude to find the source of a specific learning problem. Your acquaintance with the division of general intelligence into specific aptitudes will help you see how a learner's abilities in specific areas can directly affect the degree of learning that takes place.

Multiple Intelligences

L. L. Thurstone (1947) was among the first to advocate the use of specific as opposed to general measures of intelligence. Instead of reinforcing the idea of a single measure of intellect, Thurstone's theory led to the development of seven different abilities—verbal comprehension, general reasoning, memory, use of numbers, psychomotor speed, spatial relations, and word fluency—each measured by a separate test. For example, some learning activities require a high degree of memory, such as memorizing a long list of words in preparation for a spelling bee or a vocabulary test. Likewise, spatial relations, use of numbers, and general reasoning ability are helpful for high levels of performance in mathematics. The concept of separate abilities has the advantage that instructional methods can be adapted to learners' strengths, compensating for less well-developed abilities or being used to strengthen them.

Figure 2.1 **Factors Contributing to School Learning**

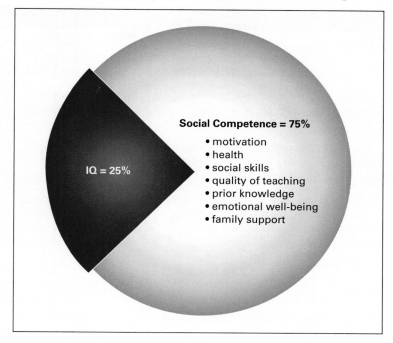

Such distinctions in ability also were more useful than general intelligence in explaining to parents why, for example, Alexis got excellent scores on math tests that emphasize number problems ($12 + 2 - 1 =$) but poor scores on math tests that emphasize word problems (If Bob rows 4 mph against a current flowing 2 mph, how long will it take him to row 16 miles?). Such apparent contradictions become more understandable in the light of specific abilities, especially if they can be improved with instruction.

Thurstone's (1947) dimensions were among the earliest, but other more recent components of ability have been proposed. For example, Gardner (2011, 2006), Gardner and Hatch (1989), and Armstrong (2009) describe eight different abilities based on skills found in modern technological society. The eight abilities identified by Gardner and the things individuals who possess high levels of these abilities would be good at are identified in Table 2.1. To these may be added a ninth intelligence, called *existential intelligence,* exemplified by a philosopher, theologian, or systems analyst, who would be good at solving problems that are not tied to any single discipline or way of thinking (Gardner, 2004, 2006). Gardner reasons that alternative forms of learning can tap into still other dimensions of ability that in the traditional classroom may go unnoticed or underutilized.

Campbell, Campbell, and Dickinson (1996), Lazear (1992), and Armstrong (2009) have put Gardner's work into practice by developing instructional materials and modules to differentiate instruction for some of these abilities. The materials and methods developed by Campbell and colleagues and by Lazear derive from the observation that many individuals who are successful in life do not score high in traditional indicators of ability, such as verbal and mathematical reasoning. Gardner (2000, 2004, 2006) suggests that these individuals use other abilities to be successful, such as those in Table 2.1, to emphasize their strengths. His theory may have particular relevance for teaching at-risk learners and students with special needs, some of whom may not learn from school in the traditional classroom setting using the traditional curriculum. Armstrong (2009), Gregory (2005), and Gregory and Chapman (2006) show how instruction in a heterogeneous classroom can be differentiated according to Gardner's multiple intelligences.

The expert in this **video** explains multiple intelligences in the classroom. Focus on the different methods employed in the classroom regarding multiple intelligences.

Table 2.1 Gardner's Multiple Intelligences

Dimension	The specific dimension may be a strength for children who:
Linguistic intelligence: Capacity with the phonology (sounds), syntax (grammar), semantics (meaning), and pragmatics (situational contexts) of language.	are described as "highly verbal," enjoy reading, like to tell stories and explain things, keep a journal, write poetry, or demonstrate strong vocabulary knowledge.
Logical-mathematical intelligence: Capacity with, not only numbers, but also patterns, and logic.	are described as having "a head for numbers," enjoy math class, or often explain their thinking mathematically (quantifying elements, using numerical symbols, relating aspects through equations, etc.).
Musical intelligence: Ability to produce and appreciate rhythm, pitch, and timbre across a variety of forms of musical expression	have an aptitude for singing or playing instruments, are interested in a variety of types of music, remember music easily, or seek out opportunities with music (playing, listening, singing, composing, etc.).
Spatial intelligence: Ability to perceive and manipulate visual and spatial elements accurately as well as abstractly	have a good sense of direction and read maps easily, demonstrate an aptitude with art, learn well with visual representations of information, or works easily with things in three-dimensions (taking apart and putting back together).
Bodily-kinesthetic intelligence: Ability to use and have fine control of the body and to manipulate objects	are athletic, enjoy being outdoors and physically active, get restless easily, demonstrate strong balance or eye-hand coordination, or learn best by "doing."
Interpersonal intelligence: Sensitivity to the temperament and motivations of others	get along easily with others, enjoy cooperative learning, are comfortable in new social situations, recognize others' accomplishments, or "read people" well.
Intrapersonal intelligence: Awareness of one's own feelings, beliefs, and thinking processes	demonstrate self-awareness, are very reflective, have a strength for self-evaluation, prefer to work independently, or are comfortable being alone.
Naturalist intelligence: Propensity to recognize and organize elements in the natural environment	enjoy learning about nature, like to take care of plants and keep pets, or seeks out opportunities to go on hikes or trips to the zoo.

Online assessments of MI sources: http://www.literacyworks.org/mi/assessment/findyourstrengths.html
http://www.bgfl.org/custom/resources_ftp/client_ftp/ks3/ict/multiple_int/index.htm

Some practical classroom applications of Gardner's theory of multiple intelligences include the following:

1. Allowing students to take differentiated paths to achieve common goals (e.g., using the Internet, reading from text, or talking to experts)
2. Allowing students to display their best, not just their average, performance (e.g., allowing multiple tries and recording their best)
3. Providing alternative ways of assessing a student's achievements and talents (e.g., allowing students to choose among an oral report, portfolio, dramatization, or written product)
4. Providing opportunities to add to the student's self-identity beyond the traditional logical/linguistic abilities required by the majority of schoolwork (e.g., allowing students to show what they know in nontraditional ways by building a scale model, completing a graphic, or newscast)

See also In Practice: Focus on Multiple Intelligences in the Classroom.

Socio-Emotional Intelligence

In addition to Gardner's contributions to the study of ability, there has been growing acknowledgment of the importance of emotions in thinking and learning. This view of ability (Goleman, 2010; Lantieri & Goleman, 2008) considers emotions as useful sources of information that can help one make sense of and navigate a learning environment. It is believed that learners vary in their ability to process information of an emotional nature and in the way they use it in completing school

In Practice

Focus on Multiple Intelligences in the Classroom

Following is a description of how one teacher organized his classroom for multiple intelligences:

To implement Gardner's theory in an educational setting, I organized my third-grade classroom in Marysville, Washington, into seven learning centers, each dedicated to one of the seven intelligences. The students spend approximately two thirds of each school day moving through the centers—15 to 20 minutes at each center. Curriculum is thematic, and the centers provide seven different ways for the students to learn the subject matter.

Each day begins with a brief lecture and discussion explaining one aspect of the current theme. For example, during a unit on outer space, the morning's lecture might focus on spiral galaxies. In a unit about the arts of Africa, one lecture might describe the Adinkra textile patterns of Ghana. After the morning lecture, a timer is set and students in groups of three or four start work at their centers, eventually rotating through all seven.

What Kinds of Learning Activities Take Place at Each Center?

All students learn each day's lesson in seven ways. They build models, dance, make collaborative decisions, create songs, solve deductive reasoning problems, read, write, and illustrate all in one school day. Some more specific examples of activities at each center follow:

- In the *Personal Work Center* (Intrapersonal Intelligence), students explore the present area of study through research, reflection, or individual projects.
- In the *Working Together Center* (Interpersonal Intelligence), they develop cooperative learning skills as they solve problems, answer questions, create learning games, brainstorm ideas, and discuss that day's topic collaboratively.
- In the *Music Center* (Musical Intelligence), students compose and sing songs about the subject matter, make their own instruments, and learn in rhythmical ways.
- In the *Art Center* (Spatial Intelligence), they explore a subject area using diverse art media, manipulatives, puzzles, charts, and pictures.
- In the *Building Center* (Kinesthetic Intelligence), they build models, dramatize events, and dance, all in ways that relate to the content of that day's subject matter.

- In the *Reading Center* (Verbal/Linguistic Intelligence), students read, write, and learn in many traditional modes. They analyze and organize information in written form.
- In the *Math & Science Center* (Logical/Mathematical Intelligence), they work with math games, manipulatives, mathematical concepts, science experiments, deductive reasoning, and problem solving.

Following their work at the centers, a few minutes are set aside for groups and individual students to share their work from the centers. Much of the remainder of the day is spent with students working on independent projects, either individually or in small groups where they apply the diverse skills developed at the centers. The daily work at the seven centers profoundly influences their ability to make informative, entertaining, multimodal presentations of their studies. Additionally, it is common for parents to comment on how much more expressive their children have become at home.

What Were the Results?

An action research project was conducted in my classroom to assess the effects of this multimodal learning format. The research data revealed the following:

1. *The students develop increased responsibility, self-direction, and independence over the course of the year.* Although no attempt was made to compare this group of students with those in other third-grade classes, the self-direction and motivation of these students was apparent to numerous classroom visitors. The students became skilled at developing their own projects, gathering the necessary resources and materials, and making well-planned presentations of all kinds.

2. *Discipline problems were significantly reduced.* Students previously identified as having serious behavior problems showed rapid improvement during the first six weeks of school. By midyear, they were making important contributions to their groups. And by year's end, they had assumed positive leadership roles that had not formerly been evident.

3. *All students developed and applied new skills.* In the fall, most students described only one center as their "favorite" and as the one where they felt confident. (The distribution among the seven centers was relatively even.) By midyear, most identified three to four

favorite centers. By year's end, every student identified at least six centers that were favorites and at which they felt skilled. Moreover, they were all making multi-modal presentations of independent projects including songs, skits, visuals, poems, games, surveys, puzzles, and group participation activities.

4. *Cooperative learning skills improved in all students.* Since so much of the center work was collaborative, students became highly skilled at listening, helping each other, sharing leadership in different activities, accommodating group changes, and introducing new classmates to the program. They learned not only to respect each other, but also to appreciate and call upon the unique gifts and abilities of their classmates.

5. *Academic achievement improved.* Standardized test scores were above state and national averages in all areas. Retention was high on a classroom year-end test of all areas studied during the year. Methods for recalling information were predominantly musical, visual,

and kinesthetic, indicating the influence of working through the different intelligences. Students who had previously been unsuccessful in school became high achievers in new areas.

In summary, many students said they enjoyed school for the first time. And as the school year progressed, new skills emerged: Some students discovered musical, artistic, literary, mathematical, and other new-found capacities and abilities. Others became skilled leaders. In addition, self-confidence and motivation increased significantly. Finally, students developed responsibility, self-reliance, and independence as they took an active role in shaping their own learning experiences.

Source: Excerpted from "Multiple Intelligences in the Classroom" by Bruce Campbell. Reprinted with permission from The Learning Revolution (*In Context* #27), Winter 1991, pp. 12–15. Copyright © 1990, 1996 by Context Institute, www.context.org.

tasks—for example, by recognizing one's own mood in order to change to best fit the task (for example, for collaborative grouping), by being able to react positively to the moods of others (for example, to control one's impulses and not overreact), by recognizing one's impact on others and changing accordingly (for example, when the consequence is desirable), by adapting to changing or stressful circumstances (for example, to recognize the inevitability of some events), and by gauging the accuracy or appropriateness of one's gut feelings in reacting to a situation (for example, to inform one's own decision making).

The concept of *emotional intelligence* has an intuitive appeal for the instructional management of learners, particularly during cooperative learning and group discussion, who may differ vastly in emotional maturity and competence. Accordingly, this concept recently has been broadened to include *social-emotional intelligence* to recognize its important role in social contexts. And, like Gardner's eight other intelligences, this intelligence, too, can be taught in the classroom (Goleman, 2000, 2008, 2010).

Characteristics of Intelligence That You Can Teach, Encourage, and Nurture in Your Classroom

Content-area specialists have identified other specific abilities following from those suggested by Gardner and Lantieri and Goleman. For example, content specialists in reading have identified no fewer than nine verbal comprehension factors, which indicate the ability to do the following:

- Know word meanings
- See contextual meaning
- See organization
- Follow thought patterns
- Find specifics
- Express ideas

- Draw inferences
- Identify literary devices
- Determine a writer's purpose

In other words, a learner's general performance in reading may be affected by any one or a combination of these specific abilities. This and similar lists point to the inevitability that once specific abilities such as "Draw inferences," "Follow thought patterns," and "Find contextual meaning" are defined, it will be possible to teach these so-called components of intelligence that were once thought to be unalterable.

We now know that many aspects of intelligence can be influenced by instruction. Sternberg suggests that confronting novel tasks and situations and learning to cope with them is one of the most important instructional goals in learning intelligent behavior. His notion of coping is expressed by 20 characteristics that he suggests are important catalysts to intelligent behavior (Sternberg, 1994, 1995). According to Sternberg you should seize opportunities presented during the natural flow of classroom activity to teach, encourage, and/or nurture your learners to:

- Be motivated
- Control their impulses
- Persevere
- Use their abilities or strengths
- Translate thought into action
- Have a product or outcome orientation
- Complete tasks and follow through
- Initiate actions on their own
- Accept momentary failure or shortcomings
- Delay gratification
- See the big picture not just the details
- Maintain a balance between critical and creative thinking
- Have a realistic level of self-confidence

And, not to:

- Procrastinate
- Attribute blame to others
- Wallow in self-pity
- Always be dependent on others
- Get stuck on personal difficulties
- Be easily distracted
- Spread oneself too thin

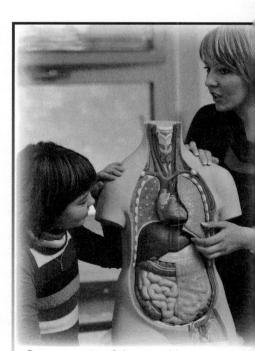

Some aspects of the age-old concept of intelligence, once thought to be unalterable, now may be taught in the classroom.

According to Sternberg and Grigorenko (2007), many social and emotional aspects of intelligence, such as these, can and should be encouraged in the classroom in the context of your instruction. Moreover, the classroom in the context of your subject matter presentations, assignments, and group work is the logical place to teach and reinforce these important catalysts to intelligent behavior. Sternberg's work is another example of the instructional value of the multidimensional approach to intelligence with which abilities, emotions, and dispositions once thought to be unalterable can be taught.

The Effects of Culture, Socioeconomic Status, and Language on Learning

In this **video**, the impact of culture on language acquisition and learning are explored. Pay close attention to how this understanding is exemplified in the classroom setting.

Although the physical school setting has remained largely unchanged over the past 75 years, the major participants—the students—have not. The typical classroom of today contains a more diverse group of learners than at any time in U.S. history. Today a large number of public school students represent non-European cultures and speak a variety of languages. For millions of students, English is not their native language. This diversity reflects not only the culture that children bring to school but also the language, learning, and motivational skills that accompany them (Bruner, 1996; Delpit, 2006; Delpit & Dowdy, 2008; Delpit, Boyd, Brock, & Rozendal, 2003; Olneck, 2001). It is no longer accurate to say that the United States is a nation and an educational system with minorities; rather, it is a nation and an educational system of minorities. Currently, nonwhite students make up over 40 percent of all students in the United States. And non-Anglo students currently make up the majority of learners in the nation's 27 largest school districts. Add to this medley of cultures in our schools an increasingly diverse assortment of family patterns and lifestyles (United States Department of Education, 2011; Sable & Hoffman, 2008).

The Effects of Culture on Learning

The result of this cultural, language, and socioeconomic diversity is an ever-increasing range of individual differences in the classroom, including populations with special learning needs. This diversity must be matched by the diversity in how teachers plan for it.

For example, the research of Bowers and Flinders (1991), Cheng (1996, 1998), Cheng, Chen, Tsubo, Sekandari, and Alfafara-Killacky (1997), Delpit (2006, 2008), Griggs and Dunn (1995), Neuliep (2008), and Tharp and Gallimore (1991) have presented convincing arguments that people from different cultures react differently to the nonverbal and verbal classroom management techniques of proximity control, eye contact, warnings, and classroom arrangement. Research suggests that students from Hispanic and Asian cultures respond more positively to quiet, private correction, as opposed to a public display, such as listing their name on the board (Banks & Banks, 2009; Cheng, 1998; Lockwood & Secada, 1999; Saito, 1999; Walqui, 2000). Furthermore, researchers cite numerous examples of how teachers from one culture interpret the behaviors of children differently than teachers from another culture (for example, with respect to the degree of unsolicited talk and movement that is accepted in the classroom). This has been called **reciprocal distancing** (Larson & Irvine, 1999) and reciprocal teaching (Oczkus, 2006, 2010).

In one form of reciprocal distancing, teachers and students (both consciously and unconsciously) use language to include or exclude various individuals from the group. For example, in an exchange between a Caucasian teacher and her African American students about Dr. Martin Luther King Jr., students used the pronoun *we* to clearly position themselves as members of a group that excluded the teacher. And the teacher, in kind, chooses a response that distances her from the class. Here are two examples of the effects of the reciprocal distancing on learners:

[An African American boy takes a picture of Dr. Martin Luther King Jr. out of his desk to color.]

> *Teacher:* Let's not look at that now! That's after lunch.
>
> *Student:* I like him. I just want to look at him.
>
> *Teacher:* Well, that's nice. Put him away. We'll do Martin Luther King after lunch.

[An African American boy across the room calls out, "*We* call him Dr. King."]

> *Teacher:* He's not a real doctor like you go to for a cold or sore throat. (Larson & Irvine, 1999, p. 395)

To capitalize on the positive aspects of group membership and encourage a sense of inclusion rather than distancing, many teachers implement discussion sessions, student teams, small groups, and the sharing of instructional materials to create opportunities for positive social interaction among their students. These various forms of cooperative learning provide alternatives to the traditional lecture/presentation format that can heighten motivation and the excitement of learning (Gillies, 2007; Jolliffe, 2007; Johnson & Johnson, 2005).

Along with this diversity comes a need to be aware of potential biases related to diversity. For example, gender-, racial-, and ethnic-specific clothing, dialects, and mannerisms can lead us to expect and look for one type of behavior more than another or to place stereotypic interpretations on classroom behavior to which gender, race, and ethnicity have no relationship (Santos & Reese, 1999). These researchers remind us that some of the teaching techniques you will study and use in your classroom will be culturally sensitive.

Antón-Oldenburg (2000), Miller (2000), Neuliep (2008), and Santos and Reese (1999) suggest a number of ways teachers can develop the ability to interact smoothly and effectively with members of various cultures—or in other words, achieve *intercultural competence* (Lustig & Koester, 2009). Walqui (2000) notes that one of the most important ways is for teachers and students to work together to construct a culture that values the strengths of all participants and respects their interests, abilities, languages, and dialects. Also important is the role of cooperative grouping, in which culturally different learners must act together to accomplish group goals. In the chapters to follow, we will discuss the important role of cooperative grouping as a tool for developing intercultural competence, as well as many other techniques for teaching in culturally diverse classrooms.

The Effects of Socioeconomic Status on Learning

Researchers have studied the relationship among social class, culture/ethnicity, and school achievement (Banks & Banks, 2006; Kincheloe & Steinberg, 2007; Howard, 2010). Their studies generally conclude that most differences in educational achievement occurring among racial and ethnic groups can be accounted for by social class, *even after the lower socioeconomic status (SES) of minority groups is considered.* In other words, if you know the SES of a group of students, you can pretty much predict their achievement with some accuracy. Information about their racial and ethnic group does little to improve the prediction.

It is now appropriate to ask, "What is it about SES that creates differences in the classroom?" and "What can I as a teacher do to lessen these differences?" Obviously, if SES plays such an important role in student achievement, it must stand for something more specific than the income and educational level of parents. Research has provided a number of more meaningful characteristics of the home and family lives of higher- and lower-SES families. These characteristics, which are the indirect results of income and education, are thought to significantly influence the achievement of schoolchildren.

The U.S. Census conducted in 2010 (U.S. Census Bureau, 2011), estimated that more than 35 million Americans may be living in poverty, including 20 percent of all children. One characteristic that seems to distinguish children of those who do and do not live in poverty is that the latter are more likely to acquire knowledge of the world outside their home and neighborhood at an earlier age. Through greater access to books, magazines, social networks, cultural events, the Internet, and people who have these learning resources, middle- and upper-class children develop their reading and speaking abilities more rapidly. This, in combination with parental teaching that tends to use more elaborated language that trains the child to think independently of the specific communication context, may give students in the middle and upper classes an advantage at the start of school. This contrasts with children who come from lower-class homes, which may emphasize obedience and conformity more than independent thinking and may emphasize rote learning (memorization, recall of facts, and so on) more than independent, self-directed learning (Christenson, Rounds, & Franklin, 1992; Grant & Ray, 2009).

Contributing to these differences is the fact that 70 percent of working-age mothers of disadvantaged students must work outside the home. In the last 30 years, the composition of the family has undergone a dramatic change. The traditional family unit is no longer the rule but the exception. In 1965, more than 60 percent of American families were traditional, or comprised of a working father and a mother who kept the house and took care of the children. Only ten percent of today's families represent the traditional family of past generations. Today's family is more likely to be a dual-career family, a single-parent family, a stepfamily, or a family that has moved an average of

14 times. All of these conditions affect the fabric of the family and the development of the school-age learners within it.

By some estimates, the majority of children now being born will live in a household where there is no adult 10 to 12 hours a day. Less time for parents to become involved in their child's education, more distracting lifestyles, and greater job and occupational stress can be expected to contribute to the growing number of disadvantaged learners. Some time ago, H. Levin (1986) estimated that the educationally disadvantaged comprise one-quarter of all school-age children. Today this proportion is even larger (U.S. Census Bureau, 2010). These learners are less likely to be immunized, more likely to be in poorer health, less ready to enter school, and more likely to experience academic failure and drop out.

The Effects of Language on Learning

Banks and Banks (2009), Delgado-Gaitan (1992, 2006), Minami and Ovando (2003), and Valencia (2010a,b) point to the important role of language in accounting for achievement difficulties of minority and immigrant learners. Many teachers are now responsible for teaching children with limited or no English-language capacity in classrooms that include students who may speak many different languages. For example, more than 100 languages are spoken in the school systems of New York City, Chicago, and Los Angeles. Spanish is the language most frequently spoken by new immigrants. Researchers point out that if language is used by a cultural group differently at home than in the classroom, members of that subculture are at a disadvantage. Children whose language at home corresponds to that expected in the classroom more easily transfer their prior experiences to the classroom in ways that facilitate their academic progress. Learners who speak another language at home than at school often experience difficulties transferring what they already know to classroom tasks and are often misunderstood. All of these differences point to the important role of differentiated instruction in the classroom.

Some have accounted for the differences between cultural minorities and mainstream learners by pointing out what minority learners lack in order to do well in school. The most prominent deficit is their lack of proficiency in English and the Standard American English dialect prominent among Anglo Americans and the middle and upper social economic classes. Using genetically or culturally inspired factors to explain these differences, such as aptitude and language, has come to be called the **cultural deficit model**. The cultural deficit model has been strongly criticized for focusing on what is missing in the child, not on what must be provided to the child for school performance to improve (Valencia, 2010a).

Although the cultural deficit model has influenced instructional practice (for example, with the practice of ability tracking), it has come to be replaced with another way of thinking about diversity called the **cultural difference model**, which also has its opponents on the grounds that it presumes ethnic differences to be inherently problematic and that even the perception of differences can channel individuals to act in a way that is problematic for minority students. Rather than focus on learners' deficits, the cultural difference model focuses on solutions that require more culturally sensitive links to and responses from the school and educational system that can improve the performance of students who are socially, economically, and linguistically different from the mainstream. In other words, the school's role is not to eliminate or diminish a child's use of his or her home language, dialect, and culturally ingrained learning style but rather to compensate for them by providing a rich and natural instructional environment that circumvents the effects these contextual factors may have on learning and uses them as a valued vehicle in which to transmit learning.

More recently, the cultural difference model has been revised and built on by Ogbu and Davis (2003) and Ogbu (1995a,b, 2008). Ogbu's research suggests that while one's cultural history may cause him or her to respond differently to school, it is the individual's **cultural frame** of reference, acquired from experience, that is the lens through which he or she interprets and responds to life's events. It is this cultural frame, not just one's cultural status, which can sometimes provide a better explanation of why different children respond to school differently. For example, when the cultural frame about schooling acquired from home is positive, differences between home and school are easily overcome. But when the cultural frame is negative, these differences are harder to overcome.

And, the cultural frame may not only derive from one's home and cultural history, but also by frames that are shared by learners independent of culture or minority status. Popular subjects, places to hang out, participation in athletics, and readiness to read may all be shared by the same individuals who do not have a common cultural history or home life, making the individual's acquired frame of reference an important addition to the cultural difference model for explaining school performance among learners.

Here are some suggestions for teachers, derived from these models, that can lessen the relationship of culture, SES, and language to school achievement:

- Provide more opportunities for learners to experience indirect and self-directed models of instruction, to which they can bring their own backgrounds and experiences to the classroom.

- Maintain high expectations for all learners, regardless of diversity. The overall learning environment should be leveled up, not scaled down.

- Include parents in the planning and implementing of important changes in curriculum, instructional techniques, and assessment aimed at eliminating the differences in performance among learners.

- Form heterogeneous groups that include culturally as well as linguistically diverse students.

- Learn and experiment with differentiated instructional techniques suitable for diverse learners, such as varying instructional modalities (listening, reading, doing), presenting content in incremental steps, grouping flexibly by need (not ability), and allowing students some choice in how they are to be assessed (writing a story, drawing a picture, telling about their experiences).

The Effects of Personality and Learning Style on Learning

Preceding sections discussed the potential influence on learning of students' general intelligence, specific aptitude, and culture. In this section, we add your students' personalities and learning styles to this equation.

When a word such as *trustworthy, creative, independent, anxious, cheerful, authoritarian,* or *aggressive* is used to describe a student, it refers to an aspect of his or her personality. *Personality* is the integration of one's traits, motives, beliefs, and abilities, including emotional responses, character traits, and even values.

Some parts of personality lie dormant until stimulated into action by some event. This is the reason a teacher is sometimes dismayed to hear, for example, that a child who is aggressive in their fifth-period social studies is shy and cooperative in someone else's seventh-period mathematics. It also is the reason that some students and teachers may never quite see eye to eye. Although such personality conflicts are rare, they can be harmful to classroom rapport if left to smolder beneath the surface. Let's look at some crises of the school years to better understand the role of personality in the classroom.

Erikson's Crises of the School Years

Some psychologists believe that different personality traits dominate at certain periods of our lives. For example, Erikson (in Mooney, 2000), who developed a theory on how personality is formed, hypothesized eight different stages of personality growth between infancy and old age that he called *crises*. Three of these stages, shown in Figure 2.2, occur during the school years:

1. The crisis of accomplishment versus inferiority
2. The crisis of identity versus role confusion
3. The crisis of intimacy versus isolation

Figure 2.2 Personal and Social Development during Erikson's Three Crises during the School Years

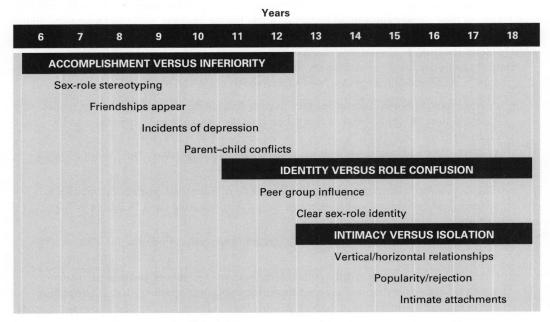

During the first crisis, *accomplishment versus inferiority,* the learner seeks ways of producing products or accomplishments that are respected by others. In this manner, the child creates a feeling of worth to dispel feelings of inferiority or inadequacy that result from competing in a world where adults appear confident and competent. At first, such accomplishments may take the easiest course—being good at sports, being good in school, or being helpful at home. For the teacher, this is a particularly challenging time, because student engagement at high rates of success is needed to keep some feelings of worth focused in the classroom. Seeing that every student has some successful experiences in the classroom can be an important vehicle for helping students through this crisis.

Erikson's second crisis during the school years, *identity versus role confusion,* is precipitated by the need to understand oneself—to find his or her identity, "the real me." One's gender, race, ethnicity, religion, and physical attractiveness can play important roles in producing or failing to produce a consistent and acceptable self-image. This is a process of accepting oneself as one truly is, apart from illusions, made-up images, and exaggerations.

Social psychologists believe that in the process of finding and accepting oneself during this second crisis, the individual must experience *recognition,* a sense of *control* over her or his environment, and *achievement.* Being a member of a group intensifies these needs. Social psychologists, such as Harpine (2008) and Patricia and Richard Schmuck (2001), urge teachers to recognize that groups help provide opportunities for recognition, control, and achievement and to use this heightened motivation to achieve academic goals. These psychologists caution that classrooms that fail to satisfy these three basic needs may contain a large number of learners who feel rejected, listless, and powerless, creating motivational and conduct problems within the classroom.

Erikson's third crisis during the school years, *intimacy versus isolation,* involves giving up part of one's identity to develop close and intimate relationships with others. Learning how to get along with teachers, parents, and classmates is one of the key developmental tasks learners must master to successfully resolve this crisis. Successful relationships with parents and teachers, referred to as **vertical relationships** (Hartup, 1989; Tremblay, Hartup, & Archer, 2005), meet a learner's needs for safety, security, and protection. Successful relationships with peers, referred to as **horizontal relationships**, are of equal developmental significance for learners. They meet learners' needs for belonging and allow them to acquire and practice important social skills.

Providing opportunities for learners to develop healthy relationships when they enter school helps them develop skills important in getting along with others, helping others, and establishing intimacy. The failure to experience healthy horizontal relationships and learn friendship-building attitudes and skills can have undesirable consequences. This failure often results in *social rejection* that encourages learners to be aggressive and disruptive in school (Bernstein, 2006; Hartup, 1989) and experience intense feelings of loneliness (Cassidy & Asher, 1992; Libal, 2007). By helping your learners construct their own well-functioning horizontal relationships, they can acquire friendship-building attitudes and skills that help create a warm and supportive classroom for all learners.

To help meet learners' needs during these three school years' crises, teachers can actively engage learners in ways that let them express themselves and their uniqueness. Here are some example activities that provide learners opportunities for recognition, control, and achievement during these critical school years:

- Art (e.g., drawing, sketching, and painting)
- Autobiographical recollections (e.g., of a major event growing up)
- Oral histories of personal experiences (e.g., of a vacation)
- Cooperative activities (e.g., team or group projects)
- Demonstrations and exhibits (e.g., use of poster boards)
- Discussions of a completed classroom activity (e.g., debriefing)
- Drama/improvisation (e.g., reenactments of personal or historical events)
- Acting/role playing (e.g., making believe you are someone else)
- Portfolios (e.g., accumulating drafts that show change or growth)
- Projects (e.g., solving a school, community, or national problem)
- Storytelling (e.g., reading aloud or in a group)

Successful relationships with peers, referred to as horizontal relationships, meet learners' needs for belonging and allow them to acquire and practice important social skills. These friendship patterns often are created through peer groups that exhibit strong commitments of loyalty, protection, and mutual benefit.

Learning Style

Another aspect of personality that will influence your learners' achievement is **learning style**, which represents the classroom conditions under which someone prefers to learn. Much has been written about how some learners are more global than analytic in how they approach learning (Irvine & York, 2001; Mshelia, 2008). Some researchers use the terms *holistic/visual* to describe global learners and *verbal/analytic* to describe the opposite style or orientation (Tharp & Gallimore, 1991). Still others prefer the term *field sensitive* to refer to the holistic/visual learning style and the term *field insensitive* to refer to the verbal/analytic learning style. To what are these researchers referring?

Basically, these terms have come to refer to how people view the world. People who are **field-dependent** tend to see the world in terms of large, connected patterns. Looking at a volcano, for example, a field-dependent person would notice its overall shape and its major colors and topographical features. A **field-independent** person, in contrast, would tend to look close up and notice the specific parts of a scene. Thus he or she might notice the individual trees, the different rocks, the size of the caldera, where the caldera sits in relation to the rest of the structure, topographical features showing the extent of lava flow, and so on.

Franklin (1992), Mshelia (2008), and Tharp (1989) believe that field dependence and independence are stable traits of individuals affecting different aspects of their lives, especially their approach to learning. Along with Sprenger (2008), they illustrate how learning style can be a useful tool for differentiating instruction. Table 2.2 summarizes some of the characteristics associated with field-dependent and field-independent learners. These researchers agree that the different traits of field-dependent and field-independent learners suggest that at least some learners think about and process information differently during classroom learning activities and that each group would benefit from some of the different instructional strategies suggested in Table 2.3.

Table 2.2 **Field-Dependent and Field-Independent Learner Characteristics**

Field-Dependent (Field-Sensitive) Learner	Field-Independent Learner
1. Perceives global aspects of concepts and materials	1. Focuses on details of curriculum materials
2. Personalizes curriculum—relates concepts to personal experience	2. Focuses on facts and principles
3. Seeks guidance and demonstrations from teacher	3. Rarely seeks physical contact with teacher
4. Seeks rewards that strengthen relationship with teacher	4. Formal interactions with teacher restricted to tasks at hand—seeks nonsocial rewards
5. Prefers to work with others and is sensitive to their feelings and opinions	5. Prefers to work alone
6. Likes to cooperate	6. Likes to compete
7. Prefers organization provided by teacher	7. Can organize information by himself or herself

Table 2.3 **Instructional Strategies for Field-Dependent and Field-Independent Learners**

Field-Dependent (Field-Sensitive) Learners	Field-Independent Learners
1. Display physical and verbal experiences of approval or warmth.	1. Be direct in interactions with learners; show content expertise.
2. Motivate by use of social and tangible rewards.	2. Motivate by use of nonsocial rewards such as grades.
3. Use cooperative-learning strategies.	3. Use more mastery learning and errorless teaching strategies.
4. Use corrective feedback often.	4. Use corrective feedback only when necessary.
5. Allow interaction during learning.	5. Emphasize independent projects.
6. Structure lessons, projects, and homework.	6. Allow learners to develop their own structure.
7. Assume role of presenter, demonstrator, checker, reinforcer, grader, or materials designer.	7. Assume role of consultant, listener, negotiator, or facilitator.

Cultural Differences in Learning Styles: Some Cautions

Is there sufficient justification to advocate a field-dependent teaching style in classrooms with significant numbers of minority learners? Should teachers make greater use of instructional practices that emphasize cooperative learning, person and movement/action-oriented activities, visual/holistic learning, and so on when teaching significant numbers of African, Hispanic, or Native American learners? Before implementing culturally responsive teaching without qualification, keep in mind the following cautions:

   1. *Beware of perpetuating stereotypes.* Valencia (2010a,b) cautions that cultural information such as that described previously may be used to perpetuate ideas from the cultural deficit hypothesis that encourages teachers to believe that these students have deficits and negative differences and, therefore, are not as capable of learning as the majority of students.

   2. *Note within-group differences.* Almost all studies of the learning style preferences of different cultural groups have shown that differences within the cultural groups were as great as the differences between the cultural groups (Cushner et al., 2008; Tharp, 1989; Waxman, Tharp, & Hilberg, 2004). On the average, the groups may differ. But around these averages are ranges of considerable magnitude. Thus using a field-dependent teaching style, even in a monocultural classroom, may fail to match the preferred learning style of at least some learners.

3. *Culturally responsive concerns may take the focus away from so-called expert practice.* Educators such as Cartledge, Gardner, and Ford (2008) and Lindsley (1992) argue that before assuming that differences in achievement are due to characteristics within the learner (for example, learning style), factors external to the learner, such as ineffective teaching practices, should be ruled out. The quality of instruction provided to minority learners should be equivalent to that provided to the majority of learners.

The Effects of the Peer Group on Learning

As a teacher, you will quickly notice that one of the most powerful influences on a student's behavior is the peer group. Often considered the source of a hidden curriculum, the peer group can influence and even teach students how to behave in class, study for tests, and converse with teachers and school administrators. In addition, the peer group can contribute to the success or failure of performance in school in many other ways. From the play group in elementary school to the teenage clique in high school, a student learns from peers how to behave in ways that are acceptable to the group and will establish status in the eyes of others (Eckmann, 2009; Prinstein & Dodge, 2008).

The power of the peer group in influencing student behavior comes from the voluntary submission of one's will to some larger cause. Teachers and parents must sometimes beg, plead, cajole, and reward to exact appropriate behavior from their students, sons, and daughters. But peer groups need not engage in any of these behaviors to obtain a high level of conformity to often unstated principles of behavior. Trendy school fashions, new slang words, places to hang out, acceptable social mates, and respected forms of out-of-school activities are communicated and learned to perfection without lesson plans, texts, or even direct verbalization. Instead, these and other behaviors are transmitted by salient others and received by those who anxiously wish to maintain membership in or gain acceptance to a particular peer group.

Friendship patterns often are created through peer groups and sometimes are adhered to with strong commitments of loyalty, protection, and mutual benefit. These commitments can create individual peer cultures or even gangs within a school. Such cultures can rival the academic commitments made in the classroom and frequently supersede them in importance. Studying for a test or completing homework frequently may be sacrificed for the benefit of the peer group. Peer groups can form on the basis of many different individual differences, such as achievement, personality, home life, physical appearance, and personal and social interests. But they commonly result from a complex combination of these factors that is not always discernible to outsiders and sometimes not even to those within the peer group (Maynard & Martini, 2005; SunWolf, 2008; Schmuck & Schmuck, 2001).

The importance of peer-group characteristics in the classroom lies in the extent to which they can be used to promote behaviors that enhance a member's engagement in the learning process. Here are several approaches for using peer relationships constructively to foster classroom goals:

1. *Stress group work in which members are from different peer groups.* When forming work or cooperative groups, be sure group members represent different backgrounds and interests, which can bring different skills and talents to an assignment. When different types of individuals are assigned to work cooperatively, group behavior tends to follow a middle ground, discouraging extreme or disruptive behavior.

2. *Conduct a group discussion of class norms, describing what class members should and should not do to be socially acceptable.* Tell group members what you expect of them, and give some examples of what they might expect of others. Glasser (1998a), Brookfield and Preskill (2005), and Sartor and Brown (2004) suggest discussing with students

An important way to positively influence peer groups in your classroom is to conduct group discussions of class norms, describing what class members should and should not do to be socially acceptable, what you expect of them, and what they should expect of each other.

ideas on how the class might be run, problems that may interfere with the group's performance, and needed rules and routines.

3. *Build group cohesiveness by promoting students' interests to one another.* Provide opportunities for your students to know one another through one or more of the following: Construct a bulletin board around the theme of friendship; have students write brief biographies about themselves for all to read on a class website; publish a class directory that includes names, hobbies, jobs, and career aspirations; and have students bring to class something they have made or really care about (a toy, tool, model, and so on).

4. *Assign older or more mature students who are more likely to be respected as role models to interact with and help younger students in a peer-tutoring situation.* Many schools have a formal peer-tutoring program called *cross-age tutoring,* in which tutors may be chosen from higher grades to help younger students who may be at risk or discouraged learners. Research has shown that tutoring is most successful when tutors have been trained and given explicit instruction on how to tutor.

The Effects of Home Life and Social Context on Learning

Closely connected with the influence of the peer group on learning is the social context in which your learners live, play, and work. Among the most prominent sources of influence in this context will be your learners' families and their relationships to the school.

In 1993, the National Governors' Conference for educational reform set forth a formidable agenda for educators. Their agenda, updated and approved by Congress (U.S. Department of Education, 1998), established the following national goals for education and set out clear and rigorous standards for what every child should know and be able to do. These goals, which have remained of paramount importance since 1998, are:

1. All children in America will start school ready to learn.

2. The high school graduation rate will increase to at least 90 percent.

3. All U.S. students will leave grades 4, 8, and 12 having demonstrated competency over challenging subject matter in the sciences and humanities.

4. United States students will be the best in the world in mathematics and science achievement.

5. Every adult American will be literate and will possess the knowledge and skills to compete in a global economy and exercise the rights and responsibilities of citizenship.

6. Every school in the United States will be free of drugs and violence and will offer a disciplined environment conducive to learning.

7. The nation's teachers will have access to programs for professional development.

8. Every school will promote parental involvement and participation in promoting the social, emotional, and academic growth of children (see also www.ed.gov/legislation/GOALS2000/TheAct).

A theme that has carried through to subsequent administrations and legislative goals has been the understanding that schools have to develop genuine partnerships with parents to achieve these goals. A singular focus on just teachers, parents, or administrators as the agents of reform will not produce the desired results. Only the active participation of parents, community groups, and educators in partnership with one another to create a learning culture will bring about the desired objectives (Epstein, 2010; DuFour, DuFour, Eaker, & Many, 2010; Dyches, Carter, & Prater, 2012).

When parents and teachers become partners, not only can student achievement increase, but in addition, parents can learn about you and your school. Research confirms that coordination and collaboration between home and school improve learner achievement, attitude toward school, classroom conduct, and parent and teacher morale (Wright, Stegelin, & Hartle, 2006). As InTASC standard 10 states, establishing genuine partnerships with the parents and guardians of your learners is as essential a teacher practice as those that involve building a cohesive classroom climate, establishing a well-managed work environment, developing goals and objectives, conducting effective instruction, and assessing student performance.

The practice of fostering parent and guardian involvement requires that throughout the school year you develop and strengthen *linking mechanisms* for parent and guardian participation and collaboration. **Family–school linking mechanisms** are opportunities for school and family involvement and may involve teacher–family conferences, home visits, participation of teachers in community events, newsletters, phone calls, personal notes, volunteering as classroom aides, and the use of home-based curriculum materials. These efforts require more than just sending a handout home to parents at the beginning of the school year, delivering an obligatory presentation during back-to-school night, or sending an occasional note home. The opportunities to develop and nurture linking mechanisms will be the culmination of your efforts to build a successful classroom workplace.

To assist in this process, Bronfenbrenner (1989, 2005) has urged us to view the family–school partnership from a **systems–ecological perspective**. Bronfenbrenner looks at the learner as a naturalist looks at nature—as an ecosystem. In the learner's ecosystem, the major systems include the family (which may be a single parent, and/or grandparent(s), foster parents, or guardians), the school, and the peer group.

One way to picture the learner's ecosystem is as a series of concentric circles, as shown in Figure 2.3. Each of these circles and its connections has a special term. The most central layer is called the *microsystem.* It includes all those settings where the child lives or spends significant portions of his or her time: the family, school, classroom, day care setting, playground, and job setting if the child is old enough. Bronfenbrenner refers to these settings as *subsystems.* Each subsystem can be viewed as a system within itself. The school system is made up of subsystems that include teachers, administrators, support personnel, school board members, and learners. The family system includes a marital, parental, sibling, and often a grandparental subsystem. The peer system includes social friendships, academic friendships, and sports or hobby friendships.

Figure 2.3 **The Child from a Systems–Ecological Perspective**

Source: Graphic originally published in *Child Development and Education,* Fifth Edition, by Teresa M. McDevitt and Jeanne Ellis Ormrod. Copyright © 2013 by Pearson Education.

Figure 2.4 **The Child's Ecosystem**

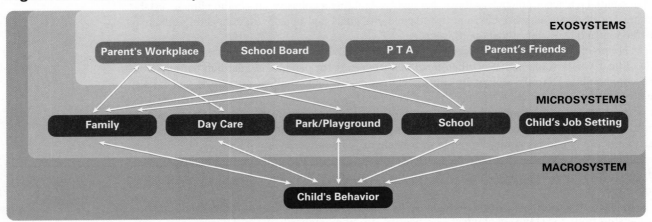

Source: From *The Developing Child,* 6th edition, by Helen Bee. Copyright © 1992 by Allyn and Bacon, Boston, MA. Adapted by permission of the publisher.

The next layer of the system includes those subsystems the child does not directly experience but that affect him or her because of the influence they exert on the microsystem. This layer is called the *exosystem*. It may include the parents' or guardian's workplace, their friends, the PTA, the school board, and so on.

Finally, both microsystems and exosystems exist in a larger setting called the *macrosystem*. This system refers to the larger culture or society in which the micro- and exosystems function. Figure 2.4 indicates some of the relationships among these systems.

A systems–ecological perspective urges us to view a learner's behavior not as a product of that individual alone but as a product of the learner and the demands and forces operating within the systems of which he or she is a member. Family experiences and the culture of the family system influence school behavior and performance, which in turn affect the family system. School adjustment problems, which may be influenced by problems within the family, may in turn exacerbate conditions within the family system. For example, the parent who never signs and returns a note from the teacher may not be an uninterested and uninvolved parent—as might be assumed. Dynamics within the family system (for example, other siblings who demand extensive care, adjustment to a new child, or work schedule) may explain the parent's apparent lack of involvement in his or her child's education.

Thus when trying to understand the behavior of parents, teachers, and learners, the systems–ecological perspective recommends that we first ask ourselves, What forces within the family–school environment impel the person to act this way? When the goal is to promote the academic and social development of the learner, the systems–ecological perspective focuses our most immediate concern on the family–school partnership.

Here are some guidelines for understanding and promoting family–school partnerships in your classroom:

1. *View the family from a systems–ecological perspective.* Avoid viewing the behavior of your learners or their mothers, fathers, or guardians as simply products of individual psychological forces. Instead recognize that the family system is made up of several subsystems, including the marital subsystem, parental subsystem, sibling subsystem, and extrafamily or exosystems, such as grandparents and employers. Changes in one subsystem inevitably bring about changes in another. Asking parents to take on greater responsibility for getting their child to bed earlier at night can result in an argument at home between husband and wife, punishment of the child, teasing by siblings, and concern and criticism by in-laws. Likewise, demands by school staff that parents do something at home to make the child complete extra homework may reverberate throughout the entire family system. These effects may be so great as to preclude any change in parental behavior.

2. *Acknowledge changes in the American family.* Most families have two working parents. Research on teacher beliefs regarding families in which both parents work shows that teachers believe working parents are less involved with their children's education (Coontz, 2008; Turner & West, 2006). However, studies by Delgado-Gaitan (1991, 1992, 2006) conclude that working and nonworking mothers spend the same amount of time in child-related activities. Furthermore, their data show that children of working mothers are just as involved in extracurricular activities as are the children of nonworking mothers.

Single-parent families make up about 27 percent of the families of schoolchildren. Yet many teachers view this family pattern as an abnormality (Hanson, 2005). Joyce Epstein, a researcher at the Johns Hopkins Center for Research on Elementary and Middle Schools, reported that teachers have lower expectations for the achievement of children from single-parent families despite the fact that no data support this (Epstein, 2010). Some researchers suggest that the requirements in single-parent families for organization, schedules, routines, and division of responsibilities better prepare children to accept such structure in schools (Aaron, 2001; Frisbie & Frisbie, 2007; Hanson, 2005).

3. *View parent participation from an empowerment model rather than a deficit model.* Delgado-Gaitan (1991, 2006) and Valencia (2010a,b) propose that we view parent participation as a process that involves giving parents both the power and the knowledge to deal with the school system. Typically, deficit model explanations have been offered for reasons culturally different parents have not become involved with schools. These perspectives sometimes have portrayed parents as passive, incompetent, or unskilled. They propose that parents are unable to become involved in their children's education because they work long hours away from the home or are simply not interested. But as Delgado-Gaitan (1992) pointed out, when examined closely, research has shown that Hispanic families who speak a different language and have a different culture from that of the school do indeed care about their children and possess the capacity to advocate for them. This holds true for African Americans, Hispanic Americans, Native Americans, and other cultural and linguistic groups, as well. The question is not whether they can become genuine partners with the school but how to empower them to do so.

4. *Recognize the unique needs of mothers and fathers when planning opportunities to involve parents.* Turnbull and Turnbull (2010) urge teachers to promote nonsexist views of parenting and parent involvement. They stress that teachers recognize the importance of mothers and fathers when designing home-school linkages. Create visiting opportunities to your classroom for both parents, and develop flexible schedules to accommodate the working schedules of both parents. Address information about the children and schooling to both parents. Seek to promote teaching skills in fathers as well as mothers. Finally, give consideration to the father's interests and needs when suggesting ways for parents to work with their children at home.

5. *Appreciate that parents are just like you: They experience periodic emotional, family, and economic problems.* Many parents may have personal, family, work, health, or other problems that remain hidden. Make a special effort to provide the benefit of the doubt, particularly when parents fail to respond to your requests in a timely manner. Hanson (2005) and Carlson (1992) document the overwhelming economic as well as custody and career problems of single parents. Their failure to monitor their children's homework, attendance, or tardiness to class may be due less to a lack of interest than to attempts to cope with day-to-day problems. When parents do not live up to your expectations, avoid trying to assign personal blame.

6. *Understand the variety of school–family linkages, and respect family preferences for different degrees of school participation.* As you are planning for parent/family involvement early in the school year, consider and evaluate the full range of ways in which parents and family members can participate. These activities can be placed on a continuum anchored on one end by activities that involve parents and family members as receivers of information (teacher–family conferences, notes home, classroom newsletter) and on the other end by activities that involve parents and family members as active educational decision makers (school and classroom advisory councils, site-based management teams, teacher aides, tutoring). As the research suggests, your learners' achievement of academic goals, adherence to rules and routines, and attitudes and expectations about school can be enhanced by having parents and family as partners.

The Teacher's Role in Improving the Academic Success of All Learners

The classroom is the logical place to begin the process of reducing some of the achievement differences that have been noted between lower-, middle-, and upper-SES and language-diverse students. Disadvantaged and language-diverse learners have an important characteristic in common: Both have difficulty expressing their past experiences and knowledge in a format that is expected by the teacher and used by other learners. This can produce a classroom of many silent learners (Nieto & Bode, 2012). Many formal interventions are trying to reduce these effects, from preschools to federally funded compensatory education programs. However, these interventions and programs are not likely to eliminate achievement differences among various groups of students who have highly divergent home and family lifestyles.

This leaves the teacher to plan for these differences as a daily fact of classroom life. The general tendencies are clear: The home and family backgrounds of lower- and higher-SES and English-language learners differently prepare them for school. For the classroom teacher, the task becomes one of differentiating and planning instruction around these differences in ways that reduce them as much as possible.

You can reduce these achievement differences in your classroom in several ways. One of these is your willingness to integrate a variety of learning aids into your lessons, such as computer instructional software, audiovisuals, learning centers, and exploratory materials along with alternative formats as to how learning is assessed. Using a variety of instructional materials and assessments will encourage your learners to use their own experiences, past learning, and preferred learning modalities to construct and demonstrate what they have learned. Lesson variety can be an important resource for those who may benefit from alternative ways of learning.

Another way in which to reduce achievement differences is to have high expectations for all your students and to reward them for their accomplishments. Sufficiently high expectations and rewards for learning outside the classroom may not be equally available to all of your learners; so your support and encouragement for learners to bring their personal experiences and culture into the classroom is important. Your role in providing opportunities to do this could be instrumental in bridging some of the differences in achievement among your learners.

Finally, as an effective teacher in a heterogeneous classroom, you will need to provide learners the opportunity to express their own sense of what they know and to build connections or relationships among the ideas and facts being taught using their own experiences. Encourage learners to construct their own meanings and express their understandings in a form that is most comfortable to them, linguistically and culturally. Doing so has two important effects in helping you attain the instructional goals of your classroom: It promotes student engagement and interest in school, and it shows them that someone thinks they have something worthwhile to say.

Other ways you can reduce the differences among learners in your classroom include the following:

1. Organize learning and instruction around important ideas that your students already know something about.

2. Acknowledge the importance of your students' prior learning by having them compare what they know to what you are teaching.

3. Challenge the adequacy of your students' prior knowledge by designing lessons that create the opportunity for them to resolve conflicts and construct new meanings for themselves.

4. Provide some tasks that make students confront ambiguity and uncertainty by exploring problems that have multiple solutions in authentic, real-world contexts.

5. Teach and encourage students how to find their own approaches or systems for achieving educational goals, for which they can take ownership.

6. Teach students that knowledge construction is a collaborative effort for creating a partnership of ideas in your classroom, rather than a solitary search of knowledge or an exclusively teacher-controlled activity.

7. Monitor and assess students' knowledge acquisition frequently and in a variety of formats (with oral responses, portfolios, demonstrations, reenactments as well as formal tests) and provide feedback in accordance with the 2004 reauthorization of the Individuals with Disabilities Education Improvement Act (IDEA) and Response to Invention legislation that will be discussed in Chapter 13.

It is evident that teachers will increasingly need to implement suggestions such as these as they face greater diversity in culture, language, social class, and ability and in a larger number of combinations than ever before. In the chapters ahead, we will present many methods and techniques that can help you meet the individual learning needs of all your students, including those with special needs.

The Teacher and Cultural, Linguistic, and Socioeconomic Bias in the Classroom

Much of what has been said about individual differences suggests that planning to eliminate bias in classroom teaching can be one of the most significant aspects of becoming an effective teacher. Pintrich and Schunk (2007) and Wolpert (2005) remind us that the way in which you interact with your students in the classroom can have a considerable influence on their motivation and attitudes toward school.

Consciously or unconsciously, everyone has biases of one kind or another. When applied in ways that affect only our own behavior and not that of others, we use the word *preference*. *Biases*, on the other hand, are not harmless. They can injure the personal growth and well-being of others and if left unchecked can significantly affect the growth and development of learners. Let's look at some of the ways you might show bias.

Many examples of teacher biases have been catalogued. For example, Good and Brophy (2007) summarize how teachers sometimes respond unequally to high and low achievers by more frequently criticizing the wrong answers of low achievers, communicating low expectations and thereby accepting and unintentionally encouraging a low level of performance among some students. Other researchers have documented how some teachers respond differently to students from various cultures and linguistic backgrounds than to those from their own background (Banks & Banks, 2009; Compton-Lilly, 2000; DeLeon, 1996; Lockwood & Secada, 1999; Schwartz, 1998). These researchers identify the following ways in which some teachers have responded differently toward low achievers and/or culturally and linguistically different learners:

• Wait longer for these students to answer.
• Give the answer after a student's slightest hesitation.
• Praise students' marginal or inaccurate answers.
• Criticize these students more frequently than other students for having the wrong answer.
• Praise students less when they give the right answer.
• Do not give students feedback as to why an answer is incorrect.
• Don't pay attention to (e.g., smile at) students and call on them less.
• Seat these students further from the teacher.
• Allow these students to give up more easily.

Generally, these findings confirm that teachers usually do not allow more response opportunities and more teacher contact for culturally different, low-achieving learners or special-needs students.

Other types of bias have been known to affect whom a teacher calls on. For example, Gage and Berliner (1998) identified several biased ways in which teachers called on their students and then analyzed the extent to which experienced teachers actually exhibited these biases in their classrooms. Their biases included calling on students disproportionately in these ways:

• Nonminority-group members versus minority-group members
• Those seated in the front half of the class versus seated in the back half of the class

- Nicer-looking students versus average-looking students
- More able students versus less able students

Gage and Berliner calculated the number of student–teacher interactions that would be expected by chance for these classifications; then from observation, they determined the actual number of interactions that occurred. Surprisingly, their results indicate that every teacher showed some bias in these categories. In other words, every teacher favored at least one student classification over another by naming, calling on, requiring information from, or otherwise interacting with those in some classification disproportionally to those not in that classification.

Bias in the way a teacher interacts with students is undesirable in any form, but it is particularly distasteful when it pertains to students who belong to a cultural, ethnic, or linguistic minority. Our nation and our educational system are based on respect for individual differences of all types. This means that our classrooms become one of the most important showplaces of democratic values. It is disturbing that researchers report frequent ethnic bias or cultural insensitivity during student–teacher interactions in mixed-ethnic classrooms. Research has pointed out that the actions of many teachers diminish the classroom participation of minority students and/or build resentment because their actions are culturally incongruent (Frawley, 2005; Kieff, 2006; Wolpert, 2005; Leiding, 2006).

These authors have contributed to the following suggestions for eliminating bias and increasing cultural sensitivity in the classroom. Each suggestion promotes the equitable distribution of power in the classroom by calling on all students—volunteers as well as nonvolunteers—to increase achievement as well as motivation:

1. Plan to spread your interactions as evenly as possible across student categories by deciding in advance which students to call on. Because the many classifications of potential bias are cumbersome to deal with, choose one or two bias categories you know or suspect you are most vulnerable to.

2. If you plan on giving special assignments only to some of your students, choose the students randomly. Place all of your students' names in a jar, and have one student draw the names of individuals needed for the special assignment. This protects you from inadvertently choosing the same students repeatedly and conveying the impression that you have favorites.

3. Consciously try to pair opposites in what you believe to be a potential area of bias for you; for example, pair minority with nonminority, more able with less able, easy to work with and difficult to work with, and so on. In this manner, when you are interacting with one member of the pair, you will be reminded to interact with the other. Frequently change one member of each pair so your pairings do not become obvious to the class.

4. When you discover a bias, plan a code to remind you of the bias and then embed it within your class notes, text, or lesson plan at appropriate intervals. For example, should you discover that you systematically favor more able learners over less able learners, place a code on the margins of your exercise to remind you to choose a less able learner for the next response.

Instead of being pulled along unconsciously by the stream of rapidly paced events in the classroom, you can be an active decision maker who influences the quality of events in your classroom by continually questioning and monitoring your interaction patterns with culturally and linguistically different, low-achieving, and special-needs learners.

A Final Word

There is no question that your students' individual differences in ability, achievement, personality, culture, peer group, and social context can dramatically affect your teaching methods and classroom achievement. So why place such diverse students in the same classroom? Would it not be more efficient to segregate students by ability and achievement level, personality type, degree of disadvantage, or even according to the most advantageous peer group? The results of such grouping might be quite astounding, if it were tried.

It is difficult to imagine life in such a segregated environment, for we live, work, and play in a world that is complex and diverse. However, our nation's founders seriously considered this very question. Their answer is in the first ten amendments to the U.S. Constitution, known as the Bill of

Rights, and in the Declaration of Independence, which gives every citizen the unqualified right to "life, liberty, and the pursuit of happiness." This constitutional guarantee specifically precludes any attempt to advance a single group at the expense of any other group. It even precludes segregating groups when "separate but equal" treatment is accorded them, because even the labeling of groups as different implies inequality, regardless of the motive for forming them.

These are important constitutional implications for the American classroom and for the diverse and special populations within it. They promote an environment that not only tolerates differences among individuals but also celebrates diversity in human potential. In a world complicated by such social and technological problems as pollution, disease, illiteracy, and environmental issues, we need divergent viewpoints, different abilities, and diverse values to address these problems. No single set of skills, attitudes, temperaments, personalities, or abilities can provide all that is needed to solve our problems.

Your willingness to be flexible in your teaching can harness the diversity needed to solve these problems by adapting your instruction to the strengths of your learners, by using different instructional approaches in teaching students of differing competencies and ethnic and racial backgrounds, and by promoting the family–school partnership. Above all, your teaching must emphasize the importance of all students working cooperatively. In the chapters ahead, we will explore ways of accomplishing these important goals.

Case History and Licensure Preparation

DIRECTIONS: *The following case history pertains to Chapter 2 content. After reading the case history, go to Chapter 2 in the Book Specific Resources section in the MyEducationLab for your course. Open the Case History and Licensure Preparation activity and complete the questions that follow. Upon completion of the test, scored answers to the short-answer question pertaining to the case history and multiple-choice questions will be provided.*

Case History

Anna Ramirez is a seventh-grader who lives with her family of five siblings and their parents in a modest house about a mile from the middle school she attends. She looks up to her two older brothers, one who is a strong athlete in high school and the other who plays the trumpet in the band. Her older sister, who dropped out of school two years ago at age 16, now has a two-year-old child. Anna helps take care of him on weekends and sometimes on school nights. She also helps with her two younger sisters, aged seven and nine, and answers their questions about their schoolwork.

Anna is very patient with her nephew and her younger sisters and creative in finding ways to keep them busy. She plays and even roughhouses with them, letting them ride her like a horse or put her on a leash as a pet dog. She likes to draw and often has all of the children coloring or painting around the kitchen table. The walls in her part of a shared bedroom are decorated with sketches she has made of her favorite singers. Her brother has nicknamed her "Leonardo" because she is always drawing something.

Anna also enjoys helping her mother and aunts prepare elaborate meals for special family dinners. While they chop and mince the fresh vegetables and herbs, they banter back and forth and tease each other. It is a very happy kitchen, and Anna feels safe and secure in its hub.

A very different Anna enters Mrs. Dodge's math classroom, unfortunately. Anna picks up her folder with a frown and goes to her assigned seat in the back of the room. Instead of doing the daily warm-up problem on the board, Anna draws in her notebook. When it is time to discuss the answer, she stares at her desk. Mrs. Dodge calls on one of several eager students who raise their hands and sends him to the board to show his work. When he is finished, she tells him he has done a good job. Meanwhile Anna has copied down the problem and its answer from the board. When Mrs. Dodge asks if there are any questions, Anna says nothing, although she does not understand the problem.

Next Mrs. Dodge has Juan, a straight-A student, read the chapter section introducing the concept of *percent* and how it relates to fractions and decimals. She stops him occasionally to ask questions.

"If you were converting ½ to a percentage, what would it be?"

Miguel is one of several in the front of the class who raises his hand, and Mrs. Dodge calls on him. "Fifty percent," he responds.

"That's very good, Miguel. You see, it is just like money, just like the change from a dollar. Fifty cents is ½ a dollar, just as 50 percent also stands for ½."

Mrs. Dodge notices that Anna is drawing on the back of her notebook and walks over to her. Mrs. Dodge picks it up and smiles sarcastically. "Oh, I thought you were graphing our work, but it only seems that you are drawing again."

The rest of the class laughs, and Anna turns red. "Anna, what is 50 percent of 200?" Mrs. Dodge asks.

Anna looks down for a second or two and is about to reply when Mrs. Dodge turns to Edgar, who is waving his hand. He gives the correct answer.

The last part of the period is labeled "Cooperative Learning" in large, bold letters on the board. Mrs. Dodge allows the students to join small, self-selected groups to work on the homework assignment. Cooperative learning

is not often used by Mrs. Dodge and even goes against her grain, because she sees it as cheating. However, many of the in-service presentations stress cooperative learning, and Mrs. Dodge knows she will not get a good evaluation if she doesn't show it in her lesson plans.

The good math students sit together in a group, although they really work separately. However, they always manage to finish before the bell rings. In many of the groups, there is interaction, but it is mainly about things other than math. Anna works with a few others she has known since early elementary school, but they seldom are able to help one another. She finishes only a few problems, and even then she is not sure they are correct.

The bell rings and Anna leaves the room. There is new vigor in her step and confidence in her stride. The next class is art.

Summing Up

This chapter introduced you to the diversity of students found in classrooms and how this diversity must be acknowledged in your teaching methods. The main points in this chapter include the following:

Not All Learners Are Alike

1. Early conceptions of teaching viewed students as empty vessels into which the teacher poured the content of the day's lesson. These conceptions failed to consider the effect of individual differences on learning.

2. A knowledge of the individual differences among learners is important (a) to adapt instructional methods to individual learning needs and (b) to understand and place in perspective the reasons behind the school performance of individual learners.

The Effects of General Ability on Learning

3. One misunderstanding that some teachers and parents have about intelligence is that it is a single, unified dimension.

4. Specific aptitude competencies are more predictive of success in school and specific occupations than is general intelligence.

5. Knowing your learners' specific strengths and weaknesses and altering instructional goals and methods accordingly will contribute to greater learning than categorizing and teaching your students according to their general intelligence.

The Effects of Specific Abilities on Learning

6. Specific definitions of intelligence and the behaviors they represent commonly are called aptitudes.

7. One of the practical classroom applications of Gardner's theory of multiple intelligences is allowing students to take differentiated paths to achieve a common goal.

8. Social-emotional intelligence is important in the classroom for recognizing one's own mood in order to change to best fit the task, to control one's impulses and not overreact, and to recognize one's impact on others and to change accordingly.

9. Sternberg suggests that confronting novel tasks and situations and learning to deal with them is one of the most important instructional goals in learning intelligence behavior.

The Effects of Culture, Socioeconomic Status, and Language on Learning

10. An important characteristic that distinguishes lower-class children from middle-class and upper-class children is that the latter more rapidly acquire knowledge of the world outside their homes and neighborhoods.

11. The cultural deficit model emphasizes what is missing in the child using genetically or culturally inspired factors, such as aptitude and language, to explain differences among culturally diverse and mainstream students. Rather than focus on a learner's deficits, the cultural difference

model focuses on solutions that require more culturally sensitive links to and responses from the school and educational system, which can improve the performance of students who are socially, economically, and linguistically different from the mainstream.

The Effects of Personality and Learning Style on Learning

12. Erikson's (1968) three crises during the school years are (a) accomplishment versus inferiority, (b) identity versus confusion, and (c) intimacy versus isolation.

13. Learning style refers to the classroom or environmental conditions under which someone prefers to learn. One of the most frequently studied learning styles is field independence/dependence.

14. Research has shown that some learners tend to be field sensitive, or holistic/visual learners, whereas others tend to be less field sensitive, or verbal/analytic learners.

15. Before implementing instructional strategies to match students' learning styles, be cautious not to perpetuate stereotypes and ignore within-group differences.

The Effects of the Peer Group on Learning

16. The peer group is an influential source of learner behavior both in and out of the classroom. Group work, group norms, group cohesiveness, and cross-age tutoring are means of using peer-group influence to foster the instructional goals of the classroom.

The Effects of Home Life and Social Context on Learning

17. Closely connected with the influence of the peer group on learning is the social context in which your learners live, play, and work. Among the most prominent sources of influence in this context will be your learners' families and their relationships to the school.

The Teacher's Role in Improving the Academic Success of All Learners

18. The home and family backgrounds of lower- and higher-SES and English-language learners differentially prepare them for school. For the classroom teacher, the task becomes one of differentiating and planning instruction around these differences in ways that reduce them as much as possible.

Cultural, Linguistic, and Socioeconomic Biases in the Classroom

19. Almost every teacher shows some type of bias in interacting with students. Bias may be avoided in these ways:

- By consciously spreading interactions across categories of students toward whom you have identified bias

- By randomly selecting students for special assignments

- By covertly pairing students who are opposite in your category of bias and then interacting with both members of the pair

- By coding class notes to remind yourself to call on students toward whom you may be biased

Key Terms

Adaptive teaching	Family–school linking mechanism	Reflective teacher
Compensatory approach	Field-dependent	Remediation approach
Cultural deficit model	Field-independent	Social competence
Cultural difference model	Horizontal relationships	Special populations
Cultural frame	Learning style	Systems–ecological perspective
Differentiated instruction	Reciprocal distancing	Vertical relationships

Discussion and Practice Questions

Questions marked with an asterisk are answered in Appendix B. Some asterisked questions may require student follow-up responses not included in Appendix B. Go to the Assignments and Activities section of the various topics on the MyEducationLab for your course to complete additional practice activities related to this chapter's content.

*1. In what two ways might you use knowledge of the individual differences in your classroom to become a more effective teacher?

*2. Describe your position as to the usefulness of intelligence tests in schools. Devise an argument you could use in responding to someone who says all intelligence is inherited.

*3. Explain the role that social competence is believed to play in school learning. If behaviors solely related to SES could be eliminated, how might differences in the tested intelligences among subgroups of learners change?

*4. Identify some of the aptitudes or factors that are likely to be more predictive than general intelligence of success in selected school subjects and occupations.

5. Using specific examples in the life of a child that you have known, explain what is meant by a systems–ecological perspective.

*6. Gage and Berliner (1998) identify a number of ways in which teachers' interactions with students can be biased. Name four, and then add one of your own not mentioned by Gage and Berliner. Why do you think the one you added is important? Describe an experience that you saw or encountered that made you add it to your list, if possible.

*7. Identify four procedures for reducing or eliminating the biases you may have when interacting with your students. Which would be the easiest to implement, and which would be the most difficult?

Professional Practice

Field Experience and Practice Activities

Questions marked with an asterisk are answered in Appendix B. Some asterisked questions may require student follow-up responses not included in Appendix B.

1. Using a school subject you will teach, identify a lesson topic in which a learner's aptitude would not be expected to predict his or her score on a classroom test on that topic. How would you explain this to a parent? What teaching strategies might account for this result?

2. Think back to some of your observations in schools. What might be some teaching practices that could be used to shrink differences in achievement due to SES?

3. Think of two learners at the grades you will teach who have different learning styles. What different types of products would each likely submit to you for their portfolio assessment as evidence of their learning?

*4. Identify two methods for dealing with a disruptive peer group that you have seen in a classroom you were observing. How might they be applied in a heterogeneous classroom?

5. Think of a child with the typical SES, learning history, and culture you will have in your classroom. Now explain in your own words what is meant by the family–school partnership. What are some things you can do with this family to strengthen this partnership in your classroom?

Digital Portfolio Activities

These digital portfolio activities relate to InTASC standards 1 and 2.

1. In this chapter you read the following:

   "Studies generally conclude that most differences in educational achievement occurring among racial and ethnic groups can be accounted for by social class. . . . In other words, if you know the SES of a group of students, you can pretty much predict their achievement with some accuracy. Information about their racial and ethnic group does little to improve the prediction."

   Given the preceding statement, outline a plan that indicates what you would do at your grade level to improve the achievement of minority learners in your classroom. Cite some of the suggestions provided in this chapter, add some of your own, and place your response in your digital portfolio in a folder labeled "Teaching the Culturally Diverse."

2. Prepare a brief outline of a lesson plan that shows that you know the difference between planning instruction from the perspective of the *cultural deficit model* versus the *cultural difference model* and its recent extensions and revisions. Be sure to indicate what specifically you would do differently in your classroom to reach diverse learners with the cultural difference model that you would not do with the cultural deficit model. Place your response in your digital portfolio in the "Teaching the Culturally Diverse" folder. Both entries will show others that you are aware of key issues in teaching culturally diverse learners.

MyEducationLab™

Go to MyEducationLab (www.myeducationlab.com) for Effective Teaching Methods: Research-Based Practice where you can:

- Find learning outcomes for the various course topics course along with national standards that connect to these outcomes.

- Complete **Assignments and Activities** that can help you more deeply understand the chapter content.

- Apply and practice your understanding of the core teaching skills identified in the chapter with **Building Teaching Skills and Dispositions** coaching activities.

- Check your comprehension of the content covered in the chapter with a book specific **Study Plan**. Here you will be able to take a chapter **pretest**, receive feedback on your answers, and then access personalized **Review, Practice, and Enrichment exercises** to enhance your understanding of chapter content. After you complete the exercises, take a **posttest** to confirm your comprehension.

- Learn how to address common classroom management issues in the **Simulations in Classroom Management**.

- Access video clips of CCSSO **National Teachers of the Year award winners** responding to the question, "Why Do I Teach?" in the Teacher Talk section.

- Create, update, and share quality lesson plans with the **Lesson Plan Builder**.

- Access state licensure test requirements, overviews of what tests cover, and sample test items in the **Certification and Licensure** section.

- Learn how to create a high quality teaching portfolio in the **Preparing a Portfolio** section.

- Access tips, advice, and other information on resume writing and interviewing, your first year of teaching, and law and public policies in the Beginning Your Career section.

3

Classroom Management I
Establishing the Learning Climate

This chapter will help you answer these questions and meet the following InTASC standards for effective teaching.

- What can I do during the first weeks of school to build a classroom climate of trust and cohesiveness?
- What can I teach my learners to help them discuss and resolve group conflicts on their own?
- How do I get my class to develop group norms?
- What types of classroom rules will I need?
- How might I use the organization of my classroom to bridge cultural gaps and reach learners with special needs?

InTASC

STANDARD 2 **Learning Differences.** The teacher uses understanding of individual differences and diverse cultures and communities to ensure inclusive learning environments that enable each learner to meet high standards.

STANDARD 4 **Content Knowledge.** The teacher understands the central concepts, tools of inquiry, and structures of the discipline(s) he or she teaches and creates learning experiences that make these aspects of the discipline accessible and meaningful for learners to assure mastery of the content.

STANDARD 9 **Professional Learning and Ethical Practice.** The teacher engages in ongoing professional learning and uses evidence to continually evaluate his/her practice, particularly the effects of his/her choices and actions on others (learners, families, other professionals, and the community), and adapts practice to meet the needs of each learner.

STANDARD 10 **Leadership and Collaboration.** The teacher seeks appropriate leadership roles and opportunities to take responsibility for student learning, to collaborate with learners, families, colleagues, other school professionals, and community members to ensure learner growth, and to advance the profession.

*E*or most teachers, confronting some sort of classroom management problem is a daily occurrence. These problems may include simple infractions of school or classroom rules, or they may involve more serious events, including showing disrespect, cheating, using inappropriate language, and openly displaying hostility.

But the management of your classroom must begin with developing trusting and nurturing relationships with your students. Without mutual feelings of trust and respect, you will be unable to assume the role of an instructional leader in your classroom. To accomplish this, this chapter discusses how you can do these things:

1. Design an orderly workplace that promotes your academic goals
2. Develop rules for the workplace that create group norms that students respect and follow
3. Change in response to unproductive rules, routines, and procedures
4. Maintain a workplace that fosters feelings of belonging, trust, and group solidarity
5. Know how to seek help from other school professionals and parents

MyEducationLab™

Visit the MyEducationLab for *Effective Teaching Methods: Research-Based Practice*, 8/e to enhance your understanding of chapter concepts with a personalized Study Plan. You'll also have the opportunity to hone your teaching skills through video-based Assignments and Activities as well as Building Teaching Skills and Dispositions lessons.

Connecting with Students

Not so long ago greater than 75 percent of students in U.S. elementary and high schools were White. In 2008, that percentage dropped below 60 percent, while during this same period there have been dramatic increases in the percentages of Hispanic, African-American, and Asian students. (Synder, Dillow, & Hoffman, 2009; U.S. Department of Education, 2011). Add to this the fact that Black and Hispanic students have a much higher rate of dropping out of school than do White students and we have a picture of continually increasing diversity in the American classroom. With this has come challenges for teachers to connect to their students to provide the emotional support needed for all students to learn (Mendler, 2001; Powell, 2010).

Aside from the many academic challenges this picture presents, especially to beginning teachers, it also presents challenges to creating a nurturing classroom and developing the tools to capture and sustain the attention of learners and to inspire them to become willing participants in the learning process. It is the nurturing context in which learning occurs that has become an important catalyst to the success of a teacher's day-to-day lessons. But, what are the ingredients of a nurturing classroom?

In a cross-cultural study of classrooms in India and the United States, researchers found three characteristics of a nurturing classroom: mutual trust and confidence between teacher and learners, unconditional acceptance of every learner's potential to learn, and opportunities for exploration and discovery (Borich, 2004). These characteristics are explored more thoroughly in the following sections.

Mutual Trust and Confidence

Mutual trust and confidence was created by alternating between lessons that were aimed at presenting knowledge, skills, and concepts in a traditional teacher to student format, while other lessons were learner-centered in which the teacher entered the learner's world by choosing topics that could be framed by their direct experiences in collaboration with one another. While the content for both paradigms were chosen from the curriculum guide, some topics were chosen to capitalize on the direct experiences of the learners. These topics followed a constructivist model emphasizing the learners' direct experience and the dialog of the classroom as instructional tools while deemphasizing lecturing and telling. Trust and confidence resulted from the shared mutual contributions of teacher and learners in a seamless pattern of moving back and forth between direct and indirect models of learning, creating a partnership of ideas connecting teacher with learner.

Unconditional Acceptance of Every Learner's Potential to Learn

Another catalyst for learning that was developed in the classrooms studied was inspired by the teachers' unconditional acceptance of the child's potential to learn. But, unconditional acceptance in these classrooms did not mean "anything goes." If a learner was asked the answer to two plus two and said five, the learner would be corrected. But, there was a difference in what followed in that, over repeated teacher questions and student answers, regardless of the nature of the responses, the teacher persisted in helping the child to learn by adjusting the question to the learner's current level of understanding; the nurturing relationship between teacher and learner remained unharmed. Over time, wrong answers that were repeatedly corrected and followed by another question, were not allowed to diminish the teacher's belief in the student's potential to learn. In other words, these teachers did not explicitly or implicitly divide learners into categories of learning potential that could weaken their supportive and nurturing role in the classroom. This made an important difference in the atmosphere of these classrooms that tended to keep all learners supported and engaged. The results showed that when wrong answers are met with a fear that their potential to learn is viewed less positively than others, the learners gave up—shutting down their future motivation to learn.

Opportunity for Exploration and Discovery

The cross-cultural study also found that both mutual trust and confidence and unconditional acceptance were instrumental in inspiring each learner to explore and discover on their own. The reason proved to be simple: Because these learners experienced mutual trust and confidence and felt unconditional acceptance throughout the entire school year, they took the initiative to explore and discover on their own without the fear of failure that many students have in venturing beyond the safe confines of what is told to them in class. It was found that disapproval by the teacher, resulting in the child's fear of failing, was one of the biggest contributors to lower academic performance in classrooms that did not use a constructivist or direct experience models that would have had the effect of inspiring the learner (a) to reach beyond the teacher, to discover knowledge and understandings on his or her own, that was (b) mediated by the teacher's unconditional belief in the child's potential to learn, and (c) that encouraged learners to take the initiative to explore and discover in authentic, real life environments.

Dyches, Carter, and Prater (2012) suggest putting into practice the above characteristics of a nurturing classroom with the following suggestions for conveying emotional support:

- Provide opportunities for learners to contribute socially to classroom tasks (e.g., hand out materials, erase the chalkboard, take attendance, etc.) that provide a sense of responsibility for everyone's well-being.
- Emphasize tasks that require cooperation while reducing reliance on competitive tasks.
- Praise students for expending the effort to succeed.
- Seek out and listen to a student's outside of school interests and experiences.
- Encourage students to use their interests, experiences, and talents in accomplishing classroom tasks, especially with collaborative work.
- Each week, choose a student who is naturally "quiet," less likely to volunteer a response or to be popular, to interact with—without drawing the attention of other students.
- Provide opportunities for students' feelings and beliefs to emerge through role playing, reading, and group assignments.
- Assign activities that encourage students to make choices and decisions on their own in directions less traveled.

What can every teacher do to create this climate for learning? This and the following chapter will introduce you to some useful ways to manage your classroom that maintain a climate of nurturance and support for your learners.

Earning Trust and Becoming a Leader the Old-Fashioned Way

According to social psychologists (French & Raven, 1959; Raven, 1974; Schmuck & Schmuck, 2001), to establish yourself as an effective leader, you have to gain your students' trust and respect the old-fashioned way: You have to earn it.

French and Raven (1959) have provided a way of looking at how you earn trust and respect by examining how you become a leader. They identified four types of leadership a teacher can strive for: expert leadership, referent leadership, legitimate leadership, and reward leadership.

Expert Leadership

Certain individuals become leaders because others perceive them as experts. Successful teachers have **expert leadership**. Their students see them as competent to explain or do certain things and as knowledgeable about particular topics. Such influence is earned, rather than conferred by virtue of having a particular title. Teachers with expert leadership explain things well, show enthusiasm and excitement about what they teach, and appear confident and self-assured before their classes.

New teachers often find it difficult to establish leadership through expert leadership. Even though they are knowledgeable and competent in their field, uncertainty and inexperience in front of a group may make them appear less so. Students are attuned to body language that suggests lack of confidence and indecision and may test the competence and challenge the authority of teachers who appear not to be in command of their subject. The best way to continue to build your expert leadership is to take advantage of in-service training opportunities and website materials connected with your subject as well as mentoring and career ladder requirements that can keep you in touch with the latest advancements in your field.

Referent Leadership

Students often accept as leaders teachers they like and respect. They view such teachers as nurturing, trustworthy, fair, and concerned about them (Glasser, 1998b; Goodlad, 2004; Levine, 2009). The term **referent leadership** describes leadership earned in this way. Ask any group of junior or senior high school students why they like particular teachers, and invariably they describe the teachers they like as "fair," "caring," and "someone you can talk to." Without referent leadership, even teachers with expert leadership may have their authority challenged or ignored.

Teachers often say they would rather be respected than liked, as if these two consequences were mutually exclusive. Research by Soar and Soar (1983) and Letts (1999) suggests that teachers can be both respected and liked. In fact, teachers who are both respected and liked are associated with greater student satisfaction and higher achievement. Glasser (1998a), Gootman (2008), and Linvine, (2009) emphasize that students' need for belonging in a classroom will more likely be met by a teacher who is perceived as both nurturing and competent. You can achieve referent leadership by creating lesson topics that can be framed by your learners' own experiences and the naturally occurring dialogue in the classroom, believing in the learning potential of all your learners, and providing opportunities for mutual exploration and discovery—creating a partnership of ideas between you and your learners.

Legitimate Leadership

Some roles carry with them influence and authority by their very nature. Police officers, legislators, and judges exert social power and leadership by their very titles. Influence in such cases may be conferred by the role itself, rather than depend on the nature of the person assuming the role. Savage (1999) refers to this type of authority as **legitimate leadership**. Teachers possess a certain degree of legitimate leadership. Our society expects students to give teachers their attention, respect them, and follow their requests. Most families also stress the importance of listening to the teacher. Every new teacher begins her or his first day of class with legitimate leadership.

Legitimate leadership therefore gives the new teacher some breathing room during the first few weeks of school. Most students will initially obey and accept the authority of new teachers by virtue of their position of authority. However, building classroom leadership solely through legitimate power may be like building a house on a foundation of sand. Teachers should use their legitimate leadership to establish referent and expert leadership and to establish a working relationship with parents and with, as needed, the guardians, extended families, and other professionals who may be providing services to the learner.

Reward Leadership

Individuals in positions of authority are able to exercise **reward leadership** in relation to the people they lead. Someone with this leadership can give out rewards in the form of privileges, titles, and responsibilities or less tangible compensation, such as approval. To the extent that students desire the rewards conferred by teachers, teachers can exert a degree of leadership and authority (Gootman, 2008).

There are, however, only a few rewards available to teachers and a great number of rewards available to students without the aid of a teacher. Students who do not care much about good grades or teacher approval are difficult to lead solely with rewards, because they can attain much of what is reinforcing to them outside school. In such cases, some teachers resort to using tangible reinforcers, such as access to desired activities, prizes, and even food. In this chapter, you will learn that rewards can be an effective tool in the classroom but cannot substitute for referent, expert, and legitimate leadership.

Although each of the preceding sources of leadership, when properly used, is a legitimate tool for managing the classroom, teachers—especially new teachers—should work quickly to achieve expert and referent leadership. You can achieve expert leadership by keeping up-to-date with developments in your teaching field, completing in-service and graduate programs, attending seminars and workshops, and completing career ladder and mentoring activities provided by your school district. From your very first day in the classroom, you can exhibit referent leadership by instilling in your students a sense of belonging and an unconditional belief in their potential to learn.

Stages of Group Development

Social psychologists, such as Schmuck and Schmuck (2001) and Curtis and Carter (2007, 2011), believe the sources of leadership you acquire are important for guiding your learners through the process of group development. They believe every successful group passes through a series of **stages of group development**, during which it has certain tasks to accomplish and concerns to resolve. The way the group accomplishes these tasks and resolves these concerns determines the extent to which you can effectively and efficiently manage the group and accomplish the goals of your classroom. Maurer (1985) describes these stages:

- *Stage 1, Forming.* Resolving concerns about acceptance and responsibilities.
- *Stage 2, Storming.* Resolving concerns about shared influence.
- *Stage 3, Norming.* Resolving concerns about how work gets done.
- *Stage 4, Performing.* Resolving concerns about freedom, control, and self-regulation.

Stage 1: Forming

When learners come together at the start of the school year, they usually are concerned about two issues: (1) finding their place in the social structure and (2) finding out what they are expected to do. This raises concerns about *inclusion,* or group membership.

During the first several days of class, learners (and teachers) naturally ask questions like these: How will I fit in? Who will accept or reject me? What do I have to do to be respected? At this time, a phenomenon called *testing* takes place. Learners engage in specific actions to see what kind of reaction they get from teachers and peers. At this stage of group formation, learners are curious

Table 3.1 Important Questions about Group Development

Stage 1: Forming	Stage 2: Storming	Stage 3: Norming	Stage 4: Performing
1. Are there activities for everyone to get to know about one another?	1. Are conflicts openly recognized and discussed?	1. Is there a process for resolving conflict?	1. Can the group evaluate its own effectiveness?
2. Has everyone had a chance to be heard?	2. Can the group assess its own functioning?	2. Can the group set goals?	2. Can the group and individuals solve their own problems?
3. Do learners interact with a variety of classmates?	3. Are new and different ideas listened to and evaluated?	3. Can learners express what is expected of them?	3. Does the group have opportunities to work independently and express themselves through a medium of their own choosing?
4. Do learners and teachers listen to one another?	4. Are the skills of all members being used?	4. Is there mutual respect between teacher and learners?	4. Can individuals evaluate themselves and set goals for personal improvement?
5. Have concerns and/or fears regarding academic and behavioral expectations been addressed?	5. Do all learners have an opportunity to share leadership and responsibility?	5. What happens to learners who fail to respect norms?	5. Is the group prepared to disband?

Source: From Richard A. Schmuck and Patricia A. Schmuck, *Group Processes in the Classroom,* 6th edition. Copyright © 2001, Wm. C. Brown Communications, Inc., Dubuque, Iowa. Reproduced with permission of The McGraw-Hill Companies.

about one another. They want to know where other class members live, who their friends are, what they like to do, and where they like to go. As students learn more about one another, they begin to see how and with whom they fit in. Castaneda (2004), Ryan (2007), and Landsman and Lewis (2011) urge teachers to engage in activities during the first few weeks of school to help learners trust one another and feel like members of a group.

Social psychologists caution teachers of the tendency during the first stage of classroom group development to concentrate almost exclusively on concerns about work and rules to the exclusion of concerns about inclusion. They warn that learners who have unresolved fears about being accepted by their teacher and fitting into their peer group will find it difficult to concentrate on academic work. They must first develop trust and feel like valued members of a group.

Table 3.1 lists questions you can ask yourself to assess group development during the forming stage.

Stage 2: Storming

The goals of the forming stage of group development are to help learners feel secure and to perceive themselves as members of a classroom group. Healthy group life at this stage occurs if learners have accepted the teacher as their leader, made some initial commitment to follow rules and procedures, and agreed to respect other members of the class.

During the storming stage of group development, students begin to test the limits of these commitments. This limit testing may take the form of amiable challenges to academic expectations and rules in order to establish under what conditions they do and do not apply. Learners may question seating arrangements, homework responsibilities, seatwork routines, and so on. Social psychologists refer to these amiable challenges to teacher authority and leadership as examples of

distancing behavior. They occur in any group where a leader initially establishes authority by virtue of his or her position, rather than through competence or credibility. This distancing behavior represents reservations learners have at this stage of group development about the commitments they made during the forming stage to class expectations and group participation.

A second type of amiable limit testing, which often accompanies distancing behavior, is called **centering behavior**. Centering occurs when learners question how they will personally benefit from being a group member. Their behavior can be described with the question, "What's in it for me?" The questions learners ask and the assertions they make reflect a preoccupation with fairness. They are quick to notice favoritism toward individual members of the group.

The distancing and centering conflicts that arise between teachers and learners, as well as among learners, are a natural part of group development. Social psychologists caution teachers about overreacting at this stage. During these types of conflicts, you will need to monitor compliance with rules and procedures but be willing to reconsider those that may not be working.

Buehl (2008), Glasser (1998b), and Kreidler (2005) urge teachers to have class discussions based on group conflict resolution. They recommend that teachers instruct their learners in how to problem solve using the following process:

1. *Agree there is a problem.* The teacher gets all members of the class to agree that there is a problem and that they will work together to solve it.

2. *State the conflict.* The teacher states concisely what the conflict is and assures all learners that they will have the opportunity to state their perspective.

3. *Identify and select responses.* Teachers and learners brainstorm and record solutions to the problem. They assess the short- and long-term consequences of the solutions, and discard those that have negative consequences.

4. *Create a solution.* The class discusses and records a solution that everyone basically agrees will resolve the conflict.

5. *Design and implement a plan.* The class discusses and works out the details of when, where, and how to resolve the conflict.

6. *Assess the success of the plan.* The students identify information they can gather to determine the success of the plan. The teacher identifies checkpoints to evaluate how the class is doing. When the conflict is resolved, the whole class discusses the value of the problem-solving process.

Table 3.1 lists questions you can ask yourself to assess group development during the storming stage.

Stage 3: Norming

The security learners develop at the forming stage provides them with a safe foundation to challenge teacher authority during the storming stage. Skilled leadership during the storming stage assures learners that they will be listened to, treated fairly, and allowed to share power and influence. This assurance leads them during the norming stage to accept academic expectations, procedures, and rules for the group and the roles and functions of the various group members.

Norms are shared expectations among group members regarding how they should think, feel, and behave. Social psychologists view norms as the principal regulators of group behavior (Di Giullio, 2006; Schmuck & Schmuck, 2001). Norms may take the form of either written or unwritten rules that all or most of the group voluntarily agree to follow. A classroom group has norms when learners, for the most part, agree on what is and is not socially acceptable classroom behavior.

Norms play an important role in governing behavior in the classroom, but their role differs from that of rules and procedures. Norms are more personally meaningful than rules, as seen in the following examples of classroom norms:

It's OK to be seen talking to the teacher.

Learners in this class should help one another.

We're all responsible for our own learning.

We shouldn't gloat when one of our classmates gives the wrong answer.

We need to respect the privacy of others.

The most important thing for this class is learning.

Social psychologists believe that positive norms serve several important functions in the classroom (Gerrig & Zimbardo, 2007; Putnam, 2006; Schmuck & Schmuck, 2001):

- Norms orient group members to which social interactions are and are not appropriate and then regulate these interactions. When norms are present, learners can anticipate how others will behave in the classroom and also how they are expected to behave.

- Norms create group identification and group cohesiveness (Gerrig & Zimbardo, 2007). Social psychologists believe the process of group formation begins when its members agree to adhere to the norms of the group. This process begins during the forming stage of group development and ends during the norming stage.

- Norms promote academic achievement and positive relationships among class members. Academic and social goals are more likely to be achieved in classrooms with consistent norms. For example, peer-group norms represent one of the most important influences on school performance (Schmuck & Schmuck, 2001; Sunwolf, 2008).

Group norms, whether in support of a teacher's goals or opposed to them, begin to develop on the first day of school during the forming stage of group development. Social psychologists have identified two basic processes by which norms develop: diffusion and crystallization. **Diffusion** takes place as learners first enter a group or class. They bring with them expectations acquired from experiences in other classes, from other group memberships, and from experiences growing up. As learners talk and mingle with each other during breaks and recess, they communicate with one another. Their various expectations for academic and social behavior are diffused and spread throughout the entire class. Eventually, as learners engage in a variety of activities together, their expectations begin to converge and form a shared perspective of classroom life. This is the process of **crystallization**.

You should do all you can to influence the development of norms that support your classroom goals. It is important that you know how to positively influence the development of class norms and to identify and alter existing ones. Here are some suggestions for developing, identifying, and altering group norms:

- Explain to the class the concept of a *group norm*. Draw up a list of norms with the class, and over time, add and delete norms that either help or impede the work of the group.

- Conduct discussions of class norms, and encourage learners to talk among themselves about norms. Glasser (1998b) and Powell (2009) suggest discussing with students ideas on how the class might be run, problems that may interfere with the group's performance, and needed rules and routines.

- Appoint or elect a class council to make recommendations for improving the class climate and productivity. Have the group assess whether the norms are working.

- Provide a model of the respect, consistency, and responsibility for learning that you want your learners to exhibit.

Healthy group development at the norming stage is characterized by group behavior that is primarily focused on academic achievement.

Stage 4: Performing

By the time the group has reached the fourth developmental stage, learners feel at ease with one another, know the rules and their roles, accept group norms, and are familiar with the routine of the classroom. The principal concern for the group at this stage is establishing its independence.

Just as the storming stage of development was characterized by a testing of limits, the performing stage is characterized by learners wanting to show they can do some things independently of the teacher. Social psychologists urge teachers to encourage the desire for independence at this stage by focusing less on classroom control and more on teaching the group how to set priorities, budget time, and self-regulate. In other words, at this stage your learners need to feel comfortable exploring and discovering on their own.

The performing stage ends when the school year or semester ends. Thus this stage represents a time of transition. Assuming all four stages of development have been successfully completed, learners will have developed relationships with one another and with their teacher. They should be able to manage themselves with the guidance and direction of the teacher. For the transition out of the group to occur successfully, you will need to establish a classroom climate of trust and confidence, unconditional acceptance, and exploration and discovery in which group development can continue to flourish. See In Practice: Focus on a Democratic Approach to Classroom Management.

In Practice

Focus on a Democratic Approach to Classroom Management

Patterned after family meetings in her own home, teacher Donna Styles's format for class meetings enables her students to share their thoughts and solve classroom issues on their own. In Styles's model, students take turns acting as a discussion leader, while the teacher promotes a respectful atmosphere and participates as a group member. Encouraged by the students' positive response to her approach, Styles decided to share her expertise with other teachers.

A teacher for more than thirty years, Styles is a veteran educator who has taught students in kindergarten through seventh grade, in both regular and multi-aged settings. She has worked as a regular classroom teacher, in English and French immersion classes, and as a thinking skills/enrichment resource teacher. She currently teaches grades five and six at Len Wood Elementary School in Armstrong, British Columbia (Canada). Styles's practical and effective approach to classroom management did not develop from her extensive teaching experience, however, but from her hands-on experience as a parent! She explains:

My husband and I had successfully used family meetings in our own family for years. We saw the positive effects of including our children in family decision-making. We saw firsthand how much more responsible our kids acted on an everyday basis, how much more an integral part of our family unit they felt, and how elevated their self-esteem became when their views were heard and considered. I realized the possible application in the classroom setting.

In her view, family-style class meetings can play a critical role in the development of students' emotional, social, moral, and intellectual development. Styles suggests that class meetings also can promote personal growth, leadership, organizational and public-speaking skills, thinking skills and cognitive gains, problem-solving skills, and interpersonal skills—creating a community of learners.

An Idea Worth Sharing

"Class meetings are most successful in classrooms that have a warm, caring, supportive environment—classrooms in which students feel comfortable to learn, feel safe to share their ideas, and feel free to ask questions and take risks," explains Styles. "Students in those kinds of classrooms are supportive of one another, work together cooperatively, encourage one another, assume responsibility for their own learning and behavior, and are allowed to make decisions."

Styles outlines several key components that make class meetings unique and effective:

Students sit on chairs in a circle.

Meetings are held every week.

A set format is followed.

Students lead the meetings.

Both problems and suggestions are discussed.

Students encourage and compliment one another.

Styles maintains that incorporating class meetings is a reasonable task if teachers prepare students for meetings in about two to three lessons during the first weeks of school. She proposes that lessons involve the teaching and practice of encouragement, creative problem solving, and circle formation. After several trial meetings, with the teacher leading and modeling the process, students become meeting leaders, with each student taking a turn as discussion leader during the school year.

Conducting Class Meetings

"Class meetings help make good classrooms even better," says Styles. "The true power of meetings lies in their ability to empower students, to motivate them to learn, and to help them discover their personal best. When both students and teachers are able to voice opinions and thoughts in a quiet, respectful atmosphere, mutual respect and understanding develops. The students realize that it is *their* classroom as much as the teacher's, and they take ownership and pride in that."

In a typical class meeting, desks are moved to the perimeter of the room and students take their designated places in a circle of chairs. The meeting leader opens the meeting. Old business is discussed and new business is dealt with. "Thank you's" and compliments are offered and the meeting is closed.

If a student wants an issue raised at a meeting, he or she places a slip of paper inside a box provided in the classroom. The papers, which include the name of the student and the date, constitute the new business of the next meeting. Typically, three types of issues are put in the box: a problem involving one or more people, a problem or issue affecting the whole class, or a suggestion for a class activity.

During class meetings, the teacher:

- Acts as a coach—providing guidance to the leader, when necessary.
- Fulfills the role of secretary.
- Performs as a group member—offering information only when needed, and making comments only when necessary to keep the tone positive and helpful.

The student leader:

- Keeps the meeting running smoothly.
- Opens and closes the meeting.
- Follows the order of steps for conducting the meeting.
- Follows steps for solving problems.
- Follows steps for discussing suggestions.

- Makes eye contact with each person speaking.
- Participates like any other member.
- Keeps discussions on topic.
- Lets students know if they are out of order.
- Asks questions, clarifies, or restates problems or ideas.
- Summarizes.
- Speaks loudly and clearly.

Accountability Made Simple

Styles has found that, with classroom meetings, discipline becomes a minor issue. Problems are discussed in meetings and students themselves determine the consequences for misbehavior. Students become highly accountable for their actions in the classroom, she observes, when their peers are taking note of their behavior and discussing poor behavior in class meetings.

"When students choose solutions to problems, they have a stake in seeing that the consequences are followed," Styles states. "Problems in the classroom are no longer just the teacher's problems to solve—they become the class's problems. Practice with the process each week enables students to become excellent problem solvers, coming up with fair and effective methods of helping classmates improve and change behaviors that interfere with others or with their learning."

Suggestions put into the box give students an opportunity to work on committees and to plan and orchestrate many interesting and fun activities during the year. This generates excitement and energy in the classroom, helping students to "buy into" coming to school and to feel a sense of belonging to the group. "As a teacher, I think there is no other tool that has such a long list of benefits. Conducting weekly class meetings with this format easily makes it one of the most powerful tools a classroom teacher can use. And it's so simple." Styles reports that—without exception—students love class meetings, and that the approach is conducive to the inclusion of students with special needs.

Styles's book, *Class Meetings: Building Leadership, Problem-Solving and Decision-Making Skills in the Respectful Classroom,* is available from Pembroke Publishing.

Source: Article by Cara Bafile, EducationWorld.com (2002). Used with permission. For more about class meetings: www.sd83.bc.ca/classmtg/classindex.html. For more about what kids say about class meetings: www.sd83.bc.ca/classmtg/quotes.html.

Establishing an Effective Classroom Climate

The *classroom climate* is the atmosphere or mood in which interactions between you and your students take place. Your classroom climate is created by the manner and degree to which you connect with your students, show warmth and support, encourage cooperation, and allow for independent judgment and choice. The climate of your classroom is of your choosing, just as your instructional methods are.

This section introduces two related aspects of an effective classroom climate: the **social environment**, determined by the interaction patterns you promote in the classroom, and the **organizational environment**, determined by the physical or visual arrangement of your classroom. Let's see how you can alter each of these to create just the right classroom climate for learning.

The Social Environment

The social environment of your classroom can vary from *authoritarian,* in which you are the primary provider of information, opinions, and instruction, to laissez-faire, in which your students become the primary providers of information, opinions, and instruction. Between these alternatives lies a middle ground, in which you and your students share responsibilities and in which your students are given freedom of choice and judgment under your direction. We have seen earlier just how important it is to frame some of your instruction around student ideas and the naturally occurring dialog of the classroom to create a partnership of ideas that connects you with your students.

For example, a group discussion might be a colossal failure in a rigid authoritarian climate, because the climate tells students that their opinions are less important than yours, that teacher talk and not student talk should take up most of the instructional time, and that the freedom to express oneself spontaneously is your right but not theirs. In a more open atmosphere, this same attempt at discussion might well be a smashing success, because the classroom climate provides all the ingredients of a good discussion—freedom to express one's opinion, a high degree of student talk, and spontaneity.

The social atmosphere you create—authoritarian, laissez-faire, or somewhere between—is determined by how you see yourself: Are you a commander in chief who carefully controls and hones student behavior by organizing and providing all the learning stimuli? Are you a translator or summarizer of the ideas that students provide? Or are you sometimes an equal partner with students in creating ideas and problem solutions? Consider the effects of each climate and how you can create it.

The effective teacher not only uses a variety of teaching strategies but also creates a variety of classroom climates. However, your ability to create a certain climate is as important as your ability to change the climate when the objectives and situation demand it. Although early research in social psychology tried to identify the type of climate most conducive to individual behavior (Lippitt & Gold, 1959), the results suggest that different climates have both advantages and disadvantages, depending on the intended goal.

Because goals change from lesson to lesson and week to week, so too must your classroom climate that supports the goals. When the goals change but your classroom climate does not, the stage is set for off-task, disruptive, and even antagonistic behavior among your students.

One aspect of an effective learning climate is the physical or visual arrangement of the classroom. This arrangement is a matter of choice that can be altered to create just the right climate for your learning objectives.

Table 3.2 Three Types of Classroom Climates

Social Climate	Example of Activity	Authority Vested in Students	Authority Vested in Teacher
Competitive: Students compete for the right answers among themselves or against a standard established by the teacher. The teacher is the sole judge of the appropriateness of a response.	Drill and practice	None	To organize the instruction, to present the stimulus material, and to evaluate the correctness of the responses
Cooperative: Students engage in dialogue that is monitored by the teacher. The teacher systematically intervenes in the discussion to sharpen and focus ideas and move the discussion to a higher level.	Small- and large-group discussion	To present opinions, to provide ideas, and to speak and discuss freely and spontaneously	To stimulate the discussion, to arbitrate differences, to organize, and to summarize student contributions
Individualistic: Students complete assignments monitored by the teacher. Students are encouraged to complete assignments with the answers they think are best. Emphasis is on getting through and testing oneself.	Independent seatwork	To complete the assignment with the best possible responses	To assign the work, and to see that orderly progress is made toward its completion

Competitive, Cooperative, or Individualistic.   We have already examined several ways you can vary your authority, as well as that of your students, in accordance with your objectives. These variations correspond not only with how much you relinquish your authority, and therefore your control of the learning process, but also how competitive, cooperative, or individualistic you wish the interactions among members of your class to be. These three conditions are illustrated in Table 3.2. You can see in the table that as you shift the classroom climate from competitive to cooperative to individualistic, you relinquish control over the learning process until, in the individualistic mode, students have almost sole responsibility for judging their own work.

Applying the Three Climates.   In addition to encouraging the proper climate for a given instructional activity, you must decide whether each climate can be applied to the full class, to groups, and to individuals with equal effectiveness. For example, as shown in Table 3.3, it is not necessary to conduct all group discussions in a cooperative climate.

Although some of the climates described in Table 3.3 may be more prevalent than others, various arrangements of students and climates are possible, depending on your instructional goals. Your job is to ensure that the degree of leadership you impose matches your instructional goal (for example, the expression of student opinion you allow, the amount of time you devote to student talk, and the spontaneity with which you want your students to respond).

The Organizational Environment

The teacher in this **video** describes how she decides to arrange the physical environment in her classroom. Pay attention to the rationale behind why she arranges the room this way.

In addition to arranging the social climate of your classroom, you also must arrange the physical climate. It goes without saying that a classroom should be attractive, well lighted, comfortable, and colorful. But aside from creating a colorful bulletin board and being neat, you may have very little influence over the external features of your classroom. It is not unusual for teachers to bring essential items at the beginning of the year—such as an alarm clock, bookcase, file cabinet, rug, and pillows for younger learners—to create a warm and efficient climate for their classroom.

What may be more important than these items, however, is the way the internal features of your classroom (desks, chairs, tables) are arranged. Students quickly get used to and accept the external features of a classroom, good or bad. But the internal arrangement of the classroom will affect your students every day of the school year.

In the upper grades, the most flexible furniture arrangement places your desk at the front of the room and aligns the student desks or tables toward you. Although it may seem strange to associate this traditional format with flexibility, it can be most flexible when you use it to create competitive,

Table 3.3 Targets for Three Types of Classroom Climates

	Competitive	Cooperative	Individualistic
Full Class	Students compete with other students by having the correct answer when it's their turn.	Students are allowed to call out hints or clues when a student is having difficulty finding the right answer.	The entire class recites the answers in unison.
Groups	Subgroups compete as opposing teams.	Subgroups work on different but related aspects of a topic, combining their results into a final report to the class.	Each subgroup completes its own assigned topic, which is independent of the topics assigned to the other subgroups. No shared report is given to the class.
Individual	Individuals compete by having to respond to the same question. The student with the quickest and most accurate response wins.	Pairs of individuals cooperate by exchanging papers, sharing responses, or correcting each other's errors.	Individuals complete seatwork on their own without direct teacher involvement.

cooperative, and individualistic environments interchangeably. This, plus the difficulty of rearranging classroom furniture every time a change in social climate is desired, makes the traditional classroom arrangement in the upper grades almost as popular today as it was 50 years ago.

There are times, however, when you will want to change the arrangement to encourage a more cooperative, interactive, and group-sharing climate. Such a classroom arrangement has many variations, depending on the external features of the classroom and available furniture. One example is shown in Figure 3.1.

Figure 3.1 Classroom Arrangement Emphasizing Positive Relations and Learning to Cooperate

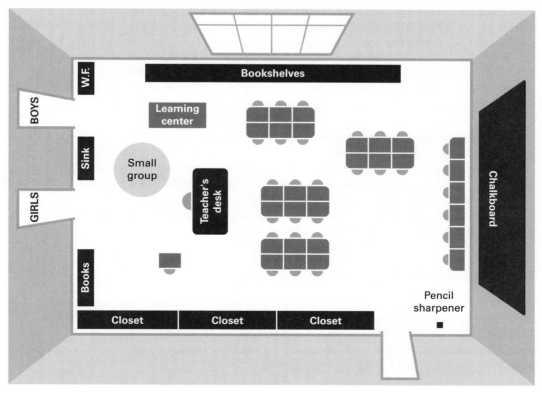

Figure 3.2 Compromise Classroom Arrangement Allowing Independent, Group, and Cooperative Learning

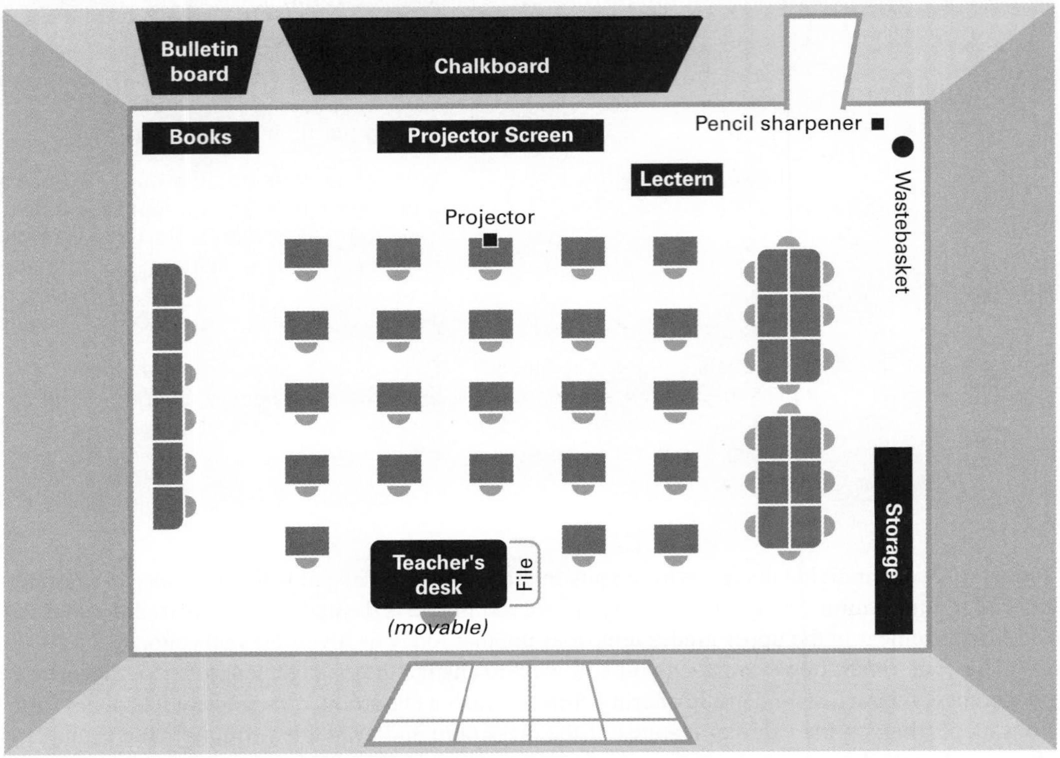

This change represents your deliberate attempt to get learners together. The barriers to interpersonal sharing and communication that sometimes result from the rigid alignment of desks can be avoided by a more informal but still systematic furniture arrangement. Because this arrangement communicates to learners that interpersonal communication and sharing are permitted, both will undoubtedly occur, whether you want them to or not.

When you group four or five student desks or tables together, you expect more expression of student opinion, increased student talk, and greater spontaneity in student responses. This emphasizes the important notion that the social climate created by your words and deeds always should match the organizational climate created by the physical arrangement of your classroom.

Of course, changing the internal arrangement of a classroom from time to time for the sake of variety is refreshing. You might compromise by maintaining the basic nature of the formal classroom but, space permitting, setting aside one or two less formal areas (for example, a learning center, group discussion table, pillow arrangement, and reading center) for times when instructional goals call for independent work or interpersonal communication and sharing. In the early grades, these elements are almost always part of the classroom arrangement and, therefore, its learning climate. A version of this arrangement is shown in Figure 3.2.

Establishing Rules and Procedures

Establishing **rules and procedures** to prevent classroom discipline problems will be one of your most important classroom management activities (Emmer & Evertson, 2012; Evertson, 1995; Evertson & Emmer, 2012; Mackenzie & Stanzione, 2010). These rules and procedures, which you should formulate before the first day of school, are your commitment to applying an "ounce of prevention" to avoid a "pound of cure."

To effectively manage a classroom, teachers need four basic types of rules and procedures:

- Rules related to academic work
- Rules related to classroom conduct
- Rules that must be communicated your first teaching day
- Rules that can be communicated later, at an appropriate opportunity

The top half of Figure 3.3 identifies some rules that may be needed during the very first days of school, either because students will ask about them or because events are likely to arise requiring their use. Notice that these rules are divided into seven conduct rules and seven work rules. For the elementary grades, it is best that you present them orally, *and* provide them on a handout, *and* post them for later reference by students. In the lower grades, learners can forget oral messages quickly—or choose to ignore them, if there is no physical representation of the rules as a constant reminder. In the later elementary grades and middle school, your recital of the rules while students copy them into their notebooks may be sufficient. For high school students, simply hearing the rules may be sufficient, as long as they are also posted for later reference.

Not all first-day rules are equally important, and other rules may have to be added as special circumstances require. But rules about responding and speaking out, making up work, determining grades, and violating rules are among the most important. It is in these areas that confusion often occurs, beginning on the very first day.

Figure 3.4 shows some of the issues you will want to consider pertaining to these four types of rules. Taking a few moments to think about these issues before they are raised in class can avoid an embarrassing pause and uncertain response when a student asks a question. Identify issues to be decided for the remaining rule areas in Figure 3.3. The bottom half of this figure identifies areas for which rules can be communicated as the situation arises. Some are specific to particular situations (for example, safety during a lab experiment, notebook completion, obtaining help for a specific assignment) and are best presented in the context to which they apply. This type of rule will be more meaningful and more easily remembered when it applies to a specific circumstance or event. Even though you may not communicate this kind of rule on the first day of school, it is usually required so soon afterward that you will want to compose a procedure for it before your first class day.

Figure 3.3 Classroom Rules Related to Conduct and Work

	Rules related to classroom conduct	**Rules related to academic work**
Rules that need to be communicated the first day	1. Where to sit 2. How seats are assigned 3. What to do before the bell 4. Responding, speaking out 5. Leaving at the bell 6. Drinks, food, and gum 7. Washroom and drinking privileges	8. Materials required for class 9. Homework completion 10. Makeup work 11. Incomplete work 12. Missed quizzes and examinations 13. Determining grades 14. Violation of due dates
Rules that can be communicated later	15. Tardiness/absence 16. Coming up to the teacher's desk 17. When a visitor comes to the door 18. Leaving the classroom 19. Consequences of rule violation	20. Notebook completion 21. Obtaining help 22. Note taking 23. Sharing work with others 24. Use of the learning center 25. Communication during group work 26. Neatness 27. Lab safety

Figure 3.4 Issues to Be Decided for Some Classroom Rules

Responding, speaking out

- Must hands be raised?
- Are other forms of acknowledgment acceptable (e.g., head nod)?
- What will happen if a student speaks when others are speaking?
- What will you do about shouting or using a loud voice?

Makeup work

- Will makeup work be allowed?
- Will there be penalties for not completing it?
- Will it be graded?
- Whose responsibility is it to know that work is missing?

Getting out of seat

- When is out-of-seat movement permissible?
- When can a student come to the teacher's desk?
- When can reference books or learning centers be visited?
- What if a student visits another student's desk?

Communicating during group work

- Can a student leave an assigned seat?
- How loudly should a student speak?
- Who determines who can talk next?
- Will there be a group leader?

Determining grades

- What percentage will quizzes and tests contribute to the total grade?
- What percentage will class participation count?
- When will notification be given of failing performance?
- How much will homework count?

Violation of due dates

- What happens when repeated violations occur?
- Where can a student learn the due dates if absent?
- What penalties are there for copying another person's assignment?
- Will makeup work be required when a due date is missed?

Early completion of in-class assignments

- Can work for other classes or subjects be done?
- Can a newspaper or magazine be read?
- Can the next exercise or assignment be worked on?
- Can students rest their heads on their desks?

Rule violation

- Will names be written on the board?
- Will extra work penalties be assigned?
- Will you have after-class detention?
- When will a disciplinary referral be made?

Here are several general suggestions for creating classroom rules:

- Specify only necessary rules. There are four reasons to have rules, and each should reflect at least one of these purposes:

> To enhance work engagement and minimize disruption
> To promote safety and security
> To prevent disturbance to others or other classroom activities
> To promote acceptable standards of courtesy and interpersonal relations

- Make your rules consistent with the classroom climate you wish to promote. As a beginning teacher, you should recognize your values and preferences for managing your classroom now, at the start of your career. Articulate your personal philosophy of classroom management, and make sure your class rules reflect it. For example, do you want your classroom climate to emphasize independent judgment, spontaneity, and risk taking, or do you want it to emphasize teacher-initiated exchanges, formal classroom rules, and teacher-solicited responses? You most likely will want your rules to allow a healthy balance of these.

- Do not establish rules you cannot enforce. A rule that says "No talking" or "No getting out of your seat" may be difficult to enforce when your personal philosophy continually encourages spontaneity, problem solving, and group work. Unfairness and inconsistency may result in applying rules you do not fully believe in.

- State your rules at a general enough level to include a range of specific behaviors. The rule "Respect other people's property and person" covers a variety of problems, such as borrowing without permission, throwing objects, and so on. Similarly, the rule "Follow teacher requests" allows you to put an end to a variety of off-task, disruptive behaviors that no list of rules could anticipate or cover comprehensively. However, be careful not to state a rule so generally that the specific problems to which it pertains remain unclear to your learners. For example, a rule stating simply "Show respect" or "Obey the teacher" may be sufficiently vague to be ignored by most of your learners and unenforceable by you. If you follow this suggestion and the preceding one, you should have prepared about four to six classroom rules for your very first day.

Unless you clearly communicate your rules and apply them consistently, all your work in making them will be meaningless. Consistency is a key reason some rules are effective while others are not. Rules that are not enforced or not applied consistently over time result in a loss of respect for the person who created the rules and is responsible for enforcing them.

Following are the most frequently occurring reasons that particular rules are not applied consistently (Emmer & Evertson, 2012; Evertson & Emmer, 2012):

1. The rule is not workable or appropriate. It does not fit a particular classroom context or is not reasonable, given the nature of the individuals to whom it applies.

2. The teacher fails to monitor students closely, and consequently, some individuals who violate the rule are called out while others are not.

3. The teacher does not feel strongly enough about the rule to be persistent about its enforcement and thus makes many exceptions to the rule.

Keep in mind that making minor deviations from a rule may not be worth your effort when (1) doing so will provide an untimely interruption to your lesson or (2) the situation is only momentary and not likely to recur. However, when problems in applying a rule persist over time, either increase your vigilance or adjust the rule to allow more flexibility in your response. (For example, coming up to the teacher's desk without permission for help may be acceptable, but coming up just to talk may not be.)

Problem Areas in Classroom Management

A primary purpose of effective classroom management is to keep learners actively engaged in the learning process. *Active engagement* means getting learners to work with and act on the material presented, as evidenced by carefully attending to the material, progressing through seatwork at a steady pace, participating in class discussions, and being attentive when called on.

This section describes four events that are particularly crucial for keeping students actively engaged in the learning process: monitoring students, making transitions, giving assignments, and bringing closure to lessons. Following are some effective classroom management practices in each area.

Monitoring Students

Monitoring is the process of observing, mentally recording, and, when necessary, redirecting or correcting students' behaviors. Monitoring occurs when you look for students' active, alert eyes during discussion sessions; their faces down and directed at the book or assignment during seatwork; their hands raised during a question-and-answer period; and, in general, signs that indicate that learners are participating in what is going on. These signs of engagement (or their absence) indicate when you need to change the pace of your delivery, the difficulty of the material, or even the activity itself.

Kounin (1970) used the term *with-it-ness* to refer to a teacher's ability to keep track of many different signs of engagement at the same time. Kounin observed that one of the most important distinctions between effective and ineffective classroom managers is the degree to which they exhibit with-it-ness. Effective classroom managers, who exhibited with-it-ness, were aware of what was happening in all parts of the classroom and were able to see different things happening in different parts of the room at the same time. Furthermore, these effective classroom managers were able to communicate this awareness to their students.

There are several simple ways to increase your with-it-ness and the extent of your students' active engagement in the learning process. One way is to increase your physical presence through

One approach to moving the entire class from one activity to another in a timely and orderly manner is to begin new activities on time and visit privately with stragglers later.

eye contact. If your eye contact is limited to only a portion of the classroom, you effectively lose with-it-ness for the rest of the classroom. It is surprising to note that a great many beginning teachers consistently do the following:

- Talk only to students in the middle-front rows.
- Talk with their backs to the class when writing on the chalkboard.
- Talk while looking toward the windows or ceiling.
- Talk while not being able to see all students because other students are blocking their view.

In each of these instances, you see only a portion of the classroom, and the students know it. Visually covering all portions of the classroom is one of the most important ingredients in conveying a sense of with-it-ness.

A second ingredient for improving with-it-ness is learning to monitor more than one activity at a time. Here the key is not only to change your eye contact to different parts of the room but also to change your focus of attention. For example, progress on assigned seatwork might be the focus of your observations when scanning students in the front of the class, but potential behavior problems might be your focus when scanning students in the back of the class.

Switch from conduct-related observations to work-related observations at the same time you change eye contact. However, as you do, be aware of the tendency to focus exclusively on one student who is having either conduct- or work-related problems. Once other students realize you are preoccupied with one of their peers, you may have problems in other parts of the classroom.

Making Transitions

The teacher in this **video** demonstrates several procedures that make transitions flow better for the students. How can you implement these strategies into your classroom to avoid this common problem of off-task behavior during transitions?

Another problem area is *transitions*. It is difficult to keep students' attention during a transition or shift from one instructional activity to another. Moving the entire class from one activity to another in a timely and orderly manner can be a major undertaking. Problems in making these transitions often occur for two reasons: (1) learners are not ready to perform the next activity or may not even know what it will be, and (2) learners have unclear expectations about appropriate behavior during the transition.

When students are uncertain or unaware of what is coming next, they naturally become anxious about their ability to perform and to make the transition. This is the time when a transition can get noisy, with some students feeling more comfortable clinging to the previous activity than changing to the next. The beginning of the school year is a time of noisy transitions, as students fumble to find the proper materials (or guess which ones are needed) and to find out what is expected of them next. They will not rush headlong into a new activity, for fear they will not like it or will be unable to do well.

In this sense, transitions are as much psychological barriers as they are actual divisions between activities. Students must adjust their psychology for the next activity, just as they must adjust their books and papers. You can help in their adjustment by telling them the daily routine you expect of them. This routine will become second nature after a few weeks, but it deserves special attention during the first days of school. This is the time for you to describe the daily activities and the order in which they will occur (for example, 10 minutes of presentation, 15 minutes of questions and discussion, 15 minutes of seatwork, and 10 minutes of checking and correcting).

Table 3.4 provides some suggestions for addressing the problems that occur during transitions.

Giving Assignments

Another crucial time for effective classroom management is when you are giving or explaining assignments. This can be a particularly troublesome time, because it often means assigning work

Table 3.4 Addressing Problems That Occur during Transitions

Problem	Solution
Students talk loudly at the beginning of transitions.	It is difficult to *allow* a small amount of talking and *obtain* a small amount. So establish a no-talking rule during transitions.
Students socialize during the transition, delaying the start of the next activity.	Allow no more time than is necessary between activities (e.g., to close books, gather materials, select new materials).
Students complete an assignment before the scheduled time for it to end.	Make assignments according to the time to be filled, not the exercises to be completed. Always assign more than enough exercises to fill the allotted time.
Students continue to work on the preceding activity after a change.	Give five-minute and two-minute warnings before the end of any activity, and use verbal markers such as "Shortly we will end this work" and "Let's finish this up so that we can begin. . ." Create definite beginning and end points to each activity, such as "OK, that's the end of this activity; now we will start . . ." and "Put your papers away and turn to . . ."
Some students lag behind others in completing the previous activity.	Don't wait for stragglers. Begin new activities on time. When a natural break occurs, visit privately with students still working on previous tasks to tell them that they must stop and change. Be sure to note the reason they have not finished (e.g., material too hard, lack of motivation, off-task behavior).
You delay the beginning of the activity to find something (file cabinet keys, materials, roster, references, etc.).	Be prepared—pure and simple! Always have the materials you need in front of you at the start of the activity.

that at least some students will not be eager to complete. Grunts and groans are common student expressions of distaste for homework and other assignments that must be completed outside the regular school day. At times like these, outbursts of misbehavior are most likely to occur.

Evertson and Emmer (1982) found that one difference between effective and ineffective classroom managers was the manner in which they gave assignments, particularly homework. The difference was attributed to several simple procedures that were commonplace among experienced teachers but not among beginning teachers.

One procedure was to attach assignments directly to the end of an in-class activity. By doing so, the teacher avoided an awkward pause and even the need for a transition, because the assignment was seen as a logical extension of what already was taking place. By contrast, imagine how you might feel being given an assignment under these conditions:

This **video** explores the lesson cycle and its importance in the classroom environment. Pay attention to the key aspects of how to implement lessons and the importance behind this practice.

Teacher A: I guess I'll have to assign some homework now, so do problems one through ten on page 61.

Teacher B: For homework, do the problems under Exercise A and Exercise B—and be sure all of them are finished by tomorrow.

Teacher C: We're out of time, so you'll have to finish these problems on your own.

In each of these assignments, there is a subtle implication that the homework may not really be needed or is being given mechanically or as some sort of punishment. Why the homework is being assigned may be a complete mystery to most students, because none of the teachers mentioned either the in-class activities to which the homework presumably relates or the benefits that may accrue from doing the assignment. Students appreciate knowing why an assignment is made before they are expected to do it.

Now consider these assignments again, this time with some explanations added:

Teacher A: Today we have talked a lot about the origins of the Civil War and some of the economic unrest that preceded it. But some other types of unrest also were responsible for the Civil War. These will be important for understanding the real

Teacher B: We have all had a chance now to try our skill at forming possessives. As most of you have found out, it's harder than it looks. So let's try Exercises A and B for tonight, which should give you just the right amount of practice in forming possessives for our next exercise.

Teacher C: Well, it looks like time has run out before we could complete all the problems. The next set of problems will give you some more practice with what we have learned today. So let's complete the rest of these tonight to see if we've got the concept. This should ensure everyone gets a good grade on the test.

causes behind this war. Questions one through ten on page 61 will help you discover some of these other causes.

Keep in mind that effective classroom managers give assignments that immediately follow the lesson or activity to which they relate and explain which in-class lesson or activity the assignment relates to. Effective classroom managers also avoid any unnecessary negative connotations (e.g., "Finish them all," "Be sure they are correct," "Complete it on time"), which may make the assignment sound more like a punishment than an instructional activity.

It is also important to convey assignments in a manner that motivates your students to complete them. Table 3.5 summarizes five different ways in which you can convey assignments positively and thus motivate your learners to continue engaging in the activity at a high level of involvement.

Finally, it is always a good idea to display prior assignments somewhere in your classroom so students who have missed an assignment can conveniently look it up without taking your time to remember or find an old assignment. A simple 24" by 30" sheet of poster board, divided into days of the month and covered with plastic, can provide a convenient and reusable way of recording and communicating past assignments on a monthly basis.

Table 3.5 Some Motivators and Their Appropriate Use

Motivator	Use Phrases Such As . . .
Using praise and encouragement	You've got it. Good work. Good try. That was quick.
Accepting diversity	That's not the answer I expected, but I can see your point. That's not how I see it, but I can understand how others might see it differently. This isn't something I'm familiar with. Where did you get that idea? That isn't a word I've heard before. Tell us what it means.
Providing explanations	The reason this is so important is . . . We are doing this assignment because . . . This will be difficult, but it fits in with . . . Experience has shown that without knowing these facts, the next unit will be very difficult.
Emphasizing reinforcement and reward	All homework completed will earn five extra points. If you get a C or better on each of the tests, I'll drop your lowest grade. Those who complete all the exercises on time can go to the learning center. If you have a C average, you get to choose any topic for your term paper.
Offering to help	Should you need help, I'll be here. Ask me for help if you need it. I'll be walking around; catch me if you have a problem. Don't be afraid to ask a question if you're having trouble.

Bringing Closure

Another time for effective classroom management is when you are bringing a lesson to its end. This is a time when students sense the impending close of the period and begin in advance to disengage from the lesson. It is a time when noise levels increase and students begin to fidget with books, papers, and personal belongings in anticipation of the next class or activity.

Closing comments also should serve a double purpose, not only ending the lesson but also keeping students actively engaged in the lesson until its very end by reviewing, summarizing, or highlighting its most important points. Closure, therefore, is more than simply calling attention to the end of a lesson. It means keeping the momentum of a lesson going by reorganizing what has gone before into a unified body of knowledge that can help students remember the lesson and place it into perspective. Following are ways you can keep your learners actively engaged at the end of your lessons and help them retain what you have taught.

Combining or Consolidating Key Points.   One way of accomplishing closure is by combining or consolidating key points into a single overall conclusion. Consider the following:

Teacher: Today we have studied the economic systems of capitalism, socialism, and communism. We have found all of these to be similar in that some of the same goods and services are owned by the government. We have, however, found them different with respect to the degree to which various goods and services are owned by the government: The least number of goods and services are owned by a government under capitalism, and the most goods and services are owned by a government under communism.

This teacher is drawing together and highlighting the single most important conclusion from the day's lesson. The teacher is doing so by expressing the highest-level generalization or conclusion from the lesson without reference to any of the details that were necessary to arrive at it. This teacher consolidated many different pieces of information by going to the broadest, most sweeping conclusion that could be made and capturing the essence of all that went before.

Summarizing or Reviewing Key Content.   Another procedure for bringing closure to a lesson is by summarizing or reviewing key content. The teacher reviews the most important content to be sure everyone understands it. Obviously, not all of the content can be repeated in this manner, so some selecting is in order, as illustrated by the following:

Teacher: Before we end, let's look at our two rules once again. Rule One: Use the possessive form whenever an *of* phrase can be substituted for a noun. Rule Two: If the word for which we are denoting ownership already ends in an *s,* place the apostrophe after, *not* before, the *s.* Remember, both of these rules use the apostrophe.

Now the teacher is consolidating by summarizing each of the key features of the lesson. The teacher's review is rapid and to the point, providing students with an opportunity to fill in any gaps about the main features of the lesson.

Providing a Structure.   Still another method for closing consists of providing learners with a structure so they can remember key facts and ideas without actually reviewing them. With this procedure, the teacher reorganizes facts and ideas into a framework for easy recall, as indicated in this example:

Teacher: Today we studied forming and punctuating possessives. Recall that we used two rules: one for forming possessives wherever an *of* phrase can be substituted for a noun and another for forming possessives for words ending in *s.* From now on, let's call these rules the *of rule* and the *s rule,* keeping in mind that both rules use the apostrophe.

By giving students a framework for remembering the rules (the *of rule* and *s rule*), the teacher organizes the content and indicates how it should be stored and remembered. The key to this procedure is giving a code or symbol system so students can more easily store lesson content and recall it for later use.

Notice that in each of the previous dialogues, the teacher accomplished closure by looking back at the lesson and reinforcing its key components. In the first instance, the teacher accomplished this by restating the highest-level generalization that could be made; in the second, by summarizing the content at the level at which it was taught; and in the third, by helping students remember the important categories of information by providing codes or symbols. Each of these closings has the potential of keeping your learners engaged when the main part of your lesson has ended. Endings to good lessons are like endings to good stories: They keep you engaged and in suspense and leave you with a sense that you have understood the story and will remember it long afterward.

Culturally Responsive Classroom Management

A number of authors have studied the effects of various styles of classroom management with diverse and special-needs learners. Researchers (Cheng, 1996; Cheng et al., 1997; Griggs & Dunn, 1995; Voltz, Sims & Nelson, 2010; Weinstein, Tomlinson-Clarke, & Curran, 2005) found connections between different cultures and the nonverbal and verbal behavioral management techniques of proximity control, eye contact, warnings, and classroom rules. For example, the greater the spatial distance between the teacher and students, the more some students became passive listeners and engaged in off-task behavior. As the teacher moved closer to students, communication tended to become more interactive, with more students following the wishes of the teacher. Standing closer to individual students promoted compliance to classroom rules, because students were drawn into nonverbal forms of communication, such as eye contact and changes in voice and body movement, that send a message of involvement.

Bowers and Flinders (1991) found that the use of space can communicate a sense of social leadership, which can promote engagement or disengagement. They report the case of a teacher who moved from student to student, checking their work while sitting on a swivel chair with casters. In this manner, the teacher was able to elicit more spontaneous and relaxed student responses, resulting in greater student involvement and compliance with classroom rules. This was especially so among students who, by virtue of their language, culture, or ethnicity, did not wish to be spotlighted in the traditional teacher-dominated manner.

Other research has studied the compatibility of various classroom management techniques with the culture and background of the teacher. Researchers (Cartledge, Gardner, & Ford, 2008; Compton-Lilly, 2000; Gay, 2010; Lockwood & Secada, 1999) present convincing arguments that teachers of different cultures interpret disruptive behaviors of children differently. For example, facial expressions during a reprimand have been found to communicate different messages concerning the importance of the reprimand. And research by Delgado-Gaitan (2006), Dillon (1989), and Putnam (2006) has pointed out that some actions of teachers may unintentionally diminish engagement among minority students and/or build resentment because the actions are culturally incongruent. For example, a teacher who constantly stands over students to monitor them can be seen as threatening. Recall the teacher who moved from student to student on a swivel chair while monitoring their work so as to be at the same level as the student. Dillon (1989) suggests that teachers examine their own value and belief systems to become more aware of how different they may be from their students. Teachers should also use the social organization of the classroom to differentiate their instruction to bridge cultural gaps in these ways:

- Establish an open, risk-free classroom climate, where students can experience mutual trust and confidence sufficiently to express their interests and individual learning needs.
- Plan and structure lessons that meet the interests and needs of students.
- Implement lessons that allow all students to be active learners through activities and responsibilities that are congruent with each learner's history, culture, and abilities.
- Differentiate instruction by adjusting the pace at which assignments are due, creating assignments and materials at graduated levels of difficulty, and providing feedback tailored to an individual learner's current level of understanding. (Haager & Klinger, 2004)

These are important considerations for establishing a culturally sensitive classroom management system and teaching to the culture, abilities, and special learning needs of students in a heterogeneous classroom.

Another classroom management challenge you are likely to face is teaching learners who are at risk academically (Overton, 2011). **At-risk learners** may struggle academically for many reasons, but among the most prevalent is becoming disengaged because the instructional resources, texts, workbooks, and learning materials that are designed for the majority of students in the classroom are not suitable for these learners. These students often need differentiated instruction, such as special instructional pacing, more feedback, supplemental instruction, or modified materials, and alternative ways of responding, all administered under conditions sufficiently flexible to keep students actively engaged in the learning process.

Learners who are at risk for poor academic performance usually are taught in one of two possible instructional arrangements: (1) a class composed mostly of average-performing students or (2) a class that is part of a **track system**, in which some sections of math, English, science, and social studies are designated for lower-performing and special-needs students.

The desirability and fairness of various tracking systems has been extensively debated (Free, 2004; Gamoran, 1992; Good & Brophy, 2007; Lou, Abrami, & Spence, 2000; Ready, Behhetto, & LoGerfo, 2005; Slavin, 1991a). The argument typically offered in favor of tracking is that it allows schools to differentiate instruction better by giving high achievers the challenge and low achievers the support they need to learn. Opponents argue that tracking is undemocratic, in that it separates learners into homogeneous groups unrepresentative of the world outside the classroom. Moreover, research has shown that tracking fails to increase learner achievement beyond what can be expected to occur in a heterogeneous classroom. Time-limited task and ability grouping within heterogeneous classes has produced superior achievement with at-risk learners compared to tracking (Gamoran, 1992; Good & Brophy, 2007; Skirtic, 1991; Slavin, 1990).

Whether you meet at-risk learners in a regular class or in a tracked class, keeping them engaged may require more than the usual variation in presentation methods (e.g., recitation, presentation), classroom climate (e.g., cooperative, competitive), and instructional materials (e.g., practice activities, learning centers).

Some characteristics of these learners that place them at risk for school failure and/or behavioral problems are their deficiency in basic skills (reading, writing, mathematics), their difficulty in dealing with abstractions, and their sometimes unsystematic or careless work habits, which may require instruction in note-taking, listening, and organization skills. When these learning strategies are not provided as part of your instruction, the result can be a performance below the child's potential, beginning a cycle of deficiencies that promotes poor self-concept, misbehavior, and disinterest in school—all of which have contributed to a particularly high dropout rate for at-risk learners (Child Trends DataBank, 2005; Brown & Garmon, 2011).

Stereotypes of at-risk learners, however, have often proven untrue, challenging broad generalizations of the perceptions of students who may be classified as at risk or assigned to lower-performing classes. These students' dispositions and actions are often surprising, as has been noted in research on resiliency (Benard, 1997; Doll, Zucker, & Brehm, 2004; Farkas & Binder, 2011). *Resilient* children are those who seem to defy the odds—becoming productive and competent individuals in spite of having a background that would suggest otherwise. Several long-term studies suggest that resilient children are more numerous than might be expected. Werner and Smith (1992) noted that between 50 percent and 70 percent of children born into extremely high-risk environments "grow up to be not only successful by societal indicators but 'confident, competent, and caring' persons" (Benard, 1997, p. 2). In other words, these students—who may be classified by a tracked class, differentiated instruction, or social and emotional behavior—are not necessarily born with the behaviors that put them at risk, nor are these behaviors necessarily unchangeable. Furthermore, many researchers and teachers believe that resiliency can be fostered in all youth.

Here are some instructional strategies that can help keep at-risk learners engaged in your classroom:

• *Develop some lessons around students' interests, needs, and experiences.* Doing so will help heighten the attention of at-risk learners and actively engage them in the learning process. Creating oral or written autobiographies at the beginning of the year or simple inventories in which students indicate their hobbies, jobs, and unusual trips or experiences can provide the basis for lesson plans, projects, and assignments that allow learners to construct their own meanings from direct experience and the interactions they have with others around them. It will also help give your classroom the all-important nurturing climate that you seek.

• *Encourage oral as well as written expression.* For at-risk learners, many writing assignments go unattempted or are begun only halfheartedly because these learners recognize their written work will not meet minimal writing standards. Consider assigning an audio- or videotaped project at the beginning of the school year; this type of project has the advantage of avoiding errors in spelling, syntax, and writing at a crucial time in the learner's development.

• *Provide study aids.* Study aids alert students to the most important problems, content, or issues in the material to be learned. They also eliminate irrelevant details that at-risk learners often study in the belief they are important. Examples of test questions or a list of topics for possible questions can help focus student effort.

• *Teach learning strategies. Learning strategies* are general methods of thinking that improve learning across a variety of subject areas. Strategies accomplish this by enhancing the way information is received, placed in memory, and activated when needed. You can increase the engagement of at-risk learners by teaching elaboration/organization (e.g., note taking and outlining), comprehension and monitoring (e.g., setting goals, focusing attention, using self-reinforcement), and problem-solving strategies (e.g., vocal and subvocal rehearsal). We will have more to say about these and other learning strategies that you can teach your learners in Chapter 11.

Notice that each of these instructional strategies provide ample opportunities for you to gain the trust and confidence of your learners, provide for your unconditional acceptance of their learning potential, and present opportunities to go beyond textbook and lecture to explore and discover—all qualities of a nurturing and successful classroom.

Planning Your First Day

If your first class day is like that of most teachers, it will include some or all of these activities (Wong, 2004):

- Keeping order before the bell
- Introducing yourself
- Taking care of administrative business
- Presenting rules and expectations
- Introducing your subject
- Closing

Because your responses in these areas may set the tone in your classroom for the remainder of the year, let's consider your first-day planning in more detail to see how you can prepare an effective routine.

Before the Bell

As the sole person responsible for your classroom, your responsibility extends not just to when your classes are in session but to whenever school is in session. Consequently, you must be prepared to deal with students before your first class begins in the morning, between classes, and after your last class has ended. Your first class day is particularly critical in this regard, because your students' before-class peek at you will set in motion responses, feelings, and concerns that may affect them long after the bell has rung. Following are a few suggestions that can make these responses, feelings, and concerns positive ones:

1. To provide a sense of with-it-ness, stand near the door as students enter your classroom. In this way, you will come in direct contact with all students and be visible to them as they take their seats. Your presence at the doorway, where students must come in close contact with you, will encourage an orderly entrance (and exit) from the classroom. Remember, your class starts when the first student walks through your classroom door.

2. Have approximately four to six rules, divided between conduct and work, clearly written on the chalkboard, bulletin board, or overhead or in the form of a handout already placed on each student's desk. You may want to prepare rules for the areas shown in the upper half of Figure 3.3 that you feel will be most critical to your classes during the first few days of school. You can formally introduce these rules later, but you should make sure they are clearly posted as students enter your class the first day.

3. Prepare a brief outline of your opening day's routine. This outline should list all the activities you plan to perform that day (or class period), in the order in which you will perform them. You can make a cue card with a simple 4 inch by 6 inch index card to remind yourself to do the following with some approximate times:

   - Greet students and introduce yourself (5 minutes).
   - Take roll (5 minutes).
   - Introduce a brief discussion topic or getting to know one another activity (15–20 minutes).
   - Assign and/or introduce needed materials and books (10 minutes).
   - Present rules (5 minutes).
   - Remind students to bring needed materials (2 minutes).
   - Introduce subject matter content (or give a brief overview of the daily schedule for the elementary grades) (0 to 10 minutes).
   - Close or transition to the normal routine for the elementary grades (3 minutes).

Introducing Yourself

Your first opportunity to meet your students up close will be while taking roll. You can begin by introducing yourself and saying something special about yourself. Your personality will and should unfold in small degrees during the first few weeks of school; so there is no need to rush it. However, providing a glimpse of the kind of person you are outside the classroom often is a nice touch for students, who would like to see you as a friend as well as a teacher. A short comment about your interests, hobbies, or special experiences—even family or home life—often is appreciated by students, who at the end of this first day will be struggling to remember just who you are (Mendler, 2001).

Preparing an Introductory Activity

After letting your students get to know some things about you, you will want to let your students tell you some things about themselves. This is when you will want to turn the tables and have your students not only identify themselves but indicate some of their own interests, hobbies, or special experiences, especially as they may relate to some of the topics you will be teaching.

To achieve this goal consider an "ice-breaking" activity that puts your learners at ease by asking them to say some things about themselves while getting to know and to interact with you and other students. On your very first day, you should begin building a classroom of support and encouragement that lays the foundation for a partnership of ideas by letting your learners know that they will be expected to interact with one another and with you in team-like fashion. Here are some example activities that can begin to build a classroom of learner support and encouragement.

• A few students (in elementary school) are asked to name what they most like to do while other students get to respond as to what they like about the activities chosen. Your job is to help the group come to a consensus as to what category to place a student's response (sport, hobby, school activity, etc.) and what makes it so enjoyable.

- A few students (in middle school) are chosen to describe something unique about themselves, such as their favorite subject, one of their talents or skills, or what they like to do most in their free time. Your role is to provide an example of how some of their responses could be related to what you will be teaching and to ask other students for additional examples.

- Students (in high school) are assigned to groups of four or five and asked to decide on one question they would like answered about the subject you will be teaching. Your job is to discuss with the full class how the question might fit the content of your course and achieve agreement on some of the things they will need to learn in order to answer their question.

While there can be many different ice-breaking activities for your grade or subject, did you notice anything in common among these three? You may have noticed that in each example the teacher started with something with which the students were already familiar and were allowed to express it in their own personal way. Then the teacher helped articulate student responses and build upon them, illustrating the beginning of a constructivist conversation and "partnership of ideas," that might well become a pattern in these classrooms for the rest of the year. Neither student nor teacher could claim exclusive ownership of the final product, yet if given sufficient time one would guess that the outcome would be pleasing to both students and teacher while advancing the goals of the curriculum.

Rules and Expectations

Plan to devote some time to discussing your classroom rules and your overall expectations about both conduct and work. This is the time to resolve student uncertainties and let your learners know what to expect. There is no better way to begin this process than by referring to the conduct and work rules that you have either posted for all to see or provided as a handout.

Introducing Your Subject

Although you may not have time to present much content on the first day, keep in mind several tips for presenting content during your first lessons:

1. Begin by talking to the whole class. This is a time when not all of your students will be eager to participate in group work or seatwork or be relaxed enough to contribute meaningfully to inquiry or problem-solving activities. These instructional approaches depend on the trust and confidence that students acquire from their experience with you over time. They will be acquiring this trust and confidence during your first days and weeks in the classroom.

2. During your initial days in the classroom, choose content activities that you believe everyone can successfully complete. At this time, you will not yet know the difficulty level most appropriate for all of your learners, so use this time to gradually try out the types of tasks and activities you eventually will ask your learners to perform. Begin with those from which you expect the most student success.

Your other tasks this first day or period can be considerable. In some cases, they can consume most of the remainder of the class period at the upper grades and a full hour or more in the lower grades. Filling out forms requested by the school and school district, checking course schedules, guiding lost students to their correct rooms, and accepting new students during the middle of the class may all be part of your first class day.

Closure

Have a definite procedure for closing in mind (for example, a preview of things to come, instructions to follow for tomorrow's class, a reminder of things to bring to class). Begin closing a full three minutes before the bell is to ring. End with a note of encouragement that all of your students can do well in your grade or class.

Follow these suggestions, and you will have a great first day!

Making Your Classroom and School a Professional Learning Community

Much of what has been said in this and the preceding chapters has been to give you some tools, understandings, and attitudes to create not just a classroom of learners but a classroom in which teacher and students live and work as a community. You already know a lot about a learning community from some of your own school experiences and reading this chapter. But, what is a "learning community?" For our purposes a *learning community* is a shared partnership of ideas with teacher and students (and teachers with other teachers) arriving at some common beliefs, values or understandings in the process of learning together.

Not long ago it would be unheard of to say that teacher and students should be learning together, since the primary role of a teacher was to "fill" the mind of the learner with what he or she needed to know. The teacher's role was to serve as an authority, "gate keeper," and information provider who would select and transfer knowledge from teacher to learner through texts and classroom presentations. At the beginning of the fifth grade, the fifth-grade student was assumed to be "empty" of fifth-grade content. And, on the first day of school the junior in high school was assumed to be empty of what was to be taught in the ensuing year. The teacher's job was to provide the necessary grade-level content.

Our common sense tells us that no learner comes to school empty of what is to be taught that year or even of some of the content taught in ensuing years. In life we naturally acquire all sorts of beliefs, understandings, and emotions that do not correspond with neatly packaged grade-level content. In other words some of the things we come to know could fit anywhere in the school curriculum, albeit sized to our developmental level. In other words, we are always constructing knowledge in wider and wider nests of embrace that eventually are enveloped by still more advanced and sophisticated nests of understanding. In other words, every child has the potential to learn and never stops learning, sometimes because and sometimes despite what is taught in more formal settings such as school. You will recognize this as one of the primary tenets of education that has come to be called "constructivism," that you briefly read about in Chapter 1 and which you will become more familiar with in the chapters ahead.

For now, you know that constructivism and learning communities go hand in hand. One cannot exist without the other. Constructivism is the creating of shared ideas framed from the learners experience and developmental level in the context of the naturally occurring dialogue of the classroom. In Chapter 1 this was called "the shared partnership of ideas." A learning community represents a dialogue between teacher and learner and learner with learner in an exchange of ideas eventually coming together to arrive at a mutually satisfying belief, understanding, or attitude. It is the back and forth discussion among teacher and students and students with students, stimulated by instructional aids, such as texts, films, computers, internet, physical models, reenactments, and human resources. Your role in a constructivist classroom is not just to guide the process but to actively play a role in creating the conditions in which to arrive at a mutually satisfying solution to a problem or dilemma. In the chapters ahead you will learn more about your active role in building and maintaining a learning community in your classroom and your classroom's role in contributing to a school wide professional learning community. For now, let's take what you have just learned about a learning community in your classroom and place it into the context of an entire school or even an entire school district.

At the school level a professional learning community (PLC) is one in which teachers participate jointly in decision making, have a shared sense of purpose, engage in collaborative work, and accept joint responsibility for the outcomes of their work—not so very different than the community of learners in your classroom. These responsibilities represent a different mindset within a traditional school by having the goal of improving both teaching and learning by maximizing teacher-to–teacher interaction and administrative talent and resources across grades.

Key to carrying out this mission are the components of a shared school vision and norms, staff collaboration, and reflective dialogue among all school personnel. The concept of collaboration among educators has been considered one of the most important elements among these. The concept of collaboration in a professional learning community implies that those who teach students should also learn and collaborate with colleagues to improve every teacher's teaching and learning (Resnick, 2010). The component of teacher collaboration is intended to build on the practice of reflective dialogue in which teachers share classroom experiences, teaching techniques, and resources that can impact and improve the entire school community not just individual classrooms. Kruse, et al. (1995, p. 30) explains the importance of reflective dialogue among school educators in establishing a professional learning community in the following way:

> Rich and recurring discourse promotes high standards of practice and both generate and reinforce core beliefs, norms, and values of the community. In other words, talk is the bridge between educational values and improved practice in schools. Reflective practice denotes self-awareness about what one does and is a condition toward which all professionals should strive. By engaging in reflection, teachers become students of their craft as they puzzle through the assumptions basic to quality practice.

You will find many opportunities to contribute to the PLC of your school and school district with the knowledge and understandings you have gained. With these opportunities, your job will be to turn the goals and aspirations of a professional learning community into practice in your classroom and school.

Case History and Licensure Preparation

DIRECTIONS: *The following case history pertains to Chapter 3 content. After reading the case history, go to Chapter 3 in the Book Specific Resources section in the MyEducationLab for your course. Open the Case History and Licensure Preparation activity and complete the questions that follow. Upon completion of the test, scored answers to the short-answer question pertaining to the case history and multiple-choice questions will be provided.*

Case History

Ms. Ford is a first-year teacher. Her third-grade class includes a large number of students who can be termed "at risk" according to a variety of standards. Many come from single-parent homes; over two-thirds qualify for reduced-price school lunches; and almost one-third speak a language other than English at home.

It is the third week of the semester, and many of Ms. Ford's worst fears have failed to materialize. Her students have not created any significant classroom management problems. On the contrary, they have been orderly, well behaved, and quiet. Ms. Ford's three classroom rules are posted neatly and clearly on the bulletin board:

Respect other people and their property.

Raise your hand before speaking.

Listen when others talk.

Even though Ms. Ford has spent a great deal of time coming up with clearly defined consequences for not following these rules, she now feels the time has been

largely wasted. The problem is not that students speak out without raising their hands; it's that they seldom speak at all. They listen quietly but only to her, because few classmates volunteer oral responses except the most simple one-word answers. The students sit in their alphabetically assigned seats, copy sentences from the board without making a sound, and spend extra effort in forming letters that are as round and perfect as the models in the handwriting exercise.

Ms. Ford had been all set to manage rambunctious 8-year-olds, but now she is at a loss about how to light the spark of engagement in her shy and passive class.

After spending most of the weekend rethinking her classroom strategies, Ms. Ford enters her class on Monday with a new plan. She stands in the doorway as her students enter the classroom, but instead of giving a stoic nod, she now greets them with a smile and a quiet reference here and there to a "pretty new sweater" or "a cool backpack." She allows herself to rub Juan's shortly cropped head and asks him if he is joining the marines. He smiles shyly up at her.

More surprises are in store for the third-graders. Gone are the neat rows of desks, and in their place are tables set in small groups to accommodate five or six students each. "Find your name at a table and be seated there," Ms. Ford tells the students.

The organization is not alphabetical but random, or at least it appears to be. It is not necessary to tell the class that the composition of each group has entailed the same attention to detail as for making a first-draft football selection. At each table are at least two students whose primary language is English, as well as one who seems conversant in both English and Spanish, which is the dominant second language in the class.

Ms. Ford explains, "All of you at the same table will be part of a team that will be working together on several projects and assignments. But first, you will need to get to know each other a little bit better. I thought today we might talk about our favorite animals, since each group will be named after the animal of its choice. Ask yourself this question: If I could be any animal for a single day, what animal would I choose and why?

"I'll start. If I could be any animal I wanted to for a day, I would be a horse—a wild, black stallion in the mountains of Wyoming. I would love to run and feel the wind in my mane, to rear up and paw at the sky, and to run like thunder through the canyons. I think it is the horse's freedom and beauty, its speed and strength, that I admire so much.

"Take a few minutes to think about this yourself, and then take turns telling your group which animal you would like to be."

Ms. Ford is amazed that after less than a minute, many students are already sharing their animal choices. And she is in for a few surprises, too. Shy Patricia, whose eyes always seem downcast, is demonstrating between giggles what her life as a monkey would be like. Romero, who knows only a few English words, is completely at home as a pouncing and growling black panther.

It is with a sly smile of satisfaction that Ms. Ford has to gently remind students, near the end of the session, to keep their voices down.

Summing Up

The main points in this chapter include the following:

Connecting with Students

1. Three characteristics of a nurturing classroom are mutual trust and confidence between teacher and learners, unconditional acceptance of every learner's potential to learn, and opportunities for exploration and discovery.

Earning Trust and Becoming a Leader the Old-Fashioned Way

2. Four types of leadership that a teacher can strive for are expert leadership, referent leadership, legitimate leadership, and reward leadership.

Stages of Group Development

3. Four stages through which a successful group passes are forming, storming, norming, and performing.

4. *Distancing* is a type of amiable limit testing, in which group members challenge academic expectations and rules to establish under what conditions they do or do not apply.

5. *Centering* is a second type of amiable limit testing, in which learners question how they will personally benefit from being a group member.

6. Two basic processes by which norms develop are *diffusion* and *crystallization*. The former occurs when different academic and social expectations held by different members spread throughout the group. The latter occurs when expectations converge and crystallize into a shared perspective.

Establishing an Effective Classroom Climate

7. The *classroom climate* is the atmosphere or mood in which interactions between you and your students take place. A classroom climate can be created by the social environment, which is related to the patterns of interaction you wish to promote in your classroom, and by the organizational environment, which is related to the physical or visual arrangement of the classroom.

8. The social climate of the classroom can range from authoritarian (in which you are the primary provider of information, opinions, and instruction) to laissez-faire (in which your students become the primary providers of information, opinions, and instruction).

9. Your role in establishing authority in the classroom and the social climate can vary. You can adopt different roles, including the following:

- Commander in chief, who carefully controls and hones student behavior by organizing and providing all the stimuli needed for learning to occur
- Translator or summarizer of ideas provided by students
- Equal partner with students in creating ideas and solving problems

10. The social climate of your classroom also can vary, depending on how competitive, cooperative, or individualistic you wish interactions among class members to be. Differences among these include the extent of opportunities for students to express opinions, the time devoted to student talk, and the spontaneity with which your students are allowed to respond.

11. The term *organizational climate* refers to the physical or visual arrangement of the classroom, determined by the positioning of desks, chairs, tables, and other internal features of a classroom.

12. The degree of competition, cooperation, and individuality in your classroom is a result of the social and organizational climate you create.

13. Rules can relate to one or more of four distinct areas:
- Academic work
- Classroom conduct
- Information you must communicate the first day
- Information you can communicate later

14. Rules can be communicated orally, on the board, on a transparency, or in a handout. Rules for the early elementary grades should be presented orally, provided as a handout, and posted for reference. Rules for the elementary grades and junior high school may be recited and copied by students. Rules for high school may be given orally and then posted.

15. The following suggestions will help you develop classroom rules:
- Make rules consistent with your climate.
- Do not make rules that cannot be enforced.
- Specify only necessary rules.
- State rules generally enough to include different but related behaviors.

16. Your inability to enforce a rule over a reasonable period of time is the best sign that you need to change the rule.

Problem Areas in Classroom Management

17. Monitoring students, making transitions, giving assignments, and bringing closure are four particularly troublesome areas of classroom management.

18. *With-it-ness* is a form of monitoring in which you are able to keep track of many different signs of student engagement at the same time.

19. You can convey assignments positively and motivate learners in the following ways:
- Use praise and encouragement.
- Provide explanations.
- Offer to help.
- Accept diversity.
- Emphasize reward, not punishment.

20. Problems during transitions occur most frequently when learners are not ready to perform the next activity and do not know what behavior is appropriate during the transition.

21. Homework assignments should be given immediately following the lesson or activities to which they relate and without negative connotations.

22. A closing statement should gradually bring a lesson to an end by combining or consolidating key points into a single overall conclusion, by summarizing or reviewing key content, or by providing a symbol system so students can easily store and later recall the content of the lesson.

Culturally Responsive Classroom Management

23. Use the following methods to bridge cultural gaps in the classroom:
- Establish an open, risk-free climate.
- Plan lessons that meet student interests and needs.
- Allow for activities and responsibilities congruent with learners' cultures.

Making Your Classroom a Learning Community

24. A learning community is a classroom with teacher and students arriving at some common beliefs, values, or understandings in the process of learning together.

25. Building and maintaining a learning community across all classrooms in a school that contributes to a school and district-wide learning community is called a professional learning community, or PLC.

Key Terms

At-risk learners
Centering behavior
Crystallization
Diffusion
Distancing behavior
Expert leadership

Legitimate leadership
Monitoring
Norms
Organizational
    environment
Referent leadership

Reward leadership
Rules and procedures
Social environment
Stages of group
    development
Track system

Discussion and Practice Questions

Questions marked with an asterisk are answered in Appendix B. Some asterisked questions may require student follow-up responses not included in Appendix B. Go to the Assignments and Activities section of the various topics on the MyEducationLab for your course to complete additional practice activities related to this chapter's content.

*1. Describe in your own words the two types of leadership beginning teachers should most quickly achieve. How would you achieve each?

*2. What is meant by the terms *diffusion* and *crystallization* of norms? In what order can you expect these two basic processes of norm development to occur?

*3. Identify three roles you can assume in your classroom that communicate different levels of authority. How will expression of student opinions, proportion of student talk to teacher talk, and spontaneity of response change as a function of these three roles?

4. Draw three diagrams of the internal features of a classroom, one each to illustrate how to promote a classroom climate that is competitive, cooperative, and individualistic.

5. Identify three academic rules and three conduct rules that you believe will be needed on your first day of class. Write out these six rules as you might show them to your students on a handout or transparency on the first day of class.

*6. Identify two rules for which retention might be improved if they were communicated in the context of a relevant circumstance or incident. Describe each circumstance or incident and why the rule would be necessary.

*7. State three guidelines for developing effective classroom rules. Identify four rules that, in your opinion, follow these guidelines.

*8. Describe a practical strategy for deciding when you should revise or eliminate a rule. Which type of rule, academic or conduct, do you feel needs to be revised most often? Why?

*9. What are four teaching practices that can help avoid misbehavior during a transition? Which one do you feel you would use the most? Why?

*10. What are two ways discussed in this chapter that out-of-class assignments can be made more meaningful and accepted by your students? What other ways can you think of?

*11. Identify three ways you can bring a lesson to a close that will help students organize the lesson in retrospect. Which one best fits the grade or subject matter you will be teaching? Why?

12. Describe what a learning community is and how you would strive to create one in your classroom.

Professional Practice

Field Experience and Practice Activities

Questions marked with an asterisk are answered in Appendix B. Some asterisked questions may require student follow-up responses not included in Appendix B.

*1. Identify the four stages of group development and provide some examples of student behavior at each stage.

*2. From your field work or observation experiences, provide some examples of classroom activities that will create (a) a competitive, (b) a cooperative, and (c) an individualistic classroom climate.

*3. How did a teacher whose class you were working in or observing try to bridge different cultures to form a productive and cohesive classroom?

Digital Portfolio Activity

The following digital portfolio activity relates to InTASC standards 3 and 5.

Place your responses to Field Experience Activities 1 and 3 into your digital portfolio in a folder titled "Classroom Management." These responses will provide examples of your skill at creating a cohesive and nurturing classroom and planning to bridge the gap between different cultures in a heterogeneous classroom.

MyEducationLab™

Go to MyEducationLab (www.myeducationlab.com) for Effective Teaching Methods: Research-Based Practice where you can:

- Find learning outcomes for the various course topics course along with national standards that connect to these outcomes.

- Complete **Assignments and Activities** that can help you more deeply understand the chapter content.

- Apply and practice your understanding of the core teaching skills identified in the chapter with **Building Teaching Skills and Dispositions** coaching activities.

- Check your comprehension of the content covered in the chapter with a book specific **Study Plan**. Here you will be able to take a chapter **pretest**, receive feedback on your answers, and then access personalized **Review, Practice, and Enrichment exercises** to enhance your understanding of chapter content. After you complete the exercises, take a **posttest** to confirm your comprehension.

- Learn how to address common classroom management issues in the **Simulations in Classroom Management**.

- Access video clips of CCSSO **National Teachers of the Year award winners** responding to the question, "Why Do I Teach?" in the Teacher Talk section.

- Create, update, and share quality lesson plans with the **Lesson Plan Builder**.

- Access state licensure test requirements, overviews of what tests cover, and sample test items in the **Certification and Licensure** section.

- Learn how to create a high quality teaching portfolio in the **Preparing a Portfolio** section.

- Access tips, advice, and other information on resume writing and interviewing, your first year of teaching, and law and public policies in the Beginning Your Career section.

4 Classroom Management II

Promoting Student Engagement

This chapter will help you answer these questions and meet the following InTASC standards for effective teaching.

- What is an effective classroom management plan?
- What techniques do effective classroom managers use?
- How do I create a learning environment that encourages positive social interaction and engagement in the learning process?
- How do I communicate with families and plan a successful teacher–family conference?
- How can I create a culturally responsive classroom management plan?

InTASC

STANDARD 2 **Learning Differences.** The teacher uses understanding of individual differences and diverse cultures and communities to ensure inclusive learning environments that enable each learner to meet high standards.

STANDARD 4 **Content Knowledge.** The teacher understands the central concepts, tools of inquiry, and structures of the discipline(s) he or she teaches and creates learning experiences that make these aspects of the discipline accessible and meaningful for learners to assure mastery of the content.

STANDARD 9 **Professional Learning and Ethical Practice.** The teacher engages in ongoing professional learning and uses evidence to continually evaluate his/her practice, particularly the effects of his/her choices and actions on others (learners, families, other professionals, and the community), and adapts practice to meet the needs of each learner.

STANDARD 10 **Leadership and Collaboration.** The teacher seeks appropriate leadership roles and opportunities to take responsibility for student learning, to collaborate with learners, families, colleagues, other school professionals, and community members to ensure learner growth, and to advance the profession.

Anyone who reads the newspaper, listens to candidates running for public office, attends school board meetings, or overhears conversations in the teachers' lounge quickly realizes that classroom order and discipline are among education's most frequently discussed topics. Inability to control a class is one of the most commonly cited reasons for dismissing or failing to rehire a teacher, and beginning teachers consistently rate classroom discipline as among their most urgent concerns (Kirsch, 2005; Rose & Gallup, 2002; Seganti, 2011).

In Chapter 3, you learned about establishing the climate for a manageable classroom. In this chapter, you will learn specific techniques for preventing disruptive behaviors from occurring and dealing with them efficiently—increasing the time your students are actively engaged in learning.

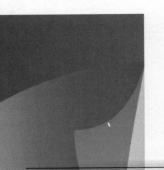

MyEducationLab™

Visit the MyEducationLab for *Effective Teaching Methods: Research-Based Practice*, 8e to enhance your understanding of chapter concepts with a personalized Study Plan. You'll also have the opportunity to hone your teaching skills through video-based Assignments and Activities as well as Building Teaching Skills and Dispositions lessons.

Systems of Classroom Management

Approaches to dealing with classroom management can be grouped into three traditions. One tradition emphasizes the critical role of communication and problem solving between teacher and students. This approach is called the **humanist tradition** of classroom management (Ginott, Ginott, & Goddard, 2003; Glasser, 1998a,b,c; Jones & Jones, 2007; Mendler, Curwin, & Mendler, 2007). The second tradition, which comes from the field of **applied behavior analysis**, emphasizes behavior modification techniques and reinforcement theory applied to the classroom (Alberto & Troutman, 2009; Canter, 2009; Landrum & Kauffman, 2006). The third and most recent approach, which emphasizes the teaching skills involved in organizing and managing instructional activities and presenting content, is called the **classroom management tradition** (Cotton, 1996; Emmer & Evertson, 2012; Evertson & Emmer, 2012). This third approach, more so than the humanistic and applied behavior analysis traditions, underscores the critical role of prevention in managing classroom behavior.

In this chapter, we briefly summarize the main features of these traditions, point out how they are used in the classroom, and show how the best features of each can be seamlessly combined into a single approach. To begin, let's identify six criteria of an effective plan for classroom management:

1. *Establish positive relationships among all learners.* A positive, supportive classroom environment that meets students' needs for building trusting relations is a necessary foundation for managing an orderly classroom. We discussed some of the ways you can build trusting relations among your learners in Chapters 2 and 3.

2. *Prevent attention-seeking and work-avoidance behavior.* The time devoted to managing the classroom should be directed to engaging students in the learning process and preventing behaviors that interfere with it. Engagement and prevention involve both the arrangement of physical space and the teaching of rules for working in this space. In Chapter 3, we considered the importance of classroom climate and provided some guidelines and examples for teaching classroom rules.

3. *Quickly and unobtrusively redirect misbehavior once it occurs.* Most classroom problems take the form of minor off-task and attention-seeking behaviors. Techniques for coping with such an event should not cause more disruption than the behavior itself.

4. *Stop persistent and chronic misbehavior with strategies that are simple enough to be used consistently.* Management systems that require responding to every act of positive or negative behavior will not likely be practical for consistent use in today's busy classrooms.

5. *Teach self-control.* Students should be allowed the opportunity to exercise internal control before the teacher imposes external control. When an external control is imposed, it should be implemented with a plan for fading it out.

6. *Respect cultural differences.* Verbal and nonverbal techniques for redirecting disruptive behavior do not mean the same thing to all cultural groups. Likewise, systematic strategies involving rewards and consequences can violate important cultural norms.

Now let's learn about the three approaches to classroom management. As you read about them, reflect on how each meets these criteria and shares some characteristics with the others.

The Humanist Tradition in Classroom Management

The principles underlying the humanist tradition come from the practice of counseling and clinical psychology. The approach is called *humanist* because it focuses primarily on the inner thoughts, feelings, psychological needs, and emotions of the individual learner. Humanist approaches emphasize the importance of allowing the student time to develop control over his or her behavior, rather than insisting on immediate behavioral change or compliance. Teachers using humanist approaches hope to achieve these ends through interventions that stress the use of communication skills, private conferences, and individual and group problem solving; an understanding of student motives; and the exercise of referent and expert leadership.

Ginott's (1995; Ginott, Ginott, & Goddard, 2003) cooperation through congruent communication (also called the *communication skills approach*), Glasser's (2003; 1998b,c) cooperative learning through individual and group problem solving, and Jones and Jones's (2009) cooperative learning and communities of support approaches are all examples of the humanist tradition. Each emphasizes a different area of skill that the effective classroom manager should possess, but all essentially represent the same underlying philosophy.

Congruent Communication

The cardinal principle underlying Ginott's (Ginott, Ginott, & Goddard, 2003) **congruent communication** skills approach is that learners are capable of controlling their own behavior if teachers allow them to do so. Teachers foster this self-control by allowing learners to choose how they wish to change their own behavior. In addition, teachers help their students deal with their inner thoughts and feelings through the use of effective communication skills.

The use of communication skills is the primary vehicle for influencing learners' self-esteem, which in turn is the primary force underlying acceptable behavior. Therefore this tradition tries first and foremost to influence student behavior by enhancing student self-esteem. According to the proponents of this approach, congruent communication is the vehicle for promoting self-esteem.

Teachers have many opportunities during the school day to engage their students in congruent communication, usually during private conferences with students who misbehave. However, such communication also can go on during problem solving with the whole class. At such times, teachers communicate congruently when they do the following:

1. *Express sane messages.* Sane messages communicate to students that their behavior is unacceptable, but they do so in a manner that does not blame, scold, preach, accuse, demand, threaten, or humiliate. Sane messages state what should be done, rather than scold what was done. Consider the statement "Rosalyn, we are all supposed to be in our seats before the bell rings" in contrast to "Rosalyn, you're always gossiping at the doorway and coming late to class."

2. *Accept rather than deny feelings.* Teachers should accept students' feelings about their individual circumstances, rather than argue about them. If a student complains "I have no friends," the teacher should accept his or her feeling of isolation and identify with the student—such as by saying "So you're feeling you don't belong to any group"—rather than try to convince the student that he or she has misperceived the social situation.

3. *Avoid the use of labels.* When talking to students about what they do well or poorly, teachers should avoid terms such as *lazy, sloppy,* and *bad attitude,* as well as *dedicated, intelligent,* and *perfectionist.* Instead teachers should describe in purely behavioral terms what they do or do not like about students—"You have a lot of erasures and white-out spots on your homework" versus "Your homework is sloppy," "You form your letters correctly" versus "You are a good writer."

4. *Use praise with caution.* Ginott believes many teachers use praise excessively and manipulatively to control student behavior, rather than to acknowledge exceptional performance. They use praise judgmentally ("Horace, you are a good student"), confuse correctness with goodness (referring to a student who completes work with a minimum of mistakes as a "good child"), praise students who perform minimally acceptable behavior as a way of influencing other students ("I like the way Joan is sitting in her seat"), and praise so often that the statements lose all significance and are not even heard by the students. Ginott urges teachers to use praise only to acknowledge exceptional performance and in terms that separate the deed from the doer—for example, "That essay showed a great deal of original thought and research."

5. *Elicit cooperation.* Once a teacher and student have identified behavioral concerns, Ginott encourages the teacher to offer the student alternatives to solving the problem, rather than use coercive power to tell him or her what to do. "Cooperate, don't legislate" is a convenient maxim for remembering this point.

6. *Communicate anger.* Teachers are people, too. They get frustrated and angry just like anyone else. Ginott believes teachers should express their feelings through the use of *"I" messages* instead of *"you" messages*. The former focus on your feelings about the behavior or situation that angered you ("I feel unhappy and embarrassed because you talked when the guest speaker was presenting"). The latter puts the focus on the students and typically accuses and blames ("You were rude to the guest speaker"). Use "I" messages when you own the problem—that is, when you are the one who is angry or upset.

If you were to resolve a classroom management problem using the humanist tradition, you might have an open discussion with your students to draw their attention to the problem. Then you would invite their cooperation in developing mutually agreed-on rules and consequences. Finally, as problems arise, you would have individual conferences with your students, during which you would use the preceding steps one through six to engage them in congruent communication.

Cooperative Learning

In this **video**, Ms. Salazar explains to her class the process for one type of cooperative learning. Pay attention to how she provides the class direction regarding cooperative learning.

Glasser (2003; 1998b,c) points out that effective classroom managers create a learning environment where students want to be, develop mutually agreed-on standards of behavior that students must follow to remain in this environment, and conduct problem-solving conferences with those who violate the standards. Jones and Jones (2009) agree with Glasser that **cooperative learning** is a way to make the classroom a place learners want to be. They believe classrooms that emphasize cooperative learning motivate all children to engage in learning activities and that whole-group instruction, in which students compete with one another for limited rewards, inevitably causes half of all students to be bored, frustrated, inattentive, or disruptive.

According to Glasser (1990) one response to disruptive behavior is discussing the problem with the student. During that time, you stress the importance of right choices and accept no excuses for wrong ones.

For Glasser (2003, 1998b,c), dealing with disruptive students is straightforward, given a classroom where students experience belonging, power, and freedom—in other words, a classroom learners would regret leaving. Faced with a student who persists in violating classroom rules the group believes are essential, Glasser recommends that the teacher should hold a brief, private conference with the student, during which the student recalls the rules and the teacher describes the disruptive behavior, asserts the need for following the rules, and makes clear the consequence for not obeying the rules—for example, removal from the room until the learner chooses to follow the rules. Glasser cautions teachers not to accept excuses from students for why they cannot control their own behavior. He disagrees with teachers who use socioeconomic or sociocultural conditions as excuses for learners not making the right choices. For Glasser, there can be no excuse for disrupting an environment designed to meet learners' needs. Furthermore, when faced with removal from such an environment, Glasser believes students will choose and thus not need be forced to behave.

Both Glasser (2003) and Jones and Jones (2009) have a clear directive for you as you begin to manage your classroom: Begin building a more friendly and nurturant workplace based on principles of cooperative learning. Here are specific recommendations:

- Develop with your students rules for the classroom.

- Get support from school administrators for having an area to which disruptive students can be removed.

- Have private conferences with disruptive students, during which you stress the importance of making right choices and accept no excuses for making wrong ones.

- Follow through when students must be removed, but always allow them the opportunity to return when they choose to follow class rules.

- Unconditionally believe in the potential of every child to learn and behave appropriately.

The Applied Behavior Analysis Tradition in Classroom Management

The tradition of applied behavior analysis in classroom management is closely linked with Skinner's (1953, 1997) theory of learning, which is called *behaviorism* or *operant conditioning*. The techniques underlying the practice of behavior modification derive from this theory. Application of behavior modification to changing socially important behaviors in the fields of education, business, and the social sciences has been called *applied behavior analysis*. To introduce both the strengths and weaknesses of this tradition, we first review the components of behavior modification that have resulted from this approach.

Behavior Modification

Behavior modification, as its name implies, focuses on changing or modifying behavior. Behavior is something a person does that is seen, heard, counted, or captured—say, in a snapshot or a home video.

Figure 4.1 summarizes some of the most important concepts of behavior modification. As the figure indicates, when you want to teach a new behavior or make an existing behavior occur more frequently (for example, spell more words correctly), you must follow the behavior with some type of reinforcement. Reinforcement can be either positive or negative. **Positive reinforcement** occurs when the frequency of a behavior is increased by providing a desired reward after the behavior has occurred. When given a desired reward after performing a behavior you will likely repeat it.

Figure 4.1 **Process of Behavior Modification**

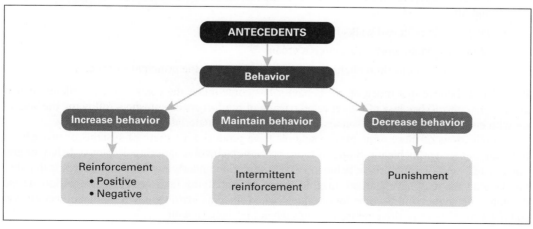

Negative reinforcement occurs when the frequency of a behavior is increased by ending or removing some painful, uncomfortable, or aversive state. In other words, the action you take to stop an annoying sound (shut off the radio), relieve a headache (take an aspirin), or end a frustrating experience (walk away) will likely be repeated again (learned) the next time you experience a similar source of annoyance, discomfort, or frustration.

Negative reinforcement refers to escape or avoidance learning to strengthen the behavior, not simply the application of discomfort or punishment. Thorndike (1913), for example, used negative reinforcement to teach cats how to escape a puzzle box. To get out of the discomfort of the box, the cat had to pull a cord hanging from the top of the box. As soon as the cat pulled the cord, the door opened and the animal escaped. The next time the cat was placed in the same box, it pulled the cord because it had learned how to escape to avoid the uncomfortable condition.

The reason negative reinforcement is important in the classroom is that learners often experience events they want to avoid: boring or difficult work, a scolding, a request to do something they do not want to do, or a direction to stop doing something they want to continue. For example, when a shy student learns that when she does not look at the teacher, the teacher stops calling on her, then this looking-away behavior becomes negatively reinforced by the teacher. The student repeats the behavior to achieve a more desirable state. Similarly, when a learner makes distracting sounds during a lesson to get the teacher to send him out of the room, the teacher negatively reinforces this sound-making behavior. The same thing happens when learners do not pay attention to get the teacher to stop the lesson; their not-paying-attention behavior becomes negatively reinforced. In other words, the teacher unknowingly has taught (negatively reinforced) these learners to pursue certain behaviors to escape or avoid an unpleasant condition.

As these examples illustrate, a teacher may inadvertently fall into the trap of negative reinforcement that learners unconsciously set. In fact, some psychologists believe more inappropriate behavior is learned through negative than positive reinforcement—that is, by learning what it takes to avoid or escape something undesirable than by being rewarded for doing something appropriate (positive reinforcement).

When you are satisfied with a particular behavior and how frequently it occurs, apply **intermittent reinforcement** to maintain the behavior at its present level. For example, consider a student who at the start of the school year was consistently late and unprepared for class but now is beginning to arrive on time. You can maintain this behavior by reinforcing the student on a random or intermittent schedule—for example, every second day, every fourth day, or on randomly selected days. An example of intermittent reinforcement is putting tokens into a slot machine long after your last win or fishing in the same spot long after your last nibble.

Behavioral antecedents are events (or stimuli) that are present when you perform a behavior that elicits or sets off the behavior. Antecedents can be any of the following:

- *Sounds.* A noisy room influences students to become more noisy, an insult from a peer influences you to give an insult back, or the tone of voice in a teacher's demand influences a child to argue back.
- *Sights.* The teacher raises a finger to the lips to indicate silence or flips the light switch on and off.
- *People.* The principal walks in and everyone gets quiet.
- *Materials.* Math worksheets elicit a groan.
- *Places.* The auditorium elicits different behaviors than the principal's office.

Behaviorists believe that much of our behavior has come under the control of antecedents (called *antecedent control*) because of the repeated pairing of reinforcers or punishers following the behavior with environmental stimuli (sounds, sights, people, and materials).

Applications of these principles to schools have produced a variety of systems or procedures for changing student behavior. Some of these procedures involve ignoring disruptive behavior and immediately reinforcing positive behavior. The assumption underlying these procedures is that disruptive students may have learned misguided ways of satisfying their need for recognition. These disruptive behaviors will become less frequent when students learn they will only gain recognition and rewards (receive positive reinforcement) when they behave well.

Other systems are built on the assumption that children learn desired behavior most efficiently when adults immediately punish inappropriate behavior and immediately reward appropriate behavior. Proponents of these systems believe that behavior will improve more rapidly when adults use both timely punishment and timely reward, rather than either punishment or reinforcement alone. These systems routinely involve such punishment procedures as *time-out,* in which the teacher immediately removes the student to an area where he or she can experience no reinforcement of any kind following a disruptive act; *response cost,* in which the teacher removes a student's privilege or reinforcer contingent on disruptive behavior (also called *fines*); and *overcorrection,* in which the student not only makes amends for what he or she did wrong but also goes beyond it by contributing something positive. For example, a student who defaces a desk not only must clean the desk he wrote on but must clean every other desk in the room as well, or a student who insults another student apologizes both to that student and to the whole class.

Although specific approaches may vary, your request to an applied behavior analyst for help with a behavior problem would likely produce the following steps for improving a learner's behavior:

1. Identify both the inappropriate behavior you wish to change and the appropriate behavior you want to take its place.

2. Identify the antecedents to both the inappropriate and appropriate behavior (for example, an influential peer), and make necessary changes in the classroom environment (for example, change the seating arrangement) to prevent the former from occurring and to increase the likelihood of the latter.

3. Identify the student's goal or purpose behind the inappropriate behavior (for example, attention seeking), and discontinue actions on your part (or those of peers) that satisfy this purpose.

4. Establish procedures for reinforcing the appropriate behavior that you want to replace the inappropriate behavior, for example, "those who finish on time can visit the learning center."

The Classroom Management Tradition

Throughout much of the latter half of the twentieth century, classroom discipline was focused on the issue of how best to respond to student misbehavior. The humanist and the applied behavior analysis approaches to classroom management shared the spotlight about equally during this period. As shown in the previous sections, both of these traditions are primarily reactive rather than preventive systems of classroom management. That is, they tend to provide solutions to misbehavior after it occurs, not before.

More recent research, however, has provided another approach to classroom management that frames the question of classroom order and discipline not in terms of reaction but prevention. This approach is based on classroom research that examined what effective teachers do to prevent misconduct and what less effective teachers do to create it. Some of this research involved observation and analysis of both experienced and inexperienced teachers while they taught. The major conclusion of this research was that more effective and less effective classroom managers can be distinguished more by what they do to prevent misbehavior than how they respond to misbehavior. In this section, we explain how the researchers came to this conclusion and the characteristics of effective classroom managers they found. But first, let's look at one study of classroom management that found some interesting principles for managing your classroom.

Emmer, Evertson, and Anderson (1980) recruited 27 third-grade teachers in eight elementary schools for a year-long observation study. During the first three weeks of school, observers gathered several types of information on each of the teachers, including room arrangement, classroom rules, consequences of misbehavior, response to inappropriate behavior, consistency of teacher responses, monitoring, and reward systems. In addition, observers counted the numbers of students who were on task and off-task at 15-minute intervals to determine the extent to which students were attending to the teacher. From these data, the researchers classified the teachers into two groups—one consisting of the more effective managers and the other consisting of the less effective managers—for more in-depth observation the rest of the year.

Those teachers who were categorized as more effective classroom managers were found to have significantly higher student engagement rates (more students actively engaged in the goals of the lesson) and significantly lower student off-task behavior (fewer reprimands and warnings) during the rest of the school year. The key to this outcome was that more effective managers established themselves as instructional leaders during the first three weeks of the school year. They worked on rules and procedures until students learned them. Instructional content was important for these teachers, but they also stressed group cohesiveness and socialization, achieving a common set of classroom norms. By the end of the first three weeks, these classes were ready for the rest of the year.

In contrast to the more effective managers, the less effective managers did not have procedures worked out in advance. This was most evident among the first-year teachers being observed. For example, the researchers described one new teacher who had no procedures for students using the bathroom, pencil sharpener, or water fountain, and as a result, the children seemed to come and go, complicating the teacher's instructional tasks. The poorer managers, like the better managers, had rules, but they presented and followed up on the rules differently. In some cases, the rules were vague: "Be in the right place at the right time." In other cases, they were introduced casually without discussion, leaving it unclear to most children when and where a rule applied.

The poorer managers were also ineffective monitors of their classes. This was caused in part by the lack of efficient routines for pupil activities. In other cases, this was the result of teachers removing themselves from active surveillance of the whole class to work at length with a single child. A major result of the combination of vague and untaught rules and poor procedures for monitoring and establishing routines was that students were frequently left without sufficient guidance to direct their own activities.

One further characteristic of the less effective managers was that the consequences of good behavior and inappropriate behavior were either not in evidence or were not delivered in a timely manner. For example, sometimes teachers issued general criticisms that failed to identify a specific offender or a particular event. Some of these teachers frequently warned children but did not follow through, even after several warnings. This tended to allow children to push the teacher to the limits, causing more problems. Other teachers issued vague disciplinary messages ("You're being too noisy") that were not adequately focused to capture the attention of any one child or subgroup of children for whom they were intended.

In sum, deficiencies in the areas of setting rules, establishing routines, monitoring, and creating a praise and reward structure clearly had a negative effect on the overall management and organization of the classroom. Most of the time, these deficiencies provided windows of opportunity for a wide range of pupil misconduct, off-task behavior, and disengagement from the goals of the classroom. In the less effective managers' classrooms, after only a few weeks had elapsed, undesirable patterns of behavior and low teacher credibility had tended to become established, and both persisted throughout the school year.

From this and related studies of classroom management (Emmer & Evertson, 2012; Evertson, 1995; Evertson & Emmer, 2012; Tauber, 1990), we learn that effective classroom managers possess three broad types of teaching behaviors:

- They devote extensive time before and during the first few weeks of school to plan and organize their classrooms to minimize disruptions and enhance work engagement.

- They approach teaching rules and routines as methodically as they approach teaching their subject areas. They provide students with clear instructions about acceptable behavior and monitor students' compliance with these instructions carefully during the first few weeks of school.

- They inform students of the consequences for breaking the rules and enforce them consistently.

As you can see, the classroom management tradition is essentially a preventive approach. It suggests ways to ensure that behavior problems do not occur. However, it offers few immediate solutions for what to do after the problem has occurred, because it emphasizes planning in anticipation of problems, not resolving them afterward. You will need a comprehensive plan incorporating elements of all three traditions to make your classroom a positive environment for learning.

An Integrated Approach
to Classroom Management

All three approaches to classroom management have advantages and limitations. Although each has made a significant contribution to our understanding of effective classroom management, teachers do not need to select one tradition over another. In fact, the research conducted and reported by Emmer, Evertson, and Anderson (1980), Emmer and Evertson (2012), Evertson and Emmer (1982, 2012), and Doyle (1986) has shown that effective classroom managers are able to blend the best parts of different approaches. Figure 4.2 summarizes the three approaches to classroom management.

Now let's look at some of the ways effective teachers put these approaches into practice.

Low-Profile Classroom Management

Logan (2003), Rinne (1997), and Leriche (1992) use the concept of **low-profile classroom management** to refer to coping strategies used by effective teachers to stop misbehavior without disrupting the flow of a lesson. These techniques are effective for so-called **surface behaviors** (Levin & Nolan, 2006), which represent the majority of disruptive classroom actions. Examples of surface behaviors are laughing, talking out of turn, passing notes, daydreaming, not following directions, combing hair, doodling, humming, tapping, and so on. They are called *surface behaviors* because they are the normal developmental behaviors that children find themselves doing when confined to a small space with a large number of other children. These behaviors do not indicate some underlying emotional disorder or personality problem. However, they can disrupt the flow of a lesson and others' engagement in work if left unchecked.

Figure 4.3 depicts the components of low-profile classroom management. Low-profile management for dealing with surface behaviors is actually a set of techniques that requires *anticipation* by the teacher to prevent problems before they occur, *deflection* to redirect disruptive behavior that is about to occur, and *reaction* to unobtrusively stop disruptions immediately after they occur. Let's look at each of these.

Anticipation.   Alert teachers have their antennae up to sense changes in student motivation, attentiveness, interest level, and excitability as these changes happen or are about to happen. These teachers are aware that at certain times of the year (before and after holidays), week (just before a

Figure 4.2 Summary of Three Approaches to Classroom Management

Humanist Tradition	Applied Research Tradition	Classroom Management Tradition
Focuses on the feelings, psychological needs, and emotions of the individual learner	Focuses on changing or modifying inappropriate behavior once it has occurred	Focuses on the prevention of misbehavior as opposed to ways of dealing with it after it has occurred
Incorporates interventions that stress communication skills, private conferences with the learner and parents, and individual and group problem-solving skills	Incorporates teacher behaviors that positively reinforce the learner, and eliminates teacher behaviors that negatively reinforce the learner	Incorporates classroom rules, consequences, and routines to keep students on task and actively engaged
Emphasizes cooperative grouping and emotional support networks composed of other learners and teachers	Emphasizes the immediate reinforcement of positive behavior and punishment together	Emphasizes time before and during the first few weeks of school to plan and organize the classroom to minimize disruptions and enhance work engagement
Advocates adherence to rules and time-out or removal for short periods, when necessary	Advocates time-out, response cost, and overcorrection	Advocates giving learners clear instructions in advance about acceptable behavior and monitoring student compliance

Figure 4.3 Characteristics of Low-Profile Classroom Management

ANTICIPATION	DEFLECTION	REACTION
Lower Profile ◄————————————————————► Higher Profile		
• Scanning • Picking up the pace • Removing temptation • Boosting interest • Changing seating arrangements	• Proximity • Eye contact • Prompting • Name dropping • Peer recognition	• Warning • Loss of privileges • Time-out • Removal • Detention

major social event), or day (right after an assembly or physical education class), students' readiness for doing work will be different from what usually can be expected. Skilled classroom managers are alert not only to changes in the group's motivational or attention level but also to changes in specific individuals, which may be noticed as soon as they enter class.

At these times, anticipation involves scanning back and forth with active eyes to quickly size up the seriousness of a potential problem and head it off before it emerges or becomes a bigger problem. For example, you may decide to pick up the pace of instruction to counter some perceived lethargy after a three-day weekend or to remove magazines or other objects that may distract students' attention before a long holiday. Some teachers maintain a reserve of activities that are likely to boost students' interest during times when it is difficult to stay focused on normal day-to-day activities. Other teachers boost interest by forcing themselves to be more positive or eager in the face of waning student enthusiasm—for example, by raising and lowering the pitch of their voice and moving to different parts of the room more frequently. At other times, it may be necessary to quickly change seating arrangements to minimize antagonism when arguments occur between students.

Anticipation involves not only knowing what to look for but also where and when to look for it. It also involves having a technique ready, no matter how small, for changing the environment quickly and without notice to prevent the problem from occurring or escalating. Here are a few reminders of what you can do to anticipate and correct emerging off-task behavior.

- Scan the classroom back and forth letting students know you are alert.
- Pick up the pace when you sense not everyone is listening.
- Change the pitch or volume of your voice to shift attention back to you.
- Keep a few interesting activities in reserve that can be used to boost attention, when needed.
- Shift seating arrangements when you anticipate off-task behavior is about to occur.

Deflection. Good classroom managers sense when disruption is about to occur. They are attuned to verbal and nonverbal cues that in the past have preceded disruptive behavior. Applied behavior analysts call these behavioral cues *antecedents* or *precursors*. They take the form of a glance, abruptly closing a book, sitting and doing nothing, squirming, asking to be excused, ignoring a request, sighing in frustration, or showing a facial expression of annoyance or anger. Although not disruptive by itself, any of these behaviors may signal that more disruptive behavior is about to follow.

Some teachers can detect the significance of antecedents and deflect them by simply moving nearer to the student who may be about to misbehave, thus preventing a more disruptive episode from occurring. Other teachers may make eye contact with the learner combined with a certain facial expression—for example, raising the eyebrows or slightly tilting the head—to communicate a warning. Both these techniques effectively use nonverbal signals to deflect a potential problem.

Verbal signals are also effective. Verbal deflection techniques include *prompting,* in which the teacher reminds the class of the rule or says, "We are all supposed to be doing math now"; *name dropping,* in which the teacher inserts the target student's name into the explanation or presentation, as in "Now if Angela were living in Boston at the time of the Boston Tea Party, she might have . . ."; and *peer recognition,* in which the teacher notices a peer engaged in appropriate behavior and acknowledges this to the class. As the potential for the problem to escalate increases, the effective manager shifts from nonverbal to verbal techniques to keep pace with the seriousness of the misbehavior that is about to occur. Here are a few reminders of what you can do to deflect and correct off-task student behavior that has begun.

- Move nearer to the student to prevent the behavior from reoccurring.
- Make eye contact with the offending student together with a displeasing or stern facial expression.
- Verbally remind the class of what they are supposed to be doing or what they are doing wrong.
- Weave the offending student's name into your instruction to catch their attention.
- Mention a student's name as an example of someone who is behaving correctly.

Reaction.   Anticipation and deflection can efficiently and unobtrusively prevent actions from disrupting the flow of a lesson. Using these techniques allows students the opportunity to correct themselves, thus fostering the development of self-control. However, the classroom is a busy place, and you will have many demands on your attention, which may make a behavior difficult to anticipate or to deflect.

When disruptive behavior occurs that you cannot anticipate or unobtrusively redirect, your primary goal should be to end the disruptive episode as quickly as possible. Effective classroom managers, therefore, must at times react to a behavior by providing a warning or incentive to promote positive self-control. Your reaction requires first that you have included among your class rules one that corresponds with the behavior in question and the consequences for violating the rule. Glasser (1998a) points out that an effective consequence for breaking a rule is temporary removal from the classroom (provided your classroom is a place that the student wants to be), school detention, or loss of privileges, recess, or some other activity the learner will miss.

When disruptive behavior occurs, your anticipation-deflection-reaction should be similar to the following:

- As soon as a student disrupts the class, acknowledge a nearby classmate who is performing the expected behavior: "Carrie, I appreciate how hard you are working on the spelling words." Then wait 15 seconds for the disruptive student to change his or her behavior.
- If the disruption continues, say, "Carlos, this is a warning. Complete the spelling assignment and leave Carrie alone." Wait 15 seconds.
- If the student does not follow the request after this warning, say, "Carlos, you were given a warning. You must now leave the room for five minutes [or you must stay inside during lunch, or you cannot go to the resource center today]. I'll talk to you about this during my free period."

Dealing with Persistent Disruptive Behavior

When used skillfully, the low-profile techniques of anticipation, deflection, and reaction should promote lesson flow. Occasionally, when these techniques do not work for a particular student or group of students, it may be a sign that the individual learning needs of the student or students are not being met. When disruptive behavior persists and you have assured yourself that you have taken low-profile steps to deal with it, you may need to increase your involvement in responding to the problem.

Responding to Misbehavior

The teacher in this **video** explains several techniques for redirecting misbehavior. Watch as she implements these techniques in the classroom environment.

You can respond to misbehavior in many ways. You may choose to ignore an infraction, if it is momentary and not likely to recur (for example, when students jump out of and back into their seats to stretch their legs after a long assignment). At the other extreme, you may call an administrator to help resolve the problem. Between these extremes are many alternative responses, listed here in order of increasing severity:

- Look at the student sternly.
- Move closer to the student.
- Call on the student to provide the next response.
- Ask the student to stop.
- Discuss the problem with the student.
- Assign the student to another seat.
- Assign an extra assignment.
- Assign the student to detention.
- Write a note to the student's parents or guardians.
- Call the student's parents or guardians.

These alternatives vary in severity from simply giving the student a look of dissatisfaction to involving the parents or guardians in resolving the problem. More important than the variety these alternatives offer, however, is your ability to match the correct response to the type of misbehavior that has occurred. One of the most difficult problems you will encounter in effectively maintaining classroom discipline will be deciding on a response that is effective in addressing the problem (Emmer & Evertson, 2012; Evertson & Emmer, 2012; Manning & Bucher, 2006; Sugai, 1996).

Although every rule violation should consistently receive a response, the severity of the consequence can and should vary according to the nature of the violation and the frequency with which it has occurred in the past. If you respond too mildly to a student who has violated a major rule many times before, nothing will likely change. If you respond too severely to a student who commits a minor violation for the first time, you will be unfair. Being flexible is important in resolving different discipline problems and should include taking into account both the context in which the violation occurs and the type of misbehavior that has occurred.

Here are some guidelines for dealing with mild, moderate, and more serious misbehavior:

- Mild misbehaviors—like talking out, acting out, getting out of seat, disrupting others, and similar misbehaviors—deserve a mild response, at first. But if they occur repeatedly, a moderate response may be appropriate. In unusual cases, such as continual talking that disrupts the class, a more serious response may be warranted.

- Moderate misbehaviors—like cutting class, being abusive toward others, fighting, and using profanity—deserve a moderate response, at first. But if these behaviors become frequent, a more serious response may be warranted.

- More serious misbehaviors—like theft, vandalism, incorrigible conduct, and substance abuse—deserve a severe response. But do not try to manage these behaviors in your classroom. Immediately bring them to the attention of school administrators.

Table 4.1 presents some responses you can make to mild, moderate, and more serious misbehavior.

Rewards and Reinforcement

There are multiple ways to use your leadership in managing discipline problems (for example, you alone decide the consequence; you have students share in the responsibility; you choose the consequence from alternatives provided by the student) and multiple levels of the seriousness of your response (from a stern glance to calling parents). But still other options are available. In this section,

Table 4.1 Examples of Mild, Moderate, and Severe Misbehaviors and Some Alternative Responses

Misbehaviors	Alternative Responses
Mild Misbehaviors	**Mild Responses**
Minor defacing of school property or the property of others	Warning
Acting out (horseplay, scuffling)	Feedback to student
Talking back	Time-out
Talking without raising hand	Change of seat assignment
Getting out of seat	Withdrawal of privileges
Disrupting others	After-school detention
Sleeping in class	Telephone call/note to parents
Tardiness	
Throwing objects	
Exhibiting inappropriate familiarity (kissing, hugging)	
Gambling	
Eating in class	
Moderate Misbehaviors	**Moderate Responses**
Unauthorized leaving of class	Detention
Abusive conduct toward others	Behavior contract
Noncompliance	Withdrawal of privileges
Smoking or using tobacco in class	Telephone call/note to parents
Cutting class	Parent conference
Cheating, plagiarizing, or lying	In-school suspension
Using profanity, vulgar language, or obscene gestures	Restitution for damages
Fighting	Alternative school service (e.g., cleaning up, tutoring)
Severe Misbehaviors	**Severe Responses**
Defacing or damaging school property or the property of others	Detention
	Telephone call/note to parents
Theft, possession, or sale of another's property	Parent conference
Truancy	In-school suspension
Being under the influence of alcohol or narcotics	Removal from school or alternative school placement
Selling, giving, or delivering to another person alcohol, narcotics, or weapons	
Teacher assault or verbal abuse	
Incorrigible conduct, noncompliance	

you will learn how learners respond to rewards and disincentives, why they respond to them differently, and how you can use each effectively in your classroom.

Many types of rewards and reinforcement can be used to increase the probability of a desirable response. A reward or reinforcement can be *external*, delivered by some other person, or *internal*, provided by the learner himself or herself. Here are some familiar external rewards commonly found in the classroom:

- Verbal or written praise
- Smile or a head nod

Rewards consistent with the goals of your classroom and matched to student interests keep learners engaged in the learning process and responding at high rates of success.

- Special privileges (for example, a visit to the learning center, library, etc.)
- Time out from regular work to pursue a special project (e.g., science exhibit)
- Permission to choose a topic or assignment
- Getting to work in a group
- Extra points toward a grade
- "Smiley face" stickers on assignments
- Note to the parents on a test or paper
- Posting a good exam or homework for others to see
- Special recognitions and certificates (for example, "Most Improved," "Good Conduct Award," "Neatest," "Hardest Worker," etc.)

Not all of these external rewards may be equally reinforcing, however. Some learners may disdain verbal praise; others will have no desire to visit the library or learning center. Some students like to be called on; shy students won't like the added attention. A reinforcement for one student may be completely irrelevant to another.

Educators have sometimes been criticized for creating a generation of learners who are hooked on artificial or extrinsic rewards and thus need them to learn and behave in classrooms. This has led to an increased interest in the use of internal rewards, also called **natural reinforcers**. An internal (natural) reward or reinforcer is one that is naturally present in the setting where the behavior occurs.

Some learners are naturally reinforced by learning to write, read, color, answer questions, play sports, solve equations, answer textbook questions, or write essays. But some are not. Many learners may require external reinforcers to begin to engage in certain classroom activities they do not find naturally reinforcing. For such children, external reinforcers have two important roles to play: (1) They allow you to shape and improve the behaviors you desire through the use of positive reinforcement, and (2) they enable you to transfer their control over the learner's behavior to natural reinforcers.

Incentives versus Punishment

Both incentives and punishment are used to decrease the probability or likelihood that a behavior will occur. For example, you can try to keep Daniel in his seat either (1) by giving him an extra assignment every time he is out of his seat or (2) by giving him a trip to the reading center for every 30 minutes he stays in his seat. In the first instance, you are giving Daniel a punishment to encourage him to do what is expected, and in the second, you are giving him a reward to achieve the same end. Punishment creates an avoidance response to an undesirable behavior. In contrast, a reward encourages the recurrence of a desirable behavior by dispensing something pleasant or rewarding immediately after the desirable behavior.

But rewards and punishments generally are not equally effective in promoting a desired behavior. Given two choices to keep Daniel in his seat—the punishment of extra homework or the reward of something interesting to work on—the reward usually will be more successful. Here are several reasons why:

- *Punishment does not guarantee the desired response will occur.* The extra homework may indeed keep Daniel in his seat the next time he thinks of moving about, but it by no means will ensure he will pursue the truly desired behavior, which is to perform some meaningful instructional activity while he is there. Instead he may daydream, write notes to friends, or even pull Rebecca's hair. All these behaviors succeed in keeping him from being punished again for getting out of his seat. Punishment in the absence of incentives can create other undesired behaviors.

- *The effects of punishment usually are specific to a particular context and behavior.* This means extra homework is not likely to keep Daniel in his seat when a substitute teacher arrives, because it was not that teacher who assigned the punishment. Also that punishment is not likely to deter Daniel from pulling Rebecca's hair, because the punishment was associated only with keeping him in his seat. Punishment rarely keeps someone from misbehaving beyond the specific context and behavior to which it was most closely associated.

- *The effects of punishment can have undesirable side effects.* If extra homework is truly aversive for Daniel, he may decide never to risk leaving his seat again, even to ask for your permission to use the restroom. Daniel may decide to take no chances about leaving his seat and not even to trust his own judgment about when an exception to the rule may be appropriate.

- *Punishment sometimes elicits a hostile or aggressive response.* Although any single punishment is unlikely to provoke a strong emotional response, keep in mind that students receive punishment in various forms all day long, both at school and at home. If your punishment is "the straw that breaks the camel's back," do not be surprised to observe an emotional outburst that is inconsistent with the degree of punishment rendered. When punishment is used, it should be used sparingly and in association with rewards and a clear delineation of the behavior that is expected.

- *The punishment can become associated with the punisher.* If you use punishment consistently as a tool for increasing the likelihood a desirable behavior will occur, you may lose the cooperation you need for managing your classroom effectively. With this cooperation gone, you will find the vital link for making management techniques work is gone as well. Plan not to solve discipline problems by using punishment; otherwise the punishment could become more strongly associated with you than the desired behavior you wish to encourage.

- *Punishment that is rendered to stop an undesired behavior but is not immediately associated with the desired behavior seldom has a lasting effect.* If the desired behavior is not clear to your students at the time you administer the punishment, they will see the punishment only as an attempt to hurt, not as an attempt to encourage the desired behavior. Punishment in the classroom should not be used as retribution for undesired behavior, but as an incentive for correctable behavior.

- *Keep in mind that the repeated use of punishment, even as a learning tool, may detract from your efforts to establish a nurturing classroom.* Take care to manage your classroom in a manner that does not deter a climate of mutual trust and confidence, unconditional acceptance of every learner's potential to learn, and a climate of exploration and discovery characteristic of a community of learners.

Warnings.   A warning can prevent a minor problem from intensifying. For the misbehaviors identified as mild in Table 4.1, it is not unusual to provide several warnings before dispensing some kind of consequence. However, after two or three warnings, you should assign some type of consequence, because waiting longer reinforces the student's belief that you are not serious about the misbehavior. This undermines the integrity of the rule being violated and your credibility.

Corporal Punishment.   Absent from the common responses to misbehavior listed in Table 4.1 is any form of corporal punishment, such as paddling a student. Such punishment, although permissible in some school districts when administered by a specifically designated school authority, generally has not proven effective in deterring misbehavior.

One reason for this is that the heightened emotion and anxiety on the part of the student (and the administrator) at the time of the punishment often prevent rational discussion of the appropriate behavior the punishment is supposed to encourage. In addition, corporal punishment can easily provoke aggression and cause hostility in both students and parents. This can outweigh any immediate benefit that might accrue from the punishment.

Generally, you should avoid physical contact with a student, because such contact is easily misunderstood. This applies whether the contact is to administer punishment or, in the case of an older student, is a reward (patting a student on the shoulder for doing a good job) or form of assistance (placing your arm around a student in times of high anxiety). Although your own judgment, the situation, and the age of the student will be your best guides, the only clear exception is a situation requiring your immediate assistance. Examples of such situations are curtailing the movement of a student who is hurting another or restraining a student from self-injury. At such times, call an administrator as quickly as possible.

The Influence of Home and Family on Classroom Behavior

It is important to note that some of the discipline problems you will face in your classroom may have their origin outside of your classroom. Living in a fast-paced, upwardly mobile society has created family stresses and strains that our grandparents could not have imagined. Their lives while growing up were not necessarily any easier than yours or your students' lives, but they were most assuredly different, particularly in the intensity and rapidity with which children experience developmental stages and life cycle changes.

For example, by some estimates, boys and girls are maturing earlier than they did 50 years ago. This means they come under the influence of the intense emotions of sex, aggression, love, affiliation, jealousy, and competitiveness earlier than their own parents may have. Teachers in the elementary grades are no longer surprised by the depth of understanding and ability of young students to emulate the media's attractively packaged images of adult behavior and lifestyles, especially as they relate to clothes, relationships, and dominance.

Although not often recognized, these generational differences sometimes are even more difficult for parents to accept than for you, the teacher. This often leads to major conflicts at home that surface in the classroom as seemingly minor but persistent misbehaviors. You can have little influence over home conflicts, except to understand they originate at home and not in your classroom. In other words, there may be times when no amount of intervention and understanding in the classroom will seem to work, since the source of the problem may lie elsewhere and may be more serious than you suppose—including marital discord, verbal or physical abuse, competition among siblings, financial distress and unemployment, and divorce. You can be sure that one or more of these family disturbances will be occurring in the lives of some of your students.

These are not trivial burdens for students, especially when combined with the social and academic demands of school, the uncertainties of their own futures, and the developmental crises that school-age children pass through between youth and adulthood (Erikson, 1968). If a problem persists and your efforts to resolve it are to no avail, consider the possibility that it may be rooted in the home life of a learner. Although there is no easy way to know what is happening in the lives of your students at home, many students welcome the opportunity to talk about the nature of their problems, when asked. For some, it will be just the opportunity they have sought to shed some of the emotional burden these events are creating in their lives.

It is not your role to resolve such problems, but knowing the reason they are occurring can explain why your solutions to a behavioral problem may not be working and what next steps may be in order to address the problem. Your active involvement in your school's professional learning community will be a valuable resource for helping you decide how to communicate to family members and other professionals who are in a position to help, such as a social worker, school nurse, special education teacher, counselor, and school psychologist. Your communication and collaboration with these professionals can be invaluable in assisting you and your learners with classroom management problems that may have their origins outside of the classroom.

Preparing for the Teacher–Family Conference

When academic or social/behavioral problems become a major impediment to a child's learning or your ability to teach others in the class, it is time for a teacher–family conference including one or both parents or, if not in the home, guardians, such as grandparents or foster parents. In this case a major infraction of a school or classroom rule has occurred, the learner is consistently ignoring classroom correctives to address a problem, or the motivation or prerequisites to learn are lacking, impeding learner progress.

In this **video**, we witness a parent-teacher conference regarding a child who has been struggling in reading. What are the components you can find regarding this conference?

The teacher–family conference provides you the opportunity to inform one or more family members of the severity of the problem and to elicit their help in removing it. Without the support of the student's family in providing the appropriate response at home, there is little chance that an intervention at school will have a lasting effect in correcting the problem and deterring its occurrence at another time (Lawrence-Lightfoot, 2003; Lightfoot, 2006). Being "grounded" for a week, having to be in at a certain time, completing extra study time in the quiet of one's bedroom, or performing extra chores around the house will have more impact than an aversive administered during the school day, as long as it is administered with a clear understanding of the desired classroom behavior.

If the request for a conference is the result of a specific problem in your classroom, notifying a family member that a conference is desired will be your responsibility. This notification should consist of a call or letter expressing to the parent(s) or guardian the following:

1. The purpose of the conference, including a statement of the joint goal of supporting the student's success in school

2. A statement or comment pointing out the integral role of the family in the academic and behavioral process of the learner (this may include a citation from the state or school policy regarding such matters)

3. Possible dates, times, and location of the conference

4. A contact person and phone number, if the family member is unable to reach you directly. If you request a conference with a student's family member by phone, be sure to ask them to record the date, time, location, and contact person for the conference at the time of the call.

Whether conducting a conference by phone (which sometimes may be the only alternative) or in person, do the following during the conference:

• Try to gain the parents' acknowledgment of the problem and participation in working toward its resolution.

• Present a doable agreed-upon plan of action for addressing the problem at home and at school.

• Identify alternatives for follow-up activities (for example, sending a note home each week indicating progress, calling immediately if the problem should recur, reviewing the situation at the next parent-teacher night).

• Write down what took place during the call or conference for future reference, including both matters of agreement and disagreement.

Conducting the Teacher–Family Conference

During the parent conference, you should briefly explain the problem, stop frequently to listen to what others have to say, and, then, express your own concerns and get across to family members your feelings.

Plain Talk. New teachers, particularly when they first meet parents or address them at group meetings, rely on familiar jargon—terms such as *norms, developmental needs, heterogeneous grouping, cognitive skills, higher-order thinking*—which may mean little to some parents. Jargon, however familiar to you, will diminish rather than increase your credibility with parents.

Listen.   Listening is your most important communication skill. Parents, particularly when they are upset, want to be heard. One of the most frequent complaints leveled by parents against teachers is that they do not listen. The following list offers hints for ensuring that parents find you a good listener.

1. Keep eye contact. Face the parent or family member and lean forward slightly to show your attention to what they are saying.
2. Acknowledge the speaker's comments to show the parent that you are listening.
3. When the parent pauses, try not to interrupt until the speaker has finished.
4. Ignore distractions, such as others seeking your attention during the conference.
5. Check your understanding by summarizing the essential aspects of what the parent seemed to say or the feeling he or she seemed to convey.
6. Seek clarification when what is said is not clear.

Suggestions 3, 5, and 6 are equally important when you are conducting a conference by phone.

Another important skill you will need is **active listening**. It is particularly valuable during *reactive* parent conferences, or conferences requested by a family member who is upset over something they perceive you said or did to or with their child. Such conferences easily can become emotionally charged. Teachers typically take a defensive or aggressive posture when confronted by an angry parent. Rather than listen to what the family member has to say—regardless of how inaccurate it may seem—the teacher follows the family member's statement with a denial, a defensive statement, or a refusal to talk further.

Active listening is when the listener provides feedback to the speaker on the message heard and the emotion conveyed and thus opens the door to further communication by letting the speaker know he or she was being understood and respected. Active listening is an essential communication skill to be used with the parents of learners and learners themselves. Before you compose a response, concentrate on what someone is saying even when you strongly object to what is being said. Like any skill, it must be practiced before you can use it naturally and automatically to compose an accurate and thoughtful response of your own.

Use "I" Messages to Express Your Feelings.   Particularly when you are upset about the words or actions of a learner or parent, you must be able to clearly communicate your feelings. However, the way to do this is not by criticizing or blaming (with a "you . . ." message) but rather by describing (1) what you find offensive, (2) the feeling or emotion you experience when the offensive condition occurs, and (3) a statement of the reason for the feeling, thus redirecting the conversation back to you and your ability to teach. Consider, for example, this statement: "When Amanda talks back to me, her behavior disrupts the entire class, and that makes me angry because I have to take time away from all the other students in the class to deal with her." This message is right on target. It focuses on the reaction to the problem, rather than what the child said or did. It opens up positive avenues to further communication.

Evaluating the Teacher–Family Conference

Following the conference, summarize what was said and agreed on, and make a list of any actions to be taken by you or the family. Make follow-up calls, send notes, and follow through on whatever you committed to. Finally, take a moment to reflect on how well you communicated with the family member(s) and achieved your goals and what you might change or do differently the next time you have a parent conference. This moment of reflection will be one of the most important aids to sharpening your parent-conferencing skills.

Expect your position as a teacher to require extensive communication with parents or extended family members. Be prepared to spend time with them and to get to know them. Active listening will be one of your most important skills that can assist you in this and in developing positive relationships with parents, learners, and with other teachers in your school's professional learning community. See In Practice: Focus on Getting Parents Involved.

In Practice

Focus on Getting Parents Involved

Active parent involvement has been associated with numerous benefits for students, including increasing student motivation and engagement in school. When it comes to homework, though, parent involvement can take many different shapes, not all of which have a positive impact on learning. When working to increase student engagement and motivation, it is important to include parents and discuss ways they can support their children's learning both at school and at home.

First, it is important that parents understand what role teachers expect them to play, especially in terms of homework. What one parent views as helping out, a teacher might perceive as interference or cheating. And what a teacher might take for granted that parents can do—such as signing off on homework or checking spelling words—a parent may not have the skills or the time to follow through on. Clearly, it is important to communicate with parents about how to best help children learn. It is also necessary for educators to be sure their expectations are realistic, given parents' skills and schedules.

It is equally important to be clear with parents about what kinds of involvement are actually beneficial to students. Studies have shown that parents who offer rewards for grades, or who punish students for poor performance, may actually decrease students' motivation to do well. Fear of punishment, anxiety about meeting parents' expectations, and worrying about being compared to siblings not only cause stress for students, but can also detract from their intrinsic motivation and interest in learning. This is not to say that parents shouldn't be invested in how their children are doing in school. Rather, it suggests that there are more productive ways for them to be involved and show their interest in students' progress.

To help children be successful with work at home and at school, parents can (Paulu, 1998):

- *Create a place at home that is conducive to studying.* Good study environments are well lit and quiet. Although every child's learning style is different, most educators agree that students do best when the television is off and the student is free from distractions.

- *Set aside a specific time for homework each day.* This might involve limiting television watching or phone calls until homework is finished. Parents should be careful, though, not to pit homework against activities students enjoy, or to create situations in which students rush through their work in order to get back to other activities. Paulu (1998) notes that family routines—which include set homework times—have been linked to higher student achievement.

- *Make sure students have all the supplies they need.* Parents should check in with students ahead of time about the kinds of projects they will be doing: It might be tough to find a calculator or a report cover at 9:00 the night before an assignment is due.

- *Be available if students have questions.* Parents can support their children by looking over homework and giving suggestions, but should not do the homework for them.

- *Make an effort to communicate regularly with teachers.* If necessary, parents should ask teachers to clarify their expectations. It is also a good idea to find out ahead of time what kinds of resources—such as tutors or services for second-language students—are available to students if they need help.

- *Avoid linking rewards or punishment to school performance.* While it is important for parents to recognize students' achievements, they should avoid external motivators for performance. Instead, parents should emphasize the value of learning and show they appreciate their child's hard work.

These expectations can be sent home to parents at the beginning of school and made available at Parent–Teacher night.

Source: Education Northwest, Formerly Northwest Regional Educational Laboratory. For more about parent involvement, see *Parent Partners: Using Parents to Enhance Education,* at www.nwrel.org /request/march99/index.html.

Some Teacher–Family Conference Topics to Be Prepared For

When the motivation to learn is seriously lacking or a major and or consistent infraction of a school or classroom rule has occurred, the most immediate effective response is the teacher–family conference, which may be with the parents, a single parent, grandparent, guardian, or foster parent. Let's look at some of the topics that teacher–family conferences may cover and that you should be prepared for. Dyches, Carter, and Prater (2012) report that typically most teacher–family conferences address one or a combination of the following issues:

- Academic performance
- Social/behavioral problems
- Child neglect or abuse
- Bullying
- School crises

Academic and Social/Behavioral Problems

Ariza (2010) points out what the classroom teacher needs to know about today's inclusive classrooms of linguistically, culturally, and ethnically diverse students and their mainstreamed peers. Among the academic challenges that some of these learners present are feelings of loneliness and isolation, not being accepted by their peers, and neglect or mistreatment due to poor language or academic skills. Students with poor academic skills frequently display behavioral problems in other areas as well, leading to incorrigible conduct and even dropping out of school. Add to these, academic challenges in reading, writing, and listening skills, especially for English as a Second Language Learners (ESL), and we have some of the more frequent conditions that will bring you into contact with the families of your learners requiring a teacher–family conference.

Child Neglect or Abuse

Child neglect or abuse includes physical, emotional, sexual, and/or psychological behavior conducted by a peer or family member that may have lifelong emotional effects on your learners. Although the seriousness of these behaviors calls for the immediate intervention by professionals in your school's professional learning community, it is your responsibility to be attentive to possible signs of child neglect or abuse in your classroom in any of the above areas and to report it to school administrators, as required by the Child Abuse, Prevention and Treatment Act of 2003. In these cases, a teacher–family conference in the presence of other professionals (e.g., social worker, child abuse officer, counseling psychologist, and school district representative) may be required to present and discuss the problem with the family.

Bullying

This **video** explores one teacher's approach to dealing with bullying. How is this approach useful and how would you improve this teacher's approach to this important topic?

A major concern in schools over the past decade has been the significant rise in reported instances of bullying. Whether this rise has been due to the actual increase in the number incidents of bullying or whether schools have become more vigilant in reporting it is unknown. But, by any account, bullying has been one of the major reasons for arranging a teacher–family conference. Bullying has been defined by Sullivan (2000) as any unprovoked act of aggression or manipulation by one child to another. Bulach, Fulbright, and Williams (2003) report that as many as a quarter of all students have been bullied at some time or another during their school years, disrupting their emotional and academic well-being. Bullying can take a number of forms that include physical and/or verbal abuse, using fear to manipulate another's behavior or to create unrest, cutting someone off from social interaction, mocking another's behavior, as well as using the Internet and smartphones to threaten or disparage another individual. Because bullying has become such a persistent problem and is noted to be on the rise, you are often the "first responder" to address this problem with a teacher–family conference.

School Crises

We have all read and heard about major school crises. And, although they occur infrequently, they usually represent high profile media accounts of violence (sometimes by students or distraught adults), acts of nature (tornados, hurricanes, and storms that disrupt school services), as well as perceived or real threats to the physical safety of school children (sometimes from threats of violence and national disasters elsewhere). These unexpected school crises, which may occur well outside the confines of your school community, can affect students, teachers, administrators, and the larger school community of family members and loved ones. While crises of this magnitude are infrequent they can be emotionally stressful to students and the school community when they hear about them or experience them. And, because they may impact so many who are part of your school, you will need to be aware of their effects and what you, as a teacher, may be expected to do.

Your responsibility during such crises is to provide the emotional support your students may need. For students who may show lingering effects of a crisis, a teacher–family conference can diminish or shorten its effects on the learner in partnership with the family. Dyches, Carter, and Prater (2012) provide suggestions that can be conveyed to parents and family members to provide the emotional support needed after the immediate crises has ended.

- Provide information as to the nature of the crisis.
- Allow the student to express their thoughts and feelings about the experience through their eyes.
- Provide assurances that things will be better, within the context of what is true.
- Reassure the student that you are there for him or her.
- Ask parents to spend additional time conversing and listening to their child that includes physical contact for young learners.

While not many teachers will face large disruptive forces within their school or community, media accounts of crises elsewhere, especially school-related crises, can affect the emotional well-being of young learners far removed from them, for which every teacher should be prepared.

Culturally Responsive Classroom Management

One of the most encouraging advances in the understanding of classroom management is the emerging field of **culturally responsive teaching**. As we saw in previous chapters, the writings and research of Bowers and Flinders (1991), Fisch and Trumbull (2008), Delpit and Dowdy (2008), Gay (2010), Tharp (1997), and Tharp and Gallimore (1991) present convincing arguments that different cultures react differently to nonverbal and verbal behavior management techniques, including proximity control, eye contact, warnings, and classroom arrangement. Furthermore, these researchers cite numerous examples of how teachers of different cultures interpret the disruptive behaviors of children differently. Therefore, be aware that many of the behavioral management techniques presented in this and Chapter 3 may or may not be culturally sensitive and that an effective classroom manager matches the technique he or she uses not only with the situation but also with the cultural history of the learner.

If the research supporting culturally responsive teaching has yet to provide explicit prescriptions for teaching culturally different learners, what does it tell us about better understanding students in multicultural classrooms? The traditional method of conducting classroom research is to study large groups of teachers, classify their teaching methods, give learners achievement tests, and try to find relationships between achievement test scores and particular teaching practices. Dillon (1989), however, used a different approach. She studied one teacher, Mr. Appleby, and his class for a year using a research method called *microethnography*. Her study has provided valuable insights into what a teacher can do to create a classroom where culturally different learners experience academic and personal success.

Dillon concluded that Appleby's effectiveness as a classroom teacher was due to his ability to assume the role of "translator and intercultural broker" between the middle-class white culture of the school and the lower-class African American culture of his students. As a cultural broker and translator, Appleby was thoroughly knowledgeable about the backgrounds of his learners, and as a result, he was able to bridge the differences between the school and community/home cultures. He had acquired a high degree of what Lustig and Koester (2009) call **intercultural competence** (DeMeulenaere, 2001). With this cultural knowledge, Appleby created a classroom with three significant attributes:

1. He created a social organization in which the teacher and learners knew one another, trusted one another, and felt free to express their opinions and feelings.

2. He taught lessons built on the prior knowledge and experiences of his learners. Because of his knowledge of the learners' backgrounds, he was familiar with their knowledge, skills, and attitudes toward the content. This knowledge allowed him to represent the subject matter in ways that encouraged students to link it with what they already knew and felt.

3. He used instructional methods that allowed learners to actively participate in lessons, to use the language and sociolinguistic patterns of their culture, and to use the language and social interaction patterns both he and his learners were familiar with.

Antón-Oldenburg (2000), Delpit and Dowdy (2008), Gay (2010), H. M. Miller (2000), and Lustig and Koester (2009) conclude that what teachers need to know to teach successfully in multicultural classrooms has more to do with knowing the values, socialization practices, interests, and concerns of their learners than with knowing about presumed learning style preferences and cognitive styles and the do's and don'ts of teaching learners with these traits. Rather, researchers believe the cultural knowledge that teachers such as Appleby have about their learners allows them to represent subject matter content in ways that are meaningful to students, to develop lessons that gain students' active participation, and to create social organizations in the classroom within which learners feel free to be themselves.

Case History and Licensure Preparation

DIRECTIONS: *The following case history pertains to Chapter 4 content. After reading the case history, go to Chapter 4 in the Book Specific Resources section in the MyEducationLab for your course. Open the Case History and Licensure Preparation activity and complete the questions that follow. Upon completion of the test, scored answers to the short-answer question pertaining to the case history and multiple-choice questions will be provided.*

Case History

Mr. Scott's tenth-grade English class has just finished a unit on Shakespeare's *Julius Caesar.* Today, he wants to have a discussion that will crystallize some of the key concepts from the play. He also hopes having a fruitful discussion will help prepare the class for the upcoming test over this material. In the past, unfortunately, discussions have been marred by many disruptions, such as students

talking out of turn, interrupting one another, and making a flurry of requests for hall passes to the bathroom because "We're not doing anything for a grade right now."

Today Mr. Scott introduces the concept of a *graded discussion.* So he can keep the discussion focused, he has selected Susan to record students' contributions. Susan is an "A" student, but she tends to dominate classroom exchanges, and students sometimes wait to hear her ideas rather than volunteer their own. Some even get resentful and refuse to answer at all. Susan will be guaranteed a 110, the highest grade, for her task of recording the contributions, but she will not be able to contribute to the discussion. The next recorder will be selected from those students who get the maximum score in today's discussion.

Susan will sit in the front of the classroom with a copy of the seating chart and make a checkmark for every comment each student makes. For the comment to be counted, the student must raise his or her hand and be acknowledged by Mr. Scott before talking. For certain responses, such as ideas that build on the comments of other students and answers to particularly hard questions, the student may receive two checkmarks. Every checkmark counts as five points.

Every student who arrives in class promptly will begin with a base score of 70. Those who are late will begin with a ten-point deduction from that base score, or 60 points. The maximum score is 110 and will count as one section of the unit test.

Mr. Scott tosses out the initial question: "Many scholars accept that the protagonist of the play is the title character, Julius Caesar, but others suggest it is really Brutus, who dominates and wrestles with the moral dilemmas that charge the action of the play. What do you think? Be sure to give reasons for your opinions."

Everyone looks to Susan, whose opinion must be the right one, and she squirms in her seat with obvious frustration. After a short pause, wherein all the students realize they cannot depend on her, Jeremy raises his hand and says, "Now that I think of it, I think the second guys are right. It's really Brutus we care about. When Caesar was killed, I didn't feel that bad. He almost deserved it the way he was acting, like he was high and mighty, but I really felt bad when Brutus killed himself."

Mr. Scott checks to see that Susan has recorded a checkmark for Jeremy and points to Juanita. Then Juanita says, "I don't know if you have to feel bad when someone dies for them to be the main character in a play, but you said something that got me thinking, Jeremy. Caesar dies in the third act. We have almost half the play without him, but Brutus sticks in there until the end."

"Juanita, you were really a good listener and built on Jeremy's idea. Make sure she gets two checkmarks for her comments, Susan."

Mack, who has been hurriedly arranging his notebook and books after his late arrival to class, raises his hand. "Sure, Caesar dies in Act III, but don't forget his ghost in Act IV. And Brutus even mentions Caesar's name when he kills himself— 'I killed not thee with half so good a will' or something like that. So I think Caesar is there in spirit throughout the whole play."

"Well, Mack," Mr. Scott replies, "your response not only built on Juanita's idea, but you even paraphrased an actual quote from the play. You have now recovered from the ten-point deduction for being late."

Andrea bursts in with a question: "What about Antony, Mr. Scott?"

Before she can continue, Mr. Scott puts his hands up to his ear, pretending not to hear. "I can't hear anyone who doesn't raise their hand."

Andrea raises her hand and waits for Mr. Scott to nod before she continues. "'Friends, Romans, Countrymen, I come to bury Caesar, not to praise him.' I mean, that is the coolest speech ever. He had the whole audience in the palm of his hand. That was really a climactic moment in the whole play."

"So now we have three candidates for protagonist: Caesar, Brutus, and Antony. Any opinions on that newest idea?"

A wave of hands goes up. No one is waiting for cues from Susan now.

Summing Up

The main points in this chapter include the following:

The Humanist Tradition in Classroom Management

1. Most classroom discipline problems are low intensity, continuous, and unconnected with any larger, more serious events.

2. The humanist tradition of classroom management focuses on the inner thoughts, feelings, psychological needs, and emotions of the individual learner. Humanist approaches emphasize the importance of allowing the student to control his or her own behavior.

3. Ginott's sane messages communicate to students that their behavior is unacceptable but do so in a manner that does not blame, scold, or humiliate.

4. Glasser's and the Joneses' cooperative learning emphasizes building a more friendly classroom that the learner will regret leaving because of misbehavior, if told to do so.

5. The humanist tradition focuses on developing rules, getting support from school administrators, holding private conferences with students, and following through when students must be removed from the classroom.

The Applied Behavior Analysis Tradition in Classroom Management

6. The applied behavior analysis tradition of classroom management applies the techniques of operant conditioning to change socially important behaviors.

7. Behavior modification focuses on changing or modifying behavior by following a behavior with some type of reinforcement.

8. Positive reinforcement occurs when a desired stimuli or reward is provided after a desired behavior to increase its frequency.

9. Negative reinforcement occurs when a painful, uncomfortable, or aversive state is avoided to achieve a more desirable state.

10. Antecedents are events or stimuli present when you perform a behavior that elicits or sets off the behavior, such as sounds, sights, and people.

11. The tradition of applied behavior analysis focuses on identifying appropriate and inappropriate behaviors, antecedents that can trigger these behaviors, the student's goal for the misbehavior, and procedures for reinforcing the appropriate behavior.

The Classroom Management Tradition

12. The classroom management tradition frames the question of classroom order and discipline not in terms of reaction but prevention.

13. The classroom management tradition focuses on planning and organizing the classroom, teaching rules and routines, and informing students of the consequences of breaking the rules.

An Integrated Approach to Classroom Management

14. The term *low-profile classroom control* refers to coping strategies used by effective teachers to stop misbehavior without disrupting the flow of a lesson.

15. Three ways to apply your authority in dealing with misbehavior are as follow:
    - You alone judge what occurred and what your response should be.
    - You provide alternative forms of a response from which the student must choose.
    - You select a response from alternatives that the student provides.

16. The level of severity with which you respond to a misbehavior should match the misbehavior that has occurred.

17. Some misbehaviors that occur in classrooms are increased unintentionally through reinforcement. In such a case, the probability of the misbehavior increases because the consequence that follows the misbehavior is perceived as desirable by the student.

18. Both reward and punishment can increase the probability of a behavior, although punishment without reward is rarely effective.

19. Punishment in the absence of reward tends to be less effective in increasing the probability of a desired behavior for the following reasons:
    - Punishment does not guarantee the desirable response will occur.
    - The effects of punishment usually are specific to a particular context.
    - The effects of punishment can have undesirable side effects.
    - Punishment can create a hostile or aggressive response.
    - The punishment can become associated with the punisher.

20. After two or three warnings have been given in response to a misbehavior, a punishment should be assigned.

21. Corporal punishment is rarely effective in deterring misbehavior.

Influence of Home and Family on Classroom Behavior

22. Realize that generational differences between child and parent can be more difficult for parents to accept than for you, the teacher, leading to problems both at home and at school.

23. Your communication and collaboration with professionals, such as a social worker, school nurse, special education teacher, counselor, or school psychologist can provide valuable assistance with classroom management problems that may have their origins with other individuals and in other contexts.

Preparing for a Teacher–Family Conference

24. One feature of the teacher–family conference that accounts for its effectiveness is the involvement of the parents in eliminating the misbehavior.

25. During the teacher–family conference, you should talk plainly, listen, and use "I" messages.

26. At the end of the conference, you should summarize what was said and agreed on, and make a list of any actions to be taken by you or the parent.

Conducting a Teacher–Family Conference

27. Effective teacher–family conferences are ones in which the teacher maintains eye contact, gives noninterruption acknowledgements, waits for family members to speak, ignores distractions, checks for understanding, and asks for clarification, when necessary.

28. Active listening is when the listener provides feedback to the speaker on the message heard and the emotion conveyed and thus opens the door to further communication.

29. "I" messages focus on the reaction to the problem, rather than what the learner said or did to open up positive avenues to further communication.

Some Teacher–Family Conference Topics to Be Prepared For

30. Typically, a teacher–family conference will address one or a combination of the following issues: academic, social, or behavioral problems, child neglect or abuse, bullying, and school crisis.

Culturally Responsive Classroom Management

31. Culturally responsive teaching represents the teacher's ability to react to different cultures with different verbal and nonverbal classroom management techniques.

32. *Intercultural competence* refers to the teacher's ability to act as a translator and intercultural broker among students of different cultures, ethnicities, and social classes.

Key Terms

Active listening
Applied behavior analysis
Behavioral antecedents
Behavior modification
Classroom management tradition
Congruent communication

Cooperative learning
Culturally responsive teaching
Humanist tradition
Intercultural competence
Intermittent reinforcement
Low-profile classroom management

Natural reinforcers
Negative reinforcement
Positive reinforcement
Surface behaviors

Discussion and Practice Questions

Questions marked with an asterisk are answered in Appendix B. Some asterisked questions may require student follow-up responses not included in Appendix B. Go to the Assignments and Activities section of the various topics on the MyEducationLab for your course to complete additional practice activities related to this chapter's content.

*1. Identify the six criteria of an effective classroom management plan. Which, in your opinion, will be the easiest to achieve in your classroom, and which will be the most difficult? Why?

*2. What specific things would Glasser have you do as you begin to manage your classroom? Which do you feel is (are) the most important? Why?

*3. How might you use both positive and negative reinforcement to stop a student from repeatedly talking? Use an example of each to support your point.

*4. Describe time-out and response cost. Give an example of a situation in which you would use each.

*5. According to research studies of classroom management, what three broad classes of preventive teaching behaviors are used by effective classroom managers? List the three in order of least to most difficult to implement at your grade level.

*6. What criteria or approaches could you use to assign consequences for misbehaving? Which approach would you feel most comfortable using? Why?

7. For the following misbehaviors, identify a consequence that reflects the severity of the offense. Do not use the same response more than once.

- Talking back
- Cutting class
- Eating in class
- Jumping out of seat
- Sleeping in class
- Obscene gesturing
- Using drugs
- Fighting

8. What reward would you provide to get a student to do each of the following?

- Homework
- Stop talking back
- Turn in assignments on time
- Be on time for class
- Remember to bring a pencil
- Not talk without raising hand

*9. Identify five reasons punishment is rarely effective in the absence of reward. Looking back at your own school days, which seems the most true for you?

*10. What two objectives for having a teacher–family conference are discussed in this chapter? What might be some other objectives?

Professional Practice

Field Experience and Practice Activities

Questions marked with an asterisk are answered in Appendix B. Some asterisked questions may require student follow-up responses not included in Appendix B.

*1. From your classroom observation and fieldwork, recall an example of what Ginott calls *sane messages*. To what extent do you think this technique was effective?

2. Using an example of teacher dialogue, provide an "I" message to communicate your disappointment to a student.

3. Give an example of a low-profile anticipation–deflection–reaction sequence that you have observed.

*4. Using a specific example from your classroom observation, identify under what conditions a punishment is or is not effective.

5. From your field experience, describe a scenario of how a teacher responded in a culturally responsive manner to a student who did poorly on an assignment. What might be a culturally unresponsive reply in this situation?

Digital Portfolio Activities

The following digital portfolio activities relate to InTASC Standards 9 and 10.

1. Imagine having to conduct a teacher–family conference concerning a student's failure to complete assignments on time. Prepare some "talking points" in an outline format that you want to be sure to bring up during the conference. Your talking points should include the following:

   • What you will do to gain the parents' acknowledgment of the problem
   • A plan of action for addressing the problem at home and at school
   • Follow-up activities that will monitor that progress is being made
   • A summary or restatement of the agreements made between you and the parents

   Place your talking points in the "Classroom Management" folder of your digital portfolio as a reminder of key issues to discuss during a conference.

2. In Field Experience Activity 5, you described a scenario of how a teacher responded in a culturally responsive manner to a student who did poorly on an assignment. Place this scenario in the "Classroom Management" folder of your digital portfolio as a reminder of a reply that is culturally responsive.

MyEducationLab™

Go to MyEducationLab (www.myeducationlab.com) for Effective Teaching Methods: Research-Based Practice where you can:

- Find learning outcomes for the various course topics course along with national standards that connect to these outcomes.

- Complete **Assignments and Activities** that can help you more deeply understand the chapter content.

- Apply and practice your understanding of the core teaching skills identified in the chapter with **Building Teaching Skills and Dispositions** coaching activities.

- Check your comprehension of the content covered in the chapter with a book specific **Study Plan**. Here you will be able to take a chapter **pretest**, receive feedback on your answers, and then access personalized **Review, Practice, and Enrichment exercises** to enhance your understanding of chapter content. After you complete the exercises, take a **posttest** to confirm your comprehension.

- Learn how to address common classroom management issues in the **Simulations in Classroom Management.**

- Access video clips of CCSSO **National Teachers of the Year award winners** responding to the question, "Why Do I Teach?" in the Teacher Talk section.

- Create, update, and share quality lesson plans with the **Lesson Plan Builder.**

- Access state licensure test requirements, overviews of what tests cover, and sample test items in the **Certification and Licensure** section.

- Learn how to create a high quality teaching portfolio in the **Preparing a Portfolio** section.

- Access tips, advice, and other information on resume writing and interviewing, your first year of teaching, and law and public policies in the Beginning Your Career section.

5 Goals, Standards, and Objectives

This chapter will help you answer these questions and meet the following InTASC standards for effective teaching.

- What are some important educational goals for the next decade?
- What are educational standards, and where do they come from?
- Why do I need behavioral objectives?
- What are the steps in writing a behavioral objective?
- What types of cognitive, affective, and psychomotor behaviors will I want to teach in my classroom?
- How can I help my learners achieve higher-order thinking skills, such as problem solving, decision making, critical thinking, and valuing?

InTASC

STANDARD 4 **Content Knowledge.** The teacher understands the central concepts, tools of inquiry, and structures of the discipline(s) he or she teaches and creates learning experiences that make these aspects of the discipline accessible and meaningful for learners to assure mastery of the content.

STANDARD 5 **Application of Content.** The teacher understands how to connect concepts and use differing perspectives to engage learners in critical thinking, creativity, and collaborative problem solving related to authentic local and global issues.

STANDARD 7 **Planning for Instruction.** The teacher plans instruction that supports every student in meeting rigorous learning goals by drawing upon knowledge of content areas, curriculum, cross-disciplinary skills, and pedagogy, as well as knowledge of learners and the community context.

STANDARD 8 **Instructional Strategies.** The teacher understands and uses a variety of instructional strategies to encourage learners to develop deep understanding of content areas and their connections, and to build skills to apply knowledge in meaningful ways.

Chapters 1 and 2 introduced some important teaching behaviors expected of you and some individual differences among your students that you can expect to see in your classroom. Chapters 3 and 4 introduced important tools and techniques for effectively managing your classroom and nurturing the learning potential of each of your students. This chapter and the next show you how to plan and organize who, what, and how you will teach in ways that reach all of your learners, whatever their differences may be. First, let's consider the distinction among goals, standards, and objectives and how establishing them can help you reach all of your students.

MyEducationLab™

Visit the MyEducationLab for *Effective Teaching Methods: Research-Based Practice*, 8e to enhance your understanding of chapter concepts with a personalized Study Plan. You'll also have the opportunity to hone your teaching skills through video-based Assignments and Activities as well as Building Teaching Skills and Dispositions lessons.

Goals, Standards, and Objectives

The words *goals, standards,* and *objectives* often are used interchangeably without recognizing their different but related meanings. **Goals** are general expressions of our values that give us a sense of direction. They are written broadly enough to be acceptable to large numbers of individuals, such as teachers, school administrators, parents, and U.S. taxpayers. When you hear your state legislator, school superintendent, or principal remark that schools need to "increase the time they devote to teaching elementary school science," "improve the problem-solving and decision-making skills of high school students," or "better integrate technology and web based learning into the classroom," they are setting goals for you to meet.

Standards are derived from goals to more specifically identify what must be accomplished and who must do what in order to meet the goals. Standards express goals from the teacher's, learner's, or school's point of view and thus identify what teachers must teach, students must learn, and schools must do. Standards also can energize and motivate teachers, students, and schools to become actively engaged in and committed to meeting the goals.

Although standards and goals can answer the question "Why am I teaching this," they do not provide a satisfactory response to what or how you will teach on any given day. Goals and standards provide little direction in determining what strategies to use in the classroom to achieve them or in determining when or if they are met. Getting satisfactory answers to these questions requires that you prepare unit and lesson **objectives** that convey the specific behaviors to be attained, the conditions under which the behaviors must be demonstrated, and the proficiency level at which the behaviors are to be performed based on the learning histories, abilities, and current levels of understanding of your learners. The examples in Table 5.1 show the purposes of and distinctions among goals, standards, and objectives.

Several approaches have been formulated to help you prepare educational objectives.

Tyler's Goal Development Approach

The idea of an educational objective can be traced to the early part of the 20th century, when Tyler (1934; 1974) first conceived of the need for goal-directed statements for teachers. His approach to establishing educational goals is illustrated in Figure 5.1. He observed that teachers were concerned far more with the content of instruction (what to teach) than with what the student should be able to do with that content (whether he or she could use it in some meaningful context).

Tyler's approach to generating educational objectives has had a major influence on curriculum development. Tyler believed that as society becomes more complex, there are more things for people to learn. But the time to learn this ever-expanding amount of knowledge and skills may actually decrease in a technologically complex society. Consequently, educators must make informed choices about which goals are worth teaching.

Tyler identified five factors to consider when establishing goals for what should be learned:

1. The subject matter we know enough about to teach (subject matter mastery)
2. Societal concerns, which represent what is valued in both the society at large and the local community
3. Student needs and interests and the abilities and knowledge they bring to school
4. What instructional theory and research tells us can be taught in the classroom

Goals are important because they express our values and give learners, their parents, and the community the reasons you are teaching the lessons you have planned, that then motivates them to become actively engaged in the learning process.

Table 5.1 **The Differences among Goals, Standards, and Objectives**

Goals	Standards	Objectives
Express our values that give us a sense of direction	Identify what will be learned—energize and motivate	Convey the specific behavior to be attained, the conditions under which the behavior must be demonstrated, and the proficiency at which the behavior must be performed
Examples	**Examples**	**Examples**
1. Every citizen should be prepared to work in a technological world.	1. Students should understand the use of the computer at home and at work.	1. Students will, using their own choice of a word-processing application, produce an edited two-page manuscript free of errors in 15 minutes or less.
2. Every adult should be functionally literate.	2. Students should be able to read and write well enough to become gainfully employed.	2. Students will, at the end of grade 12, be able to write a 500-word essay with no more than two grammatical and punctuation errors.
3. Every American should be able to vote as an informed citizen in a democracy.	3. Students should know how to choose a candidate and vote in an election.	3. Students will, at the end of an eighth-grade unit on government, participate in a mock election by choosing a candidate and giving reasons for their choice.

Figure 5.1 **Tyler's Considerations in Goal Selection**

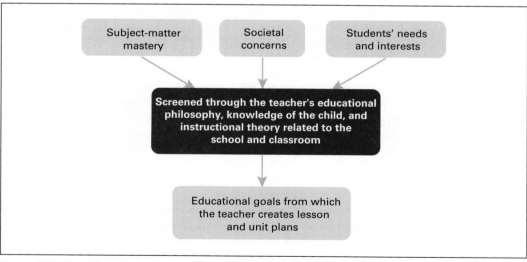

Source: R.W. Tyler, Constructing achievement tests. Ohio State University Press. Reprinted with permission.

The Origin of Educational Standards

In the past decade, several important developments have highlighted concerns about academic goals and how we measure them. In spite of the wide acceptance of *Goals 2000: Reforming Education to Improve Student Achievement* (U.S. Department of Education, 1998), which we saw in Chapter 2, professional groups and associations have also become involved in defining educational goals more

An important recommendation for curriculum reform in the next decade is that learners should be better trained to work independently and to attain more high-level thinking, conceptual, and problem-solving skills.

specifically by establishing educational standards. Many of these groups and associations have reviewed comprehensive studies of the state of education in U.S. elementary and secondary schools in an effort to identify specific criteria, or standards, by which to judge the adequacy of what students learn in their subject matter fields. These reports include: *Knowing What Students Know,* by the National Research Council (2001) and Ketterlin-Geller (2005); *Assessment Standards for School Mathematics,* by the National Council of Teachers of Mathematics (2009); *Benchmarks for Science Literacy,* by the American Association for the Advancement of Science (2009); *Expectations of Excellence: Curriculum Standards for Social Studies,* by the National Council for the Social Studies (2010); *Next Generation National Science Education Standards,* by the National Research Council (2011) and King (2006); and *Standards for the English Language Arts,* by the International Reading Association and National Council of Teachers of English (2009). Each of these reports has set forth a new framework for the curriculum in its subject area and defined the curriculum to be taught and the student outcomes be evaluated.

One outcome from the development of standards has been the awareness that instruction at all levels of schooling has been predominantly focused on memorization, drill, and workbook exercises. Therefore, these reports called for a commitment to developing a **thinking curriculum**, one that focuses on teaching learners how to think critically, reason, and problem solve in authentic, real-world contexts (Borich & Hao, 2007; Borich, 2006). These reports advocate that U.S. schools adopt such a thinking curriculum and a performance-based examination system that would adequately measure complex cognitive skills (Audit & Jordan, 2005; Burke, 2010; Borich, 2007b; Borich & Tombari, 2004; Nosich, 2012).

These new curriculum frameworks were stimulated in part by a disenchantment with the quality of public school education voiced by many segments of our society, including parents, taxpayers, legislators, business and military leaders, and some teacher groups (Council for Basic Education, 1996; Gehring, 2008). This disenchantment was not limited to matters of curriculum. It extended to the quality of teaching and teacher education, leading in some cases to recommendations for teacher competency testing and new requirements for teacher certification.

For example, the *Praxis II Series Elementary Education: Curriculum, Instruction and Assessment Test,* to be taken after completion of a bachelor's degree program in elementary/middle school education, was designed for just this purpose. Test questions cover the breadth of material a new teacher needs to know and assess knowledge of both the principles and processes of teaching. Some questions assess basic understanding of curriculum planning, instructional design, and assessment of student learning. But many other questions pose particular problems that teachers routinely face in the classroom, and, most importantly, many are based on authentic, real-world examples of student work in the context of the subject matters most commonly taught in the elementary and middle school. (See Praxis test 0011 at www.ets.org/praxis and Figure 1.5, Chapter 1.)

You have become familiar with Praxis II test questions on the principles of teaching and learning in the previous chapters and will have others available to you in this and the chapters to follow. When you study these practice questions and the skills and performances they require, keep in mind that many have come from reports representing a broad consensus among professional groups and associations that have expressed what our schools need to do to strengthen teaching and learning in the classroom. For example, several of the reports cited agreed that our schools needed to strengthen the curricula in math, science, English, foreign languages, and social studies. Also, technology was represented by a call for higher levels of computer literacy, both as separate courses and as a tool integrated into the core disciplines, which will be the topic of Chapter 7. The reports also called for renewed effort in teaching higher order thinking skills, including the teaching of concepts, problem solving, and creativity (as opposed to rote memorization and parroting of facts, lists, names, and dates divorced from a more authentic problem-solving context). These topics will be covered in Chapters 10, 11 and 12.

Not surprisingly, all the reports recommended raising both grading standards and the number of required core courses, especially at the secondary level (e.g., four years of language arts, four years of science, four years of math, and four years of social studies—the so-called "4 × 4 curriculum"). This recommendation went hand in hand with the suggestion that colleges raise their admission requirements by requiring more course work in core subjects, especially math, science, and foreign languages. Most of the reports recommended increasing school hours and homework time. For example, one report suggested a minimum seven-hour school day (some schools have fewer than six hours) and a 200-day school year (many have a 180-day year). Time spent on noninstructional activities was to be reduced accordingly, as was time spent on administrative interruptions.

By taking a broad view of our educational establishment, these reports recommended that all students meet these goals:

- Be trained to live and function in a technological world
- Possess minimum competencies in reading, writing, and mathematics
- Possess higher order thinking, conceptual, and problem-solving skills
- Be required to enroll in all the core subjects each school year, to the extent of their abilities
- Be trained to work independently and to complete assignments without direct supervision
- Improve in school attendance and be in school longer each day and year
- Be given more activities that provide practice in problem solving and decision making and that require critical thinking and making value judgments

From these broad goals prepared at the national level come standards prepared by state departments of education and professional associations that can be readily accessed by teachers. These standards provide the basis for a uniform presentation of content within a state that may be fine-tuned by schools and school districts to serve the specific populations for which they are responsible. The result is often a specific curriculum guide that covers all-important content within specific content areas. The curriculum standards that follow (also called *essential skills* in some states) are examples of several state curriculum standards at the elementary, middle school, and high school levels that identify the specific content to be taught and specific behaviors to be acquired at the classroom level in reading, science, and social studies. In the following chapter we will see how essential skills such as these are placed into a lesson plan that connects goals and standards with your classroom instruction.

Third-Grade Reading. *Reading/Word Identification.* The student uses a variety of word identification strategies. The student is expected to:

a. Decode by using letter–sound correspondences within a word
b. Blend initial letter sounds with common vowel spelling patterns to read words
c. Identify multisyllabic words by using common syllable patterns
d. Use root words and other structural cues such as prefixes, suffixes, and derivational endings to recognize words
e. Use knowledge of word order (syntax) and context to support word identification and confirm word meaning

Eighth-Grade Science. *Scientific Processes.* The student conducts field and laboratory investigations using safe, environmentally appropriate, and ethical practices. The student is expected to:

a. Plan and implement investigative procedures including asking questions, formulating testable hypotheses, and selecting and using equipment
b. Collect data by observing and measuring
c. Organize, analyze, make inferences, and predict trends
d. Communicate valid conclusions
e. Use the computer to construct graphs, tables, maps, and charts and examine and evaluate data

High School History. *U.S. History.* The student understands traditional historical points of reference in U.S. history from 1877 to the present. The student is expected to:

a. Identify the major eras in U.S. history from 1877 to the present

b. Apply absolute and relative chronology through the sequencing of significant individuals, events, and time periods

c. Analyze social issues such as the treatment of minorities, child labor, growth of cities, and problems of immigrants

The basis for state standards such as these was the perception that our schools had lost sight of their role in teaching students how to think. Traditionally, this was accomplished through the core curriculum (English, math, science, foreign languages, and social studies). However, with fewer advanced offerings in these areas and with additional time being spent in remedial and elective courses, the time devoted to teaching children how to think may have been insufficient.

Reports have suggested that schools should reverse this trend by requiring students to study both the core and more advanced content areas. Such instruction would require complex thinking skills in authentic problem-solving contexts, homework, higher assessment and grading standards, and assessment of what students can actually do with what they have learned. Mastering thinking skills—such as problem solving, decision making, and making value judgments—was considered important because these skills are required in the advanced grades, in the world of work, and to gain admittance to advanced education and training opportunities.

Figure 5.2 illustrates the translation of goals into standards and standards into objectives as a funneling or narrowing of focus in which standards, guided by our goals, are gradually translated, through subject matter curricula, into specific objectives for instruction.

The Purpose of Objectives

Objectives have two practical purposes. The first is to move standards toward classroom accomplishments by identifying the specific teaching strategies through which standards can be achieved. The second is to express teaching strategies in a format that allows you to measure their effects on

Figure 5.2 The Funneling of Standards into Instructional Objectives

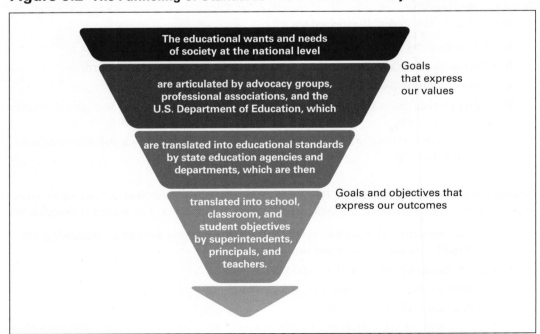

your specific learners. A written statement that achieves these two purposes is called a **behavioral objective**.

What Does *Behavioral* Mean?

When the word *behavioral* precedes the word *objective,* learning is being defined as a change in observable behavior. Therefore, the writing of behavioral objectives requires that the behavior being addressed be observable and measurable (with a test, observational checklist, student work sample, etc.). Activities occurring in the seclusion of your learners' minds are not observable and thus cannot be the focus of a behavioral objective. Unobserved activities, such as creating a mental image or rehearsing a response subvocally, can precede learning, but they cannot constitute evidence that learning has occurred because they cannot be directly observed.

Further, the behavior of your learners must be observable over a period of time during which specific content, teaching strategies, and instructional materials have been presented. This limits a behavioral objective to a timeframe consistent with the logical divisions in the school curricula that you will be teaching, such as lessons, chapters, units, and grading periods. Feedback from behavioral objectives provides data for monitoring the effects of your instructional strategies and changing them when necessary.

Steps in Preparing Behavioral Objectives

The remaining goal of this chapter is to show you how to prepare behavioral objectives for your classroom as painlessly as possible. Simply put, writing behavioral objectives involves three steps:

1. Identifying a specific goal that has an observable learning outcome
2. Stating the conditions under which a learning outcome can be expected to occur (e.g., with what materials, texts, and facilities and in what period of time)
3. Specifying the criterion level—that is, the degree of learning that will be expected from your instruction under the specified conditions

Before considering the actual written form of behavioral objectives, let's look at these three steps in more detail.

Specifying the Learning Outcomes

The first step in writing a behavioral objective is to identify a specific goal with an observable **learning outcome**. For an objective to be behavioral, it must be observable and measurable so you can determine whether the behavior is present, partially present, or absent (Gronlund & Brookhart, 2008; Mager, 1997; Kubiszyn & Borich, 2013). The key to identifying an observable outcome is choosing the right words to describe it.

Word choice in writing behavioral objectives is important because one word may have different meanings, depending on who is reading or hearing it. The endless puns heard in our culture are humorous illustrations of this: Does *well-rounded person* mean broadly educated or well fed? Words can express a concept not only accurately or inaccurately but also specifically or vaguely. It is vague usage that gives us the most trouble in writing behavioral objectives.

In a behavioral objective, learning outcomes must be expressed directly, concretely, and observably, unlike the way behaviors usually are described in the popular press, television, and even some textbooks. If you took these everyday sources as a guide for writing the behavioral expressions needed in the classroom, you would quickly find that they cannot be easily observed and probably cannot be measured, either. For example, we often hear expressions like these as desirable goals:

- Mentally healthy citizens
- Well-rounded individuals
- Self-actualized schoolchildren

- Informed adults
- Literate populace

But what do *mentally healthy, well-rounded, self-actualized, informed,* and *literate* actually mean? If you asked a large number of individuals to define these terms, you would receive quite an assortment of responses. These diverse responses would have widely divergent implications for how to achieve each desired behavior and observe its attainment. The reason, of course, is that the words are vague and open to many interpretations. Imagine the confusion such vagueness could cause in your classroom if your objective for the first grading period were simply "To inform the class about the content" or "To make them higher achievers." Johnny's parents would have one interpretation of *informed,* but Betty's parents might have quite another. (Let's hope they both don't show up on parent–teacher night!) Also, you might mean one thing by *higher achiever,* but your principal might mean another.

The point is that vague behavioral language quickly becomes a problem for those who are held accountable for bringing about the behavior in question. You can avoid this problem by writing behavioral objectives in precise language that makes their measurement specific and noncontroversial.

One way to make your behavioral objectives specific and noncontroversial is to choose behavioral expressions from a list of action verbs that have widely accepted meanings. These action verbs also allow easy identification of the operations necessary for displaying the behavior. For example, instead of expecting students to be *informed* or *literate* in a subject, expect them to do the following:

- Differentiate between . . .
- Identify the results of . . .
- Solve a problem in . . .
- Compare and contrast . . .

These action verbs describe what being *informed* or *literate* means by stating specific, observable behaviors that the learner must perform. Although we have not yet indicated how well the learner must be able to perform these behaviors, we are now closer to gathering the type of evidence that can be used to determine whether these objectives have been achieved.

Although a behavioral objective should include an action verb that specifies a learning outcome, not all action verbs are suitable for specifying learning outcomes. Some are better suited to specifying **learning activities.** Unfortunately, learning outcomes often are confused with learning activities. For example, which of the following examples represent learning outcomes and which represent learning activities?

1. The student will identify pictures of words that sound alike.
2. The student will demonstrate an appreciation of poetry.
3. The student will subtract one-digit numbers.
4. The student will show knowledge of punctuation.
5. The student will practice the multiplication tables.
6. The student will sing "The Star-Spangled Banner."

In the first four objectives, the action words *identify, demonstrate, subtract,* and *show* all point to outcomes—end products of an instructional lesson or unit. However, the action word in the fifth example, *practice,* is only a learning activity; it is not an end in itself and only can work toward a learning outcome. The sixth objective is more ambiguous. Is *sing* an outcome or an activity? It is hard to say without more information. If the goal is to have a stage-frightened student sing in public, then it is a learning outcome. However, if singing is only practice for a later performance, it is a learning activity.

Learning activities are important, but only in relation to the specific learning outcomes or end products they are attempting to achieve. Without having a learning outcome clearly in mind, there will be no way to determine the value of a learning activity for promoting desirable student outcomes.

The following illustrate some common examples that differentiate between verbs used for learning outcomes and verbs used for learning activities. Keep in mind that some behaviors that would normally be considered an activity could be a behavioral outcome, if that is all you are trying to achieve and it can be measured.

Learning Outcomes (Ends)	Learning Activities (Means)
identify	study
recall	watch
list	listen
write	read

A behavioral objective must include the end product, because you will use this end product in choosing your instructional procedures and evaluating whether you have achieved the desired result (Gronlund & Brookhart, 2008; Kubiszyn & Borich, 2013).

Identifying the Conditions

The second step in writing a behavioral objective is to identify the specific **learning conditions** under which learning will occur. If the observable learning outcome can be achieved only through use of particular materials, equipment, tools, or other resources, then these conditions should be stated in the objective. Following are some examples of objectives that state conditions:

- Create a candy store price list and use pretend money to make several purchases. Show how to add the values of different coins and how to determine and give proper change.

- Using the map of strategic resources handed out in class, identify the economic conditions in the South resulting from the Civil War.

- In the first chapter of *Charlotte's Web,* we meet Fern. Circle all the adjectives that correctly describe her: persuasive, lazy, fair-minded, emotional, hardhearted.

- Using an electronic calculator, solve problems involving the addition of two-digit, signed numbers.

- Using pictures of 14th- to 18th-century Gothic and Baroque European cathedrals, compare and contrast their styles of architecture.

If the conditions are obvious, they need not be specified. For example, it is not necessary to specify "Using a writing instrument and paper, write a short story." However, when conditions can focus learning in specific ways, eliminating some areas of study and including others, the statement of conditions can be critical to attaining the objective, and you should include it. For example, imagine that a student will be tested on the behavior indicated in the first objective in the preceding list but without the conditions indicated: "Create a candy store price list and use pretend money to make several purchases." Adding "Show how to add the values of different coins and give proper change" provides concrete examples of what is being expected that would likely produce a more specific and structured response. If students are told the conditions, they can focus their study on the precise behavior called for (e.g., relating different coins to the price of real purchases, as opposed to memorizing the values of different coins).

Note also that without a statement of conditions to focus your instruction, your students may assume different conditions than you intend. For example, in our third example, in the absence of concrete examples, some students might prepare by memorizing the definitions of the adjectives *persuasive, lazy, fair-minded, emotional,* and *hardhearted* instead of learning what characteristics of a person, such as Fern, would need to be present for each adjective to apply. And because objectives form the basis for tests, your tests might be fairer to some students than others, depending on the assumptions they make in the absence of stated conditions.

Notice in the other preceding examples that learning can take on different meanings, depending on whether students study and practice with or without the use of a map, electronic calculator, or pictures of 14th- to 18th-century cathedrals. Teaching and learning become more structured and resources more organized when you state conditions as part of your objectives. And as we have seen, objectives that specify conditions of learning lead to fairer tests.

Conditional statements within a behavioral objective can be singular or multiple. It is possible, and sometimes necessary, to have two or even three conditional statements in an objective to focus the learning. Although attaching too many conditions to an objective can narrow learning to irrelevant details, multiple conditions often are important adjuncts to improving the clarity of the behavior desired and the organization and preparation of instructional resources. Following are examples of multiple conditions, indicated by italics:

- In the first chapter of *Charlotte's Web,* we meet Fern. Circle all the words *from this list* that correctly describe her: persuasive, lazy, fair-minded, emotional, hardhearted.
- Using a *centigrade thermometer,* measure the temperature of 2 liters of *water* at a depth of 25 centimeters.
- Using a *compass, ruler,* and *protractor,* draw three conic sections of different sizes and three triangles of different types.
- Using 4 grams of *sodium carbonate* and 4 grams of *sodium bicarbonate,* indicate their different reactions in H_2O.
- *Using the list of foods provided,* fill in the blanks in the food pyramid to represent a healthy, well-balanced diet.
- *Within 15 minutes* and using the *reference books* provided, write the formulas for wattage, voltage, amperage, and resistance.
- Using a *computer* with word-processing capability, correct the spelling and punctuation errors in a *two-page manuscript in 20 minutes or less.*

It is important not to add so many conditions that learning is reduced to trivial detail. It is also important to choose conditions that are realistic—that represent authentic, real-life circumstances your learners are likely to find inside as well as outside the classroom. The idea behind stating conditions, especially multiple conditions, is not to complicate the behavior but rather to make it more natural and close to the conditions under which it will have to be performed in the real world and in subsequent instruction. Always check the conditions specified to see if they match those under which the behavior is most likely to be needed in subsequent instruction and outside the classroom.

Stating Criterion Levels

The third step in writing a behavioral objective is to specify the level of performance required to meet the objective. Specifying the outcome and conditions reveals the procedures necessary for the behavior to be observed. However, one important element is missing: How much of the behavior is required for you to consider the objective to be attained?

This element of objective writing is the **criterion level**. It is the degree of performance desired or level of proficiency that will satisfy you that the objective has been met.

Setting criterion levels is one of the most misunderstood aspects of objective writing. At the root of this misunderstanding is the failure to recognize that criterion or proficiency levels are value judgments as to what level is required for adequately performing the behavior in some later setting. The mistaken assumption is often made that a single correct level of proficiency exists and that, once established, it must forever remain in its original form. At first, criterion levels should be taken as educated guesses. They should indicate the approximate degree of proficiency needed to adequately perform the behavior in another instructional setting, in the next grade, or in the real world. But, criterion levels should be adjusted periodically to conform with how well a student or group of students are able to perform the behavior, which, as we have seen, is a major strategy of differentiated instruction.

Often criterion levels are set to establish a benchmark for testing whether an objective has been met, without recognizing that this level may not be relevant to subsequent learning tasks, instructional settings, or the learning history of an individual student. To avoid this, always consider criterion levels to be adjustable and dependent on your evaluation of how well students can adequately use the behavior at subsequent times and in contexts beyond your classroom. And remember that criterion levels need not be the same for every learner or measured in the same way for every learner.

Criterion levels come in many sizes and shapes and can be measured in different ways. For example, they can be stated in the following ways:

- Number of items correct on a test
- Number of consecutive items correct (or consecutive errorless performances)
- Essential features included (as in an essay question or research paper)
- Completion within a prescribed time limit (where speed of performance is important)
- Completion with a certain degree of accuracy
- Completion with critical sources cited

Consider the following objective:

Using one short story by John Steinbeck and another by Mark Twain, differentiate between their writing styles.

Is a criterion stated? Remember, a criterion level establishes the degree of behavior required for the objective to be met. How would the teacher know if a student's written response to this objective has demonstrated the minimum acceptable level of differentiation? With only the information given, it would be difficult and arbitrary.

Now let's add a criterion to this objective:

Using short stories by John Steinbeck and Mark Twain, differentiate their writing styles by selecting four passages from each author that illustrate differences in their writing styles.

Now there is a basis for evaluating the objective. This particular criterion level requires considerable skill in applying learned information in different contexts and allows for flexibility in the range of responses that are acceptable. Also, it allows learners to choose the passages with which they are most familiar. This type of objective is sometimes called an **expressive objective** (Eisner, 1969, 1998) because it allows for a variety of correct responses or for students to express themselves in a variety of ways for which there is no single correct answer. The amount of expressiveness in a response allowed by an objective is always a matter of degree. In other words, objectives can have more or less rigid criterion levels.

Consider another example:

Using an electronic calculator, the student will solve problems involving the addition of two-digit, signed numbers.

Is a criterion level stated for this objective? No. There is no unambiguous basis for deciding whether Angela met the objective and Bobby did not. Now, let's add a criterion level:

Using an electronic calculator, the student will correctly solve eight of ten problems involving the addition of two-digit, signed numbers.

This objective now identifies the minimum proficiency that must be observed to conclude that the desired behavior has been attained. Unlike the first version of this objective, little flexibility is allowed in the required response.

Notice that far less expression is possible in answering a question about mathematics than about literature; the former is more highly structured and more rigid in terms of possible responses. Notice also that this more structured approach to an acceptable response fits well with the nature of this particular objective; the less structured approach fits well with the literature example.

Both of these objectives illustrate that the expressiveness of an objective is established by the number of learning conditions you set, what you choose as an acceptable criterion and how you wish to measure it. Also, the level of expressiveness that fits best often is a function of the objective itself—how many acceptable answers are possible. As a teacher, you control these elements:

1. Learning outcomes
2. Conditions

3. Criterion levels

   a. Proficiency level

   b. Level of expressiveness

   c. Method of measurement

Following are some of the earlier objectives with criterion levels added in brackets (or italicized where a criterion already was included):

- In the first chapter of *Charlotte's Web,* we meet Fern. Circle [all] the words from the following list that correctly describe her: persuasive, lazy, fair-minded, emotional, hardhearted.

- Using a centigrade thermometer, measure the temperature of 2 liters of water at a depth of 25 centimeters [to within 1 degree of accuracy].

- Using a compass, ruler, and protractor, draw *three* conic sections of *different sizes* and three triangles of *different types*.

- Using 4 grams of sodium carbonate and 4 grams of sodium bicarbonate, indicate their different reactions with H_2O [by testing the alkalinity of the H_2O and reporting results in parts per million (ppm)].

- Using the list of foods provided, fill in the blanks in the food pyramid to represent a healthy, well-balanced diet [placing every food correctly].

- Within 15 minutes and using the reference books provided, find [and write correctly] the formulas for wattage, voltage, amperage, and resistance.

- Using a computer with word-processing capability, correct the spelling and punctuation errors in a *two-page manuscript in 20 minutes or less* [with 100 percent accuracy].

All these examples illustrate well-written behavioral objectives.

You have seen how to specify learning outcomes, state conditions for learning, and establish criterion levels. These are the three most important ingredients of well-written behavioral objectives. But there is one more point to know about preparing objectives: Keep them simple.

Keeping Objectives Simple

Teachers often make the mistake of being too complex in measuring learning outcomes. As a result, they resort to indirect methods of measurement. If you want to know whether Johnny can write his name, ask him to write his name—but not while blindfolded! Resist the temptation to be tricky. Consider these examples:

- The student will show his or her ability to recall the characters in the novel *Tom Sawyer* by painting a picture of each.

- Discriminate between a telephone and a television by drawing an electrical diagram of each.

- Demonstrate that you understand how to use an encyclopedia index by identifying the page on which a given subject can be found in the *Encyclopaedia Britannica.*

In the first example, painting a picture surely would allow you to determine whether the students can recall the characters in *Tom Sawyer,* but is there an easier (and less time consuming) way to measure recall? How about asking the students simply to list the characters? If the objective is to determine recall, listing is sufficient. For the second example, how about presenting students with two illustrations—one of a telephone, the other of a television—and simply asking them to tell (verbally or in writing) which is which? The third example is on target. The task required is a simple and efficient way of measuring whether someone can use an encyclopedia index.

In this chapter, you will begin writing objectives on your own. Be sure to include these three essential components in every objective you write: (1) an observable learning outcome, (2) the learning conditions, and (3) the criterion level. And, keep in mind that the learning conditions you set and the criterion level(s) you establish will determine the degree of expressiveness or flexibility you are allowing for a learner response.

The Cognitive, Affective, and Psychomotor Domains

You might have noticed that some of the example objectives shown earlier in this chapter have illustrated very different types of behaviors. For example, compare the behaviors called for in these objectives:

- Using short stories by John Steinbeck and Mark Twain, differentiate their writing styles by selecting four passages from each author that illustrate differences in their writing styles.
- Using a centigrade thermometer, measure the temperature of 2 liters of water at a depth of 25 centimeters to within 1 degree of accuracy.

Common sense tells us that the behaviors called for require different patterns of preparation and study to attain. In the former objective, study and practice would focus on analyzing the authors' writing styles and noting the differences in actual examples of their writing. Contrast this complicated process with how one might study to acquire the behavior in the second objective. Here the study and practice might consist simply of learning to accurately perceive distances between the markings on a centigrade scale. Such practice might be limited to training one's eyes to count spaces between the gradations and then assigning the appropriate number to represent temperature in degrees centigrade.

Note also the difference in study and preparation time required to achieve these two different objectives: The second could be learned in minutes, but the first might take hours, days, or even weeks. These different objectives represent only two examples of the variety of learning outcomes possible in your classroom.

Objectives can require vastly different levels of not only cognitive complexity but also affective and psychomotor complexity. The following section introduces behaviors at different levels of complexity for which behavioral objectives can be prepared. For convenience, they are organized into the following behaviors:

- **Cognitive domain**: development of intellectual abilities and skills
- **Affective domain**: development of attitudes, beliefs, and values
- **Psychomotor domain**: coordination of physical movements and performance

The Cognitive Domain

Bloom, Englehart, Hill, Furst, and Krathwohl (1984) have devised a method for categorizing objectives according to cognitive complexity. They delineate six levels of cognitive complexity, ranging from the knowledge level (least complex) to the evaluation level (most complex). As illustrated in Figure 5.3, Bloom et al. describe the levels as hierarchical; the higher-level objectives include and are dependent on the lower-level cognitive skills. Thus objectives at the evaluation level require more complex mental

This **video** demonstrates training a child in the cognitive domain. What skills are the participants exploring?

Figure 5.3 Taxonomy of Educational Objectives: Cognitive Domain

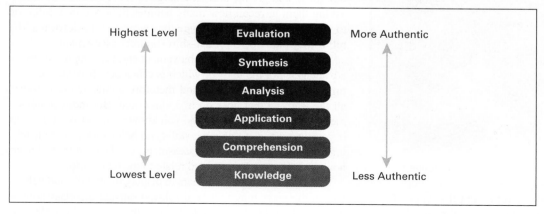

operations, or higher cognitive skills, than objectives at the knowledge level. Also notice that higher-level objectives are more authentic than lower-level objectives. Let's consider what *authentic* means.

So far in this chapter, you have seen a variety of skills and behaviors that children learn in school. Some of these require learners to acquire information by memorizing, for example, vocabulary, multiplication tables, dates of historical events, or the names of important persons. In addition, you saw some example objectives in which students had to acquire concepts, rules, and generalizations that allowed them to understand what they read, to analyze, and to compare and contrast. These types of learning outcomes represent what is called **declarative (factual) knowledge**, which contains the *facts, concepts, rules,* and *generalizations* pertaining to a specific area or topic. They include, for example, knowledge of technical vocabulary, the names of major natural resources, periods of geological time, the Pythagorean theorem, or the theory of evolution.

Other skills and behaviors involve learning *action sequences* or *procedures* to follow when, for example, using drawing materials, performing mathematical computations, operating a calculator, or practicing handwriting. These types of outcomes represent what is called **procedural knowledge**, or the knowledge of how to do things. If you know the names of the parts of a shoe, for example (lace, eyelet, tongue, and knot), you have declarative knowledge. If you know how to use this knowledge to actually tie your shoe, you have procedural knowledge.

Still other skills and behaviors require learners to think about their own thinking to determine when it is and is not leading to a desirable outcome—for example, becoming *aware* of the procedure one is using to tie one's shoe, *monitoring* the effectiveness of that procedure and, if it works, making a conscious *commitment* to use that procedure again. This type of behavior represents what is called **metacognitive knowledge**, or thinking about your thinking to become aware of your own level of understanding.

Some of these skills are best assessed with paper and pencil tests. However, skills requiring independent judgment, critical thinking, and decision making are best assessed with performance assessments. **Performance assessments** measure a skill or behavior directly, as it is used in the world outside your classroom (Borich & Tombari, 2004; Tombari & Borich, 1999). We will have more to say about the important topic of performance assessment and how you can use it in your classroom to differentiate instruction in Chapter 13.

Classroom assessment of learning, particularly beyond the early elementary grades, has been based almost exclusively on paper and pencil tests, which indicate, rather than directly measure, what children have learned. For example, you may measure an understanding of the scientific method not by having learners plan, conduct, and evaluate an experiment (a direct assessment) but by asking them to list the steps in conducting an experiment, write about the difference between a hypothesis and a theory, or choose the correct definition of a control group from a list of choices (all indirect assessment). Or you may measure children's understanding of money not by observing them buy food, pay for it, and get the correct change (direct assessment) but by asking them to recall how many pennies there are in a dollar or to write down how much change they would get back from a $10 bill if they paid $6.75 for a T-shirt (indirect assessment).

Indirect assessment of achievement and learning has obvious advantages, not the least of which is efficiency. It would be very time consuming to directly and therefore authentically measure all the learning that goes on in a classroom. But indirect assessment raises a problem: How do you know your test is telling you if your learners can *apply* the skills and behaviors you are teaching? In other words, indirect assessments can be far removed from how the behaviors being tested relate to the real world.

Authentic tests ask learners to display their skills and behaviors in the ways they will be displayed outside the classroom—in the real world. Authentic tests directly measure the skills and behaviors that teachers and learners really care about. In other

Objectives requiring higher-level cognitive, affective, and psychomotor skills are more authentic behaviors because they are more likely to represent the types of performances required of your learners in the world in which they must live, work, and play.

words, these tests ask learners to do what was modeled, coached, and practiced during classroom instruction as it would be done outside the classroom. If learners saw you demonstrate how to focus a microscope, were coached to do this, and practiced doing it, then an authentic assessment would ask them to focus a microscope, rather than label its parts on a diagram. If, however, your learners only needed to know the parts of a microscope so they could read a story about the invention of the microscope—not use one—asking them to label the parts would be an authentic assessment.

Objectives requiring higher-level cognitive, affective, and psychomotor skills—those that most closely represent the thinking curriculum introduced earlier in this chapter—represent more **authentic behaviors**. In sum, these objectives identify the types of performances required of your learners in the world in which they must live, work, and play.

Now let's look at how each behavior in the cognitive domain varies according to cognitive skill and authenticity. These behaviors are described with examples of action verbs that represent them.

Knowledge. Objectives at the knowledge level require your students to remember or recall information, such as facts, terminology, problem-solving strategies, and rules. Here are some action verbs that describe learning outcomes at the knowledge level:

define	list	recall
describe	match	recite
identify	name	select
label	outline	state

Following are examples of knowledge objectives that use these verbs:

- The student will recall the four major food groups, without error, by Friday.

- From memory, the student will match U.S. generals with their most famous battles, with 80 percent accuracy.

Comprehension. Objectives at the comprehension level require some degree of understanding. Students are expected to be able to change the form of a communication, translate or restate what they have read, see connections or relationships among parts of a communication (interpretation), or draw conclusions or see consequences from information (inference). Here are some action verbs that describe learning outcomes at the comprehension level:

convert	estimate	infer
defend	explain	paraphrase
discriminate	extend	predict
distinguish	generalize	summarize

Examples of comprehension objectives that use these verbs include the following:

- By the end of the six-week grading period, the student will summarize the main events of a story in grammatically correct English.

- The student will discriminate between the Realists and the Naturalists, citing examples from the readings.

Application. Objectives written at the application level require the student to use previously acquired information in a setting other than the one in which it was learned. Application objectives differ from comprehension objectives in that application requires the presentation of a problem in a different and often applied context. Thus the student can rely on neither the content nor the context in which the original learning occurred to solve the problem. Here are some action verbs that describe learning outcomes at the application level:

change	modify	relate
compute	operate	solve
demonstrate	organize	transfer
develop	prepare	use

Following are examples of application objectives that use these or similar verbs:

- On Monday, the student will demonstrate for the class an application to real life of the law of conservation of energy.
- Given single-digit fractions not covered in class, the student will multiply them on paper with 85 percent accuracy.

Analysis. Objectives written at the analysis level require the student to identify logical errors (e.g., point out a contradiction or an erroneous inference) or to differentiate among facts, opinions, assumptions, hypotheses, and conclusions. At the analysis level, students are expected to recognize relationships among ideas and to compare and contrast. Here are some action verbs that describe learning outcomes at the analysis level:

break down	distinguish	point out
deduce	illustrate	relate
diagram	infer	separate out
differentiate	outline	subdivide

Following are examples of analysis objectives that use these verbs:

- Given a presidential speech, the student will be able to point out the positions that attack an individual rather than that individual's program.
- Given absurd statements (e.g., A man had flu twice. The first time it killed him. The second time he got well quickly.), the student will be able to point out the contradiction.

Synthesis. Objectives written at the synthesis level require students to produce something unique or original. At this level, students are expected to solve some unfamiliar problem in a unique way or to combine parts to form a unique or novel solution. Here are some action verbs that describe learning outcomes at the synthesis level:

categorize	create	formulate
compile	design	predict
compose	devise	produce

Examples of synthesis objectives that use these or similar verbs include these:

- Given a short story, the student will write a different but plausible ending.
- Given a problem to be solved, the student will design on paper a scientific experiment to address the problem.

Evaluation. Objectives written at the evaluation level require the student to form judgments and make decisions about the value of methods, ideas, people, or products that have specific purposes. Students are expected to state the bases for their judgments (i.e., the external criteria or principles they drew on to reach their conclusions). Here are some action verbs that describe learning outcomes at the evaluation level:

appraise	criticize	justify
compare	defend	support
contrast	judge	validate

Following are examples of evaluation objectives that use these verbs:

- Given a previously unread paragraph, the student will judge its value according to the five criteria discussed in class.
- Given a description of a country's economic system, the student will defend it, basing his or her argument on the principles of democracy.

Figure 5.4 **A Taxonomy for Learning, Teaching, and Assessing**

The Knowledge Dimension	The Cognitive Process Domain					
	1. Remember	2. Understand	3. Apply	4. Analyze	5. Evaluate	6. Create
A. *Factual knowledge:* The basic facts that must be known within a discipline						
B. *Conceptual knowledge:* The interrelationships that function together to form a concept						
C. *Procedural knowledge:* How to apply skills, algorithms, techniques, and methods						
D. *Metacognitive knowledge:* Awareness and knowledge of one's own thinking						

Anderson and Krathwohl (2001) and Marzano and Kendall (2006) have prepared an updated version of Bloom and colleagues' (1984) taxonomy of educational objectives from a cognitive learning perspective, which helps teachers not only identify and assess the outcomes they desire but also the thinking processes their students must use to achieve those outcomes. Anderson and Krathwohl explore curricula from three perspectives—the cognitive learning perspective, the teaching perspective, and the assessment perspective—providing a useful framework for writing objectives that connect all three perspectives. Figure 5.4 illustrates these authors' extensions of the original taxonomy, which emphasize the distinctions among factual (declarative), conceptual, procedural, and metacognitive knowledge when writing objectives and selecting teaching strategies that can most effectively achieve those objectives. Also see In Practice: Focus on the New Field of Cognitive Science.

In Practice

Focus on the New Field of Cognitive Science

In this chapter, you have studied two taxonomies of objectives in the cognitive domain: one by Bloom and colleagues (1984), and another by Anderson and Krathwohl (2001). The development of these taxonomies represents

a gradual shift from a *behavioral model,* which emphasizes how to arrange the learning environment to bring about desired outcomes (for example, through rewards and disincentives), to a *cognitive model,* which places more emphasis on how the brain functions during problem solving, decision making, creativity, and critical thinking and the cognitive strategies that promote these outcomes. Although both taxonomies consider the acquisition of knowledge to be important, Anderson and Krathwohl have extended Bloom's taxonomy to include the cognitive and metacognitive strategies that can help learners improve their thinking and more efficiently achieve higher-order outcomes. Much of what we know about the content of thinking and assessment today we owe to advances in the cognitive science of learning.

The Behavioral Model

B. F. Skinner, considered the founder of behaviorism, generated many of the experimental data that form the basis of behavioral learning theory. He and other behavioral theorists were concerned mainly with observable indications of learning and what those observations could imply for teaching. They concentrated on observable cause-and-effect relationships.

Skinner and other behaviorists view the teacher's job as modifying the behavior of students by setting up situations to reinforce them when they exhibit desired responses. Behaviorists see learning as a sequence of stimulus and response actions in the learner. They reason that teachers can link responses involving lower-level skills and create a learning "chain" to teach higher-level skills. The teacher determines all of the skills needed to lead up to the desired behavior and makes sure students learn them in a step-by-step manner (Roblyer, Edwards, & Havriluk, 1997, p. 59).

The Cognitive Model

Many educational psychologists, however, found the behavioral approach unsatisfying. In the areas of problem solving and learning strategies, they became more concerned with what was unobservable—what was going on inside the brain.

These cognitive theories are based on the work of educational philosopher John Dewey and educational psychologists Lev Vygotsky, Jean Piaget, and Jerome Bruner. They propose that children actively construct knowledge and that this construction of knowledge happens in a social context. Vygotsky proposed that all learning takes place in the *zone of proximal development,* which is the difference between what a child can do alone versus with assistance. By building on the child's experiences and providing moderately challenging tasks, teachers can provide the *intellectual scaffolding* to help him or her learn and progress through the different stages of development.

Whereas the behavioral approach to learning emphasizes how to establish a learning environment to produce more correct answers than incorrect ones, the cognitive approach emphasizes that good thinking results from studying the cognitive processes and outcomes that underlie right and wrong answers. Cognitive psychologists believe that learners, even at the earliest grade levels, have some knowledge about nearly every topic they study (Tombari & Borich, 1999, p. 7).

Closely connected to the cognitive approach are the methods of *constructivism.* These methods emphasize students' ability to solve real-life, practical problems. Students typically work in cooperative groups, rather than individually; they tend to focus on projects that require solutions to problems, rather than on instructional sequences that require learning certain content skills. The roles of the teacher in constructivist models are to arrange for required resources and act as a guide to students while they set their own goals and teach themselves (Roblyer, Edwards, & Havriluk, 1997, p. 70).

The Affective Domain

This **video** examines how the affective domain can be implemented in the classroom. Pay attention to the strategies used by this teacher.

Another method of categorizing objectives has been devised by Krathwohl, Bloom, and Masia (1999). This taxonomy delineates five levels of affective behavior, ranging from the receiving level to the characterization level (see Figure 5.5). As in the cognitive domain, these levels are presumed to be hierarchical—that is, higher-level objectives are assumed to include and depend on lower-level affective skills. As one moves up the hierarchy, more involvement, commitment, and reliance on oneself occurs, as opposed to having one's feelings, attitudes, and values dictated by others.

The following sections contain examples of action verbs indicating each level of the affective domain.

Receiving. Objectives at the receiving level require the student to be aware of or passively attend to certain phenomena and stimuli. At this level, students are expected simply to listen or be attentive. Here are some action verbs that describe outcomes at the receiving level:

attend	discern	look
be aware	hear	notice
control	listen	share

Following are examples of receiving objectives that use these verbs:

- The student will be able to notice a change from small-group discussion to large-group lecture by following the lead of others in the class.
- The student will be able to listen to all of a Mozart concerto without leaving his or her seat.

Responding. Objectives at the responding level require the student to comply with given expectations by attending or reacting to certain stimuli. Students are expected to obey, participate, or respond willingly when asked or directed to do something. Here are some action verbs that describe outcomes at the responding level:

applaud	follow	play
comply	obey	practice
discuss	participate	volunteer

These are examples of responding objectives that use these verbs:

- The student will follow the directions given in the book without argument when asked to do so.
- The student will practice a musical instrument when asked to do so.

Valuing. Objectives at the valuing level require the student to display behavior consistent with a single belief or attitude in situations where he or she is neither forced nor asked to comply. Students are expected to demonstrate a preference or display a high degree of certainty and conviction. Here are some action verbs that describe outcomes at the valuing level:

act	debate	help
argue	display	organize
convince	express	prefer

Following are some examples of valuing objectives that use these verbs:

- The student will express an opinion about nuclear disarmament whenever national events raise the issue.
- The student will display an opinion about the elimination of pornography when discussing this social issue.

Organization. Objectives at the organization level require a commitment to a set of values. This level of the affective domain involves (1) forming a reason one values certain things and not others and (2) making appropriate choices between things that are and are not valued. Students are expected to organize their likes and preferences into a value system and then decide which ones will be dominant. Here are some action verbs that describe outcomes at the organization level:

abstract	decide	select
balance	define	systematize
compare	formulate	theorize

Examples of organization objectives that use these verbs include the following:

- The student will be able to compare alternatives to the death penalty and decide which ones are compatible with his or her beliefs.

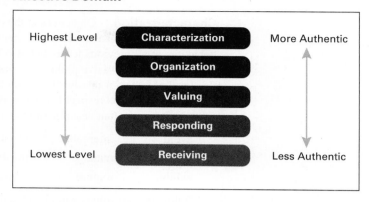

Figure 5.5 **Taxonomy of Educational Objectives: Affective Domain**

- The student will be able to formulate the reasons she or he supports civil rights legislation and be able to identify legislation that does not support her or his beliefs.

Characterization.   Objectives at the characterization level require that all behavior displayed by the student be consistent with his or her values. At this level, the student not only has acquired the behaviors at all previous levels but also has integrated his or her values into a system representing a complete and pervasive philosophy that does not allow contradictory expressions. Evaluations of this level of behavior involve the extent to which the student has developed a consistent philosophy of life (e.g., exhibits respect for the worth and dignity of human beings in all situations). Here are some action verbs that describe outcomes at this level:

avoid	internalize	resist
display	manage	resolve
exhibit	require	revise

Following are some example objectives:

- The student will exhibit a helping and caring attitude toward students with disabilities by assisting them both in and out of the classroom.
- The student will display a scientific attitude by stating and then testing hypotheses whenever the choice of alternatives is unclear.

The Psychomotor Domain

A third method of categorizing objectives has been devised by Harrow (1977) and by Moore (2006). Harrow's taxonomy delineates five levels of psychomotor behavior, ranging from the imitation level (least complex and least authentic) to the naturalization level (most complex and most authentic). Figure 5.6 illustrates the hierarchical arrangement of the psychomotor domain. These behaviors place primary emphasis on neuromuscular skills involving various degrees of physical dexterity. As behaviors in the taxonomy move from least to most complex and authentic, behavior changes from gross to fine motor skills.

Each of the levels—imitation, manipulation, precision, articulation, and naturalization— has different characteristics as described below.

Imitation.   Objectives at the imitation level require that the learner be exposed to an observable action and then overtly imitate it, such as when an instructor demonstrates the use of a microscope by placing a slide on the specimen tray. Performance at this level usually lacks neuromuscular coordination (e.g., the slide may hit the side of the tray or be improperly aligned beneath the lens). Thus the behavior generally is crude and imperfect. At this level, students are expected to observe and be able to repeat (although imperfectly) the action being visually demonstrated. Here are some action verbs that describe outcomes at this level:

align	grasp	repeat
balance	hold	rest (on)
follow	place	step (here)

Following are examples of imitation objectives that use these or similar verbs:

- After being shown a safe method for heating a beaker of water to boiling temperature, the student will be able to repeat the action.
- After being shown a freehand drawing of a triangle, the student will be able to reproduce the drawing.

Figure 5.6 Taxonomy of Educational Objectives: Psychomotor Domain

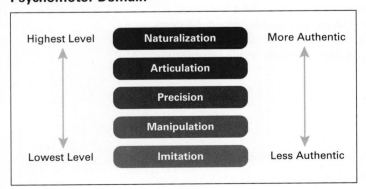

Manipulation. Objectives at the manipulation level require the student to perform selected actions from written or verbal directions without the aid of a visual model or direct observation, as in the previous (imitation) level. Students are expected to complete the action from reading or listening to instructions, although the behavior still may be performed crudely and without neuro-muscular coordination. Useful expressions to describe outcomes at the manipulation level are the same as at the imitation level, using the same action verbs, except they are performed from spoken or written instructions.

Here are examples of some manipulation objectives:

- Based on the picture provided in the textbook, type a salutation to a prospective employer using the format shown.
- With the instructions on the handout in front of you, practice focusing your microscope until you can see the outline of the specimen.

Precision. Objectives at the precision level require the student to perform an action independent of either a visual model or written set of directions. Proficiency in reproducing the action at this level reaches a higher level of refinement. Accuracy, proportion, balance, and exactness in performance accompany the action. Students are expected to reproduce the action with control and to reduce errors to a minimum. Expressions that describe outcomes at this level include the following:

accurately	independently	with control
without error	proficiently	with balance

Following are some examples of precision objectives:

- The student will be able to place the specimen accurately on the microscope tray and use the high-power focus with proficiency, as determined by the correct identification of three out of four easily recognizable objects.
- The student will be able to balance a light pen sufficiently to place it against the computer screen to identify misspelled words.

Articulation. Objectives at the articulation level require the student to display coordination of a series of related acts by establishing the appropriate sequence and performing the acts accurately, with control as well as with speed and timing. These expressions describe outcomes at this level:

confidence	integration	speed
coordination	proportion	stability
harmony	smoothness	timing

Examples of articulation objectives include the following:

- Students will be able to write all the letters of the alphabet, displaying the appropriate proportion between uppercase and lowercase, in ten minutes.
- Students will be able to complete ten simple arithmetic problems accurately on a handheld electronic calculator quickly and smoothly within 90 seconds.

Naturalization. Objectives at the naturalization level require a high level of proficiency in the skill or performance being taught. At this level, the behavior is performed with the least expenditure of energy and becomes routine, automatic, and spontaneous. Students are expected to repeat the behavior naturally and effortlessly time and again. Here are some expressions that describe this level of behavior:

automatically	professionally	with ease
effortlessly	routinely	with perfection
naturally	spontaneously	with poise

Following are some examples of naturalization objectives:

- At the end of the semester, students will be able to write routinely all the letters of the alphabet and all the numbers up to 100, each time requested.

- After the first grading period, students will be able to automatically draw correct isosceles, equilateral, and right triangles, without the aid of a template, for each homework assignment that requires this task.

The Rigor and Relevance Framework

Now that we have reviewed some levels of student outcomes you can ask of your learners, let's place your knowledge into the **rigor and relevance framework** developed by the International Center for Leadership in Education (2011). The purpose of this framework is to remind you of the continuum of thinking represented within each of the cognitive, affective, and psychomotor domains; for example, from classroom-oriented knowledge, comprehension, and application to the real life understandings and meanings that will be encountered and expected of your learners beyond your classroom and in adult life. A commitment to the rigor and relevance framework is a commitment to move from the lower to the higher levels within the cognitive, affective, and psychomotor domains with each lesson or unit you plan in order to teach increasingly authentic ways in which your learners should learn to think. The ultimate challenge of the rigor and relevance continuum is to expect of your learners an increasingly in-depth mastery of challenging tasks that require reflective thought, analysis, inquiry, problem solving, evaluation, and creativity that can be taught at every grade level and within every unit plan. Let's look at what the rigor and relevance means for your lesson and unit planning.

When a topic or task you are teaching has "rigor," it means that the content or task that you are teaching is asking learners to think deeply about a problem, analyze new situations, interpret and synthesize knowledge, bring ideas together in a new or creative way, develop and justify their own criteria for evaluation, and feel intellectually challenged. When a topic or task you are teaching is "relevant," it means that what you are teaching has some application beyond your classroom, addresses a problem of contemporary importance, builds on students' real-life experiences, and has students communicate what they have learned beyond the classroom—to the next grade, outside of school, and even to adult life. To accomplish this, some of your lessons will need to be devoted to addressing authentic problems of contemporary importance and that build upon your students' life experiences—what they already know. This will require the teaching of behaviors at the higher levels of thinking within the cognitive, affective, and psychomotor domains. In other words, a large part of a "relevant" lesson plan is being able to help your students bridge the gap between classroom knowledge and understanding and the application of that knowledge and understanding to situations outside of the classroom and to real life events.

One application of the rigor and relevance framework is to see all knowledge and understanding as a continuum of content from lesson plans that are less connected to real world applications but are necessary building blocks to more advanced thinking and lesson plans that are directly connected to life events that have easily discernable value in the life of your learners. Bybee et al. (1989) and Karplus (1975) provide a lesson planning model, called "The 5E Learning Cycle" that identifies five steps that can assist teachers in implementing the rigor and relevance framework. These steps represent teaching activities and learner behaviors in graduated steps for bridging the gap between classroom memorization, drill, and practice activities and activities that are of ostensible value to the learner beyond the immediate context in which they are learned and that also nudge the learner toward higher levels of thinking. Their outcomes and teacher activities are:

Engagement: Teacher engages students by introducing an object, event, or question.

Exploration: Teacher uses hands-on activities to explore the object, event, or question.

Explanation: Students explain their understanding of the object, event, or question while teacher expands the discussion with new concepts and skills to obtain conceptual clarity.

Elaboration: Teacher introduces activities that allow students to apply the concepts they have learned in real world contexts to extend student understanding and/or skills.

Evaluation: Teacher uses above activities to assess student application of knowledge, skills, and understandings and their relevance outside of the classroom to evaluate student progress and lesson effectiveness.

The purpose of the rigor and relevant framework and the 5E planning model is to increasingly bring your learners to the higher levels of behavior in the cognitive, affective, and psychomotor domains. We will return to this important topic in the next chapter to show how the rigor and relevant framework can be applied to your lesson and unit planning to move your learners to increasingly higher levels of thinking.

Some Misunderstandings about Behavioral Objectives

Before beginning to write objectives, you should be aware of several misconceptions about the cognitive, affective, and psychomotor domains. Following are some cautions to be mindful of when using behavioral objectives, each stated in the form of a question a parent or teacher may ask.

Are Some Behaviors More Desirable Than Others?

One misconception that often results from study of the cognitive, affective, and psychomotor domains is that simple behaviors, like the recall of facts and dates, are less desirable than more complex behaviors, requiring the cognitive operations of analysis, synthesis, and decision making. In fact, the simple–to–complex ordering of behaviors within the cognitive, affective, and psychomotor domains does not imply a continuum of desirability, because many lower-order behaviors must be learned before higher-order behaviors can be attempted.

Some teachers pride themselves on preparing objectives almost exclusively at the higher levels of cognitive complexity. But objectives at lower levels of complexity often represent the declarative knowledge base on which students build more complex behaviors. When the task-relevant prior knowledge or skills necessary for acquiring more complex behaviors have not been taught, students may demonstrate high error rates and less active engagement in the learning process at the higher levels of behavioral complexity (Alexander, 1996).

One of the most important uses of the taxonomies of behavior we have studied is to provide a menu of behaviors at different levels of complexity. As with any good diet, variety and proper proportion are the keys to good results.

What Is an Authentic Behavior?

Another misconception involves the meaning of the word *authentic*, which means "relevant to the real world." If a learner were only required to know the names of the presidents to complete a task or an assignment in the real world, that behavior could be measured authentically by asking him or her to memorize the names of the presidents, perhaps in the order in which they held office. Your measurement of this objective would be authentic because you would be asking that the behavior be displayed inside your classroom exactly as it would be performed outside. However, few occupations, courses, or programs of study will require your learners to recite the names of the presidents.

Knowledge (cognitive domain), receiving (affective domain), and imitation (psychomotor domain) are seldom sufficient in the world outside the classroom. Although they often are necessary in acquiring more complex behaviors, they are seldom important by themselves. However, behaviors representing higher cognitive skills often do take on importance outside the classroom exactly as they are taught. Evaluation (cognitive domain), characterization (affective domain), and naturalization (psychomotor domain) are examples of such behaviors. Deciding which candidate to vote for, assuming the responsibility of an informed citizen, and being able to read and complete a voting ballot are all authentic behaviors because they are necessary performances in daily life, in contrast to being able to name all the presidents. Therefore, higher cognitive skills often are more authentic than lower cognitive skills because they represent more integrated behaviors necessary for living, working, and performing in the world outside your classroom. This is one of the best reasons for a "thinking curriculum," which teaches higher cognitive skills in your classroom with the rigor and relevance framework. To help you create a thinking curriculum in your classroom, you will find in Appendix C the Higher-Order Thinking and Problem-Solving Checklist (Borich & Tombari, 2004). Use it to help you select and prioritize some of the authentic behaviors you want to teach and assess. Borich and Tombari (2004) provide subject specific examples of K–12 lesson content and objectives that illustrate higher-order thinking and problem-solving behaviors you can teach in your classroom. Write behavioral or expressive objectives for some of these, and you will be teaching a thinking curriculum.

Are Less Complex Behaviors Easier to Teach?

Another misconception is that behaviors of less complexity are easier to teach than behaviors of greater complexity. This is an appealing argument, because intuition tells us that this should be so. After all, complexity—especially cognitive complexity—often has been associated with greater difficulty, greater amounts of study time, and more extensive instructional resources.

Although simpler behaviors may be easier to teach some of the time, just the opposite can also be true. For example, consider the elaborate visual materials and mnemonic system that might be needed to recall a portion of the periodic table of chemical elements, as opposed to the simple demonstration that may be required to teach its application. In this case, the so-called less complex behavior requires greater time and instructional resources.

Whether a behavior is easier or more difficult to teach also will always depend on the learning needs of your students. Keep in mind that the ease with which a behavior can be taught is not necessarily synonymous with the level of the behavior in the taxonomy. These designations refer to the mental, or cognitive, operations required of the student, not the preparation required of the teacher to assure that learners have attained the desired outcome.

Are Cognitive, Affective, and Psychomotor Behaviors Mutually Exclusive?

Categorizing behaviors into separate cognitive, affective, and psychomotor domains does not mean that behaviors listed in one domain are not needed for attaining those listed in other domains. For example, it is not possible to think without having some feeling about what we are thinking or to feel something without thinking, which means the affective and cognitive domains are intertwined. Also putting thinking into practice can involve physical movements and performances that require psychomotor skills and abilities. For example, conducting a laboratory experiment requires not only thinking about what you are doing but also pouring liquid from one test tube to another, safely igniting a Bunsen burner, or adjusting a microscope correctly. Similarly, legible handwriting requires neuromuscular coordination, timing, and control while you are thinking about what you are writing.

Although it is convenient for an objective to contain behavior from only one of the three domains at a time, keep in mind that including one or more behaviors from the other domains also may be required. This is one of the best reasons, when appropriate, for preparing objectives in all three domains: It is evidence of your awareness of the close and necessary relationship among cognitive, affective, and psychomotor behaviors.

The Cultural Roots of Objectives

Finally, be prepared to have the source of your objectives questioned by parents, community members, and students. Some typical teacher responses to an inquiring parent question about the source of a lesson or unit objective may include "From the textbook, . . . curriculum guide, . . .

or department policies. . . ." Even though these answers may be technically correct, they miss the fundamental point, which is that objectives have roots much deeper than any single text, curriculum guide, or set of policies. Their roots lie in the educational values we espouse as a nation. Although parents, students, and other teachers may argue with the text used, the curriculum guide followed, or the department policies adopted, it is quite another matter to take exception to the values we share as a nation and that were created by many different interest groups over years of thoughtful deliberation, such as the InTASC and NBPTS standards presented in this and Chapter 1.

Texts, curricula, and policies are interpretations of the values that are shared at the broadest national level and translated into practice through goals, standards, and objectives. Texts, curriculum guides, and school district policies can no more create objectives than they can create values. Standards and their objectives, as we have seen earlier in this chapter, are carefully created to reflect our values; sources include curriculum reform committees, state and national legislative mandates, and the professional associations to which you belong.

This is why you should have knowledge of these ultimate sources from which your objectives have been derived. Without it, you may continually be caught in the position of justifying a particular text, curriculum, or policy to parents, students, and peers—some of whom will always disagree with you. Reference to any one text, curriculum, or policy cannot prove that your students should appreciate art or know how to solve an equation. But our values, as expressed through curriculum reform committees, state and national mandates, and the goals and standards of professional associations, can provide the appropriate justification and documentation for your intended learning outcomes through their publications and websites. Your attention to these values—as reported by professional papers and reports, curriculum committees, and national teacher groups—is as important to your teaching as the objectives you write.

Case History and Licensure Preparation

DIRECTIONS: *The following case history pertains to Chapter 5 content. After reading the case history, go to Chapter 5 in the Book Specific Resources section in the MyEducationLab for your course. Open the Case History and Licensure Preparation activity and complete the questions that follow. Upon completion of the test, scored answers to the short-answer question pertaining to the case history and multiple-choice questions will be provided.*

Case History

Max is a prospective teacher in the last year of his program. Today he will be observing two science classes at a middle school.

Mr. Goldthorp's Science Classroom

Mr. Goldthorp's students are working quietly at their desks. They are in the middle of a two-week field investigation unit devoted to identifying leaves. The directions for the unit are written on the handout Mr. Goldthorp has shared with Max.

Using the specimens available during school nature walks, as well as those close to home, the students will collect, identify, and label the leaves of ten trees native to their area. Work is expected to be neat and accurate and completed in ten school days.

Several students leave their desks to visit the "Reference" table, where books are available with colored pictures and detailed sketches of trees and leaves. Sometimes students help each other to decide among possible choices. Mr. Goldthorp encourages this informal cooperation and steps in with questions to guide students when needed.

Another table has a laminating machine. Aurora's eyes sparkle as she watches her dusty red oak leaf emerge, encased in shining plastic. Some students take their turns with the calligraphy pens available for labeling; others wait to use the computer to do the labeling. Four or five students make themselves comfortable on the carpet and pillow-lined library corner, where they leaf through an assortment of poetry books in hopes of finding "just the right poem" about nature to express their feelings about trees. If they recite a poem in front of the class, they can get up to ten points of extra credit.

Mr. Gonzales's Science Classroom

Across the hall, Max sees that Mr. Gonzales is also working on a unit about nature. Over the past few days, his class has been discussing the deer problem that has made the local news. Recently, a woman was seriously injured when her car ran into a deer. One of the students in class knew the injured woman and brought the topic up during a class discussion about ecology. The passion the class generated was so intense that Mr. Gonzales abandoned his usual field investigation of local stream water purity and allowed students to pursue their interest in the deer problem.

Today during Max's observation, students are debating some of the proposals brought up in the newspaper and on the radio. Mr. Gonzales is at the board, writing down the ideas. He writes each idea in a column labeled "Positives" or a column labeled "Negatives."

The class is discussing a plan that would make it illegal for residents to feed deer. Susan is animated in her disapproval of such a law. She says, "Our country is founded on freedom and property rights. You should be able to feed deer on your own property without having to ask anybody's permission." Mr. Gonzales writes "Ignores freedom and property rights" in the "Negatives" column.

"It's because people treat them like pets that causes the accidents," Carmen blurts out before she remembers to raise her hand. She is the girl who knows the injured woman. After writing her idea in the "Positives" column, as a "Safety concern," Mr. Gonzales hands out the following assignment:

> Using our class discussion, as well as ideas proposed in the newspaper or on the radio, write a proposal for dealing with the deer problem. You may combine the ideas we have read or talked about or come up with your own unique solution. Your proposal should be 300 to 400 words in length and be supported by sound reasons based on common sense and scientific principles. The final copy will be due in three days.

Summing Up

The main points in this chapter include the following:

Goals, Standards, and Objectives

1. *Goals* are expressions of societal values that provide a sense of direction broad enough to be accepted by large numbers of individuals.

2. *Standards* identify what will be learned from your instruction and energize and motivate you and your learners to achieve practical end products.

3. *Objectives* have two purposes: (1) to tie standards to specific classroom strategies that will achieve those standards and (2) to express teaching strategies in a format that allows you to measure their effects on your learners.

4. When the word *behavioral* precedes the word *objective,* the learning is being defined as a change in observable behavior that can be measured within a specified period of time.

5. The need for behavioral objectives stems from a natural preoccupation with teacher concerns for self and task, sometimes to the exclusion of concerns for the impact on students.

Steps in Preparing Behavioral Objectives

6. Simply put, behavioral objectives do the following:
   - Focus instruction on a specific goal, whose outcomes can be observed.
   - Identify the conditions under which learning can be expected to occur.
   - Specify the level or amount of behavior that can be expected from the instruction under the conditions specified.

7. Action verbs help operationalize the learning outcome expected from an objective and identify exactly what the learner must do to achieve the outcome.

8. The outcome specified in a behavioral objective should be expressed as an end (e.g., to identify, recall, list) and not as a means (e.g., to study, watch, listen).

9. If the observable learning outcome is to take place with particular materials, equipment, tools, or other resources, these conditions must be stated explicitly in the objective.

10. Conditional statements within a behavioral objective can be singular (one condition) or multiple (more than one condition).

11. The conditions stated should match those under which the behavior will be performed in the real world.

12. A *proficiency level* is the minimum degree of performance that will satisfy you that the objective has been met.

13. Proficiency levels represent value judgments, or educated guesses, as to what level of performance will be required for adequately performing the behavior in some setting beyond your classroom.

14. The *expressiveness* of an objective refers to the amount of flexibility allowed in a response. Less expressive objectives may call for only a single right answer, whereas more expressive objectives allow for less structured and more flexible responses. The expressiveness allowed is always a matter of degree.

The Cognitive, Affective, and Psychomotor Domains

15. The *complexity* of a behavior in the cognitive, affective, or psychomotor domain pertains to the operations required of the student to produce the behavior, not to the complexity of the teaching activities required.

16. Behaviors in the cognitive domain, from least to most complex, are knowledge, comprehension, application, analysis, synthesis, and evaluation.

17. Behaviors in the affective domain, from least to most complex, are receiving, responding, valuing, organization, and characterization.

18. Behaviors in the psychomotor domain, from least to most complex, are imitation, manipulation, precision, articulation, and naturalization.

Some Misunderstandings about Behavioral Objectives

19. Four important cautions in using the taxonomies of behavioral objectives are as follow:

   • No behavior is necessarily more or less desirable than any other.

   • Higher-order cognitive skills often are more authentic than lower-order cognitive skills.

   • Less complex behaviors are not necessarily easier to teach, less time consuming to teach, or dependent on fewer resources than are more complex behaviors.

   • Behavior in one domain may require achievement of one or more behaviors in other domains.

The Cultural Roots of Objectives

20. Behavioral objectives have their roots in the educational values we espouse as a nation. Texts, curricula, and department and school policies are interpretations of these values shared at the broadest national level and translated into practice through behavioral objectives.

Key Terms

Affective domain
Authentic behaviors
Authentic tests
Behavioral objective
Cognitive domain
Criterion level
Declarative (factual) knowledge

Expressive objective
Goals
Learning activities
Learning conditions
Learning outcome
Metacognitive knowledge
Objectives

Performance assessments
Procedural knowledge
Psychomotor domain
Rigor and relevance
  framework
Standards
Thinking curriculum

Discussion and Practice Questions

Questions marked with an asterisk are answered in Appendix B. Some asterisked questions may require student follow-up responses not included in Appendix B. Go to the Assignments and Activities section of the various topics on the MyEducationLab for your course to complete additional practice activities related to this chapter's content.

1. Select one of the ten InTASC standards identified in Chapter 1 and translate it into one or more objectives for your teacher preparation program. Make sure your objective is responsive to the standard from which it was derived.

*2. Identify the two general purposes for preparing behavioral objectives. If you had to choose one of these purposes as being more important to you, which would you choose? Why?

*3. Explain what three things the word *behavioral* implies when it appears before the word *objectives*.

*4. Identify three components of a well-written behavioral objective. Then give one example of each.

*5. Historically, why did the concept of behavioral objectives emerge?

*6. Why are action verbs necessary in translating goals such as producing *mentally healthy citizens, well-rounded individuals,* and *self-actualized schoolchildren* into learning outcomes?

*7. Distinguish learning outcomes (ends) from learning activities (means) by placing an O or A beside each of the following expressions:

Working on a car radio

Adding signed numbers correctly

Practicing the violin

Playing basketball

Using a microscope

Identifying an amoeba

Naming the seven parts of speech

Punctuating an essay correctly

*8. What is the definition of a condition in a behavioral objective. Give three examples.

*9. How can the specification of conditions help students study and prepare for tests?

*10. In trying to decide what condition(s) to include in a behavioral objective, what single most important consideration should guide your selection?

*11. What is the definition of *criterion level* in a behavioral objective? Give three examples.

*12. Group A below contains objectives. Group B contains levels of cognitive behavior. Match the levels in group B with the most appropriate objective in group A. Group B levels can be used more than once.

Group A: Objectives

1. Given a two-page essay, the student can identify the assumptions basic to the author's position.

2. The student will correctly spell the word *mountain.*

3. The student will convert the following English passage into Spanish.

4. The student will compose new pieces of prose and poetry according to the classification system emphasized in class.

5. Given a sinking passenger ship with 19 of its 20 lifeboats destroyed, the captain will decide, based on his or her perception of each individual's potential worth to society, whom to place on the last lifeboat.

Group B: Levels of Cognitive Behavior

a. knowledge　　**d.** analysis

b. comprehension　**e.** synthesis

c. application　　**f.** evaluation

Professional Practice

Field Experience and Practice Activities

1. Based on your experience in classrooms, provide examples of two behavioral objectives that differ in the degree of expressiveness they allow.

2. Using a topic you have observed being taught in the schools, write an objective for each level of the taxonomy of cognitive objectives: knowledge, comprehension, application, analysis, synthesis, and evaluation. Select verbs for each level from the list provided in the chapter.

3. Now exchange the objectives you have just written with a classmate. Have the classmate check each objective for (a) an observable behavior, (b) any special conditions under which the behavior must be displayed, and (c) a performance level considered sufficient to demonstrate mastery. Revise your objectives, if necessary.

4. A parent calls to tell you that based on a long talk with her son about the objectives you have written for health education, she disapproves of them, particularly those referring to the anatomy of the human body. However, you have taken the objectives almost verbatim from the teacher's guide to the adopted textbook. Compose a brief written response to this parent that shows your understanding of where objectives come from.

Digital Portfolio Activities

The following digital portfolio activities relate to InTASC Standards 6 and 7:

1. During your first teaching assignment or job interview, you may be asked to provide evidence of your ability to write behavioral objectives properly. The objectives you have written for the preceding Field Experience and Practice Activities 1 and 2 provide examples of your proficiency in writing objectives that represent (a) different degrees of expressiveness, following Eisner's (1969, 1998) view of objectives, and (b) the knowledge, comprehension, application, analysis, synthesis, and evaluation outcomes, following Bloom et al.'s (1984) view of behavioral objectives. Place these objectives in your digital portfolio in a folder titled "Behavioral Objectives."

2. To complete your knowledge of the various approaches to objectives, write objectives for a topic you are likely to teach that represent the categories of procedural knowledge and metacognitive knowledge suggested by Anderson and Krathwohl (2001). Also place these in your "Behavioral Objectives" digital portfolio folder.

MyEducationLab™

Go to MyEducationLab (www.myeducationlab.com) for Effective Teaching Methods: Research-Based Practice where you can:

- Find learning outcomes for the various course topics course along with national standards that connect to these outcomes.

- Complete **Assignments and Activities** that can help you more deeply understand the chapter content.

- Apply and practice your understanding of the core teaching skills identified in the chapter with **Building Teaching Skills and Dispositions** coaching activities.

- Check your comprehension of the content covered in the chapter with a book specific **Study Plan**. Here you will be able to take a chapter **pretest**, receive feedback on your answers, and then access personalized **Review, Practice, and Enrichment exercises** to enhance your understanding of chapter content. After you complete the exercises, take a **posttest** to confirm your comprehension.

- Learn how to address common classroom management issues in the **Simulations in Classroom Management**.

- Access video clips of CCSSO **National Teachers of the Year award winners** responding to the question, "Why Do I Teach?" in the Teacher Talk section.

- Create, update, and share quality lesson plans with the **Lesson Plan Builder**.

- Access state licensure test requirements, overviews of what tests cover, and sample test items in the **Certification and Licensure** section.

- Learn how to create a high quality teaching portfolio in the **Preparing a Portfolio** section.

- Access tips, advice, and other information on resume writing and interviewing, your first year of teaching, and law and public policies in the Beginning Your Career section.

6 Unit and Lesson Planning

This chapter will help you answer these questions and meet the following InTASC standards for effective teaching.

- How do I use state standards and curriculum guides to plan a lesson?
- How do I make a unit plan?
- What is in an effective lesson plan?
- How can I prepare lessons at or slightly above my learners' current level of understanding?
- How can my lessons provide differentiated instruction to meet the learning needs of individual students and those with special needs?

InTASC

STANDARD 4 **Content Knowledge.** The teacher understands the central concepts, tools of inquiry, and structures of the discipline(s) he or she teaches and creates learning experiences that make these aspects of the discipline accessible and meaningful for learners to assure mastery of the content.

STANDARD 5 **Application of Content.** The teacher understands how to connect concepts and use differing perspectives to engage learners in critical thinking, creativity, and collaborative problem solving related to authentic local and global issues.

STANDARD 7 **Planning for Instruction.** The teacher plans instruction that supports every student in meeting rigorous learning goals by drawing upon knowledge of content areas, curriculum, cross-disciplinary skills, and pedagogy, as well as knowledge of learners and the community context.

STANDARD 8 **Instructional Strategies.** The teacher understands and uses a variety of instructional strategies to encourage learners to develop deep understanding of content areas and their connections, and to build skills to apply knowledge in meaningful ways.

STANDARD 9 **Professional Learning and Ethical Practice.** The teacher engages in ongoing professional learning and uses evidence to continually evaluate his/her practice, particularly the effects of his/her choices and actions on others (learners, families, other professionals, and the community), and adapts practice to meet the needs of each learner.

Y ou are now ready to consider lesson planning and its relationship to the decisions you make in the classroom. Planning is the systematic process of deciding what and how your students should learn. Teachers make one such decision on an average of every two minutes they are teaching, according to an estimate by Clark and Peterson (1986). However, these "thinking on your feet" decisions represent only part of the decision-making process. Teachers also make many decisions about the form and content of their instruction, such as how much presenting, questioning, and discussing to do; how much material to cover in the allotted time; and how to differentiate instruction and reach students with special needs.

In Chapter 5, you saw the importance of establishing goals and objectives in the planning process. Now let's consider three other factors in the planning process: knowledge of your learners, knowledge of your subject matter, and knowledge of teaching methods.

Teacher as Decision Maker

As a beginning teacher, you will need four inputs to the planning process to complete your unit and lesson plans: knowledge of goals and objectives, knowledge of your learners, knowledge of the subject matter, and knowledge of teaching methods.

Knowledge of Instructional Goals and Objectives

Chapter 5 noted that before you can prepare a lesson, you must decide on your instructional goals and objectives. These planning decisions are crucial for developing effective lesson plans, because they give structure to lesson planning and, as we saw in Chapter 5, tie it to important sources of societal values and professional standards. In this chapter, we present unit and lesson plans as tools for tying these values and standards to your classroom.

Knowledge of Learners

Reviews of research on planning by Clark and Peterson (1986) and Marzano, Pickering, and Heflebower (2010) have found that teachers report spending more of their time (an average of 43 percent) planning instruction around the characteristics of their learners than around any other area of consideration (for example, assessment, classroom management, or the curriculum). Recall from Chapter 2 that some of the characteristics of your learners that will influence your instruction are their specific abilities, prior knowledge, learning styles, and home and family lives. These are the "windows" through which you will see the special needs of your learners and begin to plan for them.

Planning with respect to your learners begins by consciously noting their unique abilities and experiences that can provide you the opportunity to select content, materials, objectives, and methods that match their current level of understanding and meet their special learning needs. This knowledge will be instrumental in helping you organize, select, sequence, and allocate time to various topics of instruction.

Knowledge of Subject Matter

A third input to the planning process is knowledge of your academic discipline and grade level. As a student, you have spent much time and effort becoming knowledgeable in the subjects you will teach. You have observed and absorbed valuable information about how textbook authors, your instructors, subject-matter specialists, and your state's education standards have organized concepts in your teaching area. This information includes how parts of a subject relate to the whole, how content is prioritized, how transitions are made between topics, and which themes are major and which are minor. Consciously reflecting on this content organization—as presented by subject-matter specialists, state standards, and curriculum guides—when preparing your lessons will make learning for your students easier, more orderly, and more conducive to retention and later use. Deriving your content organization from these sources also can be instrumental in helping you select, sequence, and allocate time for what you will teach.

Knowledge of Teaching Methods

A fourth input to the planning process will be your knowledge of teaching methods. With this knowledge comes an awareness of different teaching strategies with which you can implement the key and helping behaviors introduced in Chapter 1. Also included under teaching methods are your decisions about the following:

- Appropriate pacing or tempo (the speed at which you introduce new material)
- Mode of presentation (direct presentation versus group discussion versus web based instruction)
- Class arrangement (small groups, full class, independent work)
- Classroom management (raise hand, speak out)

Your decisions pertaining to the above four inputs to planning should work together to form a well thought out plan from which you will teach your lesson objectives.

Pedagogical Content Knowledge

Shulman (1992) identified four specific sources from which you can obtain knowledge about standards and objectives, learners, subject matter, and teaching methods: from (1) practical experiences, such as viewing classroom videos, observing in classrooms, and student teaching; (2) reading case studies about what more successful teachers do in the classroom; (3) reading the professional literature about important goals and standards and paradigms for thinking about teaching; and (4) reading research studies about your subject and how to teach it. Each of these is a valuable source for extending and updating your knowledge of learners, content, and teaching methods. The chapters ahead will present key findings for effective teaching from each of these four areas.

Along with these sources of knowledge, Shulman (1987) introduced the concept of Pedagogical Content Knowledge (or PCK). Shulman noted that a teacher's subject knowledge and pedagogical (methods) knowledge were being treated as mutually exclusive domains (knowledge areas 1 and 4 above) in many teacher education programs. The consequences of such a dichotomy led to the development of teacher education programs in which the focus on subject matter and pedagogy were treated separately as different courses and subjects, and, therefore, often failed to consider the necessary relationship between the two. PCK is another type of knowledge important for effective teaching that combines these formerly separate knowledge bases into a single knowledge base that can help teachers know what teaching approaches best fit the subject matter being taught (for example, math versus science; language arts versus social studies) and know how the teaching of different elements of a subject can be enhanced with the use of certain teaching methods (for example, methods for teaching facts versus concepts versus principles). PCK focuses on the identification of pedagogical techniques that make subject matter easier to learn. It also represents the blending of content and pedagogy into an understanding of how particular topics or problems should be organized and adapted to the diverse interests and abilities of learners. These developments have led to the now widely accepted practice that specific content methods courses should follow a general methods course to better prepare teachers for the pedagogical content knowledge they will need to teach effectively in their specific fields.

Reflective Practice and Tacit Knowledge

As a beginning teacher, you probably regard your content and method knowledge as hard won during four or more long years of professional training. To be sure, it is—but you have only just begun. Your knowledge of content and methods will change with the interaction of your formal university training and your actual classroom experience.

Figure 6.1 **Inputs to the Planning Process**

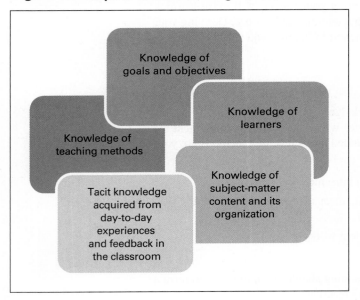

This change will result in what is called **reflective practice**, fueled by your tacit, or personal, knowledge gained from your day-to-day experience (Canning, 1991; Gill, 2000; Polanyi, 1958; York-Barr, Sommers, Ghere, & Montie, 2006). **Tacit knowledge** represents your reflection on what works in your classroom, discovered over time and through personal experience. Through everyday experiences, such as observing and consulting with other teachers as a participant in your school's professional learning community, teaching, lesson planning, and testing and grading, you will accumulate tacit knowledge and reflect on new ways of doing things that can guide your actions as effectively as knowledge from texts and formal training. This knowledge, if you take the time to reflect on it, will add to the quality of your planning and decision making by bringing variety and flexibility to your lessons, leading to revisions and refinements that can improve your unit and lesson planning. Tacit knowledge, because it comes from your own experience, can make your planning less rigid and repetitious and, over time, add fresh insights to your personal teaching style. Thus we add this fifth input to the planning process, shown in Figure 6.1.

Unit and Lesson Plans

The important process of unit and lesson planning begins with implementing the five planning inputs in Figure 6.1. This stage of the planning process takes a **system perspective**, meaning your lessons will be part of a larger system of interrelated learning, called a *unit*.

The word *system* brings to mind terms such as *school system, mental health system,* and *legal system.* Schools, mental health services, and criminal justice agencies are supposed to work as systems. This means their component parts are to interrelate and build toward some unified concept. For example, in a school system, discrete facts, skills, and understandings learned at the completion of the sixth grade are not only important in themselves but also for successfully completing the seventh grade. Seventh-grade outcomes, in turn, are important for completing the eighth grade and so on through the educational system, until the high school graduate has accumulated many of the facts, skills, and understandings necessary for adult living.

The true strength of a system, however, is that the whole is greater than the sum of its parts. Can a unit of instruction comprising individual lessons ever add up to anything more than the sum of the individual lessons? This sounds like getting something for nothing, a concept that does not ring true. But if the system of individual lessons really can produce outcomes in learners that are greater than the sum of the outcomes of the individual lessons, then another ingredient must be needed.

That missing ingredient is the relationship among the individual lessons. This relationship must allow the outcome of one lesson to build on the outcomes of preceding lessons. Knowledge, skills, and understandings evolve gradually through the joint contribution of many lessons arranged to build toward more and more complex outcomes. It is this invisible but all-important relationship among the parts of an instructional unit that allows the unit outcomes to be greater than the sum of the lesson outcomes.

Of considerable importance is the *relationship* of your district's curriculum guide to your unit and lesson plans. Units generally extend over an instructional time period of approximately one to four weeks. They usually correspond to well-defined topics or themes in the curriculum guide. Lessons, however, are considerably shorter, spanning a single class period or occasionally two or three periods. Because lessons are relatively short, they are harder to associate with particular segments of a curriculum guide. This means you can expect unit content to be fairly well structured and defined but lesson content—what you do on any given day—to be much less detailed in a curriculum guide.

Figure 6.2 **Flow of Teaching Content from the State Level to the Classroom Level**

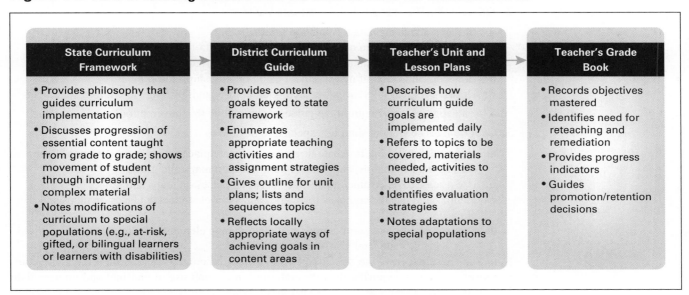

This is as it should be, because the arrangement of day-to-day content in the classroom must be flexible to meet your individual students' needs, your instructional tools and preferences, and special priorities and initiatives in your school and community. So although the overall picture at the unit level may be clear from the district's curriculum guide, at the lesson level, you must apply considerable independent thought, organization, and judgment. Figure 6.2 indicates the flow of teaching content from the state level to the classroom, illustrating the stages through which a curriculum framework is translated into unit and lesson plans.

Making Planning Decisions

Unit planning, therefore, begins with the experiences of your learners and their learning needs to inform the design of your lessons, followed by an understanding of your state's standards, the content you will teach, and the teaching methods from which you can choose. Let's take a closer look at several types of decisions you will make pertaining to these inputs to the lesson-planning process.

Standards and Objectives

State standards and **curriculum guides** derived from the grade, subject, and school district levels clearly specify the content that must be covered and in what period of time. But they may be far less prescriptive about the specific lesson activities and outcomes that students are expected to acquire. For example, an excerpt from a curriculum guide for English-language instruction might take this form:

1. *Writing concepts and skills.* The student shall be expected to learn
   a. The composing process
   b. Descriptive, narrative, and expository paragraphs
   c. Multiple paragraph compositions
   d. Persuasive discourse
   e. Meanings and uses of colloquialism, slang, idiom, and jargon

Or for a life science curriculum, the guide might provide the following:

2. *Life science.* The student shall be expected to learn

    a. Skills in acquiring data through the senses
    b. Classification skills in ordering and sequencing data
    c. Oral and written communication of data in appropriate form
    d. Concepts and skills of measurement using relationships and standards
    e. Drawing logical inferences, predicting outcomes, and forming generalized statements

And for a geography curriculum, the guide might include this information:

3. *Geography.* The student shall be expected to be able to

    a. Use cardinal and intermediate directions to locate places such as the Amazon River, Himalayan Mountains, and Washington, D.C., on maps and globes
    b. Use a scale to determine the distance between places on maps and globes
    c. Identify and use the compass rose, grid, and symbols to locate places on maps and globes
    d. Draw maps of places and regions that contain map elements, including a title, compass rose, legend, scale, and grid system

Notice in these excerpts the specificity with which the content is identified (e.g., the composing process; skills in acquiring data through the senses; and use of cardinal and intermediate directions). In contrast, note the lack of specificity concerning the learning activity and behavioral outcome (e.g., knowledge, comprehension, application, analysis, synthesis, or evaluation) to which the instruction might be directed. This is typical of many curriculum guides and provides you the flexibility of using backward lesson design to differentiate instruction by offering learners choices in the complexity of content with which a learning task will begin that matches their current level of understanding and from which every learner can experience academic success. Recalling the taxonomy of behavior in the cognitive domain in Chapter 5, you could ask the following questions:

- For which of these content areas and for which students will the simple *recall* of facts be sufficient?
- For which areas and which students will *comprehension* of those facts be required?
- For which areas and which students will *application* of what the student comprehends be expected?
- For which areas and which students will *higher-level outcomes* involving analysis, synthesis, and decision-making skills be desired?

Notice how student outcomes precede content or activity selection. As suggested by backward lesson design, your lesson planning begins with student outcomes or what you want to and can realistically achieve. Therefore, one of the most important decisions you will make will be to select the level(s) of learning outcome(s) for which an instructional unit or lesson will be prepared and to what extent differentiated activities and outcomes may be needed for individual learners, groups, and students with special needs. The flexibility afforded by most curriculum guides in selecting the learning outcomes to which instruction can be directed and from which students most benefit is both purposeful and advantageous for you. For the curriculum guide to be adapted to the realities of your classroom, a wide latitude of expected outcomes must be possible. These will depend on the unique characteristics and individual differences among your students, the content and time you can devote to a specific topic, and the overall learning outcomes desired at the unit level. Let's look at each of these more closely.

Learners

As we have seen, your lesson planning begins with what your learners know, what they can learn, and what experiences and abilities they bring to your classroom. And, as we have seen, curriculum guides typically allow you the flexibility to adapt your instruction to the individual learning needs of your students. Chapter 2 presented several categories of individual differences that will be characteristic of the learners in your classroom. These include differences in ability (including physical, learning, visual, and communication disabilities, which may represent special learning needs), prior achievement, learning style, culture, and home life. These factors can reflect entire classrooms as well as individuals. Other categories of learners—such as at-risk, bilingual, and gifted students—may add even greater diversity to your classroom. They may create the need for task-related subgroups that require individual attention, time-limited groups of higher- and lower-performing learners, or differentiated instruction for individual learners—all alternatives that will be addressed in this and chapters to come.

For now, review the suggestions that Lipson and Wixson (2012) and Wiggins and McTighe (2005) outline regarding learner factors that need to be considered in pre-lesson planning:

- Prior Content Knowledge—What prior content knowledge can be capitalized on and what knowledge needs to be taught first to maximize student engagement?
- Knowledge about Reading and Writing—Do the students have the reading and writing skills needed to be successful?
- Attitudes and Motivation—Does the instruction tap into student interests, promoting positive attitudes and motivation?
- Correlates of Reading and Writing Performance:
  - Social and Emotional Development—Is the instruction sensitive to any social or emotional issues the students may be dealing with? Do the students have the maturity level needed for the concepts addressed?
  - Language Development—Does language structure or vocabulary knowledge need to be taught before other subject matter content?
  - Physical Development—Are there any students with physical impairments (e.g., hearing) that need to be accommodated?
  - Cognitive Development—Do the students have the memory development (i.e., short term, long term, and working) to manage the content load?

Content

Perhaps foremost in the mind of the beginning teacher is the content to be taught. And, as we have seen, content follows an understanding of your learners. Your content decisions may appear easy, in that textbooks, workbooks, and curriculum guides appear to identify what you will teach before your first day in the classroom. Indeed, as you saw in the excerpts from the curriculum guides, content often is designated in considerable detail. Textbooks and workbooks carry this detail further by offering activities and exercises that define and expand upon the content in the curriculum guide. From this perspective, it may appear as if all of the content has been handed to you, if not on a silver platter, then surely in readily accessible and highly organized tests, workbooks, and curriculum materials.

Although some teachers might wish this were true, most quickly realize that as many decisions must be made about content—what to teach—as about learning needs and outcomes. You will quickly come to realize that adopted texts, workbooks, and even detailed curriculum guides identify the content to be taught but do not select, organize, and sequence content or activities according to the needs of your learners. Increasingly, school districts, textbook publishers, and software companies are providing alternative texts, instructional software, and workbooks with which teachers can better target specific populations of learners. Effective teachers know they must select from this content for some learning outcomes and learners, add to this content for others, and choose activities that engage all students in the learning process at or slightly above their current level of understanding.

Outcomes

Establishing relationships between your lessons is one of the most important planning decisions you will make to achieve your desired outcomes. How your lessons interrelate can even determine if and how well your learners achieve higher-level outcomes in the cognitive, affective, and psycho-motor domains. And this decision in turn will determine how well your unit and lesson plans reflect a thinking curriculum.

The higher levels of behavior can rarely if ever be achieved in a single lesson. Thus lessons must be placed within a unit, or system of lessons, in which individual lessons build on previously taught outcomes to achieve higher-order outcomes at the end of a unit. This is why your structuring of lesson content is so important to unit planning: Without it, the outcomes at the end of the unit may be no different from those achieved at the completion of each single lesson. Unlike miscellaneous items stored in the attic of your house or the glove compartment of your car, units should have a coherent, unified theme that rises above the cognitive, affective, and psychomotor outcomes of any single lesson.

For example, the reason you organize a particular series of lessons (e.g., on acid rain, new technologies, and conservation legislation) might be to show how several content areas can be brought together with a single theme for the purpose of solving a problem, thinking critically, or forming an independent judgment. In this case, the unit goal and needs of your learners will have played an important role in selecting this particular organization. The success of your unit will depend on the match between the level of learning outcomes you choose and your students' current level of understanding of the content you are teaching.

Now let's put your knowledge of objectives, learners, content, and organization to work in preparing unit and lesson plans.

Disciplinary and Interdisciplinary Unit Planning

The following two sections introduce unit plans and how to communicate them in a clear and orderly manner. The first approach to unit planning will show you how to plan and teach knowledge and understanding within a discipline—or vertically. **Vertical unit planning** is a method of developing units within a discipline in which the content to be taught is arranged hierarchically or in steps (e.g., from least to most complex, or from concrete to abstract) and presented in an order that ensures that all task-relevant prior knowledge required for subsequent lessons has been taught in previous lessons.

Following our discussion of disciplinary unit planning, we present a second means of communicating knowledge and understanding to your learners called *interdisciplinary unit planning,* which involves a technique called *lateral planning*. **Lateral unit planning** can be used for planning units that integrate bodies of knowledge across disciplines or content areas to convey relationships, patterns, and concepts that run across disciplines and bind different aspects of our world in some systematic way. Lateral unit plans move across the established boundaries of content areas to elicit problem solving, critical thinking, cooperative activity, and independent thought and action, emphasizing that the whole is greater than the sum of its parts. As you will see, both vertical and lateral unit planning are valuable tools for acquiring the skills of an effective teacher and meeting the unique needs of your learners.

Disciplinary (Vertical) Unit Plans

An old Chinese proverb states, "A picture is worth a thousand words." This section applies this age-old idea to unit planning by showing how you can develop a unit plan by creating a visual blueprint of your unit. This section also shows you how to use written and graphic formats to express a unit plan within a discipline, subject, or content area.

Of course, a visual device cannot substitute for a written description or outline of what you plan to teach, but it is an effective means of organizing your thinking about what you will teach. Scientists, administrators, engineers, and business executives have long known the value of visuals in the form of flowcharts, organization charts, blueprints, diagrams, and mindmaps (Buzan, 2004; Kenny, 2004; Mintzes, Wandersee, & Novak, 2000) to convey the essence of a concept, if not the details. From the beginning, teachers have used this basic method too. Pictures not only communicate the results of planning but are useful during the planning process to organize and revise a unit plan and to see the "big picture," or final outcome, you are working hard to achieve.

Although teaching parallels many other fields by using visual devices in planning, it is also a unique profession in many ways. Unlike that of a business, the product of education does not roll off an assembly line, nor does education build its product using the mathematical laws and physical materials used by the scientist and engineer. Consequently, your visual blueprints differ from those of others but at the same time reflect the qualities that have made pictures so important to planning in these other professions.

You already know about two of these qualities: the concept of *hierarchy,* which shows the relationship of the parts to the whole (lessons to unit), and the concept of *task-relevant prior knowledge,* which shows the prior knowledge necessity for a certain lesson sequence. In vertical unit planning, both concepts are put to work in creating a visual picture of a unit. Such a picture can both stimulate and organize your thoughts and communicate the results to others in an easy-to-follow graphic format.

Two simple rules are used in drawing a picture of a vertically planned unit. The first is to diagram how the unit goal is divided into specific lessons. The second is to show the sequence of these lessons and how their outcomes build on one another to achieve the unit goal. Let's look at these two rules.

Visualizing Specific Teaching Activities. Our first rule simply uses boxes to visualize areas of content—or instructional goals—at various levels of generality. In other words, any goal at the unit level can be broken into its component parts at the lesson level. Those component parts represent everything that is important for attaining the goal. This idea is illustrated in Figure 6.3.

Notice that Figure 6.3 has three levels. For now, focus on the top and bottom levels. The top shows the unit goal, which is derived from the curriculum guide and adopted textbook, which in turn are based on societal, state, and local goals. The bottom row shows content expressed at a level specific enough to prepare individual lessons.

This unit plan ends with bite-sized chunks that together exhaust the content specified at the higher levels. Just as in the story "Goldilocks and the Three Bears," the bottom of the unit plan hierarchy must end with the portion of content being served up as not too big and not too small—but

Figure 6.3 Example of a Hierarchy of Reading Content at Different Levels of Specificity

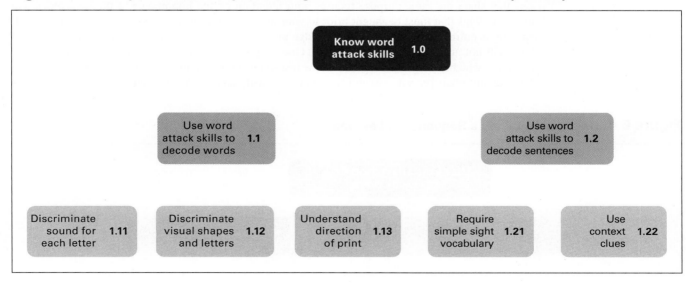

just right for individual lesson planning. How can you know whether you have achieved the right size and balance for a single lesson?

The second level of Figure 6.3 shows a logical means of getting from the general unit goal to specific lesson content. It is an intermediate thinking process that produces the lower level of just-right-sized pieces. How many intermediate levels should you have? There is no magic number; it depends on how broadly the initial goal is stated and the number of steps needed to produce content in just the right amounts for individual lesson plans. Experience and judgment are the best guides, although logical divisions within the curriculum guide and text are helpful, too.

In some cases, the route from unit to lesson content can be very direct (two levels); in other instances, several levels may have to be worked through before arriving at lesson-sized chunks. If you have trouble getting sufficiently specific for lesson-sized content, you may need to revise the unit goal by dividing it into two or more subgoals and beginning a new hierarchy from each subgoal. This was done in Figure 6.3, where the unit planner had to create two units of instruction (1.1 and 1.2) from the same goal (1.0). Notice that this is done in the same way you create an outline. This process of building a content hierarchy will guide you in making the proper distinction between unit and lesson content that is not too big and not too small that can prevent you from making false starts in lesson planning.

Visualizing the Sequence of Activities.   The second rule shows the sequence of lessons and how lesson outcomes build on one another to achieve a unit goal. This second rule, illustrated in Figure 6.4, shows the order of the individual lessons, when order is important. Notice that in Figure 6.4, we chose the first box from the second level (1.1) of the hierarchy in Figure 6.3 as our unit goal. Then, to indicate the intended unit outcome, we placed an arrow extending from the right of this top box. The outcome of all the lessons derived from it, taken together, should be the same as this unit outcome. This will always be true, regardless of whether the sequence of your lessons is important. In some instances, this sequence may be unimportant (see Figure 6.5); for others, a partial sequence may be appropriate (see Figure 6.6).

This second rule recognizes how previous lessons can modify or constrain the outcomes of subsequent lessons. It encourages you to build on previously taught learning to provide increasingly more authentic and higher-order thinking outcomes, as called for by the rigor and relevance framework presented in Chapter 5. This will be important if your unit plan is to reflect a thinking curriculum. If your lesson outcomes are unrelated, your unit outcome will not likely be at any higher level of cognitive, affective, or psychomotor complexity than your individual lesson outcomes. As an effective teacher, you should plan the interrelationships among lessons in a way that encourages higher-order thinking to emerge at the unit level. For this you will want to consult the Higher-Order Thinking and Problem-Solving Checklist in Appendix C.

Visualizing your unit plan has several advantages. Seeing a lesson in context with other lessons that share the same purpose focuses your attention on the importance of the knowledge and understandings that must be taught prior to your lesson for it to be a success. If learners have inadequately acquired the prerequisite knowledge and skills relevant to your lesson, some or most of them will not attain your lesson objective. One purpose of seeing lessons within a unit plan is to determine whether you have provided all the task-relevant prior knowledge required by each lesson. Because unit plans precede lesson plans, you can easily add the overlooked lessons and objectives

Figure 6.4 **Unit Plan Showing a Sequence of Lessons**

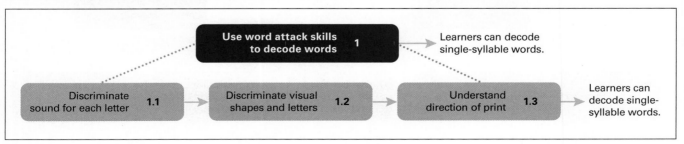

Figure 6.5 **Unit Plan without Lesson Sequence**

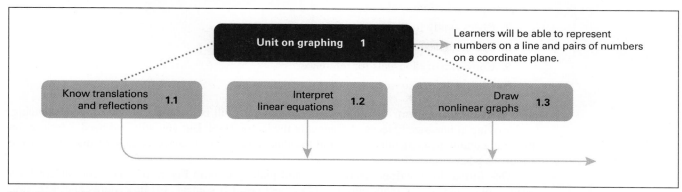

Note: Lessons 1.1, 1.2, and 1.3 can occur in any order.

Figure 6.6 **Unit Plan with Partial Lesson Sequence**

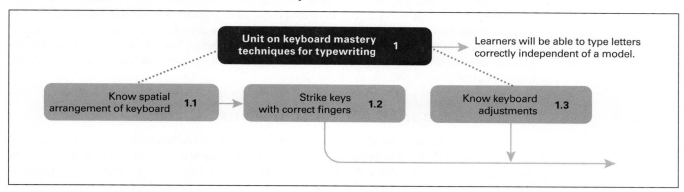

Note: Lesson 1.1 must precede Lesson 1.2.

prerequisite to later lessons. You can draw your unit plans graphically, as shown in this chapter, using the word-processing or graphics software on your personal computer or using Inspiration Software (www.inspiration.com/home.cfm).

While the graphic format of your lesson plan sequence shows what content must be taught before other content, it does not indicate the possible need to differentiate instruction for individual learners and groups or to reach special populations. Now you must ask, "What might be the role of language development, special learner needs, and even home environment on my learners' ability to profit from the lessons and exercises I have planned?" For example, would a learner's physical, hearing, communication, or visual impairment; language development; home life or culture; or prior learning history preclude his or her engagement with the lesson? When these learner characteristics are sufficiently instrumental to your transmission of content and the learner's ability to profit from it, they should be added at the bottom of your graphic unit plan to indicate the media and technology, web based resources, and supplemental materials that may be needed to differentiate instruction and reach special-needs learners.

Following is a list of some supplemental materials and strategies identified by teachers on their graphic unit plans reminding them of opportunities for differentiated instruction and how they might better accommodate special learner needs. These were added beneath the lessons to which they were relevant with codes such as 1, 2, 3, and so on:

1. Use bilingual handouts.
2. Provide extra time for students with ADHD.
3. Use small groups for G & T (gifted and talented) students.
4. Partner up for PD (physically disabled) students.

5. Assign computer lessons for remedial work.

6. Open a dictionary station.

7. Check orally for LP (lower performers).

8. Pair students for homework assistance.

9. Copy oversized visuals for reference.

10. Allow LPs to choose their own response formats.

The Written Unit Plan. Planning units graphically will be helpful in organizing, sequencing, and arriving at bite-sized pieces of content at the lesson level. But you will also need a description that will communicate details of the unit to others and that you can place in your digital portfolio for use at a later time.

One format for a written version of a unit plan appears in Figure 6.7. This format divides a written plan into its (1) main purpose, (2) objectives, (3) content, (4) procedures and activities, (5) instructional aids or resources, and (6) assessment methods. You should attach your visual blueprint to this written plan to indicate at a glance the organization, sequence, and size of the unit and to provide an introduction and overview of the written details. Together they will give you an effective tool for communicating your unit plan.

Finally, notice that in Figure 6.7, both the performance objectives (1–7) and individual learners progress from the lower levels of cognitive and psychomotor complexity (comprehension, application, imitation) to the higher levels (analysis, synthesis, precision). This illustrates how early lessons in a unit can be used as building blocks to attain higher-level outcomes, helping to achieve a thinking curriculum (Borich, 2007b; Erickson, 2006).

Interdisciplinary (Lateral) Unit Plans

Results of research indicate that teaching a unit in which different content areas are organized around a central theme and integrated with one another can lead to high levels of thinking and meaningful learning (Drake, 2007; Erickson, 2006; National Research Council, 2001; Roblyer, 2005).

An **interdisciplinary unit** is a laterally planned unit of study in which topics are integrated to provide a focus on a specific theme (Martinello & Cook, 2000; Roberts & Kellough, 2006). This approach to learning helps students make connections across subjects, themes, and concepts. The principal aim of interdisciplinary instruction is to present learners with an opportunity to discover relationships and patterns that go beyond a specific discipline and that bind different aspects of our world in some systematic way. For example, interdisciplinary units often represent themes that can be related to several different subject matter areas at the same time, such as English and reading, science, social studies, or the expressive arts. Effective interdisciplinary units also often require learners to conduct investigations that require cooperative learning and the use of reference and search tools.

Now let's return to the rigor and relevance framework and the cognitive domain presented in Chapter 5 to show how these two ideas can be brought together to help plan an interdisciplinary unit or lesson. Recall that "rigor" refers to a lesson or unit plan that makes your students think deeply about a problem, analyze new situations, and interpret and synthesize knowledge. In other words, rigor refers to a lesson or unit plan that expects your students to exhibit higher order thinking behaviors beginning with application, analysis, and synthesis and ending with evaluation. Also, recall that "relevance" refers to a lesson or unit plan that expects your students to value what you have taught beyond school, addresses a problem of contemporary importance, and builds on students' life experiences. In other words, a lesson or unit plan that has relevance expects your student to exhibit higher order thinking behaviors that are consistent with how one thinks in the context of authentic real-world events.

Interdisciplinary units provide ideal opportunities for classroom dialogue, in which learners are expected to reason critically, ask higher order questions, make predictions, and, with the aid of the teacher, evaluate the appropriateness of their own responses. Recent trends in interdisciplinary

Figure 6.7 Example of a Unit Plan

Grade: 6

Unit Topic: Making Healthy Food Choices

Course/Discipline: Health for the 21st Century

Approximate Time Required: Three Weeks

Main Purpose of the Unit Study: The purpose of this unit is to ensure students recognize how the nutritional value of food affects their ability to perform well in school and in sports and contributes to their overall well-being—physically, emotionally, socially, and mentally. Students will develop skills for making healthy food choices as well as planning for menus, shopping for nutritious foods, and preparing food safely.

Performance Objectives

The student will be able to:

1. Identify and discuss the nutritional value in the basic food groups depicted on the Food Guide Pyramid and the ChooseMyPlate guidelines.
2. Track the calories eaten daily for a period of three weeks and compare these logs to the recommended food group choices in the Food Guide Pyramid and ChooseMyPlate guidelines.
3. Review the typical diets of most pre-adolescents and plan menus for healthy eating.
4. Examine ways to shop for food that is affordable and nutritious and that align with healthy menu planning.
5. Describe ways to practice food safety.
6. Engage in hands-on food preparation that demonstrates healthy food choices.
7. Select healthy food choices from prepared menus and substitute more nutritional foods in menu samples that can be improved.

Lesson Outlines

A. Introduce the Food Guide Pyramid and Choose My Plate guidelines
   a. Review food groups
   b. Compare recommendations for daily nutrition including the Food Guide Pyramid vs. Choose My Plate

B. Food diaries
   a. Discuss caloric counts of foods
   b. Find nutritional labels on food

   c. Learn to track foods/calories/food groups with prepared template

C. Typical diets for preadolescents
   a. Review newspaper/journal articles
   b. Prepare to discuss influences on students' diets

D. Making choices when food shopping
   a. Virtual field trips and creative activities to shop for food
   b. Compare prices vs. nutritional value

E. Food safety and food preparation
   a. Small group prep
   b. Demonstrations

F. Menu comparisons

Procedures and Activities

1. Prepare template for logging individual daily food intake
2. Small collaborative group work and large group discussions
3. Individual and student pairing for online activities
4. Food safety and food prep demonstrations
5. Cutting and pasting activities for menu planning

Instructional Aids or Resources

1. Use free and accessible online materials from http://www.choosemyplate.gov/videos.html http://www.cnpp.usda.gov/Publications/MyPyramid/OriginalFoodGuidePyramids/FGP/FGPPamphlet.pdf
2. Locate current supermarket circulars with food prices including for vegetables and fruits.
3. Review food safety on http://www.foodsafety.gov/
4. Seek nutritional education materials from http://fnic.nal.usda.gov/professional-and-career-resources/nutrition-education/sources-nutrition-education-materials
5. Find examples of healthy diets for children. Example: http://www.mayoclinic.com/health/nutrition-for-kids/NU00606

Evaluation

1. Activity and small group performance
2. Project-based activity
3. Unit test

Source: Based on Copyright © 1982 by R and E Research Associates.

thematic teaching can help teachers achieve these goals but only if the themes that organize the unit are chosen carefully and in ways that help students understand how the content connects to their own lives (Ritter, 1999).

One way of accomplishing these goals is to teach how knowledge and understandings apply to and travel across different disciplines evoking increasingly higher order behaviors at the application, analysis, synthesis, and evaluation levels. For example, Roberts and Kellough (2006) describe one teacher who planned an interdisciplinary unit for her middle school students by having them read a story about a young boy who travels through time and journeys to a fantasy planet. As the boy struggles to adapt to his new culture, he experiences isolation, loneliness, domination, and imprisonment. To relate this story to several different disciplines based on students' reading, the teacher planned a unit in which the following relationships were drawn between and within disciplines, evoking higher order thinking:

- *Related to English.* The students discussed changes in the novel's setting, the development of the plot, and the author's use of the literary device of foreshadowing.
- *Related to the expressive arts.* The students made a model of the planet and a floor plan of some of the buildings, and they designed a robot that was described in the story. They also staged a dramatic reenactment of a scene in the novel.
- *Related to science.* Some students studied the flora and fauna on the planet and compared it to the plants and animals of their own state; others attempted to determine the chemical composition of the environment on the planet and identify a probable location for it in our solar system.
- *Related to social studies.* The students engaged in a map study of the planet, developed a government for the fantasy planet, compared the segregation practiced in the story with segregation elsewhere, compared the freedoms of the inhabitants on the planet with the freedoms in our own Bill of Rights, and discussed issues of prejudice and class structure.
- *Related to additional research.* The students studied popular research on dreams and experiments about the sleep of humans, which played a predominant role in the story.

Notice how the relationships and patterns and levels of thinking across subject areas in this unit did not just happen. This teacher developed her unit from a carefully constructed list of interrelated themes and behaviors that she could select from and add to that would involve students at increasingly higher order levels of thinking when determining the areas of the curriculum to be taught. To prepare her unit plan, the teacher used a set of thematic concepts, topics, and categories like that shown in Table 6.1. This information was mapped onto the existing subject matter and realms of thinking in this teacher's and other teachers' classrooms and brought to life through an interdisciplinary thematic unit.

In this manner interdisciplinary units can help you achieve the following objectives:

- Emphasize that the process of learning is sometimes best pursued as an interconnected whole, rather than as a series of specific subjects.
- Encourage students to work cooperatively in partnerships and small groups that focus on the social values of learning outside of the classroom.
- Teach students to be independent problem solvers and thinkers.
- Assist students to expand their own individual interests and learning styles.

Table 6.1 Theme Development for an Interdisciplinary Unit

Thematic Concept	Topic	Category of Literature
Freedom	Individual	Autobiographies
Cooperation	Society	Dreams
Challenge	Community	Fantasies
Conflict	Relationships	Tall Tales
Discovery	Global Concerns	Experiences
Culture	War	Firsthand Accounts
Change	Partnerships	
Perseverance		

- By focusing on higher order thinking needed in an authentic context, help students determine on their own what they need to know and what they need to learn, rather than always expect the teacher to give it to them.

A key component of **thematic units** is the varied structure of the instructional strategies used. For example, you can give your students a variety of activities and materials in several related content areas along with some challenging questions to facilitate collaboration and create a desire to learn more about a topic. Or you can have students work independently at times but also collaborate in groups to read, pose and investigate problems, and complete projects related to two or three different content areas. One group investigates a problem from one content area, while another group takes a different perspective. In this way, students interact and learn from each other. Your role is that of a facilitator or moderator of learning.

The Spectrum of Integrated Curricula.   Roberts and Kellough (2006) identify four ways you can implement **integrated thematic teaching** in your classroom, representing different degrees of involvement (Drake, 2007; Parkay & Hass, 2005).

Level 1.   At this level, you would use a thematic approach to relate content and material from various content areas during the same day. For example, the theme "Natural Disasters Cause Social Effects" could originate from the topic of "Weather," normally taught within a science or geography lesson, and the topic of "Community," normally taught within a social studies lesson. You would convey the theme of this interdisciplinary lesson to learners at the beginning of the unit in the form of a question, such as "What necessary functions in a community are often disrupted after a natural disaster?" Encourage students to suggest adding other content and questions.

Level 2.   The next level of implementation requires you to consult with other teachers and agree on a common theme. Each teacher who decides to participate in the interdisciplinary unit teaches to that theme in his or her own classroom. In this manner, students learn from a teacher in one classroom something that is related to what they are learning in another classroom. In Chapter 3 we saw this interactive interdisciplinary school dialogue to be the hallmark of a professional learning community in which teachers participate in decision-making, have a shared sense of purpose, engage in collaborative work, and accept joint responsibility for the outcome. Interdisciplinary sharing has been one of the most effective characteristics of a professional learning community and one of its most cited goals (DuFour, DuFour, Eaker, & Many, 2010). In the elementary grades a single teacher can perform this same function by referring back, say, during reading instruction to a related concept in social studies, math, or science. Display on the bulletin board a list of themes developed beforehand based on interconnections among subject areas to remind both you and your learners to identify and discuss the connections, and then have students make the connections with examples of their work.

Level 3.   At the third level, you and your students work together to form a list of common themes across subject areas. For example, in the later elementary and high school grades, you might give an assignment to search the table of contents of your text and those of other teachers for topics of thematic units you might teach in your classroom. If other teachers agree on the theme developed, they, too, can be encouraged to mutually reinforce the connections identified in their classrooms, thereby providing momentum across disciplines for your thematic unit. This level of implementation is an effective way to initiate a team approach to your interdisciplinary teaching and professional learning community.

Level 4.   At the fourth level, your students develop on their own a list of common themes or problems across disciplines. Your charge to students is to arrive at one or more themes in which a traditional subject, discipline, or content area would be inadequate for addressing the theme or resolving a problem. In other words, you instruct your students to find current, contemporary dilemmas, moral issues, and problems that defy solution in the context of any one or a small number of traditionally defined subject areas. Students may therefore be challenged to raise such a thorny problem as "How can we know when someone has really died?", requiring the simultaneous consideration of the latest advances in the fields of medicine, religion, and philosophy, or "How can we rid our planet of life-threatening pollution?", possibly requiring your class to consider knowledge from general science, physics, and chemistry and from social studies, government, and the law. At this level, your students are playing the role of independent and socially responsible thinkers, and you are playing the role of resource, guiding their thoughts and refocusing them when necessary in increasingly productive avenues for elaborating relationships, patterns, and concepts for adult living.

Notice how each of the above four levels nudges the learner up the higher order thinking ladder with real-life experiences by connecting themes and disciplines in a network of applications, concepts, and principles in nests of wider and wider embrace. This is the footprint of a unit plan with rigor and relevance.

Visualizing Your Interdisciplinary Unit. Because interdisciplinary units emphasize lateral knowledge, their graphic portrayal is different from that of disciplinary units, which emphasize vertical knowledge. The graphic technique you use for expressing lateral knowledge should allow for content to be woven in and out of lessons as the opportunity arises, without a predetermined sequence. Hence a more free-form or web-type visual format is required, sometimes called a *concept map* or *thinking map* (Buzan, 2004; Novak, 2009). This type of format shows how content is nestled within other content, how different subject areas share a common theme, how a single theme is threaded through different content areas, and how one field of study is immersed in another. Thus all important themes and issues in an interdisciplinary plan are shown simultaneously in association

Figure 6.8 Visual Representation of the Interdisciplinary Unit Theme "Adventures of Lewis and Clark"

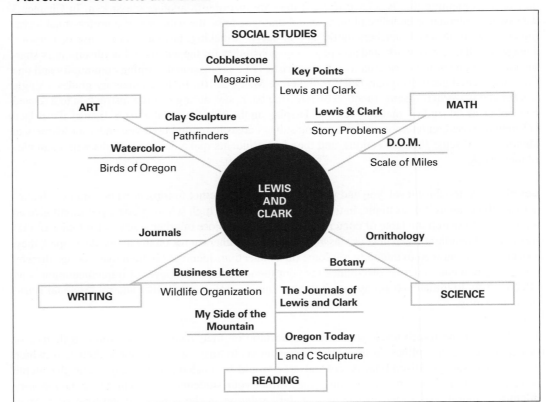

Source: From *The Classroom of the 21st Century,* by S. Kovalik, 1994. Federal Way, WA: Books for Educators. Copyright © 1994 by S. Kovalik. Reprinted with permission.

with one another. (Software, such as www.inspiration.com/home.cfm, can help you develop and visually display interdisciplinary units and lessons.)

The steps for creating graphic outlines or webs are:

1. Identify the most essential theme or idea.
2. Write this theme or idea in the center of your web.
3. Use arrows or lines going out from the main theme or idea to show relationships with other subordinate issues, topics, or content, which can become the topics of individual lessons.
4. Label the arrows and all key concepts with code words or phrases to describe the relationships you have expressed.

Figures 6.8 and 6.9 provide examples of thematic webs for expressing an interdisciplinary thematic unit. See also In Practice: Focus on Interdisciplinary Lesson Planning.

The Written Unit Plan.   The written format for an interdisciplinary unit plan is the same as that for a disciplinary unit. Recall that a written unit is divided into its (1) main purpose, (2) performance objectives, (3) content, (4) procedures and activities, (5) instructional aids and resources, and (6) assessment methods. An example of a written interdisciplinary plan appears in Figure 6.10. To this written plan, attach the visual outline or web of your theme and its interrelationships. As was the case for your disciplinary lesson plan, be sure to add those resources, materials, and strategies (e.g., groupings and resources) that you will use to differentiate your instruction for individuals or groups and to reach learners with special needs. These can be coded and added at relevant places on your interdisciplinary unit map or written unit plan.

Figure 6.9 **Visual Representation of the Interdisciplinary Unit Theme "Dimensions of Time"**

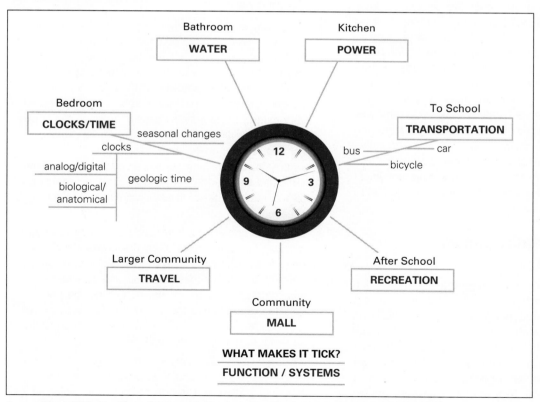

Source: From *Kid's Eye View of Science: A Teacher's Handbook for Teaching Science That Matters,* by S. Kovalik, 2002. Federal Way, WA: Books for Educators. Copyright © 2002 by S. Kovalik. Reprinted with permission.
See also *Kid's Eye View of Science: A Conceptual Integrated Approach to Teaching Science K-6* by Susan D. Olsen, Thousand Oaks, CA Corwin Press, 2010.

In Practice

Focus on Interdisciplinary Lesson Planning

In his literature class, Mr. Cline gives students the dates of the birth and death of a famous author and asks them to figure out how old the author was when she died. Silence falls over the class as students scratch their heads in frustration. One student exclaims, "It's hard to do math in English class!"

How often do we find our students reluctant or unable to recognize and use knowledge they already possess to help them solve new problems or understand new but related concepts? This phenomenon can be directly tied to the ways in which students initially learn information. In an educational era when tremendous emphasis is placed on specialized knowledge, the segregated clustering of subject-area instruction often prevents students from identifying important interconnections among the subjects they study.

The challenge for teachers is to find a healthy and meaningful balance between curricular breadth and depth. The long history of research on the ways in which students learn provides a strong rationale for the value of interdisciplinary instruction. Research in cognitive science strongly supports this view. The work of Ausubel (1968), Neisser (1976), and others in the 1980s and 1990s led to our current notion of schematic structures in the brain. These schematic structures—composed of hundreds, sometimes thousands of interconnected bits of information—serve as a framework for our knowledge. The goodness of our schematic structures is highly dependent on the way in which we initially process the information presented to us. Ausubel referred to these associations as "cognitive hooks." Instruction that provides students with links to connect otherwise discrete bits of knowledge enhances their ability to recognize and apply prior knowledge to new, related learning situations.

Obstacles to Interdisciplinary Lesson Planning

Although the development of integrated learning experiences is important, teachers often find it difficult to plan such experiences for students. The current emphasis on a whole-language orientation in the elementary curriculum assists us as we help students understand the relationships among reading, writing, and oral language, yet most school curricula retain a nonintegrated approach to subject-matter instruction. Textbooks and teachers' guides rarely emphasize the relationships between the subject

area of major concentration and other disciplines. As a result, teachers have neither the information nor the time needed to realistically include interdisciplinary experiences in curricular planning.

Although we cannot always change existing middle and high school curricular materials rapidly or directly, we can employ a planning process that will allow us to periodically incorporate cross-disciplinary ideas and activities into our repertoire of instructional strategies.

Guidelines for Planning

Each of us has particular subject matter expertise, and we have also accumulated knowledge and developed interests in other areas. Additionally, we have access to colleagues whose subject matter concentrations differ from our own. Using these resources, we can conceptualize and construct instructional lessons that help students understand important and interesting relationships between the disciplines. The following guidelines can help us as we develop interdisciplinary lessons:

- *Formulate a goal statement that indicates the principle(s) or concept(s) to be understood at the completion of the lesson.* What are the primary pieces of information or concepts that you want students to understand? Often interdisciplinary lessons do not concentrate on the mastery of specific skills. By their very nature, these lessons usually focus on the application of skills and knowledge to novel situations. For this reason, goals of interdisciplinary lessons will usually involve helping students understand how the skills and knowledge they possess can be combined to accomplish a task, discover a solution, or explain a situation.

- *Select the primary content base that will serve as the catalyst for instruction.* Often the content base will be determined by the text. There are times, however, when your goal necessitates the use of other ancillary materials. In either case, determine the primary vehicle that will drive the instruction (e.g., a work of art or literature, a scientific or mathematical principle, an event or era in history, etc.).

- *Identify events, discoveries, and writings within other disciplines that relate to the primary content base in a meaningful way.* Through talking with colleagues and brainstorming on your own, consider information in other disciplines that seems to relate to the primary content. At this point, you may find it helpful to look at the table of contents in the textbooks you will be using. However, do not discount your own expertise, the films or plays you have seen, the books or magazine articles you have read, and your life's experiences.

- *Determine the key points of intersection between the disciplines that correspond to the established terminal goal of instruction.* As you investigate each cross-disciplinary idea in more depth, keep your terminal goal well in mind. Often we become so enthralled in the idea itself that we lose sight of our major instructional intent. This is intellectually enjoyable, but it is a time-consuming luxury that few of us can afford. Some ideas will probably need to be discarded, either because they are too complex or because they do not fully address the goal. Other ideas may be so compelling and enlightening that you may want to revise the terminal goal to reflect the new insights you have gained.

- *Formulate instructional objectives.* Most interdisciplinary lessons will not focus on the mastery of specific skills. Nevertheless, it is important to determine what you expect your students to be able to do when they have completed the lesson. As in other instructional planning, objectives serve as the springboard for the development of the instructional strategies and activities you will use.

- *Identify the necessary prerequisite knowledge that students must possess in each discipline area you will address.* Interdisciplinary instruction can fall apart if students lack knowledge of the key principles or concepts within each discipline. Carefully consider the prerequisite skills students must have before they can successfully accomplish the objectives you have set forth. Sometimes missing skills or pieces of information can be taught rather quickly. However, when this is not the case, it will be necessary to revise the interdisciplinary content.

- *Formulate instructional strategies that will compel students to use their knowledge in one discipline to better understand and appreciate another.* Students are not used to activating their knowledge in one discipline while studying another. For this reason, it is important to develop activities that require this transfer in a purposeful way. Depending on the content and timeframe of instruction, you may want to use concept mapping, in-class debates, group projects, and/or a variety of discovery techniques to accomplish your goal. The critical component of an interdisciplinary lesson, as in most instruction, is active and invested participation.

Giving our students opportunities to explore interconnections among the subject areas they are studying has many advantages. Interdisciplinary instruction adds meaning and relevance to learning, as students discover fascinating and compelling relationships between disciplines.

Source: Adapted from "Planning Interdisciplinary Curriculum: A Systematic and Cooperative Approach," by Carla Mathison and Cheryl Mason, San Diego State University. Paper presented at ASCD Annual Conference, Orlando, FL.

Making Lesson Plans

To achieve a thinking curriculum in your classroom, we have emphasized the importance of choosing some unit outcomes at a higher level of thinking (for example, application, analysis, synthesis, decision making), rather than specific lesson outcomes. If you plan lessons without a higher-level unit outcome in mind, your students' attention will fall exclusively on each individual lesson, without noticing the relationship among lessons. This relationship may appear deceptively unimportant until it becomes apparent that your lessons seem to pull students first in one direction (e.g., knowledge acquisition) and then abruptly in another (e.g., problem solving), without offering instruction to guide them in the transition. The results of such isolated lesson outcomes may well be confusion, anxiety, and the lack of trust on the part of your students, regardless of how well you prepare each individual lesson and how effective your lessons are in accomplishing their stated but isolated outcomes. Because higher-level outcomes rarely can be attained within the timeframe of a single lesson, they must be achieved in the context of a unit plan.

Before you actually write a lesson plan, consider two preliminary issues that are necessary for your unit plan to flow smoothly: (1) determining where to start and (2) providing for learner diversity.

Figure 6.10 **Example of an Interdisciplinary Thematic Unit**

Grade: 5

Unit Topic: Gold Rush

Course/Subject: Interdisciplinary

Approximate Time Required: One month

1. **Main Purpose of the Unit**

   The purpose of this unit is to acquaint the students with the excitement, the hardships, and the challenges of the nineteenth-century gold rush.

2. **Performance Objectives**

   The student will be able to:

   A. *History/Social Science*—Give reasons why people came to California in the 1840s.

   B. *History/Social Science*—Describe the three routes the pioneers took to California.

   C. *History/Social Science*—Compare life in the United States in the 1840s to life in the United States now.

   D. *History/Social Science*—List supplies brought by the pioneers on the trip West.

   E. *Language Arts*—Write a journal entry to describe some of the hardships associated with the trip West.

   F. *Science*—Research and write a report on how gold is mined.

   G. *Math*—Weigh gold nuggets (painted rocks) and calculate their monetary value.

   H. *Art*—Design a prairie quilt pattern using fabric scraps.

3. **Content Outline**

   A. Reasons people came to California in the 1840s
      1. Gold
      2. Job opportunities
      3. Weather
   B. Supplies for the trip
      1. Tools
      2. Personal supplies
      3. Food
      4. Household items
   C. Life on the trip West

      1. Weather conditions
      2. Roles of men, women, children
      3. Hazards of the trail
   D. Life in California after arrival
      1. Inflated prices
      2. Staking a claim
      3. Striking it rich
      4. A typical day in the life of a miner

4. **Procedures and Activities**

   A. Read aloud
   B. Small-group reading
   C. Independent reading
   D. Discussion
   E. Journal entries
   F. Measurement
   G. Cooking
   H. Singing

5. **Instructional Aids and Resources**

   A. Literature selections
      1. *Patty Reed's Doll*
      2. *By the Great Horn Spoon*
      3. *If You Traveled West in a Covered Wagon*
      4. *Children of the Wild West*
      5. *Joshua's Westward Journal*
      6. *The Way West, Journal of a Pioneer Woman*
      7. *The Little House Cookbook*
   B. Items indicative of the period (if obtainable)
      1. Cast-iron skillet
      2. Bonnet or leather hat
      3. Old tools

6. **Assessment/Evaluation**

   Develop a rubric to grade these.

   A. Essay—Choose one route that the pioneers took to get to California and describe the journey.
   B. Gold Rush Game Board—Design a board game detailing the trip to California. The winner arrives in California and strikes it rich!

Source: Cynthia Dollins, Lecturer, Pepperdine University, Long Beach, CA.

Determining Where to Start

The teachers in this **video** are discussing ways to create lesson plans in a collaborative mode. Notice how the teachers exchange ideas.

Perhaps most perplexing to new teachers is deciding the level of learning at which a lesson should begin—for example, knowledge or comprehension or application. Do you always begin by teaching facts (instilling knowledge), or can you begin with activities at the application level or even at the synthesis and decision-making levels? Both alternatives are possible, but each makes different assumptions about the prior task-relevant knowledge and experiences of your learners and the interrelationship among your lessons. In other words your lessons should begin with where your learners are at, which then determines what you teach (DuFour, DuFour, Eaker, & Many, 2010).

Beginning a lesson or a sequence of lessons at the knowledge level (e.g., list, recall, recite, etc.) assumes that the topic you will be teaching is mostly new material. Such a lesson usually occurs at the beginning of a sequence that will progressively build this knowledge into more authentic behavior—perhaps ending at the application, synthesis, or evaluation (decision-making) level. When no task-relevant prior knowledge is required, the starting point for a lesson often is at the knowledge or comprehension level. When some task-relevant prior knowledge has been taught, the lesson can begin at a higher level of thinking. Notice from the list of objectives in Figure 6.7 that each lesson with an outcome at a higher level is preceded by a lesson with an outcome at some lower level.

As we have seen, a unit plan should attempt to teach a range of outcomes that begin at a lower level and end at a higher level. Some units might begin at the application level and end at a higher level, if a previous unit has provided the task-relevant prior knowledge and understandings required. It also is possible to progress from one level of learning outcome to another within a single lesson. This may be increasingly difficult when lessons start at higher levels, but it is possible and often desirable to move from knowledge to comprehension and on to application activities within a single lesson. This is illustrated in the flow of behaviors for the following third-grade social studies lesson:

Unit Title: Local, State, and National Geography

Lesson Title: Local Geography

Behaviors

- Student will know the geographical location of the community relative to the state and nation (knowledge).
- Student will be able to describe the physical features of the community (comprehension).
- Student will be able to locate the community on a map and globe (application).
- Student will be able to discuss how the community is similar to and different from other communities (analysis).

In this lesson, a comprehensive list of outcomes is taught in a relatively brief time (a single lesson) by using objects already known to and experienced by the students (their own community, map, globe) and by relating one outcome with another, so each new activity is a continuation of the preceding one. When the teacher plans a transition across learning levels within a single lesson, the necessary question before each new level is, "Have I provided all the required task-relevant prior knowledge?" If the answer is "Yes," the lesson will be directed at the students' current level of experience and understanding, and they will have the maximum opportunity to attain the unit objective.

Providing for Learning Diversity

A second consideration before writing a lesson plan is providing differentiated instruction for individual learners and students with special learning needs. As we have seen in this chapter and Chapter 2, not all learners share the same behavioral characteristics and task-relevant prior knowledge.

Regardless of where you position the entry level of a lesson, some students will be above it and other students will be below it. Much of the work of unit and lesson planning is playing a game of averages, in which you attempt to provide most of the instruction at the current level of understanding and experience of most of the learners. Unless an entire unit of study is individualized (as is the case with some computerized curricula), most instruction must be directed at the average learner in your classroom while attempting to meet the needs of other learners.

Many instructional methods and **tutorial and communication technologies** are available that can help you differentiate instruction and meet the needs of special learners (Gregory & Chapman, 2006; Karten, 2007, 2008; Tileston, 2010; Tomlinson, 2004, 2010; Tomlinson & McTighe, 2006). These methods and technologies share the following characteristics:

- Allow rapid movement within and across content, depending on the learners' success at any given time
- Allow students the flexibility to proceed at their own pace and level of difficulty

- Provide students immediate feedback on the accuracy of their responses
- Gradually shift the responsibility for learning from teacher to student

Before you begin your lesson plan, decide on the extent to which methods and technologies for individualizing instruction are required by the diversity of learning needs in your classroom. The following methods describe some of the options for helping all your learners achieve academic success. Be sure to include these methods in your lesson plan when they can contribute to the goals of your lesson.

Task-Ability Grouping.   You can group your class for a specific period of time by the skills required to learn the material you are presenting. For example, higher-performing readers can read ahead and work independently on advanced exercises while you direct your lesson to average- and lower-performing readers. You can divide lesson plans, objectives, activities, materials, and tests into two or more appropriate parts when learners exhibit noticeable strengths and weaknesses that cannot be bridged in a single lesson. The intent is to group learners homogeneously by learning skills relevant to a specific task or lesson for a limited amount of time, after which you should regroup when new tasks place different demands on learners.

Learning Centers.   Students tend to learn better when solving real-life problems and especially when they correspond with their experiences. As a result, many schools are working to reorganize the curriculum to support real-world problem solving and application (Baden & Mayor, 2004; Muschla & Muschla, 2006). One way to promote real-world problem solving and help individual learners apply what they have learned is through the use of a learning or activity center. A learning center can individualize a lesson by providing resources for review and practice for those who may lack task-relevant prior knowledge or skills. When a learning center can contain media, supplemental resources, and/or practice exercises directly related to applying your lesson content, include it as an integral part of your lesson plan. The more hands-on activity your learning center elicits from your learners, the more effective it will be in helping you achieve your lesson and unit goals.

Review and Follow-Up Materials.   Some of your lessons will need to stimulate the recall of task-relevant prior knowledge. An oral summary, together with a supplementary handout that asks individual learners to look up the required task-relevant information, can bring some students up to the required level while not boring others. The key to this procedure is to carefully prepare a summary and review sheet covering critically needed prerequisite knowledge for the day's lesson, such as important names, dates, concepts, themes, and formulas. Doing so lets you limit your review to the essentials that requires the least amount of time.

One way to promote real-world problem solving and help individual learners apply what they have learned is through the use of a learning or activity center.

Tutoring.   During **peer tutoring**, one student teaches another at the same grade and age level. During **cross-age tutoring**, the tutor may be one or more years and grade levels above the learner receiving the instruction. Cross-age tutoring generally has been more effective than peer tutoring, owing to the fact that older students are more likely to be familiar with the material and to be respected as role models. Tutoring has been most successful as an adjunct to regular instruction when it has provided more individual practice than can be made available in a whole-class or group setting.

Interactive Instructional CD-ROMs. Instructional CD-ROMs can provide computer-generated activities that students work through at their own level and at their own pace. CD-ROMs can also hold different soundtracks—for example, one in English and another in Spanish. These instructional CDs typically break skills down into small sub skills, such as those that might be identified in a learning hierarchy, through which students work from easy to more difficult. Questions and prompts actively engage learners in formulating responses and give them immediate knowledge of whether they are correct, providing **interactive individualized practice activities**.

Interactive CD-ROMs are now available from publishers and commercial vendors for many different grade levels and subject areas to give students practice, assess understanding, and provide remediation. These CD-ROMs can quickly assess the accuracy of students' responses to practice activities and change the sequence and difficulty of the activities to correspond with learners' current level of understanding. In this manner, practice can be tailored to individual learners, depending on how well they respond at a certain level of difficulty. Students can spend more time on a particular topic or skill, or they can return to an earlier sequence of instruction to review or relearn prerequisite knowledge. CD-ROMs also have the capability of providing color pictures, simulated motion, and charts and diagrams that can motivate learners and enhance the authenticity of the practice experience to real-world applications. As with other individualized learning methods, instructional CD-ROMs have been found most effective when providing practice opportunities for content that has already been introduced or taught.

Events of Instruction

After you have determined where to start the lesson and how to provide for diverse learning needs, you are ready to begin writing your lesson plan. At this time, you will specify the key events that occur during the lesson and for which you are responsible. By placing the responsibility for providing these events on you, we distinguish between teaching and learning. *Learning* refers to the internal events that go on inside your learners' heads. *Teaching* is the sum of the instructional activities you provide to influence what goes on in your learners' heads.

The sequence of steps you follow in lesson planning assumes that the instructional events you plan will influence learning. It is not unusual for teaching to be unrelated to learning, as when teachers teach without regard to the task-relevant knowledge and experience of their learners and students listen but nothing sinks in. The process of getting instructional events to sink in is one of planning instruction that fosters a close relationship between the external events of instruction (what you do) and the internal events of learning (what your students know and have experienced), actively engaging your learners in the learning process.

Getting Started: Some Lesson-Planning Questions

To begin, you can achieve this tightly knit relationship between what you do and what your students are thinking by considering the following questions. Your answers to these questions will serve you well in the lesson-planning steps that follow.

- Why should your students care or want to know about this topic?
- What do you want your students to know and be able to do?
- Which of their needs, experiences, and prior learnings will be a foundation for this lesson?
- To what state standards and curriculum guide content will this content relate?
- What engaging and worthwhile learning activities will you ask your students to complete that meet their needs, experiences, and prior learning?
- What instructional activities will you use to bring out these needs, experiences, and prior learning and to provide evaluative feedback?
- How will you know when your students have achieved the goal of the lesson?

In case you didn't notice, your answers to these questions will bring your students center stage into the planning process and organize in advance much of the information you will need to complete your lesson plan with the best interests, experiences, and needs of your students at heart.

You can further tighten the relationship between teaching and learning by considering seven instructional steps or events, as suggested by Gagné and Briggs (2005). To actively engage your learners in the learning process, let's consider the types of instructional activity they describe (outlined in the following sections) as a general framework. These steps include the most relevant parts of different models of lesson preparation that, when used together, can provide the foundation from which you can build your own model of lesson planning—one with which you will be most comfortable. Although not all of the events in the different models of lesson planning are applicable to every lesson, they provide a basis or menu from which you can formulate many different lesson plans. To help correlate the different models with which you may already be familiar or which you may learn about, related terms and questions from other models of lesson planning appear in parentheses and in italics.

1. Gaining Attention (Anticipatory Set)

Why should your students care or want to know about this topic?

Unless you get your students' attention, they will hear little of your lesson, let alone become actively engaged in the learning process. Thus each lesson plan begins with an instructional event to engage student interest, curiosity, and attention. In some classes, this will mean raising your students' attention from almost complete disengagement to where their vision and hearing are receptive and anticipating what is to come. In other classes, this may mean raising their attention from an already receptive mode to a higher level of anticipation, interest, and attention.

The intensity of your attention-gaining event will depend on the starting point of your learners. A fifth-period class that meets after lunch may require a more dramatic attention-getting event than an eager first-period class. You will need to find the right event for gaining your students' attention.

One of the most common attention-gaining devices is to arouse curiosity. Often this can be accomplished by asking questions:

- Have you ever wondered how we got the word *horsepower?* Who would like to guess? (from a lesson on energy)
- Can anyone think of a popular automobile with the name of a Greek god? (from an introductory lesson on mythology)
- Have you ever wondered how some creatures can live both in the water and on the land? (from a lesson on amphibious animals)

These questions, called *openers,* are designed not to have a single correct answer or even to accurately reflect the fine details of what is to follow. Instead they amuse, stimulate, or even bewilder students so that they will be receptive to the content and questions that follow and your lesson will connect with their experience. Following are other thought-provoking openers:

- Why do some scientists think that traveling to other planets will make space travelers younger? (from a lesson in general science or physics)
- Why do we have the word *i-t-s* and another word *i-t apostrophe s?* (from a lesson in punctuation)
- Why is the U.S. dollar worth more today in Mexico than in Switzerland? (from a lesson in social studies)
- Why do you think some eloquent speaking lawyers become disliked by the juries they speak to? (from a lesson in public speaking)

Another useful technique for gaining students' attention is to present any of the following:

- An apparent *contradiction:*

Why do you think the Greek empire collapsed when it was at its strongest?

- A seeming *inconsistency* in real life:

    Why do some lower forms of animal life live longer than human beings?

- Something that at first appears to be *illogical:*

    Why must one thing go backward every time something else goes forward?

For example, introducing a lesson about signed numbers by informing your learners that the multiplication of two negative numbers always results in a positive product may puzzle them, but it may also arouse their curiosity about how two negatives can result in something positive. You might continue by explaining the *number line* and mathematical rules behind this apparent contradiction.

Diagrams, pictures, illustrations, scale models, and films are other attention-getting aids. Use these devices to appeal to your learners' sense of vision while your oral presentation appeals to their sense of hearing. Graphics or visuals are particularly effective openers with students who are known to be more oriented and responsive to visual than auditory presentations. A visual opener might include samples of materials for the day's lesson, so students can touch them before the lesson begins. A visual opener also might show equipment you will use during the lesson (e.g., scales, meters, pictures, and models).

2. Informing Learners of the Objective (Anticipatory Set, Objectives, and Purpose)

What do you want students to know and be able to do?

Just because your learners have been turned on with some attention-getting device doesn't mean they will be tuned to the wavelength at which you present the lesson. To resolve this, you need to tell them the channel on which your lesson is being transmitted.

The most effective way to focus your learners' receptivity is to inform them of the behavioral outcome they will be expected to attain by the end of the lesson. You can do this by telling them early in the lesson or unit how they will be examined or expected to show competence. For example, such an expectation might be expressed in any of the following ways:

- Remember the four definitions of *power* that will be presented. (science)

- Be able to express ownership orally in a sentence to the class. (language arts)

- Correctly identify a mystery specimen of lower animal life using the microscope. (life science)

- State your true feelings about laws dealing with the death penalty. (social studies)

- Know the meaning of the italicized vocabulary words in the story "Charlotte's Web." (reading)

These statements allow learners to know the level of behavior they are expected to attain and to become selective in how to use and remember the lesson information. If your students are told they will be expected to recall four definitions of power at the end of your lesson on energy, then they will know to focus their search, retrieval, and retention processes during the lesson on the definitions or categories of power you present. Informing learners of your objective helps them organize their thinking in advance of the lesson by providing mental hooks on which to hang the key points. This activates the learning process and focuses your learners on obtaining the required behavioral outcome.

The key to the success of this instructional event is to communicate your objective clearly. To do so, choose your

Informing learners of your objective helps them organize their thinking in advance of the lesson by providing mental hooks on which to hang key points.

words with your learners' vocabulary and language level in mind, and record what you tell them as a reminder in this second part of your lesson plan.

The best way to communicate your objective is to provide examples of tasks that you expect your students to be able to perform after the lesson. This translates the action verb associated with a learning outcome into some ways this behavior might be measured on tests, in class discussions, and in question-and-answer sessions. For example, at the beginning of a unit on lower forms of animal life, you might write on the blackboard the following examples of expected outcomes and then check off the ones that most apply at the start of each day's lesson:

- ☑ Define an amoeba.
- ☑ Draw the cellular structure of an amoeba.
- ☐ Explain the reproduction cycle of an amoeba.
- ☐ Using a microscope, properly distinguish an amoeba from other single-celled animals.

Notice that these lesson outcomes range from recounting a fact to making decisions and judgments in a real biological environment.

Without knowing in advance at which of these levels they are expected to perform, your learners will have no way of selecting and focusing their attention on those parts of the instruction leading to the desired behavior. This is not to say students should ignore other aspects of the presentation. Rather, students can now see the other aspects as tools or means for gaining the highest-level outcome required, not as ends in themselves.

3. Stimulating Recall of Prerequisite Learning (Review)

What student needs, interests, and prior learning will be a foundation for this lesson?

Before you can proceed with the new lesson content, one final preliminary instructional event is needed. Because learning cannot occur in a vacuum, the necessary task-relevant prior information must be retrieved and made ready for use. This calls for some method of reviewing, summarizing, restating, or otherwise stimulating the key concepts acquired in previous lessons. This information is instrumental for achieving the level of outcome intended in the present lesson.

For example, if your goal is to have learners use a microscope to properly distinguish an amoeba from other single-celled animals, some previously acquired facts, concepts, and skills are clearly relevant to this new task. Definitions of single-celled animals, unique characteristics of an amoeba that distinguish it from other one-celled animals, and skill in using the microscope are among the task-relevant prior knowledge that will influence your learners' attainment of this outcome.

Helping students retrieve earlier information requires condensing the key aspects into a brief, easily understood form. It is not possible to summarize all of this information in a few minutes. Instead you need to use thought-provoking and stimulating techniques to focus learners on sizable amounts of prior learning and interests. Questions like these can help your students recall the most significant and memorable parts of earlier lessons:

- Do you remember why Joshua couldn't see the amoeba in the microscope? (It was on low magnification instead of high.)
- Do you remember Natasha's humorous attempt to relate the reproduction cycle of an amoeba to that of human beings? (She had equated cell division with waking up one morning to find a new baby in the family.)
- Do you remember the three-color picture Rico drew of the cellular structure of an amoeba? (Everyone had commented on how lifelike the picture was.)

Questions such as these help students retrieve task-relevant prior learning, not by summarizing that learning but by tapping into a single mental image that recalls that learning. Once the image has been retrieved, students can turn it on to search for details that may be nestled within it, achieving still greater recall. Describing how to stimulate the recall of prerequisite learning is the third entry in your lesson plan.

4. Presenting the Content (Input, Modeling)

What state standards and curriculum guide content will be taught?

Presenting the content will be the heart of your lesson plan. At first glance, this component may seem to require little explanation, but several important considerations for completing it often go unnoticed. These pertain to the authenticity, selectivity, and variety of your lesson presentation. Let's look closely at each of these.

> In this **video**, the teacher is modeling geometric concepts to her students. How can this technique help solidify learning for her students?

Authenticity.   To teach a behavior that is authentic, your lesson must present content in a way in which it will be used by your learners on assessments, in subsequent grades, and in the world outside your classroom. If your goal is to teach learners to *use* a microscope to identify single-celled animals, then teaching them to *label* the parts of a microscope will not be authentic. Although naming the parts may be a prerequisite skill and an important objective of an earlier lesson, it will not be sufficient to attain the desired goal of this lesson. In other words, how you use a behavior in daily life must always be how it is taught in order for it to be authentic. Reading in the context of a story is also an example of an authentic behavior, because the learner is being provided the opportunity to derive meaning from text, as would be expected in the real world.

You can make the behaviors you teach more authentic by changing the irrelevant aspects or context of what you are teaching as often as possible and in as many different ways as possible. Doing so prevents learning a response under only one condition but not under others that may be encountered in subsequent lessons, grades, and courses. Following are examples of changing the irrelevant aspects of a learning stimulus:

- Show both the stacked format and line format of number problems. (math)

- Introduce learners to examples of proper punctuation by using materials from popular magazines and newspapers as well as the text and workbook. (English or a foreign language)

- Show how the laws of electricity apply to lightning during a thunderstorm as well as to electrical circuitry in the laboratory. (science)

- Relate the rules of social behavior found among humans to those often found among animals. (social studies)

- Compare the central processing unit in a computer to the executive processes in the human brain. (computer science)

- Show how the reasons for a particular war also can be applied to other conflicts hundreds of years earlier. (history)

In each of these examples, the lesson designer is applying key lesson ideas in different contexts. As a result, learners are more likely (1) to focus on correct mathematical operations and not the format of the problem, (2) to notice improper punctuation when it appears in a popular publication, (3) to understand the universality of physical laws governing electricity, (4) to realize that social behavior is not a uniquely human phenomenon, (5) to distinguish the wonders of data processing from the hardware and equipment that are sometimes needed to perform it, and (6) to understand that some reasons for conflict, war, and hostility are general as well as specific.

Selectivity.   A second consideration during this stage of lesson preparation is emphasizing the content most important to your lesson. Not everything in a chapter, workbook, film, or presentation or on a handout or chalkboard will be of equal importance to the day's objective and standards. Consequently, highlighting key aspects of the material at the beginning of the lesson will help students selectively review and retain the main points of your lesson. For example, focusing your learners on the "six concepts on the bottom of page 50" or the "tables and figures at the end of Chapter 3" can help them place the day's lesson in the context of the curriculum and provide an anchor for future reference.

You will also want to highlight content during your lesson. Examples of such highlighting include verbally emphasizing the importance of certain events; telling students what to look for in a video (even stopping it to reinforce an idea); emphasizing key words on the chalkboard with underlining, circling, or color; and using verbal markers ("This is important"; "Notice the relevance of this"; "You will need this information later"). These and other methods for selectively emphasizing key parts of your lesson will be taken up in later chapters, but remember to consider them at this stage of your lesson plan.

Variety.   A key behavior of the effective teacher is instructional variety. Gaining students' attention at the start of the lesson is one thing, but keeping their attention is quite another. Variety in the modalities of instruction (for example, visual, oral, tactile) and instructional activity (large-group lecture, question and answer, small-group discussion) stimulates student thinking and interest. Shifting from visually dominated instruction to orally dominated instruction (or using both simultaneously) and breaking a lesson into several instructional activities (for example, explanation followed by question and answer) are important.

Planning changes in modality and instructional activities presents the lesson in varied contexts, giving learners the opportunity to grasp material in several different ways according to their individual learning styles. Such changes also give students the opportunity to see previously learned material used in different ways. This reinforces learned material better than simply restating it in the same mode and form. It also encourages learners to extend or expand material according to the new mode or procedure being used. For example, material learned from a presentation may be pushed to its limit in a question-and-answer period when the learner answers a question and finds out that previous understandings were partly incorrect due to the limited context in which they were learned.

In addition to keeping students attentive and actively engaged in the learning process, providing variety also creates a more memorable and conscious learning experience. Be sure to consider these and other methods of adding instructional variety to your lesson during this stage of your lesson plan.

5. Eliciting the Desired Behavior (Checking for Understanding, Guided Practice)

What engaging and worthwhile learning activities and tasks will your students complete?

After presenting the content of the lesson, provide your learners an opportunity to show that they have acquired the knowledge or understanding expected. Learning occurs in an active environment that engages the learner in the learning process at moderate to high rates of success. Therefore a fifth instructional event is needed that, when added to a lesson plan, encourages and guides learners through a process that can be expected to exhibit the outcome intended.

This fifth event—eliciting the desired behavior—differs from the four preceding ones in that it seeks the individual's covert and personal engagement in the learning process. Each learner must be placed in the position of grappling in a trial-and-error fashion with summarizing, paraphrasing, applying, or solving a problem involving the lesson content. It is not important that the learner's response be produced accurately at this stage, as long as the activity provided stimulates him or her to attempt a response. This activity guides the learner to organize a response that matches the learning outcome stated when the student was informed of the objective (the second instructional event).

The primary ways of staging this instructional event include workbooks, handouts, textbook study questions, verbal and written exercises, and oral questions that have students apply what was learned, if only in the privacy of their minds. The goal is to pose a classroom activity that encourages students to use the material taught in a nonevaluative atmosphere, as close in time as possible to the presentation of new material. Sometimes such activities can be inserted throughout the lesson with each new chunk of information, which also adds variety. In other instances, these activities occur near the end of the presentation of content.

Either way, the eliciting activity is brief, nonevaluative, and focused exclusively on posing a condition for which the learner must organize a response (e.g., from a question, problem, or exercise). This response may be written, oral, or subvocal (students respond in their own minds). An eliciting activity can be as simple as your posing a question anywhere in a lesson or as complex as the student completing a problem or exercise in a workbook at the lesson's end. The main attribute is that the activity be nonevaluative to encourage a response unhampered by the anxiety and conservative response patterns that generally occur during testing situations.

You may also want to consider some of the followings ways of eliciting the desired behavior, as suggested by Price and Nelson (2011), Rosenshine and Stevens (1986), and Zemelman, Daniels, and Hyde (2005):

- Prepare a large number of oral questions beforehand.

- Ask many brief questions on main points, on supplementary points, and on the process being taught. (Have students create their own questions.)

- Call on students whose hands are not raised in addition to those who volunteer.

- Ask students to summarize a rule or process in their own words.

- Have all students write down their answers (on paper or the chalkboard) while you circulate among them.

- Have all students write their answers and check them with a neighbor. (This is frequently used with older students.)

- At the end of a presentation/discussion (especially with older students), write the main points on the chalkboard, and then divide the class into groups to summarize the main points together.

6. Providing Feedback (Guided Practice, Closure)

What instructional practices will you use with this lesson to provide evaluative feedback?

The sixth instructional event is closely connected in time to the fifth event (eliciting the desired behavior) and is often used consecutively with it. As we have seen, eliciting the desired behavior promotes learning to the extent that learners struggle with and think about providing a correct response. The response is the individual's attempt to recall, summarize, paraphrase, apply, or problem solve in a *nonevaluative* way, which maintains his or her momentum to learn. Feedback may be provided but should be directed to the entire class or subgroups of learners who may be working at different levels. For example, after giving learners time to think on their own, the teacher can give the correct answer to the class, group several students' answers for comparison, read aloud the correct answer from where it can be found, provide a handout with the correct answer, or use an overhead projector or document camera to record volunteered answers—all nonevaluative ways of leading the learner to reengage and rethink an earlier response.

But at this sixth stage of the learning process, it is important to provide *individual* student feedback as to the correctness of a response or how to make it better. Here your response to the learner is differentiated by considering his or her ability, learning history, language and culture, and, if applicable, special needs. Responses such as "That's a good try," "That's not quite what I'm looking for at this time," and "Keep thinking" can switch the focus of a wrong answer to a more productive response and provide the opportunity to give the individual learner specific feedback without penalizing him or her for responding. If students are working silently at their seats, you can walk about the room, using a simple nod and smile to indicate the correctness of an individual performance or to encourage the revision of a wrong response. This part of the lesson plan provides the means by which evaluative feedback can be given to individual learners about the adequacy of their responses.

Some additional ways of providing feedback to individual students, small groups, and the entire class are summarized in Table 6.2.

7. Assessing the Lesson Outcome (Independent Practice)

How will you know when your students have achieved the goal of the lesson?

This final instructional event specifies the way in which you will make a final evaluation of the degree to which the learner has acquired the desired behaviors, which may include the outcomes of other lessons as well. As we have seen, eliciting activities and feedback can be immediate or delayed (an oral question or workbook problem) and nonevaluative or evaluative (a choral versus individual response). For this instructional event, you will need to identify a delayed activity that is primarily evaluative.

Table 6.2 **Some Methods of Providing Feedback**

Individual Students	Small Groups	Whole Class
Nod while walking past Point to the correct answer in the workbook or textbook Show the student the answer key Place checkmarks along incorrect answers	Sit with the group and discuss their answers Have one group critique another group's answers Give each group the answer key when finished with discussion Assign one group member the task of checking the answers of other group members	Place the answers on a transparency Provide the answers on a handout Read the answers aloud Place the answers on the chalkboard Have students grade each other's papers as you give the answers

Your assessment activities can include scored interviews, objective and essay questions, graded homework, classroom performances, and student work samples. These more formal evaluative tasks could be counterproductive to learning if required at earlier stages, when the instructional goal is to get learners to respond for the first time without limiting discovery, exploration, and risk taking—all important ingredients to meaningful learning. But, at this final stage, your assessment will be instrumental for evaluating the degree to which the learner can exhibit the desired knowledge, understandings, or behaviors at the completion of a lesson or sequence of related lessons. You will learn more about this stage of assessment in Chapter 13. But, for now, some of the assessment methods of completing this event include the following:

Tests and quizzes	Performance evaluations	Essay questions
Homework exercises	Lab assignments	Research papers
In-class workbook assignments	Presentations	Independent practice
	Oral questioning/interviews	Portfolios

Example Lesson Plans

We are now ready to collect our seven instructional events into a brief but effective lesson plan that answers our seven related questions. To be both practical and effective, a lesson plan must be short yet provide all the ingredients needed to deliver the lesson.

Following are some example lesson plans on various subjects and grade levels that show how the goals and standards in the previous chapter fit together with lesson plans in this chapter. These examples illustrate how easy lesson planning can be when the task is organized using these seven instructional events. Let's review the events and look at some lesson examples across the elementary school, middle school, and high school.

Example Lesson Plan

Reading Skills

Unit Title: Word Attack Skills (Vertically Planned Unit)

Lesson Level: Early Elementary

Subject Area: Pronunciation and Reading

Lesson Title: Sound Discrimination, Letters of the Alphabet—Lesson 2.1

The preceding titles indicate the general content of the lesson and its placement in a unit on word attack skills. The lesson identifier, 2.1, indicates this lesson is the first one in unit 2. It would appear on the graphic unit plan, as indicated in Figure 6.11.

Figure 6.11 Relationship of Lessons, Units, and a Course or Domain

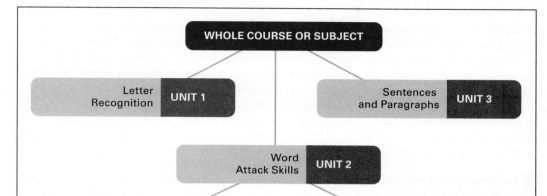

Next appears a description of how you will use each of the seven instructional events to deliver this lesson to students. To this is added some elaboration that further defines each event:

1 Gaining attention. Play an audiotape of a voice articulating the sounds.

This instructional event gains student attention and focuses learners on what is to be presented. Whatever device or procedure you use should not only gain their attention but also motivate their continued concentration well into the lesson. Keep in mind that students, especially young ones, have trouble picking up subtle transitions between classroom activities. Often their attention is focused on what has immediately preceded the lesson, and they are reluctant to change focus unless something new, interesting, or exciting is forthcoming.

Visual or auditory stimuli often are effective as attention getters, because their ability to penetrate the senses exceeds that of more neutral stimuli, like written words, verbal expressions, and pronouncements. Changing sensory modalities from listening to looking (or vice versa) often provides the incentive necessary for students to more selectively perceive and receive the message about to be communicated.

2 Informing the learner of the objective. When the tape is finished, indicate that at the end of the lesson, students will be expected to repeat the vowel sounds out loud, independently of the tape.

This instructional event translates the behavioral objective for the lesson into a form that is meaningful to students. In this example, information is being transferred from one modality (listening) to another (speaking), indicating that the objective for this lesson is written at the comprehension level of the cognitive domain, requiring a change in modalities. Your attention-getting device should be chosen to lead into the objective for the lesson. Simply clapping your hands to gain attention, followed by stating the objective, will not be as effective as having the objective actually contained within the attention-getting procedure.

In this example, the audiotape was directly related to the lesson's content, allowing these two instructional events to work together to produce a unified theme and thus enhancing learners' attention. Other simple but effective attention getters that could be made to reflect the lesson objective are a picture or chart, a question on the chalkboard, or a demonstration derived directly from lesson content.

3 **Stimulating recall of prerequisite learning.** Show how each vowel sound is produced by correctly positioning the mouth and lips.

Identifying and successfully communicating task-relevant prior knowledge to students is critical to attaining the lesson objective. Unless you paraphrase, summarize, or otherwise review this information, at least some students will be unable to comprehend what is being conveyed. Among the most frequent reasons that learners are unable to attain lesson outcomes is that they lack the skills and understandings of previously taught lessons that are necessary for subsequent learning to occur.

Prerequisite content must be recalled or stimulated into action for it to play a meaningful role in acquiring new learning. Most lessons require some previous facts, understandings, or skills, and these should be recalled and identified at this step of the lesson plan. You can achieve this by touching on the key points of the prior learning.

4 **Presenting the content.** Say each vowel sound, and then have the class repeat it twice, pointing to a chart of the positions of the mouth and lips during the articulation of each vowel sound. Do the most commonly used vowels first.

You may feel this is the heart of the lesson. You are partly right, except that there are six other "hearts," each of which could entail as much effort in planning and instructional time as this event does. Beginning teachers tend to pack their lessons with almost entirely new content. They devote far less effort to gaining learners' attention, informing learners of the objective, recalling prerequisite learning, and other instructional events that must follow the presentation of new material.

The presentation of new material is indispensable in any new lesson, but it need not always encompass most (or even a large portion) of the lesson. The result of devoting a large portion of the lesson to new material, exclusive of the other instructional events, is that the lesson is likely to present the content in pieces too big for learners to grasp. This often results in having to reteach content during subsequent lessons and ultimately less content coverage at the end of a unit. The next three instructional events will make clear that new content must itself be a stimulus for something more to come.

5 **Eliciting the desired behavior.** Have students silently practice forming the correct mouth and lip positions for each vowel sound, following the pictures in their workbooks.

For this instructional event, the learner is given guidance in how to perform the behavior and an opportunity to practice it—two activities that must go hand in hand if learning is to occur. Eliciting the desired behavior for the first time without providing an opportunity to practice could diminish the effect of this instructional event. The content described in the previous event should be presented in a form that affords the learner the opportunity to use the behavior in a nonthreatening, nonevaluative environment. Grading or performance evaluations, therefore, should not be part of the performance being elicited in this instructional event, where spontaneity, the freedom to make mistakes, and an opportunity to discover for oneself should prevail.

6 **Providing feedback.** Randomly choose students to recite the vowel sounds; correct their errors to demonstrate to the class the desired sounds.

Feedback should be given immediately after the eliciting activity. The closer the correspondence between performance and feedback, the more quickly learning will occur.

Your feedback can be part of the eliciting activity, or it can be a separate activity. In the previous instructional event, feedback was not provided and learners had no way of knowing the correctness of their behavior (mouth and lip movements). Pictures in the text guided their behavior, but because students could not see themselves performing the movements, they could not tell if they performed them accurately. In this case, feedback would have to follow the eliciting activity, making this instructional event essential for learning. The previous eliciting activity, however, might have included impersonal and nonevaluative feedback if, for example, students were asked to recite aloud the vowel sounds and the teacher provided group feedback on the accuracy of their utterances. The correspondence of an eliciting activity and feedback is a matter of degree, but these two events should occur as closely in time as possible.

7 **Assessing the lesson outcome.** The lesson outcome will be assessed as part of the unit test on word attack skills and from the exercises completed on pages 17 and 18 in the workbook.

Few lesson objectives are assessed by individual lesson tests. An amount of content larger than that contained in a single lesson usually is necessary to make a test efficient and practical. However, it is important to indicate which unit or subunit test covers the lesson content and what additional means, other than formal tests (e.g., classroom performances, projects, and portfolios), you will use to grade students' responses. The information from this assessment will provide important feedback about your students' readiness for new content and possible reasons for poor performance in later lessons for which the current material is prerequisite.

Example Lesson Plan

Literature and U.S. History

Unit Title: History of American West

Lesson Levels: Upper Elementary, Middle School

Subject Areas: History/Social Science, Language Arts, Art

Lesson Title: Westward Journals

The preceding titles indicate the general content of the lesson and the unit of which it is a part. This lesson appears on an interdisciplinary unit plan as a lesson in reading or literature titled "Westward Journals," as shown in Figure 6.12.

1 **Gaining attention.** Display items or pictures of items that pioneers may have brought with them on their trip West. These will include a diary, a bonnet, old tools, the Bible, and a cast-iron skillet.

2 **Informing the learner of the objective.** Students will be expected to choose one of the routes to California and write a diary entry from the 1840s detailing a day on the trip. Students may be creative in their presentation of this product, choosing to design a diary or journal or perhaps writing their entry on a ship or wagon made of construction paper.

3 **Stimulating recall of prerequisite learning.** As a class, students will brainstorm the main events learned about the trip West and record them on a large chart.

4 **Presenting the content.** Have students read excerpts from *The Way West: Journal of a Pioneer Woman,* by Amelia Stewart Knight, and *Joshua's Westward Journal,* by Joan Anderson. Lead a discussion of how each author details and summarizes events on the journey.

5 **Eliciting the desired behavior.** Have students pretend they are children in a wagon train or aboard a ship on the trip West in the 1840s. Tell them to write journal or diary entries about their experiences. Provide a variety of writing paper and construction paper, and invite students to be creative in designing their journals.

Figure 6.12 **Visual Representation of the Interdisciplinary Unit Theme "Gold Rush," Which Includes the Lesson "Westward Journals"**

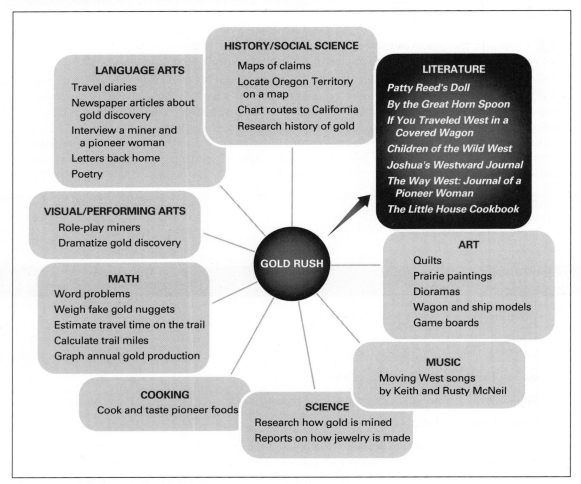

Source: Cynthia Dollins, Lecturer, Pepperdine University, Long Beach, CA.

6 **Providing feedback.** While the students are writing, ask individuals to share excerpts from their entries. Point out how the students are including the items listed on the brainstorming chart made at the beginning of the lesson.

7 **Assessing the lesson outcome.** Design a rubric describing various degrees of proficiency to grade the journal entries. Criteria may include adherence to factual events in 1840, use of descriptive language, and creativity.

Table 6.3 presents the approximate amount of time during a 50-minute class period that you might devote to each instructional event. Some periods will differ considerably from these amounts of time, such as when the entire lesson is devoted to a review or when recall of prior learning and assessing behavior is not relevant to the day's lesson. Keep in mind that experience, familiarity with content, and common sense always are your best guides for determining the percentage of time to devote to each instructional event.

From Table 6.3, it is apparent that when you emphasize one instructional event, you must deemphasize another; trade-offs always occur. Although every teacher would like to have more time than allotted for an instructional period, he or she must decide how to fit lesson content into the available time. Table 6.4 indicates some of the ways this might be accomplished when planning a typical lesson.

Table 6.3 **Approximate Distribution of Instructional Time across Instructional Events for a Hypothetical 50-Minute Lesson**

Instructional Event	Ranges in Minutes	Ranges in Percentages of Time
Gaining attention	1–5	2–10
Informing learners of the objective	1–3	2–6
Stimulating recall of prerequisite learning	5–10	10–20
Presenting the content	10–20	20–40
Eliciting the desired behavior	10–20	20–40
Providing feedback	5–10	10–20
Assessing behavior	0–10	0–20

Source: Cynthia Dollins, Lecturer, Pepperdine University, Long Beach, CA.

Table 6.4 **Integrating Technology into Different Content Areas**

Content Area	Application
Reading/Language arts	• Software programs to develop basic reading skills • Word processing to teach writing skills • Internet search engines to develop basic research skills
Math	• Tutorial and drill-and-practice software to develop math facts • Graphing calculations to illustrate abstract or hard-to-visualize relationships • Software to illustrate and explore geometry concepts
Science	• Simulations to illustrate complex relationships • Data-gathering instruments to conduct experiments in and out of the lab • Internet links to access information and communicate with other scientists
Social studies	• Simulations to explore distant places and times • Online archives to access many years of social science research • Spreadsheets and databases to organize information

The following lesson plans illustrate the seven instructional events in other content areas and for other grade levels.

Example Lesson Plan

United States History

Unit Title: United States History (Early Beginning through Reconstruction)

Lesson Level: Secondary

Subject Area: Civil War

Lesson Title: Causes of the Civil War

1 **Gaining attention.** Show the following list of wars on a transparency:

French and Indian War, 1754–1769   World War II, 1941–1945

Revolutionary War, 1775–1781   Korean War, 1950–1953

Civil War, 1861–1865   Vietnam War, 1965–1975

World War I, 1914–1918

2 **Informing the learner of the objective.** Learners will be expected to know the causes of the Civil War and to show that those causes also apply to at least one of the other wars listed on the transparency.

3 **Stimulating recall of prerequisite learning.** Briefly review the causes of both the French and Indian War and the Revolutionary War, as covered in lessons 2.1 and 2.2.

4 **Presenting the content.** (a) Summarize the major events leading to the Civil War: rise of sectionalism, labor-intensive economy, and lack of diversification. (b) Identify significant individuals during the Civil War and their roles: Lincoln, Lee, Davis, and Grant. (c) Describe four general causes of war, and explain which are most relevant to the Civil War: economic (to profit), political (to control), social (to influence), and military (to protect).

5 **Eliciting the desired behavior.** Ask the class to identify which of the four causes is most relevant to the major events leading up to the Civil War.

6 **Providing feedback.** Ask for student answers and indicate the plausibility of the volunteered responses.

7 **Assessing the lesson outcome.** Assign as homework a one-page essay that assesses the relative importance of the four causes for one of the wars listed on the transparency.

Example Lesson Plan

Language Arts

Unit Title: Writing Concepts and Skills

Lesson Level: Middle School

Subject Area: Writing Paragraphs

Lesson Title: Descriptive, Narrative, and Expository Paragraphs

1 **Gaining attention.** Read to students examples of short descriptive, narrative, and expository paragraphs from Sunday's newspaper.

2 **Informing the learner of the objective.** Students will be able to discriminate among descriptive, narrative, and expository paragraphs from a list of written examples in the popular press.

3 **Stimulating recall of prerequisite learning.** Review the meanings of the words *description, narration,* and *exposition* as they are used in everyday language.

4 **Presenting the content.** Using a headline from Sunday's newspaper, give students examples of how the story could be reported using description, narration, and exposition.

5 **Eliciting the desired behavior.** Take another front-page story from Sunday's newspaper and ask each student to write a paragraph relating the story in descriptive, narrative, or expository form, whichever he or she prefers.

6 **Providing feedback.** Call on individuals to read their paragraphs aloud; check each paragraph against the criteria for the type the student intended to write.

7 **Assessing the lesson outcome.** Provide multiple-choice questions about each form of writing on the unit test. Have students revise their paragraphs as needed and turn them in as homework the following day.

Example Lesson Plan

Mathematics

Unit Title: Consumer Mathematics

Lesson Level: Elementary

Lesson Area: Basic Mathematics

Lesson Title: Operations and Properties of Ratio, Proportion, and Percentage

1 **Gaining attention.** Display the following so all students can see: (a) can of diet soft drink, (b) one-pound package of spaghetti, (c) box of breakfast cereal.

2 **Informing the learner of the objective.** Learners will be expected to know how to determine ratios, proportions, and percentages from the information on labels of popular food products.

3 **Stimulating recall of prerequisite learning.** Review the definitions of *ratio, proportion,* and *percentage* from the math workbook.

4 **Presenting the content.** Write the information from the soft drink label on a transparency and ask students to identify the percentage of sodium.

5 **Eliciting the desired behavior.** Write on the board the list of ingredients given on the cereal box; ask students to determine (1) the percentage of daily allowance of protein, (2) the proportion of daily allowance of vitamin A, and (3) the ratio of protein to carbohydrates.

6 **Providing feedback.** Using the information on the board, point to the correct answer for behaviors 1 and 2, and show how to find the appropriate numerator and denominator for behavior 3 (in step 5) from the ingredients on the label.

7 **Assessing the lesson outcome.** Provide on the weekly quiz five problems that cover ratios (two problems), proportions (two problems), and percentages (one problem) using labels from other consumer products.

Example Lesson Plan

Science

Unit Title: Manipulative Laboratory Skills

Lesson Level: High School

Lesson Area: Biology

Lesson Title: Use of the Microscope

1 **Gaining attention.** Show the first five minutes of a video about making a lens.

2 **Informing the learner of the objective.** Learners will be expected to be able to focus correctly on a specimen of one-celled animal life, using both high and low magnification.

3 **Stimulating recall of prerequisite learning.** Review the procedures for selecting a slide from the one-celled specimen collection and mounting it on the specimen tray of the microscope.

4 **Presenting the content.** While a student demonstrates in front of the class, help position his or her posture and hands on the microscope. Gently bend his or her body and hands until the correct positioning results. Also, demonstrate the position of the eyes, and show the clockwise and counterclockwise rotation of low and then high magnification adjustment.

5 **Eliciting the desired behavior.** Have each student obtain a specimen slide, mount it on a microscope, and focus on low magnification. Randomly check microscopes, correcting the slide, position, and focus as needed with the student observing. Repeat this step for high magnification.

6 **Providing feedback.** Provide feedback in the context of the eliciting activity (step 5) to increase the immediacy of the feedback. Also refer students to the text for examples of focused and unfocused specimens.

7 **Assessing the lesson outcome.** At the completion of the unit, assess students during a practical lab exam that requires the correct mounting and identification of three unknown specimens using the microscope.

Case History and Licensure Preparation

DIRECTIONS: *The following case history pertains to Chapter 6 content. After reading the case history, go to Chapter 6 in the Book Specific Resources section in the MyEducationLab for your course. Open the Case History and Licensure Preparation activity and complete the questions that follow. Upon completion of the test, scored answers to the short-answer question pertaining to the case history and multiple-choice questions will be provided.*

Case History

A Latin student, Sean, is wearing a toga that shows his bare calves and sandaled feet. Short strips of leather dangle from his hand as he trots about Mr. Cody's tenth-grade English classroom, where he has been invited to show how the Romans dressed and acted for the Feast of the Lupercal. Sean playfully laughs and slaps his classmates on the back, as though at a party.

"That's what the Feast of the Lupercal was all about," he says. "The young Roman men ran races carrying strips of goat hide, which they considered symbols of fertility.

The race course was lined with women who wished to have children; they stood alongside the road, hoping to be touched by the leather."

A few students ask Sean for more information about the feast, and he tells them about some of the athletic games and competitions not mentioned in their current unit about Shakespeare's *Julius Caesar*. It is time for Sean to return to his Latin class, so Mr. Cody fields some of the remaining questions.

"So Caesar wanted his wife to stand in Antony's way so she could have a baby?" Lupe asks.

Instead of answering, Mr. Cody asks another question. "If that were true, Lupe, why would it be significant? What might that tell us about Caesar's ambitions?"

"That he wanted a family. Being emperor wasn't enough to make him happy." Tiffany looks up from the *Glamour* magazine inserted between the pages of her text.

"No," Lupe smiles. "It means he wanted an heir. That he wasn't content to be emperor just for life. He wanted to start his own—what do you call it—dynasty, I think."

"Exactly right, Lupe. Now you can see why some of those senators had a right to be worried." Mr. Cody adjusts his reading glasses and opens his book. "Now let's get back to that section we talked about yesterday, the part about the 'falling sickness'?" He pauses while students open their books to the designated page.

"Angelique, just what is the falling sickness?" Mr. Cody waits for a reply and then reminds her to look at the footnote.

After a few flustered attempts at pronunciation, Angelique responds, "Epilepsy."

"We were talking about that yesterday, about how the senators made such a mockery of Caesar's physical weaknesses behind his back, and some of you felt that was very mean-spirited of them. Those of you taking a history class volunteered to bring up this issue with your teachers, and I suggested that the rest of you might ask an older relative about it."

"My grandpa says that Franklin Roosevelt had polio but that he never appeared in public in his wheelchair," states Danielle.

Nathan volunteers, "Well, it's not really being mean, Mr. Cody. I mean, our president is the commander in chief. He has to be ready to lead us into war; he has to be healthy." Tim looks up from his text.

"He doesn't have to lead the troops himself, though. I mean, wheelchair or not, FDR led us to victory in World War II." Wanda has the last word, as Mr. Cody puts up his hand to quell further discussion.

He continues, "Let's take the next 20 minutes to put our thoughts into words. To what extent do we, like the Romans of Julius Caesar's time, expect our leaders to be physically vigorous? What is your personal opinion on the subject? Support it with reasons."

Summing Up

The main points in this chapter include the following:

Teacher as Decision Maker

1. Four primary inputs to the planning process are (a) knowledge of instructional goals, (b) knowledge of learner needs, (c) knowledge of subject-matter content, and (d) knowledge of teaching methods.

2. Four sources from which you can obtain information about the four inputs to planning are (a) practical experiences, such as observing in classrooms; (b) reading case studies about what successful teachers do; (c) reading the professional literature about important ideas, conceptual systems, and paradigms for thinking about teaching; and (d) reading research studies about your subject and how to teach it.

3. Another input to the planning process is tacit knowledge, representing what works, as discovered over time and through experience.

Unit and Lesson Plans

4. A unit of instruction may be thought of as a system; individual lessons within the unit are its component parts.

5. The concept of *hierarchy* tells us the relationship of the parts to the whole and the concept of *task-relevant prior knowledge* tells us what must come before what in a sequence of events.

Disciplinary and Interdisciplinary Unit Planning

6. Units can be planned vertically, emphasizing the hierarchy of the lesson content and task-relevant prior knowledge within a discipline, or laterally, emphasizing themes that integrate bodies of knowledge across disciplines to convey relationships and patterns that bind different aspects of our world.

7. In vertical planning, boxes illustrate areas of content, or instructional objectives, at various levels of generality. Lines and arrows indicate sequences among lessons and how outcomes of lessons build on one another to achieve a unit goal.

8. Three activities of vertical unit planning include the following:

   - Classifying unit outcomes at a higher level than lesson outcomes in the taxonomies of behavior

   - Planning the instructional sequence so the outcomes of previously taught lessons are instrumental in achieving the outcomes of subsequent lessons

   - Rearranging or adding lesson content to provide task-relevant prior knowledge where needed

9. In lateral, or interdisciplinary, planning, a central theme is identified, and lines or arrows are connected to it to indicate major ideas for lesson content; subordinate ideas flow outward from them.

10. Three activities of lateral, or interdisciplinary, planning are as follows:

    - Identifying an interdisciplinary theme

    - Integrating bodies of knowledge across multiple disciplines

    - Identifying relationships and patterns that bind different aspects of our world together

Making Lesson Plans

11. Before starting the preparation of a lesson plan, you should identify the learning outcome desired for the lesson (e.g., knowledge, application, evaluation, etc.) and what provisions for student diversity need to be included (e.g., time-limited ability grouping, peer tutoring, learning centers, specialized handouts, cooperative grouping).

Events of Instruction

12. The term _learning_ refers to internal events in the heads of learners that result from external teaching events you provide. Hence, the words _teaching_ and _learning_ refer to two different but related sets of activities.

13. The following external events should be specified in a lesson plan:

    - Gaining attention
    - Informing the learner of the objective
    - Stimulating recall of prerequisite learning
    - Presenting the content
    - Eliciting the desired behavior
    - Providing feedback
    - Assessing the lesson outcome

14. Gaining attention involves getting your students interested in what you will present and getting them to switch to the appropriate receptive modality for the upcoming lesson.

15. Informing learners of the objective involves telling them the learning outcome expected at the end of the lesson.

16. Stimulating recall of prerequisite learning is reviewing task-relevant prior information required by the lesson.

17. Presenting the content is delivering the desired content using procedures that stimulate thought processing and maintain interest.

18. Eliciting the desired behavior encourages the learner to attempt a response that displays the desired learning outcome.

19. Providing feedback tells the learner the accuracy of her or his elicited response in a nonthreatening, nonevaluative atmosphere.

20. Assessing the lesson outcome evaluates the learner's performance with tests, portfolios, homework, and extended assignments.

Key Terms

Cross-age tutoring
Curriculum guides
Integrated thematic teaching
Interactive individualized practice
    activities

Interdisciplinary unit
Lateral unit planning
Peer tutoring
Reflective practice
System perspective

Tacit knowledge
Thematic units
Tutorial and communication
    technologies
Vertical unit planning

Discussion and Practice Questions

Questions marked with an asterisk are answered in Appendix B. Some asterisked questions may require student follow-up responses not included in Appendix B. Go to the Assignments and Activities section of the various topics on the MyEducationLab for your course to complete additional practice activities related to this chapter's content.

*1. Identify the four primary inputs to the planning process from which the preparation of a lesson plan proceeds. When would you consult each input in the design of a lesson or unit plan?

*2. How can a unit outcome be more than the sum of its individual lesson outcomes? Give an example using content for a specific unit in your subject matter area.

*3. Explain in your own words how the concepts of *hierarchy* and *task-relevant prior knowledge* are used in unit planning.

*4. Name the levels of behavior in each of the three domains (cognitive, affective, and psychomotor) that generally are most suitable for a unit outcome.

*5. How are the boxes further down on a vertical unit plan different from the boxes higher up? Use the example you provided in question 2 to illustrate your answer.

*6. Explain how a graphic unit plan for a vertical unit is different from a graphic unit plan for a lateral unit. In your own words, why must there be a difference?

7. In your own words, what is the distinction between *teaching* and *learning?* What examples might you use to illustrate the difference with respect to a learner in your classroom?

*8. Identify the instructional event for which the key behavior of *instructional variety* would be most important.

*9. Identify the instructional event for which the key behavior of *student success* would be most important.

*10. Identify the instructional event for which the key behavior of *student engagement in the learning process* would be most important.

*11. Indicate how the instructional events of providing feedback and assessing behavior differ according to (a) the evaluative nature of the feedback provided and (b) the immediacy with which the feedback is given.

Professional Practice

Field Experience and Practice Activities

Questions marked with an asterisk are answered in Appendix B. Some asterisked questions may require student follow-up responses not included in Appendix B.

1. From a lesson you have observed, provide an example of task-relevant prior learning that would need to be taught prior to your observation. From your observation of student behavior, do you believe this knowledge was adequately taught? Why or why not?

2. For subject matter you will be expected to teach, vertically plan a three-lesson unit within a discipline in which the sequence of lessons is critical to achieving the outcome. Then laterally plan a three-lesson interdisciplinary unit in which lesson sequence is unimportant. Be sure the lesson outcomes for each unit reflect the unit outcome. In both cases, follow the graphic format shown in this chapter, drawing your lesson plan by hand or using Microsoft Word or Inspiration software (www.inspiration.com/home.cfm).

*3. From your classroom observations, identify several ways instruction was differentiated to meet individual learner needs in the context of a lesson. Which way do you believe will be most effective for your grade level or content area?

*4. From a lesson plan of a teacher you are observing, identify the seven events of instruction presented in this chapter. Which event or events, if any, could you not identify? Why?

Digital Portfolio Activity

The following digital portfolio activity relates to InTASC Standards 7, 8, and 9.

Place your unit and lesson plans for Field Experience Activities 2 and 4 into your digital portfolio in a folder titled "Lesson and Unit Plans." These will provide examples of your skill at planning disciplinary and interdisciplinary units and lessons. Add other examples of lesson and unit plans that represent your best planning as they become available.

MyEducationLab™

Go to MyEducationLab (www.myeducationlab.com) for Effective Teaching Methods: Research-Based Practice where you can:

- Find learning outcomes for the various course topics course along with national standards that connect to these outcomes.

- Complete **Assignments and Activities** that can help you more deeply understand the chapter content.

- Apply and practice your understanding of the core teaching skills identified in the chapter with **Building Teaching Skills and Dispositions** coaching activities.

- Check your comprehension of the content covered in the chapter with a book specific **Study Plan**. Here you will be able to take a chapter **pretest**, receive feedback on your answers, and then access personalized **Review, Practice, and Enrichment exercises** to enhance your understanding of chapter content. After you complete the exercises, take a **posttest** to confirm your comprehension.

- Learn how to address common classroom management issues in the **Simulations in Classroom Management**.

- Access video clips of CCSSO **National Teachers of the Year award winners** responding to the question, "Why Do I Teach?" in the Teacher Talk section.

- Create, update, and share quality lesson plans with the **Lesson Plan Builder**.

- Access state licensure test requirements, overviews of what tests cover, and sample test items in the **Certification and Licensure** section.

- Learn how to create a high quality teaching portfolio in the **Preparing a Portfolio** section.

- Access tips, advice, and other information on resume writing and interviewing, your first year of teaching, and law and public policies in the Beginning Your Career section.

7 Technology Integration in Instruction

This chapter will help you answer these questions and meet the following InTASC standards for effective teaching.

- Why teach with technology?
- What are the types of Web 2.0 technologies that can provide new contexts for learning in my classroom?
- How can I promote higher order thinking with the use of technology?
- How can technology help develop the collaborative skills of my learners?
- How will I know when technology is achieving my instructional goals?

InTASC

STANDARD 2 **Learning Differences.** The teacher uses understanding of individual differences and diverse cultures and communities to ensure inclusive learning environments that enable each learner to meet high standards.

STANDARD 3 **Learning Environments.** The teacher works with others to create environments that support individual and collaborative learning, and that encourage positive social interaction, active engagement in learning, and self motivation.

STANDARD 6 **Assessment.** The teacher understands and uses multiple methods of assessment to engage learners in their own growth, to monitor learner progress, and to guide the teacher's and learner's decision making.

STANDARD 7 **Planning for Instruction.** The teacher plans instruction that supports every student in meeting rigorous learning goals by drawing upon knowledge of content areas, curriculum, cross-disciplinary skills, and pedagogy, as well as knowledge of learners and the community context.

The previous two chapters have presented the essential skills needed for lesson planning. It is now time to complement your lesson planning skills with the many opportunities you will have to enhance your students' learning by integrating instructional technology into

your lesson plans. One of the major themes of previous chapters has been the importance of recognizing individual differences among your learners and adapting instruction to learner needs. As you will see in this chapter, your ability to integrate instructional technology into your lesson plans will be one of the major tools you will have to achieve this goal and for your learners to attain higher order outcomes in more authentic real-world environments.

Since the beginning of the twenty-first century, the Internet has been widely integrated into all walks of life, which has made a significant impact on education. Instructional technologies have become a major instructional platform for meeting learner needs. In the beginning of the Internet era, web pages were read-only, and the content could only be created by the website owner. Website visitors were information consumers but not information creators. Newer Internet technologies have revolutionized this static, one-sided, "take it" or leave it" platform for learning, replacing it with tools for dynamic online, real time interaction. Website visitors now can collaborate and create content together online. Learners can go beyond static graphical and temporal boundaries and change with whom they communicate and interact. And, teachers are increasingly becoming accustomed to interactive technological environments and integrating up-to-date technologies into instruction to evoke meaningful learning. This has become an essential complement to effective teaching methods.

Numerous research studies have found that appropriate technology integration can spark the joy of learning and provide students with cognitive tools to process information, to reflect on what they know, and to construct knowledge based on what they know (Jonassen, 1999; Lajoie, 1993). To engage students, learning tasks must be meaningful—engaging them in decision making, problem solving, and inquiry (Howland, Jonassen, & Marra, 2012). As instructional technologies have evolved, the pedagogical paradigm has changed from teacher-centered to student-centered, and technological applications have shifted their focus from users as consumers to users as creators.

In this chapter you will learn about instructional technologies and how they can benefit teachers across disciplines and grades. The content is organized around three questions: *Why* teach with technology?; *What* technologies can I use to improve my teaching effectiveness?; and, *How* can I integrate these technologies into my instruction? The answer to the *why* question will provide the underlying reasons it is important to integrate technologies into your teaching. The answer to the *what* question will describe the instructional technologies you will want to incorporate into your classroom. And, the answers to the *how* question will show you ways to implement these technologies in your classroom. In this chapter, you will also learn some guidelines for evaluating the effectiveness of your technology integration.

Why Teach with Technology?

MyEducationLab™

Visit the MyEducationLab for *Effective Teaching Methods: Research-Based* Practice, 8e to ennce your understanding of chapter concepts with a personalized Study Plan. You'll also have the opportunity to hone your teaching skills through video-based Assignments and Activities as well as Building Teaching Skills and Dispositions lessons.

With pressure from mandated curricula, Common Core State Standards, the rigor and relevance framework, and high-stakes exams, teachers have good reasons to integrate technology into their instruction. But is technology effective for teaching? This is a question that often weighs on a teacher's mind. The debate on the effectiveness of technology or media on learning has been waged by many scholars since the last century (Clark, 1983, 1994; Kozma, 1991, 1994). From this debate one point is clear: Technology is not a fix for poorly designed instruction. The effectiveness of technology depends on how teachers are able to integrate it into their instruction. In this chapter you will learn that both the teacher and the instructional design are fundamental to achieving effective technology integration.

Many studies have illuminated the educational value of technologies and justify their integration into instruction. Ogle and Beers (2009) in their text *Engaging in the Language Arts: Exploring the Power of Language* indicate that the use of technology in the classroom can:

- Increase student motivation and engagement
- Improve reading and writing skills
- Expand classroom reading materials
- Expand response and collaboration opportunities
- Expand experiences and content knowledge
- Promote imagination, critical thinking, and problem solving
- Promote multicultural understanding
- Support the learning of diverse students—those from low-income families, those with different cultural experiences, those who are English language learners, and those with physical, mental, and emotional challenges
- Increase understanding and use of the new literacies
- Promote professional development and collaboration

The research literature refers to the overall purposes for online interactions as communication, knowledge building, and learning (Joubert & Wishart, 2012). For example, technology provides students with cognitive flexibility (Spiro et al., 1991). Internet technologies now provide a manipulative media environment, called **hypermedia**, where the different learning needs of students can be met using multiple presentations of information from different sources at different levels of difficulty, along with the opportunity to create new knowledge, not just parrot back existing information. Technologies integrated with your instruction can also support **distributed cognition** (Hutchins, 1995). Distributed cognition emphasizes the thinking together aspects of cognition and advocates learning that involves the simultaneous interaction among students, computer, and the learning environment.

Because of the dynamic nature of the Internet, students have many opportunities to interpret, process, and transform information into knowledge and skills. Moreover, online technologies can help cultivate communities of practice in which students have abundant resources and facilitative tools to form their own groups, based on their interests, to exchange and create knowledge (Wenger, McDermott, & Snyder, 2002). It is expected that today's students will as adults work in jobs that do not exist today. Your classroom instruction will need to be designed to equip students with the skills of collaborative learning, inquiry, problem solving, and metacognition that can be applied in, as well as beyond, the classroom to meet these twenty-first century challenges (Knowles, 1975).

To better equip your learners to face these challenges, Anderson and colleagues (2001) revised Bloom et al.'s (1984) taxonomy in the cognitive domain with the newly added behavior of *create* (see Figure 5.4, Chapter 5, p. 147), whereby students are expected to use their previous experience to synthesize information

The use of technology in the classroom can provide a media environment in which different learning needs can be met using multiple presentations of information, from different sources and at different levels of difficulty.

and construct an original never seen before idea or product. From this framework we find that the creation of knowledge is not a completely inspirational or unplanned action but can be taught by design when teachers integrate technology into their instruction.

No matter how eloquent a teacher's presentation to an attentive and motivated class may be, it is not an easy task to solely rely on "telling" and to be able to have students engaged all the time. This is especially so with today's generation of learners who are accustomed to visual stimuli and multimedia presentations. To gain their attention and to meet their diverse learning needs, teachers will need classroom technologies that update and change the way they teach.

Most of your students today are exposed to multimedia and the Internet on a daily basis. They are "digital natives" (Prensky, 2001) or the "Net generation" (Tapscott, 1998). Most will have been born in the last 15 years depending on your grade level and they are different than learners before them. They grew up with the Internet and, for most of them, using technologies is as natural as breathing. Although these digital natives are familiar with communication and gaming technologies, they do not necessary know how to use or learn from technologies in the classroom (Bennett & Matont, 2010). While technologies integrated with your instruction may be different than some of the technologies with which they are familiar, you will need to reach them in ways that complement what they already know and build upon them. To make this happen, this chapter will present some of the most effective and efficient technologies for adoption and integration into your instruction.

Twenty-First Century Learning Technologies

The technologies in this chapter apply to Web 2.0 technologies, course management systems, and interactivity technologies that can extend and improve the clarity, depth, and scope of your lesson plans. Each of these technologies has its strengths, and you need to know how to use them at the appropriate place and time in your instruction.

Web 2.0 Technologies

In the past decade **Web 2.0 technologies** have been the most dominant information technologies on the Internet, and they have become an important means for facilitating learning and instruction in your classroom. They are dynamic, intuitively easy to use, social and collaborative, and many of them are free of charge. As a result, students can play more active roles in the learning process. Most importantly, with these technologies students can construct knowledge through social interactions with peers (Vygotsky, 1978).

Web 2.0 technologies, often called social media or social software, have been heralded as a tool for information gathering, communication, interaction, and social networking. Web 2.0 was defined as a platform without boundaries, facilitating communication, interaction, and collective intelligence through animated and refreshing display channels (O'Reilly, 2005). By creating opportunities for collaboration, these social technologies provide learners with user-friendly platforms to enhance communication with teachers and peers, and support the creation of social relationships among learners (Schroeder, Minocha, & Schneidert, 2010). Advances in Web 2.0 have brought to life constructivist approaches in which learners are expected to learn by constructing their own view of the world in concert with other learners.

Although there are many types of Web 2.0 technologies, not all of its tools were designed specifically for educational use. As a result, some teachers are hesitant to use them. They struggle to justify their use and to anchor them to their instructional objectives. The next sections will spell out the nature of these technologies to help you adopt appropriate technologies that are matched to your learners' needs. Specifically, the selection is based on the most dominant student learning needs, their current level of technology acceptance, their potential value in your classroom, and whether or not the technology (website) is free of charge.

For Web 2.0 to have maximum impact in your classroom, you will want to consider inquiry-based learning together with problem and project-based learning. With these methods, students get the opportunity to question and to be questioned while teachers use problems and projects to motivate students to investigate phenomena, create explanations, discuss their findings with peers, and reflect on their conclusions. These methods can be integrated with the different types of Web 2.0

Table 7.1 **The Focus of Inquiry Across Disciplines**

Discipline	Action of Inquiry
Social science	Engage in meaningful, integrative, value-based, challenging, and active learning to foster the "ability to make informed and reasoned decisions for the public good as citizens of a culturally diverse, democratic society in an interdependent world." (National Council for the Social Studies, 2008)
Science	"Conduct an investigation and collect evidence from a variety of sources, develop an explanation from the data, and communicate and defend . . . conclusions" to promote understanding of the natural world. (National Science Teachers Association, 2004)
Math	Participate in rigorous, high-quality mathematics instruction to develop the "level of mathematical thinking and problem solving needed" in our world today. (National Council of Teachers of Mathematics, 2000)
Language arts	Utilize reading, writing, speaking, listening, and observing for authentic purposes to "influence an individual's ability to become self-sufficient and lead a productive life." (National Council of Teachers of English, 1982)

technologies below to create learning tasks that support a commitment to inquiry in authentic learning contexts (Borich, Hao, & Aw, 2006). Table 7.1 illustrates several inquiry goals for integrating Web 2.0 technologies across the K–12 curriculum (Audet & Jordan, 2005).

Course Management Technology

During the past decade, the number of online courses has been increasing exponentially, and online learning has become commonplace at all levels of education (Hao & Borich, 2009). Studies by the Southern Regional Education Board (2007) indicate that online courses are now being used to prepare students to transition smoothly through advanced and remedial courses, improving school graduation rates and providing online discussion activities that promote higher order thinking (Bonk, 1997). When local schools face some unexpected event, such as severe weather, an incident of violence, or an epidemic that precludes or reduces class attendance, learning online becomes an alternative choice for students. In these cases course management systems are often used to construct online learning environments. Even for traditional face-to-face courses, teachers can use a course management system to enhance student learning in contexts and with experiences that exist outside of the classroom.

 The teacher in this **video** discusses the components of an online course. Pay attention to the type of technology used in this virtual classroom.

What can a course management system offer students and teachers in the traditional classroom setting? In general, course management systems can store course materials, provide discussion boards, bulletin boards, e-mail delivery, assessment tools, and, most important, develop an online learning community for motivating your learners. The strength of the system is in creating a learning environment in which students can move in and out of the formal classroom at will to retrieve and exchange online information, discuss topics, and collaborate with peers and their teacher to construct knowledge (Koschmann, 1996). To get the most out of an online learning environment you will need to promote and nurture your students' self-regulation and independent learning skills (Bonk & Graham, 2006). Research studies have indicated that students feel more comfortable and have more opportunities to learn and express themselves in online discussions when they have been introduced to and are asked to display these skills (Khan, 1997).

With a course management system teachers can message and communicate asynchronously or synchronously. **Asynchronous learning** is when information and messages are placed online for students to retrieve at their convenience or at the time they may be needed for completing an assignment (e.g., readings, finding reference and resource material, looking up course and subject outlines, seeing examples of assignments and products to be completed, learning the criteria by which they will be assessed, etc). **Synchronous learning** is when information and messages are placed online for the

In Practice

Focus on Applications of Online Learning

Graham, Allen, and Ure (2005) report that integrating online learning with traditional learning activities can transform teacher-centered instruction to student-centered learning, increase student access to learning and learning flexibility, and increase the cost-effectiveness of schooling. With the wide adoption of computer-mediated communication (CMC) technologies in education, integrating online learning activities (for example, online discussions) has become a frequent objective in K–12 classrooms.

When designing online learning activities, you will first want to examine your instructional objectives. The course management system Moodle is a good learning platform for the following objectives.

1. *To teach basic skills:* To help students acquire information or obtain knowledge about a person, place, or event (for example, learn about an event pertaining to world events), the teacher can post some website information on a discussion board to which all students would have access. Students schedule their own time to read the content on the website and identify the critical points to be discussed. Students can report what they read in class meetings or in online postings. They can paraphrase or generalize the facts from their own and each other's postings. Taking advantage of the abundance of authentic materials on the Internet, the teacher can instruct students to find readings outside of class and provide them with questions that help with comprehension. Students can then present their findings either online or in class.

2. *To teach higher-level skills:* To help students apply, analyze, synthesize and evaluate information (for example, investigate the evidence for global warming, the pros and cons of urban development, or wind power), you can upload reading materials in a course management system to have students gain background knowledge of what you will be teaching in class. In class, you can model higher levels of thinking needed to synthesize the materials and, afterwards, ask students to construct, investigate, propose, or conclude their findings in class meetings or in online discussion boards.

3. *Inquiry-based activity:* There are different types of inquiry learning, from teacher-centered to student-centered. To equip students with inquiry skills, a teacher can adopt WebQuest, an online learning activity that can transform a teacher-centered classroom to a student-centered framework (Dodge & March, 1995). WebQuest is a type of inquiry learning in which the learning is cyclical and starts with questions. Then, hypotheses are tested, answers are presented, and new questions are formed. In the scenario of WebQuest, the teacher first introduces students to some problem or activity. Then, students are required to conduct an investigation. In the process, the teacher provides specific steps or support to help students accomplish the task and provides and organizes information and resources for the students to search for the answer. Furthermore, the teacher informs students of the information on how their work will be graded. Checklists or rubrics can be created for the evaluation. Finally, the teacher concludes the WebQuest inquiry by summarizing the student's accomplishment and relating it to the learning goals. Depending on the level of inquiry, a teacher can manipulate the level of teacher-directedness and inquiry. Dodge and March (1995) have a website, which explains WebQuest process, http://webquest.org/.

4. *Online discussions:* The main activity in asynchronous online learning is the online discussion. Teachers can design an array of asynchronous online discussions by encouraging students to critique each other's work, by raising contradictory issues for students to debate, by inviting experts to share experiences and thoughts with students, or by raising some problem for students to solve or some case to discuss. Students often learn more in online discussions compared with face-to-face class meetings (Harasim, 1997). A combination of face-to-face and online discussions can provide an optimal learning environment in a heterogeneous classroom. To make online discussions a success, the teacher needs to choose topics interesting to students, stating clearly the goals and expectations for the discussion. There should be opportunities for both informal and task-oriented discussions. Furthermore, the teacher needs to facilitate online discussions by developing a social presence in the learning community, emphasizing the value of student-to-student interactions, promoting equitable collaboration, and providing constructive feedback for students in the discussion process (Rovai, 2007). Finally, the teacher needs to moderate the discussions.

5. *Online learning communities and collaborative learning:* To motivate your students in online learning, you will need to design learning tasks that get your students' attention and engages them in the learning process. You will want to engage students by having them collaborate online to develop a sense of community. To develop a sense of community, you can have students share ideas, experiences, and resources (Rovai, 2000). Palloff and Pratt I (2005) suggest developing this community by explaining the importance of collaboration, providing guidelines for the collaboration, modeling the process of collaboration online, and helping to guide and evaluate the process.

learner to receive and process immediately (e.g., instant e-mail messaging and discussion and bulletin boards for immediate student interactivity and feedback). Asynchronous and synchronous messaging provide alternative, but not mutually exclusive, ways for your students to access information and knowledge online. Their use in combination with face-to-face instruction is sometimes referred to as **blended learning**. For extended online assignments, you will want to provide some information asynchronously to provide resource material, timelines, and assessment tools that can aid assignment and project completion (Palloff & Pratt, 2003). If you want to augment your face-to-face classroom instruction with timely suggestions for your students, student-to-student and student-to-teacher feedback, idea sharing, and online discussion boards, you will want to provide some information synchronously with instant messaging. See In Practice: Focus on Applications of Online Learning.

With the emergence of Web 2.0 technologies that provide information sharing and collaboration, most course management systems tend to be embedded with the features of some social media (for example, blogs, or wikis) platform from which your students can interact. To avoid outsiders from gaining access to the identities and information being communicated by your students, course management systems provide the option of a closed system that keeps the main features of Web 2.0 (sharing, communicating, and collaborating) from being seen by others.

Moodle (https://moodle.org) is an example of a free and open source **course management system** for creating a personal communication tool by which you can maintain contact with your students in or outside of your classroom. It can be used to provide emergency announcements, resources for completing assignments, updates and timelines for work to be completed, as well as motivation for promoting higher and more in-depth levels of performance. You can use your personal computer as the server for Moodle and install it to run a personal Moodle from your classroom or home. Your school's support staff should be able to help set up Moodle to provide your classroom with access to the system and technical support.

Moodle can be regarded as an alternative to a physical classroom and is considered an ideal course management system. It is suitable for both teacher-centered and student-centered interaction. After posting course or subject content, introductory information, handouts, explanations for homework or practice exams, and so on, you can refer students to these online resources and thereby have more classroom time for teaching subject-specific content. When there is insufficient time to have a thorough discussion about a particular topic, you can open a discussion forum in Moodle. If the discussion forum is interspersed with face-to-face presentations, students can participate at their convenience, while you specify homework assignments, deadlines, and assessment criteria to ensure student participation. As an additional aid to your instruction, your course management system can include tracking tools that will record and report how much time each student spends on the online tasks that you assign.

When you try to build an online discussion community, some students might be hesitant to join. In order to break the ice and jump start a discussion, you can ask a personal question that they are motivated to answer (e.g., What do you like about school?, What are your favorite subjects?, etc.). Salmon (2004) suggests a five-stage model as a framework for moderating online discussions. The stages are:

- *Access and motivation* (the teacher welcomes and encourages students)
- *Online socialization* (the teacher helps students become familiar with one another and with the online learning environment)
- *Information exchange* (the teacher facilitates students sharing information)
- *Knowledge construction* (the teacher provides for and facilitates learning activities)
- *Student reflection* (the teacher encourages students to reflect on what they've learned)

Figure 7.1 **A Rubric for Making Students Aware of What They Are Expected to Accomplish**

Have you:

1. Selected resources?

☐ none ☐ some ☐ often ☐ many

2. Messaged with other members of your class?

☐ none ☐ a little ☐ some ☐ often

3. Checked for the accuracy of your assignment?

☐ not yet ☐ a little ☐ some ☐ finished

4. Decided on your final group product?

☐ not yet ☐ beginning to ☐ somewhat ☐ done

In addition to your moderating function, individual student assistance should be available at each stage. Your assistance should include directing how to send and receive messages (e.g., e-mails), helping with navigating the system, conferencing with groups of classmates, and searching the Internet for resources needed to complete an assignment. With your classroom management system, your students will have the opportunity to express themselves, exchange thoughts, and evaluate ideas.

When your students are required to work in groups, you can set up group norms and group member responsibilities before discussion activities begin. (See the stages of group development for which you can design online group work in Chapter 3, pp.73–77.) You can also use your course management system to help initiate a discussion by providing rubrics for communicating what your students are expected to accomplish and how they will be assessed, as suggested in Figure 7.1.

Through online discussions, you will naturally get to know more about your students, to elaborate on their ideas, and bring their thoughts into face-to-face class meetings for further structuring and elaboration. Your students can also submit assignments online by uploading files to Moodle. You can learn more about creating e-learning activities and the application of online learning tools from Bonk (2006), Shank (2007), and Simonson, et al. (2012).

Blog Technology

The teachers in this **video** are discussing the challenges they face when developing blogs for their classrooms. What techno-personal skills do you need to successfully integrate technology in the classroom?

Blogs, also called web logs, provide a platform for your students to publish text, audios, or video online (called video blog, vblog, or vlog). Students visiting blogs can leave comments or directly interact with the blog owner or with other visitors asynchronously in addition to your planned instructional content. Blogs provide a platform for self-reflection and self-expression by showing your students' work online and by publishing it for others to see. Content is displayed in reverse chronological order (latest first). Blogs functioning as personal or group journals can facilitate metacognitive and higher order thinking (Gunawardena et al., 2009). In essence, a blog is a reflective tool providing students with an effective platform for reflection (Hao, 2009). When students blog, they reflect and articulate thoughts through writing, audio recording, or video, thus enhancing their cognitive and metacognitive skills.

Podcasting, the equivalent of blogging in the audio form, and video blogging, the equivalent of blogging in the video form, are alternative types of blogs. Podcasting differs from posting audio files online in that users receive podcasts automatically—like a radio broadcast transmitted through the Internet. A podcast is a series of online audio files distributed by **Really Simple Syndication (RSS)**. An additional tool affiliated with the use of blogs is the RSS feed. It is a technology that allows your students to subscribe to a particular blog, podcast, or video blog and have it download to their electronic devices automatically, for example, a computer, an MP3 player, and even a smart phone.

For at-risk learners, many writing assignments go unattempted or are begun only halfheartedly because these learners recognize their written work will not meet minimal writing standards. To aid these students, consider assigning an audio or video podcast project at the beginning of the school year. These platforms have the advantage of avoiding errors in spelling, syntax, and writing at a critical time in the learner's development. Podcasting may consume more of the learner's time than blogging or video blogging, but it can bring a real-world flavor and enhancement to classroom teaching. For information on how to make a podcast, see Podcast for Teachers (http://www.podcastforteachers.org/).

Because blogs are accessible and provide accountability, they are suitable for developing online portfolios and learning journals. After developing online portfolios, students can assess each other and themselves with assigned rubrics to develop their digital literacy. To develop a complete digital portfolio, a student can use blogs as the portfolio platform and follow a few simple steps (Hartnell-Young & Morriss, 2007).

Google Blogger is one blogger tool that is readily available. Students can open an account at Google (http://www.blogger.com) to collect their work (especially their significant work). They can upload files to Blogger to establish personal archives. If the work is not digital, it can be photographed and/or scanned. Then, students can write a statement of their goal or vision—what they intend to accomplish—so that you will have a clear understanding of what to look for in reviewing their portfolios. Keep in mind that initial entries in a portfolio are more suitable for formative assessment, used for assessing development or progress, than summative assessment, used for selection and grading. Therefore, in your students' vision statement, they should list the specific content and steps that will form the framework of their portfolios, so that they have a guide to follow in their portfolio development. When the framework is ready, students select work from their personal archives to validate their competency. Each work should be unique. To make connections between the items of work, your students may need to create graphic organizers (for example, a chart or table). Finally, to make the portfolio comprehensive, students will need to write an introduction and a reflection for each work and a reflection on the portfolio as a whole. To help your students present their whole portfolio, there are free Web 2.0 applications for concept mapping and online presentation, which will be described later.

Blogs are especially suitable as a reflective tool. After conducting a learning task, students can reflect on their learning experience and journal about it in their blogs. However, you should not expect students to automatically know how to reflect. You can post content-related topics or raise questions in blogs to stimulate students' thinking and reflection using questions as prompts following the framework outlined below or others suggested by Schon (1987), Postholm (2008), and Smyth (1989).

- Reflection *before* action (thinking about prior experiences and theories before taking action): "What do I already know and can I use in developing my blog?"
- Reflection in action (thinking that takes place during practice): "How can I arrange my blog for maximum impact in fulfilling my purpose?"
- Reflection on action (reflection after practice has been completed): "How might I revise my blog or do things differently?"

If you want a website for your classroom, a blog should be your first choice. Your students already know or will quickly learn how to write and reply to e-mails which is all that is required in order to blog. Teachers do not need knowledge of website construction to use blogs. For safety and security reasons, it is suggested that your students write blogs in a closed system, like Moodle, with access limited just to your school.

Knowledge Organization and Construction Technology

Some Web 2.0 applications are ideally suited for knowledge organization and construction. Social bookmarking, social presentation, and concept mapping are online technologies that can facilitate your students' organization and construction of knowledge. Let's look at each of these tools to learn how they can be integrated into your instruction.

Social Bookmarking. **Social bookmarking** applications facilitate the building of an easily accessible online bookmark warehouse. After logging into a social bookmarking website, users assign descriptions (tags) to a chosen website, and then the website becomes searchable to members or to the public. Tags allow users to manage their researched knowledge (Gunawardena et al., 2009).

Users can browse their own bookmarks by time, by tag, or by topic (Farkas, 2008). This technology facilitates knowledge organization by putting together the bookmarks saved and having the connected users (through tags) share the bookmarks with each other.

Social bookmarking can be integrated into your instruction whenever you assign students to work on a project and students need to search for and organize information, especially on the Internet. Many times students find the same or related information and waste time on overlapping tasks. Social bookmarking is one of the Web 2.0 applications that can help avoid these problems to make your instruction more efficient. Del.icio.us (http://delicious.com/) is a good social bookmarking tool for the elementary and high school grades.

When a teacher starts a group project, students go to Del.icio.us to open a free account. By setting up a personal account, students can assign their peers as friends and share the bookmarks they keep at Del.icio.us. In addition to the website information friends save through bookmarks, students can look at all user-saved information of other websites that can help them learn from other related resources. With social networking, your learners are connected through common interests with a global community.

Social Presentation.   The **social presentation** tool is another application that adopts the concept of the Web 2.0 framework to help students share and work together to organize and construct knowledge. The task is to make an online presentation. To accomplish this, users log into a social presentation website, name the presentation, and start to construct the content. Friends can create slides together online, and the finished presentation content can be watched online with an accompanying website link. Through a social presentation, student presentations to the class can have a professional appearance and are easily edited during development as more knowledge is organized and constructed representing the best thinking of groups of students working collaboratively.

Web 2.0 social presentation tools can be integrated into your instruction whenever a group response or presentation is assigned. One social presentation tool is Prezi (http://prezi.com/). When students collaborate on a project and are going to present their work, they can make their presentation come "alive" with Prezi. After logging in, the students have to organize the content and sequence it in a logical way. The tool is social and collaborative; that is, students can share and work together with peers online to complete the task. Prezi also provides animation effects that make the tool especially popular with young learners.

Concept Mapping.   **Concept mapping** is a type of graphic organizer—or mind tool—for knowledge organization that can help students interpret, represent, and organize information by making a graphic in cooperation with one another. Concept mapping has been recognized as an effective way to visualize what's in one's mind and portray the organization of knowledge (Novak & Gowin, 1984; Novak & Musonda, 1991). Teachers can use any subject or grade level content with concept mapping as a mind tool to help students achieve the interrelationship among ideas and promote the higher order thinking skills called for when analyzing, synthesizing, and evaluating (Jonassen, 1999).

When teaching a set of related ideas or a concept, you can consider using concept mapping to enhance students' comprehension. One concept mapping tool, bubbl (https://bubbl.us/), is a good example of a platform for integrating concept mapping with your classroom presentation. A teacher can invite students to create a free account at bubbl. Once logged in, students can start drawing diagrams alone or with peers. Peers do not have to be online at the same time.

There are a few guidelines to making a concept map (Novak & Musonda, 1991). First, the teacher has to choose a particular question for students to answer, called a *focus question*. The question functions as the context for the concept map. Second, the teacher guides students to include *cross-links*. These are links between concepts in different domains of the concept map. Cross-links are lines or connecting points between segments of a concept that help students illustrate how a concept in one domain is related to a concept in another domain. Specific examples that help to clarify the meaning of a given concept can be added. You saw some concept maps for interdisciplinary units in Chapter 6.

In addition to helping students grasp the concepts, concept mapping can be used as an assessment tool that asks learners to graphically show their comprehension of the overall concepts or themes in what they have read. Teachers can also use bubbl to graphically illustrate lesson plans, as shown in Chapter 6.

Collaborative Writing Technology

The word "**wiki**" derives from the Hawaiian word "hurry" and represents a website where users, assigned in groups, can create content collaboratively. A wiki differs from *wikipedia,* which is an online encyclopedia. Wiki pages can be open to the public or limited to a group. The wiki is a collaborative tool because the content generation of the wiki is contributed by all participants in a shared digital space (O'Reilly, 2005). A strength of the wiki is that the content entered is continuously visible, so individual contributions of group members can be monitored. Through the mechanism of wiki participation, "communities of practice" (Wenger, 1998) can develop a collective intelligence to create knowledge and understandings while the spirit of constructivism—fostering meaningful group learning—is being carried out.

When there is insufficient class time for student collaboration, a Wiki is an efficient way for students to generate ideas together and collaborate on a project.

You will want to consider integrating a wiki into your instruction whenever you want your students to collaborate on a project or construct meanings together for a class. But sometimes there may be insufficient class time for students to collaborate and adequately develop their ideas. In this case, Wikispaces is a solution (http://www.wikispaces.com/). After you create a wiki, you can assign students to different groups and send them an invitation to open an account. Following the link, students can open an account and schedule time together to work on their group wiki; their contributions will be recorded. It's important for the group participants to take collective responsibility for knowledge construction by making complementary contributions, responding to, and building on, the ideas and contributions of others (Joubert & Wishart, 2012). You can co-create content with your students and make contributions to each group's wiki.

To make the best use of a wiki, you will want to follow a few guidelines.

1. You will need to set up clear expectations both for individual and group contributions with respect to the quality and quantity of work expected.

2. Your timeline should be limited to exert disciplined decision making to avoid some students being left behind and posting content at the last minute.

3. Ask students to cite references and sources to provide evidence of content accuracy. You will want to encourage your students to challenge each other's thoughts and contributions but respect each other's work.

4. Finally, you will want to examine each group's work regularly to check on their progress.

Keep in mind that your monitoring responsibilities include providing models of possible solutions that can lead students to the right or an acceptable solution as well as encouraging them to challenge each other's thoughts. You will also want to schedule a time for check-ups that can steer learners away from poor choices or inefficient paths of inquiry. When there is group work, the wiki is a good choice to examine each person's contribution and to monitor the quality of work while promoting the spirit of participation.

Virtual Worlds Technology

Virtual worlds provide an interactive environment, often in a two- or three-dimensional format, that is especially popular with K–12 students. They can provide the context where users are immersed in an online role-playing game for instructional purposes. In this eye-attractive, authentic world, users choose or create characters (called avatars), whose identities they assume and interact with in real time. In this imaginary world, a user plays an avatar that can be personalized to fit any role or learning context corresponding to your instructional goals (e.g., a corporate director of a space age technology company, a chairperson of a city council, or a geologist exploring uncharted territory). This simulated world can provide contexts for learning or an environment for social interaction. In this environment, users can observe, experience, and create what would be difficult or too costly in real

Watch this **video** that discusses virtual field trips. What are some of the advantages to this type of technology?

life, for example, to solve problems of pollution in a simulated city or geographic region, resolve a controversy involving the location of recreational facilities in a city park, or present arguments for and against rerouting of an oil pipeline.

Virtual worlds provide an environment ideal for role playing, simulation, work display, communication, and foreign language training. How does it do all these things? A teacher can display a problem through a virtual world, making the problem authentic and relevant to students. The environment is ideal for students to manipulate objects and to test hypotheses in an authentic context for inquiry-based learning. Whyville (http://www.whyville.net/smmk/nice) for children ages 9–16 and Woogi (http://www.woogiworld.com/) for elementary-age children provide this experience. Also see In Practice: Focus on Digital Gaming in the Classroom.

In Practice

Focus on Digital Gaming in the Classroom

Green and Hannon (2007, p. 38) capture the great wave of technology that has swept through students of the digital age with the remark, "Children are establishing a relationship to knowledge gathering which is alien to their parents and teachers."

Educators can be overwhelmed by this wave or they can ride it to a new educational level that is both dynamic and interactive. It is no secret that games and simulations have been key in the training of doctors, scientists, business people, and military personnel alike. It is now beginning to wash ashore in the classroom as well.

According to a May 2012 national survey of teachers conducted by the Joan Ganz Cooney Center, nearly 70 percent of educators reported that lower-performing students engaged more in subject matter content with the use of digital games than without them, while three-fifths reported increased attention to specific tasks and improved collaborations among all students. Sixty percent said that using digital games helped personalize instruction and better assess student knowledge and learning and that games made it easier to teach a range of learners in their classrooms.

Research (Facer, 2003) indicates that playing video games results in the development of new cognitive abilities that translate into key skills, indicating that games help learners:

- Process information quickly
- Determine what is and is not of relevance in a problem solving situation
- Process information in parallel—at the same time and from a range of different sources
- Become familiar with exploring information in a non-linear fashion

- Access information through imagery and then use text to clarify, expand, and explore the information
- Achieve the capacity to see one's environment as a form of problem-solving

The Education Arcade, a collaboration between the Comparative Media Studies Department at MIT and Microsoft iCampus, has sought ways to minimize "the sharp disconnect between the way students are taught in school and the way the outside world approaches socialization, meaning-making, and accomplishment." Of particular note is the Games-to-Teach Project featuring next-generation media for math, science, and humanities education (http://www.educationarcade.org/gtt/proto.html).

Following are some of their new-age digital games designed for the classroom.

Physical Science

Hephaestus: Students design robots, create a topology (terraform) and colonize a planet, named Hephaestus. Students study environmental variables such as distance, elevation, and surface type corresponding to physical concepts from which questions of ethics, logistics, economics, and politics can be studied.

Dreamhaus: Students learn principles of engineering and physics by investigating virtual architecture sites, solving environmental engineering puzzles, and designing buildings.

Environmental Detectives: Students play different community members investigating health problems in their city stemming from pollution problems. They develop inquiry skills and learn the science behind contaminants such as mercuric chloride and the properties of chemicals.

Physics

La Jungla de Optica: Students rescue an archeologist and his niece from a band of tomb-raiding marauders. Players work through the Temple of Light, solving optic puzzles and constructing lenses to thwart the marauders and lead Professor Carlson and Melanie to safety.

Supercharged: Students race through 3-D mazes consisting of electrostatic forces, magnetic fields, and electric fields by adopting the properties of charged particles and placing other charges in the environment.

Life Sciences

Replicate: Students role play a virus and replicate inside a host organism. They migrate through the circulation system and enter target cells in order to outwit the human immune response, without killing their host upon whom they depend for survival.

Biohazard: Students begin as junior doctors and become agents for the Center for Disease Control. They diagnose patients, identify the sources of epidemic outbreaks, and devise ways to prevent the spread of disease.

History

Revolution: Students play a citizen in Colonial Williamsburg. They experience the events of the American Revolution and negotiate their meanings with a virtual community of players. They then play out the interconnections among the social, personal, and political issues of that era.

Foreign Languages

Periodista: Students complete photographic missions in Spanish-speaking countries. They use their knowledge of cultures and language ability to negotiate with non-player characters and player characters to gain access to insider information and obtain better photographs.

Psychology

Sole Survivor: Students are kidnapped on an alien vessel and are the subject of psychology experiments.

They must use their knowledge of psychology to train a race of human prototypes and find safety.

Mathematics

The Lure of the Labyrinth: The Lure of the Labyrinth, designed at the MIT Education Arcade in collaboration with Maryland Public Television, Johns Hopkins University, and Macro International, has as its primary goal to enhance pre-algebra mathematics learning with a secondary goal of improving literacy.

Labyrinth: This is a web based adventure game played over a series of sessions. The game's storyline is a persistent narrative that evolves over time, where the player's character enters the game looking to recover a lost pet and subsequently is led by clues through a fantasy world—an underground populated by mythical monsters who are stealing pets. As a result, the player exploring this space learns how to navigate it and solves puzzles with algebra and mathematical reasoning to earn enough points to free the captive pet.

In addition to these selections offered from The Education Arcade, many commercial, off–the-shelf games also have had educational impact. *Civilization* is one example. This game originally appeared in 1991. As a result of the game's popularity, multiple versions in the series have been developed. The goal of the game is to successfully build an enduring empire. The latest version, *Civilization IV,* allows players to form teams in order to increase collaboration and plan strategy. In this turn-based strategy game, players must make decisions for their civilization around societal development and diplomacy—including when and where to build new cities, what societal advances in knowledge should be sought, and when and how to handle adversarial and nonadversarial neighboring civilizations. At the onset of the game, players even have the choice of which civilization to play—Aztecs, Romans, Mongols, and so on. As time advances in the game, new technologies emerge (such as pottery and nuclear fission), and civilization leaders have the choice to try to capitalize on these technologies.

Many other games with animated, curriculum-based content that engage students at the elementary level can be accessed at http://www.brainpop.com/video_tutorials/gameup_tutorial/.

Classroom Response Technology

The **classroom response system** (or clickers) is another type of interactivity technology. This technology was initially used in corporate training during the 1980s. But its recent miniaturization and lower cost has now made it popular in some elementary and high school classrooms. A classroom response system includes a hand-held transmitter, smaller than the size of a TV remote control, with buttons labeled A, B, C, and D. Each student can push buttons to respond to multiple-choice questions spoken or displayed by the teacher (e.g., on PowerPoint slides). Students respond to questions, and the distribution of responses from all the students are stored in a computer and displayed as a bar chart for all to see. With this technology, you can make the best use of practice test items, provide instant feedback on student learning (keeping students engaged), and immediately diagnose instructional problems to improve learning. Its most optimal use has been when a teacher may not have time for individual student feedback or for stimulating class-wide dialogue after the number responding to each alternative answer is shown to the class (Bruff, 2009). When using a classroom response system, carefully formulated and thought-provoking questions can significantly impact the effectiveness of your instruction and lead to a class-wide discussion in which all your students are participating in the inquiry process (Cheesman, Winograd, & Wehrman, 2010). Schmid (2008) indicates a few pedagogical implications for the classroom response system that can make your questioning more effective. To avoid students guessing an answer, you will want to make one of your alternative responses "I don't know." This will encourage your students to respond honestly and reduce guessing.

If your classroom response system has "confidence buttons" that allow students to indicate the confidence they have in the answer they have chosen (for example, no confidence, a little, some, a lot), you can begin the discussion and inquiry process by examining the facts and reasons individual students may have differed in degrees of confidence. You can also have your students discuss the answers with peers or in groups before choosing the confidence option. This will make your students more confident before choosing an answer and less likely to guess. Research has indicated the importance of group discussion and idea sharing before as well as after an individual or group answer is chosen. To avoid the use of your classroom response system becoming teacher-dominated, try involving your students in the selection of questions by modeling the types of test questions that might be asked.

Assessment of the Effectiveness of Technology Integration

To design your instruction and technology integration for meaningful learning, the learning tasks your students complete should be active, constructive, collaborative, authentic, and goal oriented (intentional) (Howland, et al., 2012). Following are some guidelines and websites that can help you achieve and assess these five criteria:

- Active: Students are engaged in tasks in which they manipulate the objects of the environments and observe the result. (Second Life http://secondlife.com/, Prezi http://prezi.com/)

- Constructive: Learners are engaged in tasks in which they can articulate their doings and reflect on the experience. (Blogger http://www.blogger.com/, Wikispace http://www.wikispace.com/, bubbl.us http://bubbl.us/)

- Collaborative: Learners are engaged in tasks that require discussion with others to find meanings and create understandings. (Wikispace http://www.wikispace.com/, Prezi http://prezi.com/)

- Authentic: Learners are engaged in tasks that are project or problem based, containing the complexity of real-world contexts. (Second Life http://secondlife.com/, Delicious http://delicious.com/)

- Intentional: Learners are engaged in tasks that are goal oriented. (Bubbl.us http://bubbl.us/, and Moodle http://moodle.org/)

To evaluate whether your chosen technologies are integrated into your instruction effectively, you can ask these fundamental questions:

- Did the technology address my instructional goals?

- Did the technology make an impact on my students' learning?

- In what ways did it make an impact on my students' learning?

- To what degree did my choice of technology foster the instructional goals of my pedagogical approach?

To help answer these questions, the North American Council for Online Learning (2011), a non-profit association for K–12 online learning, has provided criteria for evaluating the effectiveness of your technology integration. In Chapter 13, we will present some specific assessment tools that will help you determine the effectiveness of your technology integration on your students' learning.

While technologies for instruction abound in the market place and are being commonly used in educational settings, you should be mindful to thoughtfully select the classroom technology you chose and not be influenced by the popularity of any technology. And, although your students may already be users of digital technologies, they have not always used them as learning tools. Therefore, you should design appropriate learning tasks to model how your students can use the technologies presented in this chapter with and without your immediate assistance (Bennett, et al., 2012). The concept of assessing technology integration is simple: The design of an appropriate learning task is the key to effectively integrating technology into your lesson planning and teaching. This design should be based on your pedagogical approach and the outcomes you wish to achieve. If your technology *follows* from your pedagogical approach and outcomes, you will have achieved the effective integration of technology into your instruction.

Case History and Licensure Preparation

DIRECTIONS: *The following case history pertains to Chapter 7 content. After reading the case history, go to Chapter 7 in the Book Specific Resources section in the MyEducationLab for your course. Upon completion of the test, scored answers to the short-answer and multiple-choice questions will be provided.*

Case History

Mr. Medina teaches middle school language arts to honors students. The class is generally balanced between boys and girls whose reading scores are in the top 20 percent, although a few students have self-selected this course and may have scores in the average range. Many of them come from families with professional backgrounds, and they seem to have ready access to all the latest high tech communication devices, a situation that, at times, has caused some distraction in class.

Though cell phones are officially prohibited from the classroom, more than once Mr. Medina has had his instruction interrupted by the unique ring tones emanating from a device secretly stowed in someone's purse or backpack. And he is sure that texting goes on behind his back when he is writing on the chalkboard, not to mention the near addiction to gaming that seems to have taken the place of eating in the school cafeteria.

The class is currently reading Ray Bradbury's *The Illustrated Man,* and Mr. Medina cannot help but smile inwardly at the timeless lesson of the first short story presented there, "The Veldt." Though written in 1950, it seems to him to be fairly accurate in predicting our future fascination with technology and how it can cause human relationships to take a back seat to the comforts and the fantasy life offered by science.

The "Happylife Home" described in the futuristic short story is not that different from what is available today. "The house is filled with machines that do everything for the family from cooking meals, to clothing them, to rocking them to sleep. The two children, Peter and Wendy, become fascinated with the 'nursery,' a virtual reality room that is able to connect with the children telepathically to reproduce any place they imagine."

Mr. Medina decides that he will not be like the parents in the story, George and Lydia, who become victims of the unbridled use of technology by their children. Instead, Mr. Medina intends to use technology to engage his students.

His plan will use student blogs to teach a lesson in the importance of point of view. After having his students register at www.blogger.com for free individual accounts, he asks them to rewrite the main events of the Bradbury story, originally narrated in the third person—mostly from the father, George's, point of view—from the view point of either of the children, Peter or Wendy. The style should be informal and personal. Each student will read at least three blogs written by fellow students and post comments. These comments may concern the different feelings and interpretations evoked by changing the teller of the story.

Summing Up

The main points in this chapter include the following:

Why Teach with Technology?

1. The effectiveness of technology depends on how teachers are able to integrate it into their lesson planning.

2. Lajoie (1993) summarizes four types of cognitive tools that technologies can provide to your learners. They are:

   - Supporting students' cognitive processes, for example, memory or metacognitive processes

   - Relieving students' cognitive load by providing for lower-level cognitive skills, leaving more time and effort needed for teaching higher-level cognitive skills

   - Allowing students to engage in cognitive activities in an authentic environment that would be impossible or too costly to replicate in the classroom

   - Allowing learners to generate solutions and assess themselves in a context they will encounter in future assignments, advanced grades, and the world of work

3. The research literature refers to the purposes for online interactions as communication, knowledge building, and learning (Joubert & Wishart, 2012).

4. Internet technologies provide a manipulative media environment, called hypermedia, where the learning needs of individuals can be met using multiple presentations of information, from different perspectives, with the opportunity to create new knowledge.

5. Distributed cognition emphasizes the social aspects of cognition and advocates learning that involves the simultaneous interaction among students, computers, and the learning environment.

Twenty-First Century Learning Technologies

6. To meet the learning needs of your students in the twenty-first century, your classroom instruction will have to be designed to teach inquiry skills with pedagogies that include self-directed, problem-based, and project-based learning.

7. Moodle is an example of a free and open source classroom management system for creating a personal communication tool by which you can maintain contact with your students both in and outside of your classroom.

8. The strength of a classroom management system is its learning environment in which students can move in and out of planned instruction to retrieve and exchange information, discuss topics with the teacher, and collaborate with peers to construct knowledge (Koschmann, 1996).

9. A blended course is a traditional course of instruction incorporated with online materials and/or intermittent online discussion.

10. Web 2.0 technologies, often called social media or social software, are tools for information gathering, communication, interaction, and social networking that provide a platform for learners to learn by constructing their own view of the world in concert with others.

11. Responsibilities for teachers moderating online discussions include: welcoming and encouraging students, helping students to become familiar with one another and with the online learning environment, facilitating students' sharing of information, and designing and facilitating learning activities.

12. Web 2.0 technologies will have maximum impact in your classroom when you consider inquiry-based learning together with problem- and project-based learning.

13. Blogs, also called web logs, provide a platform for your students to publish text, audios, or video online (called video blog, vblog, or vlog) and are an ideal tool for developing portfolios.

14. Podcasting, the equivalent of blogging in the audio form, and video blogging, the equivalent of blogging in the video form, are alternative types of blogs.

15. Social bookmarking applications facilitate the building of an easily accessible online bookmark warehouse, whereby your learners can organize, tag, and store information collected from the Internet.

16. Social presentation is another Web 2.0 application for students to share and work together to organize and construct knowledge for an online presentation.

17. Concept mapping is a type of graphic organizer—or mind tool—for knowledge organization that can help students interpret, represent, and organize information by making a graphic in cooperation with one another.

18. A wiki represents a collaborative tool and website where users assigned in groups can create content collaboratively and where a teacher can monitor their work.

19. Virtual worlds is an interactive environment in which users are immersed in online role-playing games in which they choose or create characters (called avatars) whose identities they assume and interact with in real time. This simulated environment provides contexts for creating what would be impossible or difficult to do in real life.

20. A classroom response system includes a small, handheld transmitter with buttons that students can push to respond to multiple-choice questions spoken or displayed by the teacher.

Assessment of the Effectiveness of Technology Integration

21. For your instruction and technology to provide for meaningful learning, your learning tasks must actively engage your learners by having them:

    - Manipulate objects in the environment, real or virtual, and observe the result

    - Engage in tasks with which they can articulate their ideas and reflect on the experience

    - Collaborate with other learners engaged in the same or similar tasks

    - Conduct authentic inquiry that includes self-directed, problem-based, and project-based learning methods

22. You should choose and assess the effectiveness of the technologies you use by how well they meet your learners' needs and your instructional objectives.

Key Terms

Asynchronous learning
Blended learning
Blogs
Classroom response system
Concept mapping
Course management system

Distributed cognition
Hypermedia
Moodle
Podcasts
Really Simple Syndication (RSS)
Social bookmarking

Social presentation
Synchronous learning
Virtual worlds
Web 2.0 technologies
Wiki

Discussion and Practice Questions

Questions marked with an asterisk are answered in Appendix B. Some asterisked questions may require student follow-up responses not included in Appendix B. Go to the Assignments and Activities section of the various topics on the MyEducationLab for your course to complete additional practice activities related to this chapter's content.

1. Identify four types of cognitive activities that technologies can provide to learners.

*2. Provide a definition of hypermedia and an example of its use in the classroom.

*3. What is distributed cognition? Provide an example of how technologies can support distributed cognition in the classroom.

*4. What is meant by the older "take it or leave it" platform for learning? Contrast it with Web 2.0.

*5. What is Moodle and what would be an application of it in your teaching area?

*6. What is an asynchronous learning environment? Describe one for a subject you will be teaching.

*7. What are Web 2.0 technologies?

*8. What is a blog and what can it be used for?

*9. What is Really Simple Syndication (RSS)?

*10. What is the purpose of social bookmarking? Provide an example for a subject you will be teaching.

*11. What is the purpose of social presentation? Provide an example for a subject you will be teaching.

*12. What is concept mapping and how would it be used in a subject you will be teaching?

*13. What is the purpose of a Wiki and how could it be used in a subject you will be teaching?

*14. What is the major purpose of virtual world technology?

Professional Practice

Field Experience and Practice Activities

Questions marked with an asterisk are answered in Appendix B. Some asterisked questions may require student follow-up responses not included in Appendix B.

1. Prepare an instructional scenario in a subject that you will be teaching that combines traditional seat work and teacher presentations with online resources and activities to enhance and expand ongoing classroom instruction.

2. Create a classroom assignment in a subject you will be teaching that combines social bookmarking, social presentation, and group work. Provide some online resources that you and your learners could use to complete the assignment.

3. Provide an instructional objective and activity related to a problem in your subject area, such as the pollution of streams and lakes, identity theft, or a problem encountered with characters in a story being read. Cast your objective and activity in the form of a 3-D animation using virtual worlds technology in which characters (avatars) look for evidence for how to solve the problem.

4. Create a class assignment that divides your class into groups of six students each whose assignment is to create a podcast exploring different alternatives for improving student life in your school. Groups can choose improvements regarding such topics as the cafeteria, school library, sports facilities, school grounds, and so on. Your students' podcasts must be limited to ten minutes.

*5. Identify three Web 2.0 applications that are readily adaptable to small group work. Choose one of them and describe how it would be used to complete an assignment in a content area you will be teaching.

Digital Portfolio Activities

The following Digital Activities are related to InTASC Standards 5, 7, and 8.

1. In Field Experience and Practice Activity 1 you created an instructional scenario as an example of learning, combining traditional teacher presentations and seat work with online resources and activities. Place your instructional scenario in a digital portfolio folder labeled "Blended Learning" to which you can add other examples of technology integration that you observe or read about.

2. In Field Experience and Practice Activity 2 you created a 3-D animation using virtual worlds to teach about a problem with a subject you will be teaching. Place your virtual world animation in a digital portfolio folder titled "Virtual Worlds" as an example of the instructional uses of virtual worlds technology.

MyEducationLab™

Go to MyEducationLab (www.myeducationlab.com) for Effective Teaching Methods: Research-Based Practice where you can:

- Find learning outcomes for the various course topics course along with national standards that connect to these outcomes.

- Complete **Assignments and Activities** that can help you more deeply understand the chapter content.

- Apply and practice your understanding of the core teaching skills identified in the chapter with **Building Teaching Skills and Dispositions** coaching activities.

- Check your comprehension of the content covered in the chapter with a book specific **Study Plan**. Here you will be able to take a chapter **pretest**, receive feedback on your answers, and then access personalized **Review, Practice, and Enrichment exercises** to enhance your understanding of chapter content. After you complete the exercises, take a **posttest** to confirm your comprehension.

- Learn how to address common classroom management issues in the **Simulations in Classroom Management**.

- Access video clips of CCSSO **National Teachers of the Year award winners** responding to the question, "Why Do I Teach?" in the Teacher Talk section.

- Create, update, and share quality lesson plans with the **Lesson Plan Builder**.

- Access state licensure test requirements, overviews of what tests cover, and sample test items in the **Certification and Licensure** section.

- Learn how to create a high quality teaching portfolio in the **Preparing a Portfolio** section.

- Access tips, advice, and other information on resume writing and interviewing, your first year of teaching, and law and public policies in the Beginning Your Career section.

8 Questioning Strategies

This chapter will help you answer these questions and meet the following InTASC standards for effective teaching.

- What is an effective question?
- What are some different types of questions?
- What is a question-asking sequence?
- How do I ask questions at different levels of cognitive complexity?
- How do I ask questions that promote inquiry and problem solving?

InTASC

STANDARD 1 **Learner Development.** The teacher understands how learners grow and develop, recognizing that patterns of learning and development vary individually within and across the cognitive, linguistic, social, emotional, and physical areas, and designs and implements developmentally appropriate and challenging learning experiences.

STANDARD 3 **Learning Environments.** The teacher works with others to create environments that support individual and collaborative learning, and that encourage positive social interaction, active engagement in learning, and self motivation.

STANDARD 5 **Application of Content.** The teacher understands how to connect concepts and use differing perspectives to engage learners in critical thinking, creativity, and collaborative problem solving related to authentic local and global issues.

STANDARD 6 **Assessment.** The teacher understands and uses multiple methods of assessment to engage learners in their own growth, to monitor learner progress, and to guide the teacher's and learner's decision making.

STANDARD 8 **Instructional Strategies.** The teacher understands and uses a variety of instructional strategies to encourage learners to develop deep understanding of content areas and their connections, and to build skills to apply knowledge in meaningful ways.

*I*n the classroom dialogues of previous chapters, you saw the important role of asking questions in the effective teacher's menu of instructional techniques. It is a fact of classroom life that, on their very first day of school, new and experienced teachers alike begin by asking questions of their students. This is no coincidence, because most exchanges between teachers and students involve questions in some form. This chapter builds on earlier examples to define an effective question and to discuss the varied ways questions can be asked—and the types of questions you should ask more frequently than others.

Also discussed is the closely related topic of probes. Like questions, probes are effective catalysts for achieving the five key instructional goals of (1) lesson clarity, (2) instructional variety, (3) task orientation, (4) student engagement in the learning process, and (5) student success. The following chapters will show you how to combine questioning techniques with direct and indirect teaching strategies.

MyEducationLab™

Visit the MyEducationLab for *Effective Teaching Methods: Research-Based Practice,* 8e to enhance your understanding of chapter concepts with a personalized Study Plan. You'll also have the opportunity to hone your teaching skills through video-based Assignments and Activities as well as Building Teaching Skills and Dispositions lessons.

What Is a Question?

In the context of a lively and fast-paced exchange in a classroom, questions are not always obvious. As observed by Dantonio and Beisenherz (2001) and Brown and Wragg (1993), students routinely report difficulty in identifying some types of questions during a classroom dialogue—and even whether a question has been asked. For example, imagine hearing these two questions:

Raise your hand if you know the answer.

Aren't you going to *answer the question*?

The first is expressed as a command (italics), yet it contains an implicit question. The second sounds like a question, yet it contains an implicit command. Will your students perceive both of these statements as questions? Will both evoke the same response?

Voice inflection is another source of confusion; it can indicate a question even when the syntax of the sentence does not. For example, imagine hearing the following two sentences spoken with the emphasis shown:

You *said* the president can have two terms in office?

The president can have *two* terms in office?

A certain voice inflection can turn almost any sentence into a question, whether you intend it or not. In addition, a real question can be perceived as a rhetorical question because of inflection and word choice:

We all have done our homework today, *haven't we*?

Whether this is intended as a question or not, all the students who failed to complete their homework will certainly assume the question to be rhetorical.

Effective questions are those for which students actively compose responses and thereby become engaged in the learning process (Borich, 2008a; Chuska, 2003; Walsh & Sattes, 2004). The previous examples show that effective questions depend on more than just words. Their effectiveness also depends on voice inflection, word emphasis, word choice, and the context in which they are asked. Questions can be asked in many ways, and each way can determine whether the question is perceived by your students, as well as how it is perceived.

In this chapter, any oral statement or gesture intended to evoke a student response is considered a question. And if it evokes a response that actively engages a student in the learning process, it is an effective question. With this distinction in mind, let's explore the many ways of asking questions that actively engage students in the learning process.

What Consumes 80 Percent of Class Time?

In almost any classroom, at any time, you can observe a sequence of events in which the teacher structures the content to be discussed, solicits a student response, and then reacts to the response. These activities performed in sequence are the most common behaviors in any classroom. They represent the following chain of events:

1. The teacher provides structure, briefly formulating the topic or issue to be discussed.
2. The teacher solicits a response or asks a question of one or more students.
3. The student responds or answers the question.
4. The teacher reacts to the student's answer.

The teacher behaviors in this chain of events include the activities of **structuring**, **soliciting**, and **reacting**. At the heart of this chain is soliciting, or question-asking behavior. Questions are the tool for bridging the gap between your presentation of content and the students' understanding of it. The purpose of questioning should not be lost among the many forms and varieties of questions presented in this chapter. Like all the ingredients of instruction, questions are tools to encourage students to think about and act on the material you have structured.

The centerpiece of this chain—soliciting or questioning—is so prevalent that as many as 50 or more questions per class hour may be asked in the typical elementary and secondary classroom. Sometimes as much as 80 percent of all school time can be devoted to questions and answers. This enormous concentration on a single strategy attests both to its convenience and its perceived effectiveness. But as noted, not all questions are effective questions. That is, not all questions actively engage students in the learning process.

Are We Asking the Right Questions?

Some research data show that not all questions actively engage students in the learning process. Early studies estimated that 70 percent to 80 percent of all questions required the simple recall of facts; only 20 percent to 30 percent required the higher-level thought processes of clarifying, expanding, generalizing, and making inferences (Corey, 1940; Haynes, 1935). Evidently, little has changed since these early studies. More recent work in the United States and England indicates that of every five questions asked, about three require data recall, one is managerial, and only one requires higher-level thought processes (Atwood & Wilen, 1991; Brown, 2001; Brown & Wragg, 1993; Wragg, 2001).

Pay attention to the types of questions the teacher uses with his students in this **video**. How is questioning being used?

This lopsided proportion of recall questions to thought questions is alarming. The behaviors most frequently required in adult life, at work, and in advanced training—those at the higher levels of cognitive complexity involving analysis, synthesis, and evaluation—seem to be the least practiced behaviors in the classroom (Chuska, 2003; Dantonio & Beisenherz, 2001; Power & Hubbard, 1999; Wiske, 1997).

What Are the Purposes of Questions?

It would be easy to classify all questions as either *lower order* (requiring the recall of information) or *higher order* (requiring clarification, expansion, generalization, and inference). But such a broad distinction would ignore the many specific purposes for which questions are used. Most reasons for asking questions can be classified into the following general categories:

1. *Getting interest and attention.* "If you could go to the moon, what would be the first thing you would notice?"
2. *Diagnosing and checking.* "What is the meaning of the Latin word *via*?"
3. *Recalling specific facts or information.* "What are the names of the main characters in *The Adventures of Huckleberry Finn*?"
4. *Managing.* "Did you ask my permission?"
5. *Encouraging higher-level thought processes.* "Putting together all that we have learned, what household products exhibit characteristics associated with the element sodium?"

6. *Structuring and redirecting learning.* "Now that we have covered the narrative form, are we ready to go on to expository writing?"

7. *Allowing expression of affect.* "What did you like about *Charlotte's Web*?"

Most of the questions in these categories have the purpose of shaping or setting up the learner's response. In this sense, a well-formulated question serves as an advance organizer, providing the framework for the response to follow.

What Are Convergent and Divergent Questions?

Questions can be narrow or broad, encouraging either a specific, limited response or a general, expansive one. A question that limits an answer to a single or small number of responses is called a **convergent question** (*direct* or *closed*). For these questions, the learner has previously read or heard the answer and so has only to recall certain facts. Convergent questions generally ask the learner to respond at the knowledge, comprehension, or application levels.

Convergent questions set up the learner to respond in a limited, restrictive manner: "What is the meaning of the Latin word *via*?" "What are the names of the main characters in *The Adventures of Huckleberry Finn*?" The answers to these questions are easily judged right or wrong. Many convergent, or closed, questions are used in the classroom. Up to 80 percent of all questions may be of this type.

Another type of question encourages a general or open response. This is the **divergent question** (*indirect* or *open*). Divergent questions generally ask the learner to respond at the application, analysis, synthesis, and evaluation levels, requiring higher order thinking. Divergent questions, therefore, have no single right answer, although they can have wrong answers. If Carlos is asked what he liked about *Of Mice and Men* and he says "Nothing" or "The happy ending," then either Carlos has not read the book or he needs help in better understanding the events that took place and encouragement to develop a better answer.

You can expect a greater variety of responses from divergent questions than from convergent questions, which may explain why only about 20 percent of all questions are divergent. It is easier to determine the right or wrong answer to a convergent question than to sift through the range of acceptable responses to a divergent question. Divergent questions often require a follow-up response requiring more detail, new information, or a follow-up question from the teacher or other student to bring an insufficiently developed student response back into an acceptable range. In this way, divergent questions can be a rich source of lively, spontaneous classroom dialogue extending to the contributions of other students that can make your lessons fresh and interesting.

What Does Research Say about Asking Convergent and Divergent Questions?

Classroom researchers have studied the effects on student achievement of asking convergent and divergent questions (Cecil, 1995; Dillon, 2004; Gall, 1984; Hubbard & Power, 2003). As we have seen, convergent questions are best suited for developing classroom content at the knowledge, comprehension, and sometimes application levels; while divergent questions are most suited to promoting higher order inquiry, concept, and discovery types of learning (Audet & Jordan, 2005; Bransford, Brown, & Cocking, 2000; Chuska, 2003).

Interestingly, while research has supported the important role of convergent questions for knowledge, comprehension, and some application for drill, practice, and review, research has not clearly substantiated that the use of divergent questions are related to gains on tests of standardized achievement. Although some of the above studies have reported modest improvements in achievement scores with the use of divergent questioning strategies, others have not. Although these studies found a large imbalance in favor of convergent questions (a ratio of four to one), three important factors must be considered when looking at their results:

1. Tests of achievement—and particularly tests of standardized achievement—use multiple-choice items that generally test for behaviors at lower levels of cognitive complexity. Therefore, the achievement measures in these studies may have been unable to detect increases in behaviors at the higher levels of cognitive complexity that might have resulted from the use of divergent questions. Lower order behaviors (e.g., learning the multiplication tables) can be quickly elicited with convergent questioning strategies and readily detected with fill-in, matching, or multiple-choice exams at the end of a lesson. But higher order and authentic behaviors (e.g., being able to derive meaning from stories such as *Charlotte's Web*) may take longer to build to a measurable outcome.

2. The diversity of responses normally expected from divergent questions, as well as the added time needed to build on and follow up on responses, may prohibit large amounts of class time from being devoted to divergent questioning. Because less instructional time is devoted to divergent questioning than to convergent questioning, some study results may simply reflect the imbalance in instructional time, not their relative effectiveness.

3. The content best suited for teaching higher order behaviors constitutes only a small amount of the content in existing texts, workbooks, and curriculum guides. Until more curricula are written to encourage or require higher-level thought processes, the time teachers actually devote to divergent questioning may not increase.

Thus the seeming imbalance in the use and effectiveness of divergent and convergent questioning strategies may have little to do with the effectiveness of the questioning strategies themselves. Because factual recall always will be required for higher order thought processes, convergent questions always will be a necessary precondition for achieving higher-level behaviors (Bruning, Schraw, Norby, & Ronning, 2004; Mayer, 2002). Also, because more instructional time is required for higher order questioning, consistent use of moderate amounts of divergent questioning may be more practical and effective than intense but brief episodes of divergent questioning. The most appropriate convergent/divergent question ratio will be about 70:30, when lesson content emphasizes lower levels of cognitive complexity, to about 60:40, when lesson content emphasizes higher levels.

Dillon (2004) suggests that teachers who ask questions requiring analysis, synthesis, and evaluation tend to elicit these cognitive processes from their students more frequently than teachers who use fewer higher-level questions. Therefore asking divergent questions seems desirable, regardless of whether their immediate effects show up on standardized achievement tests. Most researchers would agree that the effects of higher-level questioning on the cognitive processes of learning justify its inclusion at some level in most of the lessons you will teach (Kauchak & Eggen, 2011; Ormrod, 2010a).

Who Are the Targets of Questions?

Questions at various levels of cognitive complexity can be directed to individuals, to groups, or to the entire class. Occasionally posing questions over the heads of some learners and under the heads of others will keep all students alert and engaged in the learning process (Stipek, 2003). In homogeneously grouped classes, questions can be spread across individuals, groups, and the full class but differentiated to fit the cognitive complexity most appropriate for the learners being taught. For example, general questions can be composed requiring more or less cognitive complexity and prerequisite knowledge, as illustrated in the following examples:

Less Complex	**More Complex**
"Tell me, Lupe, if you sat down to breakfast, what things at the breakfast table would most likely contain the element of sodium?"	"Lupe, what are some forms of the element sodium in our universe?"
"After the death of Lenny in *Of Mice and Men,* what happens to the other main character?"	"What is an example of dramatic irony in *Of Mice and Men*?"
"After thinking about the words *photo* and *synthesis,* what do you think *photosynthesis* means?"	"How does photosynthesis support plant life?"
"Ted, if we have the equation $10 = 2/x$, do we find x by multiplying or dividing?"	"Ted, can you solve this problem for x? $10 = 2/x$."

Notice that these examples vary not only in the cognitive processes they require but also in how they are framed, or phrased. Advance organizers, hints, and clues will be more appropriate for some types of learners than for others (Chen, 2005).

Table 8.1 **Characteristics of More and Less Complex Questions**

More Complex Questions	Less Complex Questions
Require students to generalize the content to new problems	Require students to recall task-relevant prior knowledge
Stymie, mystify, and challenge in ways that do not have predetermined answers	Use specific and concrete examples, settings, and objects with which students are familiar
Are delivered in the context of an investigation or problem that is broader than the question itself	Use a step-by-step approach, in which each question is narrower than the preceding one
Ask students to go deeper, clarify, and provide additional justification or reasons for the answers they provide	Rephrase or reiterate the answers to previous questions
Use more abstract concepts by asking students to see how their answers may apply across various settings or objects	Suggest one or two probable answers that lead students in the right direction
Are part of a sequence of questions that build to higher and more complex concepts, patterns, and abstractions	Are placed in the context of a game (e.g., 20 questions) with points and rewards

One way of framing questions for heterogeneous classes—and therefore differentiating your instruction—is to design them so different responses at various levels of complexity are required. You can accept less complex responses as being just as correct as more complex answers, if they match the level of the questions being asked. Although the responses from some learners may not be complete, you can evaluate them in terms of the cognitive complexity required by the question and the students' ability to respond to it. Therefore the elaboration given and depth of understanding required may be less for one type of learner than for another. Table 8.1 suggests specific questioning strategies.

What Sequences of Questions Are Used?

Questions also can vary according to the sequence in which they are used. Recall that the most basic **question sequence** involves structuring, soliciting, and reacting. However, many variations are possible.

One of the most popular sequences employs divergent questions that lead to convergent questions. Many teachers begin the structuring-soliciting-reacting process by starting with an open question that leads to further structuring and then asking subsequent questions that involve recall or simple deduction. This general-to-specific approach can take several twists and turns. For example, in the following dialogue, the teacher begins by encouraging speculative responses and then narrows the focus by asking a question requiring simple deduction:

Teacher: What do astronauts wear on the moon?

Students: Spacesuits.

Teacher: So what element in our atmosphere must not be present on the moon?

The same approach is used when a teacher poses a problem, asks several simple recall questions, and then reformulates the question to narrow the problem still further:

Teacher: If the native Alaskans originally came from Siberia on the Asian continent. How do you suppose they got to Alaska?

Students: [No response.]

Teacher: We studied the Bering Strait, which separates North America from Asia. How wide is the water between these two continents at the closest point?

Student: About 60 miles. The Little and Big Diomede Islands are in between.

Teacher: If this expanse of water were completely frozen, which some scientists believe it was years ago, how might Asians have come to the North American continent?

Table 8.2 Comparing Inductive to Deductive Teaching

	What Do Teachers and Students Do?
Inductive Teaching	• The teacher provides examples of certain behaviors or limited facts and a generalization is drawn that appears to apply to the circumstances regarding the behavior or specified facts given. • Students are asked to make observations of new or additional examples of similar behaviors or specified facts. Students are also given nonexamples of the behavior or specific facts. • The teacher guides students in determining pertinent or significant common data among the examples that aligns with the generalization. Students are also led to characteristics that point to nonexamples. • The teacher and students interpret the observations they have made and solidify the generalization to ensure it differentiates examples from nonexamples.
Deductive Teaching	• The teacher shares a generalization that students are to test. • The teacher identifies related facts or logical reasoning that led to the generalization. • Students test the generalization by posing a question regarding its validity, forming a hypothesis, and making a prediction that they will prove or disprove the generalization. • Students observe or collect data to test their hypothesis gathering materials and data and setting up events to make their observations. • Students analyze their data and determine if their prediction was accurate, supported by the data or events observed. • The teacher leads students to determine if they can conclude the generalization is true in the context in which it was tested. The generalization may be refined based on recorded observations and proven events.

Teachers frequently employ this type of *funneling*: adding conditions of increasing specificity to a question. However, no evidence indicates that one sequencing strategy is any more effective in promoting student achievement than any other. The specific sequence you choose should depend on your behavioral objectives, the instructional content being taught, and the ability level of your students.

Other types of questioning sequences that teachers can implement in a cycle of structuring, soliciting, and reacting are illustrated in Table 8.2. These offer useful additions to your questioning strategies menu.

What Levels of Questions Are Used?

As we have seen, as an effective teacher, you must be able to formulate divergent and convergent questions, to target questions to specific types of learners, and to arrange questions in meaningful sequences. You also must be able to formulate questions at different levels of cognitive complexity.

One of the best known systems for classifying questions according to cognitive complexity is the taxonomy of objectives in the cognitive domain that was presented in Chapter 5. This system has the advantage of going beyond the simple recall-versus-higher order thinking dichotomy frequently used in the research cited previously to provide learning outcomes at intermediate levels of cognitive complexity as well. Considering a continuum of question complexity, which fills the space between these ends of the scale, is useful in the art of asking questions.

Recall that the basic taxonomy of the cognitive domain contains six levels of cognitive complexity:

- Knowledge
- Analysis
- Comprehension
- Synthesis
- Application
- Evaluation

Table 8.3 identifies the types of student outcomes associated with each level. Look at each level to get a feel for the question-asking strategies that go along with it.

Table 8.3 **Question Classification Scheme**

Level of Behavioral Complexity	Expected Student Behavior	Instructional Processes	Key Words
Knowledge (remembering)	The student is able to remember or recall information and recognize facts, terminology, and rules.	Repetition, memorization	Define, describe, identify
Comprehension (understanding)	The student is able to change the form of a communication by translating and rephrasing what has been read or spoken.	Explanation, illustration	Summarize, paraphrase, rephrase
Application (transferring)	The student is able to apply the information learned to a context different from the one in which it was learned.	Practice, transfer	Apply, use, employ
Analysis (relating)	The student is able to break a problem down into its component parts and to draw relationships among the parts.	Induction, deduction	Relate, distinguish, differentiate
Synthesis (creating)	The student is able to combine parts to form a unique or novel solution to a problem.	Divergence, generalization	Formulate, compose, produce
Evaluation (judging)	The student is able to make decisions about the value or worth of methods, ideas, people, or products according to expressed criteria.	Discrimination, inference	Appraise, decide, justify

Knowledge

Recall from Chapter 5 that knowledge objectives require the student to recall, describe, define, or recognize facts that already have been committed to memory. Here are some action verbs you can use to formulate questions at the knowledge level:

define	identify	name
describe	list	recite

Sample questions include these:

- What is the definition of *capitalism*?
- How many digits are needed to make the number 12?
- What is the first rule for forming a possessive?
- What is the definition of a *triangle*?

Notice that each of these questions can be answered correctly simply by recalling previously memorized facts. None requires understanding what was memorized or being able to use the learned facts in a problem-solving context. However, when facts are linked to other forms of knowledge, such as those in subsequent lessons and units, they become stepping stones for gradually increasing the complexity of teaching outcomes as called for in the rigor and relevance framework presented in Chapters 5 and 6.

To avoid the overuse or disconnected use of questions at the knowledge level, ask yourself, "Do the facts required by my questions represent task-relevant prior knowledge for subsequent learning?" If your answer is "no," you might consider assigning text, workbook, or supplemental materials that contain the facts, instead of incorporating them into your question-asking behavior. If your answer is "yes," then determine in what ways learners will use the facts in subsequent lessons and raise questions that eventually will help form more complex behaviors.

Your students may not need to be able to recite the names of the presidents, the Declaration of Independence, or the elements in the periodic table, because these facts may not be task-relevant prior knowledge for more higher order outcomes. However, your learners will likely need to recite the multiplication tables, the parts of speech, and the rules for adding, subtracting, multiplying, and dividing signed numbers, because these facts will be used countless times in completing exercises and solving problems at higher levels of cognitive complexity. Always take time to ask yourself, "Are the facts I am about to teach relevant for attaining the desired outcomes of subsequent lessons?" By doing so, you will avoid asking knowledge questions that may be trivial or irrelevant.

Comprehension

Comprehension questions require some level of understanding of facts the student has committed to memory. Responses to these questions should show that the learner can explain, summarize, or elaborate on the facts that have been learned. Here are some action verbs you can use in formulating questions at the comprehension level:

convert	extend	rephrase
explain	paraphrase	summarize

Following are some sample questions:

- In your own words, what is *capitalism*?
- How many units are there in the number 12?
- In converting a possessive back to the nonpossessive form, what must be rephrased so the first rule applies?
- What steps are required to draw a triangle?

In responding to each of these questions, the student acts on previously learned material by changing it from the form in which it was first learned. For example, the teacher does not ask students to define *capitalism*; rather the request is, "In your own words, what is *capitalism?*". This requires translation or conversion of the original definition (the teacher's) into another one (the student's).

There is an important step in moving from knowledge-level questions to comprehension-level questions. Knowledge-level questions require no cognitive processing at the time of the response, but comprehension-level questions do. In the former case, the learner actually may think about the material only once—at the time it was originally learned. In the latter case, the learner must actively think about the content twice—once when the facts are memorized and again when they must be composed into a response in a different form. Although fact questions must logically precede comprehension questions, comprehension questions are superior to knowledge questions in terms of encouraging longer-term retention, understanding, and eventual use of the learned material in more authentic contexts.

Application

Application questions extend facts and understanding to the next level of authenticity. They go beyond the memorization and translation of facts. Application questions require the student to apply the facts to a problem, context, or environment that is different from the one in which the information was learned. Thus the student can rely on neither the original context nor the original content to solve the problem.

Here are some action verbs you can use in formulating questions at the application level:

apply	employ	solve
demonstrate	operate	use

Following are some sample questions:

- What countries from among those listed have a market oriented economic system?
- Can you show me 12 pencils?
- Can you apply the first rule for forming possessives to the errors in the following newspaper article?
- Can you draw a triangle for me?

Your job in forming application questions is to present your learners with a context or problem different from that in which they learned the material. Application questions encourage the transfer of newly learned material to a new and different environment.

Answering application questions requires two related cognitive processes: (1) the simultaneous recall and consideration of all the individual units (facts) pertaining to the question and (2) the composing of units into a single harmonious sequence, so that the response becomes rapid and automatic. Application questions ask students to compose previously learned responses under conditions approximating real-world problems. You can see that action sequences require two precedents: (1) learned facts and understandings acquired from knowledge and comprehension questions and (2) the use of previously learned facts and rules in new contexts. The number and quality of your application questions will determine how rapid and automatic your learners' action sequences become.

Many beginning teachers inappropriately believe that application questions should be reserved for the end of a unit or even the end of a grading period. But as you have seen, they are essential whenever a rapid, automatic response involving facts or rules is desired or when an action sequence is the lesson goal. Also remember that practice immediately following the presentation of content will better promote your learners' ability to reproduce that behavior at a later time.

The quality of your application questions will be determined largely by how much you change the problem, context, or environment in which the students learned the facts or rules. If the change is too small, transfer of learning to an expanded context will not occur, and your "parrots" will recite facts and rules from the earlier context. But if the change is too great, the new context may require a response beyond the grasp of most of your learners. The key to asking questions that require the transfer of learning to new problems or contexts is to be sure you have taught all the lower order behaviors relevant for exhibiting the behavior in a new context. The easiest way to accomplish this is to change the context only a bit at first and then gradually shift to more unfamiliar contexts.

Analysis

The teacher in this **video** is guiding her class through an analysis of literature. What language is she using to elicit responses?

Questions at the analysis level require the student to break a problem into its component parts and to draw relationships among the parts. Some purposes of questions at the analysis level are: to identify logical errors; to differentiate among facts, opinions, and assumptions; to derive conclusions; and to make inferences or generalizations—in short, to discover the reasons behind the information given.

Here are some action verbs you can use in formulating questions at the analysis level:

break down	distinguish	relate
differentiate	point out	support

Following are some sample questions:

- What factors distinguish capitalism from socialism?
- Which of the boxes do not contain 12 things?
- Can you differentiate Rule 1 possessive errors from Rule 2 possessive errors in the following essay?
- In which of the following pictures do you see a triangle?

Analysis questions tend to promote behaviors in the form of concepts, patterns, and relationships. They generally signal the start of the processes of concept learning, inquiry learning, and problem-centered learning and the beginning of the change from direct (telling) to indirect (e.g., problem-centered) instructional strategies. However, the majority of analysis questions will lack a single best answer, which is common with the teaching of facts, rules, and action sequences. Consequently, you will have to evaluate a much broader range of responses at the analysis level. Even though you may not be able to anticipate all these responses, you can prepare yourself psychologically by shifting to a less regimented, more deliberate, and slower pace, thus giving yourself more time to evaluate students' answers and to compose thoughtful responses. And you should expect some responses for which a definitive response on your part may not be possible within the confines of your question-and-answer session.

Synthesis

Questions at the synthesis level ask the student to produce something unique or original—to design a solution, compose a response, or predict an outcome to a problem for which he or she has never before seen, read, or heard a response. This level often is associated with directed creativity (Anderson & Krathwohl, 2001; Marzano & Kendall, 2006, 2008), in which not all responses may be equally acceptable. The facts, rules, and action sequences, along with any analysis questions that have gone before, may define the limits and directions of the synthesis requested.

Here are some action verbs you can use in formulating questions at the synthesis level:

compare	formulate	create
predict	devise	produce

Sample questions include:

- What would an economic system be like that combines the main features of capitalism and socialism?
- What new numbers can you make by adding by 12s?
- Can you write a paragraph showing possession without using the apostrophe *s*?
- What are some of the ways you could make a triangle without using a ruler?

Even more diversity in answers can be expected with synthesis questions than with analysis questions. Therefore, your preparation for diversity is critical to how your students receive your synthesis questions. For example, a question asking for ways to identify undiscovered elements, other than by using the periodic table of elements, opens up many possible responses. Some may not be acceptable ("Consult an astrologer"), but others may be ("Analyze minerals from the moon and other planets"). You will want to accept all reasonable answers, even though your own solutions may be limited to only a few, and keep in mind that some initially less acceptable responses can be built into more accurate, plausible, or efficient responses with additional questioning.

Recall that Table 8.2 showed different types of questioning sequences. These types of sequences can be used to expand on or restrict the initial question to better focus a student response and improve its accuracy, plausibility, or efficiency, as this dialogue illustrates:

Teacher:	In what ways other than using the periodic table might we predict the undiscovered elements?
Carlos:	We could go to the moon and see if there are some elements there we don't have.
Jessica:	We could dig down to the center of the earth and see if we find any of the missing elements.
Daniel:	We could study debris from meteorites—if we can find any.
Teacher:	Those are all good answers. But what if those excursions to the moon, to the center of the earth, and to find meteorites are all too costly and time consuming? How might we use the elements we already have here on Earth to find some new ones?
Jessica:	Oh! Maybe we could try experimenting with combinations of the elements we do have to see if we can make ones that are new and different.

This simple exchange illustrates a funneling strategy: Broad, expansive answers are accepted and then followed up with narrower questions on the next round. In this manner, multiple responses that typically result from synthesis questions can be used to gradually structure and deepen an avenue of inquiry, thereby contributing to still higher order outcomes.

Evaluation

Questions at this highest level of cognitive complexity require the student to form judgments and make decisions using stated criteria. These criteria may be subjective (when a personal set of values is used in making a decision) or objective (when scientific evidence or procedures are used in evaluating something). In each case, however, it is important that the criteria to be expressed is clearly understood, but need not be valued by everyone else.

Here are some action verbs you can use in formulating questions at the evaluation level:

appraise	decide	justify
assess	defend	judge

Following are some sample questions:

- Citing evidence, can you show whether capitalist or socialist countries have a higher standard of living?
- Which of the following numbers contain multiples of 12?
- Using Rules 1 and 2 for forming possessives and assigning one point for each correct usage, what grade would you give the following student essay?
- Given the following fragments of geometric shapes, which can be used to construct a triangle?

Evaluation questions have the distinct quality of confronting the learner with authentic problems much as they appear in the real world, as indicated by the list of higher order thinking and problem-solving behaviors in Appendix C. Because making decisions and judgments is a primary task in adult life, it is essential that classroom experiences link learners to the world in which they will live, regardless of their age or maturity.

Unfortunately, evaluation questions often are reserved for the end of a unit. Moreover, evaluation questions are sometimes considered more suitable for the middle and high school levels than the elementary grades. Both misconceptions have reduced the impact of evaluation questions on learners and reduced their opportunities to transfer what they have learned to the world outside of the classroom. If learners are to cope with real-world problems, they must learn to do so starting at the earliest grades and then throughout their schooling. Therefore your ability to ask evaluation questions that tap into the experiences of your learners can bring the world to your learners at their own level of knowledge and experience. This is one of the most valued abilities that you can have when asking questions.

This ability, however, does not come easily. To be sure, many of the characteristics of the previously addressed higher order questions—application, analysis, and synthesis—are present in evaluation questions. But with an evaluation question, criteria must be applied in deciding the appropriateness of a solution. Notice in the preceding examples that the criteria (or their source) are identified: "Citing evidence of your own choosing," "Which of the following," "Using Rules 1 and 2," "Given the following fragments." The more specific your criteria and the better your learners know them, the more actively engaged they will become in answering the question by using specified criteria from which to make a judgment.

Summary of Question Types

You now know the levels of questions that can be asked of learners and some factors to consider in selecting the appropriate type of question. To summarize:

- Questions calling for the acquisition of facts, rules, and action sequences generally are most efficiently taught with convergent questions, which have a single best answer (or a small number of easily definable answers). Convergent questions are most effective at the knowledge, comprehension, and application levels of cognitive complexity.
- Questions calling for the acquisition of concepts, patterns, and relationships generally are most efficiently taught with divergent questions, for which many different answers may be appropriate. Divergent questions are most effective at the analysis, synthesis, and evaluation levels of cognitive complexity.

Now that you are acquainted with these distinctions among these two types of questions, we turn to several specific techniques that can help you deliver these questions to your students with ease and perfection.

What Is a Probe?

A **probe** is a question that immediately follows a student's response to a question for one of these purposes:

• To elicit clarification of the student's response

• To solicit new information to extend or build on the student's response

• To redirect or restructure the student's response in a more productive direction

Use probes that elicit clarification to get students to rephrase or reword a response so you can determine its appropriateness or correctness. **Eliciting probes**—such as "Can you say that in another way?" and "How does that answer apply in the case of _____?"—encourage learners to show more of what they know, thereby exposing exactly what they understand. The brief and vague responses often given in the context of a fast-paced and lively classroom discussion can mask partially correct answers or answers that are correct but were arrived at with flawed reasoning. When you are unsure how much understanding underlies a correct response, slow the pace by probing for clarification.

Use **soliciting probes**, which ask for new information, following a response that is at least partially correct or indicates an acceptable level of understanding. This time, you are using the probe to push the learner's response to a more complex level (e.g., "Now that you have decided the laboratory is the best environment for discovering new elements, what kind of experiments would you conduct there?" or "Now that you have taken the square root of that number, how can you extend the same idea to find its cube root?").

A soliciting probe builds higher and higher plateaus of understanding by using the previous response as a stepping stone to greater expectations and more complete responses. This involves treating an incomplete response as part of the next higher-level response—not as a wrong answer. The key to probing for new information is to make your follow-up question only a small extension of your previous question; otherwise the leap will be too great and the learner will be stymied by what appears to be an entirely new question. Using this type of probe, therefore, requires much the same process for finding the right answer as does the previously correct question, only this time applied to a different and slightly more complex problem.

Use **redirecting probes** to channel the flow of ideas instead of using awkward and often punishing responses, such as "You are on the wrong track," "That's not relevant," and "You are not getting the idea." Probes for redirecting responses into more productive areas can accomplish the needed shift less abruptly and more positively, without discouraging students from offering other responses. A probe that accomplishes this purpose moves the discussion sideways, setting a new condition for a subsequent response without negating a previous response.

Probing to redirect or restructure a discussion can be a smooth and effortless way of getting learners back on track. Notice in the following example how the teacher blends the use of all three types of probes in the context of a single discussion, as indicated by the use of bold italic type:

Teacher: What do we call the grid system by which we can identify the location of any place on the globe? [To begin the questioning.]

Jason: Latitude and longitude.

Teacher: Good. What does *longitude* mean? [***To solicit*** new information.]

Jason: It's the grid lines on the globe that. . . go up and down.

Teacher: What do you mean by *up and down*? [***To elicit*** clarification.]

Jason: They extend north and south at equal intervals.

Teacher: OK. Now tell me, where do they begin? [***To solicit*** new information.]

Jason: Well, I think they begin wherever it's midnight and end where it's almost midnight again.

Teacher: Let's think about that for a minute. Wouldn't that mean the point of origin would always be changing according to where it happened to be midnight? [***To redirect***.]

Jason: I see, so the grids must start at some fixed point.

Teacher: Anybody know where they begin? [***To solicit*** new information.]

La Jonne: Our book says the first one, marked zero starts at a place called Greenwich, England.

Teacher: How can a grid that runs continuously north and south around the globe *start* anyplace, La Jonne? [***To elicit*** clarification.]

La Jonne: I meant to say that it *runs through* Greenwich, England.

Teacher: Good. Now let's return to Jason's point about time. If we have a fixed line of longitude, marked zero, how might we use it to establish time? [***To solicit*** new information.]

Jason: Now I remember. Midnight at the zero longitude—or in Greenwich, England—is called zero hours. Starting from there, there are timelines drawn around the world, so that when it's midnight at the first timeline, it will be one o'clock back at Greenwich, England, and when it's midnight at the next timeline, it will be two o'clock back at Greenwich, England, and so on.

Teacher: What does that mean? [***To elicit*** clarification.]

Jason: Each line equals one hour—so. . . so there must be 24 of them!

Teacher: It should be no surprise to learn that time determined in reference to the zero grid of longitude is called Greenwich Mean Time or Universal Time Coordinated.

How Should Wait Time Be Used?

An important consideration during questioning and probing is how long to wait before initiating another question. Sometimes your wait time can be as effective in contributing to the desired response as the question or probe itself, especially when you give students time to thoughtfully compose their answers. A wait time that is either too short or too long can be detrimental, and one that is too long also wastes valuable instructional time. Obviously, the wait time will be longer when students are weighing alternative responses (which often occurs when asking a divergent question) than when their responses must be correct, quick, and firm (which often occurs during a convergent question).

Rowe (1986, 1987) and Tobin (1987) distinguish two different wait times. **Wait-time 1** refers to the amount of time a teacher gives a learner to respond when first asked a question. In a classroom with a short wait-time 1, learners do not have much time to think before answering the question. In such a classroom, the teacher is repeating the question or calling on another learner to answer the same question after only a two- or three-second period of silence.

Wait-time 2 refers to the interval of time after a learner's first response until the teacher or other students affirm or negate the answer and the teacher then moves on. In a classroom with a long wait-time 2, the teacher waits several seconds before asking a follow-up question, correcting the answer, or otherwise commenting on what the learner said, giving that learner and others time to rethink, extend, or modify a response. A classroom with a short wait-time 2 is characterized by frequent interruptions of learners before they finish answering.

The following dialogue illustrates wait-time 1 and wait-time 2:

Teacher: From our discussion yesterday about volcanoes, what is a *caldera*?

[Wait-time 1: The teacher gives students time to think about the question and read nonverbal cues indicating the possible need

Probes follow questions and are used to clarify a student's response, solicit new information, or redirect a response in a more productive direction.

for a probe, which is especially important for divergent and higher order questions.]

> **Nelda:** I remember. It's the crater formed by the collapse of the central part of the volcano. I'm not sure, but I think it's used to vent all the steam and gases that spew out. . . .

[Wait-time 2: The teacher waits for Nelda or another student to think about and affirm or negate what was said, which is especially important for responses that are hesitant or only partially correct.]

> Yes, that's it. Now I remember the picture in the text with all the smoke coming out of it.
>
> **Martin:** She's right. That's how we drew it on the board. Everyone remember?
>
> **Teacher:** And what else did the picture on the board show?

Wait-time 1 refers to the amount of time a teacher gives a learner to respond to a question. Classrooms with short wait-time 1s do not give learners sufficient time to think before answering the question.

Increasing either type of wait time has the following effects on learner responses:

- Learners give longer answers to questions
- Learners volunteer more responses
- There are fewer unanswered questions
- Learners are more certain of their answers
- Learners are more willing to give speculative answers
- The frequency of learner questions increases

Generally, you should wait *at least 3 seconds* before asking another question, repeating the previous question, or calling on another student. Divergent questions may require thinking through and weighing alternatives that may require *up to 15 seconds* of wait time.

Research findings provide impressive testimony to the important effect that wait time can have on your learners' responses. If only one piece of advice were given to beginning teachers concerning wait time, it would be to slow down and pause longer between questions and answers. See In Practice: Focus on Effective Classroom Questioning.

Finally, remember that questioning is a principal means of engaging students in the learning process, as it gets them to think through and problem solve with the material you are presenting. Following are suggestions for using questions to promote your learners' thinking and problem solving:

- *Plan the types of questions you will ask.* Although talk-show hosts make it appear as if their questions are spontaneous and unrehearsed, this seldom is the case. In reality, ad-libbing and spontaneity can lead to as much dead time on the air as they can in your classroom. The types of questions you select, their level of difficulty, and the sequence in which you ask them should be based on your lesson objectives.

- *Deliver questions in a style that is concise, clear, and to the point.* Effective oral questions are like effective writing: Every word is needed. Pose questions in the same natural, conversational language you would use in talking with a friend.

- *Allow time for students to think (wait-time 1).* Research on question asking points to the fact that many teachers do not allow learners sufficient time to answer a question before calling on someone else or moving to the next question. Gage and Berliner (1998) report that, on average, teachers wait only about one second for learners to respond. These researchers recommend that increasing wait time to three to four seconds for lower-level questions and to as much as 15 seconds for higher-level questions.

In Practice

Focus on Effective Classroom Questioning

In 2001, the Northwest Regional Educational Laboratory conducted an extensive study of the research on teacher questioning in the classroom. This study included research that had been conducted across the K–12 grades, the majority of which was concerned with the effects on student learning produced by questions at higher and lower cognitive levels. Here are some of the major findings from a report by Kathleen Cotton, drawn from 37 research documents and reported in *School Improvement Research Series: Research You Can Use, Close-Up #5* (available at www.nwrel.org/index.html).

The Research on Classroom Questioning Findings

Researchers who have conducted general investigations of the role of classroom questioning have drawn the following conclusions:

General Findings

- Instruction that includes posing questions during lessons is more effective in producing achievement gains than instruction carried out without questioning.
- Students perform better on test items previously asked as recitation questions than on items they have not been exposed to before.
- Oral questions posed during classroom recitations are more effective in fostering learning than written questions.
- Questions that focus student attention on primary elements in the lesson result in better comprehension than questions that do not.

Placement and Timing of Questions

- Asking questions frequently during class discussions is positively related to learning facts.
- Posing questions before reading and studying material is effective for students who are older, have higher ability, and/or are known to be interested in the subject matter.
- Very young children and poor readers tend to focus on content better if questions are posed about the content before the lesson is presented.

Cognitive Level of Questions

Should we ask questions that require the literal recall of content and only very basic reasoning? Or should we ask questions that call for speculative, inferential, and evaluative thinking? When researchers looked at the cognitive level of teachers' questions in relation to the subject matter, the students, and the teachers' intent, their conclusions indicated the following:

- On average during a classroom recitation, approximately 60 percent of the questions asked are lower-level cognitive questions, 20 percent are higher-level cognitive questions, and 20 percent are procedural questions.
- Lower-level cognitive questions are more effective than higher-level questions with young (primary-level) children, particularly those who are disadvantaged.
- Lower-level cognitive questions are more effective when the teacher's purpose is to impart factual knowledge and assist students in committing this knowledge to memory.
- In settings where a high incidence of lower-level questions is appropriate, a greater frequency of questions is positively related to student achievement.
- When predominantly lower-level questions are used, their level of difficulty should be such that most will elicit correct responses.
- In most classes above the primary grades, a combination of higher- and lower-level cognitive questions is superior to the exclusive use of one or the other.
- Students whom teachers perceive as slow or poor learners are asked fewer higher-level cognitive questions than students perceived as more capable learners.
- Increasing the use of higher-level cognitive questions (to more than 20 percent) produces superior learning gains for students above the primary grades and particularly for secondary students.
- Teaching students to draw inferences and giving them practice in doing so results in higher-level cognitive responses and greater learning gains.
- For older students, increases in the use of higher-level cognitive questions (to 50 percent or more) are positively related to increases in class participation, on-task behavior, and length of student responses.

Researchers conclude their report by stating that providing better preservice training in using wait time and asking higher order questions both have the potential for increasing students' classroom participation and achievement.

Source: Education Northwest (formerly Northwest Regional Educational Laboratory).

- *Keep students in suspense.* First deliver the question, and then mention a student's name. Similarly, randomly select the students you want to answer your questions. You want your learners to anticipate that they can be called on at any time. This both increases accountability and maintains attention and alertness.

- *Give the student sufficient time to complete his or her response before redirecting the question or probing (wait-time 2).* Wait-time 2 is the time you wait following a student's answer before probing for deeper understanding or redirecting the question when the answer is incomplete or wrong. Teachers who make a deliberate effort to maintain lesson momentum often interrupt before a learner has finished responding.

- *Provide immediate feedback to the learner.* A correct answer should be acknowledged and followed by encouragement, elaboration on the response, further probing, or another question. The important point is to communicate to the learner that you have heard and evaluated the answer. Often learners (unbeknown to the teacher) perceive that their answers have been ignored. Incorrect, incomplete, or inadequate answers should be followed by a probe or redirection of the question to another student. As discussed in the following section, research suggests that learners of different achievement levels, socioeconomic levels, and cultures benefit from different questioning, redirecting, and probing techniques.

What Is Culturally Responsive Questioning?

Sociolinguistics is the study of how cultural groups differ in the courtesies and conventions of language, rather than in the grammatical structure of what is said. Sociolinguistics examines the rules of **culture-specific questioning** that govern social conversation: with whom to speak, in what manner, when to pause, when to ask and answer questions, how to interrupt a speaker, and so on. Sociolinguists study, for example, aspects of communication as revealed by the average length of utterances, time between utterances, speech rhythms, and rules for when, how, and about what people converse.

Researchers have pointed out that classrooms and schools are governed by linguistic, sociocultural, and social interaction codes that can diverge from those found in the homes, peers, and communities of immigrant children. Delgado-Gaitan (2006) and Delgado-Gaitan and Trueba (1991), for example, point out that pedagogical practices in the schools they studied in California contradicted culturally sanctioned patterns of sharing, leadership, and oral storytelling among Mexican American students. Rather than change interaction patterns to accommodate the students, teachers in mainstreamed classes attributed students' lower performance to "deficiencies" and insisted on Anglo norms of interaction that were at odds with the students' culture. Among the aspects of communication and interaction most frequently studied are wait time, rhythm, participation structure, and language (Gay, 2010; Minami & Ovando, 2003).

Wait Time

Tharp (1989) reports that different cultures often have different wait times. Navajo children, for example, are raised in a culture that allows longer responses (wait-time 2) than Anglo culture. Some studies show that Navajo children speak in longer sentences and volunteer more answers when given more time to respond. In contrast, Tharp reports that in Hawaiian culture, interrupting is a sign of interest in the speaker and in what he or she is saying. Conversely, a long wait-time 2 suggests to Hawaiian learners that the speaker is uninterested or bored with the conversation.

Other studies of Hispanic and African American learners appear to suggest that optimal wait times are culture and even context specific (Banks & Banks, 2009; Hill, 1989). Although this research does not make specific prescriptions, it does suggest that teachers must determine how to pose a question and the appropriate wait time between questions and answers within the cultural context and learning history of their learners.

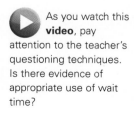 As you watch this **video**, pay attention to the teacher's questioning techniques. Is there evidence of appropriate use of wait time?

Rhythm

Conversational *rhythm* pertains to the tempo, inflections, and speed of conversations between two speakers. Young (1970) and Piestrup (1973) were among the first to observe that African American children and their mothers converse using rapid rhythms and a "contest" style of interaction. Mothers encourage their children to be assertive. Directions for household chores and children's responses to them take on an almost debate-like tone with the mother directing or calling and the children responding. Tannen (2005), Auer, Couper-Kuhlen, and Muller (1999), and Franklin (1992) suggest that this style of interaction creates a high-energy, fast-paced home environment, which contrasts with the low-energy, slow-paced environment of the typical classroom.

Franklin (1992) speculates that this contrast between the pace of conversation at home and in school may be one reason some African American children are inappropriately referred for behavior problems in the classroom. Similarly, M. G. Anderson (1992) states that many Anglo teachers overreact to the conversational style of African American adolescents, which may explain the disproportionate referral of these children to programs for learners with behavior disorders. Anderson recommends that teachers allow African American learners to use in the classroom the conversational style they bring from home. This includes speaking more rhythmically, displaying greater variation in intonation, and engaging in more fast-paced verbal interplay.

Participation Structure

The typical classroom conversation occurs in a one-to-one, question-and-answer structure or format. The teacher looks directly at a student, asks him or her a question, and waits for an answer before making a follow-up response. Tharp and Gallimore (1991) observe that such a participation structure results in very little participation by Hawaiian and Navajo children. For these children, both at home and in the community, the typical participation structure when adults are present involves a relatively small group of children together with an encouraging, participating, but nondirective adult in an informal setting. In research, when the classroom participation structures were based on those found in their cultures, both Hawaiian and Navajo children, who rarely participated in classroom discussions or question-and-answer formats, became surprisingly verbal.

Sociolinguists point out that children are more comfortable in classrooms where the sociolinguistic patterns (wait times, rhythms, participation structures, etc.) are compatible with those of their home and community. Some teachers and schools may view African American and Hispanic children as less verbal (Delgado-Gaitan, 2006; Delgado-Gaitan & Trueba, 1991). Yet when observed in a familiar home or neighborhood environment, they use vibrant, expressive, and creative language patterns. Researchers have observed that the sociolinguistic patterns of the typical U.S. classroom make certain minority-group learners uncomfortable. This in turn causes those learners to participate less in class, to participate in ways that Anglo American teachers view as deficient or inappropriate, and to achieve less. Researchers generally agree that immigrant children's school success can be explained more by a strong home culture and positive sense of ethnic identity (which should be preserved at school) than by assimilation (Schmidt & Lazar, 2011).

Language

Because much questioning is conducted in the formal language of the classroom, you should know your learners' language abilities. Approximately five million students—about 10 percent of the school-age population—have a primary language other than English. For some, English is their dominant language in the *receptive mode* (listening, reading); for others, English is their dominant language in the *expressive mode* (talking, writing).

It is not unusual to find bilingual learners who choose, for example, Spanish as their dominant means of speaking but English as their dominant means of listening (Banks & Banks, 2006; Moran & Hakuta, 2001; and Valencia, 2010a, b). This allows the teacher to speak and be understood in English, even though at least some of the learners' communications to the teacher might be in Spanish. Knowing your learners' dominant means of expression will provide more opportunities to engage all of them in the learning process. If a learner does not use English as his or her dominant language, either in the expressive or receptive mode, and you do not speak the learner's language, you can do the following:

1. Emphasize other forms of communication—including the visual, kinesthetic, and tactile modalities—to supplement your teaching objectives, thus bringing a multisensory approach to your teaching.

2. Be sensitive to cultural differences. For example, providing frequent, meaningful praise and encouragement can set the stage for learning more efficiently than repeatedly reciting rules and warnings, which may not be fully understood by some of your learners.

3. Evaluate the reading level and format of the materials you use. When selecting or differentiating materials, you may find a Spanish version of comparable content and reading level. After a trial period, evaluate the materials again and adjust the reading level accordingly.

4. Do not confuse language proficiency with subject-matter achievement or ability. Bilingual children, in comparison to monolingual children, show superior performance on tests of analytical reasoning, concept formation, and cognitive flexibility. Other research shows that learners who are fluent in two or more languages have a better knowledge of language structure and detail, understand that words are arbitrary symbols for other words and actions, and can better detect grammatical errors in written and spoken communication (Galambos & Goldin-Meadow, 1990; Portes & Rumbaut, 2006). It is also important to note that some early researchers suggested that children from economically impoverished areas who speak a nonstandard form of English (e.g., Black English) may suffer impaired cognitive development as a result. But this hypothesis has been conclusively refuted (Masahiko & Ovando, 2001; Poplack, 2000). We now know that all languages, including dialects and other forms of nonstandard English, are equally complex and equally effective for use in learning and problem solving (Oakes & Lipton, 2006). Linguists have demonstrated that languages cannot be ranked in terms of intellectual sophistication. Consequently, intellectual impairment or slow cognitive development cannot result from the primary language a learner speaks, regardless of how nonstandard that language is.

What Are Common Problems in Using Questions?

Based on classroom observations of the question-asking behavior of beginning teachers, following are some of the most frequently observed problems to watch for, along with suggested remedies.

Do You Use Complex, Ambiguous, or Double Questions?

One of the most common question-asking problems of beginning teachers involves use of the complex, ambiguous, or double question. This is a question so long and complicated that students have easily lost track of the main idea by the time they have heard the entire question. Sometimes a teacher unknowingly packs two (or even more) questions within this complicated structure.

Because such a question is delivered orally and not written, students have no way of rereading the question to gain its full intent. It is unfortunate that this type of question sometimes is so complicated that even the teacher cannot repeat it precisely when asked, thus providing different versions of the same question. Consider the following three examples of needlessly complex questions and their simpler but equally effective revisions:

Example 1
Complex form: "We all know what the three branches of government are, but where did they come from, how were they devised, and in what manner do they relate?"

This question is actually three questions in one and requires too long a response if each point in the question is to be responded to individually. In addition, the first two questions may be redundant (or are they?), and the third is sufficiently vague to bewilder most students. Finally, what if some students do not know or cannot recall the three branches of government? For those students, everything that follows is irrelevant, opening the door to inattention and off-task behavior.

Simpler form: "Recall that there are three branches of government: the executive, judicial, and legislative. What governmental functions are assigned to each branch by the Constitution?"

Example 2

Complex form: "How do single-celled animals propagate themselves and divide up to create similar forms of animal life that look like them?"

If you were to ask this question, some of your students surely would ask you to repeat it, in which case you might not remember your own complex wording. This question fails to get to the point quickly and appears to ask the same thing three times: "How do single-celled animals propagate . . . divide up . . . create similar forms of animal life?" This redundancy could easily be mistaken as asking three separate questions by students struggling to understand single-celled reproduction at an elementary level. State your question in only one way and rephrase it later, if need be, when students know the same question is being rephrased.

Simpler form: "By what process do single-celled animals reproduce?"

Example 3

Complex form: "What do you think about the Civil War, the Iraq War, or war in general?"

Depending on what part of this question students want to hear, you may get noticeably different answers. The intention is to ask a question that will provide enough options to get almost any student involved in composing a response, but unless you intend only to start a controversy, the range of responses will probably be so broad that moving to the next point will be impossible. This question may leave students arguing feverishly for the entire period, without being able to focus on the real purpose for raising the question in the first place (e.g., as an introduction to the Civil War, to unpopular wars, or to the concept of *war*). This question is too broad, too open, and too divergent to be of practical value for framing a day's lesson.

Simpler form: "What factors justify a war among groups within the same nation?"

Here are basic rules for avoiding complex, ambiguous, or double questions:

* Focus each question on only one idea.
* State the main idea only once.
* Use concrete language.
* State the question in as few words as possible.

Do You Accept Only the Answers You Expect?

Another common mistake is to accept almost exclusively the answers you expect. Recall the discussion in Chapter 2 regarding the bias that teachers sometimes have about whom they call on and interact with in classroom exchanges. Bias can extend to favorite answers as well as to favorite students. When teaching new content, you naturally strive to become more secure and confident by limiting the answers to those with which you are most familiar. Your first reaction will be to discourage responses at the edge of what you consider to be the appropriate range. This range is directly related to the openness of your questions. Open questions encourage diversity, and it is this diversity that often catches the beginning teacher off guard and forces an expansive question into a limited one. Note in the following dialogue how this teacher's supportive and nurturing posture is changed by the nature of the response:

Teacher: OK, today we will study the European settlers who came to America and why they came here. I know you already know a lot about this topic. So, why did they come to America?

Student 1: To farm.

Teacher: No, not to farm.

Student 2: To build houses and churches.

Teacher: No, that's not right either.

If this exchange were to continue for very long, it would no doubt turn off many students, if only because they know their responses cannot be entirely wrong, even if they are not what the teacher wants. What *does* the teacher want? The desired answer is probably that the early settlers came to America because of religious persecution in their European communities. The last student's response, "To build houses and churches," was a perfect opportunity for a probe that simply asked "Why churches?" Unfortunately, this teacher missed that opportunity in favor of waiting for the exact response, because he or she was unable or unwilling to build on the existing responses. This teacher may have a long wait, in which case valuable instructional time may be lost by calling on student after student in the hope that the single acceptable answer will eventually emerge.

Answers that are just what you are looking for are always desirable, but remember that partially correct answers and even unusual and unexpected ones can become effective additions to the discussion through the use of probes. The solution to this problem is to use probes that build gradually toward your targeted responses.

Why Are You Asking This Question?

Perhaps the most serious fault of all in question asking is not being certain of why you are asking a question. Remember, questions are tools that support the teaching and learning processes. Your first decision in composing questions is to determine whether your lesson is teaching facts, rules, and action sequences or concepts, patterns, and relationships. If the former is your goal, compose convergent questions at the knowledge, comprehension, and application levels. If the latter is your goal, then ask divergent questions at the analysis, synthesis, and evaluation levels. This decision strategy is summarized in Figure 8.1.

If you have not determined where you are on Figure 8.1, you will likely ask the wrong types of questions, and your questions will lack logical sequence. They may jump from convergent to divergent and move back and forth from the simple recall of facts to the acquisition of concepts and patterns. Your students will find your questions confusing, because your ideas will not be linked by

Figure 8.1 **Decision Tree for Deciding Types of Questions to Ask**

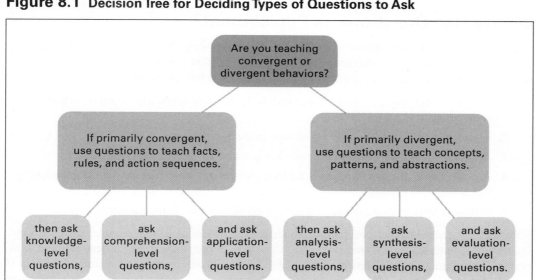

any common thread that they can follow, and you will be seen as being vague or lacking the ability to connect content in meaningful ways. Therefore it is important that you decide in advance where your questioning strategy is going and then move toward this goal by choosing appropriate questions and levels of cognitive complexity.

Finally, it is important to note that just because your goal may be convergent or divergent questions, this does not mean you cannot vary your questioning strategy across the levels shown in Figure 8.1. Questions should vary across types of learning gradually moving up the rigor and relevance framework, for example, from knowledge to application to analysis, synthesis, and evaluation, with increasing relevance to the world of your learners beyond the classroom. Keep in mind your ultimate aim is to choose the best combination of questions to reach the goal for your lesson.

Do You Answer the Question Yourself?

Another common problem is posing a question and then answering it yourself. Sometimes a student begins a response but is cut off, only to hear the remainder of the response supplied by the teacher:

Teacher: So who was the president who freed the slaves?

Student: Abraham—

Teacher: Lincoln! Yes, that's right.

Sometimes the reverse occurs: A student begins a response that the teacher knows is wrong and then is cut off by the teacher, who gives the correct response:

Teacher: So who was the president who freed the slaves?

Student: George—

Teacher: No, no! It was Abraham Lincoln.

Needless to say, both outcomes demoralize the student, who either is deprived of the chance to give a complete right answer or is shown to have a response so incorrect that it is not even worth hearing in its entirety. Neither of these outcomes may be intended, but this is how your students may see it.

Your job is to use student responses to build to other more complex outcomes. Probes to elicit new information, to go beyond an already correct answer, and to provide hints and clues after a wrong answer are particularly useful, because they extend to your students the right to give a full and deliberate response—right or wrong. Teachers who frequently interrupt student responses because of a desire for perfect answers, a dominant personality, or talkativeness may ultimately produce frustrated learners who never learn to give full and thoughtful responses or to participate voluntarily.

Do You Use Questions as Punishment?

Our final problem, and perhaps the most difficult, is the use—or rather abuse—of questions to punish or to put students on the defensive. Being asked a question can be a punishment as well as a reward. For example, questions can be used as punishment in the following ways:

1. A student who forgot to do the homework is deliberately asked a question from that homework.
2. A student who never volunteers is always asked questions.
3. A student gives a wrong response and then is asked an even harder question.
4. A student who disrupts the class is asked a question for which the answer cannot possibly be known.
5. A student who gives a careless response is asked four questions in a row.

Nearly every teacher has, at one time or another, used questions in one or more of these ways. Interestingly, some teachers do not always see these uses as punishment. Regardless of intent, however, such questions are punishment in that they (1) are unlikely to engage the student actively in meaningful learning and (2) leave the student with a worse self-image, less confidence, and more anxiety (even anger) than before. These are behaviors that can only impede the learning process and therefore have no place in your repertoire of questioning strategies. Each of the student-centered problems reflected in the preceding examples could have been handled more effectively by doing one of these things:

1. Making a list of students who do not do homework.
2. Providing example questions beforehand to students who never volunteer.
3. Giving another try and providing hints and clues to students who give wrong responses until they give partially correct answers.
4. Assigning disciplinary warnings or reprimands to students who disrupt class.
5. Passing quickly to another student after receiving a careless answer from a student.

Ample means are available for dealing with misbehavior, and such means are far more effective than using questions. Questions are instructional tools that should be prized and protected for their chosen purpose. To misuse them or to use them for any other purpose may affect how your students perceive your questions ("Did I get the hard question because the teacher thinks I'm smart or because I'm being punished?"). Such conflicts can drain students of the energy and concentration needed to answer your questions and may forever cast doubts on your motives.

Conversely, questions can be implicit rewards when used correctly. The opportunity to shine, to know and display the correct answer in front of others, and to be tested and get an approving grade are rewarding experiences for any learner. Consequently, every learner, regardless of ability level or knowledge of a correct response, should periodically have these experiences.

Do not ignore students who have difficulty responding, and do not accept wrong answers. Instead, occasionally try a broader criterion than correct/incorrect to help all students share in the emotional and intellectual rewards of answering questions. For example, try rewarding the most novel, most futuristic, most practical, and most thought-provoking answers along with the most accurate response. This will let every learner share in the challenge and excitement of answering questions.

Thus questioning is another tool that can be used to differentiate your instruction and add to your teaching menu. Because of the almost endless variety of questions, using them may well be the most flexible tool on your menu.

Case History and Licensure Preparation

DIRECTIONS: *The following case history pertains to Chapter 8 content. After reading the case history, go to Chapter 8 in the Book Specific Resources section in the MyEducationLab for your course. Open the Case History and Licensure Preparation activity and complete the questions that follow. Upon completion of the test, scored answers to the short-answer question pertaining to the case history and multiple-choice questions will be provided.*

Case History

Mr. Cole's middle school science class is heterogeneous in many ways. There is an ethnic and racial mix of Anglo, Hispanic, and African American students and a small number of Asian American students. Several are recent immigrants who understand and read English better than they speak it. Ability levels run from very low to high, with a large portion of students being in the middle. Currently, the class is studying the effects of invention and discovery on society:

Mr. Cole: My great uncle played football in college. But when he was in his twenties, he got pneumonia and died in three days. Could that happen today, Carla?

Carla: Well, my grandfather died of pneumonia last winter, but I don't think it happened that fast. I guess it could happen.

Mr. Cole: You're probably right, Carla. People still die from diseases like pneumonia, especially if they are elderly and have another illness. Maybe that was true with your grandfather?

Carla: [Her eyes wide with surprise.] He was sick for a long time.

Mr. Cole: But what about healthy athletes in their twenties? Do many of them die from pneumonia today? What do you think, Thomas?

Thomas: No, today we just give them antibiotics, and they get well pretty fast. I get your hint, Mr. Cole. Antibiotics are another invention that has really helped society.

Curtis: I had bronchitis last year, and the antibiotics didn't seem to help much at all. They aren't that great, in my opinion.

Ramona: My baby sister gets ear infections, and the medicine used to clear them up right away. But now, it doesn't help all that much.

Mr. Cole: So I see some of you have mixed experiences with antibiotics. Why do you think that is? Millie, you have your hand up. What do you think?

Millie: I saw this program on TV a couple of weeks ago that said we take antibiotics too much and that's why they don't work as well now. Some germs have gotten used to them. There are some kinds of infections now that don't go away with antibiotics anymore.

Mr. Cole: Maybe there can be too much of a good thing, then. Could it be that some inventions seem good at first, but after a while, we see that maybe they solve one problem and create another? Antibiotics cure simple pneumonia, but they can also produce what are called *resistive strains,* which are even more difficult to kill. Let's think about some other inventions that also created problems as well as solved them. I'll give you some time to think of a good example. [Thirty seconds goes by.] Jason, what have you thought of?

Jason: Well, what about cars? Sure, we can get around a lot better, but they cause a lot of pollution, too.

Curtis: Not to mention all the people who die in accidents each year.

Millie: I say computers. Some people are addicted to the Internet and don't spend time with their family anymore. Plus people get a lot of junk e-mail they don't want.

Thomas: It really creeps me out to get a phone call from a computer. I mean, people selling you stuff on the telephone is bad enough, but a computer. . .;

Millie: What about that time the computer here at school gave everybody "incompletes" by mistake? [The class groans in remembrance.]

Summing Up

The main points in this chapter include the following:

What Is a Question?

1. An effective question is one for which students actively compose a response and thereby become engaged in the learning process.

2. An effective question depends on voice inflection, word emphasis, word choice, and the context in which it is raised.

3. The three most commonly observed teacher behaviors in the classroom are structuring, soliciting, and reacting.

4. *Soliciting*—or question-asking behavior—encourages students to act on and think about the structured material as quickly as possible after it has been presented.

5. It has been estimated that 70 percent to 80 percent of all questions require the simple recall of facts, but only 20 percent to 30 percent require clarifying, expanding, generalizing, and making inferences. In other words, as few as one of every five questions may require higher-level thought processes, even though behaviors at the higher levels of cognitive complexity are among those most frequently required in adult life, at work, and in advanced training.

What Are the Purposes of Questions?

6. Common purposes for asking questions include the following:

   - Getting interest and attention
   - Diagnosing and checking
   - Recalling specific facts or information
   - Managing the class
   - Encouraging higher-level thought processes
   - Structuring and redirecting learning
   - Allowing expression of affect

What Are Convergent and Divergent Questions?

7. A question that limits possible responses to one or a small number is called a *convergent, direct,* or *closed question.* This type of question teaches the learner to respond in a limited, restrictive manner.

8. A question that has many right answers or a broad range of acceptable responses is called a *divergent, indirect,* or *open question.* Divergent questions, however, can have wrong answers.

9. The same question can be convergent under one set of circumstances and divergent under another, as when so-called creative answers to a divergent question have been memorized from a list.

10. Research has not shown that the use of higher order questions is significantly related to improved performance on standardized achievement tests. However, higher order questions have been found to elicit analysis, synthesis, and evaluation skills, which are among the skills most sought in adult life and least measured by standardized tests.

Who Are the Targets of Questions?

11. Questions can be specifically worded for cognitive complexity as well as directed to individuals, groups, or the entire class.

What Sequences of Questions Are Used?

12. Questions may be used in the context of many different sequences, such as *funneling,* where increasingly specific conditions are added to an original question, narrowing it to one that requires a simple response.

What Levels of Questions Are Used?

13. In addition to being divergent or convergent and targeted to specific types of learners, questions can be formulated at different levels of cognitive complexity, including the knowledge, comprehension, application, analysis, synthesis, and evaluation levels of the cognitive domain.

14. Knowledge questions ask the learner to recall, describe, define, or recognize facts that already have been committed to memory.

15. Comprehension questions ask the learner to explain, summarize, or elaborate on previously learned facts.

16. Application questions ask the learner to go beyond the memorization of facts and their translation and to use previously acquired facts and understandings in a new and different environment.

17. Analysis questions ask the learner to break a problem into its component parts and to recognize a relationship among the parts.

18. Synthesis questions ask the learner to design or produce a unique or unusual response to an unfamiliar problem.

19. Evaluation questions ask the learner to form judgments and make decisions, using stated criteria for determining the adequacy of the response.

What Is a Probe?

20. A *probe* is a question that immediately follows a student's response to a question; its purpose is to elicit clarification, to solicit new information, or to redirect or restructure a student's response.

21. The key to probing for new information is to make the follow-up question only a small extension of the previous question.

How Should Wait Time Be Used?

22. The time you wait before initiating another question or turning to another student may be as important in actively engaging the learner in the learning process as the question itself. Teachers should observe a wait time of at least three seconds before asking another question, repeating the previous question, or calling on another student.

23. Longer wait times have been associated with longer responses, greater numbers of voluntary responses, greater behavioral complexity of responses, greater frequency of student questions, and increased confidence in responding.

What Is Culturally Responsive Questioning?

24. Researchers point out that classrooms and schools are governed by linguistic, sociocultural, and social interaction patterns that can diverge from those found in the homes, peers, and communities of immigrant children.

25. *Cultural-specific questions* are those that take into account the wait time, rhythm, participation structure, and primary means of expression predominant in a given culture.

What Are Common Problems in Using Questions?

26. To avoid the problems commonly observed in the question-asking behavior of beginning teachers, do the following:

    • Do not ask overly complex or ambiguous questions, which may require several different answers.

    • Be prepared to expect correct but unusual answers, especially when raising divergent questions.

    • Always establish beforehand why you are asking a particular question. Know the complexity of the answer you expect as a result of asking the question.

    • Do not supply the correct answer to your own question without first probing. Never prevent a student from completing a response to a question, even if incorrect. Use a partially correct or wrong answer as a platform for eliciting clarification, soliciting new information, or redirecting.

    • Do not use questions as a form of embarrassment or punishment. Such misuse of questions rarely changes misbehavior. Moreover, questioning is an academic tool that should be prized and protected for its chosen purpose. To misuse questioning or to use it for any other purpose may affect how your students perceive your questions.

Key Terms

Convergent question
Culture-specific questioning
Divergent question
Effective questions
Eliciting probes

Probe
Question sequence
Reacting
Redirecting probes
Sociolinguistics

Soliciting
Soliciting probes
Structuring
Wait-time 1
Wait-time 2

Discussion and Practice Questions

Questions marked with an asterisk are answered in Appendix B. Some asterisked questions may require student follow-up responses not included in Appendix B. Go to the Assignments and Activities section of the various topics on the MyEducationLab for your course to complete additional practice activities related to this chapter's content.

*1. What is the definition of an *effective question,* as used in this chapter? Provide a question that you believe represents this definition.

*2. Approximately what percentage of all school time may be devoted to questions and answers? What is your opinion as to why this percentage is so high?

*3. Approximately what percentage of questions asked requires the simple recall of facts, and approximately what percentage requires clarifying, expanding, generalizing, and making inferences? What is your opinion as to why the latter percentage is so low?

*4. In your own words, what is a *convergent question* and what is a *divergent question*? Address how they are alike and different with respect to right answers and wrong answers.

5. Using the same question content, give an example of both a convergent and a divergent question.

*6. According to research, how does the asking of higher order questions affect (a) a learner's standardized achievement score and (b) a learner's use of analysis, synthesis, and evaluation skills in thinking through a problem?

7. Compose a question that is more cognitively complex and another that is less cognitively complex. How do these two questions differ in cues, hints, and advance organizers?

8. Using Table 8.2 as a guide, compose a sequence of related questions that extend and lift student responses.

9. Using the same content as in Question 8, prepare one question that elicits the appropriate level of behavioral complexity at each level of the cognitive domain—knowledge, comprehension, application, analysis, synthesis, and evaluation.

*10. What is meant by the term *wait time?* Why should beginning teachers work to increase their wait time?

*11. Identify and give examples of the five most troublesome question-asking problems for beginning teachers. Which problem is the most difficult for you?

Professional Practice

Field Experience and Practice Activities

Questions marked with an asterisk are answered in Appendix B. Some asterisked questions may require student follow-up responses not included in Appendix B.

1. From your fieldwork or observation, provide examples of what a teacher said to (a) structure a topic to be discussed, (b) solicit a student response, and (c) react to the student's response. For a topic you will be teaching, show how this chain of events would unfold using a brief teacher and student dialogue.

*2. List the seven specific purposes for asking questions. Then, give examples of questions that represent three of the most popular purposes you have observed. Identify any you have observed that are not among the seven.

*3. Write a brief classroom dialogue of teacher questions and student responses that illustrates the funneling of student responses.

4. From a classroom dialogue you have observed, provide one example each of probes that (a) elicit clarification, (b) solicit new information, and (c) redirect or restructure a student's response. In which order did these occur?

5. From your fieldwork or observation, recall three questions that you would consider culturally responsive. Explain why.

Digital Portfolio Activities

The following digital portfolio activities relate to InTASC Standards 3, 5, and 8.

1. In Field Experience and Practice Activity 2, you were asked to give examples of the seven purposes for asking questions. From this chapter, identify one example question for each of the seven purposes, and place all of the examples into your digital portfolio in a folder labeled "Questioning Strategies." Your example questions will be valuable reminders of the variety of ways in which questions can shape and set up a student's response to more accurately reveal what he or she does and does not know. These examples will also provide a future reference for you during lesson and unit planning.

2. Prepare one question each at the knowledge, comprehension, application, analysis, synthesis, and evaluation levels for a subject you will teach. Place these questions in the "Questioning Strategies" folder of your digital portfolio, and refer to them as models of questions that elicit increasingly complex learning outcomes.

MyEducationLab™

Go to MyEducationLab (www.myeducationlab.com) for Effective Teaching Methods: Research-Based Practice where you can:

- Find learning outcomes for the various course topics course along with national standards that connect to these outcomes.
- Complete **Assignments and Activities** that can help you more deeply understand the chapter content.
- Apply and practice your understanding of the core teaching skills identified in the chapter with **Building Teaching Skills and Dispositions** coaching activities.
- Check your comprehension of the content covered in the chapter with a book specific **Study Plan**. Here you will be able to take a chapter **pretest**, receive feedback on your answers, and then access personalized **Review, Practice, and Enrichment exercises** to enhance your understanding of chapter content. After you complete the exercises, take a **posttest** to confirm your comprehension.
- Learn how to address common classroom management issues in the **Simulations in Classroom Management**.
- Access video clips of CCSSO **National Teachers of the Year award winners** responding to the question, "Why Do I Teach?" in the Teacher Talk section.
- Create, update, and share quality lesson plans with the **Lesson Plan Builder**.
- Access state licensure test requirements, overviews of what tests cover, and sample test items in the **Certification and Licensure** section.
- Learn how to create a high quality teaching portfolio in the **Preparing a Portfolio** section.
- Access tips, advice, and other information on resume writing and interviewing, your first year of teaching, and law and public policies in the Beginning Your Career section.

9 Teaching Strategies for Direct Instruction

This chapter will help you answer these questions and meet the following InTASC standards for effective teaching.

- What is the direct instruction model?
- How do I organize lesson content for direct instruction?
- How can I encourage my learners to actively respond during direct instruction?
- What media and technology can I use with direct instruction?
- What are some ways of promoting the goals of direct instruction in a heterogeneous classroom?

InTASC

STANDARD 2 **Learning Differences.** The teacher uses understanding of individual differences and diverse cultures and communities to ensure inclusive learning environments that enable each learner to meet high standards.

STANDARD 4 **Content Knowledge.** The teacher understands the central concepts, tools of inquiry, and structures of the discipline(s) he or she teaches and creates learning experiences that make these aspects of the discipline accessible and meaningful for learners to assure mastery of the content.

STANDARD 5 **Application of Content.** The teacher understands how to connect concepts and use differing perspectives to engage learners in critical thinking, creativity, and collaborative problem solving related to authentic local and global issues.

STANDARD 6 **Assessment.** The teacher understands and uses multiple methods of assessment to engage learners in their own growth, to monitor learner progress, and to guide the teacher's and learner's decision making.

STANDARD 8 **Instructional Strategies.** The teacher understands and uses a variety of instructional strategies to encourage learners to develop deep understanding of content areas and their connections, and to build skills to apply knowledge in meaningful ways.

The chapter on lesson planning (Chapter 6) presented seven instructional events that form the structure of a lesson plan:

1. Gaining attention
2. Informing the learner of the objective
3. Stimulating recall of prerequisite learning
4. Presenting the stimulus material
5. Eliciting the desired behavior
6. Providing feedback
7. Assessing the behavior

This and subsequent chapters will present different instructional strategies by which these seven events of instruction can be implemented. This chapter presents strategies for direct teaching that include explanation, example, review, practice, and feedback in the context of a presentation and recitation format. In the following chapters, we will add strategies pertaining to indirect instruction, self-directed instruction, and collaborative learning.

Have you ever wondered why some teachers are more liked than others? Students cannot wait to attend the classes of some teachers but dread attending the classes of others. Teachers who are more liked often are described with phrases such as "is more organized," "has a better personality," and "is warmer and friendlier." Although these qualities may be present in teachers judged to be among the most liked, they are not the only reasons that some teachers are more interesting than others to their learners.

One of the most important factors in how interesting teachers are to their students is their use of one key behavior, **instructional variety**. In a study of experienced and inexperienced teachers (Emmer et al., 1980; Emmer & Evertson, 2012; Evertson & Emmer, 2012), experienced teachers who showed flexibility and variety in their instructional strategies were found to be more interesting, easier to listen to, and more engaging than inexperienced teachers who had no knowledge of alternative teaching strategies.

Knowledge of a variety of instructional strategies and the flexibility to change them both within and among lessons are two of the greatest assets a teacher can have. It is unlikely that any other key behavior, however well executed, will have the same effect as variety and flexibility in capturing the interest and attention of your students. This chapter provides a variety of teaching strategies you can use to compose lesson plans and to create and maintain an atmosphere of interest and variety in your classroom using a direct instruction format.

Categories of Teaching and Learning

Just as the carpenter, electrician, and plumber must select the proper tool for a specific task, you must select the proper instructional strategy for a specific learning outcome. To help determine your choice of strategies, here are two broad classifications of learning outcomes:

Type 1: Facts, rules, and action sequences

Type 2: Concepts, patterns, and relationships

Type 1 outcomes represent behaviors at lower levels of complexity in the cognitive, affective, and psychomotor domains. These include the knowledge, comprehension, and application levels of

MyEducationLab

Visit the MyEducationLab for *Effective Teaching Methods: Research-Based Practice*, 8e to enhance your understanding of chapter concepts with a personalized Study Plan. You'll also have the opportunity to hone your teaching skills through video-based Assignments and Activities as well as Building Teaching Skills and Dispositions lessons.

the cognitive domain; the awareness, responding, and valuing levels of the affective domain; and the imitation, manipulation, and precision levels of the psychomotor domain.

Type 2 outcomes represent behaviors at the higher levels of complexity in these domains. They include outcomes at the analysis, synthesis, and evaluation levels of the cognitive domain; the organization and characterization levels of the affective domain; and the articulation and naturalization levels of the psychomotor domain. Examples of Type 1 and Type 2 outcomes are shown in Tables 9.1 and 9.2.

Some important differences between instructional goals requiring these two types of learning are shown in Table 9.3.

In comparing the two columns of Table 9.3, notice that two types of learning are required. In the left column, Type 1 tasks require combining facts and rules at the knowledge and comprehension levels into a sequence of actions that can be learned by observation, rote repetition, and practice. Students can learn the correct answers by memorizing and practicing behaviors you model. In the right column, Type 2 learning is called for. The correct answers are not so closely connected to facts, rules, or action sequences that can be memorized and practiced in some limited context. Something more is needed to help the learner go beyond the facts, rules, or sequences to create, synthesize, and ultimately identify and recognize an answer that cannot be easily modeled or memorized. The missing link involves learning a concept, pattern, or relationship.

For example, to learn the concept of a *frog* involves learning the essential characteristics that make an animal a frog, as distinguished from similar animals (green chameleons). In other words, the learner needs to know not only the characteristics that all frogs have but also what characteristics distinguish frogs from other animals. If we classified frogs only on the characteristics of being green, having four legs, eating insects, and being amphibious, some turtles could be misidentified as frogs. Another category of knowledge must be learned that contains characteristics that separate frogs from similar animals (e.g., frogs have soft bodies, moist skin, and strong hind limbs, and they do not change color).

Table 9.1 Example of Type 1 Outcomes: Facts, Rules, and Action Sequences

Facts	Rules	Action Sequences
1. Recognize multiplication with two-digit numbers	Carrying with two-digit numbers	Multiplying to 1,000
2. Identify apostrophe *s*	Finding words with apostrophe *s*	Using apostrophe *s* in a sentence
3. Select multisyllable words from a list	Pronouncing multisyllable words	Reading stories with multisyllable words
4. State the chemical composition of water	Combining two parts hydrogen with one part oxygen	Writing the expression for water

Table 9.2 Example of Type 2 Outcomes: Concepts, Patterns, and Abstractions

Concepts	Patterns	Abstractions
1. Positive and negative numbers	$-3(-4) + 11 =$ $10 \times (-6) =$	Signed numbers
2. Possessive form	Police officer's daughter; Mrs. Burns's paper	Ownership
3. Vowels (v) and consonants (c)	cv order; cvc order	Vowel/consonant blends
4. Element, atomic weight, and valence	H_2O	Molecular structure

Table 9.3 Instructional Objectives Requiring Type 1 and Type 2 Outcomes

Type 1: Objectives Requiring Facts, Rules, and Action Sequences	Type 2: Objectives Requiring Concepts, Patterns, and Abstractions
1. IF The objective is to *recognize* multiplication to 1,000	BUT IF The objective is to *understand* multiplication of signed numbers
THEN TEACH the multiplication tables, and have the student *find examples.*	THEN TEACH the concept of negative and positive numbers, and *show how they are multiplied.*
2. IF The objective is to *identify* the apostrophe *s*	BUT IF The objective is to *express* ownership
THEN TEACH words using the apostrophe *s*, and have the student *find words denoting possession.*	THEN TEACH the concept of the possessive form, and have the student *practice writing paragraphs* showing forms of possession.
3. IF The objective is to *select* multisyllable words	BUT IF The objective is to *pronounce* vowel/consonant blends
THEN TEACH how to *find each word* on a list, and have the student write the words.	THEN TEACH vowels and consonants, and have the student *read the story aloud.*
4. IF The objective is to *state* the chemical composition of water	BUT IF The objective is to *determine* the molecular structure of chemical substances
THEN TEACH the symbol for two parts hydrogen and one part oxygen, and have the student *write the chemical composition of water.*	THEN TEACH the concepts of element, atomic weight, and valence, and have the student *practice balancing the atomic weights of chemical substances.*

Figure 9.1 presents an advance organizer showing the abundance of information involved in learning the concept of *frog*. Notice that to properly classify a frog among other animals that may look like frogs, both nonessential and essential frog attributes need to be learned. The nonessential attributes can be learned only by studying nonexamples, thus allowing learners to eliminate characteristics that are not unique to frogs. Finally, as learners gain more practice with both examples and nonexamples, the concept of a *frog* emerges as a tightly woven combination of characteristics. Now learners are able to disregard superficial characteristics, such as color, and to focus on characteristics unique to frogs. Given pictures of various toads, chameleons, turtles, snakes, and so on, students learn to identify correctly those animals that are frogs.

At this point, the learner has discovered at least some of the essential attributes of a frog and has formed an initial concept. Notice how different this teaching/learning process is from simply having your learners repeat some recently memorized facts about frogs: "Frogs are green, have four legs, eat insects, and can swim." This response does not tell you whether learners have acquired the *concept* of a frog, a *pattern* of which frogs are a part (e.g., can live on land and in water), or even the most general characteristics of a frog (e.g., is considered a member of the water life family). Even if students learn the considerably more complex task of how to care for frogs, they still have not

Figure 9.1 Learning the Concept of *Frog*

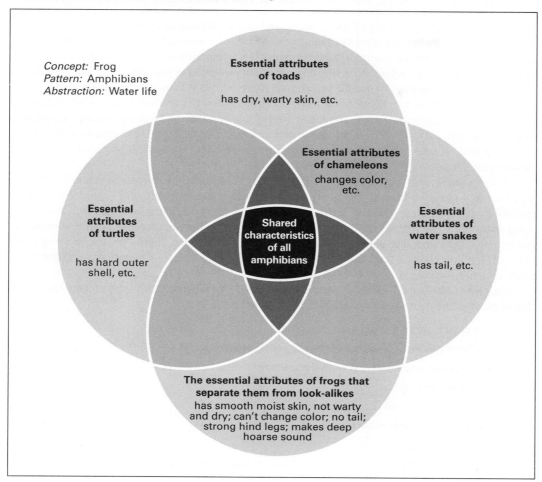

Concept: Frog
Pattern: Amphibians
Abstraction: Water life

**Essential attributes
of toads**

has dry, warty skin, etc.

**Essential attributes
of chameleons**
changes color,
etc.

**Essential
attributes
of turtles**

has hard outer
shell, etc.

**Shared
characteristics
of all
amphibians**

**Essential
attributes of
water snakes**

has tail, etc.

**The essential attributes of frogs that
separate them from look-alikes**
has smooth moist skin, not warty
and dry; can't change color; no tail;
strong hind legs; makes deep
hoarse sound

learned the concept of a *frog*. They have only learned how to arrange a constellation of facts into the action sequence of caring for frogs.

The preceding demonstrates how the processes used to learn facts, rules, and action sequences are different from those used to learn concepts, patterns, and relationships. And, just as different cognitive processes are involved in learning these different outcomes, so are different instructional strategies needed to teach them.

Facts, rules, and action sequences are most commonly taught using instructional strategies that emphasize knowledge acquisition. Concepts, patterns, and relationships are most commonly taught using strategies that emphasize inquiry or problem solving. These conclusions follow distinctions by cognitive psychologists such as J. R. Anderson (2004), Gagné, Yekovich, and Yekovich (1997), Huffman (2008), Mayer and Alexander (2010), and Ormrod (2010b) whose writings have highlighted the different instructional strategies required by learning Type 1 and Type 2 behaviors.

Knowledge acquisition and inquiry are different types of learning outcomes, so each must be linked with the specific strategies most likely to produce the desired outcome. This chapter presents a group of strategies for teaching knowledge acquisition involving facts, rules, and action sequences called **direct instruction**. The next chapter presents strategies for teaching inquiry and problem solving involving concepts, patterns, and relationships called **indirect instruction**. In subsequent chapters, both types of learning are combined to show how together they can provide a menu of teaching strategies that help your learners solve problems, think critically and independently, and work cooperatively.

Introduction to Direct Instruction Strategies

As we have seen, the teaching of facts, rules, and action sequences is most efficiently achieved through a process called the *direct instruction model*. Direct instruction is a teacher- or software-centered strategy in which you and/or the computer is the major information provider. In the direct instruction model, facts, rules, and action sequences are presented to students in the most direct way possible. At first, this usually takes a presentation and recitation format with explanations, examples, and opportunities for practice and feedback provided by the teacher. But a direct instruction presentation and recitation format employing verbal explanations and teacher-student interactions may also include software-driven questions, correction of student errors, and review and practice. Let's first look at some of the characteristics of effective direct instruction provided in a teacher presentation format.

A direct instruction presentation in the elementary and secondary classroom is not like the college lecture you may be familiar with. The typical college lecture rarely will be suitable for your classroom, because your learners' attention spans, interest levels, and motivation will not be the same as those of older students. Therefore, your presentation here is neither a lengthy monologue nor an open, free-wheeling discussion. Instead it is a quickly paced, highly organized set of interchanges that you control, focusing exclusively on acquiring a limited set of predetermined facts, rules, or action sequences.

Angelillo (2008) and Rosenshine and Stevens (1986) have equated this type of instruction with that of an effective demonstration in which the following occurs:

1. You clearly present goals and main points.
   a. State goals or objectives of the presentation beforehand.
   b. Focus on one thought (point, direction) at a time.
   c. Avoid digressions.
   d. Avoid words and phrases learners may be unsure of.
2. You present content sequentially.
   a. Present material in small steps.
   b. Organize and present material so learners master one point before you go to the next point.
   c. Give explicit, step-by-step directions.
   d. Present an outline when the material is complex.
3. You are specific and concrete.
   a. Model the skill or process (when appropriate).
   b. Give detailed and redundant explanations for difficult points.
   c. Provide students with concrete and varied examples.
4. You check for students' understanding.
   a. Make sure that students understand one point before you proceed to the next.
   b. Ask students questions to monitor their comprehension of what has been presented.
   c. Have students summarize the main points in their own words.
   d. Reteach the parts that students have difficulty comprehending—either through further teaching and explanation or by supplemental materials and students tutoring each other.

Table 9.4 provides examples of some of the action verbs that correspond to the objectives most suited for direct instruction. These outcomes are learned through application of facts, rules, and action sequences that usually can be taught in a single lesson. You can most easily and directly test them with multiple-choice, listing, matching, fill-in, and short-answer questions. Test items will call for: the listing of memorized names, dates, and other facts; the summarizing or paraphrasing of learned facts, rules, or sequences; or the connection and application of learned facts, rules, and sequences in a context slightly different from the one in which they were learned.

Table 9.4 Action Verbs That Correspond to the Objectives
Most Suited for Direct Instruction

Cognitive Objectives	Affective Objectives	Psychomotor Objectives
Recall	Listen	Repeat
Describe	Attend	Follow
List	Be aware	Place
Summarize	Comply	Perform accurately
Paraphrase	Follow	Perform independently
Distinguish	Obey	Perform proficiently
Use	Display	Perform with speed
Organize	Express	Perform with coordination
Demonstrate	Prefer	Perform with timing

Direct instruction has been referred to as "active teaching" (Angelillo, 2008; Good, 1979; Guillaume, Yopp, & Yopp, 2006; Rosenshine, 1971, 1986), which is characterized as follows:

- Full-class instruction (as opposed to small-group instruction)
- Organization of learning around questions you pose
- Provision of detailed and redundant practice
- Presenting material so learners master one new fact, rule, or sequence before the teacher presents the next
- Formal arrangement of the classroom to maximize recitation and practice

Figure 9.2 presents the teaching strategies most commonly associated with the direct instruction model. You can see that a large share of teaching time is devoted to direct instruction—that is, to providing information directly to students while interspersing explanations, examples, practice, and feedback.

Whether explaining, pointing out relationships, giving examples, or correcting errors, using strategies that follow the direct instruction model has many advantages. Research indicates that direct instruction strategies are among those that correlate highest with student achievement, as measured by standardized tests, which tend to emphasize facts, rules, and sequences (Anderson, Evertson, & Brophy, 1982; Angelillo, 2008; Marzano, Pickering, & Pollock, 2010; Rosenshine, 1997).

When Is Direct Instruction Appropriate?

When direct instruction strategies are used for the proper purpose, with the appropriate content, and at the right time, they will be an important addition to your teaching strategy menu. Most direct instruction strategies are at their best when your purpose is to disseminate information not readily available from software, texts, or workbooks in appropriately sized pieces. If such information were available, your students might well learn the material from these sources independently, with only introductory or structuring comments provided by you. However, when you must partition, subdivide, or translate textbook and workbook material into a more digestible form before it can be practiced in a workbook or software format, direct instruction is appropriate.

Another time to use direct instruction strategies is when you wish to arouse or heighten student interest. Students often fail to complete software, textbook, and workbook reading and exercises in the mistaken belief that the material is boring, is not worth their effort, or presents content already

Figure 9.2 Explicit and Systematic Instruction

1. Monitor and diagnose to gauge progress and inform reteaching:

   Closely observe student responses during instruction, addressing errors immediately.

   Use daily practice to reinforce new learning.

   Check student ability to apply knowledge, skills, and strategies in follow-up and extension activities (e.g., learning centers or homework).

   Determine targets for reteaching if errors persist.

2. Present and structure new content:

   Focus on teaching strategies that empower students to tackle a variety of content.

   Provide modeling that exemplifies the instructional target; after all, this foundation prompts the schema for structuring new learning.

   Discriminating practice is needed to inform when and when not to use new strageties.

   Sequence skills according to the following recommendations:

   - Teach preskills of a strategy before the strategy is presented
   - Introduce high-utility skills before less useful ones
   - Introduce easy skills before more difficult ones
   - Separate strategies and information likely to be confused

   Ascertain the appropriate rate for introducing new information; adjust instructional programs according to student needs.

3. Guide student practice:

   Initiate instruction with explicit information and modeling.

   Control the language used in teaching to maximize student understandings.

   Present learning one step at a time.

   Provide scaffolding that decreases as student abilities develop by:

   - Modeling expected behaviors
   - Providing prompts
   - Phasing out modeling and prompts for independent practice

4. Provide feedback and correct errors:

   Be generous with positive feedback to promote motivation and engagement.

   Feedback for errors:

   - On less complex tasks, correct the mistake, review previous items completed successfully, and then revisit the missed item.
   - On more complex tasks revisit thinking back through the serious of steps to pinpoint the source of the mistake.

   Errors inform the effectiveness of instruction, reflect student progress, and identify areas in need of review or reteaching.

5. Teach for mastery:

   Ensure sufficient practice allowing for students to apply learning independently with accuracy and fluency.

6. Review over time:

   Regularly revisit taught knowledge, skills, and strategies to assess for retention of learning.

   Reteach, if necessary.

Source: Carnine, D. W., Silbert, J., Kame'enui, E. J., Tarver, S. G., & Jungjohann, K. (2006). *Teaching Struggling and At-Risk Readers: A Direct Instruction Approach.* Upper Saddle River, NJ: Pearson.

learned. Your active participation in the presentation of content can change these misperceptions by mixing interesting supplemental or introductory information with the dry facts, by showing the application of the material to future schoolwork or world events, and by illustrating with questions and answers that the material is neither easy nor previously mastered. Your direct involvement in presenting content provides the human element that may be necessary for learning to occur in many of your students.

Finally, direct instruction strategies are indispensable for achieving content mastery and overlearning of fundamental facts, rules, and action sequences that may be essential to subsequent learning and remembering what was learned long afterwards (Gentile & Lalley, 2003; Gronlund, 2006; Lindsley, 1992). The degree of **mastery learning** that occurs is directly related to the time a student is actively engaged in the learning process. The more time spent reviewing and practicing, the greater the retention and ability to put that learning into practice at a later time. Therefore review and active student practice are important ingredients of mastery learning.

The goals of mastery learning are best achieved by the instructional sequence of review prerequisite content, present new content, practice, provide feedback, and reteach, as shown in Figure 9.3. This progressive cycle may compose nearly all of the time scheduled for a direct instruction lesson. Many examples in this chapter illustrate this type of instructional sequence. When the content to be taught represents task-relevant prior knowledge for subsequent learning, a direct instruction format provides the best assurance that this knowledge will be remembered and available for later use.

There also are times when direct instruction strategies are inappropriate. When objectives other than learning facts, rules, and action sequences are desired, direct instruction strategies become less efficient and are often far less effective than the inquiry and problem-solving strategies to be discussed in subsequent chapters. Teaching situations that need strategies other than direct instruction include (1) presenting complex material with objectives at the analysis, synthesis, and evaluation levels of the cognitive domain and (2) presenting content that must be learned gradually over a long period. Such material requires learner participation to heighten commitment to the learning process (for example, portfolios, projects, and oral performances) and to create the intellectual framework necessary for learning concepts and recognizing patterns. You can also gain your learners' participation through carefully crafted classroom dialogue, which will be illustrated in Chapters 10 and 11. See In Practice: Focus on Mastery Learning.

Figure 9.3 **Direct Instructional Sequence for Mastery Learning**

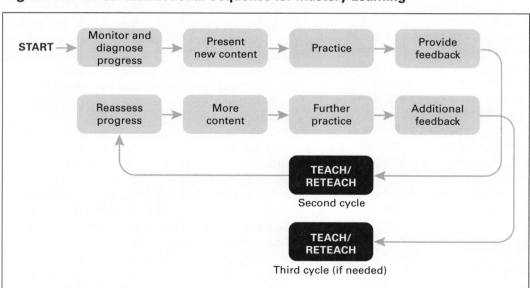

In Practice

Focus on Mastery Learning

John B. Carroll inaugurated a fundamental change in thinking about the characteristics of instruction in 1963, when he argued that student aptitudes reflect an individual's learning rate and therefore that some students need more time to learn than others. In this new paradigm, Carroll suggested that instruction should focus more on the time required for different students to learn the same material. This was in contrast with the classic model of instruction, in which the focus is on differences in ability and all students are given the same amount of time to learn.

Carroll's new theory was based on the idea that all learners have the potential to learn any content provided by the teacher but take different amounts of time to do so. Carroll identified two factors that affect the learning rate of a student: perseverance of the student and the opportunity to learn. The first is controlled by the student—that is, how much time he or she spends on learning. The latter is controlled by the teacher, who allots the time to learn.

However, it was Benjamin Bloom who fully developed the concepts now known as *mastery learning* in 1968. In the 1960s, Bloom was involved in research on the role of individual differences in learning. Impressed with Carroll's ideas, he took them further by concluding that if aptitude can predict the rate at which one learns, then the instructional variables under an instructor's control—such as the opportunity to learn and the availability of instructional materials and resources—should be able to ensure that all learners can attain mastery of any unit or lesson objective. Bloom concluded that given sufficient time and quality of instruction, nearly all students can learn. Bloom's mastery learning model also became instrumental in the nature versus nurture controversy sparked by Jensen (1969) by proposing a model in which the learning environment provided by the teacher, not heredity, accounts for most of a student's learning.

The theory of mastery learning resulted in a radical shift in responsibility for teachers; the blame for a student's failure rests with the instruction, not the student's lack of ability. In this type of learning environment, the challenges are to provide sufficient time and to employ effective instructional strategies so that all students achieve the same level of learning (Bloom, 1981; Levine, 1985). Add to this scenario curriculum-related computer software to differentiate and individualize instruction, and all learners will achieve the same level of learning but at different rates and times.

How to Instruct for Mastery

1. Clearly state the objective of the unit.
2. Divide the unit objective into lessons, each with its own objectives and assessment.
3. Identify the most effective combination of learning materials and instructional strategies for each lesson, such as presentation, recitation, modeling, questioning, discussion, and so forth.
4. Begin each unit or lesson with a brief diagnostic test or formative assessment of what students do and do not know about the topic.
5. Use the results of the diagnostic tests to provide instruction and corrective activities in the order of review, present content, practice, and provide feedback that can also be individualized with the use of curriculum-related computer software.
6. Use this cycle first with the whole class and then repeat as needed with the whole class or individuals. No student should proceed to new material until basic material has been mastered.

In summary, mastery learning is an instructional strategy based on the principle that all students can attain lesson and unit objectives with the appropriate instruction and sufficient time to learn. Mastery learning puts the techniques of tutoring and individualized instruction into a group-learning format and brings the learning strategies of successful students to nearly all the students of a given group. In its full form, it includes a philosophy, a curriculum structure, an instructional model, the alignment of student assessment, and a teaching approach.

You will have many options for integrating technology into your direct instruction lessons to ensure that all or most of your learners attain the same level of mastery. Depending on the ability level of the student and available time on the computer, more or less structure can be provided within the content of your direct instruction lesson. This provides the ability to differentiate instruction for the student who can benefit from it with regard to the level of difficulty and need for repetition, review, practice, and feedback.

Much direct instruction software is available for the elementary grades from the publishers of the textbooks and workbooks you will be using. With the Inspiration 9 software, which was introduced for lesson planning in Chapter 4, it is also possible to prepare your own tailor-made direct instruction practice sessions, review, and feedback lessons for grades and content for which commercial software may not be available. The Inspiration 9 software is organized around a template, into which can be dropped lesson content, reviews, and practice activities. It can be made available on your classroom computers, with hyperlinks to other software.

An Example of Direct Instruction

To see what direct instruction looks like in the classroom, consider the following dialogue, in which the teacher begins a direct instruction sequence to teach the acquisition of facts, rules, and action sequences for forming and punctuating possessives. She begins by informing her students of the lesson's objective. As you read, note the direct instruction strategies in bold italic from Figure 9.2.

Teacher:	Today we will learn how to avoid embarrassing errors such as this when forming and punctuating possessives. [Circles an incorrectly punctuated possessive in a newspaper headline.] At the end of the period, I will give each of you several additional examples of errors taken from my collection of mistakes found in other newspapers and magazines. I'll ask you to make the proper corrections and report your changes to the class. Who knows what a possessive is? (***Monitoring and diagnosing***)
Richard:	It means you own something.
Teacher:	Yes, a possessive is a way of indicating ownership. It comes from the word *possession,* which means "something owned or possessed." Forming possessives and punctuating them correctly can be difficult, as this newspaper example shows. [Points to paper again.] Today I will give you two simple rules that will help you form possessives correctly. But first, to show ownership or possession, we must know who or what is doing the possessing. Lucila, can you recall the parts of speech from last week's lesson? [Lucila hesitates, then nods.] What part of speech is most likely to own or possess something? (***Monitoring and diagnosing***)
Lucila:	Well, umm . . . I think . . . I think a noun can own something.
Teacher:	Yes, a noun can own something. What is an example of a noun that owns something? Brian?
Brian:	I don't know.
Teacher:	Allison?
Allison:	Not sure.
Teacher:	Yungwei?
Yungwei:	A student can own a pencil. The word *student* is a noun.
Teacher:	Good. And who can remember our definition for a noun? (***Monitoring and diagnosing***)
Damian:	It's a person, place, or thing.
Teacher:	Good. Our first rule is, Use the possessive form whenever an *of* phrase can be substituted for a noun. [Points to this rule written on board.] (*Presenting and structuring*) Let's look at some phrases on the board to see when to apply this rule. Jason, what does the first one say? (***Guided student practice***)
Jason:	The daughter of the police officer.
Teacher:	How else can we express the same idea of ownership?
Trena:	We can say "the police officer's daughter."
Teacher:	Correct. We can say "the police officer's daughter" because I can substitute a phrase starting with *of* and ending with *police officer* for the noun *police officer.* Notice how easily I can switch the placement of *police officer* and *daughter* by using the connecting word *of.* Whenever this can be done, you can form a possessive by adding an apostrophe *s* to the noun following *of.* (***Presenting and structuring***) Now we have the phrase [writes on board] *police officer's daughter.* [Points to the apostrophe.] Erica, what about our next example, *holiday of three days*? [Points to board.] (***Guided student practice***)
Erica:	We could say "three days' holiday."
Teacher:	Come up and write that on the board just the way it should be printed in the school paper. [Erica writes *three day's holiday*.] Does anyone want to change anything?

Desiree:	I'm not sure, but I think the apostrophe should go after the *s* in *days*.
Teacher:	You're right (***Feedback***), which leads to our second rule: If the word for which we are denoting ownership is a plural ending with *s,* place an apostrophe after the *s.* But if the word is a name—called a *proper noun*—ending with *s,* place an apostrophe and an *s* after the *s.* This is an important rule to remember, because it accounts for many of the mistakes that are made in forming possessives. As I write this rule on the board, copy down these two rules for use later. (***Presenting and structuring***) [Finishes writing second rule on board.] Now let's take a moment to convert each of the phrases on the overhead to the possessive form. Write down your answer to the first one. When I see all heads up again, I will write the correct answer. (***Guided student practice***) [All heads are up.] Good. Now watch how I change this first one to the possessive form. Pay particular attention to where I place the apostrophe; then check your answer with mine. [Converts *delay of a month* to *month's delay.*] Any problems? (***Monitoring***) [Pauses for any response.] OK, do the next one. [After all heads are up, converts *home of Jenkins* to *Jenkins's home.*] Any problems? [Jason looks distressed.] (***Monitoring***)
Teacher:	Jason, what did you write?
Jason:	J-E-N-K-I-N apostrophe s.
Teacher:	What is the man's name, Jason?
Jason:	Jenkins.
Teacher:	Look at what you wrote for the second rule. What does it say? (***Feedback and correcting***)
Jason:	Add an apostrophe and an *s* after the *s* when the word is a name that already ends in an *s.* Oh, I get it. His name already has the *s,* so it should be *s* apostrophe *s.* That's the mistake you showed us in the headline, isn't it?
Teacher:	Now you've got it. Let's continue. [Proceeds with the following in the same manner: *speech of the president* to *president's speech, the television set of Mr. Burns* to *Mr. Burns's television set, pastimes of boys* to *boys' pastimes.*] Now open your workbooks to the exercise on page 87. Starting with the first row, let's go around the room and hear your possessives for each of the sentences listed. Spell aloud the word indicating ownership, so we can tell if you've placed the apostrophe in the right place. Allison... [Looking at *wings of geese.*] (***Guided student practice***)
Allison:	Geeses wings'. . . spelled W-I-N-G-S apostrophe.
Teacher:	That's not correct. What word is doing the possessing? (***Feedback and correcting***)
Allison:	The geese, so it must be G-E-E-S-E apostrophe *s.*
Teacher:	Good. (***Feedback***) Practice exercises that provide a review of today's lesson are available on our computers. Before our next test, I want each of you to spend as much time as you need to be sure you get up to the 90 percent correct mark.

Direct Instruction Strategies

To help learners reach mastery, you will want to sequence your instructional strategies. Let's look at the six direct instruction strategies exemplified in the preceding classroom dialogue and outlined in Figure 9.2 including: monitoring and diagnosing students to gauge their progress, presenting and structuring new content, ensuring guided student practice, providing feedback and correcting errors, providing opportunities for reaching mastery, and conducting regular reviews of content over time.

Monitoring and Diagnosing to Gauge Progress

The first strategy in direct instruction from Figure 9.2 is **monitoring and diagnosing** to gauge progress and inform reteaching. This function emphasizes the relationship between lessons, so students remember previous knowledge and see new knowledge as a logical extension of content already mastered. Notice that early in the example lesson, the definition of a noun was brought into the presentation. This provided a review of the task-relevant prior knowledge needed for the day's lesson. It also provided students with a sense of wholeness and continuity, assuring them that what was to follow was not isolated knowledge unrelated to past lessons. This is particularly important for engaging students who do not have the appropriate level of task-relevant prior knowledge or who may be overly anxious about having to master yet another piece of unfamiliar content. Monitoring and diagnosing at the beginning of a lesson also is the most efficient and timely way of finding out if your students have mastered task-relevant prior knowledge sufficiently to begin a new lesson; if not, you may reteach the missing content, as shown in Figure 9.3.

You might think that it is common practice to begin a lesson by checking previously learned task-relevant knowledge needed for the day's lesson. Yet many teachers fail to begin a lesson by checking for this knowledge. Daily review and checking at the beginning of a lesson can be easily accomplished in one of several ways:

A major purpose of daily review and checking is to emphasize the relationships between lessons and to provide students with a sense of wholeness and continuity, assuring them that what is to follow is a logical extension of content already mastered.

1. Have students correct each other's homework at the beginning of class

2. Have students identify especially difficult homework problems in a question-and-answer format

3. Sample the understanding of a few students who are good indicators of the range of knowledge possessed by the entire class

4. Explicitly review the task-relevant information necessary for the day's lesson

Dahllof and Lundgren (1970) proposed the use of a steering group of lower- to average-performing students as a particularly effective way of determining the extent to which review and reteaching may be needed. An expanded notion of the *steering group* is a small number of low, average, and high performers who can be queried at the start of class on the task-relevant prior knowledge needed for the day's lesson. When high performers miss a large proportion of answers, this warns you that extensive reteaching for the entire class may be necessary. When high performers answer questions correctly but average performers do not, some reteaching should be undertaken before the start of the lesson. And finally, if most of the high and average performers answer the questions correctly but most of the low performers do not, you may need to consider differentiating some content or using practice exercises, summary and review sheets, or tutorial arrangements and supplementary instructional software. Doing so will ensure that large amounts of class time are not devoted to reviewing and reteaching material that may benefit only a portion of the class.

The strategy of monitoring and diagnosing to gauge progress and inform reteaching, especially when used with a carefully selected steering group, is indispensable for informing you that previous instruction was over the heads of some or most of your students and that additional review is necessary.

Presenting and Structuring

The second strategy in the direct instruction model consists of **presenting and structuring** new content. As we learned, one of the primary ingredients of the direct instruction model is presenting material in small steps. Lessons must be served in small portions that are consistent with the previous knowledge, ability level, and experience of your students. Likewise the content within the lessons must be partitioned and subdivided to organize it into small bits. No portion can be too large, or you will lose your students' attention.

The key is to focus the material on one idea at a time and to present it so learners master one point before you introduce the next point. This is most easily accomplished by dividing a lesson into easily recognizable subparts, rules, or categories. It is no coincidence that the strategy of "divide and conquer" is as appropriate in the classroom as in a military battle. Just like any great warrior, you can derive much benefit from it.

Remember that the subdivisions you use can be your own; they need not always follow those provided by the text, workbook, or curriculum guide. In fact, there is an important difference between the content divisions used in books and those needed in teaching: Content divisions in texts, workbooks, and curriculum guides generally are created for the purpose of communicating content intended to be read, not for the purpose of presenting content that must be explained orally to learners within the timeframe of a specific lesson. Consequently, published divisions such as chapter titles, subheadings, and sections identified with roman numerals in texts and even workbooks sometimes are too broad to form the bite-sized pieces that students can easily digest within a lesson.

Unfortunately, many beginning teachers stick tenaciously to these formal headings without realizing either the volume of content that falls within them or the time it takes to orally explain, illustrate, and practice this content. The truth is that you are not discarding content if you create new, more manageable organizational divisions; you only are breaking the content into smaller steps suitable for presentation in a single lesson. You can create your own subdivisions consisting of rules ("Here are some rules to follow"), steps ("We will do this, then that"), or practices ("Here is the first of five things we will cover"). These subdivisions will organize your instruction into bite-sized pieces and, most importantly, communicate this organization to your students.

Following are some ways of structuring content that are particularly relevant to direct instruction. These are the part–whole, sequential, combinations, and comparative methods of structuring content.

Part–Whole Relationships.   A part–whole organizational format introduces the topic in its most general form ("What is a possessive?") and then divides it into easy-to-distinguish subdivisions (Rule 1, Rule 2). This creates subdivisions that are easily digested and presents them in ways that always relate back to the whole.

Students should always be aware of the part being covered at any particular time ("This is Rule 2") and its relationship to the whole ("This leads to our second rule for denoting ownership"). Use verbal markers to alert students that a transition is underway ("This is Rule 1," "Here is the first part," "This is the last example of this type; now let's move to the next type").

This type of organization creates bite-sized chunks. It helps students organize and see what is being taught and informs them of what portion they are studying along the way. A part–whole organization is illustrated in Figure 9.4.

Sequential Relationships.   Another way of structuring content is by sequential ordering; you teach the content according to the way in which the facts, rules, or sequences to be learned occur in the real world. Students may already have a feel for sequential ordering from practical experience.

Figure 9.4   **Structuring a Lesson by Identifying Part–Whole Relationships**

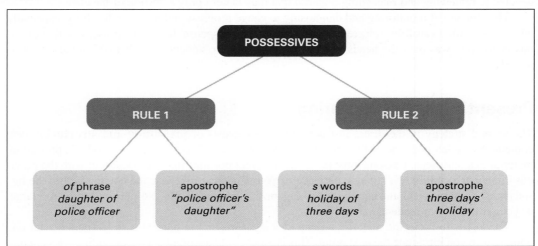

Figure 9.5 **Structuring a Lesson by Identifying Sequential Relationships**

$$y = a - b + \frac{cd}{e}$$

1. First let's determine *cd* when

$c = -1, d = 2$

$c = 0, d = -4$

$c = 2, d = -3$

2. Next let's determine $\frac{cd}{e}$ when

$cd = -2, e = -2$

$cd = 0, e = 1$

$cd = -6, e = -4$

3. Now let's determine $b + \frac{cd}{e}$ when

$b = 1, \frac{cd}{e} = 1$

$b = -2, \frac{cd}{e} = 0$

$b = 2, \frac{cd}{e} = -1.5$

4. Finally, let's determine $a - b + \frac{cd}{e}$ when

$a = 10, b + \frac{cd}{e} = 2$

$a = 7, b + \frac{cd}{e} = -3$

$a = 5, b + \frac{cd}{e} = .5$

In algebra, for example, an equation is solved by first multiplying, then dividing, then adding, and finally subtracting. This order of operations must occur for a solution to be correct. A sequentially structured lesson, therefore, might introduce the manipulation of signed numbers in the order multiplication-division-addition-subtraction. Doing so reinforces the way an equation must actually be solved, making the skill and behavior you are teaching more authentic. In other words, you would complete all examples used in teaching signed-number multiplication before introducing any examples about division, thereby teaching the correct sequence as well as the intended content. Sequential ordering is illustrated in Figure 9.5.

Combinations of Relationships. A third way you can structure lesson content is to bring together in a single format combinations of elements or dimensions that influence the use of facts, rules, and sequences. This allows an overall framework to direct the order of content by showing the logic of some combinations of facts, rules, and sequences and the illogic of other combinations.

For example, in teaching a direct instruction lesson in geography, you might develop a scheme to reveal the relationship between marketable products and the various means of transporting them to market. You could draw an organizational chart (see Figure 9.6) to structure the content. You could show the chart to your students and then teach all the relevant facts (e.g., relative weights of products), rules (the heavier the product, the more efficient the transportation system must be), and action sequences (first analyze the product's size and weight, then choose the best location). The shaded cells in Figure 9.6 identify the combinations, or dimensions of content, that are most relevant to the objectives of the lesson.

Comparative Relationships. With the comparative relationships method of structuring content, you place different categories of content or topics side by side so learners can compare and contrast them. Placing facts, rules, and sequences side by side across two or more categories enables students to observe their similarities and differences. For example, you might want to compare and contrast governmental aspects of the United States and England. You could order the instruction according to the format shown in Figure 9.7. Then you could teach the relevant economics (economic systems), politics (type of government), source of laws (U.S. Constitution versus English legal codes), and representative body (Congress versus Parliament) by moving first across the chart and then down. The chart structures the content, and students can easily use it as an advance organizer to see the structure and content to be covered as it is being taught.

Figure 9.6 Structuring a Lesson by Identifying Combinations of Relationships

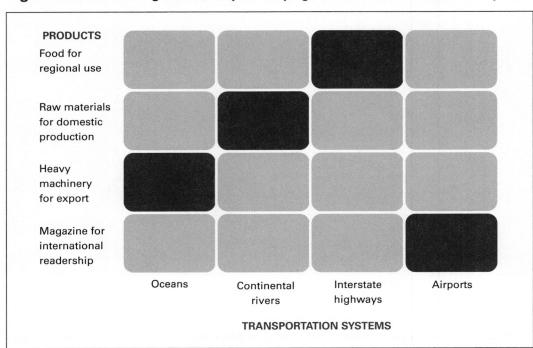

Figure 9.7 Structuring a Relationship by Identifying Comparative Relationships

Points of Comparison	United States	England
Economics	Capitalism	Capitalism
Politics	Representative democracy	Parliamentary democracy
Source of laws	U.S. Constitution	English legal codes
Representative body	Congress	Parliament

Using the Methods.   Whether you use one structuring method or a combination to organize a lesson, remember to divide the content into bite-sized pieces. To the extent these structuring techniques divide larger units of content into smaller and more meaningful units, they will have served an important purpose.

Finally, note how the teacher in our classroom dialogue combined rules and examples in organizing and presenting the content. She always presented the rule first and then followed it with one or more examples. Note also that after some examples illustrating the rule, she repeated it—either by having students write the rule after seeing it on the board or by having a student repeat it to the class. Giving a rule, then an example of the rule, followed by repetition of the rule is called the **rule–example–rule order**. It generally is more effective than simply giving the rule and then an example (rule–example order) or giving an example followed by the rule. Also learning a rule in one sensory modality (e.g., seeing it on the board) and then recreating it in a different sensory modality (e.g., writing or speaking it) will promote greater learning and retention than seeing the rule only once or reproducing it in the same modality in which it was learned.

Guided Student Practice

The third step in the direct instruction model is **guided student practice**. Recall from the structure of a lesson plan that presentation of stimulus material is followed by eliciting practice with the desired behavior. This section presents several ways of accomplishing this in the context of the direct instruction model. These elicitations are teacher guided, providing students with guided practice that you organize and direct.

Recall the important ingredients for eliciting a student response. One is to elicit the response in as nonevaluative an atmosphere as possible; this frees students to risk creating responses they may be unsure of but from which they can begin to build a correct response. Any response, however crude or incorrect, can be the basis for learning, if it is followed by nonevaluative feedback and correction.

A second ingredient for eliciting a student response is the use of covert responses. Doing so not only ensures a nonthreatening environment but also encourages student engagement in the learning task with the least expenditure of your time and effort. In the preceding example dialogue, by having students privately write their responses before seeing the correct answers on the overhead, the teacher guided each student to formulate a response; it was not necessary to call on each of them. She guided the students into responding by encouraging and later rewarding their covert responses.

An equally important aspect of eliciting a desired response is to check for student understanding. When necessary, prompt to convert wrong answers to right ones. In the example dialogue, the teacher stopped after every item to see if there were problems and prompted students to create correct answers, when necessary. Prompting is an important part of eliciting the desired behavior, because it strengthens and builds learners' confidence by encouraging them to use some aspects of the answer that have already been given in formulating the correct response (Gagné et al., 1997). In the example dialogue, Jason was encouraged to *rethink* his response, to *focus* consciously on the specific part of the problem causing the error, and to *remember* the rule that will prevent making such errors in the future.

Prompting.   One guided student practice during direct instruction is providing prompts, hints, and other types of supplementary instructional stimuli to help learners make the correct response. You can use three categories of prompts to shape the correct performance of your learners: verbal prompts, gestural prompts, and physical prompts.

Verbal Prompts.   **Verbal prompts** can be cues, reminders, or instructions to learners that help them perform correctly the skill you are teaching. For example, saying to a first-grade learner as he is writing "Leave spaces between words" reminds him what you previously said about neat handwriting. Or saying "First adjust the object lens" to a learner while she is looking at a microscope slide prompts her as she is learning how to use a microscope. Verbal prompts help guide the learner to connect performances and prevent mistakes and frustration.

Gestural Prompts.   **Gestural prompts** model or demonstrate for learners particular skills you want them to perform. For example, if you were to point to the fine adjustment knob on the microscope and make a turning gesture with your hand, you would be prompting, or reminding, the student to perform this step of the process. Gestural prompts are particularly helpful when you anticipate that the learner may make a mistake. You can use gestural prompts routinely to remind learners how to fold a piece of paper, how to grasp a pair of scissors, how to raise their hands before asking a question, or how to hold a pen properly when writing.

Physical Prompts.   Some learners may lack the fine muscle control to follow a demonstration and imitate the action being modeled. For example, you might verbally describe how to form the letter *a* and demonstrate this for the learner, and the learner may still be unable to write *a* correctly. In such a case, you might use your hand to guide the learner's hand as he writes. This is called a **physical prompt**. With a physical prompt, you use hand-over-hand assistance to guide the learner to the correct performance. You can routinely use physical prompts to assist learners with handwriting, cutting out shapes, tying shoelaces, correctly holding a dissecting tool, or performing a complex dance routine.

Least-to-Most Intrusive Prompting.   Many educators recommend that you use the least intrusive prompt first when guiding a learner's performance. Verbal prompts are the least intrusive;

physical prompts are the most intrusive (Alberto & Troutman, 2008). Thus it would be more appropriate first to say "Don't forget the fine adjustment!" when guiding a learner in the use of a microscope than to take the learner's hand and physically assist her.

The reason behind using a least-to-most intrusive order is that verbal prompts are easier to remove or fade than are physical prompts. Learners who depend on physical prompts to perform correctly will find it more difficult to demonstrate a skill independently of the teacher and to acquire authentic behavior.

Full-Class Prompting. You can also check for understanding and prompt for correct responses using the full class. The example dialogue showed one approach: The teacher asked all the students to respond privately at the same time and then encouraged them to ask for individual help ("Any problems?").

Another approach is to call on students whether or not their hands are raised, thereby seeking opportunities to prompt and correct wrong answers. One version of this is called **ordered turns**, in which you systematically go through the class and expect students to respond when their turn arrives. With small groups, this approach can be more effective in producing student achievement gains than randomly calling on students, because everyone is likely to get one or more repeated turns. But generally, the ordered turns method is less efficient when selecting students to respond during full-class instruction, because students can easily gauge the time they will have to be disengaged until their individual turns arrive. Yet another approach is to have students write out answers to be checked and perhaps corrected by a classmate.

Finally, you can develop questions beforehand to check for the most common errors and prompt when necessary. This approach has the advantage of assuming that not everyone understands or has the correct answer when no response is received. If a classroom response system is available, as presented in Chapter 7, you can place your questions on a transparency or in a digital presentation and provide your learners immediate feedback. Researchers have found this approach to be particularly effective in increasing student achievement (Angelillo, 2008; Rosenshine, 1995; Rosenshine & Stevens, 1986).

This **video** exemplifies using direct instruction with the entire class. Pay close attention to the modeling and prompting that occurs.

Modeling. Another guided student practice is modeling. *Modeling* is a teaching activity that involves demonstrating to learners what you want them to do or think. When used correctly, modeling can assist learners to acquire a variety of intellectual and social skills more effortlessly and efficiently than with verbal, gestural, or physical prompts alone. Modeling is particularly effective for younger learners, who may not be able to follow complex verbal explanations; for visually dominant learners, who may need to see how something is done before they can actually do it; and for communicating mental strategies for problem solving to all ages of learners.

Bandura and his colleagues have studied how and why we learn from models (Bandura, 1997; Griffin, 2007; Zimmerman, 1989). Their research on modeling is referred to as **social learning theory**, and it attempts to explain how people learn from observing other people. From these researchers' work, we know that children can learn not only attitudes, values, and standards of behavior from observing adults and peers but also physical and intellectual skills.

Some of this learning takes place by directly imitating what a teacher is doing; other learning takes place by inferring why the model is acting a certain way or what type of person the model is. For example, learners acquire certain values about the importance of learning, caring for others, doing work neatly, or showing respect for other cultures by observing how their parents, friends, and teachers actually behave in the real world and then inferring from their observations how they, too, should behave.

Although teachers model all the time, we know that some forms of modeling are more effective than others. Zimmerman (1989) found that teachers who were taught the practice of modeling were far more effective at helping young children to learn than teachers who were not.

Modeling is a direct teaching activity that allows students to imitate from demonstration or infer from observation the behavior to be learned. Four processes need to occur for your learners to benefit from modeling:

1. Attention
2. Retention
3. Production
4. Motivation

Let's take a brief look at each of these to discover how students learn from what they see.

Attention. Demonstrations are only of value if learners look at and/or listen to them. In other words, without attention, there can be no imitation or observational learning. Learners pay attention better under the following conditions:

1. The model is someone who is respected as an expert in his or her field.
2. The model is demonstrating something that has functional value to learners. Learners pay little attention to those things for which they see no immediate relevance.
3. The demonstration is simplified by subdividing it into component parts and presenting it in a clearly discernible step-by-step fashion.

Retention. Teachers model because they want their learners to be able to repeat their same actions when they are no longer present. Learners are more likely to remember the following types of demonstrations:

1. *Demonstrations linked to previously learned skills or ideas.* The more meaningful the demonstration, the more likely it will be retained. ("Remember how yesterday we added one-digit numbers in a column? Well, today we will use the same procedure on numbers that have two or more digits.")
2. *Demonstrations that include concise labels, vivid images, code words, or visual reminders.* These devices help learners hold new learning in memory. ("Look at how I hold my lips when I pronounce this next word.")
3. *Demonstrations that are immediately rehearsed.* This rehearsal can be overt, as when the teacher asks learners to say or do something immediately following the demonstration, or covert, as when learners visualize or mentally create an image of what the teacher demonstrated. ("Now, everyone read the next passage to themselves, repeating silently the sequence of steps I just demonstrated.")

Production. The third component of the modeling process occurs when learners actually do what the teacher demonstrated. Learners are more likely to produce what they have seen under the following conditions:

1. Production closely follows the retention phase. ("OK, now that you've practiced remembering the correct sequence of steps I demonstrated, let's use them to interpret the meaning of the following passage.")
2. The practice situation contains cues or stimuli that evoke the retained mental images or verbal codes. ("This next word requires you to position your lips exactly as you saw me do in the last example.")
3. The performance immediately follows mental rehearsal. ("Let's switch to several new examples that you haven't seen before.")

The production phase increases the likelihood that images of the demonstration learners have remembered will guide the production of newly acquired behavior. In addition, this phase allows the teacher to observe learners and give feedback on how well they have mastered the behavior. Giving learners information about the correctness of their actions—without expressing negativity or dissatisfaction—has been shown to increase the likelihood of a correct performance (Borich & Tombari, 1997, pp. 341–342).

Motivation. The final stage of the process of learning through modeling occurs when learners experience desirable outcomes following their performance. Learners are more likely to repeat the actions of a model both immediately and in new situations when the following occur:

1. Praise and encouragement, rather than criticism, immediately follow performance. ("Your answer is partly correct; think some more about what we have just discussed," as opposed to "Your answer is wrong. You were not listening again.")

2. The praise is directed at specific aspects of the performance. ("I like how you left big enough spaces between your words," as opposed to "That's neat.")

3. Directions, rather than corrections, follow an incorrect performance. ("Remember, the first step is to generate a hypothesis," as opposed to "You don't describe the research conclusions before you state the hypothesis!")

Feedback and Correcting Errors

Our next strategy in the direct instruction model is providing **feedback and correcting errors**. You will need strategies for handling right and wrong answers. Four categories of student response you will see in your classroom are (1) correct, quick, and firm; (2) correct but hesitant; (3) incorrect due to carelessness; and (4) incorrect due to lack of knowledge.

Correct, Quick, and Firm.   The student response that teachers strive most to inspire is correct, quick, and firm. Such a response most frequently occurs during the latter stages of a lesson or unit, but it can occur almost anytime during a lesson or unit if you have divided the content into bite-sized portions. A moderate to high percentage of correct, quick, and firm responses is important if students are to become actively engaged in the learning process.

Not every response from every student must be a correct one, but for most learning that involves knowledge acquisition, make the steps between successive portions of your lesson small enough to produce approximately 60 percent to 80 percent correct answers in a practice and feedback session (Bennett, Desforges, Cockburn, & Wilkinson, 1981; Brophy & Evertson, 1976; Lindsley, 1991). Once 60 percent to 80 percent right answers have been produced, you will have created a rhythm and momentum that heightens student attention and engagement and provides for a high level of task orientation. The brisk pace of providing right answers also will help minimize irrelevant student responses and classroom distractions.

Correct but Hesitant.   The second type of student response is correct but hesitant. This type frequently occurs in a practice and feedback session at the beginning or middle of a lesson. Giving positive feedback to the student who supplies a correct but hesitant response is essential. The first feedback to provide in this instance is a positive, reinforcing statement, such as "Good" or "That's correct," because the correct but hesitant response is more likely to be remembered when linked to a warm reply. The second feedback to provide is to restate the answer, assuring the student that it is correct. This will not only aid the student who is giving the correct but hesitant response, but it will also help reduce hesitant responses from other students who hear the restatement.

Incorrect Because of Carelessness.   The third type of student response is incorrect because of carelessness. As many as 20 percent of student responses fall into this category, depending on the time of day and the students' level of fatigue and inattentiveness. When this occurs and you feel a student really knows the correct response, you may be tempted to scold, admonish, or even verbally punish him or her for responding thoughtlessly (e.g., "I'm ashamed of you," "That's a dumb mistake," "I thought you were brighter than that"). You should resist temptation, however, no matter how justified it may seem at the moment. Researchers and experienced teachers agree that you can do more harm than good if you react emotionally to this type of response and verbal punishment rarely teaches students to avoid careless mistakes. The best response is to acknowledge that the answer is wrong and to move immediately to the next student for the correct response. By doing so, you will make a point to the careless student that he or she lost the opportunity for a correct response and the praise that goes with it.

Incorrect Because of Lack of Knowledge.   The fourth type of student response is incorrect because of a lack of knowledge. These errors typically occur, sometimes in large numbers, during the initial stages of a lesson or unit. When they do occur, it is better to provide hints, probe, or change the question or stimulus to a simpler one that engages the student in finding the correct response than to simply give the student the correct response. Your most important goal at this stage of the lesson or unit is to engage the learner in the process by which the right answer can be found.

In the example lesson, the teacher tried to focus Jason on the apostrophe *s* he had missed at the end of the proper noun *Jenkins* and to restate the rule concerning formation of possessives in words ending in *s*. Likewise the teacher probed Allison after her wrong answer by asking, "What word is doing the possessing?" Each of these probes led to the right answer without actually telling it to the student. When your strategy channels a student's thoughts to produce the right answer without your actually giving it, you provide a framework for producing correct responses to all similar problems.

Strategies for Incorrect Responses.   The most common strategies for incorrect responses are the following:

1. Review the key facts or rules needed to produce a correct solution.
2. Explain the steps used to reach a correct solution.
3. Prompt with clues or hints that represent a partially correct answer.
4. Use a different but similar problem to guide the student to the correct answer.

Reviewing, reexplaining, and prompting are effective until approximately 80 percent of the students respond correctly. After that point, make the correctives briefer, eventually guiding students who are making incorrect responses to helpful exercises in the text or to remedial exercises.

Researchers make a useful distinction between active and passive responding that is related to the accuracy of your learners' responses. **Active responding** includes orally responding to a question, writing out the correct answer, calculating an answer, or physically making a response (e.g., focusing a microscope). **Passive responding** includes listening to the teacher's answer, reading about the correct answer, or listening to classmates recite the right answer.

Huffman (2008) and Greenwood, Delguardi, and Hall (1984) report a strong and positive relationship between learner achievement and active responding. They also report that nearly half of a typical learner's day may be involved in passive responding. These researchers urge you to plan lessons so learners spend about 75 percent of their time engaged in active responding. They also recommend that you design practice activities to elicit correct responses about 60 percent to 80 percent of the time. Learners acquire basic facts and skills faster when their opportunities for practice result in high rates of success (Lindsley, 1991).

In summary, when providing feedback and corrections, do these things:

- Give directions that focus on the response you want learners to make.
- Chose or design instructional materials both for initial learning and practice so learners can produce correct answers 60 percent to 80 percent of the time.
- Select activities to engage your learners in active responding about 75 percent of the time.

Reaching Mastery

The fifth strategy for direct instruction is the opportunity to reach mastery through **independent practice**. Once you have successfully elicited the behavior, provided feedback, and administered correctives, give students the opportunity to practice the behavior independently. Often this is the time when facts and rules come together to form action sequences. For example, learning to drive a car requires knowledge of terminology and rules. But until the knowledge and rules are put together in an action sequence, meaningful learning has not occurred.

Independent practice provides the opportunity, in a carefully controlled and organized environment, to make a meaningful whole out of the bits and pieces. Facts and rules must come together under your guidance and example in ways that (1) force simultaneous consideration of all the individual units of a problem and (2) connect the units into a single harmonious sequence of action. Learning theorists call these two processes *unitization* and *automaticity*.

The teacher in this **video** uses several components of direct instruction. Try to match the examples with the components of independent practice.

Notice the manner in which these two processes were required in the example lesson. The individual units were the definition of a possessive (a fact) and two statements about forming possessives (Rules 1 and 2). Figure 9.8 traces the steps a student might take in translating these facts and rules into an action sequence for one sentence in the workbook. The teacher's examples of errors from newspapers and magazines provided students an opportunity to form action sequences from the facts and rules they learned. These real-life examples further increased the authenticity or relevance of their learning. In your own classroom, you can follow the rigor and relevance framework by providing opportunities for practice that increasingly resemble applications in the real world until the examples you provide are indistinguishable from those outside the classroom. Using clippings from actual newspapers and magazines was this teacher's way of doing so. Be sure to check the software available through your school and textbook and workbook publishers for other opportunities to provide your learners independent practice.

The purpose of providing opportunities for all types of independent practice is to develop automatic responses in students so they no longer need to recall each individual unit of content but can use all the units simultaneously. Your goal is to plan sufficient opportunities for independent practice to allow students' individual responses to become composed and automatic.

Keep in mind these guidelines for promoting effective practice:

- *Students should understand the reason for practice.* Practice often turns into busywork, which can create boredom, frustration, and noncompliance. Learners should approach classroom practice with the same enthusiasm with which an Olympic athlete pursues doing laps in the pool or on the track. This is more likely to occur if (1) you make known to learners the purpose of the practice ("We will need to be proficient at solving these problems in order to go on to our next activity"), and (2) practice occurs during as well as after new learning ("Let's stop right here, so you can try some of these problems yourselves").

- *Effective practice is delivered in a manner that is brief, nonevaluative, and supportive.* Practice involves more than simply saying "Take out your workbooks" or "Go to the computer terminals." Rather your introduction to a practice activity should accomplish three objectives: (1) to inform learners that they are going to practice something they are capable of succeeding at ("You've done part of this before, so this shouldn't be much different"); (2) to dispel anxiety about doing the task through the use of nonevaluative and nonthreatening language ("You've got part of it right, Anita. Now think some more and you'll have it"); and (3) to let learners know that you will be around to monitor their work and support their efforts ("I will be around to help, so let me know if you are having a problem").

Figure 9.8 **Steps Involved in Translating a Sentence into Correct Possessive Form**

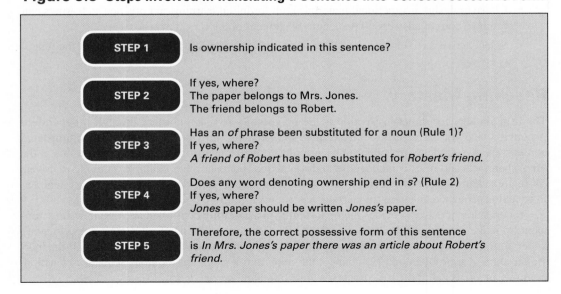

STEP 1 Is ownership indicated in this sentence?

STEP 2 If yes, where?
The paper belongs to Mrs. Jones.
The friend belongs to Robert.

STEP 3 Has an *of* phrase been substituted for a noun (Rule 1)?
If yes, where?
A friend of Robert has been substituted for *Robert's friend.*

STEP 4 Does any word denoting ownership end in *s*? (Rule 2)
If yes, where?
Jones paper should be written *Jones's* paper.

STEP 5 Therefore, the correct possessive form of this sentence
is *In Mrs. Jones's paper there was an article about Robert's friend.*

- *Practice should be designed to ensure success.* Practice makes perfect only when those who are practicing are doing so correctly. If your learners are making many math, punctuation, or problem-solving mistakes, practice is making imperfect. Design your practice to produce as few errors as possible. For example, use worksheets or software that ensures that most learners complete at least 60 percent to 80 percent of the problems correctly the first time through the material.

- *Practice should be arranged to allow students to receive feedback.* As we learned earlier in our discussion of modeling, giving feedback exerts a powerful effect on learning. Use procedures and routines for rapid checking of work so learners know as soon as possible how well they are performing. Using peers to correct one another's practice is an efficient way to give feedback. This could be efficiently accomplished with a course management system that asynchronously allows your learners to review and comment on the work of others in an online discussion board. Also having answer sheets handy so learners can check their own work is a simple and effective means of providing feedback. And don't forget to look for individual tutorial software that can detect student errors and provide additional exercises at the learner's current level of understanding.

- *Practice should have the qualities of progress, challenge, and variety.* Some have found that the key to preventing learners from becoming bored is to design practice opportunities so they actually see that they are making progress ("Don't forget to check your answers with the key on the board"). In addition, introduce practice in a challenging and enthusiastic manner ("This will really test your understanding with some new and interesting kinds of problems"). Finally, practice exercises should include a variety of examples and situations.

During independent practice, the teacher circulates around the classroom, scanning written responses, prompting for alternative answers, and reminding students of necessary facts or rules, being careful to keep interchanges short so that the work of as many students as possible can be checked.

Doing the following activities can help ensure that your students become actively engaged in the practice you provide:

1. *Walk* the class through the first few independent practice items by talking through them aloud. Doing so gives the scheduled seatwork a definite beginning, and students who are unclear about the assignment can ask questions without distracting others. This also provides a mental model for attaining a correct answer, which students can use in subsequent problems.

2. *Schedule* seatwork or computer time as soon as possible after the eliciting and feedback exercises. This helps students understand that independent practice is relevant to the guided practice provided earlier.

3. *Circulate* around the classroom while students are engaged in independent practice to provide feedback, ask questions, and give brief explanations (Emmer & Evertson, 2012). Spread circulation time equally across most of your students; don't concentrate on a small number of students. Try to average 30 seconds or less per student. Monitoring student responses during independent seatwork can be an important function of direct instruction if you keep contacts short and focused on specific issues for which a brief explanation is adequate.

Review Over Time

The sixth and final direct instruction strategy involves conducting **regular reviews**. Periodic review ensures that you have taught all task-relevant information needed for future lessons and identified areas that require reteaching of key facts, rules, and sequences. Without periodic review, you have no way of knowing whether direct instruction has been successful in teaching the required facts, rules, and sequences.

Periodic reviews have long been a part of almost every instructional strategy. In the context of direct instruction, however, periodic review and the recycling of instruction take on added importance because of the brisk pace at which direct instruction is conducted. You can establish the proper pace by noting the approximate percentage of errors that occur during guided practice and feedback; having 60 percent to 80 percent correct responses indicates a satisfactory pace.

Weekly and monthly reviews also help determine whether the pace is right or should be adjusted before covering too much content. When student responses in weekly and monthly reviews are correct, quick, and firm about 95 percent of the time, the pace is adequate. Independent practice and homework should raise the percentage of correct responses from approximately 60 percent to 80 percent during guided practice and to approximately 95 percent on weekly and monthly reviews. If the results are below these levels—and particularly if they are substantially below—your pace is too fast and some reteaching of facts, rules, and sequences may be necessary. This is especially true if the material is a prerequisite to later learning.

Another obvious advantage of weekly and monthly reviews is that they will give some learners a second chance to grasp material that they missed or only partially learned the first time around. Students often welcome these reviews; they provide a chance to go over material students may have missed, found difficult to learn the first time through, or may come across on unit tests.

Finally, having a regular weekly review (not a review "every so often") creates momentum. Momentum results from gradually increasing the coverage and depth of each weekly review until it is time for a comprehensive monthly review or exam. These reviews help sequence and pace the content you present and keeps your instruction aligned with your curriculum guide and state standards.

The objective is to create a review cycle that rises and falls in about a month, as shown in Figure 9.9. The low point of this cycle occurs at the start of a direct instruction unit, when only a week's material needs to be reviewed. The weekly review then becomes increasingly comprehensive until a major monthly assessment checks for understanding of all the content and standards covered in the previous month. The comprehensiveness of a review should build gradually, so students are not overwhelmed with a lot of unfamiliar content and always know what will be covered in the next review.

Other Forms of Direct Instruction

Finally, keep in mind that direct instruction does not only occur in a presentation–recitation format. As we have seen in Chapters 6 and 7 there are other ways of executing or assisting the direct instruction model that include course management and classroom response systems, computer-assisted instruction, peer and cross-age tutoring, various kinds of audiolingual and communication tools (e.g., recorded lessons for learning to read in the early grades), CD-ROM's, and web-accessible content—all of which can be a rich source of direct instruction and practice. These media should be included in your lesson plans. Many of them have been creatively programmed to include most of the six strategies for direct instruction and that provide opportunities to differentiate your instruction for individuals and groups of learners. Building a library of individualized courseware that covers the basic skills most frequently needed at your grade level and content area will be an important goal for differentiating your lesson plans.

Following is a lesson plan for our direct instruction dialogue following the format provided in Chapter 6.

Figure 9.9 **Cycle of Rising and Falling Action**

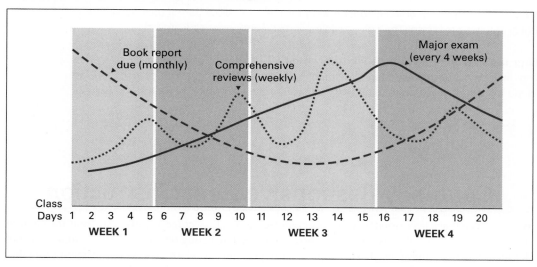

Note: The height of a cycle indicates relative amounts of instructional focus and student intensity.

Example Direct Instruction Lesson Plan

Grammar

Unit Title: Punctuation

Lesson Title: Forming and Punctuating Possessives

1 **Gaining attention.** Display the October school newspaper with a punctuation error in a headline. Point to the error.

2 **Informing the learner of the objective.** At the end of the period, students will be able to find mistakes in newspapers (in my file under "Punctuation") and make the necessary changes.

3 **Stimulating recall of prerequisite learning.** Review the part of speech most likely to own or possess something by asking students for the definition of a noun.

4 **Presenting the stimulus material.** Present two rules of possession: Rule 1. Use the possessive form whenever an *of* phrase can be substituted for a noun. Rule 2. For words that are plurals ending in *s,* place an apostrophe after the *s.* But for proper nouns ending in *s,* place an apostrophe *s* after the *s.* Write the rules on the board.

5 **Eliciting the desired behavior.** Display the following examples on a transparency, and ask students to convert them to the possessive form one at a time. See the text, pages 101–103, for other examples.

Delay of a month	The television set of Mr. Burns
Home of Jenkins	Pastimes of boys
Speech of the president	

6 **Providing feedback.** Write the correct possessive form on the transparency as students finish each example. Wait for students to finish (all heads up) before providing the answer for the next example. Probe for complete understanding by asking for the rule. Allow 30 minutes for differentiated autotutorial practices exercises for high-, middle-, and low-performance learners.

7 **Assessing the behavior.** Use the exercise on page 87 of the workbook to assess student understanding. In addition, use ordered turns recitation until about 90 percent correct responses are attained. Include ten possessives on the unit test that require the application of Rule 1 and Rule 2.

Culturally Responsive Direct Instruction

*Pay attention to how the school in this **video** is meeting the needs of their CLD students through direct instruction. What were some of the barriers?*

We have seen that a task-oriented teacher maximizes content coverage and gives students the greatest opportunity to learn. Likewise students who are involved in, acting on, and otherwise thinking about the material being presented have the greatest opportunity to learn. The key to bringing together these two important dimensions of effective teaching—task orientation and student engagement—rests with how you interact with your students to invoke a willingness to respond and apply what they have been learning. In classrooms where the range of individual and cultural differences is great, engaging students in the learning process during direct instruction can be a major challenge to achieving performance outcomes.

One facet of research dealing with cultural diversity and student engagement that can help bridge the gap has focused on differences in fluency and oral expression among learners during presentation–recitation (Delpit & Dowdy, 2008; Delpit, Boyd, Brock, & Rozendal, 2003). For example, *fluency,* or quickness to respond, can be influenced by nurturing and expressive qualities of the teacher (Lustig & Koester, 2009). The implication is that student hesitancy in responding and becoming engaged in the learning process may, for some cultural groups, be more a function of the attitude and cultural style of the teacher than of student ability. Also body posture, language, and eye contact form a pattern of **metacommunication** that is recognized by the learner and acted on according to the message being conveyed, whether intentional or not (Chen & Starasta, 2005). For example, a formal body posture and questions posed in an expressionless voice, without eye contact, may not invoke a commitment to respond. In other words, teachers must convey a sense of caring about learners before engagement can take place. Engagement techniques alone (e.g., presenting and structuring, guiding student practice, and providing feedback and corrections) will not be sufficient to actively engage students in the learning process, unless these techniques are accompanied by the appropriate metacommunication expressing nurturance and caring.

Bowers, Flinders (1991), Marzano, Pickering and Heflebower (2010), and Riggs and Gholar (2008) suggest several ways teachers can promote student engagement by conveying a sense of nurturance and caring:

- Use appropriate examples to clarify concepts and model performance. ("Let me give you an example that will help you see the relationship.")

- Accept the student's way of understanding new concepts. ("That's an interesting answer. Would you like to tell us how you arrived at it?")

- Reduce feelings of competitiveness. ("Today those who want to can work with a partner on the practice exercise.")

- Increase opportunities for social reinforcement. ("If you like, you can ask someone sitting nearby how he or she worked the problem.")

- Facilitate group achievement. ("When you're finished with your work, you can join another group to help them solve the problem.")

- Use culturally appropriate eye contact with students. ("Amanda, I'm going to sit down next to you and watch you work the first problem.")

- Recognize longer pauses and a slower tempo. ("Take your time. I'll wait for you to think of an answer.")

- Respond to unique or different questions during a response. ("You're asking about something else. Let me give you that answer, and then we'll go back to the first question.")

- Balance compliments and reinforcement equally. ("Let's not forget that both Angel and Damon got the right answer but in different ways.")

Although much still needs to be known about cultural diversity and student engagement during direct instruction, one thing is clear: Students of any culture are more likely to engage expressively in the learning process in an atmosphere that (1) emphasizes the importance of unique learner responses, (2) reduces feelings of individual competitiveness, (3) promotes a multisensory (e.g., telling as well as performing) learning environment, (4) encourages social reinforcement and peer interaction, and (5) conveys a sense of nurturance and caring.

Case History and Licensure Preparation

DIRECTIONS: *The following case history pertains to Chapter 9 content. After reading the case history, go to Chapter 9 in the Book Specific Resources section in the MyEducationLab for your course. Open the Case History and Licensure Preparation activity and complete the questions that follow. Upon completion of the test, scored answers to the short-answer question pertaining to the case history and multiple-choice questions will be provided.*

Case History

Mrs. Martinez teaches a fifth-grade class of 28 students. Recent standardized test scores at the school have been low, particularly in language and reading. Over one-half the class ranked in the lowest one-third of national norms in last year's test in either the reading or language portion. The school is making a strong effort to upgrade these skills.

Mrs. Martinez is in the middle of a lesson on teaching the appropriate use of *there, they're,* and *their*. The three words are written on the board in the following way:

There	They're	Their
a place	short for "they are"	shows ownership

She points to the first word and spells it.

"T-H-E-R-E. I mean a place when I say this word. I might say, 'Put the book over there.' T-H-E-R-E. I mean a specific place.

"Also take away the *t*" [Mrs. Martinez covers the letter *t* of *there*], "and you have *here*. That's another clue: *here* and *there*. *Here* and *there*," she repeats, this time

pointing to her desk for *here* and to a desk in the middle of the room for *there*.

"Juan, give me another sentence that uses *there* to mean a place."

Juan: I want to go out there. [He looks out the window toward the baseball diamond.]

Mrs. Martinez: Spell your word correctly.

Juan: T-H-E-R-E.

Mrs. Martinez: Well done. Susan, what is the little word inside that is our clue?

[Susan doesn't answer and looks confused. Mrs. Martinez goes to the board and covers the *t* of *there* to expose *here*.]

Susan: Here, H-E-R-E. [Mrs. Martinez points to her desk and then to a more distant desk. At first, Susan says nothing. Mrs. Martinez gestures again.] Oh, *here* and *there, here* and *there*.

Mrs. Martinez: You're good at getting clues, Susan. I bet you'd be a good detective. Now let's look at the next word.

They're—T-H-E-Y-'-R-E. It sounds the same as our first word, but it means something very different. T-H-E-Y-'-R-E is not a place; it's a short way to combine two words, *they* and *are*. The apostrophe [here she points appropriately to the board] stands for the letter *a* that we have taken out. "They are my friends." Say it fast and it becomes, "They're my friends." Matt, give us a sentence using our second word, T-H-E-Y-'-R-E.

Matt: [Matt is a high-performing student whose attention has been on a baseball game going on outside.] Their team can't even hit the ball.

Mrs. Martinez: Is Matt using our second word, T-H-E-Y-'-R-E, the one that is short for they are? What do you think, Parish?

Parish: No, he should have said, "They're not able to hit the ball." T-H-E-Y-'-R-E, short for *they are*.

Mrs. Martinez: Good, Parish. You even managed to keep the meaning of the sentence Matt used. [She pauses and walks slowly to the window.] Is Mr. Heath's class really that bad? Then I know we can beat them in next week's homeroom challenge.

Summing Up

The main points in this chapter include the following:

Categories of Teaching and Learning

1. Two broad classifications of learning are facts, rules, and action sequences (Type 1) and concepts, patterns, and abstractions (Type 2).

2. Type 1 outcomes represent behaviors at the lower levels of complexity in the cognitive, affective, and psychomotor domains; Type 2 outcomes represent behaviors at the higher levels of complexity in these domains.

3. Type 1 teaching activities require combining facts and rules at the knowledge and comprehension level into a sequence of actions that can be learned through observation, repetition, and practice. Type 1 outcomes have correct answers that can be learned by memorization and practice.

4. Type 2 teaching activities go beyond facts, rules, and sequences to help the learner create, synthesize, identify, and recognize an answer that cannot be easily modeled or memorized. Type 2 outcomes may have more than one correct answer.

5. The learning of facts, rules, and action sequences is most commonly taught with teaching strategies that emphasize knowledge acquisition; the learning of concepts, patterns, and abstractions is most commonly taught with teaching strategies that emphasize concept learning, inquiry, and problem solving.

6. The acquisition of facts, rules, and action sequences is most efficiently achieved through a process known as the *direct instruction model*. This model is primarily teacher-centered. Facts, rules, and action sequences are passed on to students in a presentation–recitation format, involving large amounts of teacher talk, questions and answers, review and practice, and the immediate correction of student errors.

Introduction to Direct Instruction Strategies

6. The direct instruction model is characterized by full-class (as opposed to small-group) instruction; by the organization of learning based on questions posed by you; by the provision of detailed and redundant practice (that may be supplemented by computer software); by the presentation of material so learners master one new fact, rule, or sequence before the teacher presents the next; and by the formal arrangement of the classroom to maximize drill and practice.

7. Direct instruction is most appropriate when the content in texts and workbooks does not appear in appropriately sized pieces, when your active involvement in the teaching process is necessary to arouse or heighten student interest, and when the content to be taught represents task-relevant prior knowledge for subsequent learning.

Monitoring and Diagnosing to Gauge Progress

8. Techniques for daily review and checking include the following:

   • Have students identify difficult homework problems in a question-and-answer format.

   • Sample the understanding of a few students who are likely to represent the class.

- Explicitly review the task-relevant prior learning required for the day's lesson.

Presenting and Structuring

9. Techniques for presenting and structuring new content include these:
   - Establishing part–whole relationships
   - Identifying sequential relationships
   - Finding combinations of relationships
   - Drawing comparative relationships

Guided Student Practice

10. Techniques for guided student practice include the following:
   - Asking students to respond privately and then be singled out for help
   - Calling on students to respond whether or not their hands are raised
   - Preparing questions beforehand and randomly asking students to respond

Feedback and Correcting Errors

11. Providing appropriate feedback and correction involves knowing how to respond to answers that are (1) correct, quick, and firm; (2) correct but hesitant; (3) incorrect due to carelessness; and (4) incorrect due to lack of knowledge.

12. For a correct, quick, and firm response, acknowledge the correct response and either ask another question of the same student or move on to another student.

13. For a correct but hesitant response, provide a reinforcing statement and restate the facts, rules, or steps needed for the right answer.

14. For an incorrect response due to carelessness, indicate that the response is incorrect and quickly move on to the next student without further comment.

15. For an incorrect response that is due to a lack of knowledge, engage the student in finding the correct response with hints, probes, or a related but simpler question.

16. For most learning involving knowledge acquisition, the steps between successive portions of your lesson should be made small enough to produce approximately 60 percent to 80 percent correct answers in a practice and feedback session.

17. Reviewing, re-explaining, and prompting are effective until approximately 80 percent of your students respond correctly; after that, correctives should be made briefer or students should be guided to individualized learning materials.

Reaching Mastery

18. Design independent practice so the learner puts together facts and rules to form action sequences that increasingly resemble applications in the real world. Provide opportunities for independent practice as soon after the time of learning as possible.

Reviews Over Time

19. Pace instruction so student responses to questions posed in weekly and monthly reviews are correct, quick, and firm about 95 percent of the time.

20. Use independent practice and homework to raise the percentage of correct responses from approximately 60 percent to 80 percent during guided practice and to approximately 95 percent on weekly and monthly reviews.

Culturally Responsive Direct Instruction

21. Student engagement in the culturally diverse classroom is promoted by accepting unique learner responses, reducing competitiveness, promoting peer interaction, and conveying a sense of nurturance and caring.

Key Terms

Active responding
Direct instruction
Feedback and correcting errors
Gestural prompts
Guided student practice
Independent practice
Indirect instruction

Instructional variety
Mastery learning
Metacommunication
Monitoring and diagnosing
Ordered turns
Passive responding
Physical prompts

Presenting and structuring
Regular reviews
Rule–example–rule order
Social learning theory
Verbal prompts

Discussion and Practice Questions

Questions marked with an asterisk are answered in Appendix B. Some asterisked questions may require student follow-up responses not included in Appendix B. Go to the Assignments and Activities section of the various topics on the MyEducationLab for your course to complete additional practice activities related to this chapter's content.

*1. Identify the learning outcomes associated with Type 1 and Type 2 teaching strategies. To what levels of behavior in the cognitive domain does each type of learning apply?

*2. What type of learning outcomes are elicited by instructional strategies that emphasize knowledge acquisition? What type of learning outcomes are elicited by instructional strategies that emphasize inquiry or problem solving?

*3. If you were to describe the direct instruction model, what characteristics would you include? What would be the topic of a lesson plan in your area that would be ideally suited to the direct instruction model and why?

*4. Provide some examples of action verbs in the cognitive, affective, and psychomotor domains that describe the type of outcomes expected from the direct instructional model. Which outcomes do you think would be hardest to achieve and why?

*5. For what instructional goals is the direct instruction model most appropriate? What other goals can you think of that are not cited in the chapter?

*6. Explain why providing guided student practice in a nonevaluative atmosphere is important for learning to occur. What would you do to encourage a reluctant student to make a first, crude response?

7. The following second-grade student responses were received by a teacher in response to the question "What does 5 plus 3 equal?"

Brooke: It could be 8.
Juan: 9.
Jason: 53.
Ashley: 8.

Provide an appropriate teacher prompt that moves each student closer to the correct or more confident answer.

8. The following tenth-grade student responses were received by a teacher who asked, "What was one of the underlying reasons for the Civil War?"

Tahnee: The South wanted the land owned by the North.
Akim: I read somewhere it was religious persecution.
Ken: Well, let me think . . . It had something to do with slavery.
Tracy: The economics of the South.

Provide an appropriate teacher prompt that moves each student closer to the correct or more confident answer.

*9. What approximate percentage of correct answers should you work toward in a practice and feedback session? What would you do to change your instructional approach if only 30% of your student responses were correct in a practice and feedback session?

*10. What is the primary purpose of independent practice in direct instruction? Choose a lesson in your teaching area, and show how you would use independent practice to fulfill this purpose. How would you vary the independent practice if more time and opportunity for practice became available?

*11. When circulating around the room to monitor independent practice, in what ways could you make your monitoring time more efficient?

*12. Approximately what percentage of student responses during weekly and monthly review sessions should be correct, quick, and firm? If you did not reach this percentage what would you do to change your teaching strategy to increase this percentage?

Professional Practice

Field Experience and Practice Activities

Questions marked with an asterisk are answered in Appendix B. Some asterisked questions may require student follow-up responses not included in Appendix B.

*1. From your fieldwork or observation, in what ways have you seen teachers review and check the previous day's work? Which ways do you feel would be the most appropriate for your classroom?

*2. Identify how a teacher you have observed structured content into small, bite-sized pieces. How would you describe this technique and do you think it naturally fits the way the subject matter you will teach is organized?

*3. After observing direct instruction, describe some of the methods you have observed for prompting a student to attain the correct response. Provide examples of prompts you would give a student after providing a wrong or partially wrong response. Indicate both the student's incorrect answer and your response.

*4. For a subject you will teach, describe a cycle of weekly and monthly reviews (for example, daily checks for understanding, weekly reviews, and comprehensive reviews monthly) that you would like to implement in your classroom to increase the percentage of students who respond correctly, quickly, and firmly. What might you change if your cycle of review was not attaining the student achievement and unit outcomes you had anticipated?

Digital Portfolio Activities

The following digital portfolio activities relate to InTASC Standards 2, 4, and 8.

1. For Field Experience and Practice Activity 3, you were asked to describe methods you have observed for prompting a student to achieve the correct response. Place your descriptions of these methods with those indicated in this chapter in a folder titled "Direct Instruction" and add them to your digital portfolio. This information will remind you of the many ways you can move a student closer to a correct answer without embarrassing him or her or expecting a response that he or she may be unable to provide at the time.

2. For Field Experience and Practice Activity 4, you were asked to describe a cycle of weekly and monthly reviews for raising the percentage of your students' responses that are correct, quick, and firm during direct instruction. Now add to your response what other instructional strategies (for example, independent practice and homework) you might use to raise the percentage of correct responses from approximately 60% to 80% during daily guided practice and feedback to approximately 95% of responses that are correct, quick, and firm on weekly and monthly reviews. Place your description in your "Direct Instruction" folder, and add it to your digital portfolio. This will remind you during unit planning how you can increase student engagement in your lessons and build momentum that keeps students focused on achieving unit outcomes.

MyEducationLab™

Go to MyEducationLab (www.myeducationlab.com) for Effective Teaching Methods: Research-Based Practice where you can:

- Find learning outcomes for the various course topics course along with national standards that connect to these outcomes.
- Complete **Assignments and Activities** that can help you more deeply understand the chapter content.
- Apply and practice your understanding of the core teaching skills identified in the chapter with **Building Teaching Skills and Dispositions** coaching activities.
- Check your comprehension of the content covered in the chapter with a book specific **Study Plan**. Here you will be able to take a chapter **pretest**, receive feedback on your answers, and then access personalized **Review, Practice, and Enrichment exercises** to enhance your understanding of chapter content. After you complete the exercises, take a **posttest** to confirm your comprehension.
- Learn how to address common classroom management issues in the **Simulations in Classroom Management**.
- Access video clips of CCSSO **National Teachers of the Year award winners** responding to the question, "Why Do I Teach?" in the Teacher Talk section.
- Create, update, and share quality lesson plans with the **Lesson Plan Builder**.
- Access state licensure test requirements, overviews of what tests cover, and sample test items in the **Certification and Licensure** section.
- Learn how to create a high quality teaching portfolio in the **Preparing a Portfolio** section.
- Access tips, advice, and other information on resume writing and interviewing, your first year of teaching, and law and public policies in the Beginning Your Career section.

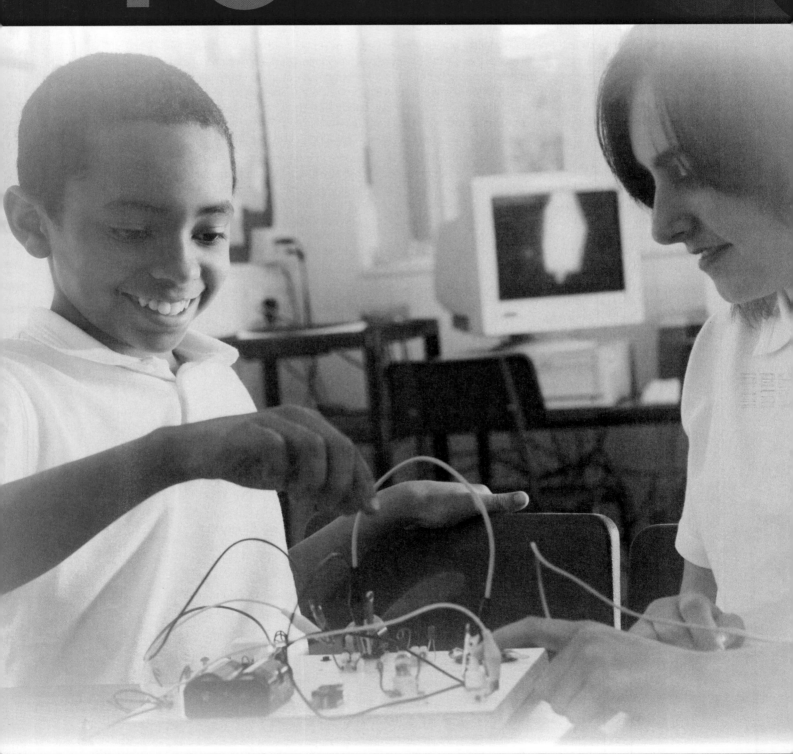

Teaching Strategies for Indirect Instruction

10

This chapter will help you answer these questions and meet the following InTASC standards for effective teaching.

- What is concept learning?
- What is inquiry learning?
- What is problem-based learning?
- What are constructivist strategies for teaching higher order learning?
- What are some ways of promoting the goals of concept learning, inquiry, and problem solving in a heterogeneous classroom?

InTASC

STANDARD 1 **Learner Development.** The teacher understands how learners grow and develop, recognizing that patterns of learning and development vary individually within and across the cognitive, linguistic, social, emotional, and physical areas, and designs and implements developmentally appropriate and challenging learning experiences.

STANDARD 3 **Learning Environments.** The teacher works with others to create environments that support individual and collaborative learning, and that encourage positive social interaction, active engagement in learning, and self motivation.

STANDARD 4 **Content Knowledge.** The teacher understands the central concepts, tools of inquiry, and structures of the discipline(s) he or she teaches and creates learning experiences that make these aspects of the discipline accessible and meaningful for learners to assure mastery of the content.

STANDARD 5 **Application of Content.** The teacher understands how to connect concepts and use differing perspectives to engage learners in critical thinking, creativity, and collaborative problem solving related to authentic local and global issues.

STANDARD 6 **Assessment.** The teacher understands and uses multiple methods of assessment to engage learners in their own growth, to monitor learner progress, and to guide the teacher's and learner's decision making.

STANDARD 8 **Instructional Strategies.** The teacher understands and uses a variety of instructional strategies to encourage learners to develop deep understanding of content areas and their connections, and to build skills to apply knowledge in meaningful ways.

hapter 9 introduced you to direct instruction for teaching facts, rules, and action sequences. Now we consider indirect instruction for teaching concepts, inquiry, and problem solving.

An old adage says, "Tell me and I forget. Show me and I remember. Involve me and I understand." The teaching of concepts, inquiry, and problem solving involves different forms of indirect instruction that actively involve your learners in seeking resolutions to questions and issues while they construct new knowledge. Indirect instruction is an approach to teaching and learning in which (1) the process is inquiry, (2) the content involves concepts, and (3) the context is a problem.

These three ideas are brought together in special ways in the indirect instruction model. This chapter presents teaching strategies you can use to compose your own indirect teaching approach that asks your learners to share the excitement of becoming actively involved in their own learning and contributing new knowledge to solve real-world problems. We begin by looking into two classrooms; one in which Tim Robbins is teaching a lesson with the direct instruction model and one in which Kay Greer is teaching the same lesson with the indirect instruction model.

Tim Robbins' Classroom

It is the third six weeks of the fall semester, and Tim Robbins is teaching a unit on fractions to his fourth-grade class. During the first 12 weeks of the year, all fourth-graders learned about the concepts of *numbers* and *number theory.* They covered such topics as odd, even, positive, and negative numbers. The fourth-graders have also become familiar with such numerical concepts as *multiples, factors,* and the *base 10 system* for writing numbers.

On this day, we observe Mr. Robbins. He is teaching a lesson on equivalent fractions as a way of representing the same amount. During the preceding four lessons, his learners have studied about fractions as quantities and learned how fractions that look different (e.g., 1/2, 2/4) actually represent the same amount. The present lesson is intended to reinforce this idea.

Mr. Robbins begins the lesson with a quick review of the previous lesson. On the overhead projector, he shows pictures of objects such as pies and loaves of bread divided to represent different fractions of the whole. In rapid-fire fashion, his learners call out the fractions. He then projects a chart with undivided whole objects and has learners come up and divide them into halves, thirds, fourths, and so on; other learners do the same on worksheets. Each learner gets immediate feedback on his or her answers.

Next Mr. Robbins signals the class to clear their desks except for a pencil and draws their attention to a large, brightly colored chart hanging on the front blackboard. (The chart is shown in Figure 10.1.) He passes out copies of the same chart to students. Mr. Robbins explains that for each row, students are to complete the fraction with a denominator of 100 that equals the fraction in the row. Then they are to fill in the third square with the decimal equivalent of that fraction.

Mr. Robbins first models how to do this. He demonstrates (pointing out that students have already learned this) how to make an equivalent fraction by multiplying the original fraction by a fraction that equals one. He works several examples to be sure his students understand the concept and then has them copy the examples onto their chart.

Mr. Robbins then calls on several students to come to the front of the room and demonstrate several more examples for the class. He has the students state as they work, for the class

Figure 10.1 Mr. Robbins's Chart for Teaching Fractions

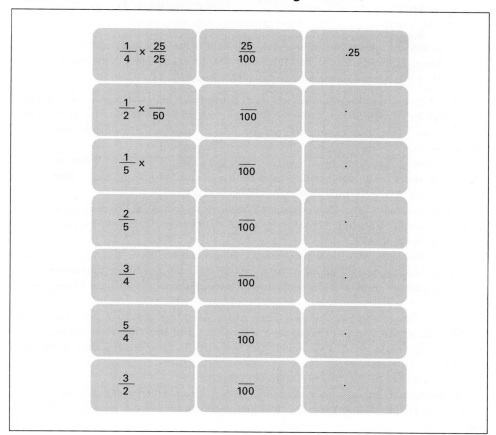

to hear, how they are solving the problems. He checks that the rest of the students correctly fill in the charts at their desks.

Finally, Mr. Robbins breaks the class into small groups and directs them to fill out the remainder of the chart. He provides each group with a key so they can immediately check their responses when finished. As the learners busily engage in their seatwork, Mr. Robbins moves from group to group, checking, giving feedback, correcting, or praising as needed. He has designed this lesson to show that fractions that look different can be equal in order to point out the relationship of decimals and fractions and to use this as a foundation for teaching the relationships between dollars, decimals, and fractions in a subsequent lesson.

Kay Greer's Classroom

In the classroom next door to Mr. Robbins, Kay Greer also is teaching a unit on fractional equivalents.* As the lesson begins, Mrs. Greer asks Denisha to tell the class what she said yesterday about fractions.

"A fraction isn't a number," she asserts, "because it isn't on the number line." Denisha points to the number line running along the top of the front blackboard. "See! There's no 1/2. Just 1, 2, 3, 4, . . . like that!"

---

*Based on information from D. L. Ball (1991), "Teaching Mathematics for Understanding: What Do Teachers Need to Know About Subject Matter?" in M. L. Kennedy (Ed.), *Teaching Academic Subjects to Diverse Learners* (pp. 67–69). New York: Teachers College Press.

"Well, class, let's think about what Denisha says. Let me give you a problem, and we'll study it and then maybe come to some conclusion about if a fraction is a number."

Mrs. Greer turns on the overhead and projects the following for all to see:

> A boy has four loaves of bread that he bought at the local supermarket. He has eight friends, and he wants each friend to get an equal part of the bread. How much bread should he give each of his friends?

Mrs. Greer draws the four loaves on the overhead and watches as the children, arranged in six groups of five, copy the drawings into their notebook. She walks around the classroom, occasionally prompting groups with the question "How much bread is each one going to get?"

The children argue among themselves: "You can't do it!" "There isn't enough bread!" "How many slices are in each loaf?" After about ten minutes, Mrs. Greer asks, "Does anyone need more time to work on this? How many are ready to discuss?"

A few raise their hands. The rest are busy drawing and redrawing loaves of bread, sketching lines across them. Several minutes go by and Mrs. Greer says, "OK, would someone like to show his or her solution?"

Frank raises his hand, walks to the overhead, and draws his solution. "I'm not sure it's right," he hedges. Frank draws four loaves of bread and divides each loaf into eight slices. (Frank's drawing appears in Figure 10.2.) He looks up and announces to the class, "Each friend gets four slices!"

"That's wrong!" challenges Rosa. "Each friend gets two slices, see?" She walks to the overhead, draws four loaves of bread, and divides each loaf into four slices. (Rosa's drawing appears in Figure 10.3.) "Each friend gets two slices," she asserts, pointing to the equal portions.

"Why not just give each friend half a loaf?" asks Albert.

"Come up here and draw your solution," says Mrs. Greer. Albert walks up to the overhead and sketches his proposal to the class. "Can you write the number that each gets?" she asks. Albert writes the number ½ on the board.

"Well, Albert's and Rosa's slices are bigger than mine," protests Frank.

"Frank," asks Mrs. Greer, "why not write the number that shows how much of the bread your eight friends get? Albert's number is 1/2. How much is one slice as Albert sees it?" she asks the class.

Figure 10.2 Frank's Drawing

Figure 10.3 Rosa's Drawing

"One-eighth," proposes Cal.

"Can you write that?" inquires Mrs. Greer. Cal comes up to the overhead and writes next to Frank's drawing.

As children write different numbers for their solutions, Mrs. Greer asks, "Well, how can we have three different numbers for each of these solutions? We have one half, two-fourths, four-eighths," pointing to the different quantities and fractions on the overhead.

After several moments of silence, several hands shoot up, and one by one, the children give explanations for the seeming discrepancy.

The lesson continues in this vein until five minutes before the bell. Then Mrs. Greer reviews what was concluded and sets the goal for the next lesson on fractions.

Now let's compare the lessons of Mrs. Greer and Mr. Robbins. Both teachers have the same goal: to help learners understand the concepts of *quantity* and *equivalence* pertaining to fractions. But they have designed two very different lessons to achieve this same end.

You may have noticed that the direct instruction approach has heavily influenced Mr. Robbins's lesson. He has designed his lesson to elicit a minimum of mistakes. His activities elicit practice of correct responses followed by immediate feedback. For Mr. Robbins, learning involves correct responding, which is best accomplished by a teacher-directed or teacher-centered lesson.

Mrs. Greer, in contrast, has a less direct approach to learning. She is less focused on correct, rapid responses than on thought processes involving concepts, inquiry, and problem solving. Her lesson takes into consideration that her learners already have information and beliefs about fractions that may or may not be correct. Mrs. Greer wants to expose students' misconceptions and challenge them to acquire new, more accurate perceptions through their own powers of reasoning. She carefully avoids providing answers. Her objective is to help learners understand fractions by influencing the cognitive processes by which they can elicit correct responses. Let's look at some of the cognitive processes around which she planned her lesson.

The Cognitive Processes of Learning

Cognitive psychologists have identified three essential conditions for meaningful learning (Anderson, 2005; Mayer, 2010): *reception, availability,* and *activation.* The reception and availability conditions are met when teachers focus their learners' attention on a problem and provide a framework or structure that organizes the content into meaningful parts, called an *anticipatory set* (Hunter, 1982; Serdvukov & Ryan, 2007) or **advance organizer** (Ausubell, 1968). Teachers fulfill the activation condition by modeling the inquiry process and using skilled questioning techniques. As learners develop greater skill at inquiry and problem solving, the teacher gradually fades out assistance and allows learners to assume more and more responsibility for their own learning.

As you may recall, supporting this approach to learning and instruction is a theory called **constructivism**. Constructivist lessons are designed and sequenced to encourage learners to use their own experiences to actively construct meaning that makes sense to them, rather than to acquire understanding through exposure to a format exclusively organized by the teacher (Fosnot, 2005; Llewellyn, 2007; Richardson, 1997). By reflecting on their own experiences, students continually change what they believe, discard old information and accept new information, and question, explore, and assess what they know. Instead of a "choo choo" train conception of learning in which knowledge is developed horizontally by sticking one train car on to the next (e.g., sixth grade knowledge on to fifth grade and seventh onto sixth, etc.), knowledge is accumulated vertically in an umbrella style conception of learning in which the learner's "umbrella" is continually opening wider and wider to capture new understandings within and across grades integrating and embracing larger amounts of information into a whole.

MyEducationLab

Visit the MyEducationLab for *Effective Teaching Methods: Research-Based Practice,* 8e to enhance your understanding of chapter concepts with a personalized Study Plan. You'll also have the opportunity to hone your teaching skills through video-based Assignments and Activities as well as Building Teaching Skills and Dispositions lessons.

For example, groups of students in a social studies class are discussing problems related to pollution and what needs to be done about them. The teacher focuses on helping students to refocus their questions in ways that will lead to practical solutions. She encourages each student to reflect on his or her current experiences with pollution. When one student comes up with a concept that links various forms of pollution and points to a single source, she seizes on it to alert the class to this important contribution, which will be a promising direction to explore. She encourages the students to consult the Web and other sources to substantiate their hypotheses and the credibility of their proposed solutions. Afterward, the class talks about what they have learned on their class's online discussion board about how their observations and documentation helped "open" them to embrace and understand a new and broader concept of *pollution.*

From examples like these, constructivists believe that knowledge results from the individual constructing reality from her or his own experiences. Learning occurs when learners create new rules and hypotheses on their own to explain what is being observed and arrive at new meanings and understandings in nests of wider and wider embrace that add a greater wholeness or completeness to what they are learning. The need to create new rules and formulate hypotheses is stimulated by classroom dialogue, problem-solving exercises, and individual projects and assignments that create discrepancies, or an imbalance, between old knowledge and new observations that must be assimilated with new conceptions that make sense to the learner. Teachers use direct experience (Piaget, 1977; Stepien, Senn & Stepien, 2008), problem- and project-based learning (Boss, Krauss, & Conery, 2008; Krauss & Conery, 2008) and social interaction (Kozulin, et al., 2003; Kumpulainen, 2001; Vygotsky, 1962) to restore the balance while deemphasizing the roles of lecturing and telling. Table 10.1 identifies some of the ways a constructivist classroom differs from a traditional classroom.

Many changes in how reading, writing, mathematics, science, and social studies are taught have followed constructivist thinking and the indirect instructional strategies that support it (Borich, 2004; Chaille, 2007; Fosnot, 2005). Let's look at some instructional strategies in these areas that have followed constructivist thinking.

Table 10.1 A Constructivist Classroom Compared to a Traditional Classroom

Traditional Classroom	Constructivist Classroom
The curriculum begins with the parts of the whole and emphasizes basic skills.	The curriculum emphasizes big concepts, beginning with the whole and expanding to include the parts.
Strict adherence to a fixed curriculum is highly valued.	Pursuit of student questions and interests is valued.
Materials are primarily textbooks and workbooks.	Materials include primary sources of information and manipulative materials.
Learning is based on repetition.	Learning is interactive, building on what the student already knows.
Teachers disseminate information to students; students are recipients of knowledge.	Teachers have a dialogue with students, helping them construct their own knowledge.
The teacher's role is directive and rooted in authority.	The teacher's role is interactive and rooted in negotiation.
Assessment is through testing; correct answers are the desired product.	Assessment includes student works, observations, and points of view, as well as tests. The process is as important as the product.
Knowledge is seen as inert.	Knowledge is seen as dynamic and ever changing with our experiences.
Students work primarily alone.	Students work primarily in groups.

Source: Based on *Concept to Classroom: A Series of Workshops.* 2004 Educational Broadcasting Corporation. Available online at www.thirteen.org/edonline/concept2class/constructivism/index.html.

Reading

For most of the twentieth century, reading curricula have taught the skills of decoding, blending, sequencing, finding main ideas, and so on outside the context of reading itself. These skills were usually practiced with contrived stories written in basal readers. Constructivist-influenced reading curricula now teach basic reading skills with a balanced approach, such as through the reading of literature while engaged in a search for meaning. Learners often work in small groups, cooperatively reading to one another and asking and answering questions based on extended reading assignments. Fact-oriented worksheets are deemphasized.

Writing

Constructivist-oriented approaches to writing instruction provide a problem-solving context by focusing learners' attention on the importance of communication. They practice writing skills not in isolation but while working on writing activities that require them to communicate ideas meaningfully to real audiences. From learners' very earliest attempts at writing, they realize that someone will read what they write. Thus what they write must be understandable. Writing instruction, then, involves a process of developing an initial draft and then revising it under the conditions that would prevail in the real world (e.g., over extended timeframes, with access to resources, with feedback from peer readers).

Mathematics and Science

Authentic problems, such as the one presented in the dialogue with Mrs. Greer at the beginning of this chapter, are the focus of constructivist approaches to math and science instruction. In such approaches, little time is spent on the rote drill and practice of individual math or science facts. Rather students are taught within a problem-solving or application context from the very beginning. The teacher attempts to have learners become actively involved in exploring, predicting, reasoning, and conjecturing, so that facts become integrated into mathematical skills and strategies that can be applied to authentic real-world problems.

Many authentic math and science problems for grades 6 through 12 are becoming available on the Internet. They provide learners the opportunity for real-time problem solving, interactivity, and connectivity with other resources. For examples of online K–12 constructivist math and science curricula, visit www.internet4classrooms.com/math_gen.htm and www.goENC.com.

Social Studies

Constructivist approaches to social studies have the goal of helping learners acquire a rich network of understandings around a limited number of topics. Parker (1991, 2009) advocates that the K–12 social studies curriculum should focus on five essential elements: the democratic ideal, cultural diversity, economic development, the global perspective, and participatory citizenship. The blending of these critical elements within a single curriculum requires a constructivist view of teaching and learning that promotes the following:

1. *In-depth study*—the sustained examination of a limited number of important topics
2. *Higher order challenge*—the design of a curriculum and instruction that requires students to gather and use information in nonroutine applications
3. *Authentic assessment*—aligning students' schoolwork with performance-oriented exhibitions of learning

These subject matter advances assume that students construct their own understanding of skills and knowledge, rather than have it told or given to them by the teacher (Sunal & Haas, 2010). Therefore constructivist lesson plans do the following:

- Present instructional activities in the form of problems for students to solve
- Develop and refine students' answers to problems from the point of view and experience of the student
- Acknowledge the social nature of learning by encouraging the interaction of the teacher with students and students with one another

Figure 10.4 Example of Spiraling Curriculum for Integrating Bodies of Knowledge

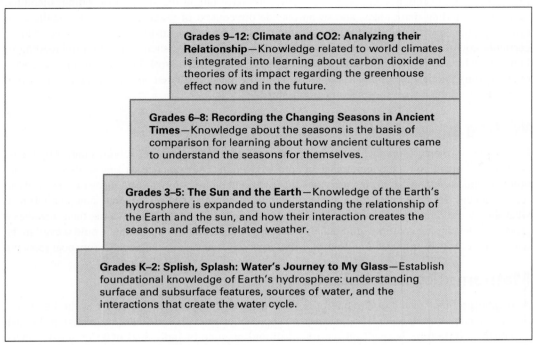

Grades 9–12: Climate and CO2: Analyzing their Relationship—Knowledge related to world climates is integrated into learning about carbon dioxide and theories of its impact regarding the greenhouse effect now and in the future.

Grades 6–8: Recording the Changing Seasons in Ancient Times—Knowledge about the seasons is the basis of comparison for learning about how ancient cultures came to understand the seasons for themselves.

Grades 3–5: The Sun and the Earth—Knowledge of the Earth's hydrosphere is expanded to understanding the relationship of the Earth and the sun, and how their interaction creates the seasons and affects related weather.

Grades K–2: Splish, Splash: Water's Journey to My Glass—Establish foundational knowledge of Earth's hydrosphere: understanding surface and subsurface features, sources of water, and the interactions that create the water cycle.

Source: Based on Renewing the Social Studies Curriculum (p. 2), by W. Parker, 1991.

Another goal of constructivist teaching is to present **integrated bodies of knowledge**. Integrated units and lessons stress the connections between ideas and the logical coherence of interrelated topics, usually in the form of interdisciplinary or thematic units of instruction (Roberts & Kellough, 2006; Ross, 2006; Wiggins & McTighe, 2005). Within a grade level, connections are made among disciplines, social studies and science, for example. Across increasingly higher grade levels, knowledge is spiraled—as students are ready to grasp greater depths of content knowledge as identified in Figure 10.4. Following the constructivist approach, the teacher presents authentic problems that naturally occur from integrated bodies of knowledge.

Comparing Direct and Indirect Instruction

The teacher in this **video** uses examples of both indirect and direct instruction. Try to differentiate the two processes.

Direct instruction strategies are best suited for the teaching of facts, rules, and action sequences, so it makes sense that indirect instruction strategies are best suited for teaching concepts, inquiry, and problem solving.

When you present instructional stimuli to your learners in the form of content, materials, objects, and events and ask them to go beyond the information given to make conclusions and generalizations or find a pattern of relationships, you are using the indirect model of instruction. *Indirect* means the learner acquires a behavior indirectly by transforming, or constructing, the stimulus material into a meaningful response that differs from both (1) the content used to present the learning and (2) any previous response given by the student. Because the learner can add to the content and rearrange it in nests of larger embrace to be more meaningful according to his or her experience, the elicited response can take many different forms. In contrast to the outcomes of direct instruction, there is rarely a single best or correct answer when using the indirect model of instruction. Instead the learner is guided to an answer that goes beyond the specific problem or content presented.

If direct instruction is so effective for teaching facts, rules, and action sequences, you might wonder why it is not used for teaching concepts, inquiry, and problem solving. The answer is that not all desired outcomes call for responses that are identical to the content taught. Direct instruction is limited to (1) learning units of the content taught so they can be remembered and (2) composing parts of the content learned into a whole, so that a rapid and automatic response can occur.

Learning at the lower levels of the cognitive, affective, and psychomotor domains relies heavily on these two processes. Both can be placed into action by content that closely resembles the desired response (e.g., "Look at this word and then say it," "Watch me form a possessive, and then you do the next one," "Read the instructions, and then focus the microscope"). The desired response need not go much beyond what is provided. The task for the learner is simply to produce a response that mirrors the form and content of the stimulus. A great deal of teaching involves these simple processes for which the direct instruction model is most efficient and effective.

Real-world activities, however, often involve analysis, synthesis, and decision-making behaviors in the cognitive domain, organization and characterization behaviors in the affective domain, and articulation and naturalization behaviors in the psychomotor domain. These behaviors complicate instruction, because they are not learned by memorizing the parts and rapidly and automatically reassembling them into a whole, as are behaviors at lower levels of complexity. Instead they must be constructed by the learner's own attempts to use personal experiences and past learnings to bring meaning to and make sense out of the content provided. As you will see in this chapter, teaching for higher order outcomes requires a different set of instructional strategies that represent the indirect instruction model.

Teaching Strategies for Indirect Instruction

Before describing the strategies that allow your learners to achieve higher order outcomes, let's consider some topics that require higher order outcomes.

Suppose you want your students to learn the following:

- Meaning of a number line (arithmetic)
- Concept of a quadratic equation (algebra)
- Process of acculturation (social studies)
- Meaning of contact sports (physical education)
- Workings of democracy (government)
- Playing of a concerto (music)
- Demonstration of photosynthesis (biology)
- Application of the law of conservation of energy (general science)

Learning these topics requires not just facts, rules, and action sequences but much more. If you teach just the facts, rules, and action sequences about the number line—"Here is the definition," "Here is how it is used," or "Follow this sequence of steps"—your students may never learn the concept that binds problems that require an understanding of the number line or how to use it in new or novel situations. Instead your students must learn to add to, rearrange, and elaborate on the content you present, using more complex cognitive processes. Let's see how this is done.

Recall from Chapter 9 (Table 9.3) the distinction between Type 1 and Type 2 behaviors. Type 1 behaviors become Type 2 behaviors by using facts, rules, and sequences to form concepts, patterns, and abstractions. As we will see in this chapter, concepts, patterns, and relationships are most effectively taught in the context of strategies that emphasize concept learning, inquiry, and problem solving.

Notice what would be required, for example, if students tried to learn the concept of a *frog* in the same way they acquired facts, rules, and action sequences about a frog. First, students would have to commit to memory all possible instances of frogs (of which there may be hundreds). Trying to retain hundreds of frog images in the same form they were presented would quickly overburden your learners' memories. Second, even after committing many types of frogs to memory, learners might confuse frogs with similar animals. The memorization process does not include the characteristics that *exclude* other animals from being frogs (e.g., has hard shell, dry skin, color changes, tail).

The processes of generalization and discrimination, if planned for in the presentation of your lesson, can help students overcome both of these problems. **Generalization** helps learners respond in a similar manner to stimuli that differ but are bound by a central concept, thereby increasing the range of instances to which particular facts, rules, and sequences apply (e.g., to all types of frogs). In addition, **discrimination** selectively restricts this range by eliminating things that appear to match the student's concept of a *frog* (e.g., a chameleon) but that differ from it in critical dimensions (e.g., has a tail).

Generalization and discrimination help students classify visually different stimuli into the same category based on critical attributes that act as magnets, drawing together all instances of the same type without requiring the learner to memorize all possible instances. The concept of a *frog,* then, becomes combined with other concepts to form larger patterns of increasing complexity. Figure 10.5 shows how concrete facts, rules, and sequences in a science curriculum (e.g., knowledge of elementary substances) must be combined with increasingly more abstract concepts and patterns (e.g., cellular forms, life functions, single-celled animals) to achieve higher order outcomes (e.g., understanding of multicellular living things and life groups). As lesson and unit goals move up the hierarchy, the teacher must move from a direct to an indirect model of instruction.

It is apparent that both your role as teacher and your organization of content need to be different for the learning of concepts, patterns, and relationships than for the learning of facts, rules, and sequences. Since the stimulus material presented to achieve higher order outcomes cannot efficiently contain all possible instances of the concept to be taught, it must provide its most critical dimensions.

The indirect instruction model uses instructional strategies that encourage the cognitive processes required both to form concepts and to combine them into larger patterns that promote inquiry and problem-solving skills. Figure 10.6 shows some of the indirect instruction strategies performed by a teacher using this model.

Figure 10.5 A Hierarchy Representing Possible Units of Instruction in a Science Curriculum

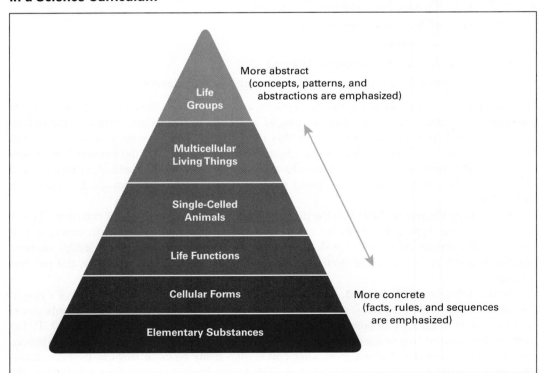

Figure 10.6 **Some Indirect Instruction Strategies**

1. *Content Organization:* Providing advance organizers that serve as "pegs" on which students
   - Hang key points
   - Focus learning in most productive areas
2. *Conceptual movement:* Induction and deduction using
   - Selected events to establish general concepts and patterns (induction)
   - Principles and generalizations that apply to specific events (deduction)
3. *Examples and nonexamples*
   - Introducing critical attributes that promote accurate generalizations
   - Gradually expanding a set of examples
   - Heightening discrimination with noncritical attributes
4. *Questions:* Raising questions that
   - Guide the search and discovery process
   - Present contradictions
   - Probe for deeper understanding
   - Point the discussion in new directions
   - Pass responsibility for learning to the student
5. *Learner experience* (Using student ideas): Encouraging students to
   - Use references from their own experience
   - Use examples to seek clarification
   - Draw parallels and associations
6. *Student self-evaluation*
   - Asking students to evaluate the appropriateness of their own responses
   - Providing cues, questions, and hints that call attention to inappropriate responses
7. *Discussion:* Promoting classroom dialogue that encourages students to
   - Examine alternatives
   - Judge solutions
   - Make predictions
   - Discover generalizations that encourage critical thinking

You can see from Figure 10.6 that indirect instruction is more complex than direct instruction. Classroom activities are less teacher-centered. This brings student ideas and experiences into the lesson and lets students begin evaluating their own responses. Because the outcomes are more complex, so, too, are your teaching strategies. To build toward these outcomes, extended forms of reasoning and questioning may be required.

The indirect instruction strategies in Figure 10.6 were among those having the highest correlation with positive student attitudes toward learning in a study by Fielding, Kame'enui, and Gerstein (1983). These also are the teaching strategies thought to be most useful in providing behaviors that students will use in subsequent grades, outside school, and in their adult lives (Hansen, 2011; Tombari & Borich, 1999; Williams, 2007).

An Example of Indirect Instruction

Now let's observe a classroom lesson in which the teacher is using indirect instructional strategies. This dialogue reflects some facts, rules, and sequences that were taught previously, but the ultimate goal is the learning of concepts and the teaching of inquiry and problem solving. As you read, note the use of bold italic type to identify indirect instruction strategies from Figure 10.6.

This dialogue provides a glimpse into a government class where a lesson on different economic systems is in progress. The teacher gets the students' attention by asking if anyone knows what system of government in the world is undergoing some changes. Marty raises his hand.

Teacher: Marty?

Marty: I think it's communism, because after the Soviet Union broke up, Russia instituted some changes.

Teacher: That's right, not unlike some countries in the Middle East that are also undergoing change. And because these changes will probably continue to affect all our lives in the years ahead, it may be a good idea to know what some different forms of government are and why some people choose to live or not live under them. To get us started, let me ask if anyone knows where the phrase "government of the people, by the people, for the people" comes from. [Rena raises her hand.] Rena?

Rena: From Lincoln's Gettysburg Address . . . I think near the end.

Teacher: That's right. Most nations have a similar statement that expresses the basic principles on which its laws, customs, and economics are based. Today we will study three systems by which nations guide and operate their economies. The three systems we will study are capitalism, socialism, and communism. They often are confused with the political systems that tend to be associated with them. A political system not only influences the economic system of a country but also guides individual behavior in many other areas, such as what is taught in schools, the relationship between church and state, how people are chosen for or elected to political office, and what newspapers can print. (***Content organization***)

For example, in the United States, we have an economic system that is based on the principles of capitalism—or private ownership of capital—and a political system that is based on the principle of democracy—or rule by the people. These two sets of principles are not the same, and in the next few days, you will see how they sometimes work in harmony and sometimes create contradictions that require changes in an economic or political system, like those occurring today in some countries around the world. (***Content organization***)

Today we will cover only systems dealing with the ownership of goods and services in different countries—that is, just the economic systems. Later I will ask you to distinguish these from political systems. Who would like to start by defining *capitalism*. What does the word *capitalism* mean to you? (***Questions***)

Robert: It means making money.

Teacher: What else, Robert?

Robert: Owning land . . . I think.

Teacher: Not only land, but . . . (***Probes for deeper understanding***)

Robert: Owning anything.

Teacher: The word *capital* means "tangible goods or possessions." Is a house tangible? (***Concept learning: deduction***)

Che-lim: Yes.

Teacher: Is a friendship tangible?

Che-lim: Yes.

Teacher: What about that, Mark? (***Asks student to self-evaluate***)

Mark: I don't think so.

Teacher: Why?

Mark: You can't touch it.

Teacher: Right. You can touch a person who is a friend but not the friendship. Besides you can't own or possess a person. So what would be a good definition of *tangible goods*?

Che-lim:	Something you own and can touch or see.
Teacher:	Not bad. Let me list some things on the board, and you tell me whether they can be called *capital*. [Writes the list.] (***Examples and nonexamples***)

        car

        stocks and bonds

        religion

        information

        clothes

        vacation

	OK. Who would like to say which of these are *capital*? [Ricky raises his hand.] (***Concept learning: deduction***)
Ricky:	Car and clothes are the only two I see.
Vanessa:	I'd add stocks and bonds. They say you own a piece of something, although maybe not the whole thing.
Teacher:	Could you see or touch it? (***Questions***)
Vanessa:	Yes, if you went to see the place or thing you owned a part of.
Teacher:	Good. What about a vacation? Did that give anyone trouble?
Mickey:	Well, you can own it . . . I mean you pay for it, and you can see yourself having a good time. [The class laughs.]
Teacher:	That may be true, so let's add one last condition to our definition of *capital*. You must be able to own it, see or touch it, and it must be durable—or last for a reasonable period of time. So now, how would you define *capitalism*? (***Concept learning: induction***)
Carey:	An economic system that allows you to have capital—or to own tangible goods that last for a reasonable period of time. And I suppose, to sell the goods, if you wanted.
Teacher:	Very good. Many different countries across the world have this form of economic system. Just to see if you've got the idea, who can name three countries, besides our own, that allow the ownership of tangible goods? (***Learner experience***)
Anton:	Canada, Japan, and . . . umm . . . Germany.
Teacher:	Good. In all these countries, capital, in the form of tangible goods, can be owned by individuals.

This dialogue illustrates one variation of the indirect model of instruction. Notice that this lesson used the naturally occurring dialogue of the classroom to encourage learners to bring their own experiences and past learning to the topic, rather than to acquire an understanding by having it presented to them in an already organized form. This lesson required learners to build an understanding of the topic collectively under the guidance of the teacher using one another's predictions, hypotheses, and experiences.

Look at Figure 10.6 again to review the teaching strategies used in indirect instruction. Now let's consider the extent to which this example lesson contains these key aspects of indirect instruction.

Content Organization

Comparing the dialogues for direct and indirect instruction, what differences do you notice? Obviously, they differ in complexity. Teaching for more complex outcomes takes more time and planning. The extensive planning needed for higher order learning is one of the most overlooked aspects of indirect instruction. With more expansive and complex content, the lesson must be introduced with a framework or structure that organizes the content into meaningful parts. This is the first step in planning for indirect instruction—organizing the content in advance.

One way of providing this framework to your learners is to use advance organizers (Ausubel, 1968; Borich & Tombari, 1997; Woolfolk, 2013). An advance organizer gives learners a conceptual preview of what is to come and helps prepare them to store, label, and package the content for retention and later use. In a sense, an advance organizer is a treelike structure with main limbs that act as pegs, or place holders, for the branches that are yet to come. Without these pegs on which to hang content, important distinctions can become easily blurred or lost.

To reinforce these distinctions, Burnette (1999) recommends concluding a lesson or unit with the same advance organizer that introduced it, so students can better envision where instruction began and ended. Advance organizers have been found especially helpful for students from diverse cultures and for English-language learners when the organizer includes links between familiar concepts and the new content to be learned (Lustig & Koester, 2009; Saunders & Goldenberg, 1999; Saunders, O'Brien, Lennon, & McLean, 1999).

For example, recall that our lesson dialogue began with an introduction about coverage of the day's lesson. To set the stage, the teacher introduced two concepts (economic systems and political systems), each comprising a complex network of relationships (*taxes, ownership, goods, services,* etc.). At the beginning of the lesson, the teacher alerted students to the reason for drawing such an early distinction between a political and an economic system. Figure 10.7 shows an advance organizer that this teacher might have used to open the lesson.

Advance organizers, especially for higher order outcomes (e.g., application, analysis, synthesis, and evaluation), represent themes or concepts at the beginning of a lesson or woven into it that provide an overview of the day's work and topics to come. Advance organizers can be presented orally or as charts and diagrams. Here are some examples with the advance organizer in italics.

- Showing a chart that illustrates the *skeletal evolution of humans* before the skeletal relationships among forms of animal life are presented (biology)
- Drawing examples of *right, equilateral, and isosceles triangles* before introducing the concept of a *right triangle* (math)
- Discussing the *origins of the Civil War* before describing its major battles (American history)
- Describing what is meant by *figures of speech* before introducing the concepts of metaphor and simile (English)

Figure 10.7 Advance Organizer for a Unit on Government

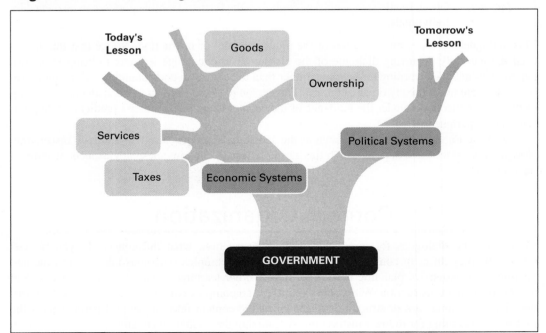

- Listening to examples of both *vowels and consonants* before teaching the vowel sounds (reading)
- Explaining the *origins of rock formations* before showing examples of igneous, metamorphic, and sedimentary rocks (science)

Notice that each of these examples presents a general theme or concept into which fits the specific content that is the subject of the day's lesson and possibly subsequent lessons. This is not accomplished by reviewing earlier content, which often is confused with the idea of an advance organizer. Instead it is done by creating a conceptual structure—skeletal evolution, various triangular shapes, Civil War origins, figures of speech, the alphabet, the evolution of rock formations—into which you can place not only the content to be taught but also that for related lessons.

Therefore, these advance organizers set the groundwork for focusing the lesson topic. They prevent every lesson from being seen as something entirely new. Finally, they integrate related concepts into larger and larger patterns that may represent unit outcomes. An advance organizer identifies the highest-level outcome to result from a lesson sequence and to which the present day's lesson will contribute. In our example dialogue, this higher order outcome was to distinguish between economic and political systems—a distinction organized in advance by the teacher's introductory remarks and graphic representation (Figure 10.7).

But before you choose an advance organizer, you will want to decide how you will organize and structure the content you will teach. For this, you will want to consider the concept learning, inquiry learning, and problem-centered approaches to learning.

Concept Learning

If the goal of your lesson is concept learning, your instruction will want to emphasize the essential attributes that bind seemingly dissimilar data, materials, objects, or events. Here students are taught a concept by seeing examples and nonexamples of an object or event, from which they learn the essential attributes that separate seemingly like objects or events.

In Chapter 9, we saw an example of concept learning and an advance organizer by diagramming the essential attributes of a frog that separates it from look-a-likes (toads, turtles, chameleons, etc.). As the learner is given more practice with examples and nonexamples of frogs, he or she recognizes a tightly woven combination of essential attributes (e.g., skin is smooth and moist, not warty and dry, can't change color; no tail, strong hind legs; makes deep hoarse sound). Concept learning is the search for the glue that holds together similar items and the attributes that can be used to distinguish examples of a given group or category from nonexamples.

The steps in a concept-learning lesson include (1) identifying the essential and nonessential attributes of the concept that you will present to students, (2) selecting positive and negative examples that distinguish the essential from the nonessential attributes, and, with the participation of your students, (3) developing decision rules that define the essential attributes for defining the concept.

Here is an example of a concept-learning lesson: "Math Facts That Equal Ten." For this lesson, the teacher does the following:

- Makes a list of both positive and negative examples of the concept *ten* and writes the examples on flash cards (positive examples, such as $6 + 4$, $12 - 2$, 10×1, etc.; negative examples, such as $7 + 2$, $15 - 4$, 2×4, etc.)
- Writes the words *Yes* and *No* as column headings on the board
- Presents the first flash card, $6 + 4$, and places it in the "Yes" column; presents the second card, $7 + 2$, and places it in the "No" column; and repeats the process with several more positive and negative examples
- Asks the class to look at the examples under each column and determine how they are the same and different
- Introduces more flash card examples and nonexamples of the concept, and asks students to choose under which column to put them; continues until most students have learned the concept

Figure 10.8 An Advance Organizer and Activity Sheet for the Concept Learning Lesson "Math Facts That Equal Ten"

What numbers can come together to make the number 10?

	Yes	No
5 + 5	5 + 5	
16 − 5		16 − 5
11 − 1		
12 − 2		
6 + 6		
6 × 2		
10 × 1		
3 + 4 + 4		
3 + 3		
12 − 4		
9 + 1		
2 + (2 × 3)		
4 × 2		
15 − 1		
3 + 4		
16 − 10		

- Asks students who have attained the concept to share their essential attributes for the concept *ten* with the remainder of the class
- Asks the class to create their own examples and come up and place them in the proper columns

By seeing numbers that do and do not form the concept, learners gradually learn to group all like instances and arrive at the essential attributes that define the concept. Figure 10.8 shows the advance organizer in the form of an activity sheet that this teacher used to introduce the concept and provide the structure for the lesson.

Inquiry Learning

The higher order goals of indirect instruction also include inquiry learning. If the goal of your lesson is to promote inquiry, you will want your instruction to emphasize how things are organized, how they change, and how they interrelate, within which concept learning may be a part of the larger inquiry process. Here the emphasis is on *how we come to know something,* more than on *what we know* (Borich & Hao, 2007; Ong & Borich, 2006).

For example, the teacher conducting the "Math Facts That Equal Ten" lesson may find that her lesson can be raised to a higher level by having students inquire into the use of a number line to show how addition, subtraction, and positive and negative numbers can be used to represent the concept *ten.* The result of this inquiry may be much less definite than the learning of a concept; in fact, the result is often more questions with which to continue the inquiry.

For example, in a physical science lesson on the internal structure of the earth, a teacher promoting facts, rules, and action sequences might give students the names and descriptions of the earth's layers—or *what we know.* But another teacher promoting inquiry might direct her students toward *how we know*—for example, "How do we know what the internal structure of the earth is like without ever having experienced it?" The former lesson requires the acquisition of facts told by the teacher, but the latter requires exploration and discovery by the students themselves. In this lesson, the inquiry process might turn to indirect measures of the internal structure of the earth and what some of these measures might be. Students might inquire about the methods used to explore beneath the earth's surface, such as the transmission and reflection of the shockwaves created by earthquakes, seismograph readings from oil exploration, and geological probes driven deep under the earth's surface to see how it has changed over time.

Using examples of shockwaves from around the world, this teacher might ask several questions of her students to organize the inquiry process that do the following:

- Go beyond immediately available information. ("What do we know from looking at these shockwaves from a recent earthquake?")
- Interpret the consequences of information or ideas. ("What do the shockwaves from these two different earthquakes tell us about how deep the earth's crust is?")
- Make predictions as a way of making students use the information they have gained from their inquiry. ("Given the shockwaves from around the world you have seen, where do you predict the next earthquake will be?")

Unlike concept learning, the inquiry approach leads to alternative paths and solutions in the process of exploring and discovering new information about a topic. Figure 10.9 shows the advance organizer that this teacher used to introduce the lesson "Beneath the Earth's Surface" with a framework or structure that organizes its content and promotes the goal of inquiry. Also see In Practice: Focus on Inquiry Learning.

Figure 10.9 **Advance Organizer for the Inquiry Lesson "Beneath the Earth's Surface"**

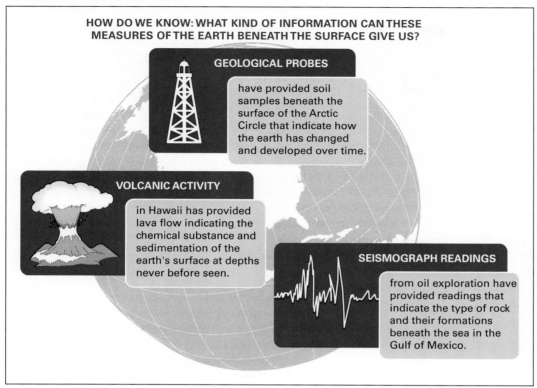

HOW DO WE KNOW: WHAT KIND OF INFORMATION CAN THESE MEASURES OF THE EARTH BENEATH THE SURFACE GIVE US?

GEOLOGICAL PROBES have provided soil samples beneath the surface of the Arctic Circle that indicate how the earth has changed and developed over time.

VOLCANIC ACTIVITY in Hawaii has provided lava flow indicating the chemical substance and sedimentation of the earth's surface at depths never before seen.

SEISMOGRAPH READINGS from oil exploration have provided readings that indicate the type of rock and their formations beneath the sea in the Gulf of Mexico.

In Practice

Focus on Inquiry Learning

In the process of inquiry, students identify problems, brainstorm solutions, formulate questions, investigate problems, analyze and interpret results, discuss, reflect, make conclusions, and present results (Bruner, 2004; Wiske, 1994). This cycle of inquiry serves as a general model for teachers planning inquiry activities that can guide students through the inquiry process. One version of the inquiry–learning cycle is the Ask, Investigate, Create, Discuss, and Reflect model illustrated in the accompanying figure. It is a five-step model for implementing an inquiry based lesson or unit.

Step 1. Ask

To promote the desire to discover, the teacher begins by raising questions and inviting students to plan the inquiry procedures and presentation of findings. The teacher initiates the inquiry process by posing the lesson topic in the form of a question and then probing,

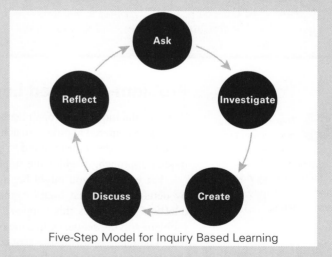

Five-Step Model for Inquiry Based Learning

prompting, and redirecting student responses to establish the inquiry climate. This is called the *teacher-initiated phase.*

When students are comfortable with the process, the teacher encourages them to raise a question of their own, to plan a procedure for answering the question, to determine how to carry out the procedure, and to decide how the results might be presented. This is called the *student-initiated phase*. This phase is a vehicle for building student-initiated questions and student-directed procedures that bring students to an independent level of inquiry. A question or a problem is the focus at this stage, which may be redefined later in the inquiry process.

Step 2. Investigate

After a student question is agreed on, the next step is to investigate it. At this stage of the inquiry, students are asked to recall prior knowledge or experiences related to the question and to brainstorm possible methods of investigating it by identifying resources and designing and carrying out a plan of action. Students also may redefine their question as new information unfolds. This information-gathering stage is a self-motivated process that is owned by the engaged students.

Step 3. Create

When the teacher and students have jointly determined that sufficient information has been gathered, students are asked to begin thinking critically about the relationship between the information (evidence) and their question—for example, how the information may or may not answer the question fully or completely. Here students synthesize the information they have uncovered to create new knowledge, which may be beyond their and possibly the teacher's prior experience. They start thinking critically about the appropriateness of their question or hypothesis, redefine their question and/or construct new ones, and decide whether to gather more data. Some interim product is expected at this stage, such as a chart synthesizing the information collected, an oral presentation that summarizes progress thus far, or a list of new or redefined questions.

Step 4. Discuss

At this stage, students discuss their findings, new ideas, and experiences with one another. Students share their experiences and investigations in their learning community, which can be a collaborative group or the entire class. When a small-group format is used, different groups may use the inquiry process to answer different questions that may have evolved from Steps 2 and 3. The task at this stage may include comparing notes, discussing conclusions, and sharing experiences across groups.

Step 5. Reflect

After discussion, students critique and communicate their results to their learning community (group or class), during which they are expected to reflect on their newly acquired knowledge. Methods for presenting findings are selected in consultation with the teacher. These methods can include a traditional written or oral report or a more extensive multimedia presentation, production, or exhibit (Martinello & Cook, 2000). Students' tasks include reflecting on the appropriateness of their question, their methods of investigation, and the accuracy of their conclusions. These tasks encourage students, either in groups or as a class, to evaluate whether a satisfactory solution was found, whether a new question is warranted, and, if so, what the new question might be by taking inventory of what has been done and making new observations. If new questions emerge, the cycle of inquiry can start again with a new lesson.

Problem-Centered Learning

There are several components to problem-centered learning. Pay close attention to this **video** and try to identify the components.

Whereas the inquiry approach leads to alternative paths and solutions in exploring new information, a problem-centered approach to achieving higher order outcomes identifies and provides for students in advance all the steps required to solve a particular problem. It is therefore less open ended than the inquiry approach, in which the steps to a task are explored and discovered through student inquiry.

For example, you might begin a general science lesson on "The Invisible Forces of Gravity" by demonstrating that liquid cannot be sucked through a straw from a tightly sealed bottle. The question "Why does this happen?" establishes the problem. You then might give your students a problem-solving sequence like the one shown in Figure 10.10 to guide their investigation of the problem. The chart, showing the sequence of events, becomes an advance organizer for the lesson that the class can follow. Each step provides an organizational branch for a particular part of the lesson.

Further content organization is provided by another advance organizer in Figure 10.11. Here the problem has been organized hierarchically to show the internal branching, or decisions, that must be followed to arrive at a conclusion. This form of content organizer can provide a particularly effective attention getter when students are asked to contribute decision points to the organizer as

Figure 10.10 **Sequential Advance Organizer for the Problem-Solving Lesson "The Invisible Forces of Gravity"**

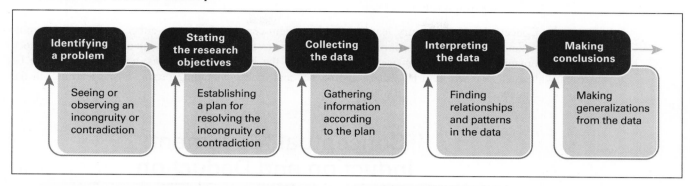

the problem is being solved and to trace each decision point (indicated by a solid line) to answer the question, "Why doesn't the liquid flow through the straw?"

A problem-centered organization of a lesson or unit recognizes the need to develop problem-solving skills as well as the knowledge and skills to respond to previously unforeseen circumstances. Problem-centered learning has several distinct characteristics that guide lesson and unit development (Delisle, 1997; Darling-Hammond, et al., 2008; Lambros, 2002; Teo, 2006). When planning a problem-centered lesson or unit, remember to do these things:

- Clearly define the problem. Although the solution may not be in sight, the problem should be described in detail and placed within a meaningful context that connects with your learners' everyday experience.

- Make clear to your learners that they are to predict how to solve the problem. Predictions should be achievable within a realistic time frame and with available resources and should be altered as new information is obtained.

- Indicate that learners will be expected to access, evaluate, and utilize data from a variety of sources. They will need to critically examine their sources and reject those that are less credible or are opinion rather than fact.

Figure 10.11 **Hierarchical Advance Organizer for the Problem-Solving Lesson "The Invisible Forces of Gravity"**

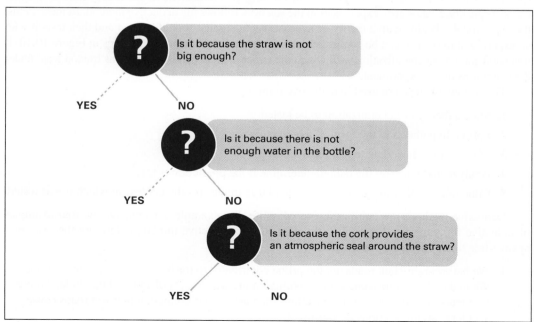

- Require that solutions fit the problem and be accompanied by clearly stated reasons as to their value or effectiveness (e.g., can be implemented more quickly, at less cost, or with superior results).

Concept learning, inquiry learning, and problem-centered learning—either singly or in combination—are useful tools for organizing your lessons for indirect instruction and providing advance organizers that communicate to your students the key steps, decisions, and relationships to be learned. We will return to these approaches and others, including project-based learning, in the chapters ahead.

Conceptual Movement: Induction and Deduction

Our next teaching strategies for indirect instruction are induction and deduction.

Induction is a form of reasoning used to draw a conclusion or make a generalization from specific instances (Stadler, 2011). It is a process in which students observe specific facts and then generalize them to other circumstances. Much of our everyday thinking proceeds in this manner, as illustrated by these examples:

1. We notice that rain-slick roads are causing accidents on the way to school, so we reduce our speed at all subsequent intersections.
2. We get an unsatisfactory grade on a chemistry exam, so we study six extra hours a week for the rest of the semester in all our subjects.
3. We see a close friend suffer from the effects of drug abuse, so we volunteer to disseminate information about substance abuse to all our acquaintances.
4. We have a math teacher who is cold and unfriendly, so we decide never to enroll in a math course again.

What these examples have in common is that they start with a specific observation of a limited set of data and end with a generalization to a much broader context. Between the beginning and end of each sequence is an interpretation of observed events and the projection of this interpretation to all similar circumstances.

Deduction is reasoning that proceeds from principles or generalizations to their application in specific instances. Deductive thinking includes testing generalizations to see if they hold in specific cases. Typically, a laboratory experiment in the sciences follows the deductive method. In these fields, the experimenter begins with a theory or hypothesis about what should happen and then tests it with an experiment to see if it can be confirmed, as was shown by the sequence of steps in Figure 10.10. If it is confirmed, the generalization with which the experiment began is accepted as true, at least under the conditions of the experiment.

The following steps are used in deductive thinking:

1. State a theory or generalization to be tested.
2. Form a hypothesis in the form of a prediction.
3. Observe or collect data to test the hypothesis.
4. Analyze and interpret the data to determine if the prediction is true.
5. Conclude whether the generalization held true in the specific context in which it was tested.

Deductive methods are familiar in everyday life. For example, let's change the four examples of inductive thinking listed previously to examples of deductive thinking. Here are the examples again—this time, illustrating deduction:

1. We believe rain-slick roads are the prime contributor to traffic accidents at intersections. We make observations one rainy morning on the way to school and find that indeed more accidents have occurred at intersections than usual. Our prediction that wet roads cause accidents at intersections is confirmed.

2. We believe that studying more will not substantially raise our grades. We study six extra hours for our math test and find that our grade has gone up. Our prediction that extra studying won't help our grades turns out to be wrong.

3. We believe that drug abuse can be detrimental to one's physical and emotional well-being. We observe and find physical and emotional effects of drug abuse in acquaintances who have admitted to using them. Our prediction that drug abuse and physical and emotional impairment are related has been confirmed.

4. We believe we will never like a math class because they are taught by cold and unfriendly teachers. We are required to take a math class and find we have just such a teacher. Our prediction that math classes are taught by cold and unfriendly teachers has been shown to be accurate—at least in this instance.

These examples of deduction have in common the fact that they begin with a general statement of belief—a theory and hypothesis—and end with some conclusion (deduction) based on an observation that tested the truth of that theory or hypothesis. Of course, our observation only entailed one instance of that theory or hypothesis; we could be wrong in some other instances. (For example, you might have no problem liking math taught by another instructor or liking sports, despite the fact that you once had a cold and unfriendly gym teacher.) As you might expect, deductive logic has been most closely associated with the scientific method.

Applying Induction and Deduction

Both induction and deduction are important tools for concept learning, inquiry learning, and problem-centered learning. Let's see how they were accomplished in our classroom dialogue on economic systems.

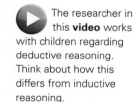

The researcher in this **video** works with children regarding deductive reasoning. Think about how this differs from inductive reasoning.

Using deduction, the teacher built a definition of tangible goods and tested it with a specific example: "Is a house tangible?" Notice how the examples increased in abstraction to better define what could be considered *tangible* (e.g., stocks and bonds). Also the teacher provided both examples and nonexamples to fine-tune this concept by showing that tangible goods in a capitalist system could exist at different levels but that some things (e.g., friendships, vacations) could not qualify as tangible goods. Also notice that a brief venture into deduction ended the teacher's introduction to capitalism. By asking students to name three countries that fit the concept of *capitalism,* he made them find specific instances that fit the general concept. This teacher also skillfully used the inductive process, beginning with specific instances of tangible goods (e.g., owning land) and increasingly broadening these instances to form a generalization (i.e., tangible goods are those things that last for a reasonable length of time).

Note that although at the end of the first part of the lesson most students understood the concept of *capitalism* as an economic system that allows the ownership of tangible goods that last, it was a rather crude interpretation that would fail subsequent tests. For example, citizens of most socialist and communist countries own tangible goods that last a reasonable period of time (e.g., a wristwatch, a car, a set of dinnerware). Recall that this crude version of the concept of *capitalism* emerged even after carefully planned examples and nonexamples were provided. This means the teacher's job was not over. Further conceptual movement would have to be made to fine-tune this concept, producing more accurate discriminations to be applied to the concept of *capitalism.*

The teaching of concepts with the indirect instructional model uses inductive and deductive thinking to

Many forms of investigation and laboratory experiments follow the deductive method in which the student begins with a prediction about what should happen in a specific instance and then conducts an investigation to see if the prediction comes true.

Table 10.2 **Comparison of Steps in Inductive versus Deductive Teaching**

Teaching Inductively	Teaching Deductively
1. The teacher presents specific data from which a generalization is to be drawn.	1. The teacher introduces the generalization to be learned.
2. Each student is allowed uninterrupted time to observe or study the data that illustrate the generalization.	2. The teacher reviews the task-relevant prior facts, rules, and action sequences needed to form the generalization.
3. Students are shown additional examples and then nonexamples supporting the generalization.	3. Students raise a question, pose a hypothesis, or make a prediction thought to be supported by the generalization.
4. Student attention is guided first to the critical (relevant) aspects of the data supporting the generalization and then to the noncritical (irrelevant) aspects.	4. Data, events, materials, and objects are gathered and observed to test the prediction.
5. A generalization is made that distinguishes the examples from the nonexamples.	5. The results of the test are analyzed and a conclusion is drawn as to whether the prediction is supported by the data, events, materials, or objects that were observed.
	6. The starting generalization is refined or revised in accordance with the observations.

develop initially crude and overly restrictive concepts into more expansive and accurate under-standings. Table 10.2 illustrates the different steps involved in inductive versus deductive teaching.

Using Examples and Nonexamples

You may learn the rule "Stop at red lights" to perfection, but until you have seen examples of when to modify the rule (e.g., when an emergency vehicle with flashing lights is behind you), you do not have the complete *concept* of a *red light,* only the *rule.*

To learn concepts, learners need to go beyond the acquisition of facts, rules, and sequences to be able to distinguish examples from nonexamples (Mayer & Alexander, 2010; Mayer & Wittrock, 1996). Observing examples and nonexamples—for example, when studying six extra hours pays off and when it does not, when disseminating drug abuse literature is likely to help and when it is not, when a cold and unfriendly teacher is likely to adversely affect your performance in a subject and when it is not—allows you to grasp concepts.

Examples represent the concept being taught by including all of the attributes essential for recognizing that concept as a member of some larger class. **Nonexamples** fail to represent the concept being taught by purposely not including one or more of the attributes essential for recognizing it as a member of some larger class. The use of examples and nonexamples defines the essential and nonessential attributes of a concept needed to identify it and make accurate generalizations about it.

Recall from our classroom dialogue some of the distinctions between the private ownership of goods and services under socialism compared to capitalism. How could this teacher develop this concept? The teacher would have to make clear that private ownership of goods and services in the context of different economic systems is always a matter of degree. That is, the system determines not only what is owned by the government but how much and therefore what is unavailable for private ownership. Accordingly, the teacher might elicit a set of interchanges to bring out these points.

Teacher:	What types of things could a group of people—say, the size of a nation—agree on that would be absolutely essential for everyone's existence?
Ronnie:	Food.
Teacher:	Good. What else?
Vanessa:	Clothes.
Teacher:	Very good.
Carey:	Cars.
Teacher:	What do you think about cars?
Ricky:	If they couldn't agree on the importance of cars for everyone, then they would have to agree on some form of public transportation, like buses and trains.
Teacher:	Yes, they would, wouldn't they? The examples show that private ownership within different economic systems is a matter of degree that depends on (a) what everyone values equally and (b) what everyone needs for everyday existence.

The teacher began the discussion by having students think about things that "a group of people—say, the size of a nation—[could] agree on that would be absolutely essential for everyone's existence"—thereby encouraging students to broaden their earlier and perhaps more narrow concepts of *capitalism* and *socialism*.

Notice also how this teacher used examples and nonexamples to sharpen distinctions and deepen understanding in these ways:

1. Using examples that vary in ways that are important to the concept being defined (e.g., a house is tangible, stocks and bonds are abstract, but both are instances of the concept of tangible goods)

2. Including nonexamples of the concept that nonetheless represent important dimensions of the concept (e.g., a vacation can be bought but is not durable and therefore not an instance of the concept of tangible goods)

3. Explaining why nonexamples *are* nonexamples, even though they may share some of the same characteristics (e.g., cars versus a public transportation system could not discriminate private ownership among economic systems)

Using Questions

Guiding concept learning, inquiry learning, and problem-centered learning with questions is the fourth indirect instruction strategy. One difference you may have noticed between the direct and indirect instruction dialogues is the way the teacher asks questions. In the direct instruction dialogue, the questions were specific and to the point, aimed at eliciting a single right answer. But in the indirect instruction dialogue, the questions steered students to seek and discover the answers with minimum assistance from the teacher. In direct instruction, answering questions is how students show what they know so you may provide clues, hints, and probes. In indirect instruction, your questions guide students into discovering new dimensions of a problem or ways of resolving a dilemma.

The indirect instruction dialogue included several questions that guided the inquiry process. The purposes of this teacher's questioning were to focus students' attention and to promote the widest possible discussion of the topic from the students' point of view, thereby connecting with the students' own experiences. In this manner, the class begins with everyone being able to participate, regardless of his or her task-relevant prior knowledge. By accepting almost any answer at the beginning, this teacher used student responses to formulate subsequent questions and begin the inquiry process to shape more accurate responses.

Small-group discussions often require the teacher to become a moderator, visiting each group periodically to answer questions, review and summarize, redirect group work, provide new or more accurate information, and achieve consensus.

The point of using questioning strategies in indirect instruction then is not to arrive at the correct answer in the quickest and most efficient manner. Rather the point is to begin an inquiry process that not only forms successively more correct answers but also forms those answers using a personal search-and-discovery process chosen by the learner and guided by the teacher. For example, the teacher followed up Robert's response that capitalism means "making money" with the question "What else?" and followed Robert's next response ("owning land") with a leading response ("Not only land but . . ."), encouraging Robert to broaden his answer.

By beginning with a broad question such as "What does the word *capitalism* mean to you?" this teacher could have been confronted just as easily with the task of narrowing, not broadening, Robert's first response. In the next interchange, this problem actually occurs, because Robert replies that capitalism means "owning anything." Now the job is to narrow or limit his response, which is accomplished by presenting the first essential attribute of the concept of *capitalism:* tangible goods.

You can see that a single guided question in the context of indirect instruction is seldom useful in itself. Questions must dovetail into other questions that continually refocus the response (e.g., broaden, then narrow, then broaden slightly again) to keep the search going. The process is much like focusing a camera, because rarely is the camera initially set at the right focus for the subject. Similarly, we could not expect Robert's first response to represent perfectly the concept of *capitalism.* Just as one begins focusing the camera in the appropriate direction, often passing the point at which the subject is in focus, so did the teacher's follow-up probe lead Robert to overshoot the mark and respond with too broad a response (e.g., "owning anything"). The teacher acknowledged the error and slightly narrowed Robert's response by noting, "The word *capital* means 'tangible goods or possessions.'"

In addition to the questions we saw earlier that can guide the inquiry process, there are others that can do the following:

- Present contradictions to be resolved ("Who owns the highways under capitalism?")
- Probe for deeper, more thorough responses ("So what would be a good definition of *tangible goods?*")
- Extend the discussion to new areas ("What things could a group of people—say, the size of a nation—agree are absolutely essential for everyone's existence?")
- Pass responsibility back to the class ("Good question. Who knows the answer to who pays for services provided under a socialist system?")

Questions like these guide the inquiry process to increasingly better responses. This process is one of the most useful for achieving higher order outcomes, where the back-and-forth (first wider, then narrower) focusing of student responses often is required to attain the appropriate level of generalization. We will have more to say about questioning strategies that can stimulate self-directed learning in the next chapter.

Learner Experience and Use of Student Ideas

The Changing View

Until recently, the use of student ideas was considered the centerpiece of indirect instruction. Using student ideas meant incorporating student experiences, points of view, feelings, and problems into the lesson by making the student the primary point of reference. A completely student-oriented lesson might be initiated by asking students what problems they were having with the content; these problems then would become the focus of the lesson. This approach was intended to heighten student interest, organize content around student problems, tailor feedback to individual students, and encourage positive attitudes and feelings toward the subject.

Although this was a laudable instructional strategy, the goals of incorporating student ideas into the lesson in this particular format often became the end itself, rather than the means by which learning could be accomplished. With this view, many forms of problem-centered learning, inquiry learning, and concept learning were thought to be synonymous with open, freewheeling discussions that began and ended with student-determined ideas and content.

Although heightening student interest, selecting content based on student problems, and increasing affect are important goals, in the indirect instruction model they are best achieved in a carefully crafted teacher-student dialogue that promotes higher order thinking. These goals can and should be achieved in the context of classroom dialogue that encourages students to connect with lesson content by using examples from, drawing parallels to and associations with their own experiences to achieve your instructional goals. Therefore, in the indirect instruction model, use of student ideas is a means of promoting inquiry, attaining essential concepts, and solving problems as a springboard to higher order thinking.

Using Student Ideas Productively

So how can teachers productively use student ideas in the context of indirect instruction? In this context, you can use student ideas in the following ways:

- Encourage students to use examples and references from their own experience, from which they can construct their own meanings.

- Share mental strategies by which the students can learn more easily and efficiently by seeing and hearing how you think through a question or problem.

- Ask students to seek clarification of, to draw parallels to, and make associations with things they already know.

- Encourage understanding and retention of ideas by relating them to students' own sphere of interests, concerns, and problems.

For examples of these uses, recall the dialogue about economic systems. By asking students to name three countries other than their own that follow a capitalistic economic system, the teacher elicited examples and references from the learners' experience.

Perhaps more important than the questions themselves was the way in which the teacher incorporated students' responses into the lesson. By asking what the word *capitalism* "means to you," this teacher was asking students to express themselves by using parallels and associations they already understood—perhaps by having a job, recalling a conversation with their parents about occupations, or by remembering television images of life in another country. Parallels and associations such as these are likely to be vastly different among students. This is desirable, both for heightening student interest and involvement and for exposing students to a variety of responses, many of which may be appropriate instances of the concept to be learned.

Finally, notice within the context of our dialogue that student ideas remained content-centered. The instruction allowed students to participate in determining the form in which learning occurred but not the substance of what was learned. This substance will usually be determined by your curriculum guide and textbook. Our example dialogue therefore contrasts with what is called **student-centered learning**, which allows students to select both the form and the substance. This is sometimes associated with **unguided discovery learning**, wherein the goal is to maintain a high level of student interest. This is accomplished largely by selecting content based on student problems or interests and by providing individually tailored feedback. Whether your approach is guided (as in this example) or unguided (as in the completion of an independent project or assignment), some preorganization and planning always will be necessary before you solicit and use student ideas.

Student Self-Evaluation

The sixth strategy for indirect instruction is to engage students in evaluating their own responses and thereby take responsibility for their own learning. You can encourage self-evaluation by gradually giving control of the evaluation function to your learners. One way of accomplishing this is by allowing learners to provide reasons for their answers so you and other students can suggest needed changes. Recall that early in the dialogue, the teacher let the students know that some of the responsibility for determining appropriate answers would fall on them. After writing a list on the board, the teacher said, "OK. Who would like to say which of these are *capital*?" The message is received when Ricky responds and Vanessa modifies Ricky's response:

> *Ricky:*   Car and clothes are the only two I see.
>
> *Vanessa:*   I'd add stocks and bonds. They say you own a piece of something, although maybe not the whole thing.

Even after Vanessa's effort to correct Ricky's response, the teacher still does not supply an answer. Instead, she keeps the evaluation of the previous responses going by responding with "Could you see or touch it?"

The goal here was to create a student dialogue focused on the appropriateness of the previous answers. The success of this self-evaluation strategy is most readily seen in the dialogue that occurs between the students and teacher. This strategy promotes a student-to-student-back-to-teacher interchange, as opposed to the more familiar teacher-to-student-back-to-teacher interchange. The teacher's role is to maintain the momentum by offering hints or focusing statements that students can use to evaluate their previous responses. Classes of students who have knowledge of the content can sustain three, four, or even five successive exchanges among themselves before some redirection becomes necessary and control returns to the teacher. This is the mark of an effective and engaging group discussion that promotes higher order thinking.

In the process of these exchanges, students learn the reasons for their answers in slow, measured steps and often from other students. And by allowing partially correct answers to become the bases for more accurate ones, the teacher can model for the class how to turn incorrect and partially correct answers into better ones. Especially during problem-centered learning, inquiry learning, and concept learning, these layers of refinement, gradually built up by student interchange, help students evaluate and refine their own responses.

Use of Group Discussion

When student-to-student-to-teacher exchanges grow into protracted interactions among a large number of students, a **full-group discussion** has begun (Burbules & Bruce, 2001). In this type of discussion, you may intervene only occasionally to review and summarize main points, or you may schedule periodic time-outs to evaluate the group's progress and to redirect, if necessary.

Group discussions can be useful for encouraging critical thinking, for engaging learners in the learning process, and for promoting the cooperative reasoning that is necessary in a democratic society (Brookfield & Preskill, 2005; Dillon, 1995; Gall & Gall, 1990; Hale & City, 2006). Because group discussion helps students think critically—to examine alternatives, judge solutions, make predictions, and discover generalizations—it is yet another approach to teaching concepts, inquiry, and problem solving. It is our seventh and last indirect instruction strategy.

When your objective is to teach content that is well structured in the text or workbook, a presentation–recitation format may be more efficient and effective than a discussion. This might be the case with topics requiring little personal opinion and judgment, for which agreement may be so high as to preclude the flexibility needed to promote alternative viewpoints and solutions.

But sometimes concept learning, inquiry learning, and problem-centered learning can take on a less formal structure. At these times, a lack of consensus can make a group discussion particularly lively and rewarding. Here are some examples of discussion-oriented questions within which concept learning, inquiry learning, and problem-centered learning can occur:

- In what ways do you believe the cities of tomorrow can accommodate our growing population?

- In time of crisis or war, how can the legislative branch of government be influenced by the executive branch?

- Do you think "Little Red Riding Hood" is fact or fiction? In what ways might it have been real in the mind of its author?

- Technology—such as computers, smart phones, and video games—can make our lives more comfortable and connected, but it has also allowed us to become so-called couch potatoes. In what ways can technology be used to help us become more fit?

- We once thought antibiotics were the magic bullet that removed the threat of infectious diseases. Now we know that the use of antibiotics has helped create new dangerous and resistant strains of bacteria. What are some other scientific advancements that have solved one problem but created another?

- Cinderella was poor and unloved but had a fairy godmother to help her out. Wilbur from *Charlotte's Web* was the runt of a litter and saved from death first by Fern and then by Charlotte. But most of us who are poor, little, or unloved do not have such magical or determined protectors. What are some ways to overcome these problems by yourself? Name people from stories, movies, or real life who tapped their own resources to make their dreams come true.

- With changes in technology and economics, many jobs have been eliminated. We no longer have elevator operators or gas station attendants, for instance. Even travel agents are in danger of losing their customers to the Internet. What are some other jobs that may fade away and some that may come into existence with new technological advancements?

Topics such as these, which are not formally structured by the text and for which a high degree of consensus may not yet exist, make good candidates for discussion sessions for solving problems, promoting inquiry, and learning essential concepts. During these discussions, you are the moderator and your **moderating tasks** are as follows:

1. *Orienting the students to the objective of the discussion* ("Today we will discuss when a nation should decide to go to war. Specifically, we will discuss the meaning of the concept of *aggression* as it has occurred in history. In the context of a war between nations, your job at the end of the discussion will be to arrive at a concept that could help a president decide if sufficient aggression has occurred to warrant going to war.")

2. *Providing new or more accurate information where needed* ("It is not correct to assume that World War II started with the bombing of Pearl Harbor. Many events occurred earlier on the European continent that some nations considered to be aggression.")

3. *Reviewing, summarizing, or putting together opinions and facts into a meaningful relationship* ("Jin, Laura, and William, you seem to be arguing that the forcible entry of one nation into the territory of another nation constitutes aggression, and the rest of the class seems to be saying that undermining the economy of another nation also can constitute aggression.")

4. *Adjusting the flow of information and ideas to be most productive for the goals of the lesson* ("Mark, you seem to have extended our concept of *aggression* to include criticizing the government of another nation through political means, such as media broadcasts, speeches at the United Nations, and so forth. But that fits better the idea of a cold war, and we are trying to study some of the instances of aggression that might have started World War II.")

5. *Combining ideas and promoting compromise to arrive at an appropriate consensus* ("We seem to have two concepts of *aggression*—one dealing with the forcible entry of one nation into the territory of another and another that has to do with undermining a nation's economy. Can we combine these two ideas by saying that anything that threatens either a nation's people or its prosperity or both can be considered aggression?")

These moderating functions can help you guide and redirect a large-group discussion without overly restricting the flow of ideas. During a large-group discussion, you should frequently perform one or more of these moderating functions to keep the groups on task and moving toward a final oral report or other group product. The more familiar the topic and the greater the consensus, the more you can relinquish authority to the group.

Small-group discussions, involving four to six students per group, may also be used during indirect instruction (Cohen, 1994; Galanes & Adams, 2009; Nash, 2008). When multiple topics must be discussed within the same lesson and time does not permit a full-class discussion of them in sequential order, try using three, four, or five small groups simultaneously.

You have three tasks in forming and guiding small group discussions: (1) to form groups whose members can work together, (2) to distribute students with diverse learning needs across groups, and (3) to move among the groups to periodically focus the discussion and resolve problems. Stopping the groups periodically, either to inform the entire class of important insights discovered by a group or to apply moderating functions, will help keep the groups close together and maintain your direction and authority (Cragan, Wright, & Kasch, 2008).

Another group format for indirect instruction is to have students work in pairs or teams. This can be an effective format when the discussion entails writing (e.g., a summary report), looking up information (in the text, encyclopedia, etc.), or preparing materials (chart, diagram, graph, etc.) (Gillies, 2007; Johnson & Johnson, 2008; Jolliffe, 2007; Slavin, 2001). In the **pair or team discussions** arrangement, your role as moderator increases in proportion to the number of pairs or teams, so only brief interchanges with each may be possible.

The pair or team approach works best when the task is more structured, when some consensus about the topic already exists, and when the orienting instructions fully define each member's role (e.g., Student A searches for the information, Student B writes a summary description of what is found, and both students read the summary for final agreement). Pairs or teams frequently become highly task oriented, so pairing or teaming tends to be most productive when the discussion objectives go beyond just delivering an oral report and include presenting a product to the class.

Gunter, Estes, and Mintz (2010) describe a pair arrangement based on the work of Lyman (1981). **Think, pair, share** is a simple technique in which students learn from one another and get to try out their ideas in a nonthreatening context before presenting them to the class. The benefits for the teacher include increased time on task in the classroom and greater quality of students' contributions to class discussions.

There are four steps to think, pair, share, and a time limit on each step is signaled by the teacher:

1. *The teacher poses a question.* The process of think, pair, share begins when the teacher poses a thought-provoking question for the entire class. Questions with single right answers are avoided. Questions must pose problems or dilemmas that students will be willing and able to think about.

2. *The students think individually.* Responding to a signal from the teacher, students are given a limited amount of time to think of their own answers to the problematic question. The time should be decided by the teacher on the basis of knowledge of the students, the nature of the question, and the demands of the schedule.

3. *Each student discusses his or her answer with a fellow student.* The end of the "think" step signals to the students that it is time to begin working with another student to reach consensus on an answer to the question. Each student now has a chance to try out possibilities. Together each pair of students can reformulate a common answer based on their collective insights to possible solutions to the problem.

4. *Students share their answers with the whole class.* In this final step, individuals present solutions individually or cooperatively to the whole class. Where pairs of students have constructed displays of their answers, as in a chart or diagram, each member of the pair can take credit for his or her specific contribution.

The success and quality of the think, pair, share activity will depend on the quality of the question posed in Step 1. If the question promotes genuine thought for students, genuine discussion and sharing will emerge from the successive steps.

Here is an example lesson plan for our indirect instruction dialogue, following the written format provided in Chapter 6.

Example Indirect Instruction Lesson Plan

Social Studies

Unit Title: Economic Systems

Lesson Title: Comparisons and Contrasts among Capitalist, Socialist, and Communist Economies

1 Gaining attention. Ask if anyone knows where the phrase "government of the people, by the people, for the people" comes from to establish the idea that the principles and rules by which a country is governed also influence its economic system.

2 Informing the learner of the objective. *This session:* To relate economic systems to the ownership of goods and services in different countries. *Next session:* To be able to distinguish economic systems from political systems and to show why some economic systems are changing.

3 Stimulating recall of prerequisite learning. Ask for a definition of *capitalism,* and then refine it with questioning and probing. Continue probing until students arrive at a definition of *capitalism* as "an economic system that allows the ownership of tangible goods that last for a reasonable period of time." Check understanding by asking for three countries (other than ours) that have capitalist economies.

4 Presenting the stimulus material.

A. Ask what the word *socialism* means. Refine the definition by questioning and probing until a definition is arrived at that defines *socialism* as "an economic system that allows the government to control and make available to everyone as many things as possible that (1) everyone values equally and that (2) are seen as essential for everyday existence." Have students compare capitalism and socialism by degree of ownership of public services and degree of taxes paid under each system.

B. Ask what the word *communism* means, and establish its relationship to the idea of *community.* Refine the definition, using the concept of degree of ownership by questioning and probing until the students arrive at still more examples of things owned and controlled by the government under communism.

5 Eliciting the desired behavior.

A. Use questions to encourage identification of the public services most commonly owned under socialism—for example, hospitals, trains, and communication systems. Some types of farms and industries will also be accepted when their relation to the public good is understood.

B. Use questions to encourage identification of the public services most commonly owned under communism—for example, food supply, housing, and industries. Emphasize those services and goods that are different from those identified under capitalism and socialism.

C. Use questions to identify the amounts and types of things owned by the government across the three systems—socialism, communism, and capitalism—to establish the concept that differences among the systems are a matter of degree of ownership and degree of taxation.

6 Providing feedback. Pose questions in a manner that encourages the student to evaluate his or her own response and the responses of other students. Probe until the student's responses approximate an acceptable answer. On the blackboard, list side by side those goods and services the students have identified as likely to be owned by the government in all three systems and those likely to be owned uniquely by any one or combination of systems. Distinguish between these goods and services and the personal items students may have mentioned, such as clothes or household goods, which cannot be used to distinguish economic systems.

7 Assessing the behavior. After students have written an essay describing the economic systems of three countries of their own choosing, each of which represents a different economic system, grade them on their comprehension of the concepts of (1) *degree of ownership* and (2) *degree of taxation,* as cited in the textbook.

Comparison of Direct and Indirect Instruction

The direct and indirect instruction models were presented in separate chapters because each includes distinctive teaching strategies. As you have seen, the models have two different purposes:

- The *direct instruction model* is best suited to the teaching of facts, rules, and action sequences and comprises six teaching strategies: monitoring and diagnosing to gauge progress and inform reteaching, presenting and structuring new content, guided student practice, feedback and correcting errors, reaching mastery through independent practice, and reviews over time.

- The *indirect instruction model* is best suited for concept learning, inquiry learning, and problem-centered learning, and comprises seven teaching strategies: advance organization of content, induction and deduction, use of examples and nonexamples, use of questions, use of student ideas, student self-evaluation, and group discussion.

Although both the direct and indirect models of instruction are significant contributions to teaching and learning, neither should exclusively dominate your instructional style because the purpose of introducing these models is to increase the variety of instructional strategies at your disposal. And, the two models can be effectively interwoven in a single lesson, as when some facts, rules, or action sequences must be acquired before introducing a concept to be learned or problem to be solved. These models and their strategies provide a variety of instructional tools that you can use in many combinations to match your particular objectives and students' learning needs. Just as different entrees have prominent and equal places on a menu, so should the direct and indirect models have prominent and equal places in your classroom. You can alternately employ and enjoy the direct and indirect models to create tantalizing combinations of educational flavors for your students.

Table 10.3 places the objectives of the direct and indirect models of instruction side by side for comparison and presents some teaching events that distinguish each model.

Culturally Responsive Indirect Instruction

Culturally sensitive teachers consider students' cultures and language skills when planning learning objectives and activities (Delpit & Dowdy, 2008). They also realize that lesson objectives should include more than just delivering content knowledge. Diverse students are often motivated by objectives that include the opportunity for affective and personal development, as well (Gay, 2010; Lustig & Koester, 2009; Rothstein-Fisch & Trumbull, 2008). Effective teachers thus consider how to include students' backgrounds, perspectives, and experiences in framing the knowledge to be gained or the activities to be accomplished.

A concept that can help foster the affective and personal nature of your classroom is **social framing**, which is the context in which a message, such as a lesson, is received and understood. Ogbu (1995a,b, 2008) defined a *social frame* as a taken-for-granted context that delimits the sources from which meaning can be derived. When a teacher announces at the start of class, "Today's lesson will expect you to know the events that led up to the Civil War," he or she has implicitly set how you are supposed to participate and respond—a social frame. A social frame can be created that can make a lesson more or less understandable to a cultural or ethnic group that may be accustomed to an alternate frame. For example, Michaels and Collins (1984) reported an example of an Anglo teacher who framed a story with linear, topic-centered patterns (e.g., "Today I will read you a series of events that happened in the lives of three characters"), whereas her African American students framed the task according to topic-associating patterns (e.g., "She's going to tell us the kinds of things that can happen to people"). While one group looked primarily for a sequential list of events that unfolded from the beginning to the end of the story, the other group made notes about the events and the memories they evoked. Thus frames that are ambiguous or less appropriate for one group versus another can alter how and what content is heard or seen.

Table 10.3 Some Examples of Events Under the Direct and Indirect Models of Instruction

Direct Instruction	Indirect Instruction
Objective: To teach facts, rules, and action sequences	*Objective:* To teach concepts, patterns, and abstractions
The teacher begins the lesson with a review of the previous day's work.	The teacher begins the lesson with advance organizers that provide an overall picture and allow for concept expansion.
The teacher presents new content in small steps, also providing explanations and examples.	The teacher focuses student responses using induction and/or deduction to refine and focus generalizations.
The teacher provides an opportunity for guided practice on a small number of sample problems and then prompts and models when necessary to attain 60 percent to 80 percent accuracy.	The teacher presents examples and nonexamples of the generalization, identifying critical and noncritical attributes.
The teacher uses questions to guide discovery and articulation of the generalization.	The teacher draws additional examples from students' own experiences, interests, and problems.
The teacher provides feedback and corrects errors according to whether the answer was correct, quick, and firm; correct but hesitant; incorrect due to carelessness; or incorrect due to lack of knowledge.	The teacher involves students in evaluating their own responses.
The teacher provides an opportunity for independent practice with seatwork and strives for automatic responses that are 95 percent correct or higher.	The teacher promotes and moderates discussion to firm up and extend generalizations when necessary.
The teacher provides weekly and monthly (cumulative) reviews and reteaches unlearned content.	

Lustig and Koester (2009) and Nieto and Bode (2012) make a case for understanding the context in which different cultures expect information to be transmitted that is particularly relevant during indirect instruction. They recommend that the teacher (1) present content from the frame most dominant in the classroom, (2) clarify the nature of the frame through which learners must see and interact with the content (e.g., as facts to be learned, skills to be performed, or concepts to think about), and/or (3) negotiate, when necessary, the frame with students at the start of the lesson. Walqui (2000) points out that using frames for which English-language learners could expect more interactive instructional approaches resulted in these students showing deeper language processing and conceptual learning. These frames also provided learners with a greater opportunity for affective and personal development.

Bowers and Flinders (1991) suggest three ways of establishing a frame at the start of a lesson that encourage students to respond in like manner: self-disclosure, humor, and dialogue. Mendler, Curwin, and Mendler (2007) suggest that each is an effective technique for adding an affective and personal dimension to your frame:

- *Self-disclosure* involves being open about your feelings and emotions that lead up to the lesson. ("I've been struggling to make this topic meaningful, and here's what I've come up with.") Doing so will encourage similar statements of self-disclosure from students, which can be used to frame the lesson.

- *Humor* at the start of a lesson establishes a flexible, spontaneous, expressive mood from which frames can become established. ("Here's a funny thing that happened to me that's connected to what we're going to study today.") Using humor will encourage students to share their own personal episodes, which can be used to provide a context for the lesson.

- *Dialogue* involves the back-and-forth discussion of lesson content and is characterized by random and simultaneous responding. Here every student can expect to be heard, and the teacher expresses lesson content idiosyncratically in the words of the learners. The teacher uses the responses of students to further structure and elaborate lesson content.

Each of these framing techniques is believed to enhance student engagement during indirect instruction. The techniques are effective with students across cultural and ethnic groups, some of whom may be less responsive to the traditional frames of prepackaged lesson plans and textbooks.

Case History and Licensure Preparation

DIRECTIONS: *The following case history pertains to Chapter 10 content. After reading the case history, go to Chapter 10 in the Book Specific Resources section in the MyEducationLab for your course. Open the Case History and Licensure Preparation activity and complete the questions that follow. Upon completion of the test, scored answers to the short-answer question pertaining to the case history and multiple-choice questions will be provided.*

Case History

Mr. Peterson's eighth-grade social studies class consists of approximately 30 students and is culturally diverse. They are currently studying a unit on economic systems. They have already established the similarities and differences between the private and public sectors of the economy. Today Mr. Peterson wants students to consider a factor that influences all economies.

Mr. Peterson: Amy, how many blacksmiths do you know?

Amy: Well, none.

Josh: What about the horseshoers who work at the racetrack?

Amy: But they don't heat up the iron like the village smithy, do they?

Mr. Peterson: You're right, Amy. Most of them just fit ready-made shoes nowadays. [Mr. Peterson pauses as he looks dramatically at the wall calendar.] Well, before we know it, it will be summer break, and I'll be needing a summer job to keep me busy. What do you think I should try this summer, Roberto? Maybe I'll be a gas station attendant. I always did like cars.

Roberto: [A bewildered pause.] A gas station attendant? You mean those guys that used to wipe your windshield and ask if you wanted regular or premium? Hey, Mr. Peterson, they're not around anymore.

Mr. Peterson: All right. What about being an elevator operator?

Rosalia: You mean like the ones in the old movies who asked, "What floor, please?" and then opened the door with a lever or something? [She smiles.] I think you're trying to have some fun with us, Mr. Peterson. Those jobs just don't exist anymore.

Mr. Peterson: Now, why do you think those jobs—the blacksmith, the gasoline attendant, and the elevator operator—have all but disappeared?

Parish: Well, we drive cars to work today. We don't ride horses except for fun.

Amber: You can just slide your credit card into the machine at the pump and get your own gas.

Rosalia: And all you have to do in an elevator is push a button for your floor—and the door opens automatically.

Mr. Peterson: So what's the common denominator? [A pause with no response.] What has made all these occupations obsolete? What do you think, Monique?

Monique: Changing times, I guess.

Mr. Peterson: But what has changed, Monique? Do you mean hairstyles or pop music or the latest shade of nail polish?

Monique: No. [She smiles as she looks down at her bright turquoise nails.] I guess I mean modern times—you know, machines and things.

Gilbert: They call it "high tech," Monique.

Mr. Peterson: Machines? High tech? Any other ideas?

Rosalia: Well, I don't know how high tech cars are. After all, Gilbert, they've been around for a century. Maybe just changing technology.

Mr. Peterson: A very good term, Rosalia. You used Monique's idea of "changing times" and Gilbert's of "high tech." Gilbert's was too narrow to include the blacksmith example, and I showed Monique that "changing times" included too much, everything from pop music to nail polish. So to summarize, we could say that . . .

Roberto: Changes in technology influence the job market by eliminating some jobs.

Mr. Peterson: I couldn't have said it better, Roberto. Now tomorrow, we'll consider the role of technology in creating new jobs.

Summing Up

The main points in this chapter include the following:

Comparing Direct and Indirect Instruction

1. Indirect instruction is an approach to teaching and learning in which concepts, patterns, and relationships are taught in the context of strategies that emphasize concept learning, inquiry learning, and problem-centered learning.

2. In indirect instruction, the learner acquires information by transforming stimulus material into a response that requires him or her to rearrange and elaborate on the stimulus material.

3. *Generalization* is a process by which the learner responds in a similar manner to different stimuli, thereby increasing the range of instances to which particular facts, rules, and sequences apply.

4. *Discrimination* is a process by which the learner selectively restricts the acceptable range of instances by eliminating things that may look like the concept but differ from it on critical dimensions.

5. The processes of generalization and discrimination together help students classify different-appearing stimuli into the same categories on the basis of essential attributes. Essential attributes act as magnets, drawing together all instances of a concept without the learner having to see or memorize all instances of it.

6. The following are instructional strategies of the indirect model:

   - Use of advance organizers
   - Conceptual movement—inductive and deductive
   - Use of examples and nonexamples
   - Use of questions
   - Use of student ideas
   - Student self-evaluation
   - Use of group discussion

Content Organization

7. An *advance organizer* gives learners a conceptual preview of what is to come and helps them store, label, and package the content for retention and later use.

8. Three approaches to organizing content and composing advance organizers are concept learning, inquiry learning, and problem-centered learning.

Conceptual Movement: Induction and Deduction

9. Induction starts with a specific observation of a limited set of data and ends with a generalization about a much broader context.

10. Deduction proceeds from theory, principles, or generalizations to their application in specific contexts.

Using Examples and Nonexamples

11. Providing examples and nonexamples helps define the essential and nonessential attributes needed for making accurate generalizations.

12. Examples represent the concept being taught by including all of the attributes essential for recognizing that concept as a member of some larger class.

13. Nonexamples fail to represent the concept being taught by purposely not including one or more of the attributes essential for recognizing it as a member of some larger class.

14. Examples and nonexamples can be used in the following ways:

    - Providing more than a single example and nonexample
    - Using examples that vary in ways that are irrelevant to the concept being defined
    - Using nonexamples that also include relevant dimensions of the concept
    - Explaining why nonexamples have some of the same characteristics as examples

Using Questions

15. In indirect instruction, the role of questions is to guide students into discovering new dimensions of a problem or new ways of resolving a dilemma.

16. Some uses of questions during indirect instruction include the following:
    - Refocusing
    - Presenting contradictions to be resolved
    - Probing for deeper, more thorough responses
    - Extending the discussion to new areas
    - Passing responsibility to the class

Learner Experience and Use of Student Ideas

17. Student-centered learning, sometimes called *unguided discovery learning*, allows the student to select both the form and the substance of the learning experience. This is appropriate in the context of independently conducted experiments, research projects, science fair projects, and demonstrations.

18. Use of student ideas can also be used to heighten student interest, to organize subject content around student problems, to tailor feedback to fit individual students, and to encourage positive attitudes toward the subject. In concept, inquiry, and problem-based learning, these goals are placed within specific unit and lesson objectives to promote higher order thinking.

Student Self-Evaluation

19. Self-evaluation of student responses occurs during indirect instruction when students are given the opportunity to reason out their answers so you and other students can suggest needed changes. Students can most easily conduct self-evaluation in the context of student-to-student-to-teacher exchanges in which you encourage students to comment on and consider the accuracy of their own and each other's responses.

Use of Group Discussion

20. A group discussion involves student exchanges with successive interactions among a large number of students. During these exchanges, you may intervene only occasionally to review and summarize, or you may schedule periodic interaction to evaluate each group's progress and redirect the discussion when necessary.

21. The best topics for discussion include those that are not formally structured by texts and workbooks and for which a high degree of consensus does not yet exist among your students.

22. Your moderating functions during discussion include the following:
    - Orient students to the objective of the discussion.
    - Provide new or more accurate information when needed.
    - Review, summarize, and relate opinions and facts.
    - Redirect the flow of information and ideas back to the objective of the discussion.
    - Combine ideas and promote compromise to reach a consensus.

Comparison of Direct and Indirect Instruction

23. Direct and indirect instruction can be used together, even within the same lesson. You should not adopt one model to the exclusion of the other. Each contains a set of strategies that can compose an efficient and effective method for the teaching of facts, rules, and sequences and to solve problems, inquire, and learn concepts.

Key Terms

Advance organizer
Constructivism
Deduction
Discrimination
Examples
Full-group discussion

Generalization
Induction
Integrated bodies of knowledge
Moderating tasks
Nonexamples
Pair or team discussions

Small-group discussions
Social framing
Student-centered learning
Think, pair, share
Unguided discovery learning

Discussion and Practice Questions

Questions marked with an asterisk are answered in Appendix B. Some asterisked questions may require student follow-up responses not included in Appendix B. Go to the Assignments and Activities section of the various topics on the MyEducationLab for your course to complete additional practice activities related to this chapter's content.

*1. What three ingredients are brought together in the indirect model of instruction? Provide a content example in which all three are present.

*2. What types of behavioral outcomes are the direct and indirect instructional models most effective in achieving?

*3. Explain use of the word *indirect* in the indirect instruction model. Provide a content example to illustrate your point.

*4. Why shouldn't direct instruction be used all the time? Give an example in which it would clearly not be appropriate.

*5. Explain what is meant by the terms *generalization* and *discrimination*. Give an example of a single learning task that requires both these processes.

*6. Identify which of the following learning tasks require only facts, rules, or action sequences (Type 1) and which require the outcomes expected from concept learning, inquiry, or problem solving (Type 2):

  a. Naming the presidents
  b. Selecting the best speech
  c. Shifting the gearshift in a car
  d. Writing an essay
  e. Describing the main theme in George Orwell's *1984*
  f. Hitting a tennis ball
  g. Winning a tennis match
  h. Inventing a new soft drink
  i. Reciting the vowel sounds
  j. Becoming an effective teacher

*7. Describe two problems that would result if a concept had to be learned using only the cognitive processes by which facts, rules, and sequences are acquired.

8. For each of the following, provide specific examples to show how the concept might best be taught inductively or deductively. Pay particular attention to whether your instruction should begin or end with a generalization.

  • Democracy
  • Freedom
  • Education
  • Effective teaching
  • Parenting

*9. For the concept of *effective teaching*, identify five essential attributes and five nonessential attributes that together could provide a definition. Using what you have written, write a paragraph explaining the concept of *effective teaching*.

*10. Using what you have learned in this and the previous chapter, identify the different purposes for asking questions in the direct and indirect models of instruction.

*11. What type of learning might be represented by group discussions that begin and end with student-determined ideas and content? How is this different from the use of student ideas in the context of concept, inquiry, and problem-based learning?

*12. For which of the following teaching objectives might you use the direct model of instruction, and for which might you use the indirect model?

  a. Sing.
  b. Use a microscope properly.
  c. Appreciate a poem.
  d. Become aware of the pollutants around us.
  e. Solve an equation with two unknowns.
  f. Read at grade level.
  g. Type at the rate of 25 words per minute.
  h. Write an original short story.
  i. Create an award-winning science fair project.
  j. Distinguish *war* from *aggression*.

  Are there any for which you might use both models?

Professional Practice

Field Experience and Practice Activities

Questions marked with an asterisk are answered in Appendix B. Some asterisked questions may require student follow-up responses not included in Appendix B.

1. Prepare a two-minute introduction to a lesson of your own choosing that provides students with an advance organizer.

2. Provide one example each of an advance organizer that reflects (a) concept learning, (b) inquiry learning, and (c) problem-centered learning in an area you will be teaching.

*3. In your own words, define *induction* and *deduction*. Give an example of each, using content from a subject you will be teaching or teacher you have observed.

*4. Think of a lesson that you have observed that promoted student ideas. What techniques did the teacher use to create this outcome? Which techniques would be most effect for the students and content you will be teaching?

5. Identify a group discussion topic in your teaching area for which moderating techniques would be needed. Describe when during the discussion each technique might be applied.

6. Provide an example of social framing using a topic you are likely to teach. Write a brief lesson introduction to indicate the words you might use to convey this frame to students at the beginning of class.

Digital Portfolio Activities

The following digital portfolio activities relate to InTASC Standards 5 and 8.

1. In Field Experience and Practice Activity 2, you provided examples of advance organizers for lessons based on concept learning, inquiry learning, and problem-centered learning that you are likely to teach. Place these example organizers in a digital portfolio folder labeled "Advance Organizers" and add other advance organizers you observe or read about that could be used in the areas you will teach.

2. In Field Experience and Practice Activity 4, you were asked to identify techniques for promoting student ideas during indirect instruction that you have observed or will be teaching. Place these in a digital portfolio folder titled "Group Discussions" as examples of the techniques to apply when you are conducting a group discussion to promote student ideas.

MyEducationLab™

Go to MyEducationLab (www.myeducationlab.com) for Effective Teaching Methods: Research-Based Practice where you can:

- Find learning outcomes for the various course topics course along with national standards that connect to these outcomes.

- Complete **Assignments and Activities** that can help you more deeply understand the chapter content.

- Apply and practice your understanding of the core teaching skills identified in the chapter with **Building Teaching Skills and Dispositions** coaching activities.

- Check your comprehension of the content covered in the chapter with a book specific **Study Plan**. Here you will be able to take a chapter **pretest**, receive feedback on your answers, and then access personalized **Review, Practice, and Enrichment exercises** to enhance your understanding of chapter content. After you complete the exercises, take a **posttest** to confirm your comprehension.

- Learn how to address common classroom management issues in the **Simulations in Classroom Management**.

- Access video clips of CCSSO **National Teachers of the Year award winners** responding to the question, "Why Do I Teach?" in the Teacher Talk section.

- Create, update, and share quality lesson plans with the **Lesson Plan Builder**.

- Access state licensure test requirements, overviews of what tests cover, and sample test items in the **Certification and Licensure** section.

- Learn how to create a high quality teaching portfolio in the **Preparing a Portfolio** section.

- Access tips, advice, and other information on resume writing and interviewing, your first year of teaching, and law and public policies in the Beginning Your Career section.

11
Self-Directed Learning

This chapter will help you answer these questions and meet the following InTASC standards for effective teaching.

- How can I get my learners to unleash their imaginative and intuitive capacities through self-directed learning?
- How do I get learners to accept responsibility for their own learning?
- How can I teach my learners to go beyond the content given—to think critically, reason, and problem solve?
- How can I engage my learners in project-based learning?
- How can I promote the goals of self-directed learning using differentiated instruction?

InTASC

STANDARD 1 **Learner Development.** The teacher understands how learners grow and develop, recognizing that patterns of learning and development vary individually within and across the cognitive, linguistic, social, emotional, and physical areas, and designs and implements developmentally appropriate and challenging learning experiences.

STANDARD 3 **Learning Environments.** The teacher works with others to create environments that support individual and collaborative learning, and that encourage positive social interaction, active engagement in learning, and self motivation.

STANDARD 4 **Content Knowledge.** The teacher understands the central concepts, tools of inquiry, and structures of the discipline(s) he or she teaches and creates learning experiences that make these aspects of the discipline accessible and meaningful for learners to assure mastery of the content.

STANDARD 5 **Application of Content.** The teacher understands how to connect concepts and use differing perspectives to engage learners in critical thinking, creativity, and collaborative problem solving related to authentic local and global issues.

STANDARD 6 **Assessment.** The teacher understands and uses multiple methods of assessment to engage learners in their own growth, to monitor learner progress, and to guide the teacher's and learner's decision making.

STANDARD 8 **Instructional Strategies.** The teacher understands and uses a variety of instructional strategies to encourage learners to develop deep understanding of content areas and their connections, and to build skills to apply knowledge in meaningful ways.

*I*n this chapter, you will study an important method for engaging your students in the learning process. Here you will learn how to teach learners to go beyond the content given—to think critically, reason, and problem solve—by using a self-directed approach to learning. You will see how to use self-directed strategies to actively engage your students in the learning process and to help them acquire the reasoning, critical-thinking, and problem-solving skills required in today's complex society.

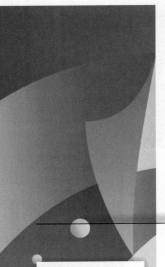

MyEducationLab™

Visit the MyEducationLab for *Effective Teaching Methods: Research-Based Practice*, 8e to enhance your understanding of chapter concepts with a personalized Study Plan. You'll also have the opportunity to hone your teaching skills through video-based Assignments and Activities as well as Building Teaching Skills and Dispositions lessons.

Self-Directed Learning

Much of today's classroom learning is focused on activities by which the learner acquires facts, rules, and action sequences. The majority of lessons require outcomes only at the lower levels of cognition: knowledge, comprehension, and application. This may explain why some national studies of the state of education in the United States and curriculum standards that have evolved from them (American Association for the Advancement of Science, 2009 National Council for the Social Studies, 2010 National Council of Teachers of English, 2011 National Council of Teachers of Mathematics, 2009) indicate that many students are unable to think independently of the teacher or to go beyond the content in their texts and workbooks. These professional associations suggest that the manner in which most schooling occurs may not be teaching students to become aware of their own learning, to think critically, and to derive their own patterns of thought and meaning from the content presented, as suggested by the cognitive outcomes identified in the Higher Order Thinking and Problem-Solving Checklist in Appendix C.

Self-directed learning is an approach to both teaching and learning that actively engages students in the learning process to acquire higher order thinking skills. Self-directed learning helps students construct their own understanding and meaning and helps them to reason, problem solve, and think critically about the content (Burke, 2006; Costa, 2009; Costa & Kallick, 2005). Self-directed learning requires you to perform this sequence of activities:

1. Provide information about when and how to use mental strategies for learning.

2. Explicitly illustrate how to use these strategies to think through solutions to real-world problems.

3. Encourage your learners to become actively involved in the subject matter by going beyond the information given—to restructure it based on their own ways of thinking and prior understandings.

4. Gradually shift the responsibility for learning to your students through practice exercises, question-and-answer dialogues, and/or discussions that engage them in increasingly complex thought patterns.

Consider the following excerpt, which illustrates how some of these teaching functions might be accomplished in a typical lesson:

Teacher: [A poem has been written on the board; the teacher reads it to the class.]

Man is but a mortal fool When it's hot, he wants it cool
When it's cool, he wants it hot
He's always wanting what is not.

Today I want to illustrate some ways to understand a poem like the one I've just read. This may seem like a simple poem, but its author put a lot of meaning into each of its words. Now let me give you an approach to studying poems like this and gaining from them the meanings intended by their authors. First let's identify the key words in this poem. Earl, what do you think are some of the most important words?

Earl:	Well, I'd say the word *man* because it's the first sentence.
Teacher:	Any others? [Still looking at Earl.]
Earl:	Not that I can see.
Teacher:	Anita?
Anita:	The words *hot* and *cool* have to be important, because they appear twice and they rhyme with the last words of the first and last lines.
Teacher:	Any other key words? Rick?
Rick:	Well, I think *a mortal fool* is supposed to be telling us something, but I don't know what.
Teacher:	Good. So now we've identified some words we think are especially important for understanding this poem. Why don't we look up in the dictionary the meanings of any of these words we don't know or are unsure of? That will be our *second* step. Ted, look up the word *mortal* for us while we begin work on our third step. The *third* step is to paraphrase what you think this author is saying. Susan, can you paraphrase what he is saying?
Susan:	I think he's saying we're always changing our minds, and that's why we look so stupid sometimes.
Teacher:	We are all human, so we certainly change our minds a lot, don't we? Rhonda looks like she wants to say something. Rhonda?
Rhonda:	Well, I'd say it's not that we're stupid that we change our minds but that it's just part of who we are. We can't help wanting what we can't have.
Teacher:	So you've added a little something to Susan's interpretation. What do you think, Susan? Do you agree?
Susan:	Yeah, we're not stupid; we're just mortals.
Teacher:	Chris, do you want to add anything?
Chris:	I'd say that we're not stupid at all. That to really enjoy something, we must have experienced its opposite. Otherwise we wouldn't know how good it is.
Teacher:	Now that brings us to our *fourth* and last step. Let's try to relate what Chris just said to our own experience. Anyone ready? Earl?
Earl:	I agree with Chris, because I remember thinking how much I welcomed winter because of how hot it was last summer.
Teacher:	[Marcia is waving her hand.] Marcia, what do you have to say about that?
Marcia:	But now that it's winter, I can't wait for the cold weather to end, so I can go swimming again. [Class nods in agreement.]
Teacher:	It looks as though Chris was right. We sometimes have to see both sides of something—hot/cold, good/bad, light/dark—to fully appreciate it. Now Ted, what did you find for *mortal* in the dictionary?
Ted:	It says "having caused or being about to cause death," "subject to death," and "marked by vulnerability."
Teacher:	Which of those do you think best fits the use of *mortal fool* in our poem?
Ted:	Well, hmm . . . the last one, because it kind of goes with what we have been saying about how we choose one thing and then another . . . like when we get too cold, we dream of summer, and then when summer comes, we think it's too hot.
Teacher:	I agree. It fits with what we all have experienced in our lives—and that means we are on the right track to interpreting the poem as the author intended. Now let's go one step further. Putting all of our ideas together, what is this poet saying? [Nodding to Alex.]
Alex:	Well, I'd say life's a kind of circle. We keep going around and around—back to where we've come and then trying to escape to where we've been. Maybe that's one kind of vulnerability—like it said in the dictionary.
Teacher:	That's good thinking, Alex. Earl, because we began with you, I'll let you have the final word.

> *Earl:* I think Alex got it, because now I understand why the author thinks we're all fools. We're like a dog going in circles chasing our tail, always wanting what we don't have. That explains the first and the last lines, doesn't it? Because we are human, we are vulnerable to always "wanting what is not." Yes, so we're mortal fools. I get it.
>
> *Teacher:* Very good. Now let's think for a moment about the four steps we just went through to understand this poem. I will repeat them slowly while you write them down. They will become your guide for reading the rest of the poems we study.

Notice how this teacher contributed something to each of the four components of self-directed learning. First she provided the learners with a mental strategy for learning—in this case, a framework of four easy-to-follow steps for interpreting poetry. These steps were sufficiently familiar and practical enough to be followed by almost any student, regardless of prior knowledge or experience. Notice that the steps were not just divisions of the task but steps that ultimately forced learners to go beyond the content presented to find their own meaning and understanding, based on personal experience and individual thinking. In other words, there were no wrong answers with this strategy—only answers that could be improved to lift the learner to the next rung of the learning ladder.

Second, the strategy provided was not just routinely given to the learners by listing its steps on the board; the steps were illustrated in the context of a real problem. The application was real world and typical of other examples to which students would be asked to apply the strategy.

Third, the learners were invited to become participants in the learning, not just passive listeners, waiting to be told what to do. Because the teacher started a question-and-answer dialogue to provide a structure for the learners' opinions and experiences, students became an active part of the process by which new knowledge was being generated. They were, in a sense, their own teachers without knowing it. This was made possible through the format of an unscripted discussion, which removed any fear of producing a wrong response that otherwise might have prevented some learners from participating.

And fourth, note that as the lesson evolved, more and more of the most important conclusions were provided by the students, not the teacher. The highest level of interpretation, with which the lesson ended, came almost entirely from the summarizing remarks of students. By the end of the lesson, the teacher's role was more that of a monitor and co-inquirer than an information provider; that role had been assumed by the students as they actively applied each of the steps given earlier in the lesson.

Now let's look more closely at some of the mental strategies that learners can actually use to acquire meaning and understanding from text.

Metacognition

One strategy for self-directed learning is **metacognition**, or mental processes that assist learners to reflect on their thinking by internalizing, understanding, and recalling the content to be learned. They include so-called invisible thinking skills—such as self-interrogation, self-checking, self-monitoring, and analyzing—as well as memory aids (called *mnemonics*) for classifying and recalling content.

Metacognitive strategies are most easily conveyed to learners through a process called *mental modeling* (Boyles, 2004; Dunlosky & Metcalf, 2008). **Mental modeling** helps students internalize, recall, and then generalize problem solutions to different content at a later time. The teacher does not just convey information but demonstrates the decision-making process as it occurs. By contrast, the mechanical memorization of steps rarely helps learners solve similar problems in other contexts or allows content to be recalled when the present topic has lost its immediate importance (e.g., no exam in sight, no homework due).

Mental modeling is particularly important when asking students to engage in complex tasks. For instance, an Internet search requires higher order thinking skills to devise a search strategy, evaluate its result, discard inapplicable items, and synthesize findings. Each of these tasks poses a challenge for learners that can be addressed through modeling ways for them to organize their thinking (Keene, 2007; Rekrut, 1999). As you observe in classrooms, you will want to watch for instances of mental modeling; note particularly effective approaches you see and how they help learners increase responsibility for their own learning by implementing and monitoring a previously modeled way of thinking.

Mental modeling involves three important steps:

1. Showing students the reasoning involved
2. Making students conscious of the reasoning involved
3. Focusing students on applying the reasoning

These steps usually are carried out through verbal statements that walk learners through the process of attaining a correct solution. They begin with verbal markers such as the following:

> Now, I will show you how to solve this problem by talking out loud as I go through it, identifying exactly what is going on in my mind. Think about each decision I make, where I stop to think, and what alternatives I choose—as though you are making the same decisions in your own mind.

Notice that the teacher is not giving learners the mechanics of getting a right answer: do step A, then B, then C. More importantly, the teacher is providing an actual live demonstration of the mental procedures that may underlie the routine completion of a problem.

Research on what makes a good demonstration (Borich & Tombari, 2004; Good & Brophy, 1995) indicates that skilled demonstrators of mental procedures do the following:

- *Focus learners' attention.* Effective demonstrators begin the demonstration only when their learners' attention is focused on them. Then they direct students' attention to the thinking or reasoning skill they want students to learn.

- *Stress the value of the demonstration.* Effective demonstrators briefly and concisely point out why their learners should observe what they are about to demonstrate. They relate the thinking skill to the content to be learned.

- *Talk in conversational language while demonstrating.* Effective demonstrators back up to cover unfamiliar concepts and repeat actions when needed, use analogies to bridge content gaps, and use examples to reinforce learning. They then probe for understanding.

- *Make the steps simple and obvious.* Effective demonstrators break complex actions into simple steps that can be followed one at a time. They point out what to do next and then describe the action as it is being performed by thinking out loud while acting.

- *Help learners remember the demonstration.* Effective demonstrators go slowly ("Stop me if I'm going too fast"), emphasize certain actions ("Now I'll ask myself a question"), highlight distinctive features ("Notice where I pause"), and give simple memory aids to help learners retain what they have seen and heard.

These mental procedures help students internalize, recall, and then generalize problem solutions to different content at a later time. Effective demonstrators do not just convey information according to the preceding steps but actually demonstrate the decision-making process as it occurs within their own thoughts. They then monitor the process as it occurs in the learner, provide feedback, and adjust the complexity and flow of content as needed. This leads to a second important concept for self-directed learning, which is *mediation*.

Teacher Mediation

The on-the-spot adjustments to content flow and complexity that you make to accommodate individual learning needs are called *teacher mediation*. Your role during **teacher-mediated learning** is to adjust the instructional dialogue to help students restructure their learning and move them closer to the intended outcome. In other words, the interactive dialogue you provide helps learners construct their own meaning from the content. This aids retention and the generalization of the reasoning process to other contexts.

The knowledge and skills that learners are to acquire are not given to them in the form of finished products. Instead you provide cognitive stimulation at just the proper times for students to acquire the end products through their own reasoning. The need to adjust both the flow and the content seldom can be anticipated. It requires mediation—your on-the-spot judgment of what new information will bring a learner's response to the next level of which he or she is capable at that moment. This next level reflects the content difficulty and cognitive complexity from which the student can most benefit at that moment.

The Zone of Maximum Response Opportunity

This level of content difficulty and cognitive complexity is the learner's **zone of maximum response opportunity** (Kozulin, Gindis, Ageyev, & Miller, 2003; Vygotsky & Kozulin, 1986).* It is the zone of behavior that, if stimulated by you, will bring a learner's response to the next level of refinement. Thus a response directed at the zone of maximum response opportunity must be at or near the learner's current level of understanding but also designed to lift his or her following response to the next higher level. Your directed response need not elicit the correct answer, because at that precise moment, the learner may be incapable of benefiting from it. It should, however, encourage the learner to refine an initially crude response.

Following are two classroom dialogues. Note that the first teacher hits the learner's zone of maximum response opportunity, but the second teacher misses it:

Teacher: When you see a proportion or ratio, such as 4/5 [writes it on board], think of the number on top as "what is" and the number on the bottom as "what could be." Think about a box of cereal that you have for breakfast. If I wrote the proportion of cereal in the box as 3/4 [writes it on board], I would say to myself, "The full box is equal to the number 4—that's the 'what could be' part. But this morning, after I fixed my breakfast, what's left is only the number 3, which is the 'what is' part. That's how I can tell the box is still pretty full, because the number for 'what is' is close to the number for 'what could be.'"

Now, Megan, explain to me what it means when it says on a label that the proportion of vitamin C for one four-ounce glass of orange juice is half the minimum daily requirement.

Megan: I'm not sure.

Teacher: OK, what words can we use to describe the number on top?

Megan: You said it's "what is."

Teacher: What does that mean?

Megan: I guess it's how much vitamin C is really in the glass.

Teacher: And now for the bottom?

Megan: You said the bottom is "what could be." Does that mean that it's all you need?

Teacher: Yes, it does—good. Now think of another example—one of your own—in which something was less than it could have been.

Megan: Well, I finished Ms. Enro's social studies test before the end of the period.

Teacher: And how long was the period?

Megan: Umm, about 40 minutes, I guess.

Teacher: Using our words, what would you call that part of the problem?

Megan: "What could be." OK, I get it. Then the time I actually took is what really happened? Yeah, I finished the test in about 20 minutes.

Teacher: So how would you express that proportion in numbers?

Megan: It would be 20, for "what is," over 40, for "what could be." The top is half of the bottom, so I guess one glass of orange juice gives you half the vitamin C you need in a day.

Teacher: OK. Let's retrace the steps you just followed for another problem.

Now let's imagine that Megan relives this episode in another classroom. After the same introductory remarks, Megan is asked the identical question:

Teacher: Now, Megan, explain to me what it means when it says on a label that the proportion of vitamin C for one four-ounce glass of orange juice is half the minimum daily requirement.

*The zone of maximum response opportunity is also called the "zone of proximal development" by Vygotsky (Kozulin, 1990).

Megan:	I'm not sure.
Teacher:	Look, if the number 1 is on the top and the number 2 is on the bottom, it must mean the top is less than the bottom. Right?
Megan:	Right.
Teacher:	So if the top number represents "what is" and the bottom number "what could be," then "what is" is one-half less than "what could be." And that can only mean the glass contains half of the minimum daily requirement of vitamin C. Get it?
Megan:	Yep.

Well, maybe Megan does "get it" and maybe she doesn't. Notice in the first example that by retracing the mental steps for Megan to recall, the teacher hit Megan's zone of maximum response opportunity, because her prior understanding and responses were taken into account in moving the dialogue closer to the intended goal of the lesson. By differentiating the questioning from that which might be given to another learner with a different zone of maximum response opportunity, the teacher provided a peg with which Megan lifted herself to the next rung of the learning ladder.

Diversity among self-directed learners can be activated by teacher interaction and the gentle interplay that taps the learner's zone of maximum response opportunity and provides appropriate stepping stones to higher levels of learning.

The second teacher simply provided the right answer. Doing so gave Megan no opportunity to construct her own response by using the mental steps provided and thereby derive a process to use for independently arriving at other right answers in similar circumstances. The first teacher focused on developing for the learner a process of reasoning—a line of thinking—that gave the content its own individual meaning yet was consistent with the intended goal of the lesson.

Through classroom dialogues such as these, you can encourage your learners to construct their own meanings and interpretations—for example, to substitute their own unique constructions for what is and what could be—and to share them with others through discussion and classroom dialogue. Such diversity among self-directed learners activates their unique learning histories, specialized abilities, and personal experiences, thus engaging them in the learning process.

Hitting the Zone of Maximum Response Opportunity

The zone of maximum response opportunity is important in self-directed learning, because you can rarely provide the most appropriate responses to all learners at all times. This is the key difference between *individualized learning* (e.g., in programmed and computerized instruction) and self-directed learning. In *individualized learning,* the content writer anticipates the most probable errors and provides remedial or alternative learning routes (called *branching*) for all learners, regardless of their zones of maximum response opportunity. Because the instruction assumes that relatively homogeneous groups of learners will work through the content, the same types of errors are anticipated for all learners. In some cases, the remedial steps or alternative branching provided may fall within a learner's zone of maximum response opportunity, but in some cases, they may not.

Because self-directed learning frequently occurs during a student response–teacher reaction sequence, it affords the opportunity to more accurately aim your spoken or written reaction at the learner's zone of maximum response opportunity. This is an important point, because aiming your reaction to a student response too sharply—to a fixed point, like "lower center field" in a baseball game—may so restrict your response that it will exclude the learning history, specialized abilities, and personal experiences of the learner. In addition, it may not consider your own content knowledge, specialized abilities, and instructional style. Figure 11.1 illustrates the zone of maximum response opportunity for a lesson in reading.

Figure 11.1 **Zone of Maximum Response Opportunity for a Reading Lesson**

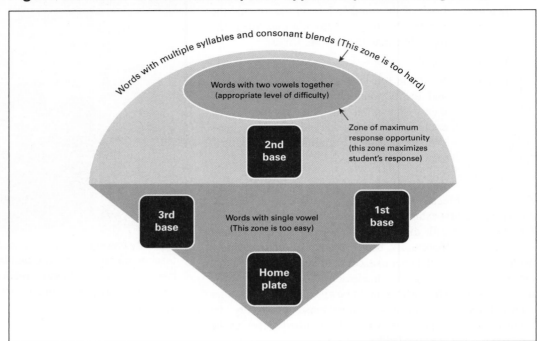

Thus the concept of a zone and the opportunity to target your instruction to fall within it afford both you and your students some latitude within which to construct and create meanings and understandings that consider individuals' unique needs. In this manner, self-directed learning promotes a gentle interplay between the minds of the learner and teacher, pulling and pushing each other in a student response–teacher reaction sequence designed to help the learner climb to the next rung of the learning ladder.

Functional Errors

Another concept important to self-directed learning is **functional errors**. Student errors play an important role in the interplay between learner and teacher (Stipek, 2001). If your reaction promotes an inaccurate and meaningless response, the interplay may not be so gentle, at least not in the learner's mind. But if your reaction creates (or even intentionally promotes) a student response that is inaccurate but *meaningful,* the interplay returns to a gentler state.

The latter condition describes a class of student errors called *functional errors.* Whether these errors are unexpected or planned for, they enhance the learner's understanding of content. Functional errors provide a logical stepping stone for climbing to the next rung of the learning ladder, which may eliminate an erroneous thought process from occurring again in the learner's mind. For example, such an error may be necessary so the student will not arrive at the right answer for the wrong reason, thereby compounding the mistake in other contexts.

Consider the following dialogue, in which a student error becomes a functional stepping stone to the next level of understanding:

Teacher: As you recall from yesterday, we were studying the reasons behind the Civil War. Under what president of the United States did the Civil War begin?

Alexis: Our book says Jefferson Davis.

Teacher: Well, it so happens Jefferson Davis was a president at the time. But that's not the right answer. Now how do you think Jefferson Davis could be a president but not the president of the United States at the time of the Civil War?

Alexis:	Well, maybe at the start of the war, there were two presidents, Jefferson Davis and someone else.
Teacher:	As a matter of fact, there were two presidents, but only one could be president of the United States.
Alexis:	Well, if he wasn't president of the United States, he must have been president of the other side.
Teacher:	What was the name of the government that represented the other side?
Alexis:	Yeah, now I remember. It was the Confederacy. It was Abraham Lincoln who was the president of the North, which must have been called the *United States,* and Jefferson Davis who must have been the president of the South, called the *Confederacy.* I guess I got confused with all the different names.

Even though the student's response was incorrect, this teacher's reaction fell within the student's zone of maximum response opportunity, because from it directly followed a correct response. Notice also how the teacher encouraged the learner to supply the correct answer, using her previous mistake as an aid to obtaining it. This strategy actually led to discussing information that went beyond the question itself—to putting Jefferson Davis in geographic perspective and in correctly naming the governments representing both the North and South.

But what if this teacher had made a less thoughtful reaction, encouraging not only another inaccurate response but worse, a dead end not useful for refining or extending the student's initial response? What might such a reaction look like?

Teacher:	Under what president of the United States did the Civil War begin?
Alexis:	Our book says Jefferson Davis.
Teacher:	I said president of the *United States,* not president of the *Confederate States of America.* See the difference?
Alexis:	I guess so.
Teacher:	Well, OK. Then let's go on to Mark.

The interplay here becomes considerably less gentle, as the specter of failure is left hanging over the learner and the teacher has no easy way out of this awkward ending. This is why self-directed learning requires teacher responses to be always at or slightly above the learner's current level of understanding and to promote a student response, correct or incorrect, that is functional for achieving the intended goal of the lesson. This is also why scripted approaches to instruction (like programmed instruction and some computer software) cannot replace the gentle interplay between student response and teacher reaction supported by the classroom dialogue and group discussion methods of self-directed learning.

Reciprocal Teaching

One way you can apply self-directed learning in your classroom is with a strategy called *reciprocal teaching* (Brown & Campione, 1994; Lubliner & Palincsar, 2001; Oczkus, 2005). **Reciprocal teaching** provides opportunities to explore the content to be learned via classroom dialogue. At the center of reciprocal teaching are group discussions, in which you and your students take turns as leader in discussing the text.

Chuska (2003) and Slavin (2001) have observed that most classroom discussions amount to little more than recitation of facts by students with the aid of question-and-answer sequences in which all or most of the answers are known. This leaves little opportunity for students to construct their own meaning and content interpretation so they can attain higher levels of understanding. In practice, many classroom discussions promote little meaningful dialogue that actually helps students struggle with the adequacy of their ideas and opinions on their way to obtaining acceptable solutions. More often, these discussions are driven by text content, with rapid-fire questions that stay close to the facts as presented in the text.

Pay attention to how reciprocal teaching is defined in this **video**. Watch how the students participate in this process.

Reciprocal teaching is a strategy that turns a typical discussion into a more productive and self-directed learning experience. It accomplishes this through four activities: predicting, questioning, summarizing, and clarifying. These unfold into the following sequence, described by Oczkus (2005) and Palincsar and Brown (1989):

1. *Predicting.* Discussion begins by generating predictions about the content to be learned from the text based on the following:

   a. Its title or subheading in the text
   b. The group's prior knowledge or information pertaining to the topic
   c. Experience with similar kinds of information

   Following the group's predictions about what they expect to learn from the text, the group reads and/or listens to a portion of it.

2. *Questioning.* The teacher chooses one individual to lead a discussion of each portion of the text that is read. Afterward the discussion leader asks questions about the information. Students respond to the questions and raise additional questions.

3. *Summarizing.* The discussion leader then summarizes the text, and the teacher invites other students to comment or elaborate on the summary.

4. *Clarifying.* If any points in the text were unclear (e.g., concepts or vocabulary), they are discussed until clarity is achieved. In this case, students may make more predictions and reread portions of the text for greater clarity.

The following dialogue illustrates the four activities of predicting, questioning, summarizing, and clarifying that comprise reciprocal teaching:

Teacher: [Reading from the text.] "The pipefish change their color and movements to blend with their surroundings. For example, pipefish that live among green plants change their color to a shade of green to match the plants."

Claire: [Leading the discussion.] One question that I had about this paragraph is, "What is special about the way the pipefish looks?"

Teacher: [Clarifying.] Do you mean the way that it is green?

Andy: [Elaborating.] It's not just that it's green. It's that it's the same color as the plants around it, all around it.

Claire: [Continuing.] Yes, that's it. My summary of this part tells how the pipefish looks and that it looks like what is around it. My prediction is that this is about its enemies and how it protects itself and who the enemies are.

Monty: [Adding to the summary.] They also talked about how the pipefish moves . . .

Keith: [Rejoining.] It sways back and forth . . .

Andy: [Adding.] . . . along with the other plants.

Teacher: [Questioning.] What do we call it when something looks like and acts like something else? The way we saw the insect called a *walking stick* yesterday? We clarified this word when we talked about the walking stick.

Angel: Mimic.

Teacher: That's right. We said we would say that the pipefish mimics the . . .

Students: [Together.] . . . plants.

Teacher: OK! Let's see if Claire's predictions come true. [The class turns to the text.]

Notice in this discussion how the teacher supports student participation in the dialogue. The teacher's aim is to engage as many students as possible in the learning process by providing reactions to student responses that are in their zones of maximum response opportunity. This is accomplished by elaborating on student responses and allowing ample opportunity for students to participate in the dialogue, from their own perspectives. This gives the teacher ample data on which to form a reaction that is within the students' zone of maximum response opportunity.

As the discussion continues, more responsibility for reading and developing the dialogue is given to the students until over time, the teacher becomes more of an adviser or coach, who refines responses instead of providing them. At that point, more and more of the discussion represents the internalization of the text by the students, who now express it through their unique learning histories, specialized abilities, and experiences.

The ultimate goal of reciprocal teaching is to sufficiently engage students in the learning process so they become conscious of their reasoning process. This occurs through their own and other students' modeling, as well as the teacher's modeling of that process, and is refined in the context of classroom dialogue. Doing so requires your continuous attention to the ongoing dialogue and to the meanings students are deriving from the text, so you can continually adjust the instructional content to meet learners' current level of understanding.

As students gradually accept the shift in responsibility from teacher to student, you reduce the amount of explaining, explicitness of cues, and prompting that may have marked the earlier part of the lesson. Figure 11.2 identifies some classroom activities that can guide the gradual shift of responsibility from teacher to learner during self-directed learning.

Oczkus (2005) and Lubliner and Palincsar (2001) offer this summary of the teacher's role during reciprocal teaching.

- The teacher and students share responsibility for acquiring the strategies employed in reciprocal teaching.

- The teacher initially assumes major responsibility for teaching these strategies ("thinks aloud" how to make a prediction, how to ask a question, how to summarize, how to clarify) but gradually transfers responsibility to the students for demonstrating use of the strategies.

- The teacher expects all students to participate in the discussion and gives all of them the opportunity to lead it.

Figure 11.2 Shifting Responsibility from Teacher to Learners

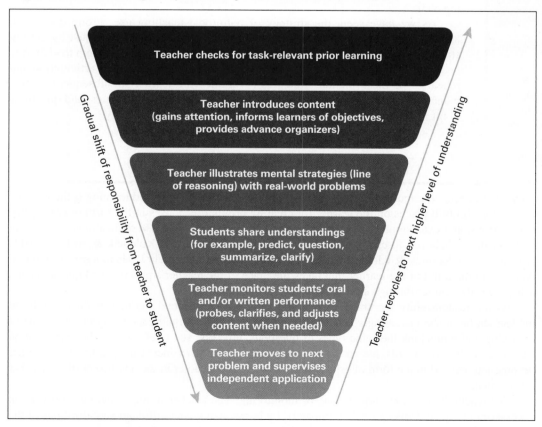

- Throughout each self-directed lesson, the teacher consciously monitors how successfully comprehension is occurring and adjusts the content as needed to the zone of maximum response opportunity.

The Social Dialogue of the Classroom

Outward verbalizations by the learner, if properly scaffolded, can be turned into inner speech that eventually replaces the teacher's prompts and self-guides the learner through similar problems.

As the preceding dialogues demonstrated, classroom conversations between the teacher and students are central to self-directed learning. The verbal interactions within a classroom are vastly different from those that occur outside it. In many classrooms, verbalizations are teacher dominated, leaving students with little alternative but to respond to teacher requests for facts and information. These traditional teaching settings may offer few opportunities for students to elaborate or comment on the topic at hand precluding any partnership of ideas between teacher and student.

However, self-directed learning strategies use classroom dialogue differently. Instead of being a verbalization intended to confirm the teacher's authority, classroom dialogue is purposefully guided to gradually shift responsibility to the learner. The teacher scaffolds knowledge, building the dialogue layer by layer and each time increasing the challenge to the learner to think independently of earlier constructions provided by the teacher.

Scaffolding must be done carefully to keep the challenge within the learner's zone of maximum response opportunity. This requires that you be aware of the learner's present level of understanding (for example, familiarity with the task) and the level at which he or she can reasonably be expected to perform (for example, from past learning performance). Attention to these details lets you scaffold the cognitive demands placed on the learner. You do so to increasingly shift the learner from just *responding* to textual material to *internalizing* its meaning by elaborating, extending, and commenting on it.

As we have seen, the strategy of reciprocal teaching uses group discussion and rotating discussion leaders to achieve this goal. It does so not just by getting students to talk, as do many traditional discussions, but by getting them to elaborate on the processes by which they are learning the content. The clear articulation and rehearsal of these mental strategies (1) guides the learner in subsequent performances and (2) helps you adjust the flow and level of prompts, cues, and questions to hit inside the learner's zone of maximum response opportunity.

The Role of Inner Speech

As we have seen, an important aspect of classroom dialogue in self-directed learning is the increasing responsibility it places on the learner for creating original responses in the form of comments, elaborations, and extensions to what is being read or being said. These verbalizations, if properly scaffolded, are believed to create an inner speech within the learner (Kolencik & Hillwig, 2011; Kozulin, 1990; Resnick & Klopfer, 1989). This **inner speech** ultimately leads to a private internal dialogue in the mind of the learner that takes the place of the teacher's prompts and questions and self-guides the learner through similar problems.

As the responsibility for unique and original productions beyond the text gradually shifts to the learner, he or she increasingly acquires the ability to speak internally, modeling the same line of reasoning and mimicking the same types of questions, prompts, and cues used by the teacher at an earlier stage. In other words, the verbal interactions that the teacher increasingly asks of the learner become internalized in the form of private speech used by the learner in the absence of direct teacher involvement.

The teacher's role now turns to one of monitoring. The teacher prompts and cues only when necessary to keep students on track. Ultimately, by internalizing the scaffolded verbalizations of the teacher and recalling them at will in private dialogue, students become their own teachers, mimicking the logic and reasoning process modeled by the teacher. Self-direction can be stimulated by many different techniques in addition to reciprocal teaching, including many forms of cooperative and group learning.

The role of inner speech in guiding the behavior of both children and adults is central to self-directed learning strategies.

Sample Dialogues of Self-Directed Learning

Now let's look at three classroom dialogues that exhibit characteristics of self-directed inquiry. In different teaching contexts, these dialogues illustrate the following:

- How a teacher models the process by which meaning and understanding can be derived from textual material
- How questions, prompts, and cues can be used to scaffold responses, gradually shifting the responsibility for learning to the student
- How the teacher thereafter can monitor student responses for continued understanding

Keep these three conditions in mind as we look at each of the three dialogues. First, we will look at a fourth-grade classroom in which Ms. Koker is teaching reading. We will observe how she models the process by which meaning and understanding can be derived from text. Our discussion begins with Ms. Koker reading an excerpt from a short story to the class from the daily reader:

Ms. Koker: [Reading from the text.] "One of the coldest climates on Earth occurs in the northern part of Alaska. In this land, a small but hardy group of Native Americans lives and prospers in small villages where hunting and fishing is a way of life. This small group of villagers . . ."

Debbie: [Interrupting.] Ms. Koker, I don't know what the word *hardy* means.

Ms. Koker: What do you think it means, Debbie? [Asking her to make a prediction.]

Debbie: Well, something that's hard—like maybe ice.

Ms. Koker: Let's see if you are right. Let's think of some other words that might mean almost the same thing as *hard*. [Introducing the idea of synonyms.]

Tim: Something that's hard is strong.

Mickey: Yeah, and it also lasts a long time.

Kim Lee: If you're strong, you can't be hurt.

Ms. Koker: OK, now let's see if any of these ideas fit with the sentence "In this land, a small but hardy group of Native Americans lives and prospers in small villages where hunting and fishing is a way of life." What do you think can be changed, Tim? [Encouraging the idea of fitting synonyms into the text to clarify meaning.]

Tim: Well, if we took out the word *hardy* and put in the word *strong,* I think it would mean the same thing.

Ms. Koker: What do you think, Itsuko?

Itsuko: It makes sense, because when you're strong you can't be hurt—say, by all the cold up north—and then you will live a long time. [Summarizing.]

Mickey: But how do we know they live a long time, just because they are strong? [Asking for clarification.]

Ms. Koker: That's a good point. We really don't know that yet, so what do you think? [Calling for a prediction again.]

Tina: I think they won't live as long as us because of all the cold weather.

Ms. Koker: So how do you think they stay warm? Let's read on to see.

Notice that Ms. Koker was modeling a strategy for deriving meaning from text. To accomplish this, she introduced the idea of synonyms; she asked Debbie what the word *hardy* meant and then asked students to insert the synonym into the text to check its appropriateness. Thus Ms. Koker was conveying a model—a mental strategy—that students can use time and again, unaided by the teacher, whenever they encounter an unknown word.

Now let's observe Mr. Willis's junior high science class to see how he uses questions, prompts, and cues to encourage self-direction. In the following discussion, Mr. Willis is teaching a fundamental law of physics by providing questions and reactions that are a scaffold to his learners' zones of maximum response opportunity:

Mr. Willis:	Here you see a balloon, a punching bag, and a tire pump. Watch carefully as I let the air out of the balloon [lets air out], punch the bag [punches it], and press down on the pump handle [pushes handle]. What did you notice about all three actions? Chet?
Chet:	You got tired. [Class laughs.]
Mr. Willis:	You're right about that, especially when I did the punching and pumping. [Reaching to Chet's current level of understanding.] Yes, you saw a reaction in me: I got tired. What other reactions did you see?
Chet:	The balloon fluttered across the room.
Mr. Willis	And what else?
Chet:	The punching bag moved forward—and, well, the pump handle went down and then a little up.
Mr. Willis:	You saw several reactions, didn't you? What were they?
Chet:	Something happened to the object you were playing with and . . . well . . . I guess something else was going on, too.
Mr. Willis:	Anita, what did you see in all three cases?
Anita:	Movement in two directions, I think.
Mr. Willis:	What were the movements?
Anita:	Well, for the balloon, it went forward, but it also pushed the air backward . . . over your face. And for the punching bag, it went forward . . . *umph* [mimics the sound] . . . and stopped. I don't know what other movement there was.
Mr. Willis:	[Pushing to the next higher level of understanding.] Think about what happened both after and before I punched the bag. To help you, make two columns on a piece of paper and label them with the words *Before* and *After.* Now write down what you saw in each of these three instances—the balloon, the punching bag, and the pump. Let's all take a minute to do this.
Anita:	[After about a minute.] Now I remember. The punching bag came back to hit your hand again. That was the second movement.
Mr. Willis:	[Checking for understanding among the others.] And what about the tire pump? Michael, you have your hand up.
Michael:	When you pushed the pump handle down to inflate the tire, it came back up.
Mr. Willis:	You're both right. There were two identifiable movements, which we will call an *action* and a *reaction.* The fundamental law of physics we have been discussing is that "Whenever there is an action, there must be a reaction." Now let's check to see if this is true for some other movements by identifying on your paper the action and reaction associated with the following. I'll say them slowly so you have time to write:

> The space shuttle taking off from Cape Canaveral
>
> An automobile moving down the street
>
> A gunshot
>
> A football being kicked over a goalpost

Notice how Mr. Willis used questions targeted to his students' current level of understanding. This allowed students to respond in some meaningful way, which gave Mr. Willis the opportunity to build on an earlier incomplete response to reach the next higher level of understanding. For example, Mr. Willis used Chet's first crude response, aided by the prompt "What other reactions did you see?" to introduce the concept of an action followed by a reaction. Each time the questioning turned to a new student, Mr. Willis targeted his question, prompt, or cue higher but still within that learner's zone of maximum response opportunity.

Also by thinking through the solution on paper—called *think sheets*—students were actively engaged in working through their responses. At the same time, this approach provided a strategy from which students might more easily derive actions and reactions for the new problems presented at the end of the dialogue. Mr. Willis's use of questions, prompts, and cues at various levels of difficulty kept this class moving through the lesson with increasingly more sophisticated responses.

Now let's look in on a third classroom. Mrs. LeFluir is teaching Spanish to a high school class not just by altering the level of questioning, as did Mr. Willis, but by altering the tasks from which learners experience the application of content firsthand. Without realizing it, Mrs. LeFluir's class is experiencing the difference between *declarative knowledge*—facts, concepts, rules, and genneralizations intended for oral or written regurgitation—and *procedural knowledge*—action sequences or procedures used in a problem-solving or decision-making task.

Mrs. LeFluir:	Today, we will study the gender of nouns. In Spanish, all nouns are either masculine or feminine. Nouns ending in *o* are generally masculine, and those ending in *a* are generally feminine. Tisha, can you identify each of the following nouns as either masculine or feminine? [Writes these words on the board.]

> *libro*
>
> *pluma*
>
> *cuaderno*
>
> *gramática*

Tisha:	[Correctly identifies each.]
Mrs. LeFluir:	Now let's see how you identified each of the words and what each word means.
Tisha:	Well, I followed the rule that if it ends in an *o*, it is masculine, but if it ends in an *a*, it is feminine. I think the words are *book, pen, notebook,* and *grammar.*
Mrs. LeFluir:	Good. Now for the next step, you have all used the indefinite articles *a* and *an* many times in your speaking and writing. In Spanish, the word *un* is used for *a* or *an* before a masculine noun, and *una* is used for *a* or *an* before a feminine noun. In Spanish, the article is repeated before each noun. Using the vocabulary words on the board, let's place the correct form of the indefinite article in front of each word. [Shifting the task demand.] Why don't you take the first one, Ted?
Ted:	It would be *un libro*.
Mrs. LeFluir:	Maria.
Maria:	*Una pluma.*
Mrs. LeFluir:	Juan and Marcos, take the next two.
Juan:	*Un cuaderno.*
Marcos:	*Una gramática.*
Mrs. LeFluir:	OK. Now we are ready to put our knowledge to work. I will give you a sentence in English, and you translate it into Spanish, being sure to include the correct form of the indefinite article. [Shifting the task demand again.] For this, you will need to remember your vocabulary from last week. If you need to, look up the words you don't remember. Mark, let's start with you. Come up to the board and write, "Do you want a book?"
Mark:	[Writes on board.] *¿Desea usted un libro?*
Mrs. LeFluir:	Good. And how did you decide to use *un* instead of *una?*
Mark:	The noun ended in *o*.

Mrs. LeFluir: [Continues with three other examples.]

Do you need grammar?

Do you want to study a language?

Do you need a notebook?

[After the students respond, she shifts the task demand again by moving to the following activity.] Now read each sentence on the transparency, and write down the correct form of the indefinite article that goes before the noun. [Shows transparency.]

Yo necesito _____ gramática.

Nosotros estudiamos _____ lengua.

¿Necesita Tomás _____ libro?

¿Es _____ pluma?

[After the students respond, she moves to a final activity and yet another task demand.] Now for each of the following sentences, I will speak in English, and I want you to repeat the same sentence entirely in Spanish. Be sure, once again, to include the correct form of the indefinite article.

Notice in this episode the different activities required of the students and how they differ in cognitive complexity. Mrs. LeFluir gradually changed the demands on her learners by shifting the tasks to which they were to respond. Her lesson began by asking only for the simple restatement of the rules (declarative knowledge) but ended by engaging students in an oral sequence of actions of the kind that might be required in having a conversation in Spanish (procedural knowledge). She gradually shifted her tasks from declarative to procedural in small enough degrees to ensure that all her students (or at least most of them) could follow.

This process also conveyed a language-learning model that will be helpful in subsequent contexts by providing a learning strategy that flows from memorization of rules and vocabulary, through completion and fill-in, to oral delivery. Notice that this sequence was completed even for this elementary lesson. This tells the learners that oral and written delivery—not the repetition of rules—is the goal to which all previous learning must contribute and toward which they must strive in their own individual learning and practice.

The systematic varying of task demands within a unit comprises an **activity structure**. Activity structures are most effective for self-directed learning when they vary the demands or problems being placed on the learner in ways that gradually require him or her to assume responsibility for learning the content at a higher level of understanding as called for in the Rigor and Relevant Framework. When needed, activity structures can be differentiated for individual or small groups of learners by giving some learners additional declarative exercises representing fewer cognitive demands while others move more quickly from declarative to procedural exercises that represent a greater range of cognitive demands. The following section describes the steps in teaching self-directed inquiry to individual learners.

Steps in Teaching Self-Directed Inquiry to Individual Learners

1. Provide a learning task, and observe how the student approaches it (e.g., reading a short selection in a history text that will be the basis for a writing assignment).

2. Ask the student to explain how he or she approaches the task of learning the textual information in preparation for the writing assignment. (This helps the student analyze his or her own cognitive approach.)

3. Describe and model for the learner an effective procedure for organizing what he or she reads. For example, explain and demonstrate how to use the study questions at the end of the selection to help focus reading; highlight the main ideas in each paragraph of the selection with a fluorescent marker; and write outline notes of key points on a separate

sheet or on note cards as a study guide for later review. This gives the student new strategies for cognitively organizing the writing assignment to come.

4. Provide the student with another similar task (e.g., another reading assignment) for practicing the new cognitive strategies. Model self-questioning behavior as you demonstrate the analysis of this similar problem—for example, "What are the key questions you will need to answer?" and "What is the main idea in this paragraph?" Write the questions on a small card for the student to use as a reminder.

5. Provide another opportunity for the student to practice the skills using self-direction, this time decreasing your role as monitor.

6. Check the result of the learner's comprehension and cognitive organization, giving reminders and corrective feedback.

Teaching Cognitive Strategies for Lifelong Learning

When you use a mental strategy to help you learn on your own, you have learned what psychologists call a **cognitive learning strategy**, or a general method of thinking that improves learning across a variety of subject areas. Cognitive learning strategies accomplish this by helping the learner to retain incoming information (*reception*), recall task-relevant prior knowledge (*availability*), and build logical connections among incoming knowledge (*activation*). These strategies (Blanton, 2005; Nessel & Graham, 2006) include the following:

- Elaboration/organization (note taking)
- Comprehension-monitoring strategies
- Problem-solving strategies
- Project-based strategies

Let's take a look at each of these.

Elaboration/Organization

Elaboration involves teaching learners how to build internal connections between new knowledge and existing knowledge. *Organization* entails showing learners how to order and systematize new information so they can remember it and use it efficiently. From Chapter 7, you learned three Internet technologies that can help your learners organize and construct knowledge, social bookmarking, social presentation, and concept mapping, that could be used independently or to assist with the activities below.

The most practical way to help your students learn how to elaborate and organize new knowledge is to teach them how to take notes (McPherson, 2011; Turkel & Peterson, 2003). Note taking can improve information processing in several ways. It enhances reception by prompting learners to attend better to what they are hearing or seeing. Furthermore, note taking assists activation by helping learners make internal connections among information and building a network of external connections with information in memory. You can give your learners several suggestions to help them take notes successfully:

- Read the text before the lesson. This provides advance organizers for the new information.
- Watch for signals that indicate important information (e.g., gestures, key words, cues to the organization of the information).
- Write down main ideas, not isolated facts. Try to be selective and not write down everything.
- When needed, use a more free-form outline format, called *webbing* (Buzan, 2004; Krasnic, 2011), using pictures, arrows, and code letters. See Figure 11.3 for an example of webbing and refer to concept mapping in Chapter 7.
- Write down examples and questions as you listen.
- Leave blanks or some other prompts to indicate what you missed.
- Review your notes as soon as possible.

Figure 11.3 **An Example of Webbing Describing Factors that Affect Weather**

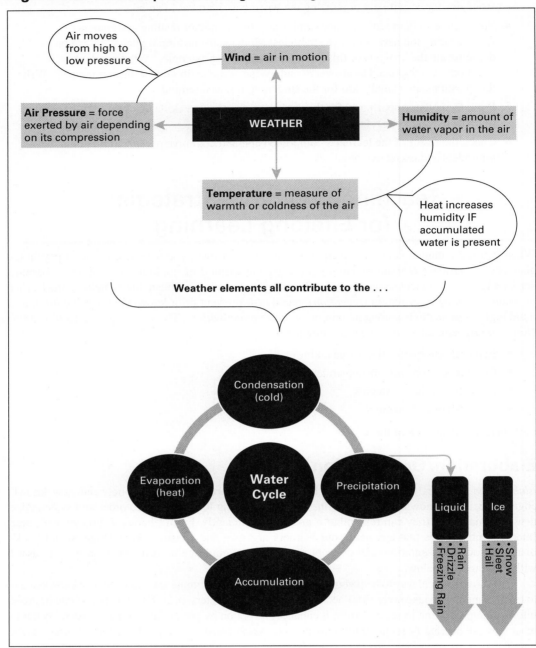

Comprehension Monitoring

Comprehension monitoring is a strategy in which students learn to evaluate their own understanding by frequently checking their own progress during the course of a lesson (Harvey & Goudvis, 2007; Rozakis & Cain, 2002). A. L. Brown (1994) used this strategy based on the reciprocal teaching method described earlier for helping both poor and good readers. Teachers modeled for learners the following three skills:

1. Survey the text and make predictions about what it says.

2. Ask questions about the main idea of the text as it is being read.

3. Become aware of unclear passages by monitoring one's own understanding, asking "Do I understand what I just read?"

Learners who used this strategy increased their reading comprehension from 50 percent to 80 percent after only four weeks of instruction. Comprehension-monitoring strategies have in common the following skills:

- *Setting goals:* "What do I have to do?" "Why am I doing this?"
- *Focusing attention:* "What am I supposed to read?" "What activity must I complete?"
- *Self-reinforcement:* "Great, I understand this. Keep up the good work." "This strategy really works."
- *Coping with problems:* "I don't really understand this. I should go back and read it again." "That's a simple mistake. I can fix that."

Problem-Solving Strategies

Cognitive learning strategists recommend that the school curriculum in most subject areas be organized around the kinds of real-life thinking that learners use not only in school but for much of their adult lives (Posamentier & Krulik, 2008). According to some strategists, curricula today are isolated by disciplines (algebra, biology, geography, etc.) that identify lists of topics, facts, and skills to be covered by the end of a semester. Such curricula sometimes can place learners in a relatively passive listening role and encourage rote or other forms of non-meaningful learning.

As an alternative to this approach, growing numbers of educators advocate the teaching of **problem-based learning skills** (Barell, 2006; Delisle, 1997; Verduin, 1996). Problem-based learning organizes the curriculum around loosely structured problems that learners solve by using knowledge and skills from several disciplines. Recall that we introduced this general approach in Chapter 6 under the topic of interdisciplinary thematic units and in Chapter 10 under the topic of indirect instruction. In both instances, we emphasized its importance as a teaching strategy. In this chapter, we highlight its importance as a cognitive lifelong learning strategy.

To benefit from problem-based learning, however, learners must know how to problem solve. Because problem solving is a cognitive learning strategy that is needed at all stages of life, teachers are increasingly being called on to teach this skill.

There are many systems for solving problems that you may teach all learners (Engel, 1998; Lambros, 2004) and for the inclusive classroom (McGrath, 2007) as well. These methods are generalizable to all curriculum areas and to a variety of problems, whether they are well-defined problems (e.g., the word problems typically seen in math curricula) or ill-defined problems with no single answer with many solution paths, and for which the nature of the problem shifts as learners are working on it.

One popular problem-solving system, called IDEAL, involves five stages for teaching problem solving (Bransford & Stein 1993):

1. *Identify the problem.* Learners must first know what the problem or problems are before they can solve them. During this stage of problem solving, learners ask themselves if they understand what the problem is and if they have stated it clearly.

2. *Define terms.* Learners check that they understand what each word in the problem statement means.

3. *Explore strategies.* Learners compile relevant information and try out strategies to solve the problem. This can involve options such as drawing diagrams, working backward to solve a math or reading comprehension problem, or breaking a complex problem into manageable units.

4. *Act on the strategy.* Once learners have explored a variety of strategies, they now select and use one.

5. *Look at the effects.* During this final stage, learners ask themselves whether they have come up with an acceptable solution.

The following sample dialogue shows how a fifth-grade teacher begins to teach her learners to use IDEAL:

Teacher: Today we are going to think a little more about the greenhouse problem. Remember what we talked about yesterday. The PTA is giving us money to build a greenhouse, but we have a problem concerning how we can get the flowers and vegetable plants to grow inside a house when they are supposed to grow outside.

Watch this **video** and differentiate the different problem-solving strategies the teacher uses in her classroom.

Student 1: First the letter *I*. You *identify* the problem.

Teacher: And what do we do when we identify a problem?

Student 2: We read about the problem and try to figure out what we are supposed to answer or solve.

Teacher: OK. I'll try to identify one of the problems with the greenhouse and then ask one of you to do the same. One of the problems I see is how the plants will get the food they will need. Anybody else?

Student 3: I see a problem: What about when it gets cold?

Teacher: So what's the problem?

Student 3: Well, it's how do you make sure they have the right temperature to live?

Teacher: Good! What was another thing we talked about when you think about problems?

Student 4: Letter *D?* You *define* any words you don't understand in the problem.

Teacher: Why is this important?

Student 4: Well, you want to make sure you really understand the problem. Sometimes we use words and think we know what they mean, but we really don't. So *D* reminds us to make sure we really know what we mean when we say something.

Teacher: Good. I'll give you an example, and then you give me one. What is a *greenhouse*? Are we all agreed on this?

Student 5: And *right temperature*. What does that mean?

Teacher: Great. Now what's the third thing we do when we think about solving a problem? (. . . teacher continues with the last three activities of the IDEAL problem solving model)

Teachers who incorporate cognitive strategies into their lessons have two broad goals: to enhance learners' (1) acquisition of knowledge (declarative, procedural, metacognitive) and (2) use of cognitive processes (reception, availability, activation). Teachers increase the likelihood of achieving these two goals and activating them throughout their learners' lives when they teach cognitive learning strategies involving elaboration/organization, comprehension monitoring, and problem solving to their students.

Project-Based Learning Strategies

Boss, Krauss and Conery (2008) and others (Harada, et al., 2008 Diffily & Sassman, 2002) propose that teachers who build their instruction around projects provide learners with thinking skills that are applicable throughout their lives. But teachers must do this in ways that assure learners that their success depends on factors they control. **Project-based learning** (1) communicates to learners the importance of the learning process and not just the product, (2) helps them set goals, and (3) uses instructional groupings to elicit the cooperation of others in completing a project.

Like problem-based learning, project-based learning makes extensive use of theories of intrinsic motivation to maintain high levels of student engagement and enthusiasm (Blackburn, 2005; Affini, 1996). However, unlike problem-based learning, project-based learning is targeted toward an achievable end product that is visualized before the process is begun.

First let's examine project-based learning and see how it promotes self-directed inquiry throughout the life cycle through intrinsic motivation. Then we will look at how it guides the inquiry process and the end product.

The Role of Tasks in Project-Based Learning

Project-based learning assigns a critical role in the development of intrinsic motivation to the nature of the classroom learning task. It asks the question, "What kinds of tasks are most likely to induce and support learner interest, effort, and persistence?"

Project-based learning advocates the use of projects as the most appropriate vehicles for engaging learners, because they can be structured around student interests. Projects have two essential components: (1) They are built around a central question that serves to organize and energize classroom activities, and (2) they require a product or outcome to answer the question successfully. Project-based learning is different from problem-based learning, however, in that it requires the development of a tangible outcome to determine if the end product has been achieved (e.g., a model, poster, skit, digital video, podcast, newspaper, demonstration, reenactment, or physical construction, such as a science exhibit or collaborative school greenhouse or garden), which because of its complexity often involves the participation of others. Both project- and problem-based learning share the same basic inquiry skills of exploration, discovery, and questioning.

Projects may be built around issues of current societal concern or questions of more historical or intellectual interest. Good projects have these critical characteristics:

- They are of extended duration, requiring several weeks or longer to complete
- They link several disciplines (e.g., involve math, reading, writing skills, etc.)
- They focus on the process as well as the product
- They involve the teacher as a coach and often require small-group collaboration

Projects should also: (1) present a real-world, authentic challenge; (2) allow for some learner choice and control; (3) be doable, or capable of being carried out within the time and resource limitations of the student and classroom; (4) require some level of collaboration; and (5) produce a tangible product. Let's look more closely at each of these characteristics.

Present a Challenge. A project meets this important criterion when it offers learners an authentic, sometimes novel, and always challenging question to investigate, resolve, and report on. This is in contrast to doing worksheets, exercise books, end-of-chapter questions, and other routine tasks, which may take up most of learners' academic time.

Allow for Learner Choice and Control. An effective project allows learners options regarding modes of investigation (reading, interviewing, observing, controlled experimentation), styles of reporting (written reports, audiotapes or videos, visual displays), solutions to problems, and types of products or artifacts to develop.

Be Doable. Learners will persevere and expend high amounts of effort if they see results. Similarly, they are more likely to believe they can see a project through to a successful conclusion if it is time limited, requires readily available resources, and includes points along the way where they can receive positive feedback, make revisions, and generate further products.

Require Collaboration. Intrinsic motivation is nurtured in classrooms that allow learners to meet their social needs. A project that cannot be completed unless a small group of learners adopt different but essential roles is an ideal vehicle for incorporating the principles of motivational theories.

Result in a Concrete Product. A project that gives learners concrete goals to work toward is more likely to sustain intrinsic motivation. Moreover, the product and the process involved in producing it allows learners to see the connection between what they do in class and what they have produced. This provides a greater sense of control over their grade, and it better meets their needs for autonomy than a grade based on a paper and pencil test alone.

The Role of the Learner in Project-Based Learning

Educators have urged school reforms that engage learners in hands-on learning activities as the best way to develop self-directed learning skills (Harada, Kirio, & Yamamoto, 2008; Viadero, 2003). Project-based learning recognizes that learners will acquire important knowledge and skills from a project only if they (1) attribute their success to effort, (2) believe they can accomplish the goals of the project, and (3) perceive themselves as competent.

The Role of the Teacher in Project-Based Learning

Students who fail to see the purpose or personal relevance of classwork to real-life activities perform more poorly than those who do see the connection between their classwork and their lives. Helping learners take ownership of their learning and allowing them some voice in class activities, as well as their evaluation, is an important part of increasing motivation and decreasing student apathy. This holds true across cultural and linguistic lines, as well as across academic disciplines (Boss, Krauss, & Conery, 2008; Curwin, 2010; Wentzel & Wigfield, 2009).

The teacher's unique role in project-based learning is that of a supporter of the learner's or group's chosen product. Consequently, proponents of project-based learning urge teachers to support their learners' interest, effort, and achievement in these ways:

- Avoid statements that imply that innate ability is all that is required to complete a project.
- Focus learners' attention both on the process of completing the project and on the product that results.
- Make encouraging statements to learners that promote commitment.

See In Practice: Focus on Project-Based Learning.

In Practice

Focus on Project-Based Learning

Teachers who practice project-based learning, or build their instructional programs around projects, provide learners with an environment ideally suited to the nurturing of motivation (Blumenfeld et al., 1991 Diffily & Sassman, 2002 Harada, Kirio, & Yamamoto, 2008). Cognitive psychologists have proposed three distinct yet overlapping theories of academic motivation: attribution theory, self-efficacy theory, and goal theory. Whether your perspective on motivation aligns with one of these theories or all three, project-based learning offers some solutions to the age-old problem of how to give energy and direction to the classroom behavior of learners.

Attribution Theory

Each of us has succeeded at some endeavors and failed at others. Think about one of your more recent successes or failures. Were you successful or unsuccessful because of the amount of effort that you exerted, your natural ability, luck, or some combination of these? Another way to ask this question is, "Do you attribute your success to internal forces, such as effort and ability, or to external forces, such as luck and the difficulty of the task?"

Forsterling (2001) and Weiner (1986), leading proponents of attribution theory, believe that people naturally seek to understand why they succeed or fail. Students, for example, when asked to explain why they received a certain grade, typically refer to their hard work or effort, innate

ability, the test being easy or hard, or luck. These causes originate either within the learner (effort, ability) or outside the learner (luck, task). A cause originating within the learner is said to have an *internal locus of causality*; one originating outside the learner has an *external locus of causality*.

Motivational theorists such as Weiner (1986) assert that only when learners attribute their success to effort are they likely to exert genuine effort to complete a project or study for a test. If learners attribute their success or failure to ability, luck, or task difficulty—all of which are out of their control—they believe that nothing they can do will improve the situation. Thus how a student thinks about or interprets success or failure, and not the experience of the outcome itself, determines the energy and direction of his or her efforts.

Self-Efficacy Theory

Self-efficacy theory holds that academic motivation hinges on the learner's beliefs that he or she can succeed at school tasks. Bandura (1986), the originator of self-efficacy theory, and Eisenberger (2005) have defined *self-efficacy* as an individual's judgment of his or her capability to organize and execute the courses of actions required to attain desired outcomes. In other words, students are more likely to begin, persist at, and master tasks that they think they are good at. This judgment is what is meant by the term *self-efficacy*.

Judgments about self-efficacy differ from attributions. *Attributions* are perceived causes of success or failure. They influence expectations and behavior, as they are one type of information that learners use when making judgments about self-efficacy. If a learner believes that success in calculus is due to being born with mathematical ability and feels that he or she possesses little of such ability, he or she will have low self-efficacy for calculus.

Bandura (1986) has identified several other sources of information that learners use to make judgments about self-efficacy. One is verbal persuasion, through which the teacher expresses faith and confidence to learners that they can be successful. Another is seeing peers succeed at a particular task. If a learner sees someone whom he or she likes and admires receive high marks or praise from a teacher for solving a difficult geometry theorem, the learner is more likely to believe that he or she can do likewise.

But the most important piece of information used by learners when making self-efficacy judgments is past experiences of success or failure with a particular task. The learner who has received high marks for three previous essays will have higher self-efficacy for the next writing project than the learner who consistently earns low grades. Thus a student weighs a variety of information in addition to attributions when coming to a judgment of self-efficacy for a particular subject. Once made, the judgment directly affects the learner's level of effort and persistence, as well as the level of achievement obtained.

Goal Theory

Goal theory, the third perspective on motivation, focuses on the learner's academic goal orientation as a source of motivation. Dweck and Reppucci's (1973) work with fifth-grade math students showed that uncontrollable failure created in learners' minds a disposition of helplessness that caused them to make no effort to solve easy problems, to which they had already given correct answers. In the late 1970s, Diener and Dweck (1980) began to investigate whether the goals for learning set by children had a more or less pronounced effect on the development of so-called learned helplessness. They administered psychological tests to groups of children to determine their academic goal orientation and found that children generally fall into two goal groups with regard to interest in learning. One group, called the *task-focused group,* focused on developing academic competence and improving their skills for purely intrinsic reasons. The other group, called the *ability-focused group,* engaged in learning tasks with the goal of "showing off their ability, outperforming others, and gaining external rewards like praise and good grades." This study showed that the two categories of goals are distinct and result in dramatically different degrees of academic motivation.

Much of the research on goal theory has shown that, in comparison to ability-focused learners, students who adopt task-focused or mastery goals are more likely to achieve in school, make more use of cognitive strategies when problem solving, and expend substantial mental effort searching their memories and relating new learning to prior learning. Researchers have documented that as children proceed through the elementary school grades, they increasingly believe that their ability sets a limit on what they can learn (Ames, 1990; Gordon & Gordon, 2006). And certain classroom activities, such as ability grouping, exacerbate this viewpoint. Thus goal theory places special emphasis on classroom practices that can enhance a student's personal goal beliefs. These goal beliefs can affect a broad range of motivational behaviors, including persistence, use of learning strategies, choices, and preferences.

Culturally Responsive Self-Directed Learning

The work of Delgado-Gaitan (2006), Gay (2010), Grant and Ray (2009), Obiakor (2006), and Weinstein et al., (2005) has underscored two important dimensions of the teacher's role in modifying classroom dialogue in the culturally diverse classroom that have become relevant to self-directed instruction. One of these is that of teacher mediation—the on-the-spot adjustments made by the teacher to extend or refocus a student's response to move him or her to the next rung on the learning ladder. The second dimension is mental modeling—the active demonstration of strategies by which students can better learn and retain the content taught.

These results have been applied in the culturally diverse classroom through various forms of social interaction to encourage students to construct their own meanings and interpretations and to revise and extend them under the guidance of the teacher. As we have seen, among the strategies for promoting teacher mediation are reciprocal teaching (Lubliner & Palincsar, 2001; Rosenshine & Meister, 1994) and problem- and project-based learning (Baden & Mayor, 2004; Berkel, et al., 2010). With each of these strategies, the teacher can elicit an individual student's responses at his or her current level of understanding based on personal experiences with and predictions about the content to be taught.

Other strategies that can help promote culturally responsive self-directed instruction include the following:

1. *Pose challenging problems.* Focus the problem so the learner must make key decisions about what is important for a solution. This feeling of responsibility and control over the inquiry is important if the learner is to become engaged and see learning as truly self-directed.

2. *Choose learning activities that allow freedom of choice and include interests.* By letting students pursue and investigate some topics of their own—choosing and constructing their own meanings and interpretations—you will be making them participants in the design of their own learning.

3. *Plan instruction around group activities during self-directed instruction.* Participating in group activities is when learners are most capable of picking up ideas from others and creating from them new and unusual variations that can be applied during self-directed learning.

4. *Include real-life problems that require problem solving.* Let learners become actual investigators in solving real-world dilemmas. Doing so will force them to place newly acquired knowledge and understanding in a practical perspective and to increase the problem-solving challenge.

5. *When testing, draw out knowledge and understanding using content that is compatible with students' culture and thus familiar to them.* Use assessments that make students go beyond knowing and remembering facts by asking them to explain, analyze, compare, contrast, hypothesize, infer, adopt, and justify as a means of indicating they can construct in their own words the meaning of what you are teaching.

With these self-directed approaches to learning, you will be able to support the participation of all your learners in the dialogue of the classroom. Your aim should be to engage as many students as possible in the learning process by providing reactions to student responses that are in their zones of maximum response opportunity. This can be accomplished in several ways:

1. Differentiating your instruction by adjusting the flow and complexity of the content to meet individual learners' needs

2. Offering ample opportunity for all students to participate in the dialogue from their own perspectives

3. Providing cognitive strategies with which students can better learn and remember the content taught

Finally, ask yourself these questions to check on the success of your efforts:

• Has my instruction been focused within my learners' zones of maximum response opportunity? Are learners bored because they have already mastered these skills, or are they frustrated because the skills are beyond what they can be expected to learn?

• Has my instruction been too solitary? Have I met my learners' social learning needs by allowing for sufficient conversation, public reasoning, shared problem solving, and cooperative projects that reproduce the cultures in which they spend the most time?

• Have I been expecting learners to acquire knowledge that is incompatible with their cultures? Do I use instructional methods that are culturally unfamiliar, irrelevant, or contradictory?

Case History and Licensure Preparation

DIRECTIONS: *The following case history pertains to Chapter 11 content. After reading the case history, go to Chapter 11 in the Book Specific Resources section in the MyEducationLab for your course. Open the Case History and Licensure Preparation activity and complete the questions that follow. Upon completion of the test, scored answers to the short-answer question pertaining to the case history and multiple-choice questions will be provided*

Case History

Mrs. Henson's culturally diverse fifth-grade class has just read a section in their science books about discoveries that challenged long-held ideas. Two of these long-held ideas were the notions of a flat Earth and an Earth-centered planetary system. The following is an excerpt from the follow-up discussion:

Mrs. Henson: Why the big smile, Nate? Was there something in our chapter that tickled your funny bone?

Nate: Well, it's just pretty weird—thinking of all those tough sailors, making it through storms without a blink but worrying all the time that they might slip off the edge of the world. I mean, that's pretty dumb, don't you think?

Mrs. Henson: I don't know. Almost everyone else at the time thought so, too. Did you ever think that centuries from now, some other "Nate" will be sitting in another classroom, laughing at us for believing in an idea that everyone else thinks is wrong?

Nate: I never thought of it that way. You mean, even though we know so much today, we might still have some things completely wrong?

Mrs. Henson: Let's think about that, class, and make some predictions. How about discussing this topic with the others at your table for a few minutes. What will students be laughing about in classrooms a couple of centuries from now? What beliefs that everyone accepts as truth today do you think will be proved false, and why?

[Mrs. Henson walks around the room as students discuss the possibilities among themselves. She pauses briefly at several tables, sometimes just to listen and sometimes to give encouragement, such as "I never would have thought of that" and "I think you're right on with that one." When she is sure that each table has at least one good suggestion, she reconvenes the full-class discussion.]

Mrs. Henson: Loretta, your group had a very interesting idea. Want to share it with us?

Loretta: Well, you know how everyone is telling us to wash our hands before we eat and to use this or that detergent or cleaner because it kills germs? Well, we predict that people in the future will know that germs are really good for us.

Mrs. Henson: But what I found most interesting as I listened to your group's conversation was the reasoning behind your prediction. Can you explain a little about that, Freeman?

Freeman: It's back to the future, I guess. My grandma, she grew up in the country, and her daddy used to say, when her mama fussed at the little ones for putting everything in their mouths, "You got to eat a bushel of dirt in your life, Addie, so don't be too hard on the little ones." According to my grandma, she and her sisters didn't have near the number of colds that we do now.

Sylvester: My uncle always says the same thing, too. "A few germs is good for you," he says.

Tiffany: I don't agree. Maybe the reason your relatives didn't get as sick was 'cause they lived in the country and they didn't come in contact with as many sick people as we do in the cities now.

Mrs. Henson: So you think the "Germs are good for you" theory fails to consider other changes, or *variables* as scientists call them?

Sylvester: No way! My uncle lived in the city, in a small apartment with six brothers and sisters.

Mrs. Henson: Besides the wisdom of your elders, what other explanations or reasons do you have for this idea?

Loretta: I guess we figured that it was something like too much of a good thing. Without any germs, we're not used to them—kind of like an only child who never has to share toys. When we meet up with germs after hardly ever having had them before, we're like my cousin when she has to share. She freaks out, and so do our bodies.

Freeman: And we really had some cool ideas about other things we could do with germs. We domesticated horses. Why not germs? Germs are so small and multiply so rapidly, we could get them to deliver some good things to our bodies—kind of like luggage that just comes along with us. Maybe things that would clear our arteries or protect us from cancer?

Mrs. Henson: I'm really impressed with your group. Not only did you come up with a prediction and an explanation for it, but you also took it to the next level and created further uses for your idea. Very good work. Now Carmen, tell us what your group chose.

Carmen: Old age. It doesn't have to happen.

Mrs. Henson: Now you have my undivided attention. [Class laughs.]

Summing Up

The main points in this chapter include the following:

Self-Directed Learning

1. *Self-directed learning* is an approach to teaching and learning that actively engages students in the learning process for the purpose of acquiring outcomes at higher levels of cognitive complexity.

2. Self-directed learning involves the following sequence of activities:
   - Provide information about when and how to use mental strategies for learning.
   - Illustrate how to use the strategies in the context of real-world problems.
   - Encourage students to restructure the content in terms of their own ways of thinking and prior understandings.
   - Gradually shift the responsibility for learning to students through practice activities (exercises, dialogues, discussions) that engage them in increasingly complex patterns of thought.

Metacognition

3. *Metacognition* is a strategy for self-directed learning that assists learners in internalizing, understanding, and recalling the content to be learned.

4. Metacognitive strategies include self-interrogation, self-checking, self-monitoring, and analyzing, along with techniques for classifying and recalling content called *mnemonics*.

5. Metacognitive strategies are taught through *mental modeling*, in which learners are walked through the process of attaining a correct solution. Mental modeling includes these stages:
   - Showing students the reasoning involved
   - Making students conscious of the reasoning
   - Focusing students on the application of the reasoning

Teacher Mediation

6. *Teacher mediation* is the teacher's on-the-spot adjustment of content flow and complexity to accommodate students' individual learning needs.

7. The role of the teacher in teacher-mediated learning is to adjust the instructional dialogue to help learners restructure their learning according to their unique abilities, learning histories, and personal experiences.

8. The *zone of maximum response opportunity* represents the level of content difficulty and behavioral complexity from which the learner can most benefit at the moment a response is given.

9. The zone of maximum response opportunity is reached through a classroom dialogue in which the teacher provides reactions to student responses that activate the unique learning history, specialized ability, and personal experience of each learner. Based on these unique characteristics, the learner can acquire individual meanings and interpretations of the content.

Functional Errors

10. *Functional errors* are incorrect or partially correct answers given by the learner that can enhance the meaning and understanding of the content and provide a logical stepping stone to the next level of learning.

Reciprocal Teaching

11. *Reciprocal teaching* involves a type of classroom dialogue in which the teacher expects students to make predictions, ask questions, summarize, and clarify when learning from text.

12. Reciprocal teaching provides opportunities to explore the content to be learned via group discussion.

13. Reciprocal teaching involves this sequence of activities:
   - Generate predictions about the content to be learned from the text and read and/or listen to a portion of it.
   - Choose a discussion leader who asks other students questions about the text; then have students respond to the questions and ask questions of their own.
   - Have the discussion leader summarize the text, and then invite other students to comment or elaborate.
   - Clarify any unresolved questions, ask for more predictions, and reread portions of the text for greater clarity, if needed.

14. The teacher's role during reciprocal teaching is to gradually shift the responsibility for learning to the students by reducing the amount of explaining, explicitness of cues, and prompting that may have marked earlier portions of the lesson.

15. During reciprocal teaching, the teacher's role is to do the following:

    • Share the responsibility for learning with the students.

    • Initially, assume responsibility for modeling how to make a prediction, how to ask a question, how to summarize, and how to clarify, but then transfer the responsibility to students for demonstrating use of these strategies.

    • Encourage all students to participate in the classroom dialogue by prompting, providing additional information, and/or altering the response demand on students.

    • Monitor student comprehension and adjust the rate and complexity of information as needed.

The Social Dialogue of the Classroom

16. In self-directed learning, the teacher scaffolds, or builds the dialogue within a discussion step-by-step, each time increasing the challenge to the learner to think independently of earlier constructions. Scaffolding must occur to the appropriate degree for each learner response to keep the challenge within the learner's zone of maximum response opportunity.

The Role of Inner Speech

17. During self-directed learning, inner (private) speech helps the learner elaborate and extend the content in ways unique to him or her. As responsibility for learning beyond the text gradually shifts to the learner, his or her ability for inner speech increases, modeling the same reasoning and using similar questions, prompts, and cues as the teacher did at an earlier stage.

Sample Dialogues of Self-Directed Learning

18. The following are the steps for teaching self-directed learning to individual learners:

    • Provide a new learning task, and observe how the student approaches it.

    • Ask the student to explain how he or she plans to learn the content (e.g., preparing for an exam).

    • Describe and model a more effective procedure for organizing and learning the content (e.g., using study questions, taking notes, or highlighting key features in the text).

    • Provide another similar task with which the student can practice the strategies provided. Model self-questioning behavior during the task to ensure the learner follows the strategies correctly (e.g., "Did I underline the key words?").

    • Provide other opportunities for the student to practice, decreasing your role as a monitor.

    • Check the result by questioning the student's comprehension and use of the strategies taught.

Teaching Cognitive Strategies for Lifelong Learning

19. Other cognitive strategies can be helpful for organizing and remembering new material during self-directed learning:

    • Elaboration/organization (note taking)

    • Comprehension monitoring

    • Problem-solving strategies

    • Project-based strategies

20. *Problem-based learning* is a problem-solving approach that organizes the curriculum around loosely structured problems that learners solve by using knowledge and skills from several disciplines.

Project-Based Learning

21. *Project-based learning* is an approach that promotes intrinsic motivation by organizing instruction around the tasks most likely to evoke and support learner interest, effort, and persistence. Key elements include a focus on the learning process (not just the product), goal setting, and instructional grouping.

Culturally Responsive Self-Directed Learning

22. Classroom dialogue can be modified to foster the goals of self-directed learning in a culturally diverse classroom by doing the following:

    • Adjusting the flow and complexity of the content

    • Offering ample opportunity for all students to participate

    • Teaching cognitive strategies

Key Terms

Activity structure	Metacognition	Teacher-mediated learning
Cognitive learning strategy	Problem-based learning skills	Zone of maximum response
Functional errors	Project-based learning	opportunity
Inner speech	Reciprocal teaching	
Mental modeling	Self-directed learning	

Discussion and Practice Questions

Questions marked with an asterisk are answered in Appendix B. Some asterisked questions may require student follow-up responses not included in Appendix B. Go to the Assignments and Activities section of the various topics on the MyEducationLab for your course to complete additional practice activities related to this chapter's content.

*1. Identify two purposes for engaging your students in self-directed learning. In which content areas that you will be teaching will these purposes most apply?

*2. What sequence of activities is involved in self-directed learning?

*3. What is *metacognition*? What are several metacognitive strategies you will want to instill in your learners?

*4. During a demonstration, what specific outcomes can mental modeling help your students acquire? Show how mental modeling could be used with a topic you will be teaching.

*5. What is your role during teacher-mediated learning? How might this role differ from that during a teacher lecture or student recitation?

*6. In your own words, describe the *zone of maximum response opportunity*. Then using the natural language of the classroom, write a short teacher-student questioning dialogue that shows that you have hit the zone of maximum response opportunity of one of your students.

*7. Explain the sequence of activities that normally occurs during reciprocal teaching. Which do you feel is the most difficult to implement and why?

*8. What should be your most important goal in promoting classroom dialogue during self-directed learning? How will you know if you have reached that goal?

*9. What is the purpose of inner (private) speech during self-directed learning? Have you ever used inner speech to increase your learning? If so, in what setting and with what results?

*10. Describe the difference between *declarative knowledge* and *procedural knowledge*. Provide an example of each for a topic you will be teaching.

*11. What are the steps for teaching self-directed learning to individual learners? What student behavior might make you decide to take the extra time to teach these skills? How will you assess whether the skills can be exhibited by your learners?

Professional Practice

Field Experience and Practice Activities

Questions marked with an asterisk are answered in Appendix B. Some asterisked questions may require student follow-up responses not included in Appendix B.

*1. What are the three stages of mental modeling? Give an example of each stage using subject matter content that you will be teaching.

2. From your classroom observations, provide some examples of verbal markers that alert learners that mental modeling is about to begin.

*3. What is the purpose of reciprocal teaching? With what content or during which instructional activities would you most likely use reciprocal teaching in your classroom and how would you assess the results?

4. Based on your experience in classrooms, create a brief excerpt to show what scaffold dialogue would look like in your teaching area. Is the scaffold dialogue at the learner's current level of understanding?

5. Provide an example from your fieldwork or classroom observation of an activity structure that varies the task demands. How would you vary the task for those learners unable to respond to the increase in complexity?

*6. Describe some cognitive strategies for lifelong learning. Considering your subject matter or grade level, which of these do you think you would find most useful and for which content areas?

Digital Portfolio Activities

The following digital portfolio activities relate to InTASC Standards 1, 3, 4, 5, 6 and 8.

1. In Field Experience and Practice Activity 4, you were asked to create a brief excerpt that represented what scaffold dialogue would be like in your teaching area. Recall that scaffold dialogue uses questions, prompts, and hints after each student's response to direct the level of discourse to his or her current level of understanding. This level, called the *zone of maximum response opportunity,* is where the student can learn and benefit from his or her own responses. Check to see if your dialogue for Activity 4 accomplishes this to your satisfaction. If not, revise it and then place it in your digital portfolio in a folder titled "Self-Directed Learning." Your dialogue will be an important reminder of the gentle interplay between teacher and student questioning that is required to move students up the learning ladder.

2. Field Experience and Practice Activity 3 asked you to identify the purpose of reciprocal teaching and the content or activities in your teaching area that might provide a desirable context for its use. Take this knowledge of reciprocal teaching, and following the example in the chapter, prepare a brief classroom dialogue in your subject area that illustrates your understanding of how to apply reciprocal teaching techniques in the classroom. Place your dialogue in your digital portfolio "Self-Directed Learning" folder as an example of your skill at applying this important concept.

MyEducationLab™

Go to MyEducationLab (www.myeducationlab.com) for Effective Teaching Methods: Research-Based Practice where you can:

- Find learning outcomes for the various course topics course along with national standards that connect to these outcomes.
- Complete **Assignments and Activities** that can help you more deeply understand the chapter content.
- Apply and practice your understanding of the core teaching skills identified in the chapter with **Building Teaching Skills and Dispositions** coaching activities.
- Check your comprehension of the content covered in the chapter with a book specific **Study Plan**. Here you will be able to take a chapter **pretest**, receive feedback on your answers, and then access personalized **Review, Practice, and Enrichment exercises** to enhance your understanding of chapter content. After you complete the exercises, take a **posttest** to confirm your comprehension.
- Learn how to address common classroom management issues in the **Simulations in Classroom Management**.
- Access video clips of CCSSO **National Teachers of the Year award winners** responding to the question, "Why Do I Teach?" in the Teacher Talk section.
- Create, update, and share quality lesson plans with the **Lesson Plan Builder**.
- Access state licensure test requirements, overviews of what tests cover, and sample test items in the **Certification and Licensure** section.
- Learn how to create a high quality teaching portfolio in the **Preparing a Portfolio** section.
- Access tips, advice, and other information on resume writing and interviewing, your first year of teaching, and law and public policies in the Beginning Your Career section.

12

Cooperative Learning and the Collaborative Process

This chapter will help you answer these questions and meet the following InTASC standards for effective teaching.

- How do I plan a cooperative learning activity?
- What roles can I assign to group members?
- What are some ways I can reward good group performance?
- What are some collaborative skills I can teach my learners?
- How can I promote the goals of cooperative learning in a culturally diverse classroom?

InTASC

STANDARD 2 **Learning Differences.** The teacher uses understanding of individual differences and diverse cultures and communities to ensure inclusive learning environments that enable each learner to meet high standards.

STANDARD 3 **Learning Environments.** The teacher works with others to create environments that support individual and collaborative learning, and that encourage positive social interaction, active engagement in learning, and self motivation.

STANDARD 4 **Content Knowledge.** The teacher understands the central concepts, tools of inquiry, and structures of the discipline(s) he or she teaches and creates learning experiences that make these aspects of the discipline accessible and meaningful for learners to assure mastery of the content.

STANDARD 5 **Application of Content.** The teacher understands how to connect concepts and use differing perspectives to engage learners in critical thinking, creativity, and collaborative problem solving related to authentic local and global issues.

STANDARD 6 **Assessment.** The teacher understands and uses multiple methods of assessment to engage learners in their own growth, to monitor learner progress, and to guide the teacher's and learner's decision making.

STANDARD 8 **Instructional Strategies.** The teacher understands and uses a variety of instructional strategies to encourage learners to develop deep understanding of content areas and their connections, and to build skills to apply knowledge in meaningful ways.

*I*n Chapter 11, you saw how self-directed learning promoted higher forms of thinking with the aid of cognitive strategies. In this chapter, you will see how these same outcomes can be extended and reinforced through various forms of peer collaboration. You will learn how indirect instruction and self-directed and cooperative learning share the complementary objectives of engaging students in the learning process and promoting the higher thought processes and more authentic behaviors required in the world of work, family, and community.

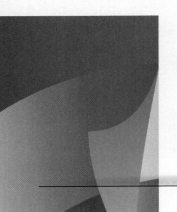

MyEducationLab™

Visit the MyEducationLab for *Effective Teaching Methods: Research-Based Practice,* 8e to enhance your understanding of chapter concepts with a personalized Study Plan. You'll also have the opportunity to hone your teaching skills through video-based Assignments and Activities as well as Building Teaching Skills and Dispositions lessons.

Outcomes of Cooperation

What good are critical-thinking, reasoning, and problem-solving skills if your learners cannot apply them in interaction with others? By bringing them together in adult-like settings to provide appropriate models of social behavior, **cooperative learning** is an instructional strategy that instills in learners important behaviors that prepare them to reason and perform in an adult world (Buehl, 2008; Gillies, et al., 2010; Johnson & Johnson, 2008; Jolliffe, 2007). Let's consider some of these behaviors.

Attitudes and Values

Adult learners form their attitudes and values from social interaction. Although we learn much about the world from books, the Internet, newspapers, and television, most of our attitudes and values are formed by discussing what we know or think with others. In this manner, we exchange *our* information and knowledge with that of others, who have acquired different information and knowledge in different ways. This exchange shapes our views and perspectives. It turns cold, lifeless facts into feelings and then into attitudes and values that guide our behavior over long periods of time.

Attitudes and values are among the most important outcomes of schooling, because they alone provide the framework for guiding actions outside the classroom, where there may be no formal sources of knowledge to fall back on. Cooperative learning is important in helping learners acquire from the curriculum the basic cooperative attitudes and values they need to think independently inside and outside your classroom.

Prosocial Behavior

During close and meaningful encounters among family members, models of **prosocial behavior** are communicated. Children learn right from wrong implicitly through their actions and the actions of others that come to the attention of adult family members. These adults are quick to point out the effects of these actions on family, friends, and the community.

With the decreasing presence of adults in the homes of working parents and single parents, the classroom has become an important vehicle for bolstering home and community values. Cooperative learning brings learners together in adult-like settings that, when carefully planned and executed, can provide appropriate models of social behavior (Stevens & Slavin, 1995). As a teacher, one of your most important roles will be to promote and model positive social interactions and relationships within your classroom (Abruscato, 1994; Kottler & Zehm, 2005).

Alternative Perspectives and Viewpoints

It is no secret that we form our attitudes and values by confronting viewpoints contrary to our own. Our likes and dislikes come from our exposure to alternatives we could not have thought of on our own, given the limitations of our immediate context and experience. These alternatives—some of which we adopt, some we modify, and some we reject—are the raw material from which we form our own attitudes and values.

Confronted with these alternatives, we are forced into the objectivity necessary for thinking critically, reasoning, and problem solving. In other words, we become less self-centered. Depending on the merits of what we see and hear, we grow more open to exchanging our feelings and beliefs with those of others. This active exchange of viewpoints and the tension it sometimes creates within us form the catalyst for our growth. Cooperative learning provides the context or meeting ground where many different viewpoints can be orchestrated, from which we form more articulate attitudes and values of our own.

Integrated Identity

One of the most noticeable outcomes of social interaction is its effect on how we develop our personalities and learn who we are. Social interaction over a long period forces us to see ourselves—our attitudes, values, and abilities—in many different circumstances. The main result is that inconsistencies and contradictions in who we are—or think we are—cannot be hidden, as might be the case in a single interaction or small number of social interactions.

If we think and act one way in one situation and another way in another situation, we cannot help but notice our own inconsistency and wonder why it exists. We attempt to resolve such contradictions, to clarify what we really believe, and to really believe what we say. Our personality becomes more coherent and integrated and is perceived by others as a more forceful and confident projection of our thoughts and feelings. Over time, repeated social interactions reduce the contradictions until our views become singular and consistent and we achieve an integrated identity.

Cooperative learning can be the start of stripping away the irrelevant, overly dramatic, and superficial appendages that mask our deepest thoughts and feelings. Thus we begin to gain an integrated sense of self.

Higher Thought Processes

If all of the preceding benefits of cooperative learning were not enough, cooperative learning has also been linked to increases in the academic achievement of learners at all ability levels (Stevens & Slavin, 1995). Simply exploring or telling may not be the most effective way of helping students achieve (Bransford et al., 2000). Cooperative learning actively engages students in the learning process and seeks to improve their critical-thinking, reasoning, and problem-solving skills (Greeno, 2006; Jacobs, Power, & Loh, 2002). Critical thinking cannot occur outside a context of attitudes and values, prosocial behavior, alternative perspectives, and an integrated identity. But together with these outcomes, cooperative learning can provide the ingredients for higher thought processes and set them to work on realistic and adult-like tasks.

These higher thought processes—required for analyzing, synthesizing, and decision making—are believed to be stimulated more by interaction with others than by books and lectures, which typically are not interactive. Books and lectures may be useful for teaching knowledge, comprehension, and application, but they seldom are sufficient to bring about the private, inner speech required for thinking critically, reasoning, and problem solving in real-life settings. These behaviors require interaction with others, as well as reflection on self, to unleash the motivation required for thinking and performing in complex ways. Therefore it should be no surprise that some of the behaviors in the Higher Order Thinking and Problem-Solving Checklist in Appendix C include cooperative behaviors.

From these outcomes, we see that cooperative learning is not just an activity that engages learners in working together but an instructional strategy for acquiring thinking skills and values that represent lifelong learning goals. These goals are illustrated in Figure 12.1.

Figure 12.1 **Outcomes of Cooperative Learning**

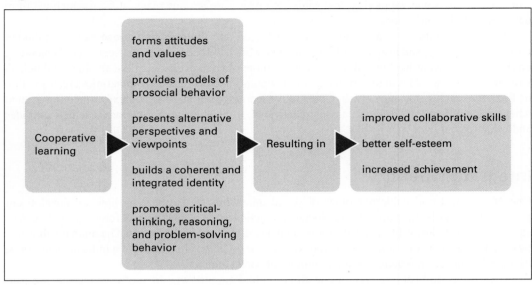

Components of a Cooperative Learning Activity

In this **video**, the teacher demonstrates how to implement the cooperative learning technique in a social studies classroom. Pay attention to the components presented.

In this chapter, you will learn how to organize your classroom for cooperative learning. In planning a cooperative learning activity, you need to decide on the following:

• The types of interactions you will have with your students
• The types of interactions your students will have with one another
• The tasks and materials you will select
• The role expectations and responsibilities you will assign

Let's look at each of these more closely.

Teacher–Student Interaction

One purpose of teacher–student interaction during cooperative learning is to promote independent thinking. Much like the student response–teacher reaction sequences during self-directed inquiry, the exchanges between you and your learners in the cooperative classroom focus on getting learners to think for themselves, independently of the text. To accomplish this goal, you will model and collaborate with learners in much the same way as in the self-directed classroom. The goals of cooperative and self-directed inquiry are complementary.

However, the way you establish teacher–student interaction during cooperative learning is different from self-directed and large-group instruction (Burbules & Bruce, 2001). In self-directed inquiry, the interaction usually is one on one, with verbal messages directed to individuals one at a time and adjusted to their zones of maximum response opportunity. In contrast, cooperative learning occurs in groups that share a common purpose and task, so you must broaden the interactions to fit the zone of maximum response opportunity that is common to most group members. Your goal is to help the group become more self-reflective and aware of its own performance.

"Think about that some more," "Why not check with the references at the learning center?" and "Be sure you have followed the guidelines I gave you" are expressions you will use frequently to address a group of four or five learners assigned a specific task. Your role is to intervene at critical junctures and then to retreat, allowing the group to grapple with the new perspective or information given. In this manner, you monitor and collaborate with the group during brief but focused interventions, keeping them on course and following a productive line of reasoning.

Student–Student Interaction

Interaction among students in cooperative learning groups is intense and prolonged. In contrast to self-directed inquiry, in cooperative learning groups, students gradually take responsibility for each other's learning. The effect may well be the same as in self-directed learning. And this is why cooperative and self-directed learning may be used as complementary learning strategies, with one reinforcing the skills acquired in the other.

During cooperative learning, the feedback, reinforcement, and support come from student peers in the group, not you. Student–student interaction constitutes the majority of time and activity during cooperative learning, unlike the modest amount of direct student–student interaction that occurs in large-group instruction. Groups of four or five—working together in the physical closeness promoted by a common task—encourage collaboration, support, and feedback from the closest, most immediate source: one's peers. An essential ingredient of cooperative learning is each learner's desire to facilitate the task performance of fellow group members.

Task Specialization and Materials

Another component of cooperative learning is the task to be learned and the materials that comprise the structure of a cooperative learning activity. Cooperative learning tasks are preplanned activities; they are timed, completed in stages, and placed within the context of the work of others. This structure promotes the sharing of ideas and/or materials and the coordination of efforts among individuals. The choices of task and supporting materials are important to promote meaningful student–student interaction.

Cooperative learning typically uses **task specialization**, or division of labor, to break a larger task into smaller subparts on which separate groups work. Eventually, these efforts come together to create the whole, to which each member of the class has contributed. Therefore, each group may be asked to specialize, focusing its efforts on a small yet meaningful part of some larger end product, for which the entire class receives credit. Groups may even compete against one another with the idea of producing the best part or highest-quality product. However, the purpose is not the competition that produces the final product but rather the cooperation within groups that the competition promotes. Cooperative task structures have the goal of dividing and specializing the efforts of small groups of individuals across a larger task, whose outcome depends on the sharing, cooperation, and collaboration of individuals within groups.

Role Expectations and Responsibilities

Assigning roles properly is important to the success of cooperative learning activities. In addition to groups being assigned specialized tasks, individuals often are assigned specialized roles to perform within their groups. Some of the most commonly assigned roles include researcher, runner, recorder, and summarizer, whose specific functions will be defined in the sections ahead.

The success of a cooperative learning activity depends on your communication of role expectations and responsibilities and your modeling of them, when necessary. This is another reason cooperative learning has little resemblance to loosely formed discussion groups. Not only must you divide labor among learners and specialized tasks, but you also must designate the roles that foster the orderly completion of a task.

If a student's duties are unclear or a group's assignment is ambiguous, cooperative learning will quickly degenerate into undisciplined discussion, in which there may be numerous uninvolved and passive participants. Uninvolved and passive participants are individuals who successfully escape sharing anything of themselves. This defeats the purpose of cooperative learning.

If a group produces an outstanding report but only a few students have contributed to it, the group as a whole will have learned no more than if each member had completed the assignment alone. And the critical thinking, reasoning, and problem solving that are so much a part of the shared effort of a cooperative learning activity will not have occurred.

Establishing a Cooperative Task Structure in Your Classroom

Now let us put to work in your classroom the four components of cooperative learning: teacher–student interaction, student–student interaction, task specialization and materials, and role expectations and responsibilities. Establishing a **task structure** for a cooperative learning activity involves five specific steps:

1. Specify the goal of the activity.
2. Structure the task.
3. Teach and evaluate the collaborative process.
4. Monitor group performance.
5. Debrief.

1. Specifying the Goal

The goal of a cooperative learning activity specifies the product and/or behaviors that are expected at the end of the activity. The outcome can take different forms:

- Written group reports
- Higher individual achievement on an end-of-activity test
- Oral performance, articulating the group consensus
- Enumeration and/or resolution of critical issues, decisions, or problems
- Critique of an assigned reading
- Collection of data, physical or bibliographical, for or against an issue

To ensure the desired outcome, your job is to identify the outcome, check for understanding, and set a cooperative tone. Each of these roles is described below.

Identify the Outcome.   As moderator and ultimate leader of the group activity, you must clearly articulate the form of the final product or performance expected of your learners in advance. For each desired outcome (for example, from the list above), illustrate the style, format, and length of the product that will constitute acceptable group work. For a written report, you might provide on a classroom blog the acceptable length and format, as well as display a sample report to guide group efforts. In each case, give your students signs of acceptable progress or milestones to be achieved and, where possible, examples of a successfully completed final product or performance.

After clearly specifying the goal, place it in the context of past and future learning. Organize the content so students will attach meaning and significance to it and see it in terms of their own experience. Typically, statements such as "Remember when we had trouble with . . ." and "Next week we will need these skills to . . ." sufficiently highlight the importance of the impending activity by linking it to past or future activities.

Check for Understanding.   Next, check for understanding of the goal and your directions for achieving it. Using a few average and high performers as a "steering group," ask for an oral restatement of your goal and directions. The entire class can benefit from hearing them again, and you can correct them if needed. Because groups typically expend so much effort during a cooperative learning activity, misinterpretation of the goal and your directions for attaining it can severely affect classroom morale by needlessly wasting a lot of learners' time and effort.

In self-directed learning, one individual can be led astray by poorly understood directives. But in cooperative learning, entire groups, not just occasional individuals, can wander off the path, leaving a significant portion of your classroom working toward the wrong goal. Having one member of each group restate the goal and your directions for attaining it is time well spent.

Set a Cooperative Tone.   Your final task in introducing the goal of your cooperative learning activity is to set a tone of cooperation. Students customarily begin cooperative learning activities as they have begun thousands of school activities before—as individuals competing against individuals. This competitive style has been ingrained in us from earliest childhood. It may be difficult for some of your learners to get the competitive spirit out of their blood, because it has become so much a part of their schooling.

Your job at the start of a cooperative learning activity is to set the tone, as captured in the saying "Two heads are better than one." Other phrases, such as "United we stand, divided we fall" and "Work together or fail together," can also remind groups of the cooperative nature of the enterprise. You might ask each group to choose or create a group motto (for example, "All for one and one for all") that provides a distinctive identity and reminds students that collaboration, not competition, is the goal.

Your role also must be one of cooperation, and this, too, must be communicated at the outset. "I am here to help . . . to answer your questions . . . to be your assistant . . . your consultant . . . your information provider." These reassuring comments can lift your classroom from the realm of competition and into the world of cooperation.

2. Structuring the Task

The structure of the task is what separates just any group activity from a cooperative learning activity. Group discussions have tasks, but they often are so generally defined (e.g., discuss the facts, raise issues, form a consensus) that they rarely allow for the division of labor, role responsibilities, collaborative efforts, and end products that promote critical thinking in a cooperative learning activity.

Kagan and Kagan (2010, 1997) identify four characteristics of an effective task structure:

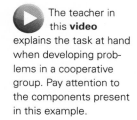

The teacher in this **video** explains the task at hand when developing problems in a cooperative group. Pay attention to the components present in this example.

1. *Positive interdependence* in which all group members are experiencing a "win-win" condition in that the success of one learner is linked to the success of other learners in the group.

2. *Individual accountability* in which there is a procedure to check that each learner individually contributes to the group effort and that there is a means of evaluating the quality of the contribution.

3. *Equal participation* in which all learners receive the same opportunities and resources to be involved in the group activity to show what they know.

4. *Simultaneous interaction* in which all students are actively engaged at the same time during the collaborative activity.

To be sure that the structure of your cooperative activity will achieve these four goals, you will need to answer several questions in advance:

- How large will the groups be?
- How will group members be selected?
- How much time will be devoted to group work?
- What roles, if any, will you assign to group members?
- What incentives/rewards will you provide for individual and group work?

Let's look at some alternatives for each of these questions and how you can choose among them.

Division of labor, often overlooked when tasks are structured, is critical to the success of group learning. Allowing students to analyze the task and identify divisions of labor can foster metacognitive growth and higher order thinking.

Group Size.   How many should be in the group? Group size is one of your most important decisions. Although influenced by the size of your class, the number of individual learners assigned to groups has far-reaching consequences for the following:

- Range of abilities within a group
- Time required for a group to reach consensus
- Efficient sharing of materials within a group
- Time needed to complete the end product

Each of these four factors will be affected by the number of members assigned to a group. This is why when subtasks are comparable, you should make groups approximately equal in size.

The most efficient group size for attaining a goal in the least time is four to six members (Cohen, 1994; Johnson, Johnson, & Holubec, 1994). Thus in a class of 25 to 30 students, about five or six groups should be formed. A smaller number of groups with more students in a group can make monitoring of group performance more difficult, because the number of times you may need to interact with each group is reduced accordingly. Groups of seven or eight generally argue more, take longer to reach consensus, have more difficulty sharing limited materials (for example, a reference that must be shared), and take longer to complete the final product.

Thus the rule of thumb is to compose groups of four or five members for single-period activities and slightly larger groups (of five or six) for activities that stretch over more than a class period, thus requiring greater task complexity and role specialization.

Group Composition.   Whom will you select for each group? Unless the task specifically calls for specialized abilities, you will form most groups heterogeneously, with a representative sample of all the learners in a class. Therefore you will assign to groups a mix of higher-/lower-performing, more verbal/less verbal, and more task-oriented/less task-oriented learners. In addition, you will monitor gender and ethnicity across groups.

Diversity contributes to the collaborative process by creating a natural flow of information from those who have it to those who need it. It also promotes the transmission of alternative perspectives and viewpoints that often sends the flow of information in unexpected and desirable directions (Buehl, 2008; Putnam, 2006).

Groups within a classroom generally should reflect the composition of the community outside it. This composition confronts learners with both differences and similarities to provide the motivation for dialogue, the need for sharing, and the natural division of interests and abilities needed to get the job done.

It also is important that groups not only represent a diversity of talents, interests, and abilities but that they also represent typically unengaged students. Social scientists long have observed that the pressure of peers working together often pulls in recalcitrant and passive learners, sweeping them up in the excitement of some larger goal. This is especially true if these learners are deprived of the support of other passive or inactive participants.

Johnson and Johnson (2008, 2005) provide additional suggestions for forming groups:

1. Choose a few higher performing students to provide encouragement and support for students who may be unengaged during group work.

2. Randomly assign students by having them count off; place the ones together, the twos together, and so forth. If five groups are desired in a class of 30, have students count off by six.

3. To build constructive relationships between majority and minority students, between children with and without disabilities, and between boys and girls, use heterogeneous groups formed with students from each category.

4. Share with students the process of choosing group members. First you select a member for a group, then have that member select another, and so on, alternating between your choice and a student's choice until the group is complete.

One approach to drawing unengaged learners into the cooperative activity is to structure the task so success depends on the active involvement of all group members. Structuring the task reduces the problems of active and passive uninvolvement. **Active uninvolvement** is when a group member talks about everything but the assigned goal of the group. **Passive uninvolvement** is when a student does not care to become involved and is a silent member of the group. Here are ways you can structure a cooperative task to increase the likelihood that all group members will be actively involved:

- Assign a product that requires a clearly defined division of labor. (For example, the division of tasks for a writing project might be looking up new words, writing a topic sentence, preparing a chart, finding examples, and so on.) Then assign specific individuals to each activity at the start of the session.

- Within groups, form pairs that are responsible for looking over and actually correcting each other's work or contribution.

- Chart the group's progress on individually assigned tasks, and encourage poor or slow performers to work harder to improve the group's overall progress. Posting a large piece of paper on a wall indicating stages of progress may be all that is needed.

- Purposely limit the resources given to a group so individual members must remain in personal contact to share materials and complete their assigned tasks (for example, one dictionary or hand calculator to share).

- Make one stage of the required product contingent on a previous stage that is the responsibility of another person. This way, group members will provide encouragement or help to those not performing adequately, so they can complete their contribution.

Time on Task.   How much time should you allot for group work? It depends on task complexity (for example, a single class period or multiple periods), but you must make some more refined estimates, as well. You need to determine the time to devote to group work and the time to devote to all groups coming together to share their contributions. This latter time may be used for group reports, a whole-class discussion, debriefing to relate the work experiences of each group to the end product, or some combination of these tasks.

Group work can easily get out of hand in the excitement, controversy, and natural dialogue that can come from passionate discussion. This possibility requires you to place limits on each stage of the cooperative learning activity, so one stage does not take time from another and leave the task disjointed and incomplete in your learners' minds.

Most time, naturally, will be devoted to the work of individual groups, during which the major portion of the end product will be completed. Individual group work normally will consume 60 percent to 80 percent of the time devoted to the cooperative learning activity. The remaining time must be divided among individual group presentations and/or whole-class discussion and debriefing that places the group work into the perspective of a single end product.

If you plan both group reports and a whole-class discussion for the same day, be aware that the discussion probably will get squeezed into a fraction of the time required to make it meaningful. To avoid this, schedule the group discussion or debriefing for the following class day, so class members have ample time to reflect on their group reports and to pull together their own thoughts about the collaborative process, which may or may not have occurred as intended. Providing 15 or 20 minutes at the beginning of class the next day is usually enough time for students to have acquired the proper distance to reflect meaningfully on their experiences of the day before—and to learn from them.

Role Assignment.   What roles should you assign to group members? As you saw earlier, division of labor within and across groups is an important dimension of cooperative learning that is not shared by most large-group discussion methods. This task specialization, as well as the division of labor it often requires, promotes the responsibility and idea sharing that mark an effective cooperative learning activity. Teachers can encourage the acceptance of individual responsibility and idea sharing in a cooperative learning experience by making role assignments within groups and by applying task specialization across groups. Teachers use these roles and responsibilities to complement group work and to interconnect the groups.

Some of the more popular **cooperative learning role functions** that teachers can assign within or across groups are suggested by Johnson and Johnson (1996, 1998):

1. *Summarizer.* This individual paraphrases and plays back to the group major conclusions to see if the group agrees and to prepare for (rehearse) the group's contribution before the whole class.

2. *Checker.* This student checks controversial or debatable statements and conclusions for authenticity against the text, workbook, or references. He or she ensures that the group will not be using unsubstantiated facts or be challenged by more accurate representations of other groups.

3. *Researcher.* This group member reads reference documents and acquires background information when more data are needed (e.g., may conduct an interview, seek a resource from the library). The *researcher* differs from the *checker* in that the former provides critical information for the group to complete its task, whereas the latter certifies the accuracy of the work in progress and/or after it has been completed.

4. *Runner.* This student acquires anything needed for the group to complete the task: materials, equipment, reference works, and so on. Far from a subservient role, this position requires creativity, shrewdness, and even cunning to find the necessary resources, which may also be diligently sought by other groups.

5. *Recorder.* This individual commits to writing the major product of the group. The recorder may require individuals to write their own conclusions, in which case he or she collates, synthesizes, and renders, in coherent form, the abbreviated work of individual group members.

6. *Supporter.* Chosen for his or her upbeat, positive outlook, the supporter praises members when their individual assignments are completed and consoles them in times of discouragement (e.g., when proper references cannot be found). He or she keeps the group moving forward by recording major milestones achieved on a chart for all the class to see, identifying progress made, and encouraging the efforts of individuals, particularly those who may have difficulty participating or completing their tasks.

7. *Observer/Troubleshooter.* This group member takes notes and records information about the group process that may be useful during whole-class discussion or debriefing. He or she reports to a class leader or the teacher when problems appear insurmountable for a group or for individual members.

Typically, a student in one of the preceding role functions also could serve as the group leader. However, because each role entails some form of leadership, the formal designation of *leader* may not be necessary. This has the desirable effect of making all role functions more equal and eliminating an authority-based structure, which can lead to arguments and disunity among members who may see themselves as more or less powerful than others. Be sure to explain and model the specific duties entailed in any of these roles that may be needed before assigning them.

In addition to these specific role functions, all group members have other responsibilities to perform. You may wish to provide students with the following reminders by writing them on the board or in a handout before beginning a cooperative learning activity:

- Ask fellow group members to explain their points clearly when you do not understand.

- Be sure to check your answers and those of others in your group against references or the text.

- Encourage members of your group to go farther—to expand on their points to surpass previous accomplishments and expectations.

- Let everyone finish what he or she has to say without interrupting, whether you agree or disagree.

- Do not be bullied into changing your mind if you really do not want to.

- Criticize ideas, not individuals.

Providing Reinforcement and Rewards. In addition to deciding on group composition, size, time, and the individual responsibilities of group members, establish a system of reinforcement and reward to keep your learners on task and working toward the goal. The following reinforcement strategies have been used effectively with cooperative learning activities:

- Grades (individual and group)
- Bonus points
- Social responsibilities
- Tokens or privileges
- Group contingencies

Grades can be used to reinforce and reward the behavior of individuals and groups during cooperative learning. However, the use of individual grades in the context of cooperative learning should stress the importance of individual effort in *achieving the group goal.*

For this reason, cooperative learning grades usually incorporate both a group member's individual performance (quality and/or extensiveness of work toward accomplishing the group goal) and the thoroughness, relevance, and accuracy of the completed group product. Individuals also can use a five-point scale to rate the active involvement of each teammate in the group process, the average of which can be each member's score for individual effort. Sample scales for measuring group and individual effort are illustrated in Figure 12.2.

Teachers may also use other types of grades as rewards:

1. Average the individual scores to determine the group grade.
2. Assign all group members the average of the highest (or lowest) half of the members' scores.
3. Average an individual's score with the group score. (For example, average an individual score of 4 with a group score of 5: $4 + 5 = 9$ divided by $2 = 4.5$).
4. Add points to the group score for each active participant within the group (or subtract points from the group score for each nonparticipant).

Another reinforcement technique you can use in combination with grades is bonus points, earned on the basis of how many group members reach a preestablished level of performance by the end of their group's activity. You might devise a group quiz (or take it from the text or workbook) and then assign an expected score for each individual member, which could vary according to previous performance or difficulty of the task. Those learners obtaining or exceeding their expected score would earn their group a bonus point.

Another popular form of reinforcement during cooperative learning is rewarding individual efforts with desirable social responsibilities, such as granting the high performer the first pick of group role next time (observer, supporter, checker, etc.). Also you can use privileges to motivate individuals and group members. You might give the highest-performing group independent study time, trips to the learning center, or use of special materials and/or resources. You can give these same privileges to the highest-performing individuals within groups.

Figure 12.2 Sample Scales for Evaluating Individual and Group Effort in a Cooperative Learning Activity

1. How active was _____ in helping the group attain its final product?	2. How complete (or accurate, or useful, or original) is this group's final product?
_____ very active	_____ very complete
_____ fairly active	_____ fairly complete
_____ somewhat active	_____ somewhat complete
_____ not too active	_____ not too complete
_____ not active at all	_____ not complete at all

Finally, teachers frequently have used group contingencies to motivate and reinforce members during cooperative learning. You may choose one of three ways of rewarding the group based on the performance of its individuals:

1. *Average-performance contingency,* in which all members are graded or reinforced based on the average performance of all group members

2. *High-performance group contingency,* in which the highest one-quarter of the group is the basis for grades, reinforcements, or privileges

3. *Low-performance group contingency,* in which the lowest one-quarter of the group is the basis for individual grades or other forms of reinforcement

3. Teaching and Evaluating the Collaborative Process

Another responsibility you have during cooperative learning is teaching the collaborative process. Most learners lack the collaborative skills needed to benefit from many cooperative learning activities. Therefore you need to identify collaborative behaviors, place them in the proper sequence, and demonstrate them. Just as self-directed learning strategies must be modeled, so must collaborative behaviors.

At the heart of collaborative skills is the ability to exchange thoughts and feelings with others at the same conceptual level. Students need to feel comfortable in communicating their ideas, beliefs, and opinions to others in a timely and efficient manner. Johnson and Johnson (2005, 2008) suggest some important cooperative learning skills and some of the ways you can teach them:

1. *Teach how to communicate one's own ideas and feelings.* Encourage the use of *I* and *my* to let students know it is their ideas and feelings that make the collaborative process work. Let students know that their personal experiences—such as events observed, problems encountered, and people met—are valued information they can use to justify their own ideas and feelings.

2. *Make messages complete and specific.* Indicate that along with the message being sent, there should be a frame of reference, perspective, or experience that led to the content of the message—for example, "I got this idea while traveling through a Pueblo Indian reservation in southern Colorado during our vacation last summer" or "I heard the president speak, and his main point reminded me of . . ." or "I read this newspaper article, and it led me to believe some things about . . ."

3. *Make verbal and nonverbal messages congruent.* Establish a sincere tone, in which hidden meanings and snide remarks are not acceptable. Indicate that one's voice and body language always reinforce the message being conveyed, but communicating serious information comically or overdramatizing will confuse both the message and the listener.

4. *Convey an atmosphere of respect and support.* Indicate that all students can contribute information, ideas, feelings, personal experiences, and reactions without fear of ridicule. Make it clear that unsupportive behaviors ("You're crazy if you think . . .") are not allowed. Also make it clear that cooperation rests on sharing both emotional and physical resources, receiving help, dividing responsibility, and looking out for one another's well-being.

5. *Demonstrate how to assess whether the message was properly received.* Instruct your learners in how to ask for interpretive feedback from listeners. Ask them to use phrases such as "What do you think about what I said?" "Does what I said make sense?" and "Can you see what I am trying to say?" The more listeners are asked to paraphrase the message, the more the sender will be sure his or her message has been received as intended.

6. *Teach how to paraphrase another's point of view.* Most learners will want to agree or disagree with the speaker without checking to see if they understand the full intent of the message. Make it known that before one can be either critical or supportive of another's

viewpoint, he or she must paraphrase the viewpoint to the satisfaction of the sender. Teach the following rules of paraphrasing:

  a. Restate the message in your own words, not those of the speaker.

  b. Introduce your paraphrased remarks with phrases such as "It seems to me that you are saying . . ." "If I understand you, you believe that . . ." and "From what I heard you say, your position is . . ."

  c. While paraphrasing, avoid any indication of approval or disapproval. For example, let it be known that responses such as "I disagree with you" and "I think you are right" should not be part of the paraphrased response, for the sole purpose of paraphrasing is to determine whether the message has been accurately received.

  7. *Demonstrate how to negotiate meanings and understandings.* Often one's understanding of a message must be corrected or fine-tuned, because the message was ambiguous, incomplete, or misinterpreted. This means that paraphrases often must be recycled to a greater level of understanding, sometimes for the benefit of both sender, and receiver. Doing so requires the use of tactful phrases from the sender, such as "What I mean to say is . . ." "What I forgot to add was . . ." and "To clarify further . . ." It also requires tactful phrases from the receiver, such as "What I don't understand is . . ." and "Can you say it some other way?" This approach is indispensable for refining the message and ensuring more accurate interpretation. The sender and receiver each must provide a graceful means for the other to correct misperceptions of what was said or heard, without emotional injury to either.

  8. *Teach participation and leadership.* Communicate the importance of the following:

  a. *Mutual benefit:* What benefits the group will benefit the individual.

  b. *Common fate:* Each individual wins or loses on the basis of the overall performance of the group.

  c. *Shared identity:* Everyone is a member of the group, emotionally as well as physically.

  d. *Joint celebration:* Satisfaction is received from the progress of the group as a whole.

  e. *Mutual responsibility:* Everyone should be concerned with underperforming group members.

See In Practice: Focus on Cooperative Learning.

In Practice

Focus on Cooperative Learning

Ms. Carter wants to build student revision groups into her writing workshop structure. Though her students are demonstrating high levels of competence with a variety of revision skills, she knows it will take additional, specific teaching to prepare to utilize those skills cooperatively.

The first day Ms. Carter introduces the concept of revision groups to the class. They draw parallels to individual writing conferences with the teacher and sharing writing with the whole class during author's chair time. Ms. Carter asks the students to generate a list of social skills that allow writing conferences and author's chair time to be effective. From that list Ms. Carter decides to target "be a good listener" and "make suggestions *nicely.*"

Ms. Carter orchestrates a mock author's chair time for the following day. She shares a selection of her own writing with the class. Before reading it aloud Ms. Carter gives select students note cards prompting them to demonstrate the opposite of "being a good listener" (e.g., Whisper to a neighbor three times while I'm reading.) and "making suggestions nicely" (e.g., When I'm done reading say, "That ending was boring, you should redo it.") Once the mock author's chair time was over Ms. Carter prompted a discussion about why those behaviors were ineffective and hurtful. Subsequently, the students produced positive examples of good listening and nice suggestions by contrasting to the negative examples and responding to the prompts: "What does [the target behavior] look like?" and "What does [the target behavior] sound like?"

A fish-bowl of a revision group in action is the next step. Ms. Carter chooses a handful of students to attempt a revision group meeting with her support. The rest of the class sits around the group to watch (like watching a fishbowl) and are provided an observation form prompting them to notice if the group uses good listening and makes suggestions nicely.

For the next two weeks during writer's workshop the class is given specific time to meet in revision groups. Ms. Carter walks around during these times to observe and make notes about how individuals and groups are demonstrating good listening and making suggestions nicely. She provides feedback to individuals and groups either at the end of the revision group meeting or during individual conferences within the next day or two.

A follow-up lesson is planned wherein the class is asked to reflect on generally how effective their work in revision groups has been and specifically how they have done with the cooperative skills of being good listeners and making suggestions nicely. From this discussion Ms. Carter creates a reflection page for revision groups to complete at the end of each meeting. The reflection page will continue to prompt students to engage in the positive cooperative skills and serve to inform Ms. Carter as she reduces her observations and direct support during revision group meeting times.

Over the next several weeks Ms. Carter notices that the students progress from a use of the target cooperative skills that is awkward and contrived to one which is more natural and integrated into the group dynamic. This is her signal that the students are ready to target a new cooperative skill.

Ms. Carter is an experienced teacher and has spent time getting students to learn to work well together in cooperative groups and in meaningful ways. Students need direction, guidance, and practice to learn to work cooperatively. Woolfolk (2011) highlights three fundamental aspects for consideration when preparing students for cooperative learning.

1. Setting Up Cooperative Groups
   - Set group size according to the learning goals.
     - Four to six students if the purpose is to review, rehearse, or practice information
     - Two to four students if the purpose is participating in discussions, problem solving, or computer learning
   - Balance the number of girls and boys.
   - Monitor to ensure all members are contributing and learning.
2. Giving and Receiving Explanations
   - All group members need to engage in asking good questions and giving clear explanations to maximize cooperative learning.
   - Giving explanations is particularly valuable for the student doing the explaining because you have to "organize the information, put it into your own words, think of examples and analogies (which connect the information to things you already know), and test your understanding by answering questions." (Woolfolk, 2011, p. 396)
3. Assigning Roles
   - Cooperation and full participation can be facilitated by assigning roles.
   - Roles should support learning by directly relating to the instructional focus.
     - A social skills focus should utilize roles that support listening, encouragement, and respect for differences.
     - A focus on practice, review, or mastery of basic skills should utilize roles that support persistence, encouragement, and participation.
     - For higher order problem solving or complex learning, groups should utilize roles that support thoughtful discussion, sharing of explanations and insights, probing, brainstorming, and creativity.
   - Emphasize the outcomes over the procedures that correspond to roles.

Source: Based on Woolfolk, A. (2011). *Educational Psychology: Active Learning Edition* (11th Ed.). Boston, MA: Pearson.

4. Monitoring Group Performance

Watch as the teacher in this **video** uses monitoring to ensure groups are on task. What components do you see presented?

To establish a cooperative learning structure, you must observe and intervene as needed to assist learners in acquiring their group's goal. Your most frequent monitoring functions will be telling students where to find needed information, repeating how to complete the task, exhibiting the form of the product to be created (in whole or part), and/or modeling the process to be used in achieving the group's goal. Your role is critical in keeping each group on track. Thus your constant vigilance of group performance is necessary to discover problems and trouble spots before they hamper group progress.

One goal of your monitoring activity should be to identify when a group needs assistance. One common need will be to remind the group of its goal. Groups can easily become disengaged or side-tracked or invent new and perhaps more interesting goals for themselves. Typically, you will move from group to group at least once at the beginning of a cooperative activity, repeating the task and the goal to be certain each group understands it.

A second goal of your monitoring activity should be to redirect groups that have discussed themselves into a blind alley. The heat of discussion and debate frequently distracts groups from productive thought, raising issues that may be only marginally relevant to accomplishing their goal. Key to your monitoring is your ability to recognize when a group is at a difficult juncture. A group might pursue an avenue of fruitless discussion and waste valuable time, when taking a different avenue could set their course productively toward an attainable goal. Your close vigilance and direction of group work can make the difference between aimless talk and productive discussion.

A third monitoring activity you will perform during cooperative learning is to provide emotional support and encouragement to overwhelmed and frustrated group members. Not all group members will gladly accept their individual assignments, nor will all groups accept their designated goal. Your encouragement and support can instill the confidence some will need to complete a task they may be unsure of and that may not be of their own choosing.

5. Debriefing

Providing feedback to the groups on how well they are collaborating is important to their progress in acquiring collaborative skills (Brookhart, 2008; Weissglass, 1996). You can accomplish **debriefing** and evaluation at the end of the collaborative activity in the following ways:

- Openly talk about how the groups functioned. Ask students for their opinions. What issues enhanced or impeded each group's performance?

- Solicit suggestions for improving the process and avoiding problems so higher levels of collaboration can be reached.

- Get viewpoints of predesignated observers. You might assign one or two individuals to record instances of particularly effective and ineffective group collaboration and to report to the full class at the time of the debriefing.

Group members also can rate each other's collaborative skills during debriefing. Individual group members might receive their ratings privately, and group averages might be discussed during the debriefing session to pinpoint strengths and deficiencies.

Figure 12.3 is a scale for rating the collaborative skills of group members. It can be used by (1) group members to rate each other, (2) one group member (e.g., an observer) who has been assigned the task of rating group members, or (3) you, the teacher. Use this scale as a checklist. On it, note the presence or absence of each skill for each group member by placing a checkmark in the appropriate box. Use *NA* ("Not applicable") for skills that do not apply for a given role or task. If you want to keep the ratings anonymous, assign each member a number instead of listing names. The whole group then can be assigned one point for each check placed on the scale, and the group with the best result or end product can be given a reward or special recognition.

Following is a summary of some obstacles to debriefing and how you can structure your cooperative learning activity to promote evaluation and feedback (based on Dishon & O'Leary, 1984):

1. *Time for debriefing.* Teachers rarely have all the time they would like to obtain information about the effectiveness of a cooperative activity. Some ways to quickly assess the effectiveness of your cooperative activity are to pose questions that your students can answer with a simple "yes" or "no" by raising their hands or by responding to a short checklist of agree or disagree questions that are prepared in advance.

2. *Vague feedback.* When students only express their satisfaction with a cooperative activity with phrases such as "We did a good job," "It was fun" or "We finished," they are not providing you information for improving the activity the next time. Try asking each group specific questions about how they arrived at their conclusions and have them identify key

Figure 12.3 Scale for Rating Collaborative Skills of Group Members

Collaborative Skills	Names of Group Members				
Provides knowledge and information to help group's progress					
Is open and candid with whole group					
Provides individual assistance and support to group members who need it					
Evaluates contributions of others in a nonjudgmental, constructive manner					
Shares physical resources—books, handouts, written information—for group to use					
Accurately paraphrases or summarizes what other group members have said					
Gives recognition to other group members when key contributions are made					
Accepts and appreciates cultural, ethnic, and individual differences					

events or incidents that occurred during the collaborative process that made their group function more or less effectively.

3. *Student engagement.* Some groups may not want to fully engage themselves in a debriefing activity. To promote their engagement, you can have each student write a paragraph or two citing specific events that describe how their group functioned. To heighten your student's engagement you can award bonus points for a well-written debriefing report.

4. *Incomplete reporting.* To help individuals and whole groups take the debriefing process seriously and turn in detailed and accurate debriefing reports, you can have group members read and check the accuracy of each other's reports. Group members can read and sign one another's debriefing reports to show that they have been checked for accuracy and completeness.

5. *Poor collaborative skills during debriefing.* During a debriefing discussion, a few group members may not to listen carefully, argue, or be disrespectful to another's ideas. You can help these learners become more effective and active contributors to the debriefing process by having them observe the debriefing process of higher functioning groups and, then, return to their own group to model these skills.

Team-Oriented Cooperative Learning Activities

Research on team oriented cooperative learning indicates that teams of learners can increase the collaborative skills, self-esteem, and achievement of individual learners (Slavin, 2001). Four **team-oriented cooperative learning** techniques have been particularly successful in bringing about these outcomes: Student Teams–Achievement Division, Teams–Games–Tournaments, Jigsaw II, and Team-Assisted Individualization. A brief summary of these follows, based on the work of Slavin (1993). These activities can be augmented by additional team oriented challenges suggested by Bordessa (2005).

Student Teams–Achievement Division (STAD)

In Student Teams–Achievement Division, the teacher assigns students to four- or five-member learning teams. Each team is as heterogeneous as possible to represent the composition of the entire class (boys/girls, higher-performing/lower-performing students, etc.).

Begin the cooperative learning activity by presenting new material via presentation or discussion and providing worksheets of problem sets, vocabulary words, questions, and such, from which students can review the main points of the presentation or discussion. When your presentation, explanation, or introduction has been completed, have team members study your worksheets, quizzing each other. They should work in pairs or in small groups, discussing the worksheet content, clarifying difficult or confusing points among themselves, and asking you questions when necessary.

Before the teams begin, give one member of each team or pair the answers to all the questions or problems on the worksheet, and assign this member the task of checking the written or oral responses of the others. Allow the teams sufficient time for everyone to complete the problems or questions on the worksheet. Make the worksheet concise enough to accommodate this.

After the teams have had sufficient time to practice with the worksheet and answer key, give individuals a written quiz over the material, in which team members may not help one another. Score the quizzes immediately, and convert individual scores into team scores (for example, by averaging all, the top half, or the bottom half). Determine the contributions of individual students by looking at how much each student's quiz score exceeds her or his past quiz average or a preset score based on his or her learning history. This way, the entire group receives a score based on all the individual members' performances, and each individual learner also receives an improvement score based on the extent to which his or her individual score exceeds past performance or a preestablished standard that recognizes the team member's learning history.

During STAD, the teacher has several roles. You act as a resource person and monitor group study activities, intervening when necessary to suggest better study techniques ("Why not choose partners now and quiz each other on the questions you have been discussing?").

Research shows that during STAD, learners gain a sense of camaraderie and demonstrate helpfulness toward fellow team members. They also pursue self-directed learning and rehearsal strategies modeled by the teacher and become self-motivated through having some control over their own learning.

Teams–Games–Tournaments

A cooperative learning activity closely related to STAD is the use of Teams–Games–Tournaments (TGT). TGT uses the same general format as STAD (four- to five-member groups studying worksheets). However, instead of individually taking quizzes at the end of a study period, students play academic games to show their mastery of the topic studied.

Jigsaw II

In the cooperative learning activity called *Jigsaw II,* you assign students to four- to six-member teams to work on an academic task broken into several subtasks, depending on the number of groups. You assign students to teams and then assign a unique responsibility to each team member. For example, assign each team member a section of the text to read. Then give each team member a special task with which to approach the reading. Assign one team member to write down and look up the meanings of new vocabulary words, another to summarize or outline the main points in the text, another to identify major and minor characters, and so on.

When all the team members have their specific assignments, break out from each original team all members with the same assignment (for example, finding and defining new vocabulary words). Have them meet as an "expert" group to discuss their assignment and to share their conclusions and results with one another. Within an expert group, members may assist each other by comparing notes (for example, definitions) and identifying points overlooked by other group members. When all the expert groups have had the opportunity to share, discuss, and modify their conclusions, members should return to their respective teams. Members should then take turns teaching their teammates about their respective responsibilities.

Jigsaw II heightens interest among team members, because the only way they can learn about the topics to which they were not assigned is to listen to the teammate who received that assignment. After each "expert" makes his or her presentation to the team telling what he or she learned from the expert group, give individual quizzes to assess how much students have learned. As in STAD, you can assign students both an overall group score and an individual improvement score based on past performance. These scores become the basis for team and individual rewards for the highest scorers.

Team-Assisted Individualization

One of the newest cooperative learning activities is Team-Assisted Individualization (TAI), which combines some of the characteristics of individualized and cooperative learning. Although originally designed for elementary and middle school mathematics classes, TAI can be used with any subject matter and grade level for which some individualized learning materials are available (e.g., computer software, self-paced texts). In TAI, you start each student working through the individualized materials at a point designated by a placement test or previous learning history. Thus students may work at different levels, depending on the heterogeneity of achievement in the classroom.

Give each student a specified amount of content to work through (for example, pages, problem sets, questions and answers) at his or her own pace. Also assign each learner to a team that represents all achievement levels and, therefore, learners who approach the individualized materials at different levels of complexity. Heterogeneity within the teams is important, because it allows you to ask team members to check one another's work. Checkers are expected to have completed portions of the material that are more advanced than those completed by others. As many group members as possible should assume the role of checker. When necessary, checkers should be given answer sheets.

Have student monitors give quizzes on each unit and then score and record the results on a master scorecard. Base team scores on the average number of units completed each week by team members and their scores on the unit quizzes. For those teams that complete a preset number of units with a minimum average quiz score, provide a reward (e.g., certificates, independent study time, learning center privileges). Assign one student monitor to each team to manage the routine checking, distribution of individualized materials, and administering and recording of the quizzes.

Because TAI uses individualized materials, it is especially useful for teaching heterogeneous classes. These classes afford you few opportunities for whole-class instruction and little time to instruct numerous small groups with diverse learning needs.

Overview of Team-Oriented Cooperative Learning Activities

The similarities and differences among the four cooperative learning methods are summarized in Table 12.1.

 Pay attention to the various cooperative learning techniques used by the teacher in this **video**.

Table 12.1 Similarities and Differences among Four Cooperative Learning Activities

Student Teams—Achievement Division (STAD)	Teams-Games-Tournaments (TGT)	Jigsaw II	Team-Assisted Individualization (TAI)
1. Teacher presents content in lecture or discussion 2. Teams work through problems/questions on worksheets 3. Teacher gives quiz over material studied 4. Teacher determines team average and individual improvement scores	1. Teacher presents content in lecture or discussion 2. Teams work through problems/questions on worksheets 3. Teams play academic games against each other for points 4. Teacher tallies team points over four-week period to determine best team and best individual scorers	1. Students read section of text and are assigned unique topic 2. Students within teams with same topic meet in "expert" groups 3. Students return to home groups to share knowledge of their topics with teammates 4. Students take quiz over each topic discussed 5. Individual quizzes are used to create team scores and individual improvement scores	1. Students are given diagnostic test/exercise by student monitor to determine placement in materials 2. Students work through assigned unit at their own pace 3. Teammate checks text against answers, and student monitor gives quiz 4. Team quizzes are averaged, and number of units completed are counted by monitor to create team scores

Many different forms of cooperative learning have been successfully used in classrooms of all grade levels and subject matters. Some of the most successful cooperative learning activities, however, have come from the ingenuity and creativity of individual teachers, who, with little formal preparation, have devised activities to promote social interaction when the subjects they are teaching encourage cooperative outcomes. Although many versions of cooperative learning can be devised from the preceding four methods, as an effective teacher, you should seize the opportunity to create a cooperative learning experience whenever the content goals lend themselves to promoting collaborative skills. This in turn can increase your learners' self-esteem, critical-thinking and problem-solving abilities that will contribute to their lifelong learning goals.

Culturally Responsive Cooperative Learning

One of the first things you will notice during cooperative learning activities is the variety of learning styles among your students. The variety in your students' independence, persistence, and flexibility during cooperative learning will be influenced, to some extent, by the predominant cultures and ethnicities in your school and classroom (Banks & Banks, 2006; Irvine & York, 2001; Price & Nelson, 2010).

For example, Bennett (2010) points out how interactions among students and between the students and teacher are influenced by learning styles that are rooted in their culture. Cushner, McClelland, and Safford (2011) describe how being a member of a subculture, minority, or ethnic

During cooperative learning, some learners may benefit more and adapt better to a task orientation that is less structured and more field dependent. Recent findings suggest that some task orientations, such as cooperative learning, may be more appropriate for some groups. Research also suggests that some of today's objectives—such as interdisciplinary thematic units and objectives pertaining to integrated bodies of knowledge—may require cooperative and collaborative activities to achieve their goals.

group can enhance the nature of interpersonal relationships within a classroom by increasing cohesiveness, informality, interpersonal harmony, and cooperation. Also Bowers and Flinders (1991) provide examples of how noise level, use of classroom space, turn taking, and negotiation can vary among social classes and ethnicities to create different but equally productive learning climates when properly managed and matched to cultural expectations.

In Chapter 2, we saw that learners can be distinguished on the basis of the cognitive processes they use to learn. But what and how they learn can also be influenced by the way a learning task is presented and if it affords them the opportunity to use their preferred learning style. Two of the learning styles that have been frequently studied are *field independence* and *field dependence* (Irvine & York, 2001; Mshelia, 2008; Wakefield, 1996).

The implications of field independence and field dependence for cooperative learning have been related to students' need for structure. From a review of the literature, Irvine and York (2001) have identified characteristics of students who need more or less structure to maximize their opportunity to learn. Some of their characteristics, which have implications for how to plan a cooperative learning activity, include the following:

Those Who Need More Structure (Field Dependent):

- Have a shorter attention span and like to move through material rapidly
- Are reluctant to try something new and do not like to appear wrong
- Tend not to ask many questions
- May need reassurance before starting a task
- Want to know facts before concepts
- Usually give only brief answers

Those Who Need Less Structure (Field Independent):

- Like to discuss and argue
- Want to solve problems with a minimum of teacher assistance
- Dislike details and step-by-step formats
- Are comfortable with abstractions and generalities
- Emphasize emotions and are open about themselves
- Tend to make many interpretations and inferences

Irvine and York (2001) also suggest specific ways teachers can orient their cooperative activities to promote particular learning styles:

For Students Who Require More Structure

- Have definite and consistent rules.
- Provide specific, step-by-step guides and instructions.
- Make goals and deadlines short and definite.
- Change pace often.
- Assess problems frequently.
- Move gradually from group work to discussion.

For Students Who Require Less Structure

- Provide topics to choose from.
- Make assignments longer and with self-imposed deadlines.
- Encourage the use of resources outside the classroom.
- Devote more time to group assignments, with the teacher serving as a resource.
- Use and encourage interest in the opinions and values of others.
- Provide opportunities for extended follow-up projects and assignments.

It has been noted that some learners within cultural and ethnic groups tend to respond better and benefit more to a task orientation that is less structured—more field dependent. For example, cooperative learning has been shown to increase the task related success of learners who are more field dependent (Losey, 1995). Other authors (Jacobs, 1999; Jacobs, Power, & Loh, 2002) provide alternatives to the notion that the most effective task orientation for the teacher is to stand in front of the classroom, lecturing or explaining to students seated in neatly arranged rows, who are assumed to have little or no expectations about or experiences with the content being taught. Cooperative teaching handbooks by Jacobs, Power, and Loh (2002), Stahl (1994, 1995, 1996), and Jolliffe (2007) suggest not only that cooperative learning may benefit some cultural and ethnic groups but also that cooperative learning may be required for all learners to help attain the problem solving and inquiry skills needed for today's curriculum objectives in social studies, science, mathematics, and the language arts.

Case History and Licensure Preparation

DIRECTIONS: *The following case history pertains to Chapter 12 content. After reading the case history, go to Chapter 12 in the Book Specific Resources section in the MyEducationLab for your course. Open the Case History and Licensure Preparation activity and complete the questions that follow. Upon completion of the test, scored answers to the short-answer question pertaining to the case history and multiple choice questions will be provided.*

Case History

Ms. Choo teaches fourth grade. Test scores for her elementary school have been lower than the state and district averages, particularly in math. Her new principal has told the staff that improvement in mathematics is a priority. Students attending the school come from lower-socioeconomic and culturally diverse backgrounds. Quite a bit of Ms. Choo's time last year was devoted to trying to manage classroom disruptions, many relating to students' petty squabbles and rude behavior toward one another.

This year, Ms. Choo is going to try to attend to her class's academic and social interaction difficulties by implementing a cooperative learning activity in math. Ms. Choo has had her students do so-called group work before, but this will be her first attempt to employ collaborative learning in a systematic way. She plans to keep it simple this time, organizing the class into assignment "help line" groups. Group members will work together to understand difficult problems. They will make corrections to mistakes by relying on a group member who understands the problems and got the correct answer. The group will also study together before each test with the goal of improving the group's average test score.

Ms. Choo knows that much of the success of her groups rests on their composition, and she has worked hard to ensure that they are heterogeneous in many ways. First of all, she looked at student achievement scores and past grades in math and made sure all levels were represented within each group. She also maintained cultural

diversity within the groups, as well as a male-female balance reflective of the class. She tried to split up cliques and special friends and to mix shy with more outgoing students.

Before the groups meet, however, Ms. Choo models and teaches the collaborative process. She tells the class that their group support and social interaction will be as important as the math content of the activity. Each group will have a "life support system," or CPR, which stands for Communication, Participation, and Respect.

To communicate properly, each group member should be able to explain the math steps necessary to reach the solution. Getting the right answer is not enough. Participation will be very important. All students must play active roles in their group; there will be mutual responsibility and benefit, shared identity, and joint celebration of success. To show respect and support for each other, students must not engage in ridicule or sarcasm. Instead they must try to say constructive things about fellow group members. Instead of saying "That was really dumb," they might say "I can understand how you might make that mistake." "Fake it till you can make it," Ms. Choo tells them, meaning that compliments may seem forced at first but will become more natural as time goes on.

To ensure that the collaborative process takes hold, Ms. Choo will give each group a grade based on her CPR model. She will spend some time with each group to see how well they communicate, participate, and show respect. For the first few weeks, the collaborative grade will be twice as important as the group average on the weekly test. Students' individual grades on the weekly tests will be recorded, as well.

With all this preparation behind her, Ms. Choo ushers in the Math Assignment Help Line with high expectations. However, she is somewhat disappointed to see Sally, who has been split up from her best friend, Teresa, sit sullenly and not participate in her group. Ricardo, usually quiet and withdrawn, seems to get along very well with the four members of his group—almost too well. He and Sam seem to talk about their after-school baseball practice as much as they do about the math problems. Troy, a very strong student, stays after class one day to complain about having his high score brought down by the group average. He also resents having to explain everything to someone else. He asks if he can work alone, because he always gets A's on the tests.

The first week's tests are averaged, and there is no improvement in two of the groups. One group's achievement is up slightly, and three groups have lower scores than before.

Summing Up

The main points in this chapter include the following:

Outcomes of Cooperation

1. Critical-thinking, reasoning, and problem-solving skills are often learned in cooperative interaction with others.

2. Indirect instruction and self-directed and cooperative learning share the complementary objectives of engaging students in the learning process and promoting higher (more complex) patterns of behavior.

3. Cooperative learning activities can instill the following in your learners:

   - Attitudes and values that guide the learner's behavior outside the classroom

   - Acceptable forms of prosocial behavior that may not be modeled in the home

   - Alternative perspectives and viewpoints on which to base attitudes and values

   - An integrated identity that can reduce contradictory thoughts and actions

   - Higher thought processes and thinking skills

Components of a Cooperative Learning Activity

4. Planning for cooperative learning requires decisions about the following:

   - Teacher–student interaction

   - Student–student interaction

   - Task specialization and materials

   - Role expectations and responsibilities

5. The primary goal of teacher–student interaction during cooperative learning is to promote independent thinking.

6. The primary goal of student–student interaction during cooperative learning is to encourage the active participation and interdependence of all members of the class.

7. The primary goal of task specialization and learning materials during cooperative learning is to create an activity structure in which the end product depends on the sharing, cooperation, and collaboration of individuals within groups.

8. The primary goal of assigning roles and responsibilities during cooperative learning is to facilitate the work of the group and to promote communication and sharing among its members.

Establishing a Cooperative Task Structure in Your Classroom

9. Establishing a cooperative task structure involves five steps:
   a. Specify the goal of the activity.
   b. Structure the task.
   c. Teach and evaluate the collaborative process.
   d. Monitor group performance.
   e. Debrief.

10. The goal of a cooperative activity may take different forms:

    - Written group reports

    - Higher individual achievement

    - An oral performance

    - An enumeration or resolution

    - A critique

    - Data collection

11. You have three responsibilities in specifying the goal of a cooperative activity:
    - Identify the outcome.
    - Check for understanding.
    - Set a cooperative tone.

12. Structuring the cooperative learning task involves the following decisions:
    - How large the groups will be
    - How group members will be selected
    - How much time will be devoted to group work
    - What roles group members will be assigned
    - What incentives and rewards will be provided for individual and group work

13. Generally, the most efficient size for a group to reach the desired goal in the least amount of time is four to six members.

14. Unless a group task specifically calls for specialized abilities, groups should be formed heterogeneously, representing the diversity of learners in the class.

15. Methods for selecting group members include the following:
    - Distribute isolated or passive learners among groups.
    - Randomly assign students to groups.
    - Choose students from each category (boys and girls, students with and without disabilities, etc.).
    - Share with students the process of choosing group members.

16. An actively uninvolved group member is one who talks about everything but the assigned goal of the group; a passively uninvolved group member is one who does not care about the work of the group and becomes silent.

17. Methods for discouraging active and passive uninvolvement include the following:
    - Assign a product requiring a clear division of labor.
    - Form pairs in which students oversee each other's work.
    - Chart group progress on individually assigned tasks.
    - Purposefully limit the resources provided to promote sharing and personal contact.
    - Make one stage of the required product contingent on a previous stage that is the responsibility of someone else.

18. Group work should make up 60 percent to 80 percent of the time devoted to a cooperative activity; the remainder should be devoted to whole-class discussion and debriefing.

19. The division of labor within a group can be accomplished with role assignments. The following are some of the most popular:
    - Summarizer
    - Recorder
    - Checker
    - Supporter
    - Researcher
    - Observer/Troubleshooter
    - Runner

20. The following types of reinforcement strategies can be used with cooperative learning activities:
    - Individual and group grades
    - Bonus points
    - Social responsibilities
    - Tokens or privileges
    - Group rewards

21. Teaching and evaluating the collaborative process involves showing your learners how to do the following:
    - Communicate their own ideas and feelings.
    - Make messages complete and specific.
    - Make verbal and nonverbal messages congruent.
    - Convey an atmosphere of respect and support.
    - Assess if the message was properly received.
    - Paraphrase another's point of view.
    - Negotiate meanings and understandings.
    - Actively participate in a group and assume leadership.

22. During the monitoring of group performance, the teacher's role is to remind each group of its goal, to redirect group efforts when needed, and to provide emotional support and encouragement.

23. During debriefing, gather feedback in a whole-class discussion about the collaborative process in these ways:
    - Openly talk about how the groups functioned during the cooperative activity.
    - Solicit suggestions for how the process could be improved.
    - Obtain the viewpoints of predesignated observers.

Team-Oriented Cooperative Learning Activities

24. Desirable outcomes have been documented for four popular team-oriented cooperative learning activities:
    - Student Teams–Achievement Division (STAD)
    - Teams–Games–Tournaments (TGT)
    - Jigsaw II
    - Team-Assisted Individualization (TAI)

Culturally Responsive Cooperative Learning

25. Task-specific outcomes of a cooperative learning activity can be related to differences in learning styles, which, for some, may be cultural in origin. Field-dependent learners tend to need a more structured cooperative learning activity than field-independent learners.

Key Terms

Active uninvolvement
Cooperative learning
Cooperative learning role functions

Debriefing
Passive uninvolvement
Prosocial behavior

Task specialization
Task structure
Team-oriented cooperative learning

Discussion and Practice Questions

Questions marked with an asterisk are answered in Appendix B. Some asterisked questions may require student follow-up responses not included in Appendix B. Go to the Assignments and Activities section of the various topics on the MyEducationLab for your course to complete additional practice activities related to this chapter's content.

*1. What two objectives are shared by self-directed and cooperative learning? Suggest an instance in which self-directed learning might occur within the context of a cooperative group.

*2. Identify five specific outcomes of a cooperative learning activity. Which will be the most important in your classroom and why?

*3. What five steps are required for establishing a cooperative task structure? To which step do you believe you will devote the most (a) planning time and (b) classroom time?

*4. What are some forms of end products or behaviors that you might require at the end of a cooperative learning activity? Which product or behavior do you think presents the biggest challenge for evaluation and assessment?

*5. About how large should a cooperative learning group be to reach a specified goal in the least amount of time? In what situation might groups be smaller or larger and still function effectively?

*6. What methods can you use to select members of a cooperative group? What might be an advantage of using one method over another?

*7. Identify three methods for minimizing passive and active uninvolvement in a cooperative learning activity. In your opinion, which method is best for drawing nonengaged learners into the cooperative activity?

*8. Identify student roles that can be assigned to group members and describe the responsibilities of each role. Think of an additional role that might be suited to the goals of a cooperative activity in your classroom.

*9. When combining scores for individual and group work into a single cooperative learning grade, what options are available? Which do you prefer and why?

*10. What three roles does the teacher perform during a cooperative learning activity to monitor and, when necessary, improve group performance? What level of difficulty would you assign to each role?

*11. What can you do to debrief your class after a cooperative learning activity? Which strategy would you prefer to use in your classroom?

*12. Identify five obstacles to debriefing, and suggest several approaches for dealing with each one. For each obstacle, identify the one you would first try to improve the debriefing process.

Professional Practice

Field Experience and Practice Activities

Questions marked with an asterisk are answered in Appendix B. Some asterisked questions may require student follow-up responses not included in Appendix B.

*1. Of the four components to consider in designing a cooperative learning activity, which, in your opinion, requires the most planning, based on your experience in classrooms? Why?

*2. Identify any reinforcers or rewards you have observed being used in classrooms to motivate or encourage group members. Which do you believe to be most effective?

*3. List the eight communication skills Johnson and Johnson (1996, 2005) identified for cooperative learning. Briefly describe and provide an example of the three you believe will be most important in your classroom.

4. Choose one of the four team-oriented cooperative learning activities suggested by Slavin (1993) that you would be willing to try out in your classroom. Describe how you would implement the

technique in your classroom in terms of the structure of the activity to be performed, the work of the teams, your role as teacher, and procedures for team scoring and recognition.

Digital Portfolio Activities

The following digital portfolio activities relate to InTASC Standards 2, 3, 4, 5, 6, and 8.

1. In Field Experience and Practice Activity 3, you were asked to describe three of the eight communication skills required for cooperative learning and to provide examples of how you would teach them to your students. Because these skills are essential for successful cooperative learning, place your response in your digital portfolio in a folder labeled "Cooperative and Collaborative Learning." Your examples of how you would teach the skills to your learners will be valuable in forming your first cooperative learning activity.

2. In Field Experience and Practice Activity 4, you were asked to choose one of the team-oriented cooperative learning activities suggested by Slavin (1993) and describe how you would implement it. Read over your response to Field Experience Activity 4 to review the specificity with which you described the structure of the activity, the work of the teams, your role as teacher, and procedures for team scoring and recognition. Make sure you will know exactly what to do at the time of your first cooperative activity. Add any details to your description that may be needed, and place it in your digital portfolio "Cooperative and Collaborative Learning" folder.

MyEducationLab™

Go to MyEducationLab (www.myeducationlab.com) for Effective Teaching Methods: Research-Based Practice where you can:

- Find learning outcomes for the various course topics course along with national standards that connect to these outcomes.

- Complete **Assignments and Activities** that can help you more deeply understand the chapter content.

- Apply and practice your understanding of the core teaching skills identified in the chapter with **Building Teaching Skills and Dispositions** coaching activities.

- Check your comprehension of the content covered in the chapter with a book specific **Study Plan**. Here you will be able to take a chapter **pretest**, receive feedback on your answers, and then access personalized **Review, Practice, and Enrichment exercises** to enhance your understanding of chapter content. After you complete the exercises, take a **posttest** to confirm your comprehension.

- Learn how to address common classroom management issues in the **Simulations in Classroom Management.**

- Access video clips of CCSSO **National Teachers of the Year award winners** responding to the question, "Why Do I Teach?" in the Teacher Talk section.

- Create, update, and share quality lesson plans with the **Lesson Plan Builder**.

- Access state licensure test requirements, overviews of what tests cover, and sample test items in the **Certification and Licensure** section.

- Learn how to create a high quality teaching portfolio in the **Preparing a Portfolio** section.

- Access tips, advice, and other information on resume writing and interviewing, your first year of teaching, and law and public policies in the Beginning Your Career section.

13

Assessing Learners

This chapter will help you answer these questions and meet the following InTASC standards for effective teaching.

- What is the difference between a *norm-referenced* and a *criterion-referenced* test?
- What are the advantages and disadvantages of different objective test formats?
- How can I grade essay tests fairly?
- How will I know if a test measures what I want it to measure?
- What is a *performance test*?
- How can I use rubrics and student portfolios to assess my learners?

InTASC

STANDARD 1 **Leadership and Collaboration.** The teacher seeks appropriate leadership roles and opportunities to take responsibility for student learning, to collaborate with learners, families, colleagues, other school professionals, and community members to ensure learner growth, and to advance the profession.

STANDARD 3 **Learning Environments.** The teacher works with others to create environments that support individual and collaborative learning, and that encourage positive social interaction, active engagement in learning, and self motivation.

STANDARD 5 **Application of Content.** The teacher understands how to connect concepts and use differing perspectives to engage learners in critical thinking, creativity, and collaborative problem solving related to authentic local and global issues.

STANDARD 8 **Instructional Strategies.** The teacher understands and uses a variety of instructional strategies to encourage learners to develop deep understanding of content areas and their connections, and to build skills to apply knowledge in meaningful ways.

STANDARD 9 **Professional Learning and Ethical Practice.** The teacher engages in ongoing professional learning and uses evidence to continually evaluate his/her practice, particularly the effects of his/her choices and actions on others (learners, families, other professionals, and the community), and adapts practice to meet the needs of each learner.

*S*ome of your strongest childhood and adolescent memories probably include taking tests in school. For that matter, test taking probably is among the most vivid memories of your college experience. If you are like most people who have spent many years in school, you have strong or mixed feelings about tests. This chapter will dispel some of the discomfort you might feel about tests and show how they can be effective tools in your classroom.

MyEducationLab

Visit the MyEducationLab for *Effective Teaching Methods: Research-Based Practice*, 8e to enhance your understanding of chapter concepts with a personalized Study Plan. You'll also have the opportunity to hone your teaching skills through video-based Assignments and Activities as well as Building Teaching Skills and Dispositions lessons.

Norm-Referenced and Criterion-Referenced Tests

To evaluate your learners' progress, what type of information do you need? That depends on your purpose. Testing can provide two types of information:

1. A student's place or rank compared to other students is revealed by a **norm-referenced test (NRT)**, so named because it compares a student's performance to that of a norm group (a large, representative sample of learners). Such information is useful when you need to compare a learner's performance to that of others at the same age or grade level.

2. A student's level of proficiency in or mastery of a skill or set of skills is revealed by a **criterion-referenced test (CRT)**, so named because it compares a student's performance with an absolute standard called a *criterion* (such as 75 percent correct). Such information helps you decide whether a student needs more instruction or an alternative instructional strategy to acquire a skill or set of skills.

Figure 13.1 illustrates when to use NRTs and CRTs. You will always want to identify the type of information needed before selecting a particular test.

Unfortunately, some teachers know little more about a student after testing than they did before. In our technically oriented society, test scores are sometimes considered ends in themselves, without the interpretation that is essential for the improvement and academic success of the learner. In such cases, teachers and parents may be quick to denounce a test, suggesting that without the proper interpretation, test data are useless. In reality, the problem might be that the teacher who selected the test either failed to identify the specific information needed before administering the test or failed to match the test carefully to his or her purpose. Let's look in on the following scenario, in which counselor John is checking his records when sixth-grade teacher Mary taps on his door.

Figure 13.1 Relationship of the Purpose of Testing and Information Desired to the Type of Test Required

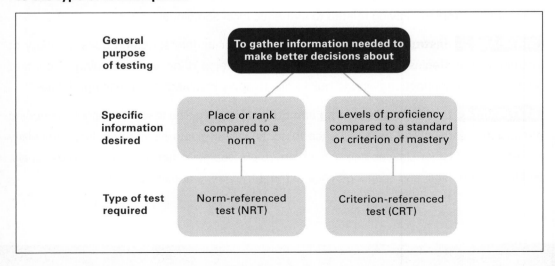

Mary: I just stopped by to see you about Danny. He's been in remedial classes for the last five years, and now he'll be in my class this year. Mrs. Rodrigues had him last year, and she said you have all the test information on him.

John: Yeah. In fact, I was just reviewing his folder. Danny's Math Cluster score on the Woodcock-Johnson is at the sixth percentile, and his Reading Cluster is at the first percentile. Good luck with him!

Mary: Boy, he sure is low. I guess that's why he's been in the remedial classroom for so long.

John: You've got it!

Mary: Well, really that's about what I was expecting. What about his skill levels?

John: What do you mean?

Mary: You know, his academic skill levels.

John: Oh, his grade levels! Umm, let's see. . . . His math grade equivalent is 2.6, and his reading grade equivalent is even lower, 1.7.

Mary: Well . . . that's not really what I need to know. I know he's way below grade level, but I'm wondering about his skills—specific skills, that is. You know, like what words he can read, what phonetic skills he has, if he can subtract two-digit numbers with regrouping . . . things like that.

John: [Becoming a bit irritated.] Mary, what more do you need than what I've given you? Don't you know how to interpret these scores?

Mary: [Frustrated.] John, I do know what these scores mean, but they only compare Danny to other students. I'm not interested in that. I want to know what he can and can't do, so I can begin teaching him at the proper skill level.

John: [Shaking his head.] Look, he's at the first-grade level in reading and the second-grade level in math. Isn't that enough?

Mary: But what level of mastery has he demonstrated?

John: Mastery? He's years behind! He's mastered very little.

There appears to be a communication problem between Mary and John. John has conveyed a lot of test information to Mary, yet she does not seem to get much out of it. John is frustrated, Mary is frustrated, and little that will help Danny has been accomplished. What is the problem?

The problem appears to be John's. Mary's questions refer to competencies or mastery of skills. Referring to Figure 13.1, we can conclude that she is interested in information about Danny's *level of proficiency*. But John's answers refer to test performance compared to other students, which means information about Danny's *rank compared to others*. Answers to Mary's questions can come only from a test designed to indicate whether Danny exceeded some state or school district standard of performance taken to indicate mastery of some skill.

If a test indicated that Danny could subtract two-digit numbers with regrouping, Mary would say he had mastered this skill if, for example, 80 percent or more correct was the criterion for mastery. In other words, he would have exceeded the standard of 80 percent mastery of subtraction of two-digit numbers with regrouping. Recall that a CRT is designed to measure whether a student has mastered a skill, where the definition of *mastery* depends on an established level or criterion of performance.

But the information John provided was normative or comparative. Danny's grade-equivalent scores allow decisions involving only comparisons between his performance and that of the typical or average performance of learners in a norm group. Danny's grade-equivalent score of 1.7 in reading indicates his reading ability equals that of the average first-grader after seven months in the first grade. It says nothing about which words Danny knows, nor does it give any information about the process he uses to read new words or how long it takes him to comprehend what he reads or to learn

The appropriateness of a given type of test depends on the purpose of testing. Criterion-referenced tests (CRTs) measure specific skills related to lesson objectives or unit content, while norm-referenced tests (NRTs) measure skills related to general categories of achievement and aptitude.

the meanings of new words. All that this score indicates is that his ability to read is well below that of the average fifth-grader and equivalent to that of an average first-grader after 7 months of school.

Grade-equivalent scores and other scores obtained from norm-referenced tests allow only general, comparative decisions, not decisions about mastery of specific skills.

Criterion-Referenced Tests

As you may have guessed, CRTs must be specific to yield information about individual skills. This is both an advantage and a disadvantage. With a specific test of individual skills, you can be relatively certain your students have either mastered or failed to master the skills in question. However, the major disadvantage is that many CRTs are necessary to make decisions about the multitude of skills taught in the average classroom.

Norm-Referenced Tests

This **video** provides an insight into the difference between norm-referenced and criterion-referenced tests. Pay attention to the advantages and disadvantages of each type of assessment.

The NRT, in contrast, tends to be general. It measures a variety of specific and general skills at once, but it cannot measure them thoroughly. Thus with NRT results, you are not as sure as you are with CRT results that your students have mastered the individual skills in question. But NRT results give you an estimate of ability in a variety of skills much faster than you could achieve with a large number of CRTs. Because of this trade-off in the uses of criterion-referenced and norm-referenced measures, there are situations in which each is appropriate. As you can see, determining the appropriateness of a given type of test depends on your purpose in testing.

The Test Blueprint

In Chapter 5, we discussed writing objectives at different levels of cognitive complexity. In this chapter, we introduce the **test blueprint**, which matches test items to your objectives. The test blueprint ensures that you will not overlook details essential to a good test. More specifically, it ensures that a test will sample learning across the range of (1) content areas covered by your instruction and (2) the cognitive and/or affective skills and processes you consider important. It ensures that your test will include a variety of items that tap different levels of cognitive complexity. Figure 13.2 illustrates a test blueprint for a unit on elementary school mathematics.

Figure 13.2 Test Blueprint for a Unit on Subtraction without Borrowing

Content Outline	Knowledge	Comprehension	Application	Total	Percent
1. The student will discriminate the subtraction sign from the addition sign.	1			1	4%
2. The student will discriminate addition problems from subtraction problems.	2			2	8%
3. The student will discriminate correctly solved subtraction problems from incorrectly solved subtraction problems.		4		4	16%
4. The student will solve correctly single-digit subtraction problems.			6	6	24%
5. The student will solve correctly subtraction problems with double-digit numerators and single-digit denominators.			6	6	24%
6. The student will solve correctly double-digit subtraction problems.			6	6	24%
Total	3	4	18	25	
Percent	12%	16%	72%		100%

To construct a test blueprint, follow these steps:

1. Classify each instructional objective for the content to be tested according to the behaviors described in Chapter 5 (for example, knowledge, comprehension, application, etc.).

2. Record the number of items to be constructed for each objective in the cell corresponding to its behavioral category.

3. Total the items for each instructional objective, and record the number in the "Total" column near the right edge of the form.

4. Total the number of items falling into each behavior, and record the number in the "Total" row near the bottom of the chart.

5. Compute the column and row percentages by dividing each total by the number of items in the test.

Constructing a test blueprint before preparing a test ensures you have adequately sampled the content area and accurately matched the test items to your instructional objectives.

Objective Test Items

Your test blueprint may call for objective test items. Objective test items have one of four formats: true/false, matching, multiple choice, and completion (short answer). Stiggins (2012) prefers the term *selected response* for these formats to emphasize that it is the system by which these formats are scored that is objective, not the selection of content they measure. In this section, we consider characteristics of each format that can make your objective, or selected-response, test items more effective.

Your first decision after completing the test blueprint will be to choose a format or a combination of formats for your test. The way you wrote the objectives may have predetermined the format, but in many instances, you will have a choice among several item formats. For example, consider the following objectives and item formats.

True/False Items

True/false items are popular because they are quick and easy to write—or at least they seem to be. True/false items really do take less time to write than good objective items of any other format, but good true/false items are not so easy to prepare.

As you know from your own experience, every true/false item, regardless of how well or poorly written, gives the student a 50 percent chance of guessing correctly, even without reading the item. In other words, on a 50-item true/false test, we would expect individuals who are totally unfamiliar with the content being tested to answer about 25 items correctly. Fortunately, there are ways to reduce the effects of guessing:

1. Encourage all students to guess when they do not know the correct answer. Because it is virtually impossible to prevent certain students from guessing, encouraging all students to guess should equalize the effects of guessing. The test scores will then reflect a more or less equal guessing factor, plus the actual level of each student's knowledge. This also will prevent test-wise students from having an unfair advantage over non-test-wise students.

2. Require revision of each statement that is false. In this approach, provide space at the end of the item for students to alter false items to make them true. Usually, the student first is asked to underline or circle the false part of the item and then to add the correct wording below the sentence, as in these examples:

T   F   High IQ children <u>always</u> get high grades in school.

　　　　　<u>tend to</u>

T   F   Panama is <u>north</u> of Cuba.

　　　　　<u>south</u>

T   F   <u>September</u> has an extra day during leap year.

<u>February</u>

With this strategy, full credit is awarded only if the revision is correct. The disadvantages of such an approach are that more test time is required for the same number of items, and scoring time is increased, as well.

Suggestions for Writing True/False Items

1. Tell students clearly how to mark *true* or *false* (e.g., circle or underline the *T* or *F*) before they begin the test. Write this instruction at the top of the test, too.

2. Make each statement definitely true or definitely false, without qualifications. If the item is true or false based on someone's opinion, identify the source of the opinion as part of the item—for example, "According to the head of the AFL-CIO, workers' compensation is below desired standards."

3. Construct true and false statements of approximately the same length, and be sure to have approximately equal numbers of true and false items.

4. Avoid using double-negative statements. They take extra time to decipher and are difficult to interpret. For example, avoid statements such as "It is not true that addition cannot precede subtraction in algebraic operations."

5. Avoid terms denoting indefinite degree (for example, *large, long time, regularly*) or absolutes (*never, only, always*). Test-wise students pick up on their vagueness and mark them "false."

6. Avoid placing items in a systematic pattern that some students might detect (for example, True-True-False-False, TFTF, and so on).

7. Don't take statements directly from the text without first making sure you are not taking them out of context.

Matching Items

Like true/false, matching is a popular and convenient testing format. Just like good true/false items, however, good matching items are not easy to write. Imagine that you are back in your ninth-grade U.S. history class, and the following matching item shows up on your test:

Directions: Match A and B.

A		**B**	
1.	Lincoln	a.	President during the 20th century
2.	Nixon	b.	Invented the telephone
3.	Whitney	c.	Delivered the Emancipation Proclamation
4.	Ford	d.	Only president to resign from office
5.	Bell	e.	Civil rights leader
6.	King	f.	Invented the cotton gin
7.	Washington	g.	Our first president
8.	Roosevelt	h.	Only president elected for more than two terms

Do you see any problems? Consider the problems you identify against the descriptions of faults that follow.

Homogeneity. The lists are not homogeneous. Column A contains names of presidents, inventors, and a civil rights leader. Unless specifically taught as a set of related individuals or ideas, this is too wide a variety for a matching exercise.

Order of Lists. The lists are reversed: Column A should be in place of Column B, and Column B should be in place of Column A. As the exercise is now written, the student reads a name and then has to read through all or many of the more lengthy descriptions to find the answer. This is a much more time-consuming process than reading a description and then finding the correct name. It also is a good idea to introduce some sort of order—chronological, numerical, or alphabetical—to your list of options. This also saves the student time in reviewing options.

Easy Guessing. Notice that there are equal numbers of options and descriptions. This increases the chance of guessing correctly through elimination. If there are at least three more options than descriptions, the chance of guessing correctly is reduced to one in four.

Poor Directions. The instructions are much too brief. Matching directions should specify the basis for matching:

> *Directions:* Column A contains brief descriptions of historical events. Column B contains the names of U.S. presidents. Indicate who was president when the historical event took place by placing the appropriate letter to the left of the number in Column A.

Multiple Correct Responses. The description "President during the 20th century" has three defensible answers: Nixon, Ford, and Roosevelt. And does "Ford" mean Henry Ford, inventor of the Model T automobile, or Gerald Ford? Always include first and last names to avoid ambiguity. Here is a corrected version of this set of matching items:

> *Directions:* Column A describes events associated with U.S. presidents. Indicate which name in Column B matches each event by placing the appropriate letter to the left of the number in Column A. Each name may be used only once.

Column A

_____ 1. Only president not elected to office
_____ 2. Delivered the Emancipation Proclamation
_____ 3. Only president to resign from office
_____ 4. Only president elected for more
       than two terms
_____ 5. Our first president

Column B

a. Abraham Lincoln
b. Richard Nixon
c. Gerald Ford
d. George Washington
e. Franklin Roosevelt
f. Theodore Roosevelt
g. Thomas Jefferson
h. Woodrow Wilson

Notice that we now have complete directions, more options than descriptions, and homogeneous lists. (All the items in Column A are about U.S. presidents, and all the items in Column B are names of presidents.) In addition, we have made the alternatives unambiguous.

Suggestions for Writing Matching Items

1. Keep both the descriptions list and the options list short and homogeneous. Both should fit on the same page. Add titles or labels to the lists to ensure homogeneity (for example, Column A, Column B).

2. Make sure all the options are plausible **distracters** (wrong-answer choices) for each description to ensure the homogeneity of lists.

3. The descriptions list should contain the longer phrases or statements; the options list should consist of short phrases, words, or symbols.

4. Number each description (1, 2, 3, etc.), and letter each option (a, b, c, etc.).

5. Include more options than descriptions, some that match more than one, or both.

6. In the directions, specify the basis for matching and whether options can be used more than once.

Multiple-Choice Items

Another popular item format is the multiple-choice question. Multiple-choice tests are more common in high school and college than in elementary school. Multiple-choice items are unique among objective test items because they enable you to measure some types of higher-level cognitive objectives. When writing multiple-choice items, be careful not to give away answers by inadvertently providing students with clues in the following ways.

Stem Clues.   The statement portion of a multiple-choice item is called the **stem**, and the answer choices are called *options* or *response alternatives*. A stem clue occurs when the same word or a close derivative occurs in both the stem and an option, thereby directing the test taker to the correct answer. Consider this example:

> In the story "Hawaiian Mystery," the name of the volcanic structure Mark and Alisha had to cross to get free was called _____.
>
> a. volcanic ridge
>
> b. tectonic plate
>
> c. caldron
>
> d. lava

In this item, the correct option and the stem both contain the word *volcanic*. Thus the wise test taker has a good chance of answering the item correctly without mastery of the content being measured.

Grammatical Clues.   Consider this item:

> U.S. Grant was an _____.
>
> a. army general
>
> b. navy admiral
>
> c. cavalry commander
>
> d. senator

Most students will pick up on the easy grammatical clue in the stem. The article *an* eliminates options b, c, and d, because "navy admiral," "cavalry commander," and "senator" do not follow grammatically. Option a is the only one that forms a grammatical sentence. A way to eliminate the grammatical clue is to replace *an* with *a/an*. Similar examples are *is/are, was/were, his/her,* and so on. Alternatively, place the article (or verb or pronoun) in the options list:

> Christopher Columbus came to America in _____.
>
> a. a car
>
> b. a boat
>
> c. an airplane
>
> d. a balloon

Redundant Words/Unequal Lengths.   Two very common faults in multiple-choice construction are illustrated in this item:

> In the story "Hawaiian Mystery," when Mark and Alisha were held hostage at the top of the volcano,
>
> a. the police could not see them to free them.
>
> b. the police called for more help.
>
> c. the police attempted to free them by going behind the volcano and risking a rescue.
>
> d. the police asked them to jump to the rock below.

The phrase *the police* is included in each option. To save space and time, it should be added to the stem: "When Mark and Alisha were held hostage at the top of the volcano, the police _____." Second, the lengths of the options could be a giveaway. Multiple-choice item writers have a tendency to include more information in the correct option than in the incorrect options. Test-wise students know that, more often than not, the longest option is the correct one. Avoid making the correct answer more than one and one-half times the length of the shortest incorrect option.

All of the Above/None of the Above. In general, use "none of the above" sparingly. Some item writers use "none of the above" only when no clearly correct option is presented. However, students catch on to this practice and guess that "none of the above" is the correct answer without knowledge of the content being measured. Also at times it may be justified to use multiple correct answers, such as "both a and c" or "both b and c." Again use such options sparingly, because inconsistencies can easily exist among alternatives that logically eliminate some from consideration. Avoid using "all of the above" entirely, because test items should encourage discrimination, not discourage it.

Higher Level Multiple-Choice Questions

A good multiple-choice item is the most time-consuming type of objective test item to write. Unfortunately, most multiple-choice items also are written at the knowledge level in the taxonomy of educational objectives. As a new item writer, you will tend to write items at this level, but you will need to write some multiple-choice items to measure higher-level cognitive objectives, as well.

First write some of your objectives to measure comprehension, application, analysis, or evaluation. This will ensure that some of your items will be at a level higher than knowledge. (Consult Appendix C and Chapter 5 for examples of higher order thinking and problem-solving behavior.) Following are some suggestions for writing higher order multiple-choice questions.

Use Justification to Assess the Reasons Behind an Answer. Add questions after a multiple-choice item to ask for specifics as to why a particular answer was chosen. Here is an example:

Directions: Choose the most appropriate answer, and cite evidence for your selection in the space below.

The principal value of a balanced diet is that it

a. increases your intelligence.

b. cures disease.

c. promotes mental health.

d. promotes physical health.

Present evidence from the text as to why you chose your answer.

Use Pictorial, Graphical, or Tabular Stimuli. Pictures, drawings, graphs, and tables can require the student to think at least at the application level in the taxonomy of educational objectives and may involve even higher-level cognitive processes. Also such stimuli often can generate several higher-level multiple-choice items, as the following questions about the content in Figure 13.3 illustrate:

Directions: Refer to the map [Figure 13.3] to answer these questions.

1. Which of the following cities would be the best location for a steel mill?

a. Li (3A)

b. Um (3B)

c. Cot (3D)

d. Dube (4B)

Figure 13.3 Use of a Pictorial Stimulus to Measure a Higher-Level Cognitive Process

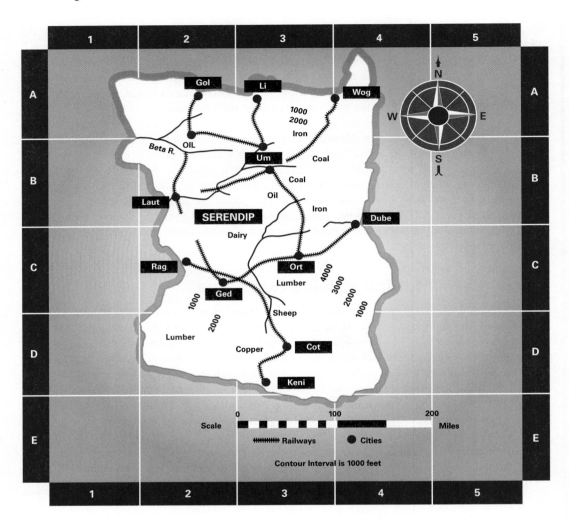

2. Approximately how many miles is it from Dube to Rag?

   a. 100 miles

   b. 150 miles

   c. 200 miles

   d. 250 miles

3. In what direction would someone have to travel to get from Wog to Um?

   a. northwest

   b. northeast

   c. southwest

   d. southeast

Use Analogies to Show Relationships between Terms. To answer analogies correctly, students must not only be familiar with the terms but also be able to understand how the terms relate to each other. For example:

Physician is to *humans* as *veterinarian* is to

a. *fruits.*

b. *animals.*

c. *minerals.*

d. *vegetables.*

Require Application of Principles or Procedures. To test whether students comprehend the implications of a procedure or principle, have them use the principle or procedure with new information or in a novel way. Doing so requires them to do more than just follow the steps in solving a problem. It asks them to demonstrate an ability to go beyond the context within which they originally learned a principle or procedure. Consider this example from a lesson that taught the computation of ratios and proportions:

> You are on vacation and want to drive from Chicago to St. Louis on your way home. The distance between these cities is 300 miles. Your car gets 20 miles per gallon on the highway.

1. How many gallons of gas will it take to make the trip?

   a. 10

   b. 15

   c. 20

   d. 25

2. How many gallons will you have left if you fill up your 23-gallon tank before leaving?

   a. 4

   b. 6

   c. 8

   d. 10

3. If you get only 15 miles per gallon instead of 20 because of some city driving, how many more driving miles will you have left before being empty after leaving St. Louis?

   a. 15

   b. 30

   c. 45

   d. 60

Suggestions for Writing Multiple-Choice Items

1. Be sure there is only one correct or clearly best answer.

2. Be sure all wrong-answer choices (distracters) are plausible. Eliminate unintentional grammatical clues, and keep the lengths and forms of all the answer choices the same. Rotate the position of the correct answer from item to item randomly.

3. Use negative questions or statements only if the knowledge being tested requires it. In most cases, it is more important for the student to know what the correct answer *is* rather than what it *is not.*

4. Include three to five options (two to four distracters plus one correct answer) to optimize testing for knowledge, rather than encourage guessing. It is not necessary to provide additional distracters for an item simply to maintain the same number of distracters for each item.

5. Use the option "none of the above" sparingly and only when all the answers can be classified unequivocally as wrong.

6. Avoid using "all of the above." It usually is the correct answer and makes the item too easy for students who have only partial information.

Completion Items

The first tests constructed by classroom teachers and taken by students often are completion tests. Like items of all other formats, there are good and bad completion items.

Suggestions for Writing Completion Items

1. Require a single-word answer or a brief, definite statement. Avoid items so indefinite that they may be logically answered by several terms:

   Poor Item: World War II ended in _____.

   Better Item: World War II ended in the year _____.

2. Be sure the item poses a problem. A direct question often is better than an incomplete statement because it provides more structure for an answer:

   Poor Item: What do you think about the main character in the story "Lilies of the Field?" _____

   Better Item: The main character in the story "Lilies of the Field" is _____.

3. Be sure the answer is factually correct. Word the question precisely in relation to the concept or fact being tested. For example, can the answer be found in the text, workbook, or class notes taken by students?

4. Omit only key words; do not eliminate so many elements that the sense of the content is impaired:

   Poor Item: The _____ type of test item usually is graded _____ than the _____ type.

   Better Item: The multiple-choice type of test item usually is graded more objectively than the _____ type.

5. Word the statement so the blank is near the end. This prevents awkward sentences.

6. If the problem requires a numerical answer, indicate the units in which it is to be expressed (for example, pounds, ounces, minutes).

Advantages and Disadvantages of Objective-Item Formats

Table 13.1 summarizes the advantages and disadvantages of each of the preceding objective-item formats.

Essay Test Items

In this section, we explain what an essay question is, describe the two major types, and provide suggestions for writing them. Essay questions are usually prepared in a written format at the middle school and high school grades but can be administered orally and responded to orally in the early elementary grades, especially when students have yet to acquire sufficient written language competency.

Like objective test items, essay questions may be well constructed or poorly constructed. The well-constructed essay question tests complex cognitive skills by requiring the student to organize, integrate, and synthesize knowledge; to use information to solve novel problems; and to be original and innovative in problem solving. The poorly constructed essay question may require the student to do no more than recall information as it was presented in the textbook or in class. Worse, the poorly constructed essay question may not inform the learner what is required for a satisfactory response.

There are two types of essay questions: the extended-response essay question and the restricted-response essay question.

Extended-Response Questions

A question that allows the student to determine the length and complexity of a response is called an **extended-response essay question**. This type of question is most useful at the analysis, synthesis,

Table 13.1 **Advantages and Disadvantages of Various Objective-Item Formats**

Advantages	Disadvantages
True/False Tests	
Tend to be short, so more material can be covered than with any other item format; thus suitable for use when extensive content has been covered	Tend to emphasize rote memorization of knowledge (although complex questions sometimes can be asked)
Fast to construct (but avoid creating items by taking statements out of context or only slightly modifying them)	Assume an unequivocally true or false answer (It is unfair to make students guess at your criteria for evaluating the truth of a statement.)
Easy to score (Tip: provide a "T" and "F" for students to circle because handwritten letters can be hard to decipher.)	Allow and may even encourage a high degree of guessing (Generally, longer examinations compensate for this.)
Matching Items	
Simple to construct and score	Tend to ask trivial information
Ideal for measuring associations between facts	Emphasize memorization
Can be more efficient than multiple-choice questions because they avoid repetition of options in measuring association	Most commercial answer sheets accommodate only five options, thus limiting the size of a matching item
Reduce the effects of guessing	
Multiple-Choice Tests	
Versatile in measuring objectives from the knowledge level to the evaluation level	Time consuming to write
Considerable course material can be sampled quickly, because writing is minimal	If not carefully written, can have more than one defensible correct answer
Scoring is highly objective, requiring only a count of correct responses	
Can be written so students must discriminate among options varying in correctness, avoiding the absolute judgments of true/false tests	
Reduce effects of guessing	
Amenable to statistical analysis, so can determine which items are ambiguous or too difficult*	
Completion Tests	
Question construction is relatively easy	Encourages a low level of response complexity
Guessing is reduced because questions require specific responses	Can be difficult to score (The stem must be general enough not to communicate the answer, leading unintentionally to multiple defensible answers.)
Less time is needed to complete than for multiple-choice items, so more content can be covered	Very short answers tend to measure recall of specific facts, names, places, and events instead of more complex behaviors

*See Kubiszyn and Borich, 2013, Chapter 11.

and evaluation levels of cognitive complexity. Because of the length of this type of item and the time required to organize and express the response, the extended-response essay question is sometimes better used as an assignment extended over a number of days or as a take-home test. Because of its length and depth, the extended-response question often is of value in assessing communication and higher-order thinking skills. Consider these examples:

- Compare and contrast the presidential administrations of George W. Bush and Ronald Reagan. Consider economic, social, and military policies. Avoid taking a position in support of either president. Your response will be graded on objectivity, accuracy, organization, and clarity.
- Now that we have studied about the gold rush, imagine that you are on a wagon train going to California. Write a letter to your relatives back home, telling them of some of the hardships you have suffered and the dangers you have experienced.

These questions, while focusing the learner, give him or her considerable latitude in formulating an answer and determining the length of the response. Now let's look at a restricted-response essay question.

Restricted-Response Questions

A question that poses a specific problem for which the student must recall the proper information, organize it in a suitable manner, derive a defensible conclusion, and express it according to specific criteria is called a **restricted-response essay question** or essay (Borich & Tombari, 2004; Kubiszyn & Borich, 2013). Restricted-response questions can be written in middle school and high school or posed orally in the early elementary grades. They usually require a minute or so of an oral response or a paragraph or two of writing. The statement of the problem given orally or as part of the written question specifies the response limitations that guide the student in responding and provides criteria for scoring. For example, the following are examples of restricted-response questions that could be delivered orally or in writing to assess student understanding:

In your own words, explain two differences between *igneous* and *sedimentary* rock, and give one example of each not given in class.

From the story "Ben Franklin's Childhood," give some examples of how Franklin was a born leader and always knew what to do.

For learners to demonstrate that they know *igneous* and *sedimentary* as concepts and not just simple knowledge, they must do two things: (1) They must use their own words to explain the differences and not simply recall what their text said or what they copied from an overhead, and (2) they must give original examples of each type of rock. If they can do this, you can correctly say they understand the concepts.

When Should You Use Essay Questions?

Although each situation must be considered individually, some situations lend themselves to essay items:

1. The instructional objectives specify high-level cognitive processes; they require supplying information, rather than simply recognizing information. These processes often cannot be measured with objective items.
2. You are only testing a few higher-level cognitive objectives. Due to time limitations, you can grade only a few essay items. If you have 30 students and design a test with six extended-response essays, you will spend a great deal of time scoring. Reserve essay questions for objectives that require higher order thinking, and/or use only one or two essay questions in conjunction with objective items.
3. Test security is a consideration. If you are afraid test items will be passed on to future students, you should use an essay test. In general, a good essay test takes less time to

construct than a good objective test. For orally prepared restricted-response questions, remember that you will need to prepare individual questions for each student in advance or assign points to other learners who contribute to another's answer.

Following are some learning outcomes and examples for which extended- and restricted-response essay questions may be used:

- *Analyze relationships.* The colors blue and gray are related to cool temperatures. What are some other colors related to? What effect would these colors have on a picture you might draw?

- *Compare and contrast positions.* Compare and contrast two characters from stories you have read to understand how the characters responded differently to conditions in the stories.

- *State necessary assumptions.* When Columbus landed on San Salvador, what did he assume about the land he had discovered? Were his assumptions correct?

- *Identify appropriate conclusions.* What are some of the reasons for and against building a landfill near homes?

- *Explain cause-and-effect relations.* What might have caused early Americans to travel west in the 1800s? Choose one of the pioneers we have studied (such as Daniel Boone), and give some of the reasons he or she traveled west.

- *Make predictions.* What can you predict about a coming storm by observing clouds? Explain what about clouds helps predict rain.

- *Organize data to support a viewpoint.* On the board, you will find the numbers of new homes built and autos purchased for each month over the past year. Use these data to support the viewpoint that our economy is getting either larger or smaller.

- *Point out strengths and weaknesses.* What is either a strength or a limitation of each of the following musical instruments for a marching band: oboe, trumpet, tuba, violin?

- *Integrate data from several sources.* Imagine that you are celebrating your birthday with nine of your friends. Two pizzas arrive, and each is cut into four pieces. What problem do you have? What method would you choose for seeing that everyone gets a piece of the pizza?

- *Evaluate the quality or worth of an item, product, or action.* What should be considered in choosing a balanced meal from the basic food groups?

Suggestions for Writing Essay Questions

1. Have clearly in mind what mental processes you want the student to use before starting to write a response to the question. Refer to the Higher Order Thinking and Problem-Solving Checklist in Appendix C and the example verbs in Chapter 5 for suggestions. Review these examples:

   Poor Item: Criticize the following speech by our president.

   Better Item: Consider the following presidential speech. Focus on the section dealing with economic policy, and discriminate between factual statements and opinions. List these statements separately, label them, and indicate whether each statement is or is not consistent with the president's overall economic policy.

2. Write the question to define the task clearly and unambiguously for the student. Tasks should be explained (1) in the overall instructions preceding the test items and/or (2) in the test items themselves. Include whether spelling and grammar will be counted and whether organization of the response will be an important scoring element. Also indicate the level of detail and supporting data required. Consider these examples:

   Poor Item: Discuss the value of behavioral objectives.

   Better Item: Behavioral objectives have enjoyed increased popularity in education over the years. In your text and in class, the advantages and disadvantages of behavioral objectives have been discussed. Take a position for or against the use of behavioral objectives in education, and support your position with at least three of the arguments covered in class or in the text.

3. Start essay questions with such words or phrases as *compare, contrast, give reasons for, give original examples of, predict what would happen if,* and so on. Do not begin with such words as *what, who, when,* and *list,* because these words generally lead to tasks that require only recall of information, which is better assessed with objective test items. Here are two more examples:

Poor Item: List three reasons behind the United States' reduction in troops in Iraq.

Better Item: After more than eight years of involvement in Iraq, the United States began reducing its military presence. Speculate on what would have happened if the United States had *not* reduced its military presence at that time and had *not* increased its military presence in prior years.

4. A question dealing with a controversial issue should ask for and be evaluated in terms of the presentation of evidence for a position, rather than the position taken. It is not defensible to demand that a student accept a specific conclusion or solution, but it is reasonable to appraise how well he or she has learned to use the evidence on which a specific conclusion is based. Consider these examples:

Poor Item: What laws should Congress pass to improve the medical care of all citizens in the United States?

Better Item: Some Americans feel the cost of all medical care should be borne by the federal government. Do you agree or disagree? Support your position with at least three logical arguments.

5. Avoid using optional items. That is, require all students to complete the same items. Allowing students to select two of three or three of four decreases the uniformity of the test across all students, which will decrease your basis for comparison among students.

6. Establish reasonable time and/or page limits for each essay item to help the student complete the entire test and to indicate the level of detail you have in mind. Indicate such limits either in the statement of the problem or close to the number of the question.

7. Be sure each question relates to an instructional objective. Check your test blueprint to see if the content of the essay item is represented.

Some Criteria for Scoring Essay Items

Essays can be difficult to score consistently across individuals. That is, the same essay answer may be given an A by one scorer and a B or C by another scorer. Or the same answer may be graded A on one occasion but B or C on another occasion by the same scorer! Following are five criteria that can help maintain the consistency of your grading across essays.

Content. Although essays are used less to measure factual knowledge than thinking processes, the content should provide material relevant to the facts and adequately cover the question being asked.

Organization. Beyond the content of a student's response, you may want to include the organization of a response among your grading criteria. For example, does the essay have an introduction, body, and conclusion? Do progressions and sequences follow a logical or chronological development? Also you will want to decide whether spelling and grammar will be included among your grading criteria, and if so, alert students to this before they take the test.

Process. If your essay item tests at the application level or above, the most important criteria for scoring will be the extent to which a particular thinking process has been carried out. In addition, each thinking process (for example, application, analysis, synthesis, and evaluation) results in a solution, recommendation, or decision. So your grading criteria should include both the adequacy of the solution, recommendation, or decision and evidence of the thinking process that led to it (for example, have the correct analytical procedures been applied?).

Completeness/Internal Consistency.   Does the essay deal adequately with the problem presented? Is there sufficient detail to support the points being made? And are these points logically related to one another to cover the topic as fully as required?

Originality/Creativity.   You may also want to recognize and encourage original and creative responses. Expect some students to develop new and creative ways of answering your questions, for which you can award credit when appropriate.

Inform your students of any of the preceding criteria you will be using. Typically, two or three of the above criteria most relevant to the focus of the exam are chosen and then weighted in terms of their importance to the overall grade—for example, 75 percent on content and 25 percent on organization, or 33 percent on content, 33 percent on process, and 33 percent on organization. Once your students know how you are going to score the test, they can prepare better and more defensible responses. Figure 13.4 illustrates a scale for scoring essays with the preceding criteria.

Figure 13.4 **Example of a Scoring Scheme for an Essay Test**

Content				
1	2	3	4	5
Very limited investigation. Little or no material related to facts.		Some investigation and attention to the facts.		Extensive investigation. Good detail and attention to the facts.

Organization				
1	2	3	4	5
Very little organization of ideas. Presentation is confusing and hard to follow.		Some organization of ideas, but logical order needs to be improved.		Good organization. Ideas are logically connected and built on one another.

Process				
1	2	3	4	5
Very little justification or support of ideas. Final solution or decision unsubstantiated.		Some justification and support of ideas. Final solution or decision needs greater substantiation.		Good justification and support of ideas. Final solution or decision is well substantiated.

Completeness				
1	2	3	4	5
Very little focus on detail. Ideas are superficial and incomplete.		Some attention to detail. Greater focus and attention to detail are needed.		Good attention to detail. Ideas are thorough and complete.

Originality				
1	2	3	4	5
Response lacks originality. Nothing new or creative.		Some originality. Greater creativity is needed.		Response is original and creative. Many novel and unexpected ideas.

Validity and Reliability

Test results are useful only if they are *valid* and *reliable*. Although it is unlikely that you will actually determine the reliability or validity of your own classroom tests, you will need to know what these terms mean when evaluating the claims made by published tests that may be purchased by your school or school district and their applicability to your classroom. These terms are defined as follows:

1. **Validity**. The test measures what it says it is measuring.
2. **Reliability**. The test yields the same or similar scores consistently.

Types of Validity

A test is *valid* if it measures what it says it is measuring. For instance, if it is supposed to be a test of third-grade arithmetic ability, it should measure third-grade arithmetic skills, not fifth-grade arithmetic skills and not reading ability. If it is supposed to measure ability to write behavioral objectives, it should measure that ability, not the ability to recognize poor objectives.

If test results will be used to make any kind of decision and if the test information is to be useful, the test must be valid. There are several ways of deciding whether a test is sufficiently valid to be useful. The three types of validity most often determined are *content validity, concurrent validity,* and *predictive validity*.

Content Validity. The content validity of a test is established by examining its content. The teacher inspects test questions to see if they correspond to what should be covered, as indicated in the test blueprint (illustrated in Figure 13.2). This is easiest when there is a test blueprint, where it may be fairly easy to specify what to include in a test. But sometimes, a test can look valid but measure something different from what is intended, such as guessing ability, reading level, or skills that learners may have acquired before your instruction. Content validity is therefore a minimum requirement for a useful test but does not guarantee a valid test.

Concurrent Validity. To establish concurrent validity, an established test must be administered at the same time as the new test you have designed. Unlike content validity, concurrent validity yields a numerical value in the form of a correlation coefficient, called a *validity coefficient* (see Kubiszyn & Borich, 2013, Chapter 16). The new test and the established test are administered to a group of students and the relationship—the correlation—between the two sets of test scores is determined. If there exists a well-established test (criterion) to which the new test can be compared (that may be shorter, more convenient, or more specific to the content you wish to measure), then concurrent validity provides a good method of determining the validity of that test.

Predictive Validity. Predictive validity refers to how well the test predicts some future behavior of the examinee that is representative of the test's content. This form of validity is particularly useful for tests that are used to predict how well the test taker will do in some future setting. Predictive validity also yields a numerical index in the form of a correlation coefficient. This time, however, it is the relationship between the test and some future behavior (for example, on-the-job performance) that is being measured.

All three types of validity—content, concurrent, and predictive—assume that some criterion exists external to the test that can be used to anchor or validate it. In the case of content validity, it is the instructional objectives (for example, in the test blueprint) that provide the anchor or point of reference. In the case of concurrent validity, it is another well-accepted test measuring the same or similar content. And in the case of predictive validity, it is some future behavior or condition we are attempting to predict.

Types of Reliability

The *reliability* of a test refers to the consistency with which it yields the same rank or score for an individual who takes the test several times. In other words, a test is reliable if it consistently yields the same, or nearly the same, scores or ranks among all individuals over repeated administrations during which we would not expect the trait being measured to have changed.

There are several ways to estimate the reliability of a test. The three methods most often used are called *test-retest, alternate form,* and *internal consistency.*

Test-Retest. Test-retest is a method of estimating reliability that is what its name implies: The test is given twice to the same individuals to determine the relationship, or correlation, between the first set of scores and the second set of scores.

Alternate Form. If two equivalent (parallel) forms of a test are available, the reliability of the test can be determined by the correlation between them. Both tests are administered to a group of students to determine the relationship (correlation) between the two sets of scores. Large differences in students' scores on two forms of a test that supposedly measure the same behavior indicate an unreliable test.

Internal Consistency. If the test measures a single concept (for example, addition), it is reasonable to assume that learners who get one item right will likely get other similar items right. In other words, items should be related or correlated with each other and therefore internally consistent. If this is the case, then the reliability of the test can be estimated by the internal-consistency method (Kubiszyn & Borich, 2013, Chapter 17).

Typically, validity coefficients for a test are lower than reliability coefficients. Acceptable validity coefficients for a test generally range between .60 and .80 or higher; acceptable reliability coefficients generally range from .80 to .90 or higher. The maximum coefficient obtainable for either validity or reliability is 1.0.

Test accuracy is in part a combined measure of validity and reliability and in part determined by how well the test content matches the prevailing educational curriculum.

Marks and Grading Systems

After you have administered your test, you will have to score it and assign marks. Often the type of symbol a teacher uses to represent a mark is determined at the school or district level, for example, A-F, Excellent-Good-Satisfactory-Poor-Unsatisfactory, or a numerical marking system, for example, 1–100. As a classroom teacher, you have considerable flexibility in determining how to assign these marks to learners.

Marks and grading systems are based on comparisons, usually comparisons of students with one or more of the following:

- Other students
- Established standards
- Aptitude
- Achievement versus effort
- Achievement versus improvement

Comparison with Other Students

The expression "grading on the curve" means your grade or mark depends on how your achievement compares with that of other students in your class. Sometimes districts or schools encourage grading on the curve by specifying the percentages of students who will be assigned various grades. For example, students in the top 10 percent will get an A.

The main advantage of such a system is that it simplifies marking decisions. There is no deliberation or agonizing over what cutoff scores should determine whether students get this grade or that. However, this type of marking system fails to consider differences in the overall knowledge or ability level of the class. Regardless of achievement, in such a system, some students always will get A's and some always will get F's.

Comparisons with other students, established standards, aptitude, effort, and improvement all can be the basis for assigning grades. Ultimately, you must decide the balance of approaches to use that best fits the goals of the classroom and school.

Comparison with Established Standards

In the marking system that uses comparison with established standards, it is possible for any student to get an A or F or any grade between. The achievements of individual students are unrelated to those of other individual students. All that is relevant is whether a student attains a defined standard of achievement or performance. We labeled this approach as *criterion referenced* earlier in the chapter. In such a system, letter grades may be assigned based on the percentages of test items answered correctly, as this distribution illustrates:

Grade	Percentage of Items Answered Correctly
A	90–100
B	80–89
C	70–79
D	60–69
F	Less than 60

In theory, this system makes it possible for all students to obtain high grades if they put forth sufficient effort (assuming the percentage cutoffs are not unreasonably high). Also grade assignment is simplified: A student either has correctly answered 90 percent of the items or has not. As with the previous method, comparison with other students, there is no deliberating or agonizing over assigning grades. Also teachers who work to improve their teaching effectiveness can observe improvement in grades with the passage of time.

As you might expect, such a system also has its drawbacks. Establishing a standard for each grade or skill attained is no small task, and what is reasonable for an A may vary from school to school and from time to time in your classroom as a result of ability levels, content, and curriculum changes. This could make grading complicated when students who vary widely in their learning histories, special needs, and abilities are assigned materials with different cognitive demands in order to differentiate your instruction.

Comparison with Aptitude

Aptitude is another term for *potential* or *ability*. In systems based on aptitude, students are compared neither to other students nor to established standards. Instead they are compared to themselves. That is, marks are assigned depending on how closely a student achieves to his or her potential. Thus students with high aptitude or potential who are achieving at high levels will get high grades, because they will be achieving at their potential. But students with average aptitude and average achievement also will get high grades, because they, too, will be considered to be achieving at their potential. And those with high aptitude and average achievement will get lower grades, because they will be achieving below their potential.

Clearly, the same grade can mean very different things in terms of absolute achievement. However, this grading system also provides reward and recognition to students who are working successfully with differentiated instructional materials at their current level of understanding (Tomlinson, 2010).

Comparison of Achievement with Effort

Systems that compare achievement with effort are similar to those that compare achievement with aptitude. Students who get average test scores but have to work hard to get them are given high marks. Students who get average scores but do not have to work hard to get them are given lower marks. The advantage cited for grading on effort is that it motivates slower or turned-off students.

However, it also may antagonize brighter students, who quickly see such a system as unfair. It may also be difficult to determine if a student has or has not worked hard.

Comparison of Achievement with Improvement

Another system compares the amount of improvement between the beginning and end of instruction. Students who show the most progress get the highest grades. An obvious problem occurs for the student who did well on a test at the beginning of the instruction, called the *pretest,* because his or her improvement will likely be less than that of a student who did poorly on the pretest.

   Which marking system should you choose? Most educators now agree that comparisons with established standards (criterion referenced) best suit the primary function of marking in the classroom, which is to provide feedback about academic progress. In reality, however, many schools, school districts, and teachers with heterogeneous classrooms have adopted multiple marking systems, such as assigning separate grades for achievement and effort—or achievement, effort, and improvement. As long as the achievement portion of the grade reflects only achievement, such systems are appropriate.

Standardized Tests

Formative versus Summative Evaluation

So far, we have limited most of our discussion to teacher-constructed tests. These tests are intended not only to provide feedback to your students as to how much they have learned but also provide feedback to you as to how well you have taught. In other words teachers employ both formal and informal assessment procedures *during* the learning process in order to modify their teaching and learning activities to improve student achievement. These types of data can involve qualitative feedback that include volunteered or solicited feedback from students and parents, observations of your teaching from peers and school administrators as well as scores from lesson and unit tests and classroom projects and activities that record the progress of your learners over time (Frey, 2007). Some formative purposes for these data might be to: (1) improve the implementation of an instructional strategy (e.g., did my students achieve the goal I set for my lesson using this strategy), (2) improve the organization of content (e.g. did they show better organization in their essays) and (3) improve their use of higher order thinking (e.g. did their portfolios show ways of viewing a problem outside the boundaries of standard conventions). The intent of these observations and student data is to provide feedback that helps you assess and modify your instructional practices, hence the phrase "formative" evaluation. The overall goal of **formative evaluation** is to improve your teaching based on data that comes directly from students and peer observation. Some examples of other information you can collect for formative evaluation would be:

- Debriefing students after a collaborative activity that asked how well their groups functioned and what arrangements enhanced or impeded group performance

- Asking students questions about the topic of an upcoming unit to see if what they already know helps in understanding the lesson

- Using lesson tests and activities to determine how well your teaching methods have achieved your unit goal

   As a result of your school's participation in the national **Response to Intervention** program, you will also have the opportunity of utilizing brief and frequently administered assessments (called curriculum-based measures—or CBM) for formative evaluation. The Response to Intervention program has the goal of improving educational opportunities for all students by frequently administering curriculum-based assessments—or probes—to assess your students' responsiveness to research-based instructional methods. We will have more to say about Response To Intervention and the important role curriculum based measures can play in the formative evaluation of your teaching practices.

   Now that we've described the role of formative assessment in improving the day to day classroom decisions you will be making, it is important to remember that at least once a year you will be asked to administer end-of-year standardized tests, evaluate their results, and interpret them for

Pay attention to the components of formative assessment presented in this **video**. Watch how the teachers collaborate in this effort.

curious and sometimes concerned parents. Because these data are used to monitor educational outcomes for purposes of accountability within and outside of your classroom, they are called "summative" evaluations. Although summative data can also be useful in modifying your teaching practices (e.g., by adjusting your teaching practices to address known deficiencies at the beginning of the year), the main intent of standardized test data is to present the overall picture or sum total of student progress from one year to the next relative to other students, hence the phrase **summative evaluation**.

Quite different from most formative assessments conducted to improve your everyday teaching, **standardized tests**, called *high-stakes* tests, are developed by test construction specialists—usually with the assistance of curriculum experts, teachers, and school administrators—to determine a student's performance level relative to that of others of similar age and grade. These tests are standardized because they are administered and scored according to specific and uniform (standard) procedures.

When schools use standardized tests, administrators can more easily and confidently compare test results from different students, classes, schools, and school districts than is the case with teacher-made tests. For the most part, schools use standardized tests for comparative purposes. This is quite different from the purposes of teacher-made tests, which are to determine pupil mastery or skill, to assign grades, and to provide specific feedback to you to reflect upon and, when needed, modify your teaching practices. Table 13.2 compares standardized and teacher-made tests on several important dimensions.

The results of standardized tests are reported as *percentile ranks*. Percentile ranks enable you to determine how a student's performance compares with that of others of the same grade or age. Keep in mind that when interpreting percentile ranks:

1. Percentile ranks often are confused with *percentage correct*. In using percentile ranks, be sure you communicate that a percentile rank of, for example, 62 means the individual's score was *higher* than 62 percent of all those who took the test (called the *norming sample*). Or you could say that 62 percent of those who took the test scored lower than this individual. (Commonly, a score at the 62nd percentile is misinterpreted to mean the student answered only 62 percent of the items correctly. But a score at the 62nd percentile might be equivalent to a B or a C, whereas a score of 62 percent likely would be an F.)

2. Equal differences between percentile ranks do not necessarily indicate equal differences in achievement. In a class of 100 pupils, the difference in achievement between the 2nd

Table 13.2 A Comparison of Standardized and Teacher-Made Achievement Tests

Dimension	Standardized Achievement Tests	Teacher-Made Achievement Tests
Learning outcomes and content measured	Measure general outcomes and content appropriate to the majority of U.S. schools; tend not to reflect specific or unique emphasis of local curricula.	Well adapted to the specific and unique outcomes and content of local curriculum; adaptable to various amounts of content, but tend to neglect complex learning outcomes.
Quality of test items	Quality of items is generally high; items are written by specialists, pretested, and selected on the basis of results from quantitative item analysis.	Quality of item is often unknown; quality is typically lower than standardized tests due to limited time available to the teacher.
Reliability	Reliability is high, commonly between .80 and .95, and frequently above .90 (highest possible is 1.0).	Reliability is usually unknown, but can be high if items are carefully constructed.
Administration and scoring	Procedures are standardized; specific instructions are provided.	Uniform procedures are possible, but usually are flexible and unwritten.
Interpretation of scores	Scores can be compared to norm groups; test manual and other guides aid interpretation and use.	Score comparisons and interpretation are limited to local class or school situation; few if any guidelines are available for interpretation and use.

percentile and 5th percentile is substantial, whereas the difference between the 47th and 50th percentile is negligible. Interpreting the differences in percentile ranks must take into consideration that percentiles toward the extreme or end points of the percentile distribution tend to be spread out (like a rubber band) and thus represent much greater changes in achievement than differences in the middle of the scale, where the amount of change between percentiles tends to be small.

Helping Students Prepare for Standardized Tests

Standardized tests can be used to determine whether a student receives access to Advanced Placement (AP) and honors courses, is promoted to the next grade, or even graduates from high school. Likewise these tests have high stakes for principals and teachers when they receive recognition or reprimands depending on the test's outcome. Regardless of how you personally may feel about these tests, they are used in all 50 states and are likely to be around for some time to come. So here are some suggestions from Kubiszyn and Borich (2013) that may relieve some of the frustration you feel about these tests and help your students perform better on them.

Focus on the Task, Not Your Feelings about It.   Because your students' promotion and your teaching position can be affected by your state's standardized assessment program, it makes sense to focus less on your feelings about the test and more on the demands of the task before you. So it will be critical for you to obtain your state's academic standards at your grade level, which are usually available from the website of your state education agency. Ensuring that you target state standards in your classroom is the single most important thing you can do to prepare your students to perform well on these tests. To do so, you may have to modify your instructional methods some to match the content and processes identified in the state standards.

Inform Students and Parents about the Importance of the Test.   Although some students will already understand the purpose and relevance of the test, some will not. To get students to try their best, some educators advocate warning students or issuing rewards. Others say such strategies send the wrong message and only increase the stress and pressure that can impair student performance. Neither of these approaches will be as effective as taking the time to explain to your students the reason the test is being administered, how the results will be used, and how the test is relevant to their learning. With this approach, you are more likely to engage and motivate your students to do well and to take the test seriously. Instead of presenting a lecture on the pros or cons of tests, be straightforward and simple: Let your students know that they have learned what will be necessary to do well on the test and that you expect them to do well.

Teach Test-Taking Skills from the First Day of School as Part of Your Regular Instruction.
Some students seem to perform better on tests than other students. This may seem to be because of luck, aptitude, confidence, or some other factor. However, there also is an element of skill in test taking that affects student performance. If all the students in your class have basic test-taking skills, their overall performance will increase. For example, you can teach your students to do the following:

1. *Follow directions carefully.* Some students, especially those who are impulsive or have difficulty reading, may neglect to read directions carefully or not read them at all. You can address this critical point frequently during your daily classroom routine and remind students about it during your regular classroom tests.

2. *Read test items, passages, and related information carefully.* Who has not rushed through a test item only to find that he or she missed or misread a word and lost credit for the item as a result? You can reduce the likelihood your pupils will do this by providing practice in highlighting key words, rereading items, and double-checking answers during in-class and homework assignments and regular tests. For multiple-choice questions, remind students to read each option before selecting the answer. This may be especially important for pupils who have come from cultures where standardized tests are not used or used less frequently than they are in the United States.

3. *Manage test-taking time.* Students must work quickly to complete standardized tests, but they must also work accurately. This skill, too, can be improved with practice in the classroom. Instead of giving students as much time as they need to answer questions on a classroom test, impose a time limit for practice. For a lengthy test, have students plan the number of minutes they will spend on each phase of the test.

4. *Attempt easier items first.* Many teacher-made tests begin with easy items and end with the most difficult items. But the items in standardized tests typically have a more random order to their difficulty level. Unprepared students may encounter a difficult question early in the test—one that even many of the best students may miss—and spend an inordinate amount of time on it. When you administer classroom tests, encourage students to answer all the items they know the answers to before they attempt the more difficult items.

5. *Eliminate options before answering.* Test-wise students know they can increase their chance of answering correctly if they eliminate one or two multiple-choice or matching options before attempting to choose the correct one. Have your students practice this in class, and remind them to follow this strategy during your objective tests.

6. *Teach students to check their answers after completing the test.* Some pupils have such an aversion to tests or take them so lightly that they do not check their answers after they finish a test—even if they have time. You can practice this by reminding your students to use the full testing time to go over their answers when giving classroom tests.

As the Day of the Standardized Test Approaches, Respond to Student Questions Openly and Directly. Days before a standardized test, you can expect that some children will begin to wonder or worry about it (e.g., What will it look like? Will I be the last one finished? What if I get a bad grade? What can I do if I have a question during the test?). This sense of uncertainty is a common cause of test anxiety, too much of which will interfere with students' performance.

To prevent anxiety before the test day, provide your pupils with as much information as you can about the test's format and administration procedures. This can include basic information such as the test days and times; the subjects, format, and style of response; and how their questions may be scored. You may also want to role-play various scenarios with the class to ensure they are clear on the procedures.

Take Advantage of Whatever Preparation Materials Are Available. In many states, the state education agency or school district will provide some helpful practice tests and exercises designed to familiarize students with the style, format, and subject matter of the test. Although these exercises take classroom time, they will improve students' test-taking efficiency and manage their stress by minimizing their uncertainty and increasing the time they spend focusing on the test items, rather than wondering how they fill in the answer sheets. Take full advantage of the preparation materials provided, and supplement them with materials of your own, when available.

Performance Assessment

Some skills—particularly those involving independent judgment, critical thinking, and decision making—are best assessed by asking learners to show what they can do. In the field of athletics, diving and gymnastics are examples of performances that show what students can do with what they have learned. Their scores are used to decide, for example, who earns a medal; who wins first, second, third, and so on; or who qualifies for district or regional competition. These are called *performance assessments.* For examples of performance assessment see In Practice: Focus on Performance Assessment.

Teachers use performance assessments to assess complex cognitive processes, as well as attitudes and social skills in academic areas such as science, social studies, and math (King, 2009; National Research Council, 2001). When doing so, teachers establish situations that allow them directly to observe and rate learners as they analyze, problem solve, experiment, make decisions, measure, cooperate with others, present orally, or produce a product (Burke, 2010). These situations simulate real-world activities, as might be expected in a job, in the community, or in various forms of advanced training.

In Practice

Focus on Performance Assessment

Performance tests can be assessments of processes, products, or both. For example, at the Darwin School in Winnipeg, Manitoba, teachers assess the reading process of each student by noting the percentage of words read accurately during oral reading, the number of sentences read that are meaningful within the context of the story, and the percentage of story elements the learner can talk about in his or her own words after reading.

At the West Orient School in Gresham, Oregon, fourth-graders assemble portfolios of their writing products. These portfolios include both rough and polished drafts of poetry, essays, biographies, and self-reflections. Several math teachers at Twin Peaks Middle School in Poway, California, require their students to assemble math portfolios, which include the following products of their problem-solving efforts: long-term projects, daily notes, journal entries about troublesome test problems, written explanations of how they solved problems, and the problem solutions themselves.

Social studies learning processes and products are assessed in the Aurora, Colorado, public schools by engaging learners in a variety of projects built around this question: "Based on your study of Colorado history, what current issues in Colorado do you believe are the most important to address, what are your ideas about the resolutions of those issues, and what contributions will you make toward the resolutions?" Learners answer this question in a variety of ways involving individual and group writing assignments, oral presentations, and exhibits.

These teachers and others across the United States are using performance tests to assess not only higher-level cognitive skills but also noncognitive outcomes, such as self-direction, ability to work with others, and social awareness (Marzano, Pickering, & Pollock, 2004). This concern for the affective domain of learning reflects an awareness by educators that the skilled performance of complex tasks involves more than the ability to recall information, form concepts, generalize, and problem solve. It also involves habits of mind, attitudes, and social skills (Costa & Kallick, 2004a,b).

The public school system in Aurora, Colorado, has developed a list of learning outcomes and their indicators for learners in grades K–12 (see Figure 13.5). For each of these 19 indicators, a four-category rating scale

serves as a guide for teachers who are unsure of how to define "Assumes responsibility" or "Demonstrates consideration." While observing learners during performance tests in, for example, social studies, science, art, or economics, teachers are alert to recognize and rate those behaviors that suggest learners have acquired the desired outcomes.

Teachers in the Aurora public schools are encouraged to use this list of outcomes when planning their courses. They first ask themselves, What key facts, concepts, and principles should all learners remember? In addition, teachers try to fuse this subject-area content with the five district outcomes (see Figure 13.5) by designing special performance tests. For example, a third-grade language arts teacher who is planning a writing unit might choose to focus on Indicators 8 and 9 to address the district outcomes related to "A Collaborative Worker," Indicator 1 for the outcome "A Self-Directed Learner," and Indicator 13 for the outcome "A Quality Producer." The teacher would then design a performance assessment that allows learners to demonstrate learning in these areas. He or she might select other indicators and outcomes for subsequent units and performance tests.

Likewise a ninth-grade history teacher, having identified the important content for a unit on civil rights, might develop a performance test to assess district outcomes related to "A Complex Thinker," "A Collaborative Worker," and "A Community Contributor." A performance test might take this form: "A member of a minority in your community has been denied housing, presumably on the basis of race, ethnicity, or religion. What steps do you believe are legally and ethically defensible, and in what order do you believe they should be followed?" (adapted from Redding, 1992, p. 51). This performance test could require extensive research, group collaboration, role playing, and recommendations for current ways to improve minority rights.

Performance tests represent an addition to paper-and-pencil objective-type tests, which are the most efficient, reliable, and valid instruments available for assessing knowledge, comprehension, and certain applications. But when it comes to assessing complex thinking skills, attitudes, and social skills, performance tests can, if properly constructed, do a better job. If not properly constructed, however, performance assessments can have some of the same problems with authenticity, scoring

Figure 13.5 **Learning Outcomes of Aurora Public Schools**

A Self-Directed Learner

1. Sets priorities and achievable goals.
2. Monitors and evaluates progress.
3. Creates options for self.
4. Assumes responsibility for actions.
5. Creates a positive vision for self and future.

A Collaborative Worker

6. Monitors own behavior as a group member.
7. Assesses and manages group functioning.
8. Demonstrates interactive communication.
9. Demonstrates consideration for individual differences.

A Complex Thinker

10. Uses a wide variety of strategies for managing complex issues.
11. Selects strategies appropriate to the resolution of complex issues and applies the strategies with accuracy and thoroughness.
12. Accesses and uses topic-relevant knowledge.

A Quality Producer

13. Creates products that achieve their purpose.
14. Creates products appropriate to the intended audience.
15. Creates products that reflect craftsmanship.
16. Uses appropriate resources/technology.

A Common Contributor

17. Demonstrates knowledge about his or her diverse communities.
18. Takes action.
19. Reflects on his or her role as a community contributor.

Source: © Aurora Public Schools, 1993. Reprinted with permission.

efficiency, reliability, and validity as traditional approaches to testing. Borich and Tombari (2004) and Stiggins (2007) emphasize that performance assessments of affect must adhere to the same standards of evaluation and scoring as assessments of achievement, or the results may prove too subjective to be of value. Borich and Tombari (2004) outline the step-by-step procedures for constructing performance assessments in your classroom.

One of the best ways of getting your learners to exhibit what they know and can do is through creating a portfolio. Although some traditional paper and pencil tests strive to measure complex cognitive outcomes, a portfolio is a performance assessment that measures them in more authentic contexts. With a portfolio, the teacher observes and evaluates student abilities to carry out the complex activities used and valued inside as well as outside the classroom.

The Portfolio

Rationale for the Portfolio

As you know from building your own digital portfolio during this course, a portfolio is a collection of accomplishments over time. Creating this collection is one of the best ways learners can show their final achievement and the effort they put into getting there. (Lightfoot, 2006; Reynolds & Rich, 2006).

Portfolios are not new. Painters, fashion designers, artisans, and writers traditionally have assembled portfolios that embody their best work. Television and radio announcers compile video- and audiotaped excerpts of their best performances, which they present when interviewing for a job. A portfolio shows others what they can really do.

A portfolio in the classroom serves a similar purpose. It shows off the learner's best writing, artwork, science projects, historical thinking, or mathematical achievement. And it also shows the steps the learner took to get there. A portfolio compiles the learner's best work and also includes works-in-progress: early drafts, test runs, pilot studies, and preliminary trials. Thus the portfolio offers an ideal way to assess final mastery, effort, reflection, and growth in learning. In sum, it tells the learner's story of achievement.

There are three types of portfolios—working portfolios, display or show portfolios, and assessment portfolios—each of which has its own purpose:

1. A w*orking portfolio* represents works in progress. It serves as a depository for student accomplishments that are on the way to being selected and polished for a more permanent assessment or display portfolio.

2. A student selects his or her best works from a working portfolio for a *display* or *show portfolio*. With the aid of the teacher, the student learns to critically judge the works, focusing on those qualities that make some stand above others.

3. An *assessment portfolio* may contain all or some of the selections in a display portfolio as well as some of those that began in a working portfolio. Although the purpose of the working portfolio is to develop good products and the purpose of the display portfolio is to show off finished products, some of the contents of these collections are often used for the purpose of assessment. The teacher, therefore, is the primary audience of the **assessment portfolio**.

Working, display, and assessment portfolios can be organized and presented digitally or in a binder, accordion file, or box file format. A *digital portfolio* displays the student's work with the click of a mouse, utilizing all the multimedia capabilities of the computer, such as audio, video, graphics, and text transformed into computer-readable formats. This type of portfolio has the special advantage of presenting information instantly and interactively, instead of linearly, to emphasize connections and relationships among entries, which a typical binder or file presentation can obscure. Commercially available portfolio design software for students (www.aurbach.com), as well as commonly available software such as Microsoft PowerPoint, provides a template for facilitating the development of portfolios. For more information about digital portfolios, see Adams-Bullock and Hawk (2009).

Many school districts use portfolios and other types of exhibitions to help motivate students and document their growth and achievement in learning. The reliability and validity of a classroom teacher's judgment is always a matter of concern, but it is less so when the teacher has multiple opportunities to interact with learners and numerous occasions to observe their work and confirm evaluations of their achievement.

Many educators believe a portfolio's greatest value is for showing teachers, parents, and learners a richer array of what learners know and can do than is possible with paper and pencil tests and other snapshot assessments. If designed properly, a portfolio can show a learner's ability to think and problem solve, to use strategies and procedural-type skills, and to construct knowledge. But in addition, it also tells something about a learner's persistence, effort, willingness to change, skill in monitoring his or her own learning, and ability to be self-reflective or metacognitive. In this sense, a portfolio can give the teacher information about a learner that no other measurement tool can provide.

There are also other reasons for using portfolios. Creating a portfolio is an ideal way to motivate reluctant learners (Gronlund & Engel, 2002). Portfolios also provide a means to communicate to parents and other teachers the level of achievement that a learner has reached. Report card grades give us some idea of this, but portfolios supplement grades by showing the supporting evidence.

Portfolios are not an alternative to paper and pencil tests, essay tests, or performance tests. Each of these tools has validity. If you want to assess a learner's factual knowledge, an objective-type test is appropriate. If you are interested in a snapshot assessment of how well a learner uses a cognitive strategy, you can use an extended- or restricted-response essay, which will not involve the work required for **portfolio assessment**. But if you want to assess both achievement and growth in an authentic context, you should consider using a portfolio.

Building a Portfolio

There are five steps to building a portfolio for your teaching area.

The teacher in this **video** explains the required components of the portfolio for his class. Listen carefully to how he integrates the portfolio assessment during the course of the year.

Step 1: Decide on the Purposes for a Portfolio.   Have your learners think about their purposes in assembling a portfolio. Having learners identify for themselves the purposes of the portfolio is one way to increase the authenticity of the task. However, your learners' purposes (e.g., getting a job with the local news station) will not necessarily coincide with yours (e.g., assessing learners). So be clear about your purposes at the outset of portfolio design.

Classroom-level purposes that portfolios can achieve include the following:

- Monitoring student progress
- Communicating what has been learned to parents
- Passing on information to subsequent teachers
- Evaluating how well something was taught
- Showing off what has been accomplished
- Assigning a course grade

Step 2: Identify Cognitive Skills and Dispositions.   A portfolio, like any performance assessment, is a measure of deep understanding and genuine achievement. It can measure the growth and development of competence in areas such as knowledge construction and organization, cognitive strategies (analysis, interpretation, planning, revising), procedural skills (clear communication, editing, drawing, speaking, building), metacognition (self-monitoring, self-reflection), and certain dispositions or habits of mind (flexibility, adaptability, acceptance of criticism, persistence, collaboration, and desire for mastery).

Throughout this text, you have practiced how to specify different types of cognitive outcomes, identify aspects of these learning types, and plan to assess them. Apply this same practice to specifying what you want to know about your learners from their portfolios. So as part of your teaching strategy, decide the types of products, processes, or outcomes you will be expecting of your learners:

- *Products:* Poems, essays, charts, graphs, exhibits, drawings, maps, and so forth
- *Complex cognitive processes:* Skills in acquiring, organizing, and using information
- *Observable performances:* Physical movements, as in dance, gymnastics, or typing; oral presentations; and use of specialized procedures, as when dissecting a frog, bisecting an angle, or following a recipe
- *Attitudes and social skills:* Habits of mind, group work, and recognition skills

Step 3: Decide Who Will Plan the Portfolio.   When deciding who will plan the portfolio, consider what is involved in preparing gymnasts or skaters for a major tournament. The parent hires a coach. Then together, the coach, pupil, and parent plan the routines, costumes, practice times, music, and so on. They are a team whose sole purpose is to produce the best performance possible. The gymnast or skater wants to be the best he or she can be. These young athletes also want to please their parents and coaches and meet their expectations. The atmosphere is charged with excitement, dedication, and commitment to genuine effort.

This is the atmosphere you are trying to create when using portfolios. You, the learner, and the parents are a team for helping the learner improve writing, math reasoning, or scientific thinking and to assemble examples of this growing competence. Learners want to show what they can do and to verify the trust and confidence that you and their parents have placed in them. The portfolio is their recital, their tournament, their competition.

Figure 13.6 Example of a Teacher Letter to Parents Introducing a Portfolio Project

I am your child's 8th grade English teacher. I would like your help with an exciting project we are about to begin in our class. The project will be to have all students create during the semester portfolios of their writing that they can show to you, me, and their classmates. The examples of writing that they may choose to put in their portfolios can include letters, essays, writing to persuade someone, criticism, poetry, autobiography, fiction, and even dramatic scripts. Your son or daughter can choose from among these combinations the writing he or she would most like to place in the portfolio.

What I would like to ask of you is your assistance in helping your son or daughter revise and edit his or her writing so that the very best samples of work are placed in the portfolio. I have found that one of the best ways to become a good writer is to have someone else read what is written and provide suggestions as to what to edit and revise. Your willingness to read what your child writes and to suggest improvements in spelling, grammar, and content would be invaluable in encouraging your child's best work. At the end of the semester, we will display everyone's portfolio of writing in the classroom, at which time you will be invited to see your child's and other children's portfolios.

May I ask you to initial each sample of writing that you read to indicate that your son or daughter has sought your assistance in improving it?

Thank you for your help, and I look forward to seeing you at our exhibition of writing skills at the end of the semester.

The principal stakeholders in the use of portfolios are you, your learners, and their parents. Therefore you should involve parents by sending home an explanation of portfolio assessment and asking that they and their children discuss its goals and content. See Figure 13.6 for an example of a letter one teacher wrote to parents introducing a portfolio project.

Step 4: Decide Which Products and How Many Samples to Put in the Portfolio. When determining what and how much to include in the portfolio, you must make two key decisions about ownership and instruction. *Ownership* refers to your learners' perception that their portfolios contain what they want them to. You already considered this issue in Step 3. By involving learners and their parents in the planning process, you enhance their sense of ownership. You also do this by giving them a say in what goes into the portfolio. The task is to balance your desire to enhance ownership with your responsibility to see that the content of the portfolio measures the cognitive skills and dispositions you identified in Step 3.

In terms of *instruction,* both learners and their parents need to see that you are focusing on teaching the skills necessary to fashion the portfolio's content. You should not require products in math, for instance, that you did not prepare learners to create. If students are creating writing portfolios, your instructional goals must include teaching skills in writing poems, essays, editorials, or whatever your curriculum specifies. The same holds for science, social studies, geography, and history portfolios. Thus, in deciding what to include in learners' portfolios, ensure that you only require products your learners were prepared to develop.

The most satisfactory way to satisfy the learner's need for ownership and your need to measure what you teach is to require certain categories of products that match your instructional purposes and cognitive outcomes and to allow the learner and parents to choose the samples within each category. For example, you may require an eighth-grade math portfolio to contain materials that represent the following categories of math content:

1. *Number and operation,* in which the learner demonstrates the understanding of the relative magnitude of numbers, the effects of operations on numbers, and the ability to perform those mathematical operations

2. *Estimation,* in which the learner demonstrates understanding of basic facts, place value, and operations; mental computation; tolerance of error; and flexible use of strategies

3. *Predictions,* in which the learner demonstrates abilities to make predictions based on probabilities; to organize and describe data systematically; to make conjectures based on data analyses; and to construct and interpret graphs, charts, and tables

Learners and their parents would have a choice of which assignments to include for each category listed. For each assignment, the learner would include a brief statement about what the sample says about his or her development of mathematical thinking skills.

Another example could be a high school writing portfolio. The teacher might require that the following categories of writing be in the portfolio: persuasive editorial, persuasive essay, narrative story, autobiography, and dialogue. Learners would choose the samples of writing for each category. For each sample, they would include a cover letter that explains why they chose this sample and what the sample shows about their development as a writer.

You will also have to decide how many samples of each content category to include in the portfolio. For example, do you require two samples of persuasive writing, one of criticism, and three of dialogue? Shavelson, Gao, and Baxter (1991) suggest that as many as eight products or tasks representing different topics or categories may be needed to obtain a reliable estimate of performance from portfolios. Make this decision after eliciting suggestions from your students.

Step 5: Build the Portfolio Rubrics.   In Step 2, you identified the major cognitive skills and dispositions that your portfolio will measure. In Step 4, you specified the content categories that your portfolio will contain. Now you must decide what good, average, and poor performance look like for each entry in the portfolio and the portfolio as a whole.

You already have had some experience doing this. For each dimension on which you will rate the content in a portfolio, list the primary traits or characteristics you think are important. Figure 13.7 shows how this was done for an essay portfolio for which the teacher felt the cognitive outcomes of quality of reflection, writing conventions, organization, planning, and quality of revision were important criteria by which to judge the portfolio entries. Next, construct a rating scale that describes the range of student performance that can occur for each of these dimensions (e.g., 1–5), as noted in Figure 13.7. These rating scales, called **rubrics**, express an explicit set of criteria for assessing a particular product or performance. A rubric includes levels of potential achievement for each desired outcome that, then, are given numerical values (Arter & Chappuis, 2006; Burke, 2010). Figure 13.8 shows how this was done for a math problem-solving portfolio for which the teacher wants to assess the cognitive outcomes of quality of reflection, mathematical knowledge, strategic knowledge, and communication.

Once you design rubrics for the specific contents of the portfolio, you may want to design scoring criteria for the portfolio as a whole product (Burke, 2010). Some traits to consider when developing a scoring mechanism for the entire portfolio are thoroughness, variety, growth or progress, overall quality, self-reflection, flexibility, organization, and appearance. Choose from among these traits or include others, and build a five-point rating scale for each characteristic.

Portfolio Assessment and Report Card Grades

Portfolio assessments require a substantial commitment of teacher time and learner engagement. Consequently, the teacher who decides to use them should ensure that the performance or portfolio grade has substantial weight in the six-week or final report card grade. One way to accomplish this is to score quizzes, tests, homework assignments, performance tests, and portfolios on the basis of 100 points. Computing the final grade simply involves averaging the grades for each component, multiplying these averages by the weights assigned, and adding these products to determine the total grade. Figure 13.9 provides examples of three formulas for accomplishing this.

Plan a Portfolio Conference

Plan to have a final conference at the end of the year or term with each learner and, if possible, his or her parents to discuss the portfolio and what it says about the learner's development and final achievement. The learner can be responsible for conducting the conference, with a little preparation from you on how to do it. This final event can be a highly motivating force for the learner to produce an exemplary portfolio.

Figure 13.7 **Essay Portfolio Rating Form**

_____ First Draft
_____ Second Draft
_____ Final Draft

To Be Completed by Student:

1. Date submitted: _____

2. Briefly explain what this essay says about you. _____
   _____

3. What do you like best about this piece of writing? _____
   _____

4. What do you want to improve in the next draft? _____
   _____

5. If this is your final draft, will you include this in your portfolio? Why? _____
   _____
   _____

To Be Completed by Teacher:

Rating	Description

1. Quality of Reflection

5	States very clearly what he or she likes most and least about the essay. Goes into much detail about how to improve the work.
4	States clearly what he or she likes and dislikes about the essay. Gives detail about how to improve the work.
3	States his or her likes and dislikes but could be clearer. Gives some detail about how the work will be improved.
2	Is vague about likes and dislikes. Gives few details about how the essay will be improved.
1	No evidence of any reflection on the work.

2. Writing Conventions

5	The use of writing conventions is very effective. No errors are evident. These conventions are fluid and complex: spelling, punctuation, grammar usage, sentence structure.
4	The use of writing conventions is effective. Only minor errors are evident. These conventions are nearly all effective: punctuation, grammar usage, sentence structure, spelling.
3	The use of writing conventions is somewhat effective. Errors do not interfere with meaning. These conventions are somewhat effective: punctuation, grammar usage, sentence structure, spelling.
2	Errors in the use of writing conventions interfere with meaning. These conventions are limited and uneven: punctuation, grammar usage, sentence structure, spelling.
1	Major errors in the use of writing conventions obscure meaning. Lacks understanding of punctuation, grammar usage, sentence structure, spelling.

(*continued*)

Figure 13.7 **Continued**

Rating	Description

3. Organization

5	Clearly makes sense.
4	Makes sense.
3	Makes sense for the most part.
2	Attempted but does not make sense.
1	Does not make sense.

4. Planning (1st draft only)

5	Has clear idea of audience. Goals are completely clear and explicit. An overall essay plan is evident.
4	Has idea of audience. Goals are mostly clear and explicit. Has a plan for the essay.
3	Somewhat clear about the essay's audience. Goals are stated but somewhat vague. Plan for the whole essay is somewhat clear.
2	Vague about who the essay is for. Goals are unclear. No clear plan is evident.
1	Writing shows no evidence of planning.

5. Quality of Revision (2nd draft only)

5	Follows up on all suggestions for revision. Revisions make definite improvements.
4	Follows up on most suggestions for revision. Revisions improve the previous draft.
3	Addresses some but not all suggested revisions. Revisions create some improvement over earlier draft.
2	Ignores most suggestions for revision. Revisions do not improve the earlier draft.
1	Made only a minimal attempt to revise, if at all.

Sum of ratings: _____

Average of ratings: _____

Comments: _____

_____

_____

_____

_____

_____

_____

_____

_____

Figure 13.8 Math Problem-Solving Portfolio Rating Form

Content Categories:

____✔____ Problem solving   Problem _____ 1

_____ Numbers and operations   ____✔____ 2

_____ Estimation   _____ 3

_____ Predictions

To Be Completed by Student:

1. Date submitted: _____

2. What does this problem say about you as a problem solver? _____
_____
_____

3. What do you like best about how you solved this problem? _____
_____
_____

4. How will you improve your problem-solving skill on the next problem?_____
_____
_____

To Be Completed by Teacher:

Rating   *Description*

1. Quality of Reflection

      5   Has excellent insight into his or her problem-solving abilities and clear ideas of
                    how to get better.

      4   Has good insight into his or her problem-solving abilities and some ideas of how
                    to get better.

      3   Reflects somewhat on problem-solving strengths and needs. Has some idea of
                    how to improve as a problem solver.

      2   Seldom reflects on problem-solving strengths and needs. Has little idea of how
                    to improve as a problem solver.

      1   Has no concept of him- or herself as a problem solver.

2. Mathematical Knowledge

      5   Shows deep understanding of the problems, math concepts, and principles.
                    Uses appropriate math terms, and all calculations are correct.

      4   Shows good understanding of math problems, concepts, and principles. Uses
                    appropriate math terms most of the time. Few computational errors.

      3   Shows understanding of some of the problems, math concepts, and principles.
                    Uses some terms incorrectly. Contains some computation errors.

      2   Makes errors in many problems. Uses many terms incorrectly.

      1   Makes major errors in problems. Shows no understanding of math problems,
                    concepts, and principles.

(continued)

Figure 13.8 Continued

Rating	Description

3. Strategic Knowledge

5 Identifies all the important elements of the problem. Reflects an appropriate and systematic strategy for solving the problem; gives clear evidence of a solution process.

4 Identifies most of the important elements of the problem. Reflects an appropriate and systematic strategy for solving the problem, and gives clear evidence of a solution process most of the time.

3 Identifies some important elements of the problem. Gives some evidence of a strategy to solve the problem, but the process is incomplete.

2 Identifies few important elements of the problem. Gives little evidence of a strategy to solve the problem, and the process is unknown.

1 Uses irrelevant outside information. Copies parts of the problem; makes no attempt at solution.

4. Communication

5 Gives a complete response with a clear, unambiguous explanation; includes diagrams and charts when they help clarify the explanation; presents strong arguments that are logically developed.

4 Gives good response with fairly clear explanation, which includes some use of diagrams and charts; presents good arguments that are mostly but not always logically developed.

3 Explanations and descriptions of the problem solution are somewhat clear but incomplete; makes some use of diagrams and examples to clarify points, but the arguments are incomplete.

2 Explanations and descriptions of the problem solution are weak; makes little, if any, use of diagrams and examples to clarify points; the arguments are seriously flawed.

1 Uses ineffective communication; diagrams misrepresent the problem; arguments have no sound premises.

Sum of ratings: _____

Average of ratings: _____

Comments: _____

_____

_____

_____

_____

_____

_____

_____

_____

_____

Figure 13.9 **Three Examples of Different Ways to Compute and Weight Grades**

Grading Formula Example #1 ("One, Two, Three Times Plan")

Homework and Classwork: All grades for homework and classwork are totaled and averaged. The average grade will count once.

Homework and classwork grades followed by the average:

84, 81, 88, 92, 96, 85, 78, 83, 91, 79, 89, 94 = 1040 ÷ 12 = 86.6 = 87 average

Quizzes: All of the quizzes are totaled and averaged. This average grade will count two times.

Quiz grades followed by the average:

82, 88, 80, 91, 78, 86 = 505 ÷ 6 = 84.2 = 84 average

Tests and Major Projects: All of the tests and major projects are totaled and averaged. This average grade will count three times.

Test and major project grade followed by the average:

81, 91, 86 = 258 ÷ 3 = 86 average

The 6 weeks' grade is computed as follows:

87 (one time) + 84 + 84 (two times), + 86 + 86 + 86 (three times) = 513 ÷ 6 = 85.5 = 86 as the grade

Grading Formula Example #2 ("Percentages Plan")

A teacher determines a percentage for each area. For example, homework and classwork count 20 percent of the grade; quizzes count 40 percent of the grade; and tests and major projects count 40 percent of the grade.

Using the same scores as listed above, a student's grade is computed as follows:

20 percent of the 86.6 for homework and classwork is 17.3; 40 percent of the 84.2 for quizzes is 33.7; and 40 percent of the 86 for tests and major projects is 34.4.

The six weeks' grade is 17.3 + 33.7 + 34.4 = 85.4 = 85. (The average is different because the weight put on each area varies in the two examples.)

Grading Formula Example #3 ("Language Arts Plan")

A language arts teacher determines that the publishing, goal meeting, journal, and daily process grades each count one-fourth (25 percent) of the six weeks' grade.

A language arts grade is computed as follows:

The publishing grade is issued only at the end of the six weeks = 88

The goal meeting grade is issued only at the end of the six weeks = 86

The journal grades are 82 + 92 + 94 + 90 + 88 + 86 = 532 ÷ 6 = 88.7 = 89

The daily process grades are 78 + 82 + 86 + 94 + 94 + 91 = 532 ÷ 6 = 87.5 = 88

The six weeks' grade is 88 + 86 + 89 + 88 = 351 ÷ 4 = 87.75 = 88

Assessing the Academic Progress of Special Learners in the Regular Classroom

You should know about three important pieces of legislation that regulate the instruction and assessment of special learners in the regular classroom. These are the No Child Left Behind Act (NCLB), the Individuals with Disabilities Education Improvement Act (IDEIA), and Response to Intervention.

The No Child Left Behind Act

The reauthorization of the Elementary and Secondary Education Act (ESEA) was signed into law in January 2002 and renamed the No Child Left Behind Act (NCLB). The intent of NCLB is to "improve educational opportunities for every American child—regardless of ethnicity, income, or background." The law specifically intends to raise the academic achievement of traditionally low-performing, economically disadvantaged students. To accomplish its objectives, the law was built on "four common-sense pillars":

- Accountability for results
- An emphasis on doing what works based on scientific research
- Expanded parental options
- Expanded local control and flexibility

NCLB is a wide-ranging act and includes several important federal education programs that are relevant to the general education teacher. These include Education for the Disadvantaged, Reading First/Early Reading First, Safe and Drug-Free Schools, and Bilingual and Migrant Education. Your school district's federal funding for these programs is closely linked to state, district, and school compliance with annual assessments that determine whether the learners in your classroom attain *adequate yearly progress (AYP)*.

The 2004 Reauthorization of the Individuals with Disabilities Education Improvement Act

A second large-scale federal program that you will be involved with is the Individuals with Disabilities Education Improvement Act (IDEIA-04), passed in November 2004. Congress's intent in passing IDEIA-04 was to reaffirm that children with disabilities are entitled to a free and appropriate public education (FAPE) and to ensure that special education students have access to all the potential benefits that regular education students have from the general curriculum, including the reforms initiated by NCLB in 2002. IDEIA-04 requires that the instruction for students with disabilities follows the curriculum in the regular classroom, except in the most severe cases. In addition, IDEIA-04 requires that students with disabilities be assessed with the same measures used to assess regular education students, with the exception that extreme cases be assessed with appropriate accommodations or alternate assessments.

Under IDEIA-04, regular education teachers are required to be members of the individualized education program (IEP) team for each child with a disability. The IEP team—consisting of the regular education teacher, the special education teacher, and the parents—determines how the performance and progress of the special learner in the general curriculum will be assessed. The team also must collect the data necessary to make such determinations, including behavioral data when the behavior of a child with a disability impedes progress in the general curriculum. Testing of children with disabilities within the regular classroom by the classroom teacher will be required to help determine whether a student is in need of special education and the extent to which his or her behavior is impeding progress in the general curriculum. In-class testing is also necessary to evaluate the progress of each child with a disability toward the annual objectives established in the IEP and to meet the accountability requirements of IDEIA-04 and NCLB.

Congress's intent in passing both IDEIA-04 and NCLB is clear: Children with disabilities must be instructed within the general curriculum, their progress within the general curriculum must be assessed regularly, and, except where an IEP can justify an accommodation or alternate assessment, they must participate in the same annual academic assessment required for their nondisabled peers. Because the general education teacher will be the professional on the IEP team most familiar with the general curriculum and the annual academic assessment in the regular classroom, he or she should expect to play an important role in IEP team meetings. And because the progress of a child with a disability can often be hampered by behavioral and social needs that result from the disability, this, too, will have to be assessed regularly to determine whether it impedes progress in the general curriculum, whenever called for in the IEP.

One of the tasks expected of the regular education teacher is to assess children with disabilities to help determine whether they can participate appropriately in the annual academic assessment required by NCLB. The techniques and tools covered in this chapter (e.g., teacher-made objective and essay tests and performance and portfolio assessments) and in Chapter 5 (goals, standards, and objectives) will be needed for this purpose. Because the case of each child with a disability may be unique, assessment modifications appropriate for one learner may or may not be appropriate for others, such as providing additional time to complete tests and assessments, using stimuli with large print or Braille, limiting distractions, and allowing more frequent breaks. To evaluate the academic performance and progress of a child with a disability in the general curriculum, the IEP team will rely largely on data gathered in the regular classroom. The general education teacher, therefore, will be expected to provide performance and progress data for the special learner and any assessment accommodations that might be necessary for annual assessments of his or her progress.

Algozzine and Ysseldyke (2006) and Ysseldyke and Algozzine (1990) have identified the ways in which the regular classroom teacher may be involved in the assessment process. The flowchart shown in Figure 13.10 illustrates how the testing and assessment skills of the regular education teacher are instrumental in each step of the special education process of identification, instruction,

Figure 13.10 **Teacher Participation throughout the Identification, Instruction, and Evaluation Process for Special Learners**

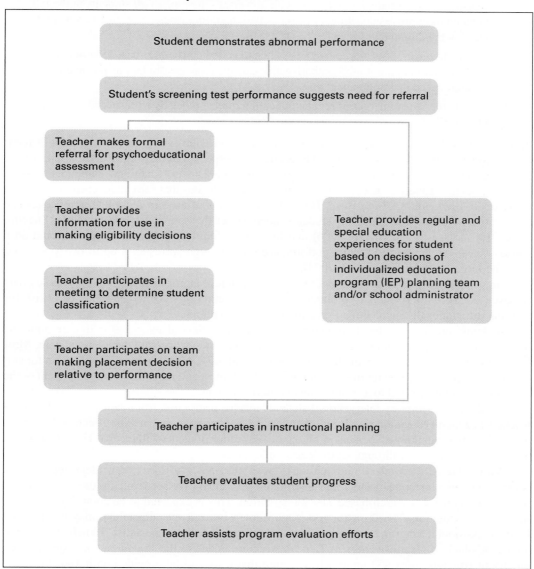

Source: Ysseldyke, J., & Algozzine, R. (1990) *Instructor's resource manual, Introduction to special education,* 2nd edition. Reprinted with permission.

and evaluation of special learners in the regular classroom. This chart also portrays the responsibilities for assessment of special learners that the general education teacher can be expected to assume. Each of these programs emphasize the ongoing monitoring of the progress of all student to enable early identification of learning problems and the need for specialized and/or intensified instruction to students identified as struggling.

Response to Intervention (RTI)

In addition to your knowledge of NCLB and IDEIA, you will need to know about Response to Intervention, not only because it is required but because it can have a significant impact on your school and classroom. Earlier we saw how RTI could help initiating research-based practices and with their frequently administered formative assessments with specially constructed curriculum-based measures. Although implementation of RTI in the regular education classroom has been uneven, there is little doubt that RTI will have a significant impact on every future teacher.

RTI can be characterized as:

- A system-wide initiative, that begins with universal screening of all students in the fall, intended to improve educational outcomes by integrating assessment, instruction, and decision making, that

- Utilizes frequent, brief, formative assessments (called curriculum-based measures—or CBM) rather than one-time summative assessments to assess student responsiveness to research-based instruction, and that

- Reflects the recent merger of regular education reform (NCLB) with special education reform (IDEIA)

Taken together, IDEIA, NCLB, and RTI are expected to provide even greater integration of regular and special education in the future. All teachers are expected to be trained in the basics of the RTI approach and understand how it differs from and complements traditional summative assessment approaches. Evidence is beginning to emerge that indicates that formative, curriculum-based measures (CBM) (Jones, 2008; Hosp, Hosp, & Howell, 2006) used in most RTI approaches can be effective in identifying struggling students much earlier than previously was possible (Shapiro, Keller, Edwards, Lutz, & Hintze, 2006) and that curriculum-based measures, administered on a weekly basis, can be used to predict performance on state high-stakes tests up to two years later (Keller-Margulis, Shapiro & Hintze, 2008).

Simply put, Response to Intervention is a multi-tiered approach to help struggling learners (Hoover, 2011). Its purpose is to promote early identification of students who may be at risk for learning difficulties through a three-tiered model of intervention.

Students' progress is closely monitored at each stage (tier) of intervention to determine the need for further instruction or intervention in general education, special education, or both. Most RTI applications are based on a model of increasingly intensive research-based intervention for students with increasingly greater intervention needs. The largest and most common component of the three-tier model is referred to as primary intervention (Tier 1).

Within Tier 1 (primary intervention) students receive instruction from their regular classroom teachers in general education classrooms that research studies have shown to be effective. It is anticipated that approximately 80 percent of all regular education students will receive Tier 1 instruction and will remain at Tier 1 throughout their academic careers.

Within Tier 2 (secondary intervention), those students who have been identified through screening to be nonresponsive to Tier 1 instruction (i.e., at risk for academic failure) are provided with more intensive research-based Tier 2 instruction. This is expected to be about 15 percent of the school population. Tier 2 instruction is more intensive and specialized and may be provided by the classroom teacher in small groups or on a pullout basis by a specialist. To help ensure that a student's lack of responsiveness to Tier 1 instruction is due to the student and not simply poor quality instruction, most RTI approaches require that a student be provided with Tier 2 instruction only if the majority of the student's classmates have made adequate progress with Tier 1 instruction.

Within Tier 3 (tertiary intervention), the student may be referred for a comprehensive special education evaluation to determine whether the student qualifies for special education services as a student with a specific learning disability. Failure to respond to Tier 2 instruction is considered the primary criterion for a student to qualify for special education services. IDEIA requires that student responsiveness to Tier 2 or Tier 3 instruction must be repeatedly monitored with formative, curriculum-based measures on a weekly basis, known as progress monitoring. Progress monitoring provides the teacher with the information needed for informed, data-based instructional decision making, allowing for the quick adjustment of the level of instruction provided to students. Curriculum-based measures shifts the focus for progress monitoring from a summative evaluation (e.g., determining what a student has learned on end-of-year standardized tests) to a formative evaluation (e.g., determining what a student is learning continuously throughout the year during instruction).

The promise of RIT is that general education teachers will be able to enhance learning for all students and more quickly and accurately identify struggling learners to provide targeted instruction that enables a greater number of learners to benefit from the regular classroom. For an extensive review of RTI see Kubiszyn and Borich (2013, Chapter 3).

Table 13.3 shows the three RTI tiers beginning with universal screening for all students. Tier 2 is shown with two alternative approaches, one in which students are presented with a variety of interventions based on their individual needs and responsiveness to previous instruction and a second approach in which students with a similar difficulty or skill sets are presented with one standard, research-based intervention. As a general or special education teacher your knowledge of these two approaches will be important for the effective and immediate remediation of Tier 2 struggling learners.

NCLB, IDEIA, and RTI should be seen as complementary pieces of educational legislation, rather than specific remedies directed to either regular education or special education. IDEIA, in

Table 13.3 Comparing Problem-Solving and Standard Protocol Approaches to RTI

Comparison of RTI Approaches		
	Problem-Solving	**Standard Treatment Protocol**
Universal screening	Class-wide assessment/universal screening is administered to identify students who are potentially struggling.	
Tier 1	All students receive high-quality instruction. Frequent progress monitoring is conducted to assess struggling students' performance levels and rates of improvement.	
Tier 2	Students whose progress in Tier 1 is not adequate receive additional individual support. 1. A team makes instructional decisions based on an individual student's performance. The team identifies the academic problem; determines its cause; and then develops, implements, and evaluates a plan to address the problem. 2. Students are presented with a variety of interventions, based on their unique needs and performance data. 3. Interventions are flexible and individualized to meet a student's needs.	Students whose progress in Tier 1 is not adequate receive additional group support. 1. The person delivering the intervention makes instructional decisions following a standard protocol. 2. Students with similar needs are presented with one standard, research-validated intervention. 3. The intervention is delivered in a predetermined format that may address multiple skill sets. This allows for greater quality control (i.e., treatment fidelity is easier to monitor given the ease of implementing a single intervention).
Tier 3	Students whose progress is still insufficient in Tier 2 may receive even more intensive intervention. Depending on a state's or district's policies, some students may qualify for special education services based on their progress monitoring data. In some states or districts, they may receive either an abbreviated or comprehensive evaluation for the identification of a learning disability.	

Source: Materials created by the IRIS Center (http/iris.peabody.vanderbilt.edu) for the National Association of State Directors of Special Education IDEA Partnership. Sponsored by the U.S. Department of Education Office of Special Education Programs, 2007.

particular, was specifically intended to break down the barriers between regular and special education. Its emphasis on formative assessment and progress monitoring complements the primary intention of NCLB and RTI, which is to improve educational opportunities for all students with frequently administered curriculum-based assessments followed by the use of research-based instructional methods.

Case History and Licensure Preparation

DIRECTIONS: *The following case history pertains to Chapter 13 content. After reading the case history, go to Chapter 13 in the Book Specific Resources section in the MyEducationLab for your course. Open the Case History and Licensure Preparation activity and complete the questions that follow. Upon completion of the test, scored answers to the short-answer question pertaining to the case history and multiple choice questions will be provided.*

Case History

Ms. Velchek was happy when she was hired for her current teaching job. The middle school was newly built and featured state-of-the-art facilities, including computer, language, and biology labs. When she looked at the standardized test scores of her sixth-grade social studies class, she was pleased. Most of the class was functioning above grade level in critical areas such as science, vocabulary, reading comprehension, and mathematics, as well as in her own area of social studies. On Back-to-School Night, her classroom was packed with parents who seemed concerned and supportive.

But just six weeks into the year, Ms. Velchek was discouraged. She was having every bit as much trouble with this seemingly ideal class as she had had the year before with a crowded class of inner-city students considered to be at-risk learners. Even though her current students excelled on their weekly quizzes and objective tests, she suspected they earned their high grades with only cursory reading of the assignments. Most were earning A's and B's, yet none seemed really interested in class. Moreover, she doubted students remembered much of the information they provided on tests over the long run.

Reading students' essays had been exhilarating at first. They wrote well-constructed sentences, their thoughts were fairly well organized, and they made few spelling errors. But now Ms. Velchek wondered if their writing ability was disguising a rather superficial understanding of the concepts she was teaching.

Ms. Velchek thought that by changing her tests and maybe even her grading system, she could help promote and test for higher levels of understanding. She decided to eliminate the true/false quizzes, in which students could

get half of the items correct by guessing. She would continue using multiple-choice items but would write them to elicit her students' skill at applying what they learned, not just memorizing.

The class had just finished a unit on world geography, and students expected an exam that would emphasize facts about climate and topography. As usual, they would come prepared with freshly memorized facts—this time, about annual rainfall and the proper names of bodies of water, mountain ranges, and desert regions.

Mark hoped that all the facts and figures he had crammed for while watching TV last night would remain in his memory until midmorning. He had given the chapters a quick once-over during breakfast, so he felt as well-prepared as he always did. But his mouth dropped when he saw the first question.

None of the memorized information—the knowledge of rainfall, temperature, and terrain—was of help now. What lay before Mark was an invented country, complete with data on mineral deposits, vegetation, rainfall, and temperature and details about fictitious rivers, lakes, and mountains. One question asked, "Given your knowledge of geography and its influence on economics and population growth, answer the following items concerning this hypothetical country. Here are four possible sketches showing population distributions. Using the data given, which of these populations do you believe these data best represent?" Another question asked about economic development, showing four maps with different areas sketched in for livestock ranching, commercial grain, mining, and industry.

Mark swallowed hard and flipped to the last page, the essay question, which he usually could easily answer. With most tests, his paraphrasing of the textbook passages was sufficient for a high score. He "had a way with words" and made up for forgotten details by using well-chosen adjectives. But his narrative ability was not of much help today. This essay question asked, "Write a paragraph explaining in detail the reasoning behind each of your multiple-choice map selections."

It was close to the end of the period, and no one had finished the test early this time. The puzzled expressions of the students at the beginning of the test had been replaced by looks of determination and, on some faces, subtle satisfaction.

Summing Up

The main points of this chapter include the following:

Norm-Referenced and Criterion-Referenced Tests

1. A test that determines a student's place or rank among other students is called a *norm-referenced test (NRT)*. This type of test conveys information about how a student performed compared to a large sample of learners at the same age or grade.

2. A test that compares a learner's performance to a standard of mastery is called a *criterion-referenced test (CRT)*. This type of test conveys information about whether a student needs additional instruction on some skill or set of skills.

3. The major advantage of an NRT is that it covers many different content areas in a single test; its major disadvantage is that it is too general to be useful in identifying specific strengths and weaknesses tied to individual texts or workbooks.

4. The major advantage of a CRT is that it can yield highly specific information about individual skills or behaviors. Its major disadvantage is that many such tests would be needed to make decisions about the range of skills and behaviors typically taught in school.

The Test Blueprint

5. A *test blueprint* is a table that matches the test items to be written with the content areas and levels of behavioral complexity taught. The test blueprint helps ensure that a test samples learning across (a) the range of content areas covered and (b) the cognitive and/or affective processes considered important.

Objective Test Items

6. Objective test item formats include the following:
   - True/false
   - Matching
   - Multiple choice
   - Completion or short answer

7. Two methods for reducing the effects of guessing in true/false items are (a) to encourage all students to guess when they do not know the answer and (b) to require the revision of statements that are false.

8. Guidelines for constructing matching items include the following:
   - Make lists homogeneous, representing the same kind of events, people, or circumstances.
   - Place the shorter list first, and list options in chronological, numbered, or alphabetical order.
   - Provide approximately three more options than descriptions to reduce the chance of guessing correctly.
   - Write directions to identify what the lists contain and specify the basis for matching.
   - Closely check the options for multiple correct answers.

9. Avoid the following flaws when writing multiple-choice items:
   - Stem clues, in which the same word or a close derivative appears in both the stem and an option
   - Grammatical clues, in which an article, verb, or pronoun eliminates one or more options from being grammatically correct
   - Repeating the same words across options that could have been provided only once in the stem
   - Making response options of unequal lengths, indicating that the longest option may be correct
   - The use of "all of the above," which discourages response discrimination, and "none of the above," which encourages guessing

10. Suggestions for writing higher-level multiple-choice items include use of the following:
    - Pictorial, graphical, or tabular stimuli
    - Analogies that demonstrate relationships among items
    - Application of previously learned principles or procedures

11. The following are suggestions for writing completion items:
    - Require single-word answers.
    - Pose each question or problem in a brief, definite statement.
    - Check to be sure the response is factually correct.
    - Omit only one or two key words in the item.
    - Word the statement so the blank is near the end.
    - If the question requires a numerical answer, indicate the units in which the answer is to be expressed.

Essay Test Items

12. An extended-response essay question allows the student to determine the length and complexity of a response.

13. A restricted-response essay question poses a specific problem for which the student must recall and organize the proper information, derive a defensible conclusion, and express it within a stated time or length.

14. Essay items are most appropriate when (a) the instructional objectives specify high-level cognitive processes, (b) relatively few test items (students) are necessary, and (c) test security is a consideration.

15. Suggestions for writing essay items include the following:
    - Identify beforehand the mental processes you want to measure (e.g., application, analysis, decision making).
    - Define the task to be accomplished by the student clearly and unambiguously.
    - Begin the essay question with a key word or phrase, such as *compare, give reasons for,* or *predict.*
    - Require the presentation of evidence for a controversial question.
    - Avoid using optional items.
    - Establish reasonable time and/or page limits.
    - Be sure each essay question relates to an objective on the test blueprint.

16. Use of the following criteria will help increase consistency and accuracy when scoring essay items:
    - Content: Essay questions should be used for measuring thinking processes.
    - Organization: Essay questions should have an introduction, body, and conclusion.
    - Process: Essay questions should result in a solution, recommendation, or decision.
    - Completeness/Internal consistency: Essay questions should have sufficient detail to support the points being made.
    - Originality/Creativity: Essay questions should offer new and creative alternatives.

Validity and Reliability

17. *Validity* refers to whether a test measures what it says it measures. Three types of validity are *content, concurrent,* and *predictive.*

18. *Content validity* is established by examining a test's content. *Concurrent validity* is established by correlating the scores on a new test with the scores on an established test given to the same set of individuals. *Predictive validity* is established by correlating the scores on a new test with some future behavior of the examinee that is representative of the test's content.

19. *Reliability* refers to whether a test yields the same or similar scores consistently. Three types of reliability are *test-retest, alternate form,* and *internal consistency.*

20. *Test-retest reliability* is established by giving the test twice to the same individuals and correlating the first set of scores with the second. *Alternate form reliability* is established by giving two parallel but different forms of the test to the same individuals and correlating the two sets of scores. *Internal consistency reliability* is established by determining the extent to which the test measures a single concept.

Marks and Grading Systems

21. Marks and grading systems are based on comparisons, usually comparisons of students with one or more of the following:
    - Other students
    - Established standards
    - Aptitude
    - Achievement versus effort
    - Achievement versus improvement

Standardized Tests

22. *Standardized tests* are developed by test construction specialists to determine a student's performance level relative to that of others of similar age and grade. They are standardized because they are administered and scored according to specific and uniform procedures.

Performance Assessment

23. A *performance assessment* asks learners to show what they know by measuring complex cognitive skills using authentic, real-world tasks.

The Portfolio

24. A *portfolio* is a planned collection of materials that documents what a student has accomplished and what steps he or she took to get there.

Assessing the Academic Progress of Special Learners in the Regular Classroom

25. The intent of No Child Left Behind (NCLB) is to improve the educational opportunities of every learner—regardless of ethnicity, income, or background.

26. The intent of the Individuals with Disabilities Education Improvement Act (IDEIA) is to provide children with disabilities a free and appropriate public education (FAPE) and to ensure that special education students have access to all the potential benefits that regular education students have from the general curriculum.

27. The intent of Response To Intervention (RTI) is to promote early identification of students who may be at risk for learning difficulties through a three-tiered intervention model.

Key Terms

Assessment Portfolio
Criterion-referenced test (CRT)
Distracters
Extended-response essay question
Formative evaluation
Individuals with Disabilities Education
 Improvement Act (IDEIA)

Marks and grading systems
No Child Left Behind Act (NCLB)
Norm-referenced test (NRT)
Portfolio assessment
Reliability
Response to Intervention
Restricted-response essay question

Rubrics
Standardized tests
Stem
Summative evaluation
Test blueprint
Validity

Discussion and Practice Questions

Questions marked with an asterisk are answered in Appendix B. Some asterisked questions may require student follow-up responses not included in Appendix B. Go to the Assignments and Activities section of the various topics on the MyEducationLab for your course to complete additional practice activities related to this chapter's content.

*1. Identify the characteristics of a norm-referenced and a criterion-referenced test and the purpose for which each is best suited.

*2. What two instructional dimensions are measured by a test blueprint? Give an example of how the two dimensions are used with real data for a test you might construct.

*3. Identify four formats for objective test items, and give two advantages and two disadvantages of each format.

*4. What are four things to avoid in writing good multiple-choice test items? Which do you feel is the hardest to avoid?

*5. What three devices may be used to prepare multiple-choice questions at higher levels of cognitive complexity? Prepare examples of a multiple-choice items using each one.

*6. Identify the reasons discussed in this chapter for preparing an essay test as opposed to an objective test. What might be some other reasons or situations in which you might choose to prepare an essay test?

*7. Describe three advantages and three disadvantages of essay items. What, in your opinion, is the biggest advantage and biggest disadvantage?

*8. Identify five criteria for scoring essay items. What percentage weight of 100 would you assign to each?

*9. Define the concepts of *validity* and *reliability*, and discuss each in terms of a recent test you have taken. Were you aware of the reliability and validity of the test? If not, did you know where you might obtain this information?

*10. Provide the approximate ranges for an acceptable validity coefficient and an acceptable reliability coefficient. What is the maximum possible size of a validity or reliability coefficient?

*11. What is a standardized test? Name one you have taken most recently and comment why or why not you thought the test accurately measured what you knew.

*12. What does a *percentile rank* indicate for a given individual? What two points should be kept in mind in interpreting a percentile rank?

13. Describe the procedure you would use to aggregate scores for a number of portfolio ratings. By providing hypothetical ratings for the entries on your rating form, indicate with actual numbers and averages how you will (a) calculate weights, (b) take the average score for each entry, (c) add up all the entries to get an overall score, and (d) assign a grade (e.g., A to F) to the average score.

Professional Practice

Field Experience and Practice Activities

Questions marked with an asterisk are answered in Appendix B. Some asterisked questions may require student follow-up responses not included in Appendix B.

*1. Compare and contrast the characteristics of extended-response and restricted-response essay items. Provide an example of each from your field experience or classroom observations.

*2. What is a *scoring rubric*? Construct a scoring rubric for a portfolio essay question using the examples in Figure 13.7.

*3. What are the three types of test validity? What information would each provide about a test given that you would give in your classroom?

*4. What three methods can be used to determine the reliability of a test? What information would each provide for a test given in your classroom?

*5. Identify five procedures for assigning marks and one advantage and one disadvantage of each. Which approach or combination of approaches have you observed in your field work or classroom observations?

6. Develop a portfolio rating form using Figures 13.7 and 13.8 as guides. Be sure to include definitions of all the scale alternatives (e.g., 1 to 5) being rated.

7. Describe in your own words the distinct focus and value to your classroom of each of the following: NCLB, IDEIA, and Response to Intervention.

Digital Portfolio Activities

The following digital portfolio activities relate to InTASC Standards 6 and 9.

1. In Field Experience and Practice Activities 1 and 2, you were asked to write an example of an extended-response and a restricted-response essay question and to prepare a scoring rubric identifying the criteria by which one of the responses would be assigned a grade. Examine your rubric for completeness, and place it into your digital portfolio in a folder titled "Learner Assessment."

2. In Field Experience and Practice Activity 6, you were asked to develop a portfolio rating form that includes definitions of all the scale alternatives (e.g., 1 to 5) being rated. This rating form will serve as a general template from which you can prepare other scales and criteria to match the portfolio products being rated. Place your rating form in your "Learner Assessment" portfolio folder for future reference.

MyEducationLab™

Go to MyEducationLab (www.myeducationlab.com) for Effective Teaching Methods: Research-Based Practice where you can:

- Find learning outcomes for the various course topics course along with national standards that connect to these outcomes.

- Complete **Assignments and Activities** that can help you more deeply understand the chapter content.

- Apply and practice your understanding of the core teaching skills identified in the chapter with **Building Teaching Skills and Dispositions** coaching activities.

- Check your comprehension of the content covered in the chapter with a book specific **Study Plan**. Here you will be able to take a chapter **pretest**, receive feedback on your answers, and then access personalized **Review, Practice, and Enrichment exercises** to enhance your understanding of chapter content. After you complete the exercises, take a **posttest** to confirm your comprehension.

- Learn how to address common classroom management issues in the **Simulations in Classroom Management.**

- Access video clips of CCSSO **National Teachers of the Year award winners** responding to the question, "Why Do I Teach?" in the Teacher Talk section.

- Create, update, and share quality lesson plans with the **Lesson Plan Builder**.

- Access state licensure test requirements, overviews of what tests cover, and sample test items in the **Certification and Licensure** section.

- Learn how to create a high quality teaching portfolio in the **Preparing a Portfolio** section.

- Access tips, advice, and other information on resume writing and interviewing, your first year of teaching, and law and public policies in the Beginning Your Career section.

Appendix A

Teacher Concerns Checklist

Francis F. Fuller and Gary D. Borich
The University of Texas at Austin

This checklist explores what teachers are concerned about at different stages of their careers. There are no right or wrong answers, because each teacher has his or her own concerns.

Below and on the following page are statements of concerns you might have. Read each statement, and ask yourself, "When I think about teaching, am I concerned about this?"

- If you are not concerned or the statement does not apply, write a 1 on the line.
- If you are a little concerned, write a 2 on the line.
- If you are moderately concerned, write a 3 on the line.
- If you are very concerned, write a 4 on the line.
- And if you are totally preoccupied with the concern, write a 5 on the line.

1 Not concerned
2 A little concerned
3 Moderately concerned
4 Very concerned
5 Totally preoccupied

___ 1. Having insufficient clerical help
___ 2. Whether students respect me
___ 3. Having too many extra duties and responsibilities
___ 4. Doing well when I'm observed
___ 5. Helping students to value learning
___ 6. Having insufficient time for rest and class preparation
___ 7. Not having enough assistance from specialized teachers
___ 8. Managing my time efficiently
___ 9. Losing the respect of my peers
___ 10. Not having enough time for grading and testing
___ 11. The inflexibility of the curriculum
___ 12. Too many standards and regulations set for teachers
___ 13. My ability to prepare adequate lesson plans
___ 14. Having my inadequacies become known to other teachers

___ 15. Increasing students' feelings of accomplishment
___ 16. The rigid instructional routine
___ 17. Diagnosing students' learning problems
___ 18. What the principal may think if there is too much noise in my classroom
___ 19. Whether each student is reaching his or her potential
___ 20. Obtaining a favorable evaluation of my teaching
___ 21. Having too many students in a class
___ 22. Recognizing the social and emotional needs of students
___ 23. Challenging unmotivated students
___ 24. Losing the respect of my students
___ 25. Lack of public support for schools
___ 26. My ability to maintain the appropriate degree of class control
___ 27. Not having sufficient time to plan
___ 28. Getting students to behave

___ 29. Understanding why certain students make slow progress

___ 30. Having an embarrassing incident occur in my classroom for which I might be judged responsible

___ 31. Not being able to cope with disruptive students in my classes

___ 32. That my peers may think I am not doing an adequate job

___ 33. My ability to work with disruptive students

___ 34. Understanding ways in which student health and nutrition problems can affect learning

___ 35. Appearing competent to parents

___ 36. Meeting the needs of different kinds of students

___ 37. Seeking alternative ways to ensure that students learn the subject matter

___ 38. Understanding the psychological and cultural differences that can affect my students' behavior

___ 39. Adapting to the needs of different students

___ 40. The large number of administrative interruptions

___ 41. Guiding students toward intellectual and emotional growth

___ 42. Working with too many students each day

___ 43. Whether students can apply what they learn

___ 44. Teaching effectively when another teacher is present

___ 45. Understanding what factors motivate students to learn

The following items on the Teacher Concerns Checklist represent dimensions of *self*, *task*, and *impact*.

Self: 2, 4, 8, 9, 13, 14, 18, 20, 24, 26, 28, 30, 32, 35, 44

Task: 1, 3, 6, 7, 10, 11, 12, 16, 21, 25, 27, 31, 33, 40, 42

Impact: 5, 15, 17, 19, 22, 23, 29, 34, 36, 37, 38, 39, 41, 43, 45

To determine your score, total the number of responses in each of the three categories of concern—self, task, and impact. The higher your score in the category (out of a maximum 75 points), the more you are identified with that stage of concern. Also, by summing responses to items in each category and dividing by the number of items completed, you can compute an average rating for each of the three stages of concern. Shifts of concern from self to task are typical of student teachers after a semester in a field experience. Larger shifts, particularly from task to impact, are frequently noted for in-service teachers during their first two to three years of teaching.

Appendix B

Answers to Chapter Questions and Activities

Here are the answers to the questions marked with asterisks for the Discussion and Practice Questions and the Field Experience and Practice Activities at the end of each chapter.

Chapter 1
Discussion and Practice Questions

1. 1, 2, 1 (or 2), 1 (or 2), 2, 3, 2, 3, 2 (or 1), 3, 2, 3, 3

Chapter 2
Discussion and Practice Questions

1. **a.** Match instructional methods to individual learning needs.
   b. Understand the reasons behind the school performance of individual learners.

2. Environmentalists believe that differences in IQ scores among groups can be attributed to social class or environmental differences. Hereditarians believe that heredity rather than the environment is the major factor determining intelligence.

3. By some estimates, social competence accounts for about 75 percent of school learning, leaving only about 25 percent to the influence of intelligence. If the influence of socioeconomic status on learning could be removed, differences in IQ among learners could be expected to become smaller.

4. Factors that are likely more predictive of school learning than general IQ are specialized abilities such as those suggested by Thurstone and by Gardner and Hatch, which may include verbal intelligence (English), spatial intelligence (art), and interpersonal intelligence (social studies, drama).

6. Front half/back half, girls/boys, more able/less able, nonminority/minority.

7. Spread interactions across categories of students; select students randomly; pair students; code class notes.

Field Experience and Practice Activities

4. Form heterogeneous groups composed of members of different peer groups. Conduct a group discussion of class norms.

Chapter 3
Discussion and Practice Questions

1. Expert and referent power. You can achieve each type of power by keeping up with developments in your field and giving your students a sense of belonging and acceptance.

2. *Diffusion* occurs when different academic and social expectations, held by different members, spread throughout the group. *Crystallization* occurs when expectations converge and crystallize into a shared experience. Diffusion precedes crystallization.

3. The three roles are sole provider of information (commander in chief), translator or summarizer of student ideas, and equal partner with students in creating ideas and problem solutions. Student opinion, student talk, and spontaneity will increase from the former role to the latter.

6. **a.** Stay seated and quiet when there is a visitor at the door.
   b. Line up single-file when exiting the classroom.

7. **a.** Make rules consistent with your classroom climate.
   b. Make rules that can be enforced.
   c. State rules generally enough to include specific behaviors.

8. Revise or eliminate a rule when it cannot be consistently reinforced over a reasonable period of time.

9. **a.** Allow no talking.
   b. Allow no more time than is absolutely necessary.
   c. Make assignments according to the time to be spent, not the exercises to be completed.
   d. Give a five-minute and a two-minute warning.

10. Give reasons for the assignment, and give the assignment immediately following the presentation of content to which it is related.

11. **a.** Restate the highest-level generalization.
    b. Summarize the key aspects of the content.
    c. Provide codes or symbols for remembering the content.

Field Experience and Practice Activities

1. Forming, storming, norming, and performing.

2. **a.** Drill and practice
   b. Group discussion
   c. Seatwork

3. Possible answers include the following: He or she established an open, risk-free climate; planned lessons that match student interests and needs; and allowed for activities and responsibilities congruent with the learners' cultures.

Chapter 4
Discussion and Practice Questions

1. **a.** Establish positive relationships.
   b. Prevent attention seeking and work avoidance.
   c. Quickly and unobtrusively redirect misbehavior.
   d. Stop persistent and chronic misbehavior.
   e. Teach self-control.
   f. Respect cultural differences.

2. **a.** Develop classroom rules.
   b. Get support from school administrators to create an area where disruptive students can be moved temporarily.
   c. Hold private conferences with disruptive students.
   d. Follow through by giving students an opportunity to return to the classroom.

3. *Positive:* Give a reward immediately following a desirable behavior. *Negative:* End an uncomfortable state when a desirable behavior occurs.

4. *Time-out:* Remove the student to an area where he or she can receive no reinforcement. *Response cost:* Remove a reinforcer or privilege contingent on disruptive or inappropriate behavior.

5. (a) They devote extensive time to organizing their classroom to minimize disruptions and enhance work engagement. (b) They methodically teach rules and routines and monitor their compliance. (c) They inform students of the consequences for breaking the rules and enforce the consequences.

6. (a) You alone judge what occurred, what the proper punishment is, and whether the punishment has been met. (b) You provide alternative forms of punishment from which the student must choose. (c) You select a punishment from alternatives provided by the student.

9. **a.** Punishment does not guarantee the desirable behavior will occur.

   b. The effects of punishment usually are specific to a particular context and behavior.

   c. The effects of punishment can have undesirable side effects.

   d. Punishment can elicit a hostile or aggressive response.

   e. The punishment can become associated with the punisher.

10. (a) Gain support of the parents for assuming some of the responsibility for the behavior management process. (b) Design a plan of action for addressing the problem at home and at school.

Field Experience and Practice Activities

1. Sane messages communicate to students that their behavior is unacceptable in a manner that does not blame, scold, or humiliate.

4. Punishment is effective when the desired behavior is made clear at the time of the punishment and when it is used in conjunction with rewards.

Chapter 5
Discussion and Practice Questions

2. (a) Tie general aims and goals to specific classroom strategies that will achieve those aims and goals. (b) Express teaching strategies in a format that allows you to measure their effects on your learners.

3. The behavior is observable, measurable, and occurs in a specific period of time.

4. The components are the observable behavior, the conditions under which it is to be observed, and the level of proficiency at which it is to be displayed.

5. Teachers tended to focus their concerns on self and task, sometimes to the exclusion of their impact on students.

6. Action verbs point toward the goal of achieving the desired behavior and observing its attainment.

7. A, O, A, A, A, O, O, O

8. A *condition* is the circumstances under which the behavior is to be displayed.

9. Specifying the conditions establishes the setting under which the behavior will be tested, which guides students in how and what to study.

10. Your selection should be guided by the extent to which the conditions are similar to those under which the behavior will have to be performed in the real world.

11. The criterion level is the level of proficiency at which the behavior must be displayed.

12. (1) b, (2) a, (3) b, (4) e, (5) f

Chapter 6
Discussion and Practice Questions

1. Knowledge of aims and goals, knowledge of learners, knowledge of subject-matter content and organization, knowledge of teaching methods, and tacit knowledge.

2. A unit outcome can be more than the sum of individual lesson outcomes because of how individual lessons are sequenced and build on one another to produce a unit.

3. The concept of *hierarchy* helps us see the relationship between individual lesson outcomes and the unit outcome. It also helps us identify lessons that are not too big or too small but rather just right. Teachers use *task-relevant prior learning* to identify the proper sequence of lessons needed to teach the unit outcome. Both concepts help us picture the flow and sequence of a lesson plan.

4. *Cognitive:* analysis, synthesis, evaluation. *Affective:* valuing, organization, characterization. *Psychomotor:* precision, articulation, naturalization.

5. The boxes further down represent smaller, more detailed portions of content.

6. The former must show hierarchy and sequence; the latter does not.

8. Present the content.

9. Assess the behavior.

10. Elicit the desired behavior.

11. Providing feedback is immediate and nonevaluative, whereas assessing the behavior is delayed and evaluative.

Field Experience and Practice Activities

3. Ways of differentiating instruction include ability grouping, peer tutoring, learning centers, review, and follow-up materials.

4. The seven events are gain attention, inform the learner of the objective, stimulate recall of prerequisite learning, present the stimulus material, elicit the desired behavior, provide feedback, and assess the behavior.

Chapter 7
Discussion and Practice Questions

1. Supporting students' cognitive processes; reducing students' cognitive load for lower level cognitive skills; allowing students to engage in cognitive activities in authentic environments; and allowing learners to generate problem solutions and assess their performance.

2. Using multiple presentations of information from different sources to create new knowledge.

3. Distributed cognition emphasizes the social aspects of cognition that involves the simultaneous interaction among students, computer, and the learning environment.

4. Take it or leave it refers to the older Web 1.0 read-only platform in which content could only be created by the website owner. Web 2.0 provides the opportunity for website visitors to collaborate and create content together online.

5. Moodle is a free and open source classroom management system for keeping in touch with your students in and outside of the classroom.

6. An asynchronous learning environment is one in which students can move in and out of the formal classroom routine to retrieve and exchange information to discuss topics and collaborate.

7. Web 2.0 technologies represent a platform for learning that facilitates communication, interaction, and collective intelligence through dynamic, animated, and refreshing display channels.

8. A blog is a platform for self-expression and self-reflection that can show your learner's work online for others to see.

9. RSS allows your students to subscribe to a particular blog or podcast and have it download to their computer, MP3 player, or smart phone.

10. Social bookmarking is used to manage and archive researched knowledge from a variety of Internet sources by putting together the bookmarks saved and having connected users share the bookmarks.

11. Social presentation applications allow a community of learners to share and work together to organize and construct knowledge for an online presentation

12. Concept mapping is a type of graphic organizer for knowledge organization that can help students interpret, represent, and organize information in cooperation with one another.

13. It can be used in any group sharing activity, such as a report or portfolio, in which it is desirable to have all the content continuously visible and available to all group members for the purpose of developing a collective intelligence to create knowledge and understanding.

14. Virtual world technology provides a three-dimensional format that immerses users in an instructional online role-playing activity in which they create and interact with characters in real time.

Field Experience and Practice Activities

5. Among the Web 2.0 applications that are conducive to group work are blogs, podcasting, social bookmarking, social presentation, wiki, and virtual worlds.

Chapter 8
Discussion and Practice Questions

1. An *effective question* is one that actively engages a student in the learning process.

2. As much as 80 percent of school time may be devoted to questions and answers.

3. Lower order questions comprise as much as 80 percent of all questions, and higher order questions comprise as little as 20 percent.

4. A *convergent question* has only a single or small number of correct responses and thus many wrong answers. A *divergent question* has no single best answer and generally has multiple answers; however, divergent questions can have wrong answers.

6. Higher order questions are (a) unlikely to affect standardized achievement but (b) likely to increase the learner's analysis, synthesis, and evaluation skills.

10. *Wait time* is the time the teacher waits for a student to respond to a question. Generally, beginning teachers should work to increase their wait time to encourage a student response that can be built on by the teacher and other students for further learning.

11. Raising overly complex questions, not being prepared for unexpected answers, not knowing the purpose underlying a question, providing answers to questions before students can respond, using questions as a form of punishment. Examples will vary.

Field Experience and Practice Activities

2. Interest and attention getting, diagnosing and checking, recalling specific facts or information, managing, encouraging higher-level thought processes, structuring and redirecting learning, and allowing expression of affect.

3. The dialogue should demonstrate funneling, which begins with open questions and proceeds to narrow down questions to require making simple deductions and recall or reasoning and problem solving.

Chapter 9
Discussion and Practice Questions

1. Type 1: facts, rules, action sequences. Type 2: concepts, patterns, abstractions. Type 1 outcomes generally apply to the knowledge, comprehension, and application levels; Type 2 outcomes generally apply to the analysis, synthesis, and evaluation levels.

2. Knowledge acquisition: facts, rules, action sequences. Inquiry or problem solving: concepts, patterns, and abstractions.

3. Characteristics would include full-class instruction; questions posed by the teacher; detailed and redundant practice; one new fact, rule, or sequence mastered before the next is presented; arrangement of classroom to maximize drill and practice.

4. Cognitive: recall, describe, list. Affective: listen, attend, be aware. Psychomotor: repeat, follow, place.

5. Instructional goals include (a) to disseminate information not readily available from texts or workbooks in appropriately sized pieces; (b) to arouse or heighten student interest; and (c) to achieve content mastery.

6. Providing guided practice results in creating a response, however crude, that can become the basis for learning.

9. Teachers should work toward 60 percent to 80 percent correct answers. Ways to change the instructional approach include reducing content coverage and increasing opportunities for practice and feedback.

10. The primary purpose of independent practice is to form action sequences. The lesson and discussion will vary. The independent practice should increasingly resemble applications in the real world.

11. Keep contacts to a minimum (an average of 30 seconds), and spread contacts across most students, avoiding concentrating on a few students.

12. About 95 percent of answers should be correct, quick, and firm.

Field Experience and Practice Activities

1. **a.** Have students correct each other's work.

   b. Have students identify difficult homework problems.

   c. Sample the understanding of a few students who represent the range of students in the class.

   d. Explicitly review the task-relevant information necessary for the day's lesson.

2. Techniques include part–whole, sequential, combinations, and comparative.

3. Methods include to review key facts, explain the steps required, prompt with clues or hints, and walk student through a similar problem.

4. For example, you might gradually increase the coverage and depth of weekly reviews until the time for a comprehensive monthly review arrives.

Chapter 10
Discussion and Practice Questions

1. The three ingredients are inquiry, discovery, and a problem.

2. *Direct instructional model:* facts, rules, and action sequences. *Indirect instructional model:* concepts, patterns, and abstractions.

3. The learner indirectly acquires a behavior by transforming stimulus material into a response or behavior that differs (a) from the stimulus used to present the learning and (b) from any previous response emitted by the learner.

4. Direct instruction is not generally efficient or effective for attaining outcomes at the higher levels of complexity involving concepts, patterns, and abstractions.

5. *Generalization* involves classifying apparently different stimuli into the same category on the basis of criterial attributes. *Discrimination* involves distinguishing

examples of a concept from nonexamples. An example of a learning task requiring both processes is learning the meaning of *democracy*.

6. **a.** Type 1
   b. Type 2
   c. Type 1
   d. Type 2
   e. Type 2
   f. Type 1
   g. Type 2
   h. Type 2
   i. Type 1
   j. Type 2

7. (a) Our memories would become overburdened trying to remember all the possible instances of the concept. (b) Instances of the concept would easily be confused with noninstances.

9. *Essential attributes:* lesson clarity, instructional variety, task orientation, engagement in the learning process, moderate to high success rate. *Nonessential attributes:* number of credit hours attained, degree held, number of in-service workshops attended, college grades, years of teaching experience.

10. In direct instruction, the purposes for asking questions are to elicit a single right answer or to reveal the level of understanding. In indirect instruction, the purpose is to help the student search for and discover an appropriate answer with a minimum of assistance.

11. The type of learning might be student-centered or unguided discovery learning. In indirect instruction, student ideas are used as a means of accomplishing the goals of the prescribed curriculum.

12. **a.** direct
    b. direct
    c. indirect
    d. indirect
    e. direct
    f. direct
    g. direct
    h. indirect
    i. indirect
    j. indirect

Both models might be used for topics c, d, h, and j.

Field Experience and Practice Activities

3. *Induction* is the process of thinking in which a set of specific data is presented or observed and a generalization or unifying pattern is drawn from the data. *Deduction* is the process of thinking in which the truth or validity of a theory is tested in a specific instance.

4. **a.** Encourage students to use examples and references from their experience.
   b. Ask students to draw parallels and associations from things they already know.
   c. Relate ideas to students' interests, concerns, and problems.

Chapter 11
Discussion and Practice Questions

1. **a.** To actively engage them in the learning process.
   b. To help them acquire reasoning, critical-thinking, and problem-solving skills.

2. **a.** Provide information about when and how to use mental strategies.
   b. Illustrate how to use the strategies.
   c. Encourage learners to restructure the content.
   d. Gradually shift the responsibility for learning to the student through practice activities.

3. *Metacognition* refers to the mental processes used by the learner to understand the content being taught. Using metacognitive strategies assists learners in internalizing, understanding, and recalling the content to be learned.

4. Mental modeling can help students internalize, recall, and generalize problem solutions to different content at a later time.

5. During mediation, the teacher helps students restructure what they are learning to move them closer to the intended outcome.

6. The *zone of maximum response opportunity* is the content difficulty and behavioral complexity from which the student can most benefit at the moment. Sample dialogues will vary.

7. **a.** Ask students to make predictions about the text, and then read from the text.
   b. Choose a discussion leader to ask questions about the text, to which the other students respond.
   c. Ask the discussion leader to summarize the text, and invite other students to comment.
   d. Discuss points that remain unclear, invite more predictions, and reread the text, if needed.

8. Your primary goal should be to gradually shift the responsibility for learning to the students.

9. The purpose of inner speech is to model the same line of reasoning and to use the same types of questions, prompts, and cues as the teacher did at an earlier stage.

10. _Declarative knowledge_ is intended only for oral and verbal repetition. _Procedural knowledge_ is used in some problem-solving or decision-making task.

11. **a.** Provide a new learning task.

    b. Ask the student to explain how he or she will complete the task (e.g., learn the content).

    c. Describe and model a more effective approach to learning the content.

    d. Provide another learning task with which the student can try the new approach. Model self-questioning behavior for the student as the new material is being learned.

    e. Provide other opportunities for practice, decreasing your role as monitor.

    f. Check the result by questioning the student's comprehension and use of strategies.

Field Experience and Practice Activities

1. (a) Show students the reasoning involved. (b) Make students conscious of it. (c) Focus them on the application of the reasoning.

3. Reciprocal teaching provides opportunities to explore the content to be learned via group discussion.

6. **a.** Jingles or trigger sentences

   b. Narrative chaining

   c. Number rhyme or peg word

   d. Chunking

Chapter 12

Discussion and Practice Questions

1. The shared objectives are (a) engaging students in the learning process and (b) promoting higher, more complex patterns of thought.

2. **a.** Attitudes and values

   b. Prosocial behavior

   c. Alternative perspectives and viewpoints

   d. Integrated identity

   e. Higher thought processes

3. **a.** Specify the goal.

   b. Structure the task.

   c. Teach and evaluate the collaborative process.

   d. Monitor group performance.

   e. Debrief.

4. Forms of products or behaviors include written group reports, higher individual achievement, an oral performance, an enumeration or resolution, a critique, and data collection.

5. The most efficient group size is four to six members.

6. **a.** Build groups around isolated students.

   b. Randomly assign students.

   c. Form groups heterogeneously.

   d. Share with students the selection process.

7. The answer should include three of the following six methods:

   a. Assign a product that requires a clear division of labor.

   b. Form pairs in which students oversee each other's work.

   c. Chart the group's progress on individually assigned tasks.

   d. Limit the resources provided to promote sharing and contact.

   e. Make one stage of product contingent on a previous stage completed by someone else.

8. **a.** Summarizer

   b. Checker

   c. Researcher

   d. Runner

   e. Recorder

   f. Supporter

   g. Observer/Troubleshooter

9. (a) Average the individual scores to determine the group grade. (b) Assign all group members the average of the highest (or lowest) half of the members' scores. (c) Average an individual's score with the group score.

10. The teacher's roles are (a) to remind each group of its assigned role, (b) to redirect the group's efforts, and (c) to provide emotional support and encouragement.

11. (a) Openly talk about how the groups functioned. (b) Solicit suggestions for how the process could be improved. (c) Get viewpoints of predesignated observers.

12. **a.** There is not enough time.

    b. Debriefing stays vague.

    c. Students stay uninvolved.

    d. Written reports are incomplete.

    e. Students use poor collaborative skills.

Field Experience and Practice Activities

1. **a.** Teacher–student interaction

   b. Student–student interaction

   c. Task specialization and materials

   d. Role expectations and responsibilities

2. **a.** Grades—individual and group

   b. Bonus points

   c. Social responsibilities

   d. Tokens or privileges

   e. Group contingencies

3. **a.** Communicate one's own ideas and feelings.

   b. Make messages complete and specific.

   c. Make verbal and nonverbal messages congruent.

   d. Convey an atmosphere of respect and support.

   e. Assess whether the message was properly received.

   f. Paraphrase another's point of view.

   g. Negotiate meanings and understandings.

   h. Participate and lead.

Chapter 13

Discussion and Practice Questions

1. A norm-referenced test compares a student's performance to that of a large sample of pupils (called the *norm group*) representative of those being tested. It is useful when you need to compare a learner's performance to that of others of the same age or grade level. A criterion-referenced test compares a student's performance to a standard of mastery (called a *criterion*). It is useful when you need to decide if a student requires more instruction in a certain skill or content area.

2. A test blueprint measures (a) level of cognitive complexity and (b) area of instructional content.

3. **a.** True/false

   b. Matching

   c. Multiple choice

   d. Completion or short answer

4. **a.** Stem clues

   b. Grammatical clues

   c. Redundant words/unequal response lengths

   d. Use of "all of the above" and "none of the above"

5. The three devices are (a) pictorial, graphical, or tabular stimuli; (b) analogies that demonstrate relationships among terms; and (c) application of previously learned principles or procedures.

6. Reasons for using an essay test are that (a) higher-level cognitive processes have been taught, (b) relatively few items can be graded, and (c) test security is a consideration.

7. *Advantages:* Essay tests require students to use higher-level cognitive processes, are well-suited to certain topics and objectives, and can measure communication skills pertinent to a subject area. *Disadvantages:*

Essay tests are tedious to read and score, may be influenced by the learner's communication skills, and may involve some degree of subjectivity on the part of the scorer.

8. **a.** Content

   b. Organization

   c. Process

   d. Completeness/Internal consistency

   e. Originality/Creativity

9. *Validity* refers to whether the test measures what it is supposed to measure. *Reliability* refers to whether the test yields the same or similar scores consistently.

10. An acceptable validity coefficient ranges between .60 and .80 or higher. An acceptable reliability coefficient ranges between .80 and .90 or higher. The maximum possible size of either a validity or reliability coefficient is 1.0.

11. A *standardized test* is constructed by specialists to determine a student's level of performance relative to that of other students of similar age and grade.

12. A *percentile rank* indicates that the student's score was higher than the scores of that percentage of individuals in the norming sample. That is, in the norming sample, the percentage of students indicated scored lower than this individual. Two points to keep in mind in interpreting a percentile rank are as follows:

    a. The percentile rank is not the percentage of correct answers.

    b. The extreme or end points of a percentile distribution tend to be spread out, whereas percentiles toward the center tend to be compressed. This makes comparisons between the same number of points at different portions of the scale difficult.

Field Experience and Practice Activities

1. An extended-response essay question allows students to determine the length and complexity of the response. It is most useful when the problem provides little or no structure and outcomes at the analysis, synthesis, and evaluation levels are desired. A restricted-response essay question poses a specific problem for which the student must recall proper information, organize it, derive a defensible conclusion, and express it according to specific criteria. It is most useful when the problem posed is structured and when outcomes at the application and analysis levels are desired.

2. A *scoring rubric* is a guide written in advance that indicates the criteria or components of an acceptable answer.

3. The three types of validity are (a) content, (b) concurrent, and (c) predictive.

4. The three methods of testing reliability are (a) test-retest, (b) alternate form, and (c) internal consistency.

5. Marks and grading systems are based on comparisons with the following:

   a. Other students
   b. Established standards
   c. Aptitude
   d. Achievement versus effort
   e. Achievement versus improvement

Appendix C

Higher Order Thinking and Problem-Solving Checklist

Check each column below indicating (1) the extent to which your curriculum *requires* students to achieve the following outcomes and (2) the extent to which *you are teaching* your students to achieve these outcomes.

Assign the number 5 to each checkmark under "Great Extent," a 4 to "Fair Extent," a 3 to "Some Extent," a 2 to "A Little," and a 1 to "Not at All." Subtract your assigned rating or value for the "Degree of Implementation" column from that in the "Degree of Importance" column for each behavior to arrive at your highest priorities.

	Degree of Importance					Degree of Implementation				
	Does your curriculum require students to achieve the following? (Check one)					Are you teaching your students to achieve the following? (Check one)				
	1	2	3	4	5	1	2	3	4	5
Application of Knowledge										
1. Search one's memory for what he or she already knows about a problem.										
2. Draw a picture or diagram that shows what was learned or observed.										
3. Construct and interpret graphs, charts, and tables.										
4. Classify/categorize things according to definable attributes.										
5. Communicate the results of what was observed in written and oral format.										
6. Apply given rules to reach a conclusion.										
7. Consult a variety of knowledge sources to gather information.										
Analytical Skills										
8. Identify the similarities and differences among various elements.										
9. Compare a problem to problems encountered previously.										

435

	Degree of Importance					Degree of Implementation				
	1	2	3	4	5	1	2	3	4	5
10. Understand the relationship of each component to the whole.										
11. Draw reasonable conclusions from the observation or analysis of data.										
12. Identify and articulate errors in one's own thinking or in that of others.										
13. Explain the reasons for a conclusion.										
14. Predict what will happen given the information one has.										
15. Plan a way to test one's prediction.										
16. Distinguish the most important elements of a problem.										
17. Organize the conclusion about a problem in a logical fashion.										
18. Identify the criteria for evaluating a problem solution.										
19. Gather information or evidence to solve a problem.										
20. Find corroborating evidence from among different data sources.										
21. Determine the reliability of the evidence.										
22. Place an interpretation of a problem in the context of prevailing circumstances.										

Synthesis/Creativity

	1	2	3	4	5	1	2	3	4	5
23. Generate new ways of viewing a situation outside the boundaries of standard conventions.										
24. Reformulate a problem to make it more manageable.										
25. Brainstorm new applications of content.										
26. Anticipate potential problems.										
27. Accurately summarize what is read or others have said, orally and in writing.										

Evaluation/Metacognition

	1	2	3	4	5	1	2	3	4	5
28. Ask oneself what was learned.										
29. Make appropriate revisions on the basis of feedback.										
30. Assess the risks involved in a solution.										

	Degree of Importance					Degree of Implementation				
	1	2	3	4	5	1	2	3	4	5
31. Monitor the outcome and revise a strategy, where appropriate.										
32. Judge the credibility of evidence.										
33. Evaluate and revise what is written.										
34. Ask oneself questions about ideas one is unsure of.										
35. Catch fallacies and contradictions.										

Dispositions

	Degree of Importance					Degree of Implementation				
36. Meaningfully praise the performance of others.										
37. Share and take turns.										
38. Help keep others on task.										
39. Provide assistance to others when needed.										
40. Engage in tasks even when the answers or solutions are not immediately apparent.										
41. Seek accuracy.										
42. Be flexible to change one's viewpoint to match the facts.										
43. Demonstrate restraint over impulsive behaviors.										
44. Compose drafts and tryouts in attempts to solve a problem.										
45. Demonstrate persistence in tackling difficult tasks.										
46. Use a constructive tone when responding to others.										
47. Display enthusiasm for learning.										
48. Ask for feedback when needed.										
49. Collaborate with others in teams.										
50. Provide assistance to others when asked.										
51. Demonstrate independence in completing a project.										
52. Listen attentively to others.										
53. Ignore distractions that interfere with goal attainment.										
54. Keep a record of one's own progress toward important goals.										

	Degree of Importance					Degree of Implementation				
	1	2	3	4	5	1	2	3	4	5
55. Realistically evaluate one's own performance.										
56. Set goals that are achievable within a specific time span.										
Values										
57. Demonstrate awareness of ethical concerns and conflicts.										
58. Adhere to codes of conduct.										
59. Show an ability to resolve ethical dilemmas and conflicts.										
60. Maintain self-discipline in dealing with difficult situations.										
61. Behave in a manner that communicates care and concern for others.										
62. Act responsibly in dealing with tasks and people.										

Glossary

A

Active listening The listener provides feedback to the speaker about the message heard and the emotion conveyed and lets the speaker know he or she is being understood and respected.

Active responding Orally responding to a question, writing out the correct answer, calculating an answer, or physically making a response (e.g., focusing a microscope).

Active uninvolvement When a group member talks about everything but the assigned goal of the group.

Activity structure The systematic varying of task demands within a unit.

Adaptive teaching Applying different instructional strategies to different groups of learners so they all can achieve success.

Advance organizer A framework or structure that organizes the content into meaningful parts.

Affective domain Behaviors that relate to the development of attitudes, beliefs, and values: receiving, responding, valuing, organizing, and characterizing.

Applied behavior analysis Classroom management emphasizing behavior modification techniques and reinforcement theory.

Asynchronous learning A system of learning in which students can move in and out of the formal classroom routine to retrieve and exchange information, discuss topics, and collaborate with peers and their teachers.

At-risk learners Those who are most often off task and disengaged and who have difficulty learning at an average rate.

Authentic behaviors The types of performances required in the real world.

Authentic tests Tests that ask learners to display their skills and behaviors in the way they would be displayed in the real world, outside the classroom.

B

Behavioral antecedents Events or stimuli that are present when a behavior is performed that elicit or set off the behavior.

Behavioral objective A written statement that identifies specific classroom strategies to achieve desired goals and expresses these strategies in a format that allows their effects on learners to be measured.

Behavior modification Changing or modifying a behavior by following the behavior with some type of reinforcement.

Blended learning A traditional course of instruction incorporating online materials and intermittent online discussion.

Blogs A platform for students to publish text, audios, or video online with which they can reflect and articulate thoughts through writing, audio recording or video, enhancing their cognitive and metacognitive skills.

C

Centering behavior A type of amiable limit testing, during which learners question how they will personally benefit from being group members.

Class management system A personal communication tool by which you can maintain contact with your students in and outside of the classroom by using your personal computer and Moodle.

Classroom management tradition Focuses on planning and organizing the classroom, teaching rules, and routines, and informing students of the consequences of breaking the rules.

Classroom response system A teacher–learner interactive system in which students can by remote control respond to teacher questions posed in a multiple-choice format, the answers to which can be immediately displayed for all to see.

Coercive power Asserting authority by punishing misbehavior.

Cognitive domain Behaviors that relate to the development of intellectual abilities and skills: knowledge, comprehension, application, analysis, synthesis, and evaluation.

Cognitive learning strategy General methods of thinking that improve learning by helping the learner to retain incoming information (reception), recall task-relevant prior knowledge (availability), and build logical connections among incoming knowledge (activation).

Compensatory approach The teacher chooses an instructional method to compensate for learners' lack of information, skills, or ability and alters content presentation to circumvent learners' weaknesses and promote their strengths.

Concept mapping A type of graphic organizer—or mind tool—for knowledge organization that can help learners interpret, represent, and organize information by making a graphic in cooperation with others.

Congruent communication Using communication skills to promote learners' self-esteem, which influences them to choose acceptable behavior.

Constructivism Designing and sequencing lessons to encourage learners to use their own experiences to actively construct meaning that makes sense to them, rather than to acquire understanding through exposure to a format organized by the teacher.

Constructivist teaching strategies Instructional tools that emphasize the learner's direct experience and the classroom dialogue while deemphasizing lecturing and telling.

Convergent question One that limits an answer to a single or a small number of responses.

Cooperative learning An arrangement in which students work in groups and are rewarded on the basis of the success of the group. According to Glasser, cooperative learning builds an environment that makes the classroom a place learners want to be.

Cooperative learning role functions Summarizer, checker, researcher, runner, recorder, supporter, and observer/troubleshooter.

Criterion level The degree of performance required to achieve a learning objective.

Criterion-referenced test (CRT) Compares a student's performance with an absolute standard of mastery, or criterion.

Cross-age tutoring One student teaches another; the tutor may be one or more years or grade levels above the learner.

Crystallization Learners' expectations converge into a shared perspective of classroom life as they engage in activities together.

Cultural deficit model Using genetically or culturally inspired factors to explain differences in such things as aptitude and language between cultural minorities and mainstream learners.

Cultural difference model Focusing on solutions that require culturally sensitive links to and responses from the school to improve the performance of students who are socially, economically, and linguistically different from the mainstream.

Cultural frame The individual's frame of reference, acquired from experience, that is the lens through which he or she interprets and responds to events.

Culturally responsive teaching The teacher's ability to react to students of different cultures with different verbal and nonverbal classroom management techniques.

Culture-specific questioning Rules that govern social conversation among different cultural groups, which can be used to better target questions to specific populations of learners.

Curriculum guides Grade, department, or school district specifications about what content must be covered in what period of time.

D

Daily review and checking A direct instruction strategy that emphasizes the relationship between lessons so students remember previous knowledge and see new knowledge as a logical extension of content already mastered.

Debriefing Gathering feedback about an activity by discussing it, soliciting suggestions for improving it, and getting observers' viewpoints about it.

Declarative (factual) knowledge Facts, concepts, rules, and generalizations pertaining to a specific area or topic; intended to be spoken or written.

Deduction Reasoning that proceeds from principles or generalizations to their application in specific instances.

Differentiated instruction Maximizing each student's academic success and personal growth as a learner by meeting the student where he or she is and providing the needed instruction and resources that lift him or her to the next step on the learning ladder.

Diffusion The process by which learners' different academic and social expectations spread through the class as they communicate with one another.

Direct instruction A teacher-centered, knowledge acquisition, presentation-recitation model for teaching facts, rules, and action sequences.

Discrimination Selectively restricting a range of instances by eliminating things that appear to match the concept but that differ from it in critical dimensions.

Distancing behavior A type of amiable limit testing, during which group members challenge academic expectations and rules to establish under what conditions they do and do not apply.

Distracters The wrong answer choices in a multiple-choice or matching test item.

Distributed cognition Media emphasizing the social aspects of cognition advocating learning that involves the simultaneous interaction among student, computer, and the learning environment.

Divergent question One that has many or a broad range of acceptable responses.

E

Effective questions Questions for which students actively compose responses, thereby becoming engaged in the learning process.

Eliciting probes Questions asked to seek clarification of the student's response to determine its appropriateness or correctness.

Engaged learning time The amount of time students devote to learning in the classroom.

Enviromentalist position The belief that social class and the environment, rather than heredity, are the major factors in determining intelligence.

Examples Representations of a concept that include all the attributes essential for recognizing it as a member of a larger class.

Expert power Being seen as competent to explain or do certain things and as knowledgeable about particular topics.

Expressive objective A learning objective that may have a variety of correct responses.

Extended-response essay question One that allows the student to determine the length and complexity of the response.

F

Family-school linking mechanisms Opportunities for school and family involvement, such as parent–teacher conferences, home visits, teachers' participating in community events, newsletters, phone calls, personal notes, parents' volunteering as classroom aides, and using home-based curriculum materials.

Feedback and correctives The direct instruction strategy for handling right and wrong answers.

Field dependent Seeing the world in terms of large, connected patterns.

Field independent Seeing the world in terms of its specific parts.

Formative evaluation Data collection practices for improving classroom instruction using curriculum-based measures (CBM) applied continuously throughout the school year to measure student progress.

Full-group discussion Student exchanges, with successive interactions among large numbers of students.

Functional errors Incorrect or partially correct answers that can enhance the meaning and understanding of content and provide a logical stepping stone for climbing to the next rung of the learning ladder.

G

Generalization Responding in a similar manner to stimuli that differ but are bound by a central concept.

Gestural prompts Modeling or demonstrating for learners the skill being taught.

Goals Derived from standards to more specifically identify what must be accomplished and who must do what for standards to be met.

Guided student practice The direct instruction strategy of presenting stimulus material and then eliciting practice, directed by the teacher, of the desired behavior.

H

Helping behaviors Behaviors used in combinations to implement key effective teaching behaviors, including using student ideas and contributions, structuring, questioning, probing, and teacher affect (developing the teacher–learner relationship).

Hereditarian position The belief that heredity, rather than environment, is the major factor in determining intelligence.

Horizontal relationships Successful relationships with peers that meet learners' need for belonging and allow them to acquire and practice important social skills.

Humanist tradition Classroom management focusing on the inner thoughts, feelings, psychological needs, and emotions of individual learners.

Hypermedia Media with which learning needs are met by using multiple presentations of information from different sources or perspectives along with the opportunity to create new knowledge.

I

Independent practice The direct instruction strategy in which the teacher brings facts and rules together in ways that force simultaneous consideration of all the individual units of a problem and connect the units into a single harmonious sequence of action.

Indirect instruction Teaching strategies that emphasize concept learning, inquiry, and problem solving to teach concepts, patterns, and abstractions.

Individuals with Disabilities Education Improvement Act (IDEA) A legislative mandate affirming that children with disabilities are entitled to a free and appropriate public education and ensuring that special education students have access to all the potential benefits that are available to regular education students.

Induction Reasoning used to draw a conclusion or make a generalization from specific instances.

Inner speech A learner's private internal dialogue that takes the place of the teacher's prompts and questions and self-guides the learner through similar problems.

Instructional variety The teacher's variability or flexibility of delivery during the presentation of a lesson.

InTASC standards The ten principles describing what teachers should know and be able to do, according to the Interstate New Teacher Assessment and Support Consortium.

Integrated bodies of knowledge Units and lessons that stress the connections between ideas and the logical coherence of interrelated topics.

Integrated thematic teaching Relating content and material from various subject areas.

Interactive individualized practice activities Lessons on CD-ROM that use questions and prompts to actively engage learners and give them immediate feedback.

Intercultural competence The teacher's ability to act as a translator and intercultural broker between students of different cultures, ethnicities, and socioeconomic levels.

Interdisciplinary unit A laterally planned unit of study in which topics are integrated to focus on a specific theme.

Intermittent reinforcement Reinforcing a behavior at random or on an intermittent schedule to maintain it at its present level.

K

Key behaviors The five behaviors essential for effective teaching: lesson clarity, instructional variety, teacher task orientation, engagement in the learning process, and student success rate.

L

Lateral unit planning Planning units that integrate knowledge across disciplines or content areas to convey relationships, patterns, and abstractions.

Learning activities The means of achieving learning outcomes.

Learning conditions The specific conditions under which learning will occur.

Learning outcome An observable and measurable behavior; the end product of an instructional lesson or unit.

Learning structures The logical progression of ideas with which a lesson is conveyed, identifying what the learner needs to know at each step before new learning can take place.

Learning style The instructional and classroom conditions under which an individual prefers to learn.

Legitimate power Having influence because of one's title or role, rather than one's nature.

Lesson clarity The notion that the teacher's presentation to the class should make points clear to learners at different levels of understanding and explain concepts in logical, step-by-step order; the oral delivery should be direct, audible to all students, and free of distracting mannerisms.

Living curriculum Using multimedia, often over the Internet, to create a fluid and personalized learning environment.

Low-profile classroom management Coping strategies teachers use to stop misbehavior without disrupting the flow of a lesson.

M

Marks and grading systems Based on comparison, usually of students with one or more of the following: other students, established standards, aptitude, achievement versus effort, and achievement versus improvement.

Mastery learning An instructional strategy based on the principle that all students can attain lesson and unit objectives given appropriate instruction and sufficient time to learn.

Mental modeling Demonstration of the decision-making process to help students internalize, recall, and generalize problem solutions to different content at a later time.

Metacognition Mental processes that assist learners to reflect on their thinking by internalizing, understanding, and recalling the content to be learned.

Metacognitive knowledge Thinking about one's thinking to become aware of one's level of knowledge.

Metacommunication The pattern of the teacher's body posture, language, and eye contact that is recognized by the learner and acted on according to the message being conveyed, intentionally or not.

Moderating tasks The means by which the teacher orients students to the objective of the discussion; provides new or more accurate information; reviews, summarizes, and relates opinions and facts; and redirects the flow of information and ideas back to the objective.

Monitoring The process of observing, mentally recording, and, when necessary, redirecting or correcting students' behaviors.

Moodle A free and open source class management system for creating a personal communication tool by which the teacher can maintain contact with students in or outside of the classroom.

N

Natural reinforcers Internal rewards or reinforcers that are naturally present in the setting where a behavior occurs.

Negative reinforcement Avoiding a painful, uncomfortable, or aversive state to achieve a more desirable state.

No Child Left Behind Act (NCLB) A legislative mandate to improve educational opportunities for every child—regardless of ethnicity, income, or background.

Nonexamples Items that fail to represent the concept being illustrated by purposely not including one or more of the attributes essential for recognizing them as members of a larger class.

Norm-referenced test (NRT) Compares a student's performance to that of a norm group, or a large, representative sample of learners.

Norms Shared expectations among group members regarding how they should think, feel, and behave.

O

Objectives Statements that convey to learners the specific behaviors to be attained, the conditions under which the behaviors must be demonstrated, and the proficiency at which the behaviors must be demonstrated.

Operant conditioning Transferring from external to internal control of behavior.

Ordered turns Systematically going through the class and expecting each student to respond when his or her turn comes.

Organizational environment The teacher's visual or physical arrangement of the classroom.

P

Pair or team discussions   Best used when the task is highly structured, some consensus about the topic already exists, and the orienting instructions fully define each member's role.

Passive responding   Listening to the teacher's answer, reading about the correct answer, or listening to classmates recite the right answer.

Passive uninvolvement   When a group member does not care about the goal of the group and becomes silent.

Peer tutoring   One student teaches another at the same grade and age level.

Performance assessments   Learners show what they know by using complex cognitive skills to perform authentic, real-world tasks; tests that measure a skill or behavior directly, as they are used in the world outside the classroom.

Physical prompts   Using hand-over-hand assistance to guide the learner to the correct performance.

Podcasting   A video blog that students can download to their computer or mobile phones to view the content.

Portfolio assessment   A collection of work that shows a learner's growth in proficiency, long-term achievement, and significant accomplishments in a given academic area.

Positive reinforcement   Providing a desired stimulus or reward after a behavior increases in frequency.

Praxis   A series of assessments for entering a teacher-training program, becoming licensed, and/or for the first year of teaching.

Presenting and structuring   The direct instruction strategy for presenting new material in small steps consistent with students' previous knowledge, ability level, and experience, so learners master one point before the teacher introduces the next point.

Probe   A question that immediately follows a student's response to a question.

Problem-based learning   Organizing instructional tasks around loosely structured or ill-defined problems that learners solve by using knowledge and skills from several disciplines.

Procedural knowledge   Action sequences or procedures used in a problem-solving or decision-making task; learning action sequences or procedures to follow; knowledge of how to do things.

Project-based learning   Promoting intrinsic motivation by organizing instruction around the tasks most likely to induce and support learner interest, effort, and persistence.

Prosocial behavior   Appropriate attitudes and values that children learn from close and meaningful encounters among family members and in the classroom.

Psychomotor domain   Behaviors that relate to the coordination of physical movements and performance: imitation, manipulation, precision, articulation, and naturalization.

Q

Question sequence   Structuring, soliciting, and reacting, with many possible variations.

R

Reacting   The teacher's responding to students' answering of questions.

Really Simple Syndication   A technology that allows users to subscribe to a particular blog, podcast, or video blog and have it automatically downloaded to their electronic devices, for example, computer, MP3 player, or smart phone.

Reciprocal distancing   The effect of teachers from one culture interpreting children's behaviors differently than teachers from another culture.

Reciprocal teaching   A type of classroom group dialogue in which the teacher expects students to make predictions, ask questions, summarize, and clarify the text.

Redirecting probes   Questions that restructure a discussion with follow-up to get students back on track.

Referent power   Being seen as trustworthy, fair, and concerned about students.

Reflective practice   Teaching that is inspired by the tacit or personal knowledge gained from day-to-day experiences.

Reflective teacher   A teacher who is thoughtful and self-critical about his or her teaching.

Reliability   Refers to whether a test consistently yields the same or similar scores.

Remediation approach   One in which the teacher provides learners with the prerequisite knowledge, skill, or behavior needed to benefit from planned instruction.

Response to Intervention   A legislative mandate intended to improve educational outcomes for all students by integrating assessment, instruction, and decision making by using repeated curriculum-based measures rather than once-a-year summative assessments to assess student progress.

Restricted-response essay question   One that poses a specific problem for which the student must recall proper information, organize it suitably, derive a defensible conclusion, and express it according to specific criteria.

Reward power   Being able to confer privileges, approval, or tangible compensation.

Rigor and relevance framework   A framework for the continuum of thinking in the cognitive, affective, and psychomotor domains encountered and expected of learners beyond the classroom and in adult life.

Rubrics   Rating scales that express criteria for assessing essay or portfolio content.

Rule–example–rule order   Giving a rule, then an example of the rule, and then a repetition of the rule.

Rules and procedures   Rules related to academic work, classroom conduct, information the teacher must communicate the first day, and information that can be communicated later.

S

Small-group discussions   About four to six students per group.

Social bookmarking   An application that facilitates building an easily accessible online bookmark warehouse that becomes searchable to members or the public.

Social competence   The factors that, in addition to intelligence, contribute to learners' success, including motivation, health, social skills, quality of teaching, prior knowledge, emotional well-being, and family support.

Social environment   The interaction patterns the teacher promotes in the classroom.

Social framing   The context in which a message such as a lesson is received and understood.

Social learning theory   The study of how people learn from observing others.

Social presentation   A Web 2.0 application that helps learners share and work together to organize and construct knowledge for online presentation.

Social power   Being an effective leader; having students' trust and respect.

Socioeconomic status (SES)   An approximate index of one's income and education level.

Sociolinguistics   The study of how cultural groups differ in the courtesies and conventions of language, rather than in the grammatical structure of what is said.

Soliciting   Question-asking behavior that encourages students to act on and think about the material.

Soliciting probes   Questions that ask for new information after a response that is partially correct to push the learner to a more complex level of understanding.

Special populations   Groups of learners with physical, learning, visual, psychological, and/or communication disabilities that may impair learning.

Stages of group development   A series of stages—forming, storming, norming, and performing—during which the group has certain tasks to accomplish and concerns to resolve.

Standardized tests   Administered and scored according to specific and uniform procedures; used to determine a student's performance level relative to that of others of similar age and grade.

Standards   General expressions of educational values that provide a sense of direction in decision making.

Stem   The statement part of a multiple-choice item.

Structuring   How the teacher uses questions to direct learning.

Student-centered learning   Allows the student to select the form and substance of the learning experience.

Student success rate   The rate at which students understand and correctly complete exercises and assignments.

Summative evaluation   Data collection practices for presenting the overall progress of students, usually from one year to the next, using standardized tests.

Surface behaviors   The normal developmental behaviors that children perform when confined to a small space with a large number of other children.

Synchronous learning   Placing information and messages online for the learner to receive and process immediately.

System perspective   Planning lessons to be part of the larger system of interrelated learning, or the unit.

Systems-ecological perspective   Viewing the learner as an ecosystem in which the major systems include the family, school, and peer group; behavior is considered a product of the learner and the demands and forces operating within the systems of which he or she is a member.

T

Tacit knowledge   The teacher's reflection on what works in the classroom, as discovered over time and through personal experience.

Task specialization   Breaking a larger task into smaller subparts on which separate groups work.

Task structure   In cooperative learning, specifying the goal, structuring the task, teaching and evaluating the collaborative process, monitoring group performance, and debriefing.

Teacher-mediated dialogue   An exchange in which the teacher helps learners restructure what is being learned using their own ideas, experiences, and thought patterns.

Teacher-mediated learning   Adjusting the instructional dialogue to help students restructure their learning and construct their own meanings from the content.

Teacher task orientation   How much classroom time the teacher devotes to the task of teaching an academic subject.

Teaching concerns   The concerns with which teachers most strongly identify at different periods in their careers.

Team-oriented cooperative learning   Using teams of heterogeneous learners to increase the collaborative skills, self-esteem, and achievement of individual learners.

Test blueprint   A table that matches the test items to be written with the content areas and levels of behavioral complexity taught.

Thematic unit   A variety of activities and materials focused in several related content areas and taught using different instructional strategies.

Think, pair, share   A technique in which students working in pairs learn from one another and get to try out their ideas in a nonthreatening context before presenting them to the class.

Thinking curriculum One that focuses on teaching learners how to think critically, reason, and solve problems in authentic, real-world contexts.

Track system A system in which some sections of instruction are allocated to lower- and/or higher-performing students.

Tutorial and communication technologies Methods that are flexible, allow rapid movement within and across content, provide immediate feedback on accuracy of responses, and gradually shift responsibility for learning from the teacher to student.

U

Unguided discovery learning To maintain high levels of student interest, selecting content based on student problems or interests and providing individually tailored feedback.

V

Validity Refers to whether a test measures what it says it measures.

Verbal prompts Cues, reminders, or instructions to learners that help them correctly perform the skill being taught.

Vertical relationships Successful relationships with parents and teachers that meet learners' needs for safety, security, and protection.

Vertical unit planning A method of developing units in a discipline by arranging the content to be taught hierarchically or in steps and in an order that ensures that all task-relevant prior knowledge required for subsequent lessons has been taught in previous lessons.

Virtual worlds An interactive Internet environment in two- or three-dimensional format in which learners are immersed in an online role-playing for instructional purposes.

W

Web 2.0 Communication Technology The most dominant information and communication technology on the Internet that is an important means for facilitating learning and instruction in the classroom.

Wait-time 1 The amount of time a teacher gives a learner to respond when first asked a question.

Wait-time 2 The amount of time that passes after a learner's first response until the teacher or another student affirms or negates the answer.

Weekly and monthly reviews The direct instruction strategy of conducting periodic reviews to ensure that all task-relevant information needed for future lessons has been learned and to see whether reteaching is necessary.

Wiki A website where users assigned in groups can create content collaboratively.

Z

Zone of maximum response opportunity The level of content difficulty and behavioral complexity from which the learner can most benefit.

References

Aaron, K. (2001). *Single parents can raise great children.* New York: Mass Market Paperback.

Abruscato, J. (1994). Boost your students' social skills with this 9 step plan. *Learning, 22*(5), pp. 60–61, 66.

Adams-Bullock, A., & Hawk, P. (2010). *Developing a teaching portfolio: A guide for preservice and practicing teachers* (3rd ed.). Upper Saddle River, NJ: Prentice Hall.

Affini, J. (1996). *150 ways to increase intrinsic motivation in the classroom.* Boston: Allyn & Bacon.

Akhavan, N. (2008). *The teacher's guide to teaching reading.* Portsmouth, NH: Heinemann.

Alberto, P. A., & Troutman, A. C. (2009). *Applied behavior analysis for teachers* (8th ed.). Upper Saddle River, NJ: Pearson.

Aldrich, C. (2005). *Learning by doing: A comprehensive guide to simulations, computer games, and pedagogy in e-learning and other educational experiences.* Hoboken, NJ: Wiley.

Alexander, P. (Ed.). (1996). The role of knowledge in learning and instruction [Special issue]. *Educational Psychologist, 31*(2), pp. 89–145.

Algozzine, R., & Ysseldyke, J. (2006). *The fundamentals of special education: A practical guide for every teacher.* Thousand Oaks, CA: Corwin.

Allen, I. E., & Seaman, J. (2006). Making the Grade: Online Education in the United States, 2006. Needham, MA: Sloan, C. Retrieved April 17, 2012, from http://sloanconsortium.org/publications/survey/pdf/Making_the_Grade.pdf

American Association for the Advancement of Science. (1993). *Benchmarks for science literacy: Project 2061.* New York: Oxford University Press.

American Association for the Advancement of Science. (2009). *Benchmarks for science literacy.* New York: Oxford University Press.

Ames, C. (1990). Motivation: What teachers need to know. *Teachers College Record, 91,* pp. 409–421.

Anderman, E. M., & Maehr, M. L. (1994). Motivation and schooling in the middle grades. *Review of Educational Research, 64*(20), pp. 287–309.

Anderson, J. R. (2005). *Cognitive psychology and its implications* (6th ed.). Cranbury, NJ: Worth.

Anderson, L., Evertson, C., & Brophy, J. (1982). *Principles of small group instruction in elementary reading.* East Lansing: Michigan State University, Institute for Research on Teaching.

Anderson, L., & Krathwohl, D. (Eds.). (2001). *Taxonomy for learning, teaching, and assessing: A revision of Bloom's taxonomy of educational objectives.* New York: Longman.

Anderson, L., Stevens, D., Prawat, R., & Nickerson, J. (1988). Classroom task environments and students' risk-related beliefs. *The Elementary School Journal, 88,* pp. 181–296.

Anderson, M. G. (1992). The use of selected theater rehearsal technique activities with African-American adolescents labeled "Behaviorally Disordered." *Exceptional Children, 59,* pp. 132–140.

Anderson, L. W., Krathwohl, D. R., Airasian, P. W., & Cruikshank, K. A. (2001). *Taxonomy for learning, teaching, and assessing: A revision of Bloom's Taxonomy of Educational Objectives.* New York: Longman.

Angelillo, J. (2008). *Whole-class teaching: Minilessons and more.* Portsmouth, NH: Heinemann.

Antón-Oldenburg, M. (2000, September). Celebrate diversity! *Scholastic Instructor,* pp. 46–48.

Armstrong, T. (2009). *Multiple intelligences in the classroom.* Alexandria, VA: ASCD.

Atwood, V., & Wilen, W. (1991). Wait time and effective social studies instruction: What can research in science education tell us? *Social Education, 55,* pp. 179–181.

Audet, R., & Jordan, L. (Eds.). (2005). *Integrating inquiry across the curriculum.* Thousand Oaks, CA: Corwin.

Auer, P., Couper-Kuhlen, E., & Muller, F. (1999). *Language in time: The rhythm and tempo of spoken interaction.* Oxford, UK: Oxford University Press.

Ausubel, D. P. (1968). *Educational psychology: A cognitive view.* New York: Holt, Rinehart & Winston.

Baden, M., & Mayor, C. (2004). *Foundations of problem-based learning.* Berkshire, UK: Open University Press.

Ball, L., Lubienski, S., & Mewborn, D. (2001). Research on teaching mathematics: The unsolved problem of teachers' mathematical knowledge. In V. Richardson (Ed.), *Handbook of research on teaching* (pp. 433–456). Washington, DC: American Educational Research Association.

Bandura, A. (1986). *Social foundations of thought and action: A social cognitive theory.* Upper Saddle River, NJ: Prentice Hall.

Bandura, A. (1997). *Self-efficacy.* New York: W. H. Freeman.

Banks, J. (1997). *Teaching strategies for ethnic studies* (6th ed.). Boston: Allyn & Bacon.

Banks, J. (2000). *Cultural diversity and education: Foundations, curriculum, and teaching* (4th ed.). Boston: Allyn & Bacon.

Banks, J. (2005). *Cultural diversity and education: Foundations, curriculum, and teaching* (5th ed). Boston: Allyn & Bacon.

Banks, J., & Banks, C. (Eds.). (2001). *Handbook of research on multicultural education.* San Francisco: Jossey-Bass.

Banks, J., & Banks, C. (2009). *Multicultural education: Issues and perspectives.* Hoboken, NJ: Wiley.

Barell, J. (2006). *Problem-based learning: An inquiry approach.* Thousand Oaks, CA: Corwin.

Barr, R. (2001). Research on the teaching of reading. In V. Richardson (Ed.), *Handbook of research on teaching* (pp. 360–415). Washington, DC: American Educational Research Association.

Baum, S., Viens, J., & Slatin, B. (2005). *Multiple intelligences in the elementary classroom: A teacher's toolkit.* New York: Teachers College Press.

Benard, B. (1997). Turning it around for all youth: From risk to resilience. *ERIC/CUE Digest,* Number 126. Washington, DC: ERIC Clearinghouse on Teaching and Teacher Education. (ERIC Document Reproduction Service No. ED 412 309)

Bennett, C. (2010). *Comprehensive multicultural education: Theory and practice* (7th ed.). Boston: Allyn & Bacon.

Bennett, S., Bishops, A., Dalgarno, B., Kennedy, G., & Waycott, J. (2012). *Implementing Web 2.0 technologies in higher education: A collective case study.* Computers and Education.

Bennett, N., & Desforges, C. (1988). Matching classroom tasks to students' attainments. *The Elementary School Journal, 88,* pp. 221–224.

Bennett, N., Desforges, C., Cockburn, A., & Wilkinson, B. (1981). *The quality of pupil learning experiences: Interim report.* Lancaster, UK: University of Lancaster, Centre for Educational Research and Development.

Bennett, S., & Matont, K. (2010). Beyond the 'digital natives' debate: Towards a more nuanced understanding of students' technology experiences. *Journal of Computer Assisted Learning, 26,* pp. 321–331.

Berliner, D. (1979). Tempus educare. In P. Peterson & H. Walberg (Eds.), *Research on teaching: Concepts, findings, and implications* (pp. 120–135). Berkeley, CA: McCutchan.

Berliner, D., & Biddle, B. (1995). *The manufactured crisis: Myth, fraud, and the attack on America's public schools.* New York: Addison-Wesley.

Bernstein, J. (2006). *10 days to a less defiant child: The breakthrough program for overcoming your child's difficult behavior.* Cambridge, MA: Da Capo Press.

Besnoy, K. & Clarke, W. (2009). *High-tech teaching success! A step-by-step guide to using innovative technology in your classroom.* Waco, TX: Prufrock Press.

Bettencourt, E., Gillett, M., Gall, M., & Hull, R. (1983). Effects of teacher enthusiasm training on student on-task behavior and achievement. *American Educational Research Journal, 20,* pp. 435–450.

Bitter, G. & Lagacy, J. (2007). *Using technology in the classroom.* Boston: Allyn & Bacon.

Black, S. (1996). The truth about homework. *American School Board Journal,* 183(10), pp. 48–51.

Blackburn, B. (2005). *Classroom motivation from A to Z: How to engage your students in learning.* Larchmont, NY: Eye on Education

Blanton, B. (2005). The application of the cognitive learning theory to instructional design. *International Journal of Instructional Media,* 25(2), pp. 171–180.

Bloom, B. (1981). *All our children learning.* New York: McGraw-Hill.

Bloom, B., Englehart, M., Hill, W., Furst, E., & Krathwohl, D. (1984). *Taxonomy of educational objectives: The classification of educational goals. Handbook I: Cognitive domain.* New York: Longman Green.

Blumenfeld, P. C., Soloway, E., Marx, R. W., Krajcik, J. S., Guzdial, M., & Palincsar, A. (1991). Motivating project-based learning: Sustaining the doing, supporting the learning. *Educational Psychologist, 26,* pp. 369–398.

Bonk, C. J. (1997). Learner-centered Web instruction for higher-order thinking, teamwork, and apprenticeship. In B. H. Khan (Ed.), *Web-Based Instruction.* New Jersey: Educational Technology Publication, Inc. (pp. 167–178).

Bonk, C. J., & Graham, C. R. (Eds.) (2006). *The Handbook of Blended Learning.* San Francisco, CA: Pfeiffer.

Bordessa, K. (2005). *Team challenges: 170+ group activities to build cooperation, communication, and creativity.* St. Paul, MN: Zephyr Press.

Borich, G. (1993). *Clearly outstanding: Making each day count in your classroom.* Boston: Allyn & Bacon.

Borich, G. (2004). *Vital impressions: The KPM approach to children.* Austin, TX: The KPM Institute.

Borich, G. (2007a). Introduction to thinking. In A. Choo & G. Borich (Eds.), *Teaching strategies to promote thinking skills.* Singapore: McGraw-Hill.

Borich, G. (2007b). Introduction to the thinking curriculum. In A. Ong & G. Borich (Eds.), *Teaching strategies that promote thinking.* Singapore: McGraw-Hill.

Borich, G. (2008a). Characteristics of effective teaching. In N. Salkind (Ed.), *Encyclopedia of educational psychology.* Thousand Oaks, CA: Sage Publications.

Borich, G. (2008b). *Observation skills for effective teaching* (5th ed.). Upper Saddle River, NJ: Merrill/Prentice Hall.

Borich, G., & Hao, Y. (2007). Inquiry-based learning: A practical example. In A. Ong & G. Borich (Eds.), *Teaching strategies that promote thinking.* Singapore: McGraw-Hill.

Borich, G., Hao, Y., & Aw, W.L. (2006). Inquiry-based learning: A practical application. In A. C. Ong & G. D. Borich (Eds.), *Teaching Strategies that Promote Thinking: Models and Curriculum Approaches* (pp. 29–52).

Borich, G., & Tombari, M. (1997). *Educational psychology: A contemporary approach* (2nd ed.). Boston: Allyn & Bacon.

Borich, G., & Tombari, M. (2004). *Educational assessment for the elementary and middle school classroom* (2nd ed.). Upper Saddle River, NJ: Merrill/Prentice Hall.

Boss, S., Krauss, J., & Conery, L. (2008). *Reinventing project-based learning: Your field guide to real-world projects in the digital age.* Washington, DC: International Society for Technology in Education.

Bowers, C., & Flinders, D. (1991). *Culturally responsive teaching and supervision: A handbook for staff development.* New York: Teachers College Press.

Boyles, N. (2004). *Constructing meaning through kid-friendly comprehension strategy instruction.* Gainesville, FL: Maupin House Publishing.

Bransford, J. D., & Steen, B. (1994). *The IDEAL problem solver* (2nd ed.). New York: Worth.

Bronfenbrenner, V. (1989). Ecological systems theory. In R. Vasta (Ed.), *Annals of child development* (Vol. 6, pp. 187–251). Greenwich, CT: JAI Press.

Brofenbrenner, V. (2005). *The ecology of human development: Experiments by nature and design.* Cambridge, MA: Harvard University Press.

Brookfield, S., & Preskill, S. (2005). *Discussion as a way of teaching: Tools and techniques for democratic classrooms.* San Francisco: Jossey-Bass.

Brookhart, S. (2008). *How to give feedback to your students.* Alexandria, VA: Association for Supervision and Curriculum Development.

Brophy, J. (2010). Motivating students to learn. New York, NY: Routledge.

Brophy, J. (1981). Teach praise: A functional analysis. *Review of Educational Research, 51,* pp. 5–32.

Brophy, J. (1992). Probing the subtleties of subject-matter teaching. *Educational Leadership, 49*(7), pp. 4–8.

Brophy, J. (1996). *Teaching problem students.* New York: Guilford Press.

Brophy, J. (2002). *Teaching: Educational practices series—1.* United Nations Educational, Social, and Cutural Organization (UNESCO). Geneva, Switzerland: International Bureau of Education. Available from www.ibe.unesco.org.

Brophy, J., & Evertson, C. (1976). *Learning from teaching: A developmental perspective.* Boston: Allyn & Bacon.

Brophy, J., & Good, T. (1986). Teacher behavior and student achievement. In M. C. Wittrock (Ed.), *Handbook of research on teaching* (3rd ed., pp. 328–375). Upper Saddle River, NJ: Merrill/Prentice Hall.

Brookhart, S. (2008). *How to give effective feedback to your students.* Alexandria, VA: ASCD.

Brown, A. L. (1994). The advancement of learning. *Educational Researcher, 23,* pp. 4–12.

Brown, A., & Campione, J. (1994). Guided discovery in a community of learners. In K. McGilly (Ed.), *Classroom lessons: Integrating cognitive theory and classroom practice* (pp. 81–132). Norwood, NJ: Ablex.

Brown, G. (2001). *Questioning in the secondary school.* New York: RoutledgeFalmer.

Brown, G., & Wragg, E. (1993). *Questioning.* London: Routledge.

Bruner, J. (2004). *Toward a theory of instruction.* Cambridge, MA: Belknap Press.

Bruner, J. S. (1996). *The culture of education.* Cambridge, MA: Harvard University Press.

Bruning, R., Schraw, G., Norby, M., & Ronning, R. (2004). *Cognitive psychology and instruction* (4th ed.). Upper Saddle River, NJ: Merrill/Prentice Hall.

Bruff, D. (2009). *Teaching with classroom response systems: Creating active learning environments.* San Francisco: Jossey-Bass.

Buehl, D. (2008). *Classroom strategies for interactive learning.* Newark, DE: International Reading Association.

Bulach, C., Fulbright, J., & Williams, R. (2003). Bullying behavior: What is the potential for violence at your school? *Journal of Instructional Pschology, 30,* pp. 156–165.

Bullough, R. (1989). *First-year teacher: A case study.* New York: Teachers College Press.

Burbules, N., & Bruce, B. (2001). Theory and research on teaching as dialogue. In V. Richardson (Ed.), *Handbook of research on teaching* (4th ed.). Washington, DC: American Educational Research Association.

Burden, P. (1986). Teacher development: Implications for teacher education. In J. Raths & L. Katz (Eds.), *Advances in teacher education* (Vol. 2). Norwood, NJ: Ablex.

Burke, K. (2010). *From standards to rubrics in six steps: Tools for assessing student learning, K-8.* Thousand Oaks, CA: Corwin.

Burnette, J. (1999). *Critical behaviors and strategies for teaching culturally diverse students.* ERIC/OSEP Digest E 584. Reston, VA: ERIC Clearinghouse on Disabilities and Gifted Education. (ERIC Document Reproduction Service No. ED 435 147)

Buzan, T. (2004). *How to mind map.* New York: HarperCollins.

Bybee, R. (1989). *Science and technology education for the elementary years: Frameworks for curriculum and instruction.* Washington, D.C.: The National Center for Improving Instruction.

Bybee, R., & Loucks-Horsely, S. (2001). National science education standards as a catalyst for change. In J. Rhoton & P. Bowers (Eds.), *Professional development planning and design: Issues in science education.* Arlington, VA: National Science Teachers Association.

Campbell, B., Campbell, L., & Dickinson, D. (1996). *Teaching and learning through multiple intelligences.* Boston: Allyn & Bacon.

Canning, C. (1991). What teachers say about reflection. *Educational Leadership, 48*(6), pp. 69–87.

Canter, L. (2009). *Assertive discipline: Positive behavior management for today's classroom.* Bloomington, IN: Solution Tree.

Cantrell, S. C. (1998/1999). Effective teaching and literacy learning: A look inside primary classrooms. *The Reading Teacher, 52*(4), pp. 370–378.

Carlson, C. (1992). Single parenting and stepparenting: Problems, issues and interventions. In M. J. Fine & C. Carlson (Eds.), *The handbook of family-school intervention: A systems perspective* (pp. 188–214). Boston: Allyn & Bacon.

Carpenter, T., Dossey, J., & Koehler, J. (Eds.). (2004). *Classics in mathematics education research.* Reston, VA: National Council of Teachers of Mathematics.

Carroll, J. B. (1963). A model of school learning. *Teachers College Record, 64,* pp. 723–733.

Cartledge, G., Gardner, R., & Ford, D. (2008). *Diverse learners with exceptionalities: Culturally response teaching in the inclusive classroom.* Upper Saddle River, NJ: Prentice Hall.

Cassidy, J., & Asher, S. R. (1992). Loneliness and peer relations in young children. *Child Development, 63,* pp. 350–365.

Castaneda, C. (2004). *Teaching and learning in diverse classrooms: Faculty reflections on their experiences and pedagogical practices of teaching diverse populations.* New York: Routledge.

Cecil, N. (1995). *The art of inquiry: Questioning strategies for K–6 classrooms.* Iowa City, IA: Portage & Main Press.

Chaffee, J. (2010). *Thinking critically* (9th ed.). Boston: Houghton Mifflin.

Chaille, C. (2007). *Constructivism across the curriculum in early childhood classrooms.* Boston: Allyn & Bacon.

Cheesman, E. A., Winograd, G. R., & Wehrman, J. D. (2010). Clickers in teacher education: Student perceptions by age and gender. *Journal of Technology and Teacher Education, 18*(1), pp. 35–55.

Chen, B. (2005*). Effects of advance organizers on learning and retention.* London, England: Springer-Verlag.

Chen, G., & Starasta, W. (2005). *Foundations of intercultural communication.* Lanham, MD: University Press of America.

Cheng, L. (1996, October). Enhancing communication: Toward optimal language learning for limited English proficient students. *Language, Speech and Hearing Services in Schools, 28*(2), pp. 347–354.

Cheng, L. (1998). *Enhancing the communication skills of newly-arrived Asian American students. ERIC/CUE Digest,* Number 136. New York: ERIC Clearinghouse on Urban Education. (ERIC Document Reproduction Service No. ED 420 726)

Cheng, L., Chen, T., Tsubo, T., Sekandari, N., & Alfafara-Killacky, S. (1997). Challenges of diversity: An Asian Pacific perspective. *Multicultures,* 3, pp. 114–145.

Child Abuse Prevention and Treatment Act (2003) P.L. pp. 100–294

Child Trends DataBank. (2005). Retrieved from www.child trends%2databank.org/indicators/1HighSchoolDropout.cfm.

Christenson, S. L., Rounds, T., & Franklin, M. J. (1992). Home-school collaboration: Effects, issues and opportunities. In S. L. Christenson & J. C. Conoley (Eds.), *Home-school collaboration: Enhancing children's academic and social competence.* Silver Spring, MD: National Association of School Psychologists.

Chuska, K. (2003). *Improving classroom questions: A teacher's guide to increasing student motivation, participation and higher-level thinking* (2nd ed.). Bloomington, IN: Phi Delta Kappa Educational Foundation.

Clark, C., & Peterson, P. (1986). Teachers' thought processes. In M. R. Wittrock (Ed.), *Handbook of research on teaching* (3rd ed., pp. 255–296). Upper Saddle River, NJ: Merrill/Prentice Hall.

Clark, R. E. (1983). Reconsidering research on learning from media. *Review of Educational Research* 53, pp. 445–59.

Clark, R. E. (1994). Media will never influence learning. *Educational Technology Research and Development,* 42(2), pp. 21–29.

Cohen, E. (1994). Restructuring the classroom: Conditions for productive small groups. *Review of Educational Research,* 64(1), pp. 1–35.

Compton-Lilly, C. (2000). "Staying on children": Challenging stereotypes about urban parents. *Language Arts,* 77(5), pp. 420–427.

Conant, A., & Carin, J. (2008). *Activities for teaching science as inquiry* (7th ed.). Hobogen, NJ: Prentice-Hall.

Coontz, S. (2008). *American families: A multicultural reader.* Oxford, UK: Routledge.

Cooper, J. O., Heron, T. E., & Heward, W. L. (1987). *Applied behavior analysis.* Upper Saddle River, NJ: Merrill/Prentice Hall.

Corey, S. (1940). The teachers out-talk the pupils. *School Review,* 48, pp. 745–752.

Corno, L. (1996). Homework is a complicated thing. *Educational Researcher,* 25(8), pp. 27–30.

Corno, L., & Snow, R. (1986). Adapting teaching to individual differences among learners. In M. C. Wittrock (Ed.), *Handbook of research on teaching* (3rd ed., pp. 605–629). Upper Saddle River, NJ: Merrill/Prentice Hall.

Costa, A. (2009) *Habits of mind across the curriculum: Practical and creative strategies for teachers. Alexandria,* VA: ASCD.

Costa, A., & Kallick, B. (2003). *Assessment strategies for self-directed learning.* Thousand Oaks, CA: Corwin.

Costa, A. & Kallick, B. (2008). *Learning and leading with habits of mind: 16 essential characteristics for success.* Alexandria, VA: ASCD.

Costa, A., & Kallick, B. (Eds.). (2003). *Activating and engaging habits of mind.* Cheltenham, Australia: Hawker Brownlow Education.

Costa, A., & Kallick, B. (Eds.). (2004). *Assessing and reporting on habits of mind.* Arlington, VA: Association for Supervision and Curriculum Development.

Costantino, P., De Lorenzo, M., & Tirrell-Corbin, C. (2008). *Developing a professional teaching portfolio: A guide for success* (3rd ed.). Boston: Allyn & Bacon.

Cotton, K. (1996). Affective and social benefits of small-scale schooling. *ERIC Digest.* Charleston, WV: ERIC/Cooperative Research & Extension Services for Schools.

Council for Basic Education. (1996). *What teachers have to say about teacher education.* New York: Council for Basic Education.

Cragan, J., Wright, D., & Kasch, C. (2008). *Communication in small group discussions: Theory, process and skills.* Florence, KY: Wadsworth.

Cronbach, L., & Snow, R. (1981). *Aptitudes and instructional methods.* New York: Irvington/Naiburg.

Crook, C., Fisher, T., Graber, R., Harrison, C., Lewin, C., Cummings, J., Logan, K., Luckin, R., Oliver, M., & Sharples, M. (2008). *Implementing Web 2.0 in secondary schools: Impacts, barriers and issues.* Becta: Coventry.

Cruickshank, D., & Metcalf, K. (1994). Explaining. In T. Husen & T. N. Postlewaite (Eds.), *International encyclopedia of education* (2nd ed.). Oxford: Pergamon.

Curtis, D., & Carter, M. (2011). *Reflecting children's lives: A handbook for planning your child-centered curriculum* (2nd ed.). St. Paul, MN: Redleaf Press.

Curtis, D., & Carter, M. (2007). *Learning together with young children: A curriculum framework for reflective teachers.* St. Paul, MN: Redleaf Press.

Curwin, R. (2010). *Meeting students where they live: Motivation in urban schools.* Alexandria, VA: ASCD.

Curwin, R. L., & Mendler, A. N. (1997). *As tough as necessary: Countering violence, aggression, and hostility in our schools.* Alexandria, VA: Association for Supervision and Curriculum Development.

Cushner, K., McClelland, A., & Safford, P. (2011). *Human diversity in education: An intercultural approach.* New York: McGraw-Hill.

Dahllof, U., & Lundgren, U. P. (1970). *Macro- and micro-approaches combined for curriculum process analysis: A Swedish educational field project.* Goteborg, Sweden: University of Goteborg, Institute of Education.

D'Amico, J., & Gallaway, K. (2008). *Differentiated instruction for the middle school math teacher: Activities and strategies for an inclusive classroom.* Hoboken, NJ: Wiley.

Daniels, H. , Zelelman, S. & Hyde, A. (2005). *Best practice: Today's standards for teaching and learning in America's schools.* New York, NY: Heinemann.

Dantonio, M., & Beisenherz, P. (2001). *Learning to question, questioning to learn: Developing effective teacher questioning practices.* Boston: Allyn & Bacon.

Darling-Hammond, L., et al. (2008). *Powerful learning: What we know about teaching for understanding.* San Francisco, CA: Jossey-Bass.

Darling-Hammond, L., & Bransford, J. (Eds.). (2005). *Preparing teachers for a changing world: What teachers should learn and be able to do* (pp. 169–201). San Francisco: Jossey-Bass.

Delgado-Gaitan, C. (1991). Involving parents in the schools: A process of empowerment. *American Journal of Education,* 100(1), pp. 20–46.

Delgado-Gaitan, C. (1992). School matters in the Mexican-American home: Socializing children to education. *American Educational Research Journal,* 29(3), pp. 495–516.

Delgado-Gaitan, C. (2006). *Building culturally responsive classrooms: A guide for K–6 teachers.* Thousand Oaks, CA: Corwin.

Delgado-Gaitan, C., & Trueba, H. (1991). *Crossing cultural borders: Education for immigrant families in America.* London: Falmer Press.

Delisle, R. (1997). *How to use problem-based learning in the classroom.* Alexandria, VA: Association for Supervision and Curriculum Development.

Delpit, L., Boyd, F., Brock, C., & Rozendal, M. (2003). *Multicultural and multilingual literacy and language: Contexts and practices (Solving problems in teaching of literacy).* New York: Guilford Press.

Delpit, L. (2006). *Other people's children: Cultural conflict in the classroom.* New York: New Press.

Delpit, L., & Dowdy, J. (2008). *The skin that we speak: Thoughts on language and culture in the classroom.* New York: New Press.

DeMeulenaere, E. (2001, April). Constructing reinventions: Black and Latino students negotiating the transformation of their academic identities and school performance. Paper presented at the annual meeting of the American Educational Research Association, Seattle, WA.

Dev, P. C. (1997). Intrinsic motivation and academic achievement: What does their relationship imply for the classroom teacher? *Remedial and Special Education, 18*(1), 12–19.

Dewey, J. (1938). *Logic: The theory of inquiry.* New York: Holt.

Diaz-Rico, L. (2012). *A course for teaching English learners* (2nd ed.). Boston: Allyn & Bacon.

Diener, C., & Dweck, C. (1980). An analysis of learned helplessness II: The processing of success. *Journal of Personality and Social Psychology, 39,* pp. 940–952.

Diffily, D., & Sassman, C. (2002). *Project-based learning with young children.* Portsmouth, NH: Heineman.

Di Giullo, R. (2006). *Positive classroom management: A step-by-step guide to helping students succeed.* Thousand Oaks, CA: Corwin.

Diller, D. (1999). Opening the dialogue: Using culture as a tool in teaching young African American children. *The Reading Teacher, 52*(8), pp. 820–828.

Dillon, D. (1989). Showing them that I want them to learn and that I care about who they are: A microethnography of the social organization of a secondary low-track English reading classroom. *American Educational Research Journal, 26,* pp. 227–259.

Dillon, J. (1990). *The practice of questioning.* New York: Routledge.

Dillon, J. (1995). Discussion. In L. W. Anderson (Ed.), *International encyclopedia of teaching and teacher education* (2nd ed., pp. 251–255). Tarrytown, NY: Elsevier Sciences.

Dillon, J. T. (2004). *Questioning and teaching: A manual of practice.* San Jose, CA: Resource Publications.

Dilworth, M., & Brown, C. (2001). Consider the difference: Teaching and learning in culturally rich schools. In V. Richardson (Ed.), *Handbook of research on teaching* (pp. 643–667). Washington, DC: American Educational Research Association.

Dishon, D., & O'Leary, P. (1984). *A guidebook for cooperative learning.* Kalamazoo, MI: Learning Publications.

Doll, B., Zucker, S., & Brehm, K. (2004). *Resilient classrooms: Creating healthy environments for learning.* New York: Guilford Press.

Doyle, W. (1983). Academic work. *Review of Educational Research, 53,* pp. 159–200.

Doyle, W. (1986). Classroom organization and management. In M. Wittrock (Ed.), *Handbook of research on teaching* (3rd ed., pp. 392–431). Upper Saddle River, NJ: Merrill/Prentice Hall.

Drake, S. (2007). *Creating standards-based integrated curriculum: Aligning curriculum, content, assessment, and instruction.* Thousand Oaks, CA: Corwin.

DuFour, R., DuFour, R., Eaker, R., & Many, T (2010). *Learning by doing: A handbook for professional learning communities at work.* Bloomington, IN: Solution Tree.

Dunkin, M., & Biddle, B. (1974). *The study of teaching.* New York: Holt, Rinehart & Winston.

Dunlosky, J., & Metcalf, J. (2008). *Metacognition.* Thousand Oaks, CA: Sage.

Dunn, R., & Griggs, S. (1995). *Multiculturalism and learning styles: Teaching and counseling adolescents.* Westport, CT: Praeger.

Dweck, C., & Reppucci, N. (1973). Learned helplessness and reinforcement responsibility in children. *Journal of Personality and Social Psychology, 25,* pp. 109–116.

Dyches, T., Carter, N., & Prater, M. (2012). *A teacher's guide to communicating with parents: Practical strategies for developing successful relationships.* Boston: Pearson.

Echevarria, J., & Graves, A. (2011). *Sheltered content instruction: Teaching English learners with diverse abilities* (4th ed.). Boston: Allyn & Bacon.

Egbert, J., & Ernst-Slavit, G. (2010). *Access to academics: Planning instruction for K–12 classrooms with ELLs.* Boston: Allyn & Bacon.

Eggen, P., & Kauchak, D. (2006). *Educational psychology: Windows on classrooms* (7th ed.). Upper Saddle River, NJ: Merrill/Prentice Hall.

Eisenberger, J. (2005). *Self-efficacy: Raising the bar for all students.* Larchmont, NY: Eye on Education.

Eisner, E. (1969). Instructional and expressive educational objectives: Their formulation and use in curriculum. In W. Popham, E. Eisner, H. Sullivan, & L. Tyler (Eds.), *Instructional objectives: AERA monograph series on curriculum evaluation* (No. 3, pp. 1–18). Chicago: Rand McNally.

Eisner, E. (1998). *The enlightened eye: Qualitative inquiry and the enhancement of educational practice.* Upper Saddle River, NJ: Merrill/Prentice Hall.

Emmer, E., & Evertson, C. (2012). *Classroom management for middle and high school teachers* (8th ed.). Upper Saddle River, NJ: Pearson/Merrill.

Emmer, E., Evertson, C., & Anderson, L. (1980). Effective classroom management at the beginning of the school year. *The Elementary School Journal, 80*(5), pp. 219–231.

Engel, A. (1998). *Problem-solving strategies.* New York: Springer.

English, L. (Ed.). (2002). *Handbook of international research in mathematics education.* Mahwah, NJ: Erlbaum.

Epstein, J., (2010). *School, family, and community partnerships: Preparing educators and improving schools.* Eagan, MN: Westview Press.

Erikson, H. (2006). *Concept-based curriculum and instruction for the thinking classroom.* Thousand Oaks, CA: Corwin.

Evertson, C. (1995). Classroom rules and routines. In L. Anderson (Ed.), *International encyclopedia of teaching and teacher education* (2nd ed., pp. 215–219). Tarrytown, NY: Elsevier Science.

Evertson, C., & Emmer, E. (1982). Effective management at the beginning of the school year in junior high classes. *Journal of Educational Psychology,* 74, pp. 485–498.

Evertson, C., & Emmer, E. (2012). *Classroom management for elementary teachers* (8th ed.). Upper Saddle River, NJ: Pearson/Merrill.

Falk, B., & Blumenreich, M. (2005). *The power of questions: A guide to teacher and student research.* Portsmouth, NH: Heinemann.

Farkas, M. (2008). Isn't it del.icio.us?. *American Libraries,* April. p. 32.

Farkas, P., & Binder, J. (2011). *Resilient children.* Llumina Press: www.llumina.com.

Fasset, D., & Warren, J. (2010). *Communication and instruction.* Thousand Oaks, CA: Sage.

Federal Education Budget Project: Individuals with Disabilities Act Overview. Retrieved from Internet at: febp.newamerica. net/background-analysis/individuals-disabilities-education-act-overview.

Federal Interagency Forum on Child and Family Statistics (2001). *America's children: Key national indicators of well-being 2001.* Washington, DC: U.S. Government Printing Office.

Ferdig, R. E. (2007). Editorial: Examining social software in teacher education. *Journal of Technology and Teacher Education,* 15(1), pp. 5–10.

Ferster, C., Skinner, B., Cheney, C., & Morse, W. (1997). *Schedules of reinforcement.* Acton, MA: Copley Publishing Group.

Fielding, G., Kame'enui, E., & Gerstein, R. (1983). A comparison of an inquiry and a direct instruction approach to teaching legal concepts and applications to secondary school students. *Journal of Educational Research,* 76, pp. 243–250.

Fisch, C., & Turnbull, E. (2008). *Managing diverse classrooms: How to build on students' cultural strengths.* Alexandria, VA: ASCD.

Fletcher, D. (2010). Facebook: Friends without border. *Time,* 175(21), pp. 16–22.

Flanders, N. (1970). *Analyzing teacher behavior.* Reading, MA: Addison-Wesley.

Forsterling, F. (2001). *Attribution: An introduction to theories: Research and applications.* Philadelphia: Psychology Press.

Fosnot, C. (2005). *Constructivism: Theory, perspectives and practice.* New York: Teachers College Press.

Franklin, M. E. (1992). Culturally sensitive instructional practices for African-American learners with disabilities. *Exceptional Children,* 59, pp. 115–122.

Frawley, T. (2005). Gender bias in the classroom: current controversies and implications for teachers. *Early Childhood Education Journal,* July, 2005, pp. 1–18.

Free, J. (2004, August). Race and school tracking: From a sociological perspective. Paper presented at the annual meeting of the American Sociological Association, San Francisco, CA.

French, J., Jr., & Raven, B. (1959). The bases of social power. In D. Cartwright (Ed.), *Studies in social power* (pp. 150–168). Ann Arbor: University of Michigan Press.

Fuller, F. (1969). Concerns of teachers: A developmental conceptualization. *American Educational Research Journal,* 6, pp. 207–226.

Gage, N., & Berliner, D. (1998). *Educational psychology* (6th ed.). Boston: Houghton Mifflin.

Gagné, E., Yekovich, C., & Yekovich, F. (1997). *The cognitive psychology of school learning.* Boston: Allyn & Bacon.

Gagné, R., & Briggs, L. (2005). *Principles of instructional design* (5th ed.). Florence, KY: Wadsworth.

Gaillard, L. (1994, December 14). Hands off homework? *Education Week,* 14(5), p. 4. Retrieved September 19, 2000, from www.edweek.org/ew/1994/15gaill.h14.

Galambos, S. J., & Goldin-Meadow, S. (1990). The effects of learning two languages on levels of metalinguistic awareness. *Cognition,* 34, pp. 1–56.

Galanes, G., & Adams, K. (2009). *Effective group discussion: Theory and practice.* Boston: McGraw-Hill.

Gall, J., & Gall, M. (1990). Outcomes of the discussion method. In W. W. Wilen (Ed.), *Teaching and learning through discussion: The theory and practice of the discussion method.* Springfield, IL: C. C. Thomas.

Gall, M. (1984). Synthesis of research on questioning in recitation. *Educational Leadership,* 42(3), pp. 40–49.

Gamoran, A.(1992). Synthhesis of research: Is ability grouping equitable? *Educational Leadership,* 50(2), pp. 11–13

Garcia, R. L. (1991). *Teaching in a pluralistic society: Concepts, models, strategies* (2nd ed.). New York: HarperCollins.

Gardner, H. (2000). *Intelligence reframed: Multiple intelligences for the 21st century.* New York: Basic Books.

Gardner, H. (2004). The theory of multiple intelligences revisited. Invited address presented to the International Conference on Multiple Intelligences, Beijing, China, May 21, 2004.

Gardner, H. (2006). *Multiple intelligences: New horizons in theory and practice.* New York: Basic Books.

Gardner, H. (2011). *Frames of mind: The theory of multiple intelligences.* New York: Basic Books.

Gardner, H., & Hatch, T. (1989). Multiple intelligences go to school. *Educational Researcher,* 18(8), pp. 4–10.

Gay, G. (2010). *Culturally responsive teaching: Theory, research, and practice.* New York: Teachers College Press.

Gehring, A. (2008). *Back to basics: A complete guide to traditional skills* (3rd ed.). New York: Skyhorse Publishing.

Gentile, J., & Lalley, J. (2003). *Standards and mastery learning.* Thousand Oaks, CA: Corwin.

Gerrig, R., & Zimbardo, P. (2007). *Psychology and life.* Boston: Allyn & Bacon.

Gill, J. (2000). *The tacit mode: Michael Polunya's postmodern philosophy.* Albany, NY: SUNY Press.

Gillies, R., Ashman, A., & Terwei, J. (2010). *The teacher's role in implementing cooperative learning in the classroom.* New York: Springer.

Ginott, H. (1995). *Teacher and child: A book for parents and teachers.* New York: Collier.

Ginott, H., Ginott, A., & Goddard, W. (2003). *Between parent and child.* New York: Three Rivers Press.

Glasser, W. (2003). *For parents and teenagers: Dissolving the barrier between you and your teen.* New York: Harper.

Glasser, W. (1998a). *Choice theory in the classroom.* New York: HarperPerennial.

Glasser, W. (1998b). *Quality School: Managing students without coercion.* New York: HarperPerennial.

Glasser, W. (1998c). *The Quality School teacher: Specific suggestions for teachers who are trying to implement the lead-management ideas of the Quality School in their classrooms* (rev. ed.). New York: HarperPerennial.

Goldhaber, D., & Anthony, E. (2003). *Indicators of teacher quality.* New York: ERIC Clearinghouse on Urban Education. (ERIC Document Reproduction Service No. ED 478 408)

Goleman, D. (2000). *Working with emotional intelligence.* New York: Bantam.

Goleman, D. (2008). *The caring teacher's guide to discipline: Helping students learn self-control, responsibility and respect, K-6.* Thousand Oaks, CA: Corwin.

Goleman, D. (2010). *Emotional intelligence.* London: Bloomsbury.

Good, T. (1979). Teacher effectiveness in the elementary school. *Journal of Teacher Education, 30,* pp. 52–64.

Good, T., & Brophy, J. (1995). *Contemporary educational psychology* (5th ed.). New York: Longman.

Good, T., & Brophy, J. (2007). *Looking in classrooms* (10th ed.). Boston: Allyn & Bacon.

Goodlad, J. (2004). *A place called school.* New York: McGraw-Hill.

Gootman, M. (2008). *The caring teacher's guide to discipline: Helping students learn self-control, responsibility, and respect, K–6.* Thousand Oaks, CA: Corwin.

Gordon, R., & Gordon, M. (2006). *The turned-off child: Learned helplessness and school failure.* Pittsburgh, PA: American Book Publishing.

Grabe, M., & Grabe, C. (2006). *Integrating technology for meaningful learning.* Boston: Houghton Mifflin.

Graham, C. R., Allen, S., & Ure, D. (2005). Benefits and challenges of blended learning environments. In M. Khosrow-Pour (Ed.), *Encyclopedia of information science and technology* (pp. 253–259). Hershey, PA: Idea Group.

Grant, K., & Ray, J. (2009). *Home, school, and community collaboration: Culturally responsive family involvement.* Thousand Oaks, CA: Sage.

Green, H., & Hannon, C. (2007). Their Space: Education for a digital generation, online version, accessed September 4, 2011, http://www.demos.co.uk/files/Their space web.pdf.

Greenwood, C. R., Delguardi, J. C., & Hall, R. V. (1984). Opportunity to respond and student academic achievement. In W. L. Heward, T. E. Heron, D. S. Hill, & J. Trap-Porter (Eds.), *Focus on behavior analysis in education* (pp. 58–88). Upper Saddle River, NJ: Merrill/Prentice Hall.

Gregory, G. (2005). *Differentiating instruction with style: Aligning teacher and learner intelligences for maximum achievement.* Thousand Oaks, CA: Corwin.

Gregory, G., & Chapman, C. (2006). *Differentiated instruction: One size doesn't fit all.* Thousand Oaks, CA: Corwin.

Griffin, C. (2007*). The theory and practice of learning.* Boca Raton, FL: Taylor & Francis.

Griggs, S., & Dunn, R. (1995). Hispanic-American students and learning style. *Emergency Librarian, 23*(2), pp. 11–16.

Gronlund, G. (2006). *Make early learning standards come alive: Connecting your practice and curriculum to state guidelines.* St. Paul, MN: Redleaf.

Gronlund, G., & Engel, B. (2002). *Focused portfolios: A complete assessment for the young child.* St. Paul, MN: Redleaf.

Gronlund, N. (2003). *Gronlund's writing instructional objectives.* Upper Saddle River, NJ: Prentice Hall.

Gronlund, N., & Brookhart, S. (2008). *Gronlund's writing instuctional objectives* (8th ed.). Upper Saddle River, NJ: Prentice Hall.

Grouws, D. A. (Ed.). (1992). *Handbook of research on mathematics teaching and learning.* New York: Macmillan.

Guillaume, A., Yopp, R. & Yopp, H. (2006). *50 Strategies for active teaching: Engaging K–12 learners in the classroom.* Upper Saddle River, NJ: Pearson/Prentice Hall.

Gunawardena, C. N., Hermans, M. B., Sanchez, D., Richmond, C., Bohley, M., & Tuttle, R. (2009). A theoretical framework for building online communities of practice with social networking tool. *Educational Media International, 46*(1), pp. 3–16.

Gunter, M., Estes, T., & Mintz, S. (2006). *Instruction: A Model's Approach* (5th ed.). Boston: Allyn & Bacon.

Haager, D. & Klinger, J. (2004). *Differentiating instruction in inclusive classrooms: The special educator guide.* Boston, MA: Allyn & Bacon.

Hale, M., & City, E. (2006). *The teacher's guide to leading student-centered discussions: Talking about texts in the classroom.* Thousand Oaks, CA: Corwin.

Hanson, E. (2011). *Idea-based learning: A course design process to promote conceptual understanding.* Sterling, VA: Stylus Publishing.

Hanson, W. (2005). *Raising you alone.* Golden Valley, MN: Tristan Publishing.

Hao, Y. (2009). Integrating blogs in teacher education. In T. Kidd & J. Keengwe (Eds.), *Adult learning in the digital age: Perspectives on online technologies and outcomes* (pp. 134–147). Hershey, PA: IGI Global.

Hao, Y., & Borich, G. (2009). A practical guide to evaluate quality of online courses. In H. Song & T. Kidd (Eds.), *The handbook of research on human performance and instructional technology* (pp. 324–343). Hershey, PA.

Harada, V., Kirio, C., & Yamamoto, S. (2008). *Collaborating for project-based learning in grades 9–12.* Columbus, OH: Linworth Publishing.

Harasim, L. M. (1997). Teaching and learning on-line: Issues in computer-mediated graduate courses. *Canadian Journal of Educational Communication, 16*(2), pp. 117–135.

Harpine, E. (2008). *Group interventions in schools: Promoting interventions for at-risk and children and youth.* New York: Springer.

Hartnell-Young, E., & Morris, M. (2007). *Digital portfolios: Powerful tools for promoting professional growth.* Thousand Oaks, CA: Corwin Press.

Harrow, A. (1977). *A taxonomy of the psychomotor domain: A guide for developing behavioral objectives.* New York: David McKay.

Hartman, H. (2009). *A guide to reflective practice for new and experienced teacher.* New York: McGraw-Hill.

Hartup, W. W. (1989). Social relationships and their developmental significance. *American Psychologist, 44,* pp. 120–126.

Harvey, S. & Goudvis, A. (2007). *Strategies that work: Teaching comprehension for understanding and engagement.* Portland, ME: Stenhouse Publishers.

Hassard, J. *Science as inquiry: Active learning, project-based, web-assisted and active assessment strategies to enhance student learning: Grades 5–8.* Good Year Books. Culver City, CA.

Haynes, H. (1935). *The relation of teacher intelligence, teacher experience and type of school to type of questions.* Unpublished doctoral dissertation, George Peabody College for Teachers, Nashville, TN.

Henson, K. (2009). *Curriculum Planning: Integrating multiculturalism, constructivism, and education reform* (4th ed.). Long Grove, IL: Waveland Press Inc.

Hennessy, S. (2011). The role of digital artefacts on the interactive whiteboard in supporting classroom dialogue. *Journal of Computer Assisted Learning, 27*, pp. 463–489.

Hilliard, A. (1992). The pitfalls and promises of special education practice. *Exceptional Children, 59*(2), 162–172.

Horcones, J. (1991). Walden Two in real life: Behavior analysis in the design of the culture. In W. Ishag (Ed.), *Human behavior in today's world.* New York: Praeger.

Horcones, J. (1992). Natural reinforcement: A way to improve education. *Journal of Applied Behavior Analysis, 25*(1), pp. 71–76.

Howard, T. (2010). *Why race and culture matter in schools: Closing the achievement gap in America's classrooms.* New York: Teachers College Press.

Howland, J. L., Jonassen, D., & Marra, R. M. (2012). *Meaningful learning with technology.* Boston, MA: Pearson.

Hubbard, R., & Power, B. (2003). *The art of classroom inquiry: A handbook for teacher-researchers.* Portsmouth, NH: Heinemann

Huffman, K. (2008). *Psychology in action: Active learning edition* (9th ed.). Hoboken, NJ: Wiley.

Hunter, M. (1982). *Mastery teaching.* El Segundo, CA: Instructional Dynamics.

Hutchins, E. (1995). *Cognition in the wild.* Cambridge, MA: MIT Press.

International Reading Association and National Council of Teachers of English (2009). *Standards for the English language arts.* Washington, DC: Author.

Irvine, J., & York, D. (2001). Learning styles and culturally diverse students: A literature review. In J. Banks & C. Banks (Eds.), *Handbook of research on multicultural education* (pp. 484–497). San Francisco: Jossey-Bass.

Jackson, P. (1968). *Life in classrooms.* New York: Holt, Rinehart & Winston.

Jacobs, E. (1999). *Cooperative learning in context: An educational innovation in everyday classrooms.* Albany: State University of New York Press.

Jacobs, E., Power, M., & Loh, W. (2002). *Teacher's source book for cooperative learning.* Thousand Oaks, CA: Corwin.

Johnson, D., & Johnson, R. (1996). Cooperative learning and traditional American values: An appreciation. *NASSP Bulletin, 80*(579), pp. 63–65.

Johnson, D., & Johnson, R. (1998). *Learning together and alone: Cooperative, competitive, and individualistic learning* (5th ed.). Boston: Allyn & Bacon.

Johnson, D., & Johnson, R. (2005). Learning groups. In S. Weelan (Ed.), *The handbook of group research and practice* (pp. 441–461). Thousand Oaks, CA: Sage.

Johnson, D., & Johnson, R. (2008). *Joining together: Group theory and group skills* (8th ed.). Upper Saddle River, NJ: Merrill/Prentice Hall.

Johnson, D. W., Johnson, R. T., Holubec, E. J., & Roy, P. (1994). *The new circles of learning: Cooperation in the classroom.* Alexandria, VA: Association for Supervision and Curriculum Development.

Jolliffe, W. (2007). *Cooperative learning in the classroom: Putting it into practice.* Thousand Oaks, CA: Sage.

Jonassen, D. H. (1999). *Computers as mindtools for schools, engaging critical thinking.* Englewood Cliffs, NJ: PrenticeHall.

Jonassen, D. H. (2010). *Learning to solve problems: A handbook for designing problem-solving learning environments.* New York: Routledge.

Jones, F., Jones, P., Jones, J., & Jones, B. (2007). *Fred Jones tools for teaching: Discipline, instruction, motivation* (2nd ed.). [DVD]. Available from www.fredjones.com.

Jones, K. (1995). *Simulations: A handbook for teachers and trainers.* East Brunswick, NJ: Nichols.

Jones, V., & Jones, L. (2009). *Comprehensive classroom management: Creating communities of support and solving problems* (9th ed.). Boston: Allyn & Bacon.

Jordan, J. (1988). Nobody mean more to me than you and the future life of Willie Jordan. *Harvard Educational Review, 58*, pp. 363–374.

Joubert, M., & Wishart, J. (2012). Participatory practices: Lessons learnt from two initiatives using online digital technologies to build knowledge. *Computers and Education*, pp. 110–119.

Kagan, S. & Kagan, M. (1997). *Cooperative learning structures for teambuilding.* San Clemente, CA: Kagan Cooperative Learning.

Kagan, S. & Kagan, M. (2010). *Frequent Questions (Kagan Cooperative Learning).* Amazon Digital Services: Kindle Edition.

Kaplan, P., Rogers, V., & Webster, R. (2008). *Differentiated instruction made easy: Hundreds of multi-level activities for all learners.* Hoboken, NJ: Wiley.

Karplus, R. (1975). The learning cycle. In F. Collea, et al., Workshop on physics teaching and the development of reasoning. Stonybrook, NY: American Association of Physics.

Karten, T. (2007). *More inclusive strategies that work: Aligning student strengths with standards.* Thousand Oaks, CA: Corwin.

Karten, T. (2008). *Facilitator's guide to more inclusion strategies that work.* Thousand Oaks, CA: Corwin.

Karweit, N., & Slavin, R. (1981). Measurement and modeling choices in studies of time and learning. *American Educational Research Journal, 18*, pp. 157–171.

Kauchak, D., & Eggen, P. (2011). *Learning and teaching: Research-based methods* (6th ed.). Boston: Allyn & Bacon.

Keene, E. (2007). *Assessing comprehension thinking strategies.* Huntington Beach, CA: Shell Education.

Keirns, J. (1998). *Designs for self-instruction: Principles, processes, and issues in developing self-directed learning.* Boston: Allyn & Bacon.

Keller-Margulis, M., Shapiro, E., & Hintze, P. (2008). Long term diagnostic accuracy of curriculum-based measures in reading and mathematics. *School Psychology Review,* Fall, pp. 1–13.

Kennedy, M. (Ed.). (1991). *Teaching academic subjects to diverse learners.* New York: Teachers College Press.

Kenny, J. (2004, June). Mind-mapping: Cortical clobber. *Times Educational Supplement Online*, 4588, p. 29.

Ketterlin-Geller, A. (2005). Knowing what all students know: Procedures for developing universal design for assessment. *The Journal of Technology, Learning and Assessment, 18*, pp. 1–22.

Khan, B. H. (Ed.) (1997). *Web-based instruction.* Englewood Cliffs, NJ: Educational Technology Publication, Inc.

Kieff, J. (2006). Let's talk about friendship: An anti-bias unit on building classroom community. *Early Childhood Education Journal.* January, 2006, pp. 1–8.

Kilpatrick, J., Martin, W. G., & Schifter, D. (2003). *A research companion to principles and standards for school mathematics.* Reston, VA: National Council of Teachers of Mathematics.

Kincheloe, J. & Steinberg, S. (2007). *Cutting class: socioeconomic status and education.* Lanham, MD: Rowman & Littlefield.

King, B. (2009). Authentic intellectual work: Common standards for teaching social studies. *Social Education.* Silver Spring, MD: National Council for the Social Studies.

King, K. (2006). *Integrating the National Science Education Standards in classroom practice.* Upper Saddle River, NJ: Prentice-Hall.

Kirsch, T. (2005, April). President's message: Seniority and transfers are under attack. *The PFT Reporter: Official Publication of the Philadelphia Federation of Teachers.* Retrieved from www.pft.org/archrept/rep0404/presrep.html.

Knapczyk, D., & Rodes, P. (2001). *Teaching social competence.* Verona, WI: Attainment Company.

Knapp, M., & Woolverton, S. (2001). Social class and schooling. In J. Banks & C. Banks (Eds.), *Handbook of research on multicultural education* (pp. 548–569). San Francisco: Jossey-Bass.

Knowles, M. (1975). *Self-directed learning: A guide for learners and teachers.* New York: Association Press.

Koschmann, T. (Ed.) (1996). *CSCL: Theory and practice of an emerging paradigm.* Hillsdale, NJ: Lawrence Erlbaum Associates, Inc.

Kottler, J., & Zehm, S. (2005). *On being a teacher: The human dimension.* Thousand Oaks, CA: Corwin.

Kounin, J. (1970). *Discipline and group management in the classroom.* New York: Holt, Rinehart & Winston.

Kozma, R. B. (1991). Learning with media. *Review of Educational Research, 61,* pp. 179–211.

Kozma, R. B. (1994), The influence of media on learning: The debate continues. *School Library Media Research, 22*(4), pp. 233–239.

Kozulin, A. (1990). *Vygotsky's psychology: A biography of ideas.* Cambridge, MA: Harvard University Press.

Kozulin, A., Gindis, B., Ageyev, V., & Miller, S. (Eds.). (2003). *Vygotsky's educational theory in cultural context.* New York: Cambridge University Press.

Krasnic, T. (2011). *How to study with mind maps: The concise learning method.* Amazon Digital Services: Concise Books Publishing.

Krathwohl, D., Bloom, B., & Masia, B. (1999). *Taxonomy of educational objectives book 2/Affective domain.* Boston: Addison-Wesley.

Krauss, J. & Conery, L. (2008). *Reinventing project-based learning: Your field guide to real-world projects in the digital age.* Washington, DC: International Society for Technology in Education.

Kreidler, W. (2005). *Creative conflict resolution* (2nd ed.). Tucson, AZ: Good Year Books.

Kubiszyn, T., & Borich, G. (2013). *Educational testing and measurement: Classroom applications and practice* (10th ed.). Hoboken, NJ: Wiley.

Kuh, G., Kinzie, J., Smith, J., & Whitt, E. (2005). *Assessing conditions to enhance educational effectiveness: The inventory for student engagement and success.* San Francisco: Jossey-Bass.

Kumpulainen, K. (2001). *Classroom interaction and social learning: From theory to practice.* New York: RoutledgeFalmer.

Lajoie, S. (1993). Computer environments as cognitive tools for enhancing learning. In S. Lajoie & S. J. Derry (Eds.), *Computers as Cognitive Tools.* Hillsdale, NJ: Lawrence Erlbaum Associates, Inc. (pp. 261–288).

Lambros, A. (2002). *Problem-based learning in middle and high school classrooms: A teacher's guide to implementation.* Thousand Oaks, CA: Corwin.

Landrum, T., & Kauffman, J. (2006). In C. Evertson & C. Weinstein (Eds.), *Handbook of classroom management.* Mahwah, NJ: Lawrence Erlbaum Associates.

Landsman, J. & Lewis, C. (2011). *White teachers/diverse classrooms: Creating inclusive schools, building on students' diversity, and providing true educational equity* (2nd ed.). Sterling, VA: Stylus Publishing.

Lankes, A. (1995). Electronic portfolios: A new idea in assessment. *ERIC Digest, 95*(9), pp. 1–4. (ERIC Document Reproduction Service No. ED 390 377)

Lantieri, L., & Goleman, D. (2008). *Building emotional intelligence: Techniques to cultivate inner strength in children.* Boulder, CO: Sounds True.

Larson, J., & Irvine, P. D. (1999). "We call him Dr. King": Reciprocal distancing in urban classrooms. *Language Arts, 75*(5), pp. 393–400.

Lavin, J., & Nolan, J. (2003). *Principles of classroom management: Professional decision-making model.* Boston: Allyn & Bacon.

Lawrence-Lightfoot, S. (2003). *The essential conversation: What parents and teachers can learn from each other.* New York: Random House.

Lazear, D. (1992). *Teaching for multiple intelligences. Fastback No. 342.* Bloomington, IN: Phi Delta Kappa Educational Foundation.

Leiding, D. (2006). *Racial bias in the classroom: Can teachers reach all children?* Lanham, MD: R&L Education.

Leriche, L. (1992). The sociology of classroom discipline. *The High School Journal, 75*(2), pp. 77–89.

Letts, N. (1999). *Creating a caring classroom (Grades K–6).* New York: Scholastic.

Levin, H. (1986). *Educational reform for disadvantaged students: An emerging crisis.* Washington, DC: National Education Association.

Levin, J., & Nolan, J. F. (2006). *Principles of classroom management: A hierarchical approach.* Boston: Allyn & Bacon.

Levine, D. (1985). *Improving student achievement through mastery learning programs.* San Francisco: Jossey-Bass.

Levine, D. (2009). *Building classroom communities: Strategies for developing a culture of caring.* Bloomington, IN: Solution Tree.

Levine, D., & Lezotte, L. (2001). Effective schools research. In J. Banks & C. Banks (Eds.), *Handbook of research on multicultural education* (pp. 525–549). San Francisco: Jossey-Bass.

Levis, D. S. (1987). Teachers' personality. In M. J. Dunkin (Ed.), *Encyclopedia of teaching and teacher education* (pp. 585–588). New York: Pergamon.

Lewin, L. (2009). *Teaching comprehension with questioning strategies that motivate middle school readers.* New York: Scholastic Teaching Resources.

Libal, A. (2007). *Runaway train: Youth with emotional disturbance (Youth with special needs).* Broomall, PA: Mason Crest Publishers.

Lightfoot, P. (2006). *Student portfolios: A learning tool.* Bloomington, IN: BookSurge Publishing.

Lindsley, O. R. (1991). Precision teaching's unique legacy from B. F. Skinner. *Journal of Behavioral Education, 1,* pp. 253–266.

Lindsley, O. R. (1992). Why aren't effective teaching tools widely adopted? *Journal of Applied Behavior Analysis,* 25(1), pp. 21–26.

Lippitt, R., & Gold, M. (1959). Classroom social structure as a mental health problem. *Journal of Social Issues, 15,* pp. 40–58.

Llewellyn, D. (2007). *Inquire within: Implementing inquiry-based science standards.* Thousand Oaks, CA: Corwin.

Lockwood, A. T., & Secada, W. G. (1999, January). Transforming education for Hispanic youth: Exemplary practices, programs, and schools. *NCBE Resource Collection Series, No. 12.* Washington, DC: National Clearinghouse for Bilingual Education.

Logan, J. (2003). Classroom management: Techniques, policies, procedures, and programs to ensure that discipline "rules" your classroom. Education Resources Information Center. (ERIC Document Reproduction Service No. ED 479 639)

Losey, K. (1995). Mexican American students and classroom interaction: An overview and critique. *Review of Educational Research,* 65(3), pp. 283–318.

Lou, Y., Abrami, P., & Spence, J. (2000). Effects of within-class grouping on student achievement: An exploratory model. *Journal of Educational Research, 94,* pp. 101–112.

Lubliner, S., & Palincsar, A. (2001). *A practical guide to reciprocal teaching.* New York: McGraw-Hill.

Lustig, M., & Koester, J. (2009). *Intercultural competence: Interpersonal communication across cultures* (6th ed.). Boston: Allyn & Bacon.

Lyman, F. (1981). The responsive classroom discussion. In A. Anderson (Ed.), *Mainstreaming digest.* College Park: University of Maryland College of Education.

Lysakowski, R., & Walberg, H. (1981). Classroom reinforcement and learning: A quantitative synthesis. *Journal of Educational Research, 75,* pp. 69–77.

Mackenzie, R. & Stabzuibe, L. (2010). *Setting limits in the classroom: A complete guide to effective classroom management with a school-wide discipline plan* (3rd ed.). New York: Three Rivers Press.

Mager, R. (1997). *Preparing instructional objectives.* Atlanta, GA: CEP Press.

Manning, L., & Bucher, K. (2006). *Classroom management: Models, applications, and cases.* Upper Saddle River, NJ: Prentice Hall.

Martinello, M., & Cook, G. (2000). *Interdisciplinary inquiry in teaching and learning* (2nd ed.). Upper Saddle River, NJ: Merrill/Prentice Hall.

Marx, R., & Walsh, J. (1988). Learning from academic tasks. *The Elementary School Journal,* 88(3), pp. 207–219.

Marzano, R. (2009). *On excellence in teaching.* Bloomington, IN: Solution Tree.

Marzano, R., & Kendall, J. (2006). *The new taxonomy of educational objectives.* Thousand Oaks, CA: Corwin.

Marzano, R. & Kendall, J. (2008). *Designing and assessing educational objectives: Applying the new taxonomy.* Thousand Oaks, CA: Corwin.

Marzano, R., Pickering, J., & Heflebower, T. (2010). *The highly engaged classroom (classroom strategies).* Centennial, CO: Marzano Research Laboratory.

Marzano, R., Pickering, J., & Pollock, J. (2004). *Classroom instruction that works: Research-based strategies for increasing student achievement.* Alexandria, VA: Association for Supervision and Curriculum Development.

Masahiko, M., & Ovando, C. (2001). Language issues in multicultural contexts. In J. Banks & C. Banks (Eds.), *Handbook of research on multicultural education* (pp. 427–444). San Francisco: Jossey-Bass.

Maurer, R. E. (1985). *Elementary discipline handbook: Solutions for the K–8 teacher.* West Nyack, NY: The Center for Applied Research in Education.

Mayer, R. & Alexander, P. (2010). *Handbook of research on learning and instruction.* New York: Routledge.

Mayer, R. E., & Moreno, R. (2003). Nine ways to reduce cognitive load in multimedia learning. *Educational Psychologist,* 38(1), pp. 43–52.

Mayer, R., & Wittrock, M. (1996). Problem-solving transfer. In D. Berliner & R. Calfee (Eds.), *Handbook of educational psychology* (pp. 47–62). New York: Macmillan.

Maynard, A., & Martini, M. (Eds). (2005). *Learning in cultural context: Family, peers and school.* New York: Springer.

McGrath, C. (2007). *The inclusion-classroom problem solver: Structures and supports to serve all learners.* Portsmouth, NH: Heinemann.

McNary, S., Glasgow, N., & Hicks, C. (2005). *What successful teachers do in inclusive classrooms: 60 research-based teaching strategies that help special learners succeed.* Thousand Oaks, CA: Corwin.

McPherson, F. (2011). *Effective notetaking.* Wellington, New Zealand: Wayz Press.

Means, B. & Haertel, G. (2004) *Using technology evaluation to enhance student learning.* New York: Teachers College Press.

Medrich, E. A., Roizen, J. A., Rubin, V., & Burkley, S. (1982). *The serious business of growing up: A study of children's lives outside school.* Berkeley: University of California Press.

Megnin, J. (1995). Combining memory and creativity in teaching math. *Teaching PreK–8,* 25(6), pp. 48–49.

Meichenbaum, D., & Biemiller, A. (1998). *Nurturing independent learners: Helping students take charge of their learning.* Cambridge, MA: Brookline.

Mendler, A. (2001). *Connection with Students.* Alexandria, VA: ASCD.

Mendler, B., Curwin, R., & Mendler, A. (2007). *Strategies for successful classroom management.* Thousand Oaks, CA: Corwin.

Mercado, C. (2001). The learner: "Race," "ethnicity," and linguistic difference. In V. Richardson (Ed.), *Handbook of research on teaching* (pp. 668–694). Washington, DC: American Educational Research Association.

Messick, S. (1995). Cognitive styles and learning. In L. Anderson (Ed.), *International encyclopedia of teaching and teacher education* (2nd ed., pp. 387–390). Tarrytown, NY: Elsevier Science.

Michaels, S., & Collins, J. (1984). Oral discourse styles: Classroom interaction and the acquisition of literacy. In D. Tamen (Ed.), *Coherence in spoken and written discourse.* Norwood, NJ: Ablex.

Miller, H. M. (2000). Teaching and learning about cultural diversity: All of us together have a story to tell. *The Reading Teacher,* 53(6), pp. 666–667.

Miller, M. J. (1992). *Model standards for beginning teacher licensing and development: A resource for state dialogue.* [Online]. Available at www.ccsso.org.

Minami, M., & Ovando, C. (2003). Language issues in multicultural contexts. In J. Banks & C. Banks (Eds.), *Handbook of research on multicultural issues* (pp. 427–444). San Francisco: Jossey-Bass.

Mintzes, J., Wandersee, J., & Novak, J. (2000). *Assessing science understanding.* San Diego, CA: Academic Press.

Mislevy, R., Steinberg, L., Almond, R., Haertel, G., & Penuel, W. (2000, February). Leverage points for improving educational assessment. Paper prepared for the Technology Design Workshop, Stanford Research Institute, Menlo Park, CA.

Mooney, C. (2000). *Theories of childhood: An introduction to Dewey, Montessori, Erikson, Piaget and Vygotsky.* St. Paul, MN: Redleaf Press.

Moore, K. (2006). *Classroom teaching skills* (6th ed.). New York: McGraw-Hill.

Moran, C., & Hakuta, K. (2001). Bilingual education: Broadening research perspectives. In J. Banks & C. Banks (Eds.), *Handbook of research on multicultural education* (pp. 445–462). San Francisco: Jossey-Bass.

Moran-Ellis, J. (2007). *Children and social competence.* London, UK: Taylor & Francis

Mshelia, A. (2008). *Cognition, culture and field dependence-independence.* Bloomington, IN: Authorhouse.

Muijs, D., & Reynolds, D. (2005). *Effective teaching: Evidence and practice* (2nd ed.). Thousand Oaks, CA: Sage.

Muschla, J., & Muschla, G. (2006). *Hands-on math projects with real-life applications: Grades.* San Francisco: Jossey-Bass.

Nash, R. (2008). *The active classroom: Practical strategies for involving students in the learning process.* Thousand Oaks, CA: Corwin.

National Board for Professional Teaching Standards. (2001). *Five core propositions.* [Online]. Available at www.nbpts.org.

National Center for Leadership in Education. (2011). *Rigor/Relevance Framework.* Rexford, NY: Author.

National Council for the Social Studies. (2010). *National curriculum standards for social studies teachers.* Silver Springs, MD: Author.

National Council of Teachers of English. (2011). *Standards for the English language arts.* Urbana, IL: Author.

National Council of Teachers of English. (2009). *Guidelines for the preparation of teachers of English language arts.* Urbana, IL: Author.

National Council of Teachers of Mathematics. (2009). *Assessment standards for school mathematics.* Reston, VA: National Council of Teachers of Mathematics.

National Council of Teachers of Mathematics. (2009). *Illuminating NCTM's principles and standards for school mathematics.* Reston, VA: Author.

National Mental Health Information Center, U.S. Department of Health and Human Services. (2005). *Tips for teachers.* Available at www.mentalhealth.org/cmhs/TraumaticEvents/teachers.asp.

National Research Council. (2011). *Next generation national science education standards.* Washington, DC: National Academies Press.

National Research Council. (1999). *Knowing what your students know.* Washington, DC: National Academies Press.

National Research Council. (2001). *Knowing what students know: The science and design of educational assessment.* Washington, DC: National Academies Press.

Neisser, U. (1976). *Cognition and reality.* San Francisco: W. H. Freeman.

Nessel, D., & Graham, J. (2006). *Thinking strategies for student achievement.* Thousand Oaks, CA: Corwin.

Neuliep, J. (2008). *Intercultural communication: A contextual approach.* Thousand Oaks, CA: Sage.

Nieto, S., & Bode, P. (2012). *Affirming diversity: The sociopolitical context of multicultural education* (6th ed.). Boston: Allyn & Bacon.

North American Council for Online Learning. (2011). *National standards for quality online teaching.* Vienna, VA: Author. Retrieved April 23, 2012, from http://www.inacol.org/research/nationalstandards/iNACOL_TeachingStandardsv2.pdf.

Nosich, G. (2012). *Learning to think things through: A guide to critical thinking across the curriculum* (4th ed.). Upper Saddle River, NJ: Prentice-Hall.

Novak, J. (2009). *Learning, creating, and using knowledge: Concept maps as facilitative tools in schools and corporations.* Mahwah, NJ: Lawrence Erlbaum.

Novak, J. D., & Gowin, D. B. (1984). *Learning how to learn.* New York and Cambridge, UK: Cambridge University Press.

Novak, J. D., & Musonda, D. (1991). A twelve-year longitudinal study of science concept learning. *American Educational Research Journal, 28*(1), pp. 117–153.

Nunn, G., & Kimberly, R. (2000, December). "IDEAL" problem solving using a collaborative effort for special needs and at-risk students. *Education,* pp. 10–16.

Oakes, J., & Lipton, M. (2006). *Teaching to change the world.* Boston: McGraw-Hill.

Obiakor, F. (2006). *Multicultural special education: Culturally responsive teaching.* Upper Saddle River, NJ: Prentice Hall.

Oczkus, L. (2005). *Reciprocal teaching at work: Strategies for interpreting reading comprehension.* Newark, DE: International Reading Association.

Oczkus, L. (2010). *Reciprocal teaching at work: Powerful strategies and lessons for improving reading comprehension* (2nd ed.). Newark, DE: International Reading Association.

Ogbu, J. (1995a). Cultural problems in minority education: Their interpretations and consequences—Part one: Theoretical background. *The Urban Review, 27*(3), pp. 189–205.

Ogbu, J. (1995b). Cultural problems in minority education: Their interpretations and consequences—Part two: Case studies. *The Urban Review, 27*(4), pp. 271–297.

Ogbu, J. (2008). *Minority status, oppositional culture and schooling.* New York: Routledge.

Ogbu, J., & Davis, A. (2003). *Black American students in an affluent suburb: A study of disengagement.* Mahwah, NJ: Lawrence Erlbaum.

Olneck, M. (2001). Immigrants in education. In J. Banks & C. Banks (Eds.), *Handbook of research on multicultural education.* San Francisco: Jossey-Bass.

Ong, A., & Borich, G. (Eds.). (2006). *Teaching strategies that promote thinking.* Boston: McGraw-Hill.

Ormrod, J. (2010a). *Educational psychology: Developing learners* (7th ed.). Upper Saddle River, NJ: Prentice Hall.

Ormrod, J. (2010b). *Human learning* (6th ed.). Upper Saddle River, NJ: Prentice Hall.

O'Reilly, T. (2005). What is Web 2.0? Retrieved May 9, 2010, from http://oreilly.com/web2/archive/what-is-web-20.html.

Palincsar, A., & Brown, A. (1989). Classroom dialogues to promote self-regulated comprehension. In J. Brophy (Ed.), *Advances in research on teaching* (Vol. 1, pp. 35–71). Greenwich, CT: JAI Press.

Palloff, R. M., & Pratt, K. (2003). *The virtual student: A profile and guide to working with on line learners.* San Francisco: Jossey-Bass.

Palloff, R. M., & Pratt, K. (2005). *Collaborating online: Learning together in community.* San Francisco: Jossey-Bass.

Parkay, F., & Hass, G. (2005). *Curriculum planning: A contemporary approach* (7th ed.). Boston: Allyn & Bacon.

Parker, W. (1991). *Renewing the social studies curriculum.* Alexandria, VA: Association for Supervision and Curriculum Development.

Parker, W. (2009). *Social studies today: Research and practice.* New York: Routledge.

Patton, J. R. (1994). Practical recommendations for using homework with students with learning disabilities. *Journal of Learning Disabilities,* 27(9), 570–578.

Paul, R. (1990). *Critical thinking.* Rohnert Park, CA: Center for Critical Thinking and Moral Critique, Sonoma State University.

Paulu, N. (1998). *Helping your students with homework: A guide for teachers.* Washington, DC: U.S. Department of Education, Office of Educational Research. Retrieved September 19, 2000, from www.ed.gov/pubs/HelpingStudents.

Phillips, D. (2000). *Constructivism in education.* Chicago: National Society for the Study of Education, University of Chicago Press.

Piaget, J. (1977). Problems in equilibration. In M. Appel & L. Goldberg (Eds.), *Topics in cognitive development: Vol. 1. Equilibration: Theory, research and application* (pp. 3–13). New York: Plenum.

Piestrup, A. (1973). *Black dialect interference and accommodation of reading instruction in first grade* (Monograph No. 4). Berkeley: University of California, Language Behavior Research Laboratory.

Pintrich, P., & Schunk, D. (2007). *Motivation in education: Theory, research, and applications* (3rd ed.). Upper Saddle River, NJ: Merrill/Prentice Hall.

Pitler, H., Hubbel, E., Kuhn. M., & Malenoski, K. (2007). *Using technology with classroom instruction that works.* Alexandria, VA: ASCD.

Polanyi, M. (1958). *Personal knowledge.* Chicago: University of Chicago Press.

Pollock, J. E. (1992). Blueprints for social studies. *Educational Leadership,* 49(8), 52–53.

Popham, J. (2009) *Instruction that measures up: Successful teaching in the age of accountability.* Alexandria, VA: ASCD.

Poplack, S. (2000). *The English history of African-American English.* Hoboken, NJ: Wiley.

Portes, A., & Rumbaut, R. (2006). *Immigrant America: A portrait.* Berkeley: University of California Press.

Posamentier, A., & Krulik, S. (2008). *Problem-solving strategies for efficient and elegant solutions, Grades 6–12: A resource for the mathematics teacher.* Thousand Oaks, CA: Corwin.

Postholm, M. B. (2008). Teachers developing practice: Reflection as key activity. *Teaching and Teacher Education,* 24, pp. 1717–1728.

Powell, E. (2009). *Friends and peer pressure: Junior high group study.* Ventura, CA: Gospel Light.

Powell, S. (2010). *Wayside teaching: Connecting with students to support learning.* Thousand Oaks, CA: Corwin.

Power, B., & Hubbard, R. (1999). *Living the questions: A guide for teacher-researchers.* Portland, ME: Stenhouse.

Prensky, M. (2001). Digital natives, digital immigrants. *On the Horizon,* 9, pp. 1–6.

Price, K. & Nelson, K (2011). *Planning effective instruction: Diversity responsive methods and management.* Florence, KY: Wadsworth.

Prinstein, N., & Dodge, K. (2008). *Understanding peer influence in children and adolescents.* New York: Guilford Press.

Putnam, J. (2006). *Organizing and managing classroom learning communities.* New York: McGraw-Hill.

Raven, B. H. (1974). The comparative analysis of power and power preference. In J. T. Tedeschi (Ed.), *Perspectives on social power* (pp. 172–198). Chicago: Aldine.

Ready, D., Beghetto, R., & LoGerfo, L. (2005, August). Race and social learning: Ability grouping and contextual effects. Paper presented at the annual meeting of the American Sociological Association, Chicago.

Redding, N. (1992). Assessing the big outcomes. *Educational Leadership,* 49(8), pp. 49–53.

Rekrut, M. (1999). Using the Internet in classroom instruction: A primer for teachers. *Journal of Adolescent and Adult Literacy,* 42(7), pp. 546–557.

Resnick, L., & Klopfer, L. (Eds.). (1989). *Toward the thinking curriculum: Current cognitive research.* Arlington, VA: Association for Supervision and Curriculum Development.

Reynolds, N., & Rich, R. (2006). *Portfolio keeping: A guide for students.* New York: Bedford/St. Martin's Press.

Richardson, V. (1997). Constructivist teaching and teacher education: Theory and practice. In V. Richardson (Ed.), *Constructivist teacher education: Building new understandings* (pp. 3–14). Washington, DC: Falmer Press.

Riggs, E. & Gholar, C. (2008). *Strategies that promote student engagement.* Thousand Oaks, CA: Corwin.

Rinne, C. (1997). *Excellent classroom management.* Belmont, CA: Wadsworth.

Ritter, N. (1999). Teaching interdisciplinary thematic units in language arts. *ERIC Digest D142.* Bloomington, IN: ERIC Clearinghouse on Reading, English, and Communication. (ERIC Document Reproduction Service No. ED 436 003)

Roberts, P., & Kellough, R. (2006). *A guide for developing interdisciplinary thematic units* (3rd ed.). Upper Saddle River, NJ: Merrill/Prentice Hall.

Roblyer, M. (2003). *Integrating educational technology into teaching.* Upper Saddle River, NJ: Merrill/Prentice Hall.

Roblyer, M. (2005). *Integrating educational technology into teaching* (4th ed.). Upper Saddle River, NJ: Merrill/Prentice Hall.

Roblyer, M., Edwards, J., & Havriluk, M. (1997). *Integrating educational technology into teaching* (3rd ed.). Upper Saddle River, NJ: Merrill/Prentice Hall.

Rogan, J., Borich, G., & Taylor, H. P. (1992). Validation of the stages of concern questionnaire. *Action in Teacher Education,* 14(2), pp. 43–49.

Rogoff, B. (1990). *Apprenticeship in thinking: Cognitive development in social context.* New York: Oxford University Press.

Rohrkemper, M., & Corno, L. (1988). Success and failure on classroom tasks: Adaptive learning and classroom teaching. *The Elementary School Journal,* 83, pp. 335–351.

Ronis, D. (2007). *Problem based learning for math and science: Integrating inquiry and the internet.* Thousand Oaks, CA: Corwin.

Rose, L., & Gallup, A. (2002). The 32nd annual Phi Delta Kappa/Gallup poll of the public's attitudes toward the public schools. *Phi Delta Kappan,* 84, pp. 41–46, 51–56.

Rosenshine, B. (1971). *Teaching behaviors and student achievement.* London: National Foundation for Educational Research in England and Wales.

Rosenshine, B. (1983). Teaching functions in instructional programs. *The Elementary School Journal,* 83, pp. 335–351.

Rosenshine, B. (1986). Synthesis of research on explicit teaching. *Educational Leadership,* 43(7), pp. 60–69.

Rosenshine, B. (1995). Advances in research on instruction. *Journal of Educational Research,* 88(5), pp. 262–268.

Rosenshine, B. (1997, March). The case for explicit, teacher-led, cognitive strategy instruction. Paper presented at the annual meeting of the American Educational Research Association, Chicago.

Rosenshine, B., & Meister, C. (1992). The use of scaffolds for teaching higher-level cognitive strategies. *Educational Leadership,* 49(7), pp. 26–33.

Rosenshine, B., & Meister, C. (1994). Reciprocal teaching: A review of the research. *Review of Educational Research,* 64, pp. 479–530.

Rosenshine, B., & Stevens, R. (1986). Teaching functions. In M. C. Wittrock (Ed.), *Handbook of research on teaching* (3rd ed., pp. 376–391). Upper Saddle River, NJ: Merrill/Prentice Hall.

Ross, W. (2006). *The social studies curriculum: Purposes, problems, and possibilities.* Albany: State University of New York Press.

Rothstein-Fisch, C. & Trumbull, E. (2008). *Managing diverse classrooms: How to build on students' cultural strengths.* Alexandria, VA: ASCD.

Rovai, A. P. (2000). Building and sustaining community in asynchronous learning networks. *Internet and Higher Education,* 3, pp. 285–297.

Rovai, A. P. (2007). Facilitating online discussions effectively. *Internet and Higher Education,* 10, pp. 77–88.

Rowe, M. B. (1986, January-February). Wait time: Slowing down may be a way of speeding up. *Journal of Teacher Education,* 23, pp. 43–49.

Rowe, M. B. (1987). Wait time: Slowing down may be a way of speeding up. *American Educator,* 11(1), pp. 38–43, 47.

Rozakis, L., & Cain, D. (2002). *Super study skills.* New York: Scholastic.

Ryan, M. (2007). *Ask the teacher: A practitioner's guide to teaching and learning in the diverse classroom.* Boston, MA: Allyn & Bacon.

Ryan, K. (1992). *The roller coaster year: Essays by and for beginning teachers.* New York: HarperCollins.

Sable, J., & Hoffman, L. (2008). *Characteristics of 100 largest public elementary school districts in the United States: 2005–2006.* Washington, DC: National Center for Educational Statistics, U.S. Department of Education.

Sacks, S. R., & Harrington, C. N. (1982, March). Student to teacher: The process of role transition. Paper presented at the meeting of the American Educational Research Association, New York.

Saito, L. T. (1999). Socio-cultural factors in the educational achievement of Vietnamese American students (Doctoral dissertation, University of California, Irvine, 1999). *Dissertation Abstracts International,* 60 (08), 2802A.

Salmon, G. (2004). *E-moderating: The key to teaching and learning online.* London: Taylor & Francis.

Santos, R. M., & Reese, D. (1999). Selecting culturally and linguistically appropriate materials: Suggestions for service providers. *ERIC Digest.* Washington, DC: Office of Educational Research and Improvement & U.S. Department of Education. (ERIC Document Reproduction Service No. ED 431 546)

Sartor, L., & Brown, M. Y. (2004). *Consensus in the classroom: Fostering a lively learning community.* Mt. Shasta, CA: Psychosynthesis Press.

Saunders, P. (2005). *Characteristics of effective teaching.* Kalamazoo: Western Michigan University, Center for Teaching and Learning.

Saunders, W., & Goldenberg, C. (1999). *The effects of instructional conversations and literature logs on the story comprehension and thematic understanding of English proficient and limited English proficient students.* Washington, DC: Center for Research on Education, Diversity and Excellence.

Saunders, W., O'Brien, G., Lennon, D., & McLean, J. (1999). *Successful transition into mainstream English: Effective strategies for studying literature.* Washington, DC: Center for Research on Education, Diversity and Excellence.

Savage, T. (1999). *Teaching self-control through management and discipline.* Boston: Allyn & Bacon.

Savery, J. R., & Duffy, T. M. (1995). Problem-based learning: An instructional model and its constructivist framework. *Educational Technology,* 35(5), pp. 31–38.

Scarr, S. (1981). Testing for children: Assessment and the many determinants of intellectual competence. *American Psychologist,* 36(10), pp. 1159–1166.

Schargel, F. (2003). *Dropout prevention tools.* Larchmont, NY: Eye on Education.

Schargel, F. (2005). *Best practices to help at-risk learners.* Larchmont, NY: Eye on Education.

Schmid, E. C. (2008). Using a voting system in conjunction with interactive whiteboard technology to enhance learning in the English language classroom. *Computers & Education,* 50, pp. 338–356.

Schmidt, P. & Lazar, A, (2011). *Practicing what we teach: Culturally responsive literacy classrooms make a difference.* New York: Teachers College Press.

Schmuck, R., & Schmuck, P. (2001). *Group processes in the classroom* (6th ed.). New York: McGraw-Hill

Schon, D.A. (1987). *Educating the reflective practitioner.* San Francisco: Jossey-Bass.

Schwartz, W. (1998, November 13). The identy development of multiracial youth. *ERIC/CUE Digest.* New York: ERIC Clearinghouse on Urban Education.

Schroeder, A., Minocha, S., & Schneidert, C. (2010). The strengths, weaknesses, opportunities and threats of using social software in higher and further education teaching and learning. *Journal of Computer Assisted Learning,* 26, pp. 159–174.

Seganti, C. (2011). *Classroom discipline 101.* Amazon Digital Services: Kindle Education

Serdvukov, P., & Ryan, M. (2007). *Writing effective lesson plans: The 5-star approach.* Boston: Allyn & Bacon.

Shade, B. J. (1982). Afro-American cognitive style: A variable in school success. *Review of Educational Research,* 52, pp. 219–244.

Shalaway, L. (1999). *Learning to teach.* New York: Scholastic.

Shank, P. (2007). *The online learning idea book: 95 proven ways to enhance technology-based and blended learning.* Hoboken, NJ: John Wiley & Sons, Inc.

Shapiro, E., Keller, M., Edwards, I., Lutz, G., & Hintze, J. (2006). General outcome measures and performance on state assessment and standardized tests. Reading and math performance in Pennsylvania. *Journal of Psychoeducational Assessment,* 42(1), 19–35.

Shavelson, R. J., & Baxter, G. P. (1992). What we've learned about assessing hands-on science. *Educational Leadership,* 49(8), pp. 20–25.

Shavelson, R. J., Gao, X., & Baxter, G. (1991). *Design theory and psychometrics for complex performance assessment.* Los Angeles: UCLA Center for Research on Evaluation, Standards and Student Testing.

Shifflet, M., & Brown, J. (2006). The use of instructional simulations to support classroom teaching: A crisis communication case study. *Journal of Educational Multimedia and Hypermedia,* 15(4), pp. 377–396.

Shlomo, S. (Ed.). (1999). *Handbook of cooperative learning methods.* Westport, CT: Praeger.

Shulman, L. S. (1992). Toward a pedagogy of cases. In J. H. Shulman (Ed.), *Case methods in teacher education* (pp. 72–92). New York: Teachers College Press.

Shulman, L. S. (1987). Knowledge and teaching: Foundations of the new reform. *Harvard Educational Review,* 57(1), pp. 1–22.

Simonson, M., Smaldino, S. E., Albright, M., & Zvacek, S. (2011). *Teaching and learning at a distance: Foundations of distance education.* Boston: Allyn & Bacon.

Skinner, B. F. (1953). *Science and human behavior.* Upper Saddle River, NJ: Merrill/Prentice Hall.

Skirtic, T. (1991). The special education paradox: Equity as the way to excellence. *Harvard Educational Review,* 61(2), pp. 148–206.

Slavin, R. (1990). Achievement effects of ability grouping in secondary schools: A best evidence synthesis. *Review of Educational Research,* 60, pp. 471–499.

Slavin, R. (1991). *Educational psychology: Theory into practice.* Upper Saddle River, NJ: Prentice Hall.

Slavin, R. (1993). *Student team learning: An overview and practical guide.* Washington, DC: National Education Association.

Slavin, R. (2001). Cooperative learning and intergroup relations. In J. Banks & C. Banks (Eds.), *Handbook of research on multicultural education.* San Francisco: Jossey-Bass.

Smilansky, M. (1979). *Priorities in education: Preschool, evidence and conclusions.* Washington, DC: World Bank.

Smyth, J. (1989). Developing and sustaining critical reflection in teacher education. *Journal of Teacher Education,* 40(2), pp. 2–9.

Soar, R., & Soar, R. (1983). Context effects in the learning process. In D. C. Smith (Ed.), *Essential knowledge for beginning educators* (pp. 156–192). Washington, DC: American Association of Colleges of Teacher Education.

Spiro, J., Feltovich, P.J., Jacobson, M.J., & Coulson, R.L. (1991). Cognitive flexibility, constructivism and hypertext: Random access instruction for advanced knowledge acquisition in ill-structured domains. *Educational Technology,* 31(9), pp. 22–25.

Southern Regional Education Board (2007). *Five academic reasons: Why state virtual schools are important to your state.* Atlanta, GA: Author. Retrieved August 15, 2008, from http://www.sreb.org/programs/EdTech/pubs/2007pubs/07T07_Five_acad_reas.pdf.

Sprenger, M. (2008). *Differentiation through learning styles and memory.* Thousand Oaks, CA: Corwin.

Stadler, F. (2011). *Induction and deduction in the sciences.* New York: Springer.

Stahl, R. (Ed.). (1994). *Cooperative learning in social studies: A handbook for teachers.* Menlo Park, CA: Addison-Wesley.

Stahl, R. (Ed.). (1995). *Cooperative learning in language arts: A handbook for teachers.* Menlo Park, CA: Innovative Learning Publications.

Stahl, R. (Ed.). (1996). *Cooperative learning in science: A handbook for teachers.* Menlo Park, CA: Innovative Learning Publications.

Steffe, L., & Gale, J. (Eds.). (1995). *Constructivism in education.* Mahwah, NJ: Lawrence Erlbaum.

Stepien, W. (2008). *Problem-based learning with the Internet, grades 3–6.* Waco, TX: Prufrock Press.

Sternberg, R. (1994). *Thinking and problem solving.* San Diego, CA: Academic Press.

Sternberg, R. (1995). *The nature of insight.* Cambridge, MA: MIT Press.

Sternberg, R., & Grigorenko, E. (2007). *Teaching for successful intelligence: To increase student learning and achievement.* Thousand Oaks, CA: Corwin.

Stevens, R., & Slavin, R. (1995). The cooperative elementary school: Effects on students' achievement, attitudes and social relations. *American Educational Research Journal,* 32(2), pp. 321–351.

Stiggins, R. & Chappuis, J. (2012). *An introduction to student-involved assessment for learning* (6th ed.). Boston: Pearson.

Stipek, D. (1996). Motivation and instruction. In D. C. Berliner & R. C. Calfee (Eds.), *Handbook of educational psychology* (pp. 85–113). New York: Simon & Schuster/Macmillan.

Stipek, D. (2003). *Motivation to learn: Integrating theory and practice* (4th ed.). Boston: Allyn & Bacon.

Stone, R. (2007). *Best practices for teaching mathematics: What award-winning classroom teachers do.* Thousand Oaks, CA: Corwin.

Sugai, G. (1996, Fall-Winter). UO and public schools design just-in-time learning approaches to find solutions to rising student discipline problems. *Education Matters,* 3(1), pp. 10–11.

Sullivan, K. (2000). *The anti-bullying handbook.* New York: Oxford University Press.

Sunal, C., & Haas, M. (2010). *Social studies for the elementary and middle grades: A constructivist approach* (4th ed.). Boston: Allyn & Bacon.

Sunwolf, T. (Ed.) 2008. *Peer Groups: Expanding our study of small group communication.* Thousand Oaks, CA: Corwin.

Synder, T., Dillow, S., & Hoffman. C. (2009). *Digest of education statistics 2008* (NCES 2009). National Center for Educational Statistics, Institute of Education Sciences, U.S. Department of Education, Washington, D.C.

Tannen, D. (2005). *Conversational style: Analyzing talk among friends.* Oxford, UK: Oxford University Press.

Tapscott, D. (1998). *Growing up digital: the rise of the Net generation.* New York: McGraw-Hill.

Tauber, R. (1990). *Classroom management from A to Z.* Chicago: Holt, Rinehart & Winston.

Taylor, B. M., Pearson, P. D., Clark, K. F., & Walpole, S. (1999). Effective schools/accomplished teachers. *The Reading Teacher,* 53(2), pp. 156–159.

Teddlie, C., & Stringfield, S. (1993). *Schools make a difference: Lessons learned from a 10-year study of school effects.* New York: Teachers College Press.

Teo, N. (2006). Problem-based learning. In A. Ong & G. Borich (Eds.), *Teaching strategies that promote thinking* (pp. 68–83). Boston: McGraw-Hill.

Tharp, R. (1997). *From at-risk to excellence: Research, theory, and principles for practice.* Santa Cruz, CA: Center for Research on Education, Diversity and Excellence.

Tharp, R., & Gallimore, R. (1991). *Rousing minds to life: Teaching, learning and schooling in social context.* New York: Cambridge University Press.

Tharp, R. G. (1989). Psychocultural variables and constants: Effects on teaching and learning in schools. *American Psychologist,* 44, pp. 349–359.

Thorndike, R. L. (1913). *The psychology of learning (Educational psychology II).* New York: Teachers College Press.

Thurstone, L. (1947). *Primary mental abilities, Form AH.* Chicago: Science Research Associates.

Tileston, D. (2010). *What every teacher should know about diverse learners.* Thousand Oaks, CA: Corwin.

Tileston, D. (2010). *What every teacher should know about student motivation.* Thousand Oaks, CA: Corwin.

Tischler, M. (2005). *Magnetizing the learner: How teachers can impart enthusiasm to students.* Alexandria, VA: Association for Career and Technical Education.

Tobin, K. (1987). The role of wait-time in higher cognitive level learning. *Review of Educational Research,* 57, pp. 69–95.

Tombari, M., & Borich, G. (1999). *Authentic assessment in the classroom: Practice and applications.* Upper Saddle River, NJ: Merrill/Prentice Hall.

Tomei, L. (Ed.). (2006). *Integrating information and communications technologies into the classroom.* Hershey, PA: IGI Global.

Tomlinson, C. (2010). *Leading and managing a differentiated classroom.* Alexandria, VA: ASCD.

Tomlinson, C. (2004). *How to differentiate instruction in mixed ability classrooms* (2nd ed.). Alexandria, VA: Association for Supervision and Curriculum Development.

Tomlinson, C., & McTighe, J. (2006). *Integrating differentiated instruction and understanding by design.* Alexandria, VA: Association for Supervision and Curriculum Development.

Tremblay, R., Hartup, W., & Archer, J. (2005). *Developmental origins of aggression.* New York: Guilford Press.

Troutman, A., & Alberto, P. (2009). *Applied behavior analysis for teachers.* Upper Saddle River, NJ: Pearson.

Turkel, J., & Peterson, F. (2003). *Note-taking made easy.* Madison: University of Wisconsin Press.

Turner, L. & West, R. (2006). *The family communication sourcebook.* Thousand Oaks, CA: Sage.

Turnbull, A. P., & Turnbull, H. R. (2010). *Families, professionals and exceptionality: Positive outcomes through partnerships and trust* (6th ed.). Upper Saddle River, NJ: Prentice Hall.

Tyler, R. W. (1934). *Constructing achievement tests.* Columbus: Ohio State University Press.

Tyler, R. W. (1974). Considerations in selecting objectives. In D. A. Payne (Ed.), *Curriculum evaluation: Commentaries on purpose, process, product.* Lexington, MA: D.C. Heath.

Tzitzikas, Y., Christophides, V., Flouris, G., Kotzinos, D., Markkanen, H., Plexousakis, D., & Spyratos, N. (2006). Trialogical e-learning and emergent knowledge artifacts. In E. Tomadaki & P. Scott (Eds.), *Innovative approaches for learning and knowledge sharing, ECTEL 2006 Workshops Proceedings.* Greece: University of Patras (pp. 385–399).

U.S. Census Bureau. (2011). *United States Census 2010.* Retrieved from http://2010.census.gov/Press-Release/www/2010/sumfile1.html.

U.S. Department of Education (2011). Characteristics of the 100 Largest Public Elementary and Secondary School Districts in the United States: 2000-2001. Washington, DC: BiblioGov.

U.S. Department of Education, Office of Educational Research and Development, Education Resources Information Center. (1998). *Goals 2000: Reforming education to improve student achievement.* Washington, DC: Author.

Valencia, R. (2010a). *Dismantling contemporary deficit thinking.* New York: Routledge.

Valencia, R. (2010b). *Chicano school failure and success: Past, present, and future.* New York: Routledge.

Verduin, J. (1996). *Helping students develop investigative problem solving and thinking skills in a cooperative setting.* Springfield, IL: C. C. Thomas.

Voltz, L., Sims, M. & Nelson, B. (2010). *Connecting teachers, students, standards: Strategies for success in diverse and inclusive classrooms.* Alexandria, VA: ASCD.

Vygotsky, L. (1978). *Mind in society: the development of higher psychological process.* Cambridge, MA: Harvard University Press.

Vygotsky, L. (1962). *Thought and language.* Cambridge, MA: MIT Press.

Wakefield, J. (1996). *Educational psychology: Learning to be a problem solver.* Boston: Houghton Mifflin.

Walberg, H. (1986). Syntheses of research on teaching. In M. C. Wittrock (Ed.), *Handbook of research on teaching* (3rd ed., pp. 214–229). Upper Saddle River, NJ: Merrill/Prentice Hall.

Walqui, A. (2000). Access and engagement: Program design and instructional approaches for immigrant students in secondary school. In *Topics in immigrant education 4. Language in education: Theory and practice, 94.* Washington, DC: Center for Applied Linguistics.

Walsh, J., & Sattes, B. (2004). *Quality questioning: Research-based practice to engage every learner.* Thousand Oaks, CA: Corwin.

Watkins, R. (2005). *75 e-learning activities: making online learning interactive.* Hoboken, NJ: John Wiley & Sons, Inc.

Waxman, H., Tharp, R., & Hilberg, R. (Eds.). (2004). *Observational research in U.S. classrooms: New approaches for understanding cultural and linguistic diversity.* Cambridge, UK: Cambridge University Press.

Webb, N., Trooper, J., & Fall, R. (1995). Constructive activity and learning in collaborative small groups. *Journal of Educational Psychology,* 87(34), pp. 406–423.

Weinberg, R. (1989). Intelligence and IQ. *American Psychologist,* 44, pp. 98–104.

Weiner, B. (1986). *An attribution theory of motivation and emotion.* New York: Springer-Verlag.

Weinstein, C., Tomlinson-Clarke, S., & Curran, M. (2005). Toward a conception of culturally responsive classroom management. *Journal of Teacher Education, 55*(1), pp. 14–25.

Weisner, T., Gallimore, R., & Jordan, C. (1988). Unpackaging cultural effects on classroom learning: Native Hawaiian peer assistance and child-generated activity. *Anthropology and Education Quarterly, 19,* pp. 327–353.

Weiss, E. M., & Weiss, S. G. (1998). New directions in teacher evaluation. *ERIC Digest.* Washington, DC: ERIC Clearinghouse on Teaching and Teacher Education. (ERIC Document Reproduction Service No. ED 429 052)

Weissglass, J. (1996). Transforming schools into caring learning communities. *Journal for a Just and Caring Education, 2*(2), pp. 175–189.

Wentzel, K., & Wigfield, A. (2009). *Handbook of motivation at school.* New York: Routledge.

Wenger, E. (1998). *Communities of practice.* New York: Cambridge University Press.

Wenger, E., McDermott, R., & Snyder, W. M. (2002). *Cultivating communities of practice.* Boston: Harvard Business School Press.

Werner, E., & Smith, R. (1992). *Overcoming the odds: High-risk children from birth to adulthood.* New York: Cornell University Press.

White, B., & Frederiksen, J. (2000). Metacognitive facilitation: An approach to making science inquiry accessible to all. In J. Minstrell & E. Van Zee (Eds.), *Teaching in the inquiry-based classroom.* Washington, DC: American Association for the Advancement of Science.

Wiggins, G., & McTighe, J. (1998). *Understanding by design.* Alexandria, VA: Association for Supervision and Curriculum Development.

Wilen, W. (1991). *Questioning skills for teachers* (3rd ed.). Washington, DC: National Education Association.

Williams, R. (2007). *Higher order thinking skills: Challenging all students to achieve.* Thousand Oaks, CA: Corwin.

Willis, J. (2006). *Research-based strategies to ignite student learning.* Alexandria, VA: Association for Supervision and Curriculum Development.

Wilson, M., & Bertenthal, M. (2005). *Systems for state science assessment.* Washington, DC: National Academies Press.

Wiske, M. (Ed.). (1997). *Teaching for understanding: Linking research with practice.* San Francisco: Jossey-Bass

Wolpert, E. (2005). *Start seeing diversity: The basic guide to an anti-bias classroom.* St. Paul, MN: Redleaf Press.

Woolfolk, A. (2013). *Educational psychology* (12th ed.). Boston: Allyn & Bacon.

Wong, H. K. (2004). *The first days of school: How to be an effective teacher.* Mountain View, CA: Author.

Wormeli, R. (2004). Summarization in any subject: 50 techniques to improve student learning. Alexandria, VA: ASCD.

Wragg, C. (2001). *Questioning in the primary school.* New York: RoutledgeFalmer.

Wright, K., Stegelin, D., & Hartle, L. (2006). *Building family, school and community partnerships.* Upper Saddle River, NJ: Prentice Hall.

York-Barr, J., Sommers, W., Ghere, G., & Montie, J. (2006). *Reflective practice to improve schools: An action guide for educators.* Thousand Oaks, CA: Corwin.

Young, V. H. (1970). Family and childhood in a Southern Georgia community. *American Anthropologist, 72,* pp. 269–288.

Ysseldyke, J., & Algozzine, R. (1990). *Instructor's resource manual: Introduction to special education* (2nd ed.). Boston: Houghton Mifflin.

Zemelman, S., Daniels, H., & Hyde, A. (2005). *Best practice: Today's standards for teaching and learning in America's schools* (3rd ed.). Portsmouth, NH: Heinemann.

Zimmerman, B. (1989). A social cognitive view of self-regulated academic learning. *Journal of Educational Psychology, 81,* pp. 329–339.

Zubizarreta, J., & Seldin, P. (2004). *The learning portfolio: Reflective practice for improving student learning.* San Francisco: Jossey-Bass.

Name Index

Aaron, K., 59
Abrami, P., 91
Abruscato, J., 354
Adams, K., 312
Affini, J., 342
Ageyev, V., 290, 328
Airasian, P. W., 207–208
Akhavan, N., 24
Alberto, P. A., 104
Albright, M., 212
Alexander, P., 153, 257, 306
Alfafara-Killacky, S., 48, 90
Algozzine, R., 415
Allen, S., 210
Ames, C., 345
Anderson, J., 257, 289
Anderson, L., 12, 109, 111, 147, 148, 235, 254, 259
Anderson, L. W., 207–208
Anderson, M. G., 242
Angelillo, J., 258, 259, 270
Antón-Oldenburg, M., 49, 124
Archer, J., 52
Armstrong, T., 43
Asher, S. R., 53
Ashman, A., 354
Atwood, V., 227
Audet, R., 209, 228
Auer, P., 242
Ausubel, D. P., 178, 298
Aw, W. L., 208–209

Baden, M., 182, 346
Bafile, C., 78
Ball, D. L., 287
Ball, L., 22
Bandura, A., 270, 344, 345
Banks, C., 48–50, 61, 241, 242, 371
Banks, J., 48–50, 61, 241, 242, 371
Barell, J., 341
Barr, R., 22
Baum, S., 12
Baxter, G., 408
Bee, H., 58
Beghetto, R., 91
Beisenherz, P., 17, 226, 227
Benard, B., 91
Bennett, C., 371
Bennett, N., 12, 272

Bennett, S., 208, 219
Berliner, D., 11, 13, 61, 62, 239
Bernstein, J., 53
Bettencourt, E., 21
Biddle, B., 7, 11
Biemiller, A., 12, 14, 16
Binder, J., 91
Bishops, A., 219
Blackburn, B., 342
Blanton, B., 339
Bloom, B., 143, 147–149, 207–208, 262
Blumenfeld, P. C., 13, 344
Blumenreich, M., 8, 17
Bode, P., 22, 23, 25, 60, 315
Bohley, M., 212, 213
Bonk, C. J., 209, 212
Bordessa, K., 369
Borich, G., 7, 9, 12, 18, 28, 42, 70, 134, 136, 137, 139, 144, 148, 154, 172, 208–209, 226, 271, 290, 295, 298, 300, 327, 391, 392, 397, 401, 404, 417, 425
Boss, S., 290, 342, 344
Bowers, C., 22, 23, 48, 90, 123, 278, 315, 372
Boyd, F., 48, 278
Boyles, N., 326
Bradbury, R., 219
Bransford, J., 39, 228, 341, 355
Brehm, K., 91
Brewster, C., 121
Briggs, L., 184
Brock, C., 48, 278
Bronfenbrenner, V., 57
Brookfield, S., 55–56, 310
Brookhart, S., 22, 137, 139, 367
Brophy, J., 4, 7, 8, 11–14, 16, 22, 23, 61, 91, 259, 272, 327
Brophy, J. E., 5–7
Brown, A., 17, 331, 332
Brown, A. L., 340
Brown, C., 22
Brown, G., 8, 226, 227
Brown, M. Y., 55–56
Bruce, B., 310, 356
Bruff, D., 218
Bruner, J., 148, 301
Bruner, J. S., 48
Bruning, R., 229
Bucher, K., 114

Buehl, D., 75, 354, 360
Bulach, C., 122
Bullough, R., 28
Burbules, N., 310, 356
Burden, P., 28
Burke, K., 134, 324, 402, 408
Burnette, J., 298
Buzan, T., 169, 176, 339
Bybee, R., 152

Cain, D., 340
Campbell, B., 43, 46
Campbell, L., 43
Campione, J., 331
Canning, C., 164
Canter, L., 104
Cantrell, S. C., 7
Carin, J., 20
Carlson, C., 59
Carnine, D. W., 260
Carpenter, T., 24
Carroll, J. B., 262
Carter, M., 73
Carter, N., 56, 71, 122, 123
Cartledge, G., 55, 90
Cassidy, J., 53
Castaneda, C., 74
Cecil, N., 228
Chaffee, J., 14
Chaille, C., 14, 15–16, 18, 19, 25, 290
Chapman, C., 43, 181
Chappuis, J., 41, 383
Cheesman, E. A., 218
Chen, B., 229
Chen, G., 278
Chen, T., 48, 90
Cheng, L., 48, 90
Christenson, S. L., 49
Chuska, K., 8, 226–228, 331
City, E., 310
Clark, C., 162
Clark, K. F., 7
Clark, R. E., 207
Cockburn, A., 272
Cohen, E., 312, 360
Collins, J., 314
Compton-Lilly, C., 61, 90
Conant, A., 20
Conery, L., 290, 342, 344

Miller, S., 290, 328
Minami, M., 50, 241
Minocha, S., 208
Mintzes, J., 169
Montie, J., 38, 164
Mooney, C., 51
Moore, K., 150
Moran, C., 242
Morriss, M., 213
Mshelia, A., 53, 372
Muijs, D., 8
Muller, F., 242
Muschla, G., 182
Muschla, J., 182
Musonda, D., 214

Nash, R., 312
Neisser, U., 178
Nelson, B., 90
Nelson, K., 189, 211
Nessel, D., 339
Neuliep, J., 48, 49
Nickerson, J., 12
Nieto, S., 22, 23, 25, 60, 315
Nolan, J. F., 111
Norby, M., 229
Nosich, G., 134
Novak, J., 169, 176
Novak, J. D., 214

Oakes, J., 243
Obiakor, F., 345
O'Brien, G., 298
Oczkus, L., 48, 331–333
Ogbu, J., 50, 314
O'Leary, P., 367
Olneck, M., 48
Ong, A., 300
O'Reilly, T., 208, 215
Ormrod, J., 57, 229, 257
Ovando, C., 50, 241, 243

Palincsar, A., 13, 17, 331–333, 344, 346
Palloff, R. M., 211
Parkay, F., 175
Parker, W., 291, 292
Paul, R., 20
Paulu, N., 121
Pearson, P. D., 7
Peterson, F., 339
Peterson, P., 162
Phillips, D., 15–16, 18, 25
Piaget, J., 19, 148, 290
Pickering, J., 7, 8, 13, 15, 162, 259, 278, 403
Piestrup, A., 242
Pintrich, P., 61
Polanyi, M., 164
Pollock, J., 7, 8, 15, 259, 403
Popham, J., 8
Poplack, S., 243

Portes, A., 243
Posamentier, A., 341
Postholm, M. B., 213
Powell, E., 76
Powell, S., 70
Power, B., 17, 227, 228
Power, M., 355, 373
Prater, M., 56, 71, 122, 123
Pratt, K., 211
Prawat, R., 12
Prensky, M., 208
Preskill, S., 55–56, 310
Price, K., 189, 371
Prinstein, N., 55
Putnam, J., 76, 90, 360

Raven, B., 72
Raven, B. H., 72
Ray, J., 49, 345
Ready, D., 91
Redding, N., 403
Reese, D., 49
Rekrut, M., 326
Reppucci, N., 345
Resnick, L., 95–96, 334
Reynolds, D., 8
Reynolds, N., 404
Rich, R., 404
Richardson, V., 14, 15–16, 18, 25, 289
Richmond, C., 212, 213
Riggs, E., 12, 278
Rinne, C., 111
Ritter, N., 172–173
Robbins, T., 286–289
Roberts, P., 172, 173, 175, 292
Roblyer, M., 148, 172
Rogers, V., 22
Rogoff, B., 16
Rohrkemper, M., 8, 14
Ronis, D., 24
Ronning, R., 229
Rose, L., 103–104
Rosenshine, B., 7, 13, 14, 16, 189, 258, 259, 270, 346
Ross, W., 292
Rothstein-Fisch, C., 314
Rounds, T., 49
Rovai, A. P., 210, 211
Rowe, M. B., 238
Rozakis, L., 340
Rozendal, M., 48, 278
Rumbaut, R., 243
Ryan, K., 28
Ryan, M., 74, 289

Sable, J., 48
Sacks, S. R., 28
Safford, P., 371–372
Saito, L. T., 48
Salmon, G., 211

Sanchez, D., 212, 213
Santos, R. M., 49
Sartor, L., 55–56
Sassman, C., 342, 344
Sattes, B., 226
Saunders, P., 7, 15
Saunders, W., 298
Savage, T., 72
Savery, J. R., 19
Schifter, D., 24
Schmid, E. C., 218
Schmidt, P., 242
Schmuck, P., 52, 55, 72–76
Schmuck, R., 52, 55, 72–76
Schneidert, C., 208
Schon, D. A., 213
Schraw, G., 229
Schroeder, A., 208
Schunk, D., 61
Schwartz, W., 61
Secada, W. G., 48, 61, 90
Seganti, C., 103–104
Sekandari, N., 48, 90
Serdvukov, P., 289
Shalaway, L., 120
Shank, P., 212
Shapiro, E., 416
Shavelson, R. J., 408
Shulman, L. S., 163
Silbert, J., 260
Simonson, M., 212
Sims, M., 90
Skinner, B. F., 107, 148
Skirtic, T., 91
Slatin, B., 12
Slavin, R., 13, 91, 312, 331, 354, 355, 369
Smaldino, E. S., 212
Smith, J., 12, 21
Smith, R., 91
Smyth, J., 213
Snow, R., 39
Snyder, W. M., 207
Soar, R., 72
Soloway, E., 13, 344
Sommers, W., 38, 164
Spence, J., 91
Spiro, R.J., 207
Stabzuibe, L., 82
Stadler, F., 304
Stahl, R., 373
Starasta, W., 278
Stegelin, D., 56
Stein, B. S., 341
Steinbeck, J., 141, 143
Steinberg, S., 49
Sternberg, R., 47
Stevens, D., 12
Stevens, R., 189, 258, 270, 354, 355
Stiggins, R., 41, 383, 404
Stipek, D., 229, 330

Subject Index

extended-response, 390, 392, 393
as helping behavior, 17–19
as indirect instruction strategy, 307–308
knowledge, 232–233
levels of, 231–236
probes as, 237–238
problems related to, 243–247
process, 18–19
as punishment, 246–247
purpose of, 227–228
research on, 240
restricted-response, 392, 393
sequences of, 230–231
synthesis, 235
targets of, 229–230
task-oriented, 10
wait time between, 238–239, 241

Reaction, to destructive behavior, 113
Reading
constructivist approach to, 291
educational standards for, 135
Reading lesson plan, 190–193
Really Simple Syndication (RSS), 212
Receiving, objectives for, 148–149
Reciprocal distancing, 48
Reciprocal teaching
explanation of, 48, 331–332
self-directed learning and, 332–334
Redirected probes, 237, 238
Referent leadership, 72
Reflective practice, 164
Reflective teaching, 38
Reinforcement/reinforcers. *See also* Rewards
application of, 114–116
behavior modification and, 107–108
in cooperative learning settings, 362–364
intermittent, 108
natural, 116
negative, 108
positive, 107
Relationships
direct instruction and, 265–268
horizontal, 52–53
vertical, 52
Reliability, test, 396–397
Remediation approach, 39–40
Resilient children, 91
Response cost, 109
Responses, objectives for, 149
Response to Intervention (RTI), 399, 416–418
Restricted-response questions, 392, 393
Retention, 271
Review materials, 182
Reviews, periodic, 276
Reward leadership, 73

Rewards. *See also* Reinforcement/reinforcers
in cooperative learning settings, 362–364
explanation of, 114–116
Rhythm, conversational, 242
Rigor and relevance framework, 152–153

Schools
crises in, 123
linking mechanisms between families and, 57, 59
Science instruction
constructivist approach to, 291
educational standards for, 135
lesson plan for, 198
Selectivity, 187–188
Self-directed learning
classroom dialogue and, 334–335
cognitive learning strategies for, 339–342
culturally-responsive, 345–346
explanation of, 324–326
functional errors and, 330–331
inner speech and, 334–335
metacognition and, 326–327
methods to teach, 338–339
project-based learning strategies for, 342–345
reciprocal teaching and, 331–334
sample dialogues for, 335–338
teacher mediation and, 327
zone of maximum response opportunity and, 328–330
Self-disclosure, 315
Self-efficacy theory, 344–345
Self-evaluation, 310
Sequential ordering, 266–267
SES. *See* Socioeconomic status
Single-parent families, trends in, 59
Small-group discussions, 312
Social bookmarking, 213–214
Social competence, 42
Social context, learning and, 56–59
Social environment, 79–80
Social framing, 314
Social presentation, 214
Social studies instruction, 291–292
Socioeconomic status (SES)
effective teaching and variations in, 22, 23, 39, 61
effect on learning, 49–50
explanation of, 22
Socio-emotional intelligence, 44, 46
Sociolinguistics, 241
Solicited probes, 237
Soliciting, 227. *See also* Questions/ questioning
Special learners
assessment of, 413–418
classroom management and, 90

Special populations, 39
Standardized tests
explanation of, 400
formative evaluation and, 399–400
helping students prepare for, 401–402
questions on, 228–229
summative evaluation and, 400–401
teacher-made vs., 400
Standards
explanation of, 132, 133
InTASC, 25–26
for lesson and unit plans, 166–167
origin of, 25–26, 133–136
Storming stage of group development, 74–75
Strategies. *See* Teaching strategies
Structuring
function of, 227
lesson content, 16–17
Student-centered learning, 309
Student engagement, 278–279
Students. *See* Learners
Student Teams-Achievement Division (STAD), 369
Study aids, 92
Subject matter, teacher knowledge of, 162–163
Summarizing, 89–90
Summative evaluation, 400
Surface behaviors, 111
Synchronous learning, 209, 211
Synthesis, 146
Synthesis questions, 235
System perspective, for planning, 164
Systems–ecological perspective, 57–58

Tacit knowledge, 164
Task orientation, teacher, 10–11
Task specialization, 357
Task structure
characteristics of, 359–364
debriefing and, 367–368
goal specification and, 358–359
group performance monitoring and, 366–367
teaching collaborative process and, 364–365
Teacher behaviors
helping, 7, 15–21
key, 7–15
Teacher concerns checklist, 425–426
Teacher-mediated dialogue, 15–16
Teacher-mediated learning, 327
Teacher-parent conferences
evaluation of, 120–121
preparation for, 119
strategies for, 119–120
topics for, 122–123